BusinessObjects® XI:
The Complete Reference

Cindi Howson

McGraw-Hill

New York Chicago San Francisco
Lisbon London Madrid Mexico City
Milan New Delhi San Juan
Seoul Singapore Sydney Toronto

Sponsoring Editor
Lisa McClain

Editorial Supervisor
Jody McKenzie

Project Editor
Carolyn Welch

Contributing Author
Elizabeth Newbould

Acquisitions Coordinator
Alexander McDonald

Technical Editors
David Taylor
Richard Foster

Copy Editor
Bob Campbell

Proofreaders
Paul Tyler
Susie Elkind

Indexer
Claire Splan

Production Supervisor
Jean Bodeaux

Composition
Apollo Publishing Services

Art Director, Cover
Jeff Weeks

Cover Designer
Jeff Weeks

This book was composed with Adobe® InDesign®.

To BONYMAUG, a dedicated bunch

About the Author

Cindi Howson is the President of ASK, a BI consultancy. She has worked with Business Objects since 1994, helping customers around the world implement and optimize their deployments. As an industry analyst, she authors the BIScorecard ™ product reviews, teaches for TDWI, and writes for *Intelligent Enterprise*. You can contact her at cindihowson@askcindi.com.

About the Contributing Author

Elizabeth Newbould is the practice principal for Business Intelligence at Dataspace, Incorporated (www.dataspace.com), one of the U.S.'s foremost data warehousing consultancies. With more than 15 years' experience implementing complex data warehousing and business intelligence solutions for Fortune 500 companies, Elizabeth has contributed to the success of her customers by applying proven methods and expertise in a range of industries including automotive, legal, manufacturing, and health care. Elizabeth can be reached at enewbould@dataspace.com.

About the Technical Editors

David Taylor has been an employee of Business Objects (through the acquisition of Crystal Decisions) for five years. He is based in Atlanta and is currently a senior sales consultant in their Telecommunications practice. He has been in the information technology sector for more than 15 years, working with Fortune 500 companies in an ERP, product development, and business intelligence capacity.

Richard Foster has been an Atlanta based employee of Business Objects for eight years and is currently a principal sales consultant. He has been in the information technology sector for more than 25 years in various capacities including software sales support, software development, post sales implementation, hardware sales support, and several roles within corporate IT organizations.

Contents at a Glance

Contents

Foreword

Business Objects launched the modern business intelligence (BI) industry 16 years ago with a simple but profound idea: a "semantic layer" that would make it easy for nontechnical business users to access data from various databases and applications and create reports from their business systems without requiring programming help from the IT or IS department. In the years since, BI has evolved far beyond this modest goal into a comprehensive set of technologies that are, organization by organization, changing the way the world does business.

BusinessObjects XI Release 2 is the latest BI platform from Business Objects and represents a major evolutionary step in the BI industry. It brings together all the tools a company needs, from enterprise information management (EIM) to analytics, to create a complete platform for business success. BusinessObjects XI makes it easier for more people throughout an organization to glean deep insight into the business, discover one version of the truth, and make better decisions.

Cindi Howson is a highly respected consultant in the BI industry and an experienced writer of BI books. In *BusinessObjects XI: The Complete Reference*, she has created the ultimate BusinessObjects XI reference guide. It deserves an initial careful reading and then a permanent place within easy reach. *BusinessObjects XI: The Complete Reference* lays the groundwork for starting any BI initiative, presenting the key strategies and implementation considerations. It also offers excellent information on key concepts and features, and can save you time in planning your projects and help you navigate through a maze of choices. *BusinessObjects XI: The Complete Reference* is valuable for organizations of all shapes and sizes in both the public and private sectors, including large organizations, departments within large organizations, as well as small and medium-sized businesses.

BusinessObjects XI: The Complete Reference also provides a look at the power of BusinessObjects XI to deliver ongoing business value far beyond any initial implementation. As Howson writes, "A business intelligence implementation is a project that you will never finish and is one in which the best you can do is to provide a starting point for users to make more informed decisions and discover opportunities." In fact, BI is a never-ending process of discovering new ways to use BI and implementing solutions that lead to even more ways to use it.

In all, more than 37,000 organizations and millions of individuals use solutions from Business Objects for this ongoing—and endlessly rewarding—journey, and many now recognize that BusinessObjects XI is the perfect vehicle for finding greater business value around every corner. One Business Objects customer, Emergency Medical Associates, a physician's group that contracts to staff hospital emergency departments, first bought solutions from Business Objects for reporting on its operational systems. Once the BI system was deployed, however, the BI team recognized they could use BI to create a fully functional system-wide bio-surveillance system. Most recently they have implemented dashboards for performance management, and they believe they are just getting started. Companies that use BusinessObjects are some of the most innovative organizations in business today.

Beyond the many features covered in *BusinessObjects XI: The Complete Reference*, BusinessObjects XI offers organizations substantial strategic benefits. It was developed with a focus on simplicity and enables organizations to offer business intelligence functionality to all types of users throughout the organization. BusinessObjects XI is also a robust BI platform that enables standardization on a single BI system and encourages continuing customer innovation beyond reporting or query and analysis.

Simplicity has always been a core design principle at Business Objects, and recently greater usability has become a driving force in the development of our products. BusinessObjects XI breaks new ground in this area, making it easier than ever to provide access to business intelligence throughout an organization. For example, new interface innovations, such as Intelligent Question, make it easy for even nontechnical business users to query data and get the vital business information they need when they need it.

We also architected BusinessObjects XI to be the most complete BI platform with solutions for the entire BI lifecycle, from data integration and data quality to performance management and forecasting. It offers customers the ability to standardize on a single platform from a single vendor. With standardization, you have the opportunity to reap huge benefits that include much lower software licensing and hardware costs, far greater integration across all systems for greater accuracy and more confidence in a single version of the truth, and significantly less risk when it comes to regulatory compliance. By standardizing on one vendor, you also have one support path and a shorter learning curve, leading to higher productivity and faster time to benefit.

Finally, BusinessObjects XI allows you to deploy a business intelligence environment that can be forever expanded and molded to foster continued innovation. As you implement your first project with reporting and drill-downs, then move on to another project that adds complex queries across multiple data sources, *BusinessObjects XI: The Complete Reference* will provide the concepts, strategies, and details you need to be successful. You can then take off on your own and explore even more sophisticated initiatives, using analytics for forecasting, or creating dashboards and scorecards for performance management.

While BusinessObjects XI is the most complete and powerful BI suite on the market today, we at Business Objects know our task is far from finished. Howson's comment that a BI project is never finished is based on the fact that our customers' requirements continue to evolve very quickly, so our product must as well, with continual enhancements and innovations. With the wealth of information that exists outside the corporation, we see a different paradigm for accessing information. It is a Global Network of Business Intelligence that allows us to query data across multiple sources no matter where they exist on the Internet. We will also be delivering advanced solutions related to searching through unstructured data, processing both persistent and nonpersistent data, and managing the billions of bits of data that will be collected by RFID technologies. Our customers are pushing for these innovations, and we are right there with them.

No doubt countless other innovations will be inspired by the latest technological advances. The years ahead will be exciting ones for anyone creating or using business intelligence systems, and in the same way that Business Objects pioneered the industry 16 years ago, we intend to continue to shape its future and provide our customers with solutions that make them smarter, more productive, and more competitive.

As you turn the pages of this excellent reference guide, recognize that you are just beginning your journey through all the possible ways that Business Objects can change every aspect of the way you do business. Fortunately, Cindi Howson takes you on this journey one step at a time, so sit back, relax, and enjoy the ride.

Bernard Liautaud
Founder, Chairman of the Board, and Chief Strategy Officer
Business Objects

Acknowledgments

First and foremost, I must thank the readers of the first *BusinessObjects: The Complete Reference*. If you hadn't helped to make the first book successful, the publisher and I would not have embarked on this second edition. Your e-mails, questions, kind words, constructive criticisms, and suggestions have helped shape this edition.

Thank you to the McGraw-Hill publishing team for pulling everything together. When I see everything that goes on behind the scenes in bringing a book to a reader, I am sometimes astounded that this book was completed at all. Thank you to Lisa McClain who pushed hard for a second edition, despite my declarations that I could never survive another such endeavor. Thank you to copy editor Bob Campbell for ensuring all those product names were right and for teaching me multiple times how to spell dialog. Thank you to Carolyn Welch for moving the product along in editorial and production, and to Jody McKenzie for making it all look nice in print. Thank you Alex for keeping track of all the moving parts.

Thank you to the power house of an analyst relations team at Business Objects—Rebecca Adams, Danielle Guinebertière, and Tracy Eiler—who supported me through this process by ensuring I had access to multiple software versions and channeling dozens of nit-picky, sometimes obscure questions to product marketing and management. Thank you to those who provided the answers: Paul Ross, Darren Cunningham, James Thomas, Howard Jung, Steve, and others. Thank you to the demo team, particularly John Kreisa and Alexis Guinebertière, who urgently provided new keys and beta software that allowed this book to be brought to market sooner. Thank you to Bernard Liautaud for writing the Foreword at the 11th hour, and, of course, for creating a successful company and product that I have been fortunate to work with.

With so many sweeping changes in this software release, both the publisher and I thought that using a technical editor internal to Business Objects might give us a leg up on software changes. I thank David Taylor and Richard Foster for taking on such a difficult and thankless task, and John Care for recommending them. David, in particular, thank you for continuing to argue with me and quadruple test aspects that we disagreed on. Thank you to Elizabeth Newbould at Dataspace, technical editor extraordinaire for the first edition, who came to my rescue in writing Chapter 22.

I would be lost without my colleagues and business partners who make working in this space simply more fun: Wayne Eckerson, Mark Myers, Knute Holum, and Al Hughes. Thank you to Nigel Pendse for his wit and contribution to Chapter 2. Thank you to my clients who keep me grounded in reality and who give meaning to all this work. I am grateful when customers willingly share their insights, in particular Chris Sieverts, Jonathan Rothman, Paul Zanis, and Tom Nather.

As with any book, much of it is written at crazy times, and I once again thank my family for their unwavering support, personal sacrifices, and for always believing in me. Keith, I promise, I won't start on another book, oh, for at least six weeks ☺, as long as SOFFC wins the cup again! Megan, ready for that butterfly race? And Sam, let's go throw that football (better yet, you throw it, I'll just cheer). Teresa, are you still free for lunch?

Introduction

Early in this project, the publisher and I thought this book would be based on BusinessObjects XI Release 1. When the vendor accelerated the timeline for XI Release 2, we decided to rewrite the book for this version, initially using a beta version of the software and then revising against the production version of XI Release 2.

Software Modules Covered Business Objects' product line is ever expanding, and herein lies a dilemma with the publishing industry: The Complete Reference brand does not imply the complete XI product line. Although I would have been glad if this book were published under a different title (lest you think it covers every module within XI), the reality is that you then would not be able to find the book via major booksellers. To manage expectations, please be aware that the following modules are not covered in-depth in this book: building reports with Crystal Reports (there are numerous other books that cover this topic), Data Integrator, Dashboard Manager, Performance Manager, Planning, and Live Office. As many of you have made excellent suggestions to cover some of these modules, lack of coverage simply became a matter of scope and time.

Sample Data For the first edition of this book, I tried to make your learning experience more exciting by using BusinessObjects 5i to provide interesting insights about wine prices and ratings (New Zealand Sauvignon Blancs are your best buy!). Because there were so many changes in the product with XI Release 2, I have relied mainly on the familiar, vendor-supplied eFashion and Island Resorts Marketing universes for the current edition of this book. Both use Microsoft Access databases and are part of the standard installation routine. The eFashion universe is based on fictional data from a retail-clothing store. It contains three years of sales and promotion costs for 211 fashion products and 13 stores. The Island Resorts Marketing universe contains reservation and sales information by customer and resort. When I wanted to demonstrate specific Oracle RDBMS or Microsoft SQL Server capabilities, I used sample data installed as part of these RDBMS. For Oracle, I used 9i and predominantly the Sales History (SH) tables. For SQL Server, I used SQL Server 2000 and the Northwind Products database.

What's Inside

Part I, "Getting Ready for BusinessObjects XI," introduces Business Objects (the company), the history of business intelligence, and key aspects of the product line. Project managers in particular will find Part I useful in understanding the people and communication issues that affect a business intelligence implementation. With the myriad product choices and deployment approaches, Part I will help you stay focused on the users and business values of your implementation. For existing customers, Chapter 5 is an essential read in understanding changes in the architecture and planning your migration.

Part II, "A Better Universe," covers universe design, maintenance, and securing content through the Central Management Console. As you deploy BusinessObjects XI across the enterprise, there are choices about where to build the intelligence in relational tables, OLAP databases, the universe, and the reports. As well, the larger your company's deployment, the greater the need for test and production environments, a quality assurance process, and usage monitoring. Part II explains the tools to do this. Even if you are an end-user, you will want to skim Part II to better drive your business requirements into the universe design.

Part III, "Reporting and Analysis," covers the end-user tools: InfoView portal, Web Intelligence in depth, and advanced features of Desktop Intelligence. Part III is when you finally get the return on your business intelligence investment as users explore and analyze data in ways never before possible. Part III covers the basics of accessing standard reports and exploring the data, as well as the advanced techniques of creating queries, formatting documents, defining powerful report formulas, and leveraging advanced features.

Conventions

This book uses the following conventions:

Convention	Used For
Bold	Information you enter in a dialog box
SMALL CAPS	Keys such as DELETE or BACKSPACE
Courier font	SQL syntax, Designer and Web Intelligence formula functions, or data source table and column names
Italics	Classes and object names as well as input variables
Business Objects	The company
BusinessObjects	The full client product
BusinessObjects XI	The platform and suite of products

PART

Getting Ready for BusinessObjects XI

Introduction to Business Intelligence

"Study the past if you would divine the future"—Confucius

Business intelligence is a way of exploring data to improve business performance, whether to drive profitability or to manage costs. It is not a technology you implement and then put in maintenance mode; it is an approach that evolves, morphs, and starts over again as the business climate changes, the users discover new opportunities to leverage information, and technology changes. When you implement business intelligence tools, the focus of the project is not to finish, but rather to deliver a certain amount of value and functionality within a predefined period. Never has this been more true than now with BusinessObjects XI, as a broader set of functionality, serving diverse user needs, has been brought onto a common platform. As you implement XI, you will need to prioritize which applications and interfaces you will leverage most. Will your project be bottom up: sort out the infrastructure to lower BI costs? Or top down: deliver scorecards to align and measure business performance?

Much of your implementation approach will depend upon where you are on the business intelligence lifecycle and whether or not you are completely new to BusinessObjects XI, a long-time Business Objects customer, or a long-time Crystal customer. The purpose of this chapter is to provide some insight as to how business intelligence evolved and is still evolving, so that you can assess where your company is in the BI lifecycle, where your users are today, and where they are heading. You'll see how Business Objects, the company and the product, have evolved with their customers and the industry, bringing the dream of business intelligence to more users and beyond traditional corporate boundaries. In many cases, Business Object's innovations have shaped and redefined the market.

The Background of Business Intelligence

The need to access information is not new. After all, people have always needed data to make informed decisions, although a number of errors in decision-making processes are still prevalent, including gut feel. As a type of technology, though, business intelligence is relatively young and emerged as a distinct market in the early 1990s. Pre–business intelligence, it was expensive and time-consuming to get access to the right data. If you are just starting out on the journey of business intelligence, you may find it hard to believe there was a time when information access was more painful than it is today. There are signs that BI has not quite delivered everything we hoped it would. For example, according to a TDWI survey, less than 20 percent of company employees use a BI tool on a regular basis. As BI technology evolves, and with a number of innovations in BusinessObjects XI, I expect this BI penetration to improve dramatically in the next few years. Customers are equally optimistic, expecting the percentage of active BI users to increase to 40 percent in the next three years.

Prior to business intelligence, decision-makers predominantly relied on the following sources of information:

- Printed reports, generated on a periodic basis by mainframe-based systems. If a critical measure were missing from the printed report, you had to wait months for IT to create a custom report.

- Manually populated spreadsheets, which provided a bit more flexibility than printed reports. Unlike today, when users may export data from a report, or better yet, use BusinessObjects Live Office to dynamically import data into a spreadsheet, in the late 1980s, field personnel would call in their sales figures to an analyst, who would manually enter data into a spreadsheet. This allowed for some form of analysis on monthly data at best. With manual data entry, there was enormous room for human error and a higher degree of data discrepancies, as rarely did the manually populated spreadsheet match the source system.

- Gut feel still provided the best form of decision-making, as managers were close to the markets and the customers, and markets did not change at the pace they do today. If a manager had access to quantitative numbers, there was a high degree of distrust of the numbers, and rightly so. After all, the data was stale and the manual collection processes fallible.

CAUTION *As you deploy BusinessObjects XI, never underestimate the role and "hold" these legacy reporting systems continue to have over users. If you make BusinessObjects XI appear any more difficult than legacy reporting systems, your project risks failure. You are trying to change in a matter of months decision-making processes that have existed for decades.*

Custom-developed decision support systems (DSSs) and executive information systems (EISs) attempted to overcome some of the limitations of these original information sources. Decision support systems took the data from mainframe-based transaction systems and presented the results to users in a parameterized form. Users would enter a couple of parameters, such as time period, customer, country, and product. The DSS then displayed results in a tabular format. The beauty of this was that it was easy to use, significantly more so than wading through pages of paper-based reports. If you wanted to graph something, however, you had to re-key the data into a spreadsheet.

If you wanted to view a different data subject, this was generally not possible. Decision support systems generally provided insight into only one subject of data at a time. Each function generally had its own custom transaction system (see Figure 1-1), making it almost impossible to share information across functions. When a customer placed an order, the order entry system maintained its own customer codes. To generate an invoice, the accounts receivable department would have to reenter the order into its own accounting system, which most likely used a different set of customer codes. If you wanted to combine actual sales data (accounts receivable) with shipment dates (orders), it was generally not possible.

Early decision support systems with their proprietary nature gave way to executive information systems (EISs) in the late 1980s. Executive information systems were expensive to implement but provided graphical dashboards based on a broader set of information, sometimes with feeds from external data sources. At the time, products such as Lightship by Pilot Software, Inc., Forest and Trees by Platinum Technology, and Commander Decision by Comshare, Incs, were breakthrough applications and in high demand.

The fundamental problem with EIS systems was that *E* stood for executive. Companies soon realized that not only executives but all decision-makers needed access to information. Some savvy marketing companies later would tout their products as *everyone's* information system. However, until organizations fixed the back-end data, the stale, silo-based information could not be actionable, regardless of how pretty it looked in a dashboard or a briefing book. At the time, data warehousing was not a generally accepted technology, so moving beyond silo-based information systems was mission impossible. What surprises me is that even today, the most often cited barrier to a successful enterprise BI deployment is lack of an integrated data architecture. Fail to address the back-end systems, and your BusinessObjects XI implementation will fail.

Potentially, the latest approaches to dashboards (and other innovations) make the concept of *everyone's* information system a greater reality. I find Business Objects' recent advertising campaign both appropriate and amusing, since it highlights some of the historical mistakes in the BI industry. One ad shows a warehouse employee with a tag line "Meet the CEO of shocks and spokes." The ad emphasizes that BI belongs in the hands of every employee in an organization, not just in the hands of a few executives.

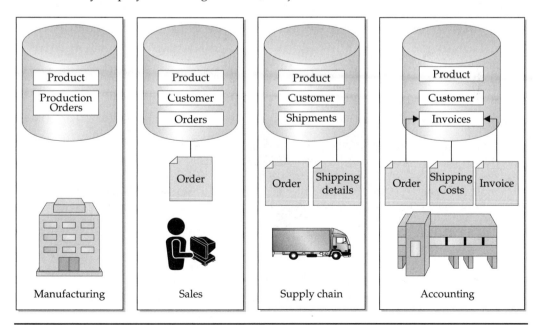

FIGURE 1-1   Each function had its own custom-built transaction system and corresponding DSS.

Business Intelligence Is Born

In the early 1990s, a number of business and technological factors merged to drive and enable the creation of a new breed of tools, business intelligence, as shown in Figure 1-2.

Several factors drove the need for more information, faster. With the fall of the Berlin wall, the signing of NAFTA, the endless possibility of emerging markets, and economic prosperity, growth and globalization were the mantra for many organizations. However, to operate a global company, companies need access to global or multiregional data. The function- and region-based DSSs could no longer satisfy users' needs. Silo-based EISs broke. At the same time, PCs were becoming common office tools. Users were increasingly analyzing data via spreadsheets or PC-based graphics programs. With this limited data analysis, users put pressure on IT to deliver more robust reports. IT could not keep pace with the demand. Personal computing both drove business intelligence and enabled client/server computing.

A number of technological advances became enablers for business intelligence. First, large corporations began implementing enterprise resource planning (ERP) systems, such as SAP, PeopleSoft, and Oracle Financials. With these implementations, companies hoped to: (1) reduce the number and complexity of custom transaction systems, (2) meet the business demands for growth and globalization, and (3) derive the productivity and cost benefits of business process reengineering. With ERP systems (Figure 1-3), companies implement modules that share common business data. Each module includes rules that ensure a company is following its intended business processes. For example, in generating

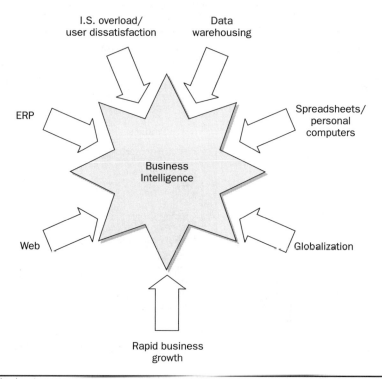

FIGURE 1-2 The business intelligence explosion

a customer order, the shipment is not scheduled until a price has been agreed upon and inventory is available. Modules share information with one another. The same customer information used to process the order is used to invoice the customer. When a customer places the order and the product is shipped, this information is integrated with the accounts receivable module to generate an invoice. With the proprietary transaction systems shown in Figure 1-1, data was double-entered, and customer IDs were specific to each system. With an integrated ERP system, an accountant no longer re-keys the information into a separate system; all reference data is shared across the multiple modules. (See Figure 1-3.) If the productivity and business process reengineering savings were not enough to incite a company to replace their legacy systems with an ERP, then the threats of year 2000 issues were.

Initially, ERP vendors promised they would provide insight into a company's business. It was a false promise. ERP systems provide the infrastructure that makes the insight *possible*,

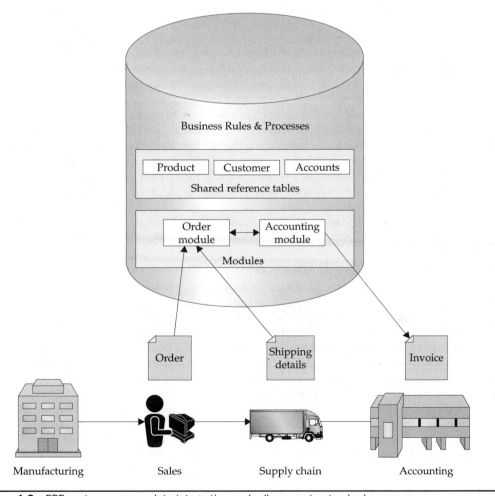

FIGURE 1-3 ERP systems ensure data integration and adherence to standard processes.

but the insight comes only when business intelligence tools and a data architecture are implemented in *conjunction with* the ERP system. System integrators and consultants, eager to assist with ERP implementations, only fueled this misconception. Some companies recognized that the newly implemented ERP system would not be able to replace all the information requirements that custom reports and DSS systems provided. Although ERPs helped streamline operations and eliminate duplicate data entry, they did nothing to simplify data access.

The second key enabler to business intelligence was client/server computing. With PCs on many users' desktops, companies could shift much of the processing power from mainframes to PCs, at a significantly lower cost. All of the sexy charts that made EISs so appealing could easily be rendered on an MS Windows or Apple desktop. The user interface was much more intuitive than mainframe-based reports and programming languages. For the first time, companies could purchase best-of-breed products and the components worked together. Okay, so they needed some brute force and perhaps some aggressive vendor sessions, but they did work, a shock for many who previously had single-vendor solutions.

While client/server computing placed greater demands on BI, the Web has brought BI to even more users. In some respects, the client/server computing that was once a catalyst for BI can now be an obstacle (that and a general resistance to change). With client/server computing, BI software and database connectivity had to be installed on every user's desktop. With the Web, BI users only need access to a browser. Customers have been rethinking their corporate intranets and BI infrastructure to better leverage the Web. In some circumstances, the Web has both expedited and hindered broader BI adoption. Because many Crystal Report consumers required little report-based interactivity, the Web became the perfect delivery vehicle for those reports. Meanwhile, the huge installed base of BusinessObjects classic users has slowed the adoption of Web Intelligence. Also, prior to XI Release 2, there was significantly more functionality in the BusinessObjects desktop interface than in Web Intelligence. Despite some strong selling points of the Web-based interface, few BusinessObjects classic report users were willing to give up the familiarity and robustness of the desktop tool.

Data Warehouse Speeds BI Adoption

The data warehouse was the biggest enabler for powerful reporting and BI's initial wave of success. A data warehouse extracts information from the ERP and aggregates it to allow for fast analysis of vast amounts of data. Some initial data warehouse projects were deemed failures, costing millions of dollars and producing no measurable benefits after years of effort. Fortunately, industry consultants quickly remedied the data warehouse approach, proposing subject-oriented data marts that can be built in smaller time frames. Ideally, a central data warehouse still acts as the platform to populate the data marts. As a technology, data marts and data warehousing allow IT to safely isolate the transaction system from the reporting system. A slow query does not halt order processing. As a business application, data warehousing allows users to analyze broader sets of data with dimensional hierarchies. When analyzing data in either an ERP or a proprietary transaction system, the queries are still limited to a particular module or set of tables. I suspect that one reason that BusinessObjects is so widely deployed without a data warehouse is that it provides unique capabilities to report authors to circumvent these constraints. With BusinessObjects, report authors can query multiple subject areas and stitch the results together seamlessly, locally. Synchronized multiple data providers is probably the single most anticipated feature in Web Intelligence XI Release 2.

With a data warehouse, the data is combined into one subject area or business view, allowing users to perform analyses that cut across multiple business processes. This approach puts significantly less strain on the BI application and is more scalable than attempting to put so much logic within one report. As the data is aggregated, data warehouses can contain years of history, allowing users to analyze trends; ERP and transaction systems often contain only current data at the most granular level of detail preventing any kind of trend analysis. Table 1-1 compares some of the different purposes and features of a transaction system with those of a data warehouse.

The Internet Influence

With the Internet boom of the late 1990s, the Web has had a dramatic impact on BI. A large deployment in a client/server deployment may have been in the thousands; in a Web deployment, it's tens of thousands. What once was viewed as a departmental application is now considered an enterprise resource. In some cases, the corporate intranet is no longer the deployment boundary, as customers and suppliers can also access rich BI content from a browser.

ERP/Transaction System	Data Warehouse / Data Mart
Goal is to process orders, post journal entries	Goal is to provide access to information to improve revenues, manage costs, improve customer service, achieve strategic goals
Current information with very little history	Larger amounts of history allow multiyear trend analysis, this year versus last year comparisons
Real-time information	Information extracted on a periodic basis (hourly, daily, weekly, and so on)
Detailed data down to the line item or level of data entry	Aggregated data but increasingly granular
Fast inputs, but slow queries	Read-only; tuned for fast queries
Normalized tables in thousands	Denormalized star or snowflake schemas with fewer tables
Rarely hierarchical groupings	Hierarchical groups give level of time, chart of accounts, product groupings, customer groups, and so on
Fixed reports by one detailed dimension (cost center, plant, order number)	Fixed or ad hoc reporting and analysis by multiple dimensions across all business functions

TABLE 1-1 Comparison of Transaction Systems with Data Warehouses

To leverage the Web, many BI vendors have re-architected their products. The industry still hotly debates Web delivery and authoring approaches. A browser interface is not always as intuitive as a Windows environment and lacks the maturity and consistent design of Windows-based applications. For this reason, Business Objects is continuing to provide a desktop authoring tool, Crystal Reports, for high-fidelity production-style reports, developed by professional report authors. Web Intelligence, meanwhile, is a purely Web-based authoring tool, ideally for business users who may not need all the advanced design tools that an IT developer requires. Yet to provide a certain amount of intuitiveness, Web Intelligence has two interfaces: an applet that has a richer design experience and a zero-footprint HTML version that is more wizard-like for basic reports. Desktop Intelligence, formerly called BusinessObjects classic, allows long-time customers to preserve their report development investments while offering a migration strategy.

The user interface is only one aspect of a Web-based BI deployment that the industry and customers alike need to rethink. The other is clearly the architecture. BusinessObjects XI Release 1 (released December 2004) certainly was about integrating the Crystal and BusinessObjects product lines, but it was also about providing a scalable architecture for Web-based BI. As deployments grow increasingly larger, with 24 by 7 access, and no downtime, the architecture must be more fault-tolerant and use shared services (discussed more in Chapter 5).

A Broader BI Suite

Since its inception, the BI market has been highly fragmented. In the last couple of years, many vendors, including Business Objects, have offered innovations or acquisitions to span multiple BI market segments. While customers may be willing to integrate a database from one vendor with a query tool from a different vendor, they may not be willing to do the same for, say, a dashboard tool and query tool. Customers have moved from departmental, à la carte purchases of multiple BI components to centralized purchases of tightly integrated suites. The degree to which you must understand individual BI market segments is dependent upon the stage of your implementation and your company's philosophy of seeking best-of-breed solutions versus an integrated solution. It's also important to understand the vendor's partnership strategy for those segments in which Business Objects is less of a market leader.

The sections that follow describe some of the main BI market segments. Figure 1-4 shows how some of the market segments relate to components of a BusinessObjects XI architecture.

Data Integration

Data integration or extract, transform, and load (ETL) tools used to be distinct from the BI suite, and with some vendors, they still are. Their job is to take the data from the source ERP or transaction system and then to cleanse and aggregate it to load in a data warehouse or data mart. Simply getting the data into an OLAP database or RDBMS does not in itself provide business value. As business users attempt to answer questions with the data, the ETL process often changes to extract more data, clean the data, or transform it to add robust business calculations.

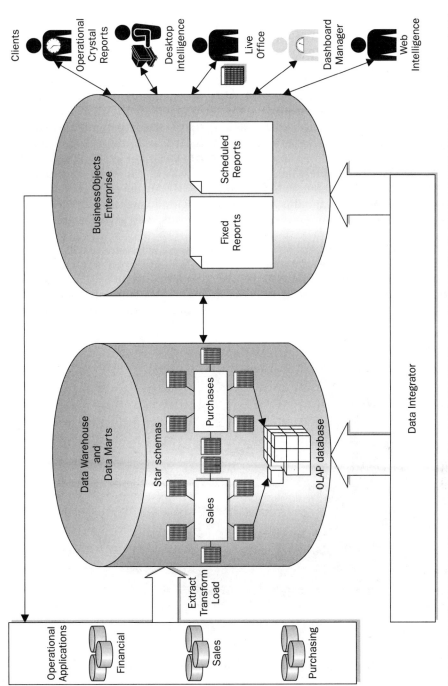

FIGURE 1-4   Components of a BusinessObjects XI deployment

In 2002, Business Objects acquired Acta Technology, a leading ETL vendor, and rebranded the product as BusinessObjects Data Integrator. The company increasingly views data quality and integrity as key to the success of any BI or EPM deployment and a component of its Enterprise Information Management (EIM) strategy. With any BI implementation, much of the success rests with the information architecture. Provide users with bad data, and the BI tool that is the window to this bad data will take the blame; provide users with good data, and the BI tool will enjoy the credit. In the company's official product line diagram, EIM is central (see Figure 1-5). To this end, the company continues to enhance Data Integrator, acquiring EII vendor Medience (Q4 2005) as a way of providing access to distributed data sources in real time, and launched Data Federator in Q2 2006. In April 2006, Business Objects acquired privately held Firstlogic as a way of improving data quality.

As of 2004, sales from Data Integrator accounted for less than 5 percent of Business Objects' total license revenues, but this increased to roughly 10 percent in 2005. Data Integrator is one of the company's fastest growing segments, with sales increasing 51 percent year-over-year.

As an ETL solution, Data Integrator continues to compete with pure-play ETL vendors such as Informatica as well as ETL solutions from RDBMS vendors such as Oracle Warehouse Builder or Microsoft Integration Services (formerly DTS). It's perfectly reasonable to use a third-party ETL solution as part of your BusinessObjects XI deployment. However, because Business Objects also owns not just the ETL piece of the BI architecture shown in Figure 1-4

FIGURE 1-5   BusinessObjects XI product line diagram. Reproduced with permission of Business Objects.

but also the front-end pieces, the vendor has extended the ETL integration to the business users. In this regard, while viewing any report, a business user can see the data lineage, transformations, and business descriptions. This information is taken directly from Data Integrator and populated into the universe. This integration allows for a broader type of impact analysis. When the source information changes, an administrator can identify which data warehouse table columns, which universes, and ultimately which business reports are affected. In cases in which Crystal Report instances have been used for maintaining historical data, Data Integrator can access these report instances to populate a data warehouse.

Query and Reporting

Query and reporting is the process of querying a database and then formatting it for readability and analysis. This is the segment in which BusinessObjects initially was launched in the early 1990s, and its origins help explain why its SQL generation is so robust. Over the years, the prevalence of query and reporting tools has led this market segment to become synonymous with business intelligence, even though business intelligence encompasses so much more. With query and reporting, users may query a data mart or a data warehouse, or they may query a transaction system.

Some define "reporting" as the process of formatting a report to enable analysis, while others define reporting as the delivery and distribution of standard reports throughout an organization. In 2003, Business Objects acquired Crystal Decisions, traditionally considered an enterprise reporting vendor. Hmmm, but wasn't BusinessObjects used for reporting as well? Yes, and herein lies a potential source of confusion that you must manage as part of your deployment. For sake of clarity, I'll refer to Crystal Reports as a "production" reporting tool and Web Intelligence as a "management" reporting tool. But don't pigeonhole these tools as reserved for certain users or data sources. As I'll explain next, while there are some clear differentiators between the two, there also is potential for overlap.

The needs within production reporting are often different than the needs within management reporting. Yet sometimes, the needs blur and the lines cross—and just as you can use a hammer to get a screw into the wall, you can use a production reporting tool for management reporting. The converse, however, is not true: rarely can you use a management-style query and reporting tool to develop production-style reports. The tool may not support the pixel-perfect layouts, normalized data sources, or programmability that IT developers demand.

With management-style query and reporting, the source is more often a data warehouse (though not always). Whereas IT develops production reports, power users and casual business users develop their own reports. The following table compares some additional characteristics that help distinguish production-style reports from management-style reports. These characteristics are by no means absolutes. Neither of these segments is precise. For example, Web Intelligence reports can be used individually, departmentally, or enterprise-wide. Crystal Reports would rarely be developed for an individual user and are more often enterprise-wide. Similarly, bursting a report and pushing it to numerous recipients is often considered a strong point of Crystal Reports, yet this is also possible with Web Intelligence reports (although it requires different processes and server resources).

Characteristic	Production	Management
User interface	Crystal Reports	Web Intelligence
Primary author	IT developer	Power user or business user
Purpose	Complete an operational task, fulfill regulatory reporting requirement	Decision-making and analysis
Report delivery	Portal, paper, or e-bill, embedded in application	Portal, e-mail
Report bursting	Burst to thousands	Schedule individually
Print quality	Pixel-perfect	Presentation quality
Number of report authors	Few	100s or 1000s
Number of report consumers	10s of 1000s	100s or 1000s
Predominant data source	OLTP—real time	Data warehouse or mart, occasionally OLTP
Level of data detail	Granular	Aggregated
Scope	Operational	Tactical, strategic
Usage	Fixed reports	Fixed or interactive reports, ad hoc queries

(Source: BIScorecard.com)

Production-style query and reporting is the process of querying an OLTP database and then formatting it to create a document, perhaps an invoice, a bank statement, a check, a list of open orders, or a fixed report consumed by thousands of users. In creating these reports, developers often require dynamic and programmatic control over the layout. These are some reasons that Crystal Reports is embedded in so many applications, with native connectivity to dozens of data sources. When the reporting is not against the transaction system, it may be against an operational data store or detailed data within a data warehouse. An invoice looks the same month to month; users have little desire to tailor its appearance (unlike a management report). This is Crystal Reports' sweet spot.

Management-style query and reporting is intended for users who want to author their own reports. They are less concerned with the precise layout (since they aren't trying to generate an invoice) but do want charts and tables quickly and intuitively. This is Web Intelligence's sweet spot.

Most organizations have the need for both types of tools, although in smaller organizations, you may choose one or the other.

Analysis

BusinessObjects XI provides query, reporting, and analysis in one interface, Web Intelligence, that generates a dynamic microcube based on the query results. Online Analytical Processing

(OLAP) has historically been a distinct market segment of BI. OLAP databases were often implemented as separate solutions from a query and reporting tool. With OLAP-aware universes (new in XI Release 2), Web Intelligence users can analyze data in OLAP databases such as Hyperion Essbase, Microsoft Analysis Services, IBM DB2 Cube Views, or SAP BW. Crystal Reports can also access OLAP databases natively for richer report design against these data sources. OLAP Intelligence offers users access to OLAP databases as well.

In its broadest sense, OLAP provides multidimensional analysis with different dimensions and different levels of detail. Capabilities such as drill-down, rotate, and swap are OLAP features. OLAP, though, has some clear definitions set forth by E.F. Codd (the father of the RDBMS) in 1993. OLAP itself can be further divided into different approaches: relational (ROLAP), multidimensional (MOLAP), hybrid (HOLAP), or dynamic (DOLAP).

NOTE *DOLAP used to be an acronym for Desktop OLAP because the processing initially occurred on the desktop. However, Dynamic OLAP is a more appropriate acronym, as the processing can occur in either a desktop environment or a mid-tier application server, but in either case, the cache is built dynamically without any explicit user or administrative tasks.*

These approaches differ in where the aggregations, calculations, and processing are performed. The following table compares some of the vendors and their different approaches to OLAP:

Architecture	Primary Difference	Vendor
ROLAP	Calculations done in a relational database.	IBM DB2 Cube Views, SAP/BW, and Microsoft Analysis Services can also act as ROLAP but most often use MOLAP
MOLAP	Calculations performed in a server-based multidimensional database. Cubes provide write-access for inputting budget data or performing what-if analysis.	Hyperion Essbase, Microsoft Analysis Services
HOLAP	Aggregations in a cache but with seamless drill-through to relational.	Microsoft Analysis Services
DOLAP	Calculations performed on the desktop or Enterprise Server to build a microcube. Cubes are read-only.	Web Intelligence

Given these traditional OLAP architectures, it's not surprising that many customers are not sure where to classify Web Intelligence or Desktop Intelligence. I often call it a DOLAP solution because the cache is built dynamically, either on the desktop in the case of Desktop Intelligence or on the Enterprise Server in the case of Web Intelligence. However, it is also a ROLAP approach because it provides automatically drill-through to detail, server-based ranking, aggregate navigation, and other capabilities while leveraging the data storage of the RDBMS. The only architecture you can say it is not is MOLAP. You might deploy BusinessObjects XI *instead of* a MOLAP solution or *in addition to* a MOLAP solution.

Analytic Applications

Henry Morris of International Data Corporation (IDC) coined the term *analytic application*. For software to be considered an analytic application, IDC says it must have the following characteristics:

- It must function independently of the transaction or source systems.
- It must extract, transform, and integrate data from multiple sources and allow for time-based analysis.
- It must automate a group of tasks related to optimizing particular business processes.

At one point, analytic applications seemed to be the next big wave of BI, and yet many vendors who dove headfirst into the segment later retrenched. Business Objects has always had a much stronger "build" than "buy" mentality. I hesitate to use the term "build," as it is reminiscent of developing an application from scratch, coding in a programming language. The "build" approach with analytic applications is more appropriately described as "customize," in which developers and users assemble objects and templates to deliver an application.

With Application Foundation (initially released in 1999), Business Objects provided a development platform for companies to build their own analytic applications and management dashboards, specifying their own process rules and best practices. The initial product met with mixed success and was largely constrained by the full-client BusinessObjects. With the release of XI, the company rebranded its analytic applications as Performance Management Applications. This solution has a number of prebuilt applications such as Customer Intelligence, Finance Intelligence, and Supply Chain Intelligence, to name a few, all rewritten leveraging Web Intelligence XI. Analytic Solutions are prepackaged data models built with Data Integrator that are available for retail, CPG, and finance.

One of the larger segments of analytic applications involves budgeting, planning, and financial consolidation software. In the past, Business Objects preferred to partner with vendors of such solutions even as part of its Performance Manager product. In August 2005, the company acquired SRC software. SRC uses relational storage for planning data, allowing customers to readily integrate SRC within a BusinessObjects XI deployment. The vendor plans to provide prebuilt planning universes and greater security integration in the future. Business Objects continues to partner with other vendors in this segment, including Geac Computer and Cartesis.

Dashboards and Scorecards

The terms *dashboard* and *scorecard* are often used interchangeably, although there is a difference. In its simplest terms, a dashboard is a collection of information, similar to a dashboard in your car. It might include

- A map that color codes where sales are performing well or poorly
- A gauge chart that shows if expenses are over/under budget
- A trend line that tracks stock outs

Whereas dashboards present multiple numbers in different ways, a scorecard focuses on a given metric and compares it to a target. In analyzing performance versus the target, a scorecard may provide a strategy map (see Figure 1-6) and track accountability. Scorecard products are often certified by the Balanced Scorecard Collaborative.

Business Objects offers Dashboard Manager as a dashboarding solution and Performance Manager as a scorecard solution (not to be confused with Performance Management Applications! ☺). Across the industry, a dashboard solution can be anything, including a complex document you create in Web Intelligence or Crystal Reports, a customized portal such as My InfoView, or a more robust solution such as Dashboard Manager (see Figure 1-7). Where Dashboard Manager is most different from a complex document is that it has several integrated analytic engines (Segmentation, Metrics, Rules and Alerts, Predictive, and Statistical Process Control) that allow for more sophisticated analysis. It has built-in "analytics" or controls to facilitate visual analysis and interaction with the dashboard. For example, a map analytic allows you to display data geographically. A thermometer analytic allows you to display a metric against a target value.

Data Mining

Data mining is a particular kind of analysis that discovers patterns in data using specific algorithms such as decision trees, neural networks, clustering, and so on. Data mining is used for predictive analytics and is forward-looking, whereas query and reporting tools

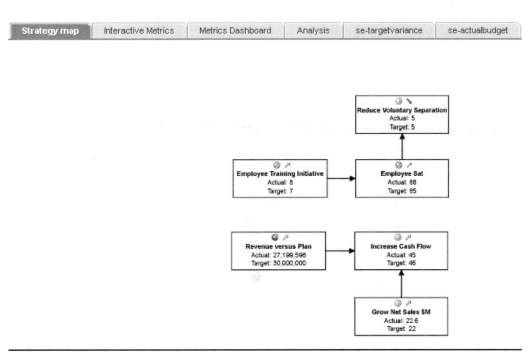

Figure 1-6   Strategy map within Performance Manager

FIGURE 1-7   Dashboard Manager

are more typically used for analyzing historical data. Another difference is that, whereas standard query and reporting tools require you to ask a specific question, data mining does not. For example, an interesting data mining discovery is that beer and diaper sales are closely correlated (one theory: a quick stop to the store to pick up more diapers is a good time to pick up more beer); a standard query tool would force a user to ask a more precise question such as, "What do beer consumers purchase in the same store visit?" With a data mining solution, users only need to say, "Here is some data, now show me what's related." Okay, I'm simplifying it. The truth is that building models and interpreting them is a sophisticated task demanding a highly skilled statistician.

Business Objects does not compete in the data mining space that is dominated by SAS, SPSS, IBM, Fair Issac, and others. Business Objects does, however, provide OEM data mining capabilities from KXEN as part of its Performance Management, Predictive Analytics module. Models from other data mining packages, such as SAS and IBM, can also be passed via Predictive Markup Modeling Language (PMML) to Performance Management.

The History of Business Objects the Company

Bernard Liautaud cofounded Business Objects in France in 1990. In Q3 2005, Liautaud assumed the role of Chief Strategy Officer. John Schwarz, previously President of Symantec, became CEO. Business Objects has dual headquarters in both Paris, France, and San Jose, California. While such a multicultural split in headquarters can create a "not invented here" attitude, Business Objects sees its transnational identity as a competitive advantage in a global marketplace.

At one point in BI history, Business Objects might have been viewed as a niche player or underdog. Today, it is considered the industry leader on a number of fronts. Its revenues, once in the millions, reached the one billion dollar mark in 2005. Part of what has helped it reach this mark has been its acquisition of Crystal Decisions, but clearly, the other aspect has been a history of innovation.

Product Innovation

It's difficult to say whether XI Release 2 or XI Release 1 is the company's biggest release to date as they both contain significant innovations. Many observers predicted that XI Release 1 would never happen. The key innovation in XI Release 1 was the integration and re-architecting of the product line to leverage the service-oriented, proven architecture of Crystal Enterprise. This re-architecting allows for open and more fine-grained security, greater scalability, and a broader suite of capabilities on a common platform.

In XI Release 2, there are numerous innovations, but the one that will have the biggest impact on long-time customers is support for Desktop Intelligence (or full client documents) within the new platform. As well, Web Intelligence now provides a richness in authoring, analysis, and report consumption that will make it the preferred interface going forward. Customers can optionally convert documents to Web Intelligence (see Chapter 24 for a comparison of capabilities).

Figure 1-8 provides a timeline of some of the company's major product innovations and key acquisitions.

- **1990**   Patented semantic layer allows users to generate SQL using familiar business terminology.

- **1995**   BusinessQuery for Excel (now discontinued) allowed users to launch a query directly from a spreadsheet and analyze the results in the spreadsheet. Live Office replaces this product in XI Release 2, supporting content from both Crystal Reports and Web Intelligence.

- **1996**   BusinessObjects is rearchitected as a 32-bit application and introduces the microcube technology for Dynamic OLAP.

- **1997**   Web Intelligence thin client is first introduced.

- **2000**   InfoView Portal is released, along with BusinessObjects 5i, which offers full-client capabilities in three-tier mode.

- **2001**   Auditor is launched, allowing administrators to track use of documents, universes, and objects by users and groups.

- **2001**   Application Foundation and BusinessObjects Analytics are launched, providing companies with prebuilt applications as well as a development

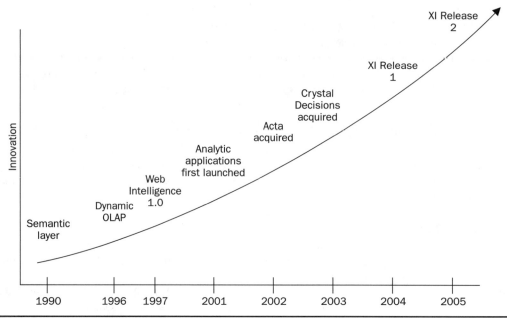

FIGURE 1-8   Major product innovations

environment for analytic applications. These products are later rebranded Dashboard Manager and Performance Management Applications.

- **2002**   Acta is acquired to provide ETL capabilities and packaged data marts, later rebranded as Data Integrator and Rapid Marts.
- **2003**   Crystal Decisions is acquired for its pixel-perfect reporting solution, enterprise architecture, and huge base of OEM partners and customers.
- **2004**   BusinessObjects XI Release 1 provides a new architecture that integrates Crystal Enterprise and the classic BusinessObjects suite. The product includes several major enhancements such as collaboration and guided analysis through the Encyclopedia.
- **2005**   BusinessObjects XI Release 2 closes the parity gap between Web Intelligence and Desktop Intelligence. It includes a new patented interface Intelligent Question to garner more casual users.
- **2005**   SRC Software is acquired as part of the company's performance management strategy, providing budgeting, planning, and financial consolidation software.
- **2006**   FirstLogic is acquired to embed data quality capabilities in Data Integrator.

The Future

At the time of this writing, Business Objects is considered the leading BI vendor in terms of revenues, product capabilities, and market presence as defined by a number of analyst firms, including IDC, Forrester, and Gartner. Although there has been recent consolidation, the market remains relatively fragmented, and competition is fierce. While nobody can predict the future, it's relevant to consider some of the vendor's strategies that will shape future product directions and determine continued success:

- **SMB and Enterprise Customers**   While many BI vendors (including Business Objects) continue to pursue enterprise customers and expand the footprints in these accounts, Business Objects further extends its reach to small to medium-sized businesses. In the last year, it has released special versions of Crystal Reports to provide a complete entry-level reporting solution. Also, the release of Crystal Xcelsius gives these customers highly visual, Excel-based dashboards.

- **Enterprise Information Management**   As discussed elsewhere in this chapter, lack of a robust data architecture can lead a business intelligence implementation to fail. While other BI vendors have largely left these issues to be addressed by database vendors, Business Objects has made information management a core part of its strategy.

- **Enterprise Performance Management**   Business intelligence is about empowering users to access the information they need to do their jobs effectively; enterprise performance management is about ensuring the company focuses on those things that most determine business performance. It provides the tools and processes to enable individual business units to measure progress toward goals that are aligned with strategic objectives of the company as a whole. An effective EPM solution requires an enterprise business intelligence platform and robust data architecture.

Beyond these strategies, the momentum of the BI market clearly contributes to Business Objects' success. Business intelligence spending continues to be cited as the number one or two IT investment for companies in 2006. Product innovations, including the easy interactivity of Web Intelligence, the intuitive power of Dashboard Manager, and the integration of spreadsheet-based BI in Live Office, together extend the reach of BI.

Summary

To borrow a phrase from a data warehouse vendor, business intelligence is not a destination but a journey. While this book focuses on the company's core query and analysis products, Business Objects now offers much more, extending its capabilities into ETL on the back end and analytic applications on the front end.

A business intelligence implementation is a project that you will never finish and is one in which the best you can do is to provide a *starting point* for users to make more informed decisions and discover opportunities. With so much product capability, you must stay focused on the business value of BusinessObjects XI. Your challenge will be to understand how the history of business intelligence in your company influences your users' attitudes, understanding, and receptiveness toward BusinessObjects XI. Perhaps you are still fighting some of the battles of just having implemented a new ERP. Perhaps your initial goal is a modest one of simply weaning users from printed reports to online reports. Perhaps your company will be one of the industry innovators which many aspire to be, using BusinessObjects XI in ways never before anticipated and directly contributing to your firm's market position and profitability. Enjoy the journey!

CHAPTER 2

Goals of Deploying BusinessObjects XI

Whether you are first implementing BusinessObjects XI or expanding an existing implementation, it's important to be clear about the goals of your deployment. You may be implementing BusinessObjects XI as part of an IT effort or as part of a specific business initiative. The goals of these two groups can be quite different. The goals may be driven by the following:

- **IT** to reduce infrastructure costs, limit custom report development, or replace a legacy reporting system
- **A business unit** to provide access to data to manage and measure the day-to-day business activities
- **The corporation** as part of a larger enterprise performance management initiative, as a strategic tool that provides competitive advantage

The goals of different stakeholders may collide and impede progress or merge to make the implementation more successful. You may start out on the implementation with one set of goals only to discover a more important goal as you proceed. In some cases, good scope management will help the project stay on track. In other cases, recognize that business intelligence is not as exact as other technology projects and requires a degree of flexibility. Capabilities are delivered on an iterative basis rather than a traditional waterfall project lifecycle. Often, you may feel that a BI project never ends, and in fact, it doesn't and shouldn't. However, focusing on the goals of the project will help minimize the risk that the technology and latest product innovations become all-consuming (as fun as they may be!) and ensure resources are aligned to deliver value within a defined timeframe.

DILBERT: © Scott Adams/Dist. by United Feature Syndicate, Inc.

IT Goals

Although BusinessObjects XI provides business insight, it is still a tool purchased primarily by the IT organization as the enabler to information access. IT controls the source systems and the data warehouse. The challenge here is in making sure the IT goals are a starting point and not an end point. For example, let's assume that your current approach to reports is for a custom programmer to develop them against the source system. Crystal Reports may be the tool of choice for creating such custom reports. The business users are reasonably happy because each report is customized with their view of the data; it's easy (no training required), and it's correct because the data came directly from the transaction system/ERP.

However, this approach to information access poses several problems:

- The report developer generally has to know the detailed ERP/OLTP schema and programming language.

- The cost to develop and maintain one report is high. Because the report developer is several steps removed from the business, it may take multiple iterations to get the report right. By the time it is right, however, the user requirements change.

- Reporting directly against the OLTP can affect response time both for inputting transactions and for executing a report.

- Without a data warehouse, a significant amount of business logic is built into each individual report.

Some users, though, are not satisfied, because IT can't develop custom reports fast enough. IT has become a bottleneck. Your company decides it needs to complement the Crystal Reports deployment with Web Intelligence as an ad hoc query and reporting tool with the primary goal of reducing the time and cost to develop custom reports and ideally providing end users with more flexibility. You enable the Web Intelligence module, build a few universes, and train the users on the tool. Users will now be able to create their own reports, and the IT department can focus on a smaller set of canned, enterprise-wide reports. Goal accomplished?

No. First, the skill set to build a BusinessObjects universe is often quite different than the programming skills to develop an ERP-based custom report. The roles of the existing report developers must be redefined, or they will impede implementation (see Chapter 3, under the heading "Influencers"). Is there still a need for custom reports against the ERP? Probably, yes, but ideally for a much smaller number. Second, you just went from a business user's having access to a fixed report (easy to use) to the user's starting at a blank query panel with no data. Part of such a deployment effort must include an evaluation of which reports should remain as fixed reports, which should be eliminated, and which should be re-developed as standard Web Intelligence reports. IT may still develop these initial Web Intelligence reports, since they know the data and current reporting requirements, or power users within the business may become the initial report authors. Don't let this step discourage you—providing standard reports is a *starting point* only. With all the Web-based interactivity in Web Intelligence, end users (not IT developers) can easily fine-tune a report to resort, format, filter, and drill. Creating a set of standard reports ensures that users do not perceive Web Intelligence as a step backward: theoretically empowered, but overwhelmed and with no data and certainly no business insight.

Author and researcher Jeremy Hope suggests in his book, *Reinventing the CFO*, that IT is a culprit in CFOs being increasingly overwhelmed. He suggests that IT has provided finance users with so much unfiltered data that CFOs should be "more wary of implementing new tools and IT systems that soak up valuable time and money but fail to provide reasonable value." At first blush, his case seems to put unfair blame on IT. IT often provides users with more unfettered access to data, because they ask for it . . . or because the users don't and can't adequately define their requirements. Users must accept some culpability in the overwhelming amount of data (but little business insight) that many data warehouse and business intelligence implementations provide. Yet in support of Hope's contention, IT can do much more to ensure value is provided. Standard reports are certainly a way of accomplishing this. Dashboards are yet another. In this regard, IT knows what is possible and needs to work in concert with the business to ensure both constituents achieve their goals.

Over time, as both power users and casual users work with the standard Web Intelligence reports, they can move on to modify, customize, and finally, create their own reports. It is this phase of the implementation in which IT realizes the cost benefit, and the business gains a lot of other benefits. Had you stayed in custom development mode with only a handful of Crystal Report experts, the programmers would still be hard-coding inflexible reports and users would see only a limited amount of data. While the goal to limiting custom report development may not sound as glorious and strategic as "enterprise performance management," it is valid, with a measurable benefit of reduced costs and overtime, along with improved business insight.

Reporting Directly Against a Transaction System

When you implement an ad hoc query tool, you may reduce report development costs, but you do nothing to improve query response time or provide meaningful context to the data. In fact, you run a high risk that you will make response time significantly worse for both the end user queries and transaction system inputs. The simple answer is to build a data warehouse or a data mart. After all, the fundamental difference between these two platforms is their sole purpose in life: automating a process versus providing business insight (see Table 1-1 in Chapter 1). Yet many companies still elect to implement BusinessObjects XI directly against the OLTP (or a copy of it) for several reasons:

- **Timing**   A data warehouse may be a long-term goal, but under budget constraints, companies need to achieve immediate benefits. They don't have the time or resources to develop an enterprise information strategy. If you recently implemented a new OLTP, then you need reports right now, immediately, not six months from now. This kind of approach also gives you a relatively quick way of communicating the value of deploying a business intelligence solution.

- **Lack of sponsorship**   A successful data warehouse project requires strong business sponsorship and agreement across departments and functions. In contrast, OLTP-based reporting is often deemed an IT responsibility, since IT programs the reports. IT can implement and control reporting in this environment, without having to gain the buy-in necessary for a data warehouse; the politics of a data warehouse project are deferred.

- **Cost and complexity**   Data warehouse implementations range in price from $50,000 to millions of dollars. Poorly managed projects can take years to achieve measurable benefits, and even well-managed ones will take several months. In addition to selecting a BI tool, you will face a number of other choices in terms of architecture, servers, databases, data integration and ETL tools, approach, and design. A data warehouse is a long-term investment, but be careful not to ignore the hidden costs associated with implementing Web Intelligence against the OLTP. Lack of dimensional or cross-functional data may limit the data's usability; data will remain just "data" and not "information." The universes will be significantly more complex and take longer to develop, as transformations normally done in the ETL process must be performed to a degree in the universe.

- **Real-time access**   Real-time BI continues to generate a fair bit of hype, and new buzzwords such as "Operational BI" add to both hype and confusion. The real-time debate is both a technology issue and a business requirements issue: what do users need, and what technology can best meet those needs. Certain technologies allow a data warehouse to be updated in near real time as source data changes. For some applications (such as stock traders and risk management), users indeed need access to real-time data with data feeds from multiple processes and functions. Here, EII technologies (note Business Objects' recent acquisition of Medience) are compelling. However, real-time BI also touches a nerve with OLTP users who need flexible access to transaction-level data. ERP vendors may excel in business process automation, but they have generally been weak at providing intuitive reporting tools. As long as the transaction processing time does not suffer, it makes perfect sense to integrate BusinessObjects XI with the OLTP, whether embedding Crystal Reports within an OLTP application or using Data Integrator and Web Intelligence against an ERP-centric data mart. The vendor provides a number of solutions to facilitate this. Rapid Marts are prepackaged data models for specific ERP solutions such as PeopleSoft, Oracle Financials, Siebel, SAP, and J.D. Edward. Further, some BusinessObjects XI features such as multipass SQL, derived tables, and multiple data providers per report make real-time BI against the OLTP achievable.

Whatever your reason for using BusinessObjects XI directly against the OLTP, you will need to take some precautions to ensure a successful deployment. Killer queries can cripple a system and prevent orders from being processed. It takes only a few times for this to happen before you will either (a) fund a data warehouse or (b) limit ad hoc access.

If BusinessObjects XI is to become a strategic application, you do not want to limit access. However, you do want to deploy in a highly managed way, even more so when you are accessing an OLTP. Pay particular attention to the universe design, ensuring optimal joins and removing the ability to use nonindexed fields as condition objects (see Chapter 9, the section "Modify a Dimension"). Ensure the standard reports use prompts to limit the amount of data returned and to guarantee that the conditions are based on indexed fields. With custom OLTP reports, each user executes the query, placing an additional load on the OLTP. With BusinessObjects XI, use the Public Folders for users to access one pre-run, cached report. Use the integrated scheduling to run more resource-intensive reports during nonworking hours and possibly push certain reports to individual users. Finally, ensure you use the integrated auditing capabilities to understand who is using certain reports, universes, or objects; when; and how they are being used (see Chapter 16).

Business Goals

Regardless whether you are starting out with a departmental implementation or with the simple goal of automating a legacy report process, the sweet spot of business intelligence is when it is aligned with the business goals. This is when BusinessObjects XI is not merely a productivity tool (for example, to get the same data faster) but a strategic tool that measurably affects company profitability, competitiveness, and market share. Even if you start out implementing BusinessObjects XI to fulfill IT goals, the road does not end there. Its uses will evolve, and in support of this evolution, IT must realize that much of the BusinessObjects deployment is iterative.

Those initial starter reports should be modified as the business environment changes. Documents in Public Folders (or in version 6 and earlier, Corporate Documents) should be modified as the business uses BusinessObjects XI more effectively, drivers of performance are measured, or the business environment changes. If these reports and/or universes remain static for an extended period of time, it's an indication that your deployment is not closely aligned with the business needs. Arguably, there will be some universes and reports that are more operational in nature and that support work processes that may not change all that often.

If you are a project manager or sponsor, then it's easier for you to keep the project aligned with the business goals. If you are a lone power user or universe developer, you may be thinking, "Not me, that's for the higher-ups to do!" Perhaps. However, as the BusinessObjects XI expert, you are best suited to understand how the various modules can be leveraged to fulfill the business goals. Too often there is a disconnect between the opportunities and the technical capabilities. Keep your ear to the ground, and you will discover the opportunities. Read the company newsletters, and you will discern the company goals and come up with new ideas on how BusinessObjects XI can help achieve those goals. Most business units have individual business plans. Take a look at them. Which reports can you design to measure implementation of the business plan? Don't forget that some of the world's greatest innovations have come from the rank and file, not the executives!

Given the volume and breadth of data needed to fulfill broad company goals, BusinessObjects XI is often implemented in conjunction with a data warehouse or data mart. If the data warehouse is being implemented at the same time, many of the business goals in implementing and justifying the warehouse will be the same for implementing BusinessObjects XI.

The business goals may be fairly broad, such as

- Providing front-line managers with direct access to data that shows the health of the day-to-day business

- Gaining insight into what was previously a black hole, caused by a closed transaction system that lacks robust reporting capabilities

- Providing data to support company-wide initiatives such as enterprise performance management, business process reengineering, Sarbanes-Oxley compliance, and Six Sigma

Even when the goals are this broad, to achieve measurable benefits, you need to develop more precise goals and tie them in with the BusinessObjects XI development and implementation. Table 2-1 provides some typical goals by process. With each broad goal, as you implement BusinessObjects XI, identify what information elements help achieve or measure the goal. If the elements are in the data warehouse, then ensure these elements are exposed in the universe along with the necessary dimensions to provide context to the data.

While the goals in Table 2-1 are company-oriented, other business goals may be more narrowly defined yet still provide a measurable benefit. As you implement BusinessObjects XI in phases or by departments, look to align the implementation with achieving these specific business goals.

Process	Goals	Measures
Sales and Marketing	Improve customer loyalty	• Customer sales over time • Customers who buy both products A and B • Customer purchases by channel • Share of wallet • Customer churn
	Manage prices	• Price trend over time • Retail price versus manufacturing costs
	Increase market share	• Revenue versus competitors • Revenue trend versus industry trend
Supply Chain	On-time delivery	• Number/volume shipments shipped by requested data • Number of early, on-time, late orders over time • Inventory levels for top-selling products • Ratio of number of days of sales versus inventory to fulfill those sales (DSI)
	Low freight costs	• Orders fulfilled from most cost-effective shipping point • Freight costs • Volumes and discounts with freight suppliers
Finance	Reduce aging of accounts receivable Reduce budget variance	• Accounts receivable over time • Actual expense versus budget
Human Resources	Reduce employee turnover Competitive pay	• Employee turnover over time • Salary versus job level, job history, market salaries

TABLE 2-1   Use BusinessObjects XI to Monitor and Achieve Business Goals

Following are some examples from Business Objects customers and how they use the suite to achieve specific business goals:

- T-Mobile as a way of improving call center operations and staffing levels to ensure high service levels for its 20 million subscribers
- Emergency Medical Associates (EMA) to help physicians improve clinical diagnosis, track trends in flu-related illnesses, provide early identification of disease outbreaks, and monitor the number of patients treated in a given hour
- Blue Cross Blue Shield of Kansas City as a way of controlling rising health care costs
- Dow Chemical to enable all managers to control individual business unit expenses, as well as to improve supply chain efficiencies by measuring order performance and inventory levels
- Simon and Schuster to track sales of particular books and determine the effectiveness of cooperative advertising
- An oil and gas company to ensure contract compliance and to reduce the number of days between product shipment and invoice issuance
- A manufacturing company to determine the performance of various distribution channels

In some cases, the elements may not be in the data warehouse, but you can still provide them via objects in a universe or a variable in a report. In this respect, implementing a data warehouse and BusinessObjects XI simultaneously poses a challenge for the data warehouse not to become a constraint that limits your ability to leverage functionality provided by the product suite. Just because data isn't in the data warehouse, that doesn't mean you can't and shouldn't deliver data to users. If it helps achieve a business goal, do it. For example, many companies need access to external market data for benchmarking. Unless the data can be coded to conform to existing dimensions, third-party data often cannot be stored in the data warehouse. BusinessObjects XI, on the other hand, is much more flexible. It provides a number of ways to incorporate structured or unstructured external data:

- The repository allows users to store non-BusinessObjects documents, so if the data comes in the form of an Excel spreadsheet or PDF document, it can be stored in the repository.
- The microcube architecture allows users to merge corporate data with external data and display the results via one report or chart.
- Universe designers or report authors can embed HTML and web site addresses into standard reports, providing navigation through a thought or problem-resolution process.
- BusinessObjects Live Office allows users to store external data in a spreadsheet and refresh other parts of the spreadsheet from either a Crystal Report document or a Web Intelligence document.

Designing and building the dimensional models, ETL process, and warehouse infrastructure is resource intensive and complex. Short-staffed and nearing (or past) a project milestone, it's easy to devote 90 percent of the time of a BI project to delivering the physical tables or star schemas and only 10 percent of the time to delivering universes, reports, and dashboards. For the business, though, the reports and dashboards are the primary window to the data warehouse. Make it unwieldy, and the business will not be able to focus on analyzing data for business benefit; they'll spend an inordinate amount of time figuring out how to use the tool. Fail to provide standard reports or dashboards, and the business may feel nothing was delivered.

For each of the business goals, you must develop a corresponding standard report as part of the BI deployment effort. This standard report may act as a template that users then refresh with their own view of the data, or it may be automatically refreshed and sent to them. This all sounds pretty obvious, doesn't it? It should be! The issue is that while these business goals are often used to get project funding, with all the technological and organizational issues involved in delivering a BI solution, it's easy to forget why you started on this endeavor. The project team gets so focused on setting up the infrastructure, they leave it for the users to figure out what to do with these newfangled tools. In some rare organizations, where computer and data literacy is high, it may be a valid approach simply to deliver the tools. The business runs with it and exploits the value. Usually, though, users accustomed to no data or to inflexible, custom-developed reports do not immediately know how to approach a flexible BI tool. It's up to you as the BusinessObjects project manager, team leader, power user, or internal expert to show them the possibilities!

BI Standardization: A Joint Goal

As BI deployments have evolved and matured over the years, both IT and the business increasingly recognize a joint goal: to reduce the number of disparate BI tools so that business users have access to one version of the truth and IT can better support a smaller number of tools. With XI Release 2, Business Objects offers a complete toolset that serves one of the broadest ranges of users needs, all on a common platform.

Chapter 3 discusses the different user segments in a BI implementation and how you may tailor your solution, training, and promotion efforts to each of these user segments. With BI standardization, the goal is not to create a "one size fits all" solution. Instead, it's to ensure that for each BI segment, there is only one standard tool that shares a common server, security, and metadata environment: for example, one ad hoc query tool for power users, one dashboard interface for executives, one production reporting tool for IT developers.

With a smaller number of tools to support, IT reaps enormous cost savings in terms of reduced software licensing and maintenance fees, lower hardware costs, and lower support costs, while still improving service levels. For the business, it reduces their training time and ensures one version of the truth. Even when companies implement a data warehouse to achieve a single version of truth, if different BI tools access the same data in the data warehouse, measures can be recalculated and represented in each BI tool in a slightly different way.

Although BI standardization is crucial for an enterprise solution, there are often insurmountable obstacles to achieving standardization. First, many companies still allow individual business units to purchase BI solutions themselves; such solutions are not necessarily purchased by a central IT or purchasing department. Second, when IT fails to partner with the business and views itself as the "gatekeeper" to data access rather than an enabler, the business must take matters into its own hands. At risk for IT is control and, for some, job protection; at risk for the business is competitiveness and eventually viability. Ideally, both stakeholders share a common goal, and I would suspect that those who don't will ultimately fail, causing IT to be outsourced or the business to go bankrupt. Finally, standardization takes a high degree of executive sponsorship, as standardization often means some users will need to make sacrifices, either in terms of shutting down other BI applications or in giving up customized or specialized functionality that may be important to a few but not to the enterprise as a whole.

With so many barriers to standardization, I was pleasantly surprised to find in a TDWI survey I co-authored, "Enterprise Business Intelligence: Strategies and Technologies for Deploying BI on an Enterprise Scale," a relatively high success rate: 58 percent consider their standardization efforts highly to very highly successful (based on 594 respondents from a mixture of company sizes and geographic locations). A third of organizations surveyed say they plan to standardize on an integrated suite of BI tools within two years, and another 24 percent have already standardized.

Measures of Success

How you measure success is determined, in part, by the goals you wish to achieve. On an intangible level, you know your implementation is successful when

- People have heard of BusinessObjects (or the name of your BI project/application).
- The business sees IT as a partner and not as a gatekeeper who holds the key to corporate data.
- Users feel empowered to get to the information they need to do their jobs.
- Business and financial analysts feel they spend less time collecting data and more time analyzing data, using it to make informed decisions.

It's a paradox that a tool that allows quantitative measurement of business goals is seldom measured itself. In some respects, this is true of many IT projects in which the measure of success is simply whether the application is delivered on time and on budget.

As part of the annual OLAP Survey (www.survey.com/olap/), Nigel Pendse has surveyed customers each year to determine what benefits they obtained (or failed to achieve) by deploying a BI solution and whether or not those benefits were quantified. As shown in Figure 2-1, the most proven and quantified benefits are the least tangible: faster, more accurate reporting and better business decisions. The number of companies quantifying these benefits has also increased from 2002 to 2005. The more tangible benefits of saving headcount, increasing revenues, and so on are suspected but not formally measured. The chart in Figure 2-1 uses the following weighting:

Level of Benefit Reported	Weighting
Proven and quantified	10
Proven but not measured	8
Formally claimed but not verified	5
Informally suspected	3
Not achieved	–2
Got worse/more expensive	–6
Don't know	0

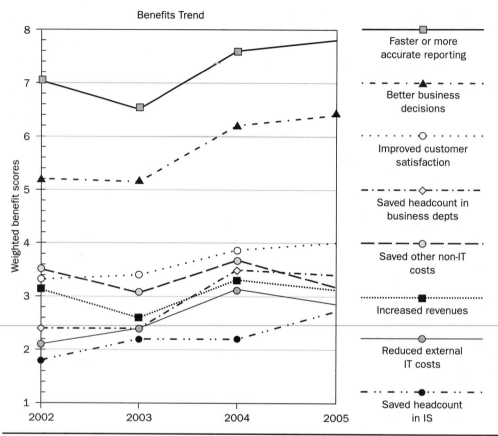

FIGURE 2-1   Benefits trend from The OLAP Surveys by Nigel Pendse. Reprinted with permission.

In achieving IT goals, there are a number of ways to measure success:

- The number of custom OLTP reports eliminated
- Reduction in IT overtime or contract programmers for developing custom reports
- Elimination of duplicate, competing report systems
- Number of users trained versus number of users who log in to BusinessObjects on a regular basis
- Number of queries executed each month
- Number of standard reports accessed

TIP   *Refer to Chapter 16 for approaches to tracking BusinessObjects XI usage.*

In measuring achievement of business goals, the great debate is over how much can be attributed to implementing BusinessObjects XI versus other variables that help achieve the goal. I suspect this is one reason why the OLAP Survey shows it is a benefit that is less often measured. For example, in Table 2-2, one of the company's goals is to improve market share. This can be measured by changes in revenue over time or for particular market segments.

Action to Improve Market Share	Percent Contribution
Increased promotion and modified ad campaign	30%
Improved product line	25%
Better employee training, customer service, reduced turnover	30%
BusinessObjects' access to information to focus marketing efforts on most likely buyers, ensure order compliance, reduce product defect	15%

TABLE 2-2   Estimates for How Much Cost Savings / Revenue Improvement Can Be Attributed to the BusinessObjects Implementation

BusinessObjects provides the *information* to measure progress and to do more targeted marketing. However, *achieving the goal* may require increased promotion, improved product support and innovation, better training of customer service personnel, reduced employee turnover, and so on. Exogenous change may remove a competitor from the market, allowing a company to improve market share without having taken any other action. When several variables contribute toward achieving that goal, then assign a reasonable percentage for how much BusinessObjects contributes toward achieving the goal. In the following table, BusinessObjects contributed 15 percent to increased market share. Is this an exact number? No. Can it ever be precisely measured? No. It is merely one measure of success. Thus if a five-billion-dollar company increases its revenues by 10 percent in an otherwise flat market, you can say BusinessObjects contributed $500,000 toward achieving this goal (10% x $5B x 15% = $500K).

With the more specific goals described earlier, the measure of success may be an improvement over the initial situation.

Some companies that have implemented BusinessObjects can cite individual cases where BusinessObjects directly affected the bottom line. For example, a manufacturing company used BusinessObjects to do a gap analysis of production costs between two similar facilities; they identified $1 million in operating inefficiencies. Without BusinessObjects, they would not have had the data to identify this opportunity. So perhaps you would say BusinessObjects is 50 percent responsible for the cost savings; the remaining 50 percent can be attributed to eliminating the inefficiencies. The beauty of this example is that the company started implementing BusinessObjects as a follow-on to an ERP implementation. The goal was for IT to eliminate custom, disparate reporting systems, and now, BusinessObjects is a strategic asset that has helped the company achieve a number of business goals and measurable business benefit.

Owens and Minor was one of the early adopters of Web Intelligence and has won numerous awards for its use of business intelligence. As a medical supplies distributor, the company's data warehouse contains information on suppliers' delivery performance and hospitals' purchasing volumes. By providing both the hospitals and distributors access to this intermediary data, the company attributes millions of dollars in new business to their BusinessObjects extranet implementation. Their BusinessObjects implementation provides a competitive advantage and holds strategic value. Yet, it too had humble beginnings. According to Don Stoller, the director of information management, the original goal was to improve productivity of the field sellers who needed access to information while visiting clients. Several years after the initial implementation, BusinessObjects not only offers a competitive advantage but is its own revenue stream, as external customers pay for access.

Emergency Medical Associates (EMA) was an early adopter of Web Intelligence, Dashboard Manager, and XI Release 2. They've received extensive media coverage for their innovative use of business intelligence in an industry that lags others in IT innovation. When EMA added several hospitals as new clients, it attributed the advanced business intelligence infrastructure as a major selling point. Their long-term goal is to be able to offer their BI product to other emergency departments as a template.

ROI as a Measure of Success

Return on investment (ROI) is another measure of success and one that is often used to fund the project. While it is fairly easy to measure the cost of the BusinessObjects implementation (the investment portion), it is not easy to measure the return. As you saw in the preceding section, it's debatable how much of a revenue increase you can attribute to BusinessObjects versus other factors. Even when ROI is used to fund a project, companies rarely go back and measure the actual ROI. It is a precise number derived from imprecise inputs. IDC first published a study on the ROI for data warehouses in 1996. IDC determined the average three-year ROI was 401 percent for the 62 projects measured. The Data Warehousing Institute (TDWI) published a study in 2000, showing an ROI of 300 percent. While 47 companies participated in the study, less than a quarter measured ROI. In December 2002, IDC released another ROI study focusing on the value of business analytics, the applications that reside on top of a data warehouse. The average ROI was 431 percent, and the median was 112 percent, with less than a year payback period. Some companies had returns of more than 2000 percent, and IDC reported that the most successful projects were when the business analytics implementation corresponded with business process improvements.

As business intelligence moves from departmental solutions to enterprise applications, some companies have measured the ROI for efforts to standardize on a single BI platform. According to the TDWI survey I co-authored, mentioned previously, only 9 percent of companies surveyed (43 out of 460 respondents) have measured the ROI for standardizing on a BI platform. The estimated average three-year ROI is 60 percent, with an annual savings of $781,724. Blue Cross and Blue Shield of Kansas City, an early adopter of XI Release 2, estimated its ROI for standardizing and migration to the new platform at 150 percent for a three-year period.

With ROI being such an imprecise measure, it's not surprising many companies never go back and calculate it for a business intelligence implementation.

You know your project is successful according to all the other measures of success described in the preceding sections. Nonetheless, it is a number that provides a basis for comparison to other BI implementations and IT initiatives. It also is a measure well understood by finance users, a significant group of BusinessObjects users. In this respect, knowing your approximate ROI is a useful tool in promoting BusinessObjects.

The basic formula for calculating ROI over a three-year period is

ROI = [(NPV Cost Reduction + Revenue Contribution)/Initial Investment] x 100

Net Present Value (NPV) considers the time value of money. In simplistic terms, if the company had one million dollars to deposit in a bank today, next year, assuming a meager five-percent interest, it would be worth $1,050,000. The formula to calculate NPV of a three-year cost or revenue is

$$NPV = F/(1 + r) + F/(1 + r)^2 + F/(1 + r)^3$$

F is the future cash flow from the cost reductions and revenue contributions. r is the discount rate for your company. Five percent may be the interest a bank is willing to pay, but companies will have a different rate that takes into account the expected return for other investments and opportunity costs from investing in BusinessObjects versus other capital projects.

To take the earlier example of improved market share (Table 2-2), assume

- $500,000 revenue contribution each year
- $400,000 annual savings by eliminating two custom report programmers @ 2 x 2,000 hours x $100 an hour
- 10 percent discount rate
- $1 million initial investment in hardware, software, training, and consulting to implement BusinessObjects

The projected ROI for a three-year period is

$$223\% = \left[\frac{\frac{400,000 + 500,000}{1.10} + \frac{400,000 + 500,000}{1.10^2} + \frac{400,000 + 500,000}{1.10^3}}{1,000,000} \right] \times 100$$

For additional information on evaluating the ROI for your implementation, Jonathan Wu, a principal of Knightsbridge Solutions LLC, teaches a course for TDWI on measuring the value of your BI implementation. You can access his ROI calculator and white paper at www.knightsbridge.com/news/white.php.

Summary

You may have multiple goals in deploying BusinessObjects XI. These goals change over time as your use of information and your BI deployment matures. Recognize that the goals of IT and business users may sometimes conflict. When IT and the business partner together and a BI deployment is aligned with the business objectives, then expect to achieve greater success. Measuring the benefits of your implementation is useful for project funding and promoting the BI application. In absence of these measurements, look for a number of other indicators that show progress toward achieving these goals.

Understanding Your Users

With any BI deployment, there are different groups of users, all with distinct information and functional needs. The ways they want to access BusinessObjects XI will also vary. One group of users may be logged in to InfoView 90 percent of the workday and will actively ask for more data, more resources, faster query time, and more functionality. Another group may never directly log in to InfoView yet will make decisions from data delivered through BusinessObjects XI, whether via a pushed e-mail report, a spreadsheet populated from Live Office, or data quoted by an analyst. Both groups of users are your customers, yet they will have very different needs that affect how you develop, promote, and deploy the various products. Using the marketing concept of customer segmentation will help you identify your user groups, understand their different needs, and develop a better deployment strategy. Chapter 3 defines possible user segments, and Chapter 4 describes what you customize per segment.

What Is Segmentation?

Segmentation is a way of looking at one large user base—for example, all employees in a company—and dividing it into smaller groups. Each segment, or smaller group, has similar characteristics, needs, or benefits. In different chapters in this book, I refer to two common segments: report authors and information consumers. Your company may have more than these two segments. Segmentation provides you a way of better understanding your users and why their requirements are different. It will help you prioritize target user groups and provide the appropriate information and functionality to achieve the highest business value. As you define different segments, you will want to tailor your product offering, promotion, implementation schedule, and training for each segment. You also may use the segments to define groups and permissions in the Central Management Console, which replaces Supervisor (see Chapter 13). Following are some characteristics that will help you segment potential BusinessObjects XI users.

Computer Literacy Level   Potential BI users who have worked with personal computers and the Internet since their inception will greet BusinessObjects XI differently than those who did not. Users who primarily surf the Web but who are not proficient with spreadsheets and other Windows-based programs fall somewhere in the middle. Computer literacy today is much higher than in the early 1990s, when Business Objects and business intelligence as an industry first emerged. Information sharing is much more prevalent, yet boundaries still exist and many employees still greet computers with a degree of trepidation. Recognize that such users still may need information to do their jobs, yet they may not see BusinessObjects XI as their primary resource. These users still may request scheduled, printed reports or, in the absence of such automation, may rely on gut-feel decision-making.

Primary vs. Secondary   Some users log in to InfoView to develop their own reports, refresh queries, and interactively analyze the data. These are *primary* users whom you will grant access to in the CMC.

However, you will also have a *secondary* segment of users who consume the information provided by report authors and analysts. These secondary users may never log directly in to BusinessObjects XI; in fact, they may not even know BusinessObjects XI exists (unless you do some proactive promotion, covered in Chapter 4). They know only that they get a report via e-mail or a corporate intranet. For all they know, the data came directly out of one ERP screen. It will be hard for you to estimate the size of this "secondary" user segment, but in many instances, some of your most important customers are in this secondary user segment. Let's say the VP of Marketing receives BusinessObjects-generated PDF files via e-mail on a regular basis. These standard reports are critical for the VP. The VP's administrative assistant is the one who developed the initial reports and scheduled them via InfoView. The assistant makes sure the reports are generated and delivered as needed. Meanwhile, as more users access the system, the Job Server is getting overloaded. Some reports run much later than requested; some fail to execute. The primary user, the administrative assistant, may be the one to shout, but it is the secondary user, the VP of Marketing, that can most likely approve funding for an additional server. Also, it is this secondary customer—who has never logged directly in to InfoView—who will most likely see the business potential of products you have not yet implemented, such as Dashboard Manager or Enterprise Performance Manager.

Job Level   A user's job level will affect the breadth of data the user wants to access (number of reports and universes) and the level of detail. Executive-level jobs may need a broad set of data but without a lot of detail. Analyzing the data is a minor part of these jobs, so these may be the people for whom you want to develop a dashboard with key performance indicators, whether a My InfoView page or an interactive dashboard via Dashboard Manager. Mid-level jobs may still need a broad set of data but with more detail. The combination of broad data requirements and more detailed data may make it hard to deliver only dashboards. They may need access to multiple InfoView folders, multiple documents, and ad hoc access. Entry-level accounts payable clerks or customer service representatives may want to see only very detailed data. As their information requirements are narrow, these users may need only a few standard reports with interactive prompts; they may access BusinessObjects XI often, constantly refreshing a document for a particular account, customer, date range, and so on.

Job Function   You also can segment users according to job function. Supply chain users will all have similar information needs, which will be different from the information needs of users in the finance department. Functional requirements also may vary by function: consider how many spreadsheet power users there are in any finance department. This group of users then may not care about dashboards as much as they care about spreadsheet integration. Marketing personnel will have different information requirements, and with respect to functionality, they may ask for things such as predictive analysis that other groups have not requested. Administrative assistants may not be decision-makers, but in many companies, their exceptional computer literacy and multitasking skills have led them to become expert users of Web Intelligence.

In many companies, certain job functions also have varying degrees of influence and power. Ideally, the degree of influence would be commensurate with the degree of value added to the company, but that's not always the case. The challenge for you as a BusinessObjects project manager or administrator is to

- Recognize that the different functions will have different requirements, thus demanding certain modules and capabilities more than other groups
- Prioritize fulfillment of those requirements

Degree of Analytic Job Content   Some jobs require a significant amount of data analysis. The analytic component also may relate to either the job level or the job function, or sometimes to both. For example, financial analysts may be fairly senior in a business; these jobs have a high analytic component. These are the number crunchers who will pound the system. They understand the different data nuances and even the potential data sources. It's easy to assume that these people are your only users, since they may have solutions implemented first, complain loudest when something is wrong, live and die by access to information, and control the information flow to secondary users. This may in fact be you! With all your demands for access to information, the company rewarded you with being a universe designer, report author, or BusinessObjects XI subject matter expert. Congratulations! Remember, though, that not everyone can spend all day collecting, manipulating, and exploring data. Some users need access to standard reports simply to know what is going on. They log in to InfoView for ten minutes a day (or week) just to make sure the business is running smoothly . . . or to find out if there is enough inventory to fulfill an order . . . or to identify customers with outstanding invoices. When the information indicates a problem area, it may not be their job to sift through the data to identify the underlying cause. Instead, they may call the business or financial analyst to figure out why there is a problem.

In BI, we seem to have a tendency to want all end users to become experts. It's a profound difference to *empower* a user—to provide them with easy tools to access and explore information when they need to—and an altogether different scenario to assume accessing and analyzing data is their primary job.

Users whose job content requires a fair bit of data analysis often demand more features and functions. Do not let their demands fool you into thinking all your users need these advanced capabilities. Jobs with a high analytic content may use more capabilities such as Live Office, report variables, multiple data providers, and ad hoc queries; on the other hand, users with jobs with minimal analytic content may only refresh a standard report on a periodic basis. At most, they might evolve to Web Intelligence Interactive or Intelligent Question users.

ERP or Source System Use   Some of your users may also enter data into the transaction or ERP system. Regardless whether your company uses BusinessObjects XI directly against the transaction system or an ERP-populated data warehouse, these users will be more familiar with the precise meanings of individual objects. At the same time, dimensional groupings and hierarchies that don't exist in the source system may be a completely new concept. These users may need additional explanation as to why there is a data warehouse and how the data has been transformed.

Level of Data Literacy   Data literacy and computer literacy are two entirely different things. I may be computer literate, but if you ask me to decipher the meaning of baseball statistics, I'm clueless (RBIs maybe, but ERA and SO, forget it!); I don't know the data. So too with corporate data. Source system users and users whose jobs have a high analytic content may understand the data well and have a high level of data literacy. Certain users may understand the finer points of "price." Is it list price, average selling price, price net of returns? However, you cannot assume that users with high levels of data literacy have equally high computer literacy. A transaction system user may know the data but be comfortable entering data only by following the exact same screens every time. Change the user interface and such users are lost.

An often-minimized part of a BusinessObjects implementation is regarding training users on the data. You can train users where to click to build certain queries, but training them to interpret the data and simply to know what the data is and means requires separate attention. The context panel in Web Intelligence XI Release 2 can go a long way to helping with data literacy. Object descriptions are finally displayed to report consumers, not just to report authors. This assumes that the universe designer has populated the object descriptions. If you are a long-time BusinessObjects user and never bothered to complete this part of the universe before, this latest release makes it well worth the effort. The Encyclopedia also can help users understand what the data elements mean and which reports are most appropriate for a given decision-making process.

Level of Spreadsheet Usage   Spreadsheet users deserve their own segment and, thus, sometimes their own BI interface. They are loyal to the spreadsheet and think everything should be delivered in a spreadsheet. I used to underestimate the importance of this but was cured of my oversight in the early 1990s. After spending months developing a DSS system for a new transaction system, I waited with bated breath finally to train the users. The users balked at these inflexible, ugly mainframe-based reports and asked, "Why do we need these reports? Just dump all the data into Excel." Indeed!

Fortunately, Business Objects has a couple of solutions for such users. First introduced in BusinessObjects Version 6.0, users can save a report directly to Excel; the save nicely preserves the charts, formatting, and breaks. Further, with the integrated scheduling in XI, you can schedule a report to be automatically exported to an Excel file format. Finally, Live Office allows users to execute queries directly from a spreadsheet. Links to the Web Intelligence or Crystal Reports documents are maintained in the spreadsheet, allowing users to access new data in real time.

There are a number of challenges with BI and spreadsheet integration. Volume of data is one thing; multiple versions of the truth when the data is manipulated locally is another. So do consider why users want the spreadsheet integration at all. For a discussion of valid and less valid reasons, see BIScorecard.com, Spreadsheet Integration Criteria. Regardless of such challenges, do recognize this user segment and develop a strategy to meet their distinct needs while simultaneously ensuring that the spreadsheets do not get out of hand and become mini–data marts.

Amount of Travel   Certain job types require more travel than others. Some users may access the system only from their desktop or a corporate browser; users who travel may want access via a BlackBerry or a notebook computer. They may want information broadcast to them or may want to work in offline mode, exploring previously refreshed queries and drilling in local microcubes.

With a greater number of reports being authored in Web Intelligence, you must consider the disconnected aspect of users who travel frequently. There are a number of solutions to address these users' needs. Perhaps a PDF document or spreadsheet is sufficient. Or they may want to drill and sort offline via a Desktop Intelligence document. Longer-term, the vendor plans to provide a Web Intelligence viewer for this kind of disconnected access.

Implementation Phase   As you ramp up your BusinessObjects XI implementation, you will offer different users access to the system at different points in time. As described in Chapter 4, many tasks, including levels of communication, content, resource planning, and so on, will be tailored according to different user groups and their implementation phase.

Internal vs. External Users   Consider the different needs of employees of the company and customers that you may provide information to via an extranet. Internal employees may be allowed to access whatever software module you have licensed, whereas external customers often will have more restrictions on content and functionality. External users have different requirements from your internal users. Authentication in large extranets can be one challenge if you will have thousands of potential extranet users. Do they all need a unique login, or will you use a guest login? If you allow certain customers to create new queries, their own security policies may not allow applets to cross firewalls, thus requiring the use of the HTML interface. Internal employees may have access to more data, whereas external users will only be allowed to see their data. For these users, you may use the row restrictions and object security levels in Designer.

Others Who Affect Implementation Efforts

In addition to your target users (either primary or secondary), you need to be aware of gatekeepers, influencers, and deciders (Figure 3-1). These people may or may not be eventual BusinessObjects XI users, but they do affect project funding and your implementation efforts. For each type of stakeholder, I have provided an archetype. The individual job titles and dynamics will vary company to company. The important thing is to recognize that it is more than just the users that affect the success of your implementation and whose needs you must consider.

Gatekeepers

Gatekeepers control access to potential data sources, existing reports, or even other users. Gatekeepers can either help your implementation be a wild success or sabotage your efforts. Let's assume you want to use BusinessObjects XI to access a central data warehouse. IT had a vision of the central data warehouse being used to populate dependent data marts. Unfortunately, due to budget constraints, lack of understanding, and political issues, your individual business unit or function never built a dependent data mart. The central data warehouse owner/project manager is a gatekeeper. The gatekeeper will either grant you ad hoc access, knowing you will only complain about the lousy response time (that's why they wanted you to sponsor a data mart!), or do everything to impede the BusinessObjects implementation. Thus, the infighting begins. Ideally, the two stakeholders work together to

- Implement BusinessObjects XI in a controlled way.
- Understand usage to educate users/sponsors on the value of BI.
- Analyze access patterns and problems to fund and develop the dependent data mart.

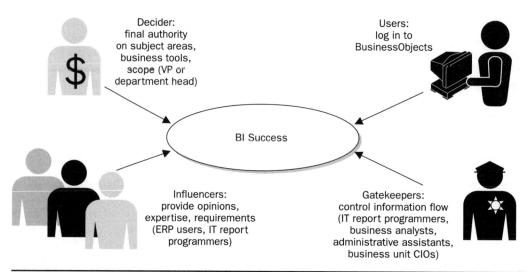

FIGURE 3-1   Many people besides direct users affect the success of a BusinessObjects implementation.

The administrative assistant discussed in the preceding major section in connection with primary versus secondary status can also be a gatekeeper. As the BusinessObjects XI expert, you want to better understand the information flow and business value of the reports the assistant schedules on a regular basis. A conversation with the VP of Marketing would be invaluable. The assistant sees no need for such a meeting (nor does the VP of Marketing, since the VP has never even heard of BusinessObjects XI), as the assistant can tell you everything you want to know about how the department uses the tool anyway. At this point, you can rely exclusively on the feedback the assistant gives you, or you can ask the assistant for help by having a joint conversation with both the primary and secondary users. To make the BusinessObjects XI implementation more successful,

- Understand what the gatekeepers want.
- Recognize their efforts and role in the business intelligence process; look for ways to involve them or make them part of the implementation team.
- Identify the mutually exclusive goals.
- Identify the common goals.
- Build allegiances with the gatekeepers so that they work with you, not against you.
- Understand if there are any job protection issues involved here.

Influencers

Influencers are another set of people that affect how well your implementation proceeds. Influencers provide input to your users about how good the solution is, whether it will really be useful, and how it is being deployed. The influencers often have some role in an existing reporting process and may have a vested interest in keeping the old reporting process running. They may be source system report programmers (why do we need a BI tool when we can hand-code everything?), source system experts (why do we need a data warehouse, anyway?), business analysts who have developed departmental databases, or power users. *Positive* influencers expedite your implementation and provide a lot of positive word-of-mouth promotion. *Negative* influencers impede your efforts by spreading fear and doubt.

Unfortunately, you may encounter a degree of job protection or "not invented here" syndrome with negative influencers. These are the hurdles to overcome. If a business analyst has spent an inordinate amount of time creating queries to populate departmental databases and spreadsheets, then the BusinessObjects XI implementation will be perceived as a threat. It renders their data sources obsolete. Negative influencers may slow your implementation by seeding your new users with doubt by saying, "Look how slow it is! The data is wrong!" For this reason, you need influencers on your side. If they know the data requirements, then get them to have a stake in BusinessObjects XI's success. While they may be proud of the departmental system they created, they will know too well the manual processes and reconciliation time they go through to keep the data current and accurate. If they cannot be directly part of the project team, ensure they are a focal point for implementation or a designated BusinessObjects expert.

Many companies have more than one BI tool for a variety of reasons: departmental autonomy to buy their own BI solution, merger and acquisition, best of breed capabilities in several tools, to name a few. Of all the applications IT must deliver, BI standardization is the most contentious (next to spreadsheets, that is). If you are charged with reducing the number of different BI tools and converting users to the corporate standard of BusinessObjects XI, then the competing BI tool experts will be powerful influencers. They will be the first to spot how their tool is better and argue for standardizing on their BI tool. In some cases, competing BI tools may have better functionality in specific areas, so give them credit and save your breath. If you have followed an objective selection process, you should be able to articulate how the standard was selected and by what criteria BusinessObjects XI was the best fit for your company. You may have to do this multiple times before you gain acceptance. If the decision to implement BusinessObjects XI as a corporate standard was autocratic, blame the decision-maker and march onward. The bottom line is that the measure of success is not who agrees with the decision, but rather, that the standard is adopted and how well you use it to achieve a measurable business benefit.

Deciders

Deciders are the final decision-makers. A decider may be a project sponsor or an end user or both. Deciders are in a position of authority and can cast the final vote on funding the project, establishing an implementation strategy, or approving the initial set of modules to deploy. In the preceding examples, the decider could be

- The CIO who overrules the central data warehouse project manager and allows individual business units to proceed with their own implementation efforts of certain modules, regardless of what can be supported via a BI competency center

- The VP of Marketing who requires all marketing staff to at least be report consumers who log in to the InfoView portal to retrieve their own reports, while the administrative assistant and business analyst are designated as the report authors

- The CFO who commits to phasing out the departmental spreadsheets/databases after an agreed-upon period of running BusinessObjects XI reports in parallel

Pre–business intelligence, I focused on work group computing tools. A new business unit VP was looking to improve productivity and computer literacy. In the late 1980s, this was the first time some people had ever seen a PC. Managers would scribble messages onto pieces of paper that secretaries typed and sent as e-mails. The secretaries printed incoming e-mails and manually distributed them. The new VP instructed managers to do their own e-mails and forbade the secretaries to type or print them anymore. People were dismayed and aggravated (hard to imagine today, with e-mail being so commonplace). At the time, though, his decisions were considered radical, and many wondered if it was a waste of time to expect mid-management to be "typists." After everyone got over the shock of this radical change, productivity and computer literacy improved, and this same business unit eventually became an early adopter of business intelligence tools. I'd like to think that the Internet has drastically boosted everyone's enthusiasm for BI tools and direct access to information, but there are still so many information boundaries in corporations. In those cases where users, gatekeepers, and influencers are resistant to business intelligence, it helps to have a strong *decider* to champion your implementation efforts.

When to Analyze Segments

Ideally, the market segments should be identified early in the development process. As you will see in Chapter 4, market segments help you tailor deployment choices. Failure to agree on the target users or segment can quickly derail your project. As an example, a mid-sized maintenance supply company started out with a very clear scope: to enable senior marketing people to track monthly gross margin and sales by product, time, and region. They wanted a highly graphical tool with a dashboard. They selected a leading OLAP database and visualization tool, at the time a good decision for this user segment. At some point, field sellers voiced their information requirements. Field sellers needed a different level of detail than the senior marketing people, requiring daily sales figures down to the customer and order number. They didn't want graphics; they needed the detail numbers in a tabular report. Field sellers are a different user segment than senior marketing people, with different needs. Unfortunately, the scope of this project was not well managed. The right tools were used for the wrong applications and user segments. Neither user segment was satisfied with the end product. Although the project had strong business sponsorship and was driven by business goals, it failed because the target user group was not well understood.

If the market segments had been clearly defined at the project scoping stage, the project manager would have recognized the diverse needs and could have either declared the requirements out of scope or more appropriately matched the solution with each user segment.

Project Roles

To deliver BI functionality, the project team should include both IT and business personnel. As discussed in Chapter 1, a business intelligence project never ends and your company's ability to leverage it to a competitive advantage is evolutionary. Therefore, many of these roles will continue beyond the project completion to provide ongoing support. You may decide to roll some of the responsibilities into a BI competency center, or conversely, you may staff certain project phases with people who are part of an existing BI competency center.

- **Sponsor**   When business goals drive the implementation, the sponsor is usually from the business. It may be the CFO if you are trying to measure financial performance, the VP of Marketing if you are trying to improve customer penetration and retention, the VP of Supply Chain if you are trying to improve order fulfillment and reduce inventory costs, and so on. If the goals of your implementation are IT-related (see Chapter 2), then the sponsor may be a senior person in the IT organization, such as the CIO, ERP manager, or data warehouse manager. The sponsor provides the funding for the project and resolves any scope issues the project team cannot resolve themselves.

- **Program manager**   The program manager ensures that BusinessObjects XI is deployed consistently across multiple projects and applications. The program manager sets the priorities for projects that vie for the same resources.

- **Project manager**   The project manager controls the budget, resources, and time to implement BusinessObjects. The project manager ensures that the deliverables are within the agreed-upon scope of the project and that the project stays focused on the intended goals.

- **Security administrator**   A security administrator defines users to the CMC or to groups in the directory server and grants access to the BusinessObjects XI modules, universes, and folders. The security function can be centralized or decentralized to allow one security administrator for each department or function. The security administrator must understand the groups, permissions, and data sources, as well as staying informed about personnel changes to revoke or add access when employees change departments. Within the CMC, you can create groups that have permissions to access certain interfaces and capabilities; these groups and permissions should correspond to the different user segments you've identified.

- **Universe designer**   The universe designer provides the business view to the relational data in a transaction system or a data warehouse. The designer must understand SQL from a query and analysis viewpoint, database performance issues, and business requirements. It can be a challenge to find one person with these diverse skill sets. Some companies will train business analysts or power users in the more technical skills, finding this an easier approach than trying to teach an IT developer the business skills. The technical aspects required to build a universe sometimes leads a DBA to become the universe designer. The role of universe designer can also be split between two people, one who physically develops the universe and another who ensures the universe fulfills the business requirements. With larger deployments, there may be several designers across the organization, one for each business unit or function. This division has been hotly debated by customers and consultants alike. Who should own universe development—central IT or individual business units? It's clear to me that central IT should own the BusinessObjects Enterprise Server infrastructure. At the other end of the spectrum, it's clear to me that the business should own the report development (assuming that IT provides some starter templates). The universe lies squarely in the middle. In an ideal deployment and organization in which IT and the business are closely aligned and IT is keenly focused on helping the business accomplish its goals, IT should develop the universes, with the business defining the requirements and having ultimate say over what goes in a universe and what does not. Where this centralization of the universe fails is when the universe does not meet the business requirements. When the universe doesn't fulfill the business requirements, it forces the users to build more report formulas, create increasingly complex reports with multiple data providers, or in the end, model their own solutions in spreadsheets and departmental databases. If the universe is monolithic and inflexible, then from a company point of view, let the business build their own universe, ideally following agreed-upon design principles, utilizing shared dimensions via linked universes (see Chapter 15). In either circumstance, it's important to have an "ultimate" designer or quality assurance process to ensure the universes are deployed consistently (see Chapter 16). The design principles and quality assurance process belong in the BI competency center, as this role continues beyond implementation.

- **Report author/pilot user** A report author is typically a power user who both understands the data and is computer literate. Report authors may be business analysts who require ad hoc access to information or who previously created and maintained departmental data sources. They also may be professional developers who previously coded reports. Be careful to manage this, though: the goal is not to code complex reports, but rather, to leverage the common business definitions and power built into the universe. Administrative assistants who are computer literate and who provide printed reports or compiled spreadsheets may also become report authors. When first deploying a new universe, pilot the universe with report authors. Only a minority of total users will be report authors.

- **Information consumers** Information consumers, also called report readers and report recipients, access fixed reports that may include prompts to filter the data. Report authors may prepare and distribute reports to readers via e-mail, InfoView, printouts, and so on. Information consumers may not have a high degree of computer or data literacy, or the job type may have minimal information requirements. With Web Intelligence interactive, these report readers can also dynamically sort, filter, and drill within a predefined report. While I wholeheartedly believe that all users should *not* evolve into report authors, I do wholeheartedly hope that the majority of information consumers *will* evolve to interactive report consumers. With the vendor's current licensing model, this evolution does have an implication on product licensing and server platform.

- **BusinessObjects XI expert** BusinessObjects XI experts know the end-user tool sets and the different modules available, but they do not necessarily understand the data. They are good with software and technology. Report authors may become BusinessObjects XI experts as they work more with the tool. Such experts should be part of an ongoing BI competency center.

- **Data expert** A data expert may be a business analyst, data modeler, or source system expert who knows where the data comes from, the quality of the data, and its different meanings and may be the champion for a metadata repository. The data expert may not necessarily use BusinessObjects but can help resolve data discrepancies that are discovered when users start analyzing it with BusinessObjects. A data modeler designs the underlying star or snowflake schema in a data warehouse or data mart. That person can provide expertise on advanced business calculations and certain universe components such as aliases, shortcut joins, how to use derived tables, and so on. When you introduce aggregate awareness into the universe, the data modeler provides the dimensions by which to aggregate.

- **Database administrator (DBA)**   A DBA may be the universe designer or may review the universe for optimal SQL. DBAs resolve query performance problems, build aggregate tables, or correct password synchronization problems between different data sources. The DBA will also help decide the technical deployment of the BusinessObjects Enterprise repository.

- **Administrator or architect**   You may have a BusinessObjects Enterprise administrator who installs and maintains the software applications (Web Intelligence, Crystal Reports, Desktop Intelligence, Dashboard Manager, and so on). In small deployments, the BusinessObjects Enterprise administrator and the designer are often one and the same. In larger deployments, there may be multiple administrators. Whereas universe designers require a business background and SQL skills, administrators and architects require more technical skills and may be systems engineers. In addition to software issues, the administrator deals with server performance and load balancing. They will decide when to deploy BusinessObjects Enterprise in a distributed environment, which processes to run on dedicated servers, and how to provide failover protection.

- **Trainer**   The BusinessObjects XI trainer knows both the software and the data to a degree. Often, two people may provide the training to cover these two different aspects. Internal BusinessObjects XI experts may train end users, or they may use a Business Objects training partner.

- **Communication/marketing specialist**   This person provides expertise on effective ways to communicate project plans, deliverables, and goals to the different user segments. He or she may write or review articles for company newsletters, coordinate internal user conferences, design logos used in project gifts or application screens, and help ensure that key messages are stated in terms of business benefits rather than technical features.

Summary

Segmentation is a way of grouping your users according to their needs and skill sets. These groupings will help you tailor deliverables and messages. Certain user groups will want only standard reports on an intermittent basis; others will need the flexibility of ad hoc access on a daily basis. Not all users will greet BusinessObjects XI with enthusiasm. Understanding these users' roles and objectives can help you minimize the users' disruption to your implementation efforts and enlist them as advocates to ensure a more successful deployment.

Marketing BusinessObjects XI

In looking at this chapter title, you might respond, "Marketing BusinessObjects XI? That's something the vendor does! Nothing to do with my implementation." Yet it's got everything to do with your implementation and is the one technique that will help you boost usage, user satisfaction, and ROI with little to no cash investment. It does, however, require an investment in attitude and in making sure a marketing approach gets incorporated into your project plan.

Many BI project managers assume they do not need to market BusinessObjects XI. It's easy to assume the tool should sell itself, especially if you are implementing it in response to users' requests. Keep in mind, though, that only a handful of users may have specifically requested BusinessObjects XI and been involved in a BI tool selection or standardization. For all the other users, you need a strategy of defining what you will deliver and how you will communicate those deliverables to your different user segments.

Marketing can be an uncomfortable concept for many IT people, so while this chapter will introduce you to some key marketing concepts, be sure to enlist help from your company's internal marketing or public relations department.

When to Develop a Marketing Plan

It is surprising to me (and perhaps to you as well) that one of the most popular courses I teach for The Data Warehouse Institute (TDWI) is on marketing the BI application. Amid so many other technical subjects, a soft skills course still garners high attendance. Also, when I tell people I teach a course on marketing the data warehouse, they often laugh and say, "What's to teach? Marketing means just say yes." Ever the gullible consumer, I respond with, "That's selling!" Perhaps it's a minor distinction. The essence of marketing is first and foremost *understanding* what users want and only then *developing* what they want. This sounds like the mantra of many IT organizations who want to be more aligned with the business. A marketing plan can give you the techniques to better accomplish this dialogue and level of understanding. At a minimum, a marketing plan will help you develop a communication strategy and manage user expectations.

Therefore, you want to draft a market plan early in the project, often before project funding. A marketing plan will help you articulate what you intend to deliver and why. As discussed under "Product" in this chapter, a marketing approach ensures you get used to describing what you deliver in terms of the *benefits,* not the *features.* This difference in emphasis makes the funding and implementation process easier. What would your project sponsors rather invest in?

- **Feature**   A BI tool with synchronized multiple data providers that leverages a Java application server
- **Benefit**   A BI tool that will help improve profitability

As you architect the BusinessObjects XI deployment and develop the various components such as universes, reports, and dashboards, update the marketing plan to reflect changes in functionality. As you work with users to define requirements and preview the functionality, you can gauge which elements of the plan are effective.

Elements of a BI Marketing Plan

A BI marketing plan consists of the following elements:

- **Situation analysis**   Covers your current situation; offers competitive analysis; and includes a strengths, weaknesses, opportunities, and threats (SWOT) analysis.
- **Marketing mix**   Involves the four *P*s of marketing: product, price, promotion, and place.
- **Groups of users**   Defines your BI customer segments. Divide your users into different groups as described in Chapter 3. Once you have determined your user segments, tailor the marketing mix (product, promotion, price, and place) to each segment.
- **Objectives**   Includes how you will measure your marketing and project effectiveness. Some of this may involve measurement of the goals described in Chapter 2, or it may include the marketing objectives: number of users trained, number of promotional efforts, and so on.

Situation Analysis

What is the current situation in your company? Have you just begun implementing BusinessObjects, or has it been available for a while but your implementation efforts have stalled? Are you trying to standardize on BusinessObjects XI, although you have multiple BI tools? If you have only just begun to implement BusinessObjects XI, then the current situation may include these concerns:

- How users currently access information (Is information contained only in the transaction system, or have departments created their own spreadsheets and databases?)
- How information is shared and distributed throughout the organization
- If you develop custom reports, the number of existing reports and the time backlog to fulfill new requests
- Attitudes toward the existing information flows (Are users frustrated, or do they think it's generally okay?)

If BusinessObjects has been used in the company for a while, the current situation addresses

- What data sources are available and which universes are in use
- How much users create their own reports or the degree to which standard reports have been used
- Typical query response time
- System availability
- Number of defined, trained, and active users
- Product architecture and end-user tools to access the data (Desktop Intelligence or BusinessObjects classic, Crystal Reports, InfoView, Web Intelligence, Dashboard Manager, and so on)
- How business-oriented is the universe versus too much intelligence built into individual reports
- The degree to which the universe and standard reports can answer common business questions versus users having to create user-defined objects and report variables
- User satisfaction with the current situation

Even if BusinessObjects XI is the only BI tool in your company, it faces competition. Your job is to identify and understand the competition to articulate why and in what circumstances BusinessObjects XI is a better solution. Recall from Chapter 1 the history of business intelligence. You are trying to change years of decision-making processes within a short time frame. Resistance to change is an automatic barrier. Users may be accustomed to accessing information via paper-based reports, hand-delivered to their desk. When information is difficult to get to, gut-feel decision-making is the competition. If you are deploying BusinessObjects XI against a data warehouse, then the ERP or transaction system may be the competition. If you are trying to get decision-makers to retrieve their own reports or to access key indicators via a dashboard, the competition is the phone call to a business analyst or to an assistant who can print the reports for them.

A SWOT analysis (strengths, weaknesses, opportunities, and threats) is an effective tool in evaluating the current situation in terms of BusinessObjects XI's internal competition. It is also a necessary first step in determining what product capabilities you can and should deliver and what benefits you will emphasize in promotions. Tables 4-1 and 4-2 give two sample SWOT analyses. The first one is for a young data warehouse deployment in which BusinessObjects is not the only BI tool. The second one is for a mature BusinessObjects deployment that has stalled.

The purpose of the situation analysis is to understand where you are today so that you can identify opportunities for improvement over the current situation and/or the competitive information sources. In both SWOT analyses, slow queries are a weakness that has caused a number of threats. Slow queries can be a major barrier for a successful implementation and are often identified as a reason for low BI adoption.

With the ever greater immediacy the Internet provides, users want answers to business questions instantaneously, at the speed of thought. Explanations regarding indexes or query complexity are deemed irrelevant. The fact that you are providing them with more flexibility than did previous information systems is quickly forgotten.

SWOT	Analysis
Strengths	• Universes are small and focused, with access to global data. • Business definitions are consistent. • Self-serve access is available.
Weaknesses	• Queries are slow. • New terminology from a recent ERP implementation is confusing to users; universes contain no bridge to old transaction system terminology. • Standard reports are unavailable. The budget and IT mandate was to build the universe; users must develop their own reports. While some may have done so, they are not shared in a consistent way, so nobody knows about them. • The data warehouse is updated weekly; users want daily updates.
Opportunities	• Create summary tables in data warehouse; include aggregate awareness in universe design to improve query performance. • Enable scheduling for slow queries. • Update objects' descriptions and modify training materials to bridge new and old terminology. • Ensure standard user reports are available via public folders in InfoView. • Evaluate target user group, business goals for daily updates.
Threats	• To avoid slow response time, the department assistant prints reports and manually distributes them. • Another department is implementing a MOLAP server for faster queries, with a different BI tool as the front end.

TABLE 4-1   SWOT Analysis for New Implementation

While it is true that the majority of response time issues in a BI deployment can be blamed on the data warehouse and not specifically on BusinessObjects XI, failure to fix these problems directly affects the success of BusinessObjects XI. Users will blame the tool they see, not the technology behind the scenes. Further, while it is up to the DBA to ensure the database is well tuned with efficient indexes and summary tables, it is up to the universe designer to leverage them. Ensure universe objects frequently used in conditions do not contain advanced SQL commands that cause the index to be bypassed. Report authors must ensure standard reports use condition objects from indexed fields. When you can't improve the data source performance, then use other deployment methods to bypass the problem. Use the integrated scheduling capabilities in XI to cache and/or distribute reports. Based on the SWOT analysis in Table 4-2, implementing a MOLAP database may be a good approach for response time issues as well as complex calculations. Some companies have reported drastic performance improvements with a relatively new product, HyperRoll.

SWOT	Analysis
Strengths	• Complete data with three years of history is available. • A number of initial ETL problems have finally been resolved. • There are multiple subject areas.
Weaknesses	• Queries are slow. • The large universe is unwieldy for users to navigate. Users inadvertently create incorrect queries when they use the wrong objects.
Opportunities	• Evaluate universe joins to improve query response time. • Evaluate the indexing strategy in data warehouse for most frequently used access paths. • Promote resolution of ETL problems and improved data quality. • Create smaller, more targeted universes.
Threats	• Since users perceive the data warehouse is always wrong, custom reports continue to be built against the ERP. • To avoid slow response time and the unwieldy universe, business units extract data into multiple MS Access databases and create custom dashboards and front ends.

TABLE 4-2   SWOT Analysis for a Mature but Stalled Deployment

In Table 4-2, one of the identified weaknesses was a large, unwieldy universe. In this real-world example, even IT professionals struggled to know which object to use when. Once the deployment team developed a more targeted universe, offered some standard reports, and promoted the resolutions and enhancements, usage increased significantly within a short period.

Marketing Mix: The Four *P*s

Marketing mix is a set of interdependent tools for increasing BusinessObjects XI usage and the impact it has within your company. If you speak to one of your internal marketing experts, he or she may give you a couple more *P*s to add to the mix, but for business intelligence the most important *P*s are product, price, promotion, and place.

Product

If you think the choice of product is predetermined, think again! First, consider that the BusinessObjects XI platform has multiple user interfaces, each targeted at a different user group requiring slightly different capabilities. The delineation for when to use a given product is not an absolute. Different user groups may overlap in requirements and therefore in product usage. Table 4-3 lists some of the BusinessObjects XI modules and the corresponding user group.

Product	Primary User Group
Crystal Reports	IT developers to design pixel-perfect reports that may need to be bursted to multiple recipients or embedded within an application
Web Intelligence	Business authors to design shared reports or ad hoc queries and analyses
Intelligent Question	Executives who want fast answers to common business questions
Desktop Intelligence	Power users who want to design more complex reports for disconnected access
Live Office	Power users who prefer the Excel interface
Dashboard Manager	Executives and managers who want an overview of key metrics
InfoView only	Information consumers who want to view and refresh standard reports but who don't need to build their own. Reports can include those built in Crystal Reports, Web Intelligence, Desktop Intelligence
Performance Manager	Managers who wish to set and manage goals and understand cause and effect of performance indicators.

TABLE 4-3   Match the Product Module with the Needs of the User Group

Also, realize that in some circles and with some user segments, these individual product names may have meaning and recognition. Many users, however, may have never heard of them. In this respect, you will have to repeat, within your own organization, all the selling Business Objects, the company, had to go through to persuade you to buy their tool set.

As you do so, focus as much as possible on the *benefits* your implementation will deliver, not the technical *features* of the products. Consider some of the products you buy as a consumer. For example, Disney World emphasizes the magic and memories (the benefits), not the number of rides and attractions (the features). Particularly with business intelligence, a number of technical features will have little meaning to users, yet clearly, IT professionals are comfortable focusing on features. Restating the features in terms of the benefits is one of the hardest language barriers for the project team to overcome. Table 4-4 highlights some features that are better described to users in terms of the benefits they provide.

In a few instances, the feature and related benefit will be clear; but these instances are in the minority. For example, if you emphasize the ability to create graphs, spreadsheet users who have used graphs in their analysis will recognize that graphs provide the benefit of visual analysis and a faster ability to spot trends, problems, and opportunities. When you buy a car, you know that four-wheel or front-wheel drive (feature) will allow you to control your car better in snow (the benefit). When the benefit is not immediately clear, document it as part of your project plan. Then have the project team practice articulating the benefits so that they (1) stay focused on why you are implementing BusinessObjects XI and (2) can more effectively promote your efforts in both formal and casual conversations with users.

A second aspect to the product component of the market mix is what to call the product. Will you refer to it by the vendor-provided product names, or will you give it a different

Feature	Benefit
Aggregate awareness	Fast queries
InfoView Public Folders	Immediate access to key performance indicators; one version of the truth with no loss in time reconciling different reports
Disconnected access	Ability to work with reports while on the plane or at a customer site
Ad hoc queries	Explore the root cause of a problem, without waiting for an IT report developer
Exception-based reporting	Proactively manage the business when indicators fall below a certain threshold; fix a problem before it is out of control

TABLE 4-4   Emphasize Benefits, Not Features

name that also reflects the business goals and data sources? The benefit of including the vendor-provided name is that you can leverage some of the vendor's marketing efforts. The downside is if the vendor changes product names, it can cause confusion. If you are suffering from a stalled implementation or if there were negative impressions early in the implementation, change the name! When you develop your own BI product name, be sure to consider the acronym created. If it is a global deployment, take into account the cultural impact of acronyms. Following are some clever product names:

- **WISDOM**   Web Intelligence Supporting Decisions, from Owens & Minor. WISDOM Gold is an enhanced extranet version.

- **OASIS**   Online Analysis Sales Information System

- **Risk Intelligence**   Used by Zurich North America for insurance claims and losses

- **Inventory Workbench**   Used by Lands' End for inventory information delivered via Application Foundation

- **Honeycomb**   Used by Burt's Bees to brand information accessed via BusinessObjects XI. A tag line displayed in InfoView, "A Bee's Eye View", also conveys the message that this information helps the "worker bees" in the company.

- **Business Intelligence Center of Excellence (BICE)**   Used by Cingular Wireless, which has also developed a catchy logo and slogan, "Don't leave your BI decisions to chance."

Don't leave your BI decisions to chance!

Price

With business intelligence, there is the price you paid to license the Business Objects software, but there is also the price you may charge your internal users. Such pricing policies often depend in large part on what you have done in the past with reporting systems and what you do with other information systems. Many companies do not charge end users for using BusinessObjects XI. It is reflected as an indirect cost, part of corporate overhead. Some companies will charge a flat fee when a user is first granted access to BusinessObjects XI. This approach may help you manage the implementation to ensure that the people who need access the most will also pay for it. However, let's assume your company has already bought 1000 licenses. The company has already incurred the expense. Re-charging business units may help move the costs from the IT department to the business unit, but it has no material effect on company expenses. Your goal is to get the information closer to the decision-makers. You also need to recover your expenses, so you charge per trained user. This per-user fee may inadvertently cause the business unit manager to restrict the number of BusinessObjects users. Their budget is tight; they need to control expenses, no matter that it has no effect on company cash flow. The business stays stuck in the information flow of one central person running and distributing reports. The pricing strategy just caused you to fail to bring the information closer to the decision-maker.

Although BusinessObjects XI allows you to create usage reports for billing, the risk with direct charges that relate to usage is that you may also inadvertently discourage usage. The more expensive it is to analyze data, the less likely users are to explore information. In determining a direct-billing approach, you need to evaluate how advanced your company is in terms of information literacy and where you want to get to. If the data warehouse or Enterprise Servers are overloaded, then charging for usage may help you recover costs to pay for increasing capacity. If the servers are underutilized, don't charge by usage.

Companies are more likely to charge users directly when the customers are external. Owens & Minor, for example, charges external customers for access to WISDOM. Here, the Web Intelligence extranet is a source of revenue and the charges indicate WISDOM has exceptional value; if Owens & Minor offered it as a free service, customers might not have appreciated its value. An insurance company told me they began charging external customers only when they moved from mainframe reports to a data warehouse. Customers balked. They had never paid for reports in the past; why should they pay now? It didn't matter to them that they finally had more data and more flexibility than before. Nobody likes a price increase, especially if it has been forced upon them. If users had a free DSS or mainframe reports before, then don't charge for access to fixed reports. You can deploy the reports via InfoView, granting such users interactive access to fixed reports. When users want the additional capabilities to create new reports, only then would you charge them for the new capability.

Place

The "place" within your marketing mix is where you plan to deliver BusinessObjects XI capabilities or reports. Somehow the place is a seldom-considered aspect of a business intelligence project, yet it is a component of the marketing mix that greatly affects which of the vendor's products you use or which features are important. With BI, a push approach versus a pull approach has been a pendulum in which many companies initially thought pushing reports to users was a good way to manage scalability. According to some recent surveys, though, this approach is on the decline, and allowing users self-service pull access is on the rise. I suspect this is in part a backlash against information overload. Too many pushed reports can quickly be perceived as spam.

Table 4-5 lists some of the places you may deliver standard reports or interactive analysis; each of these places affects the product functionality you will teach the users as well as the interfaces you choose to deploy.

Promotion

Many BI deployments focus on the product and capabilities they want to deliver and pay little attention to promotion. The project team, staffed primarily with IT people, focuses on development efforts and not on the promotion activities that should accompany an

Place	Product or Functionality
E-mail to Inbox, BlackBerry, or other handheld device	InfoView, scheduled as PDF
E-mail with personalized, bursted report	Crystal Reports or Desktop Intelligence with scheduling
Corporate intranet	InfoView
Disconnected laptop computer	Desktop Intelligence offline mode, Live Office, or PDF-based reports
Remote dial-in	Web Intelligence with Citrix
Corporate extranet	InfoView or Web Intelligence HTML Report panel

TABLE 4-5 The Place for Delivering BI Affects Which Modules and Features You Deploy

implementation plan. Changing from an old reporting environment or decision-making process to a new one requires promotion.

Users will go through an evolution as you promote your business intelligence solution. During the funding and development stages of the project, you want to build *awareness* about what is coming. You want everyone—not just the power or primary users described in Chapter 3—to have heard of BusinessObjects XI or your BI product name. As you get closer to delivering capability, you want to increase *knowledge* as your target user segment learns when and how to use BusinessObjects XI. The third phase of promotion is to increase *usage,* in which people within all levels of the organization are *aware* of BusinessObjects XI, *know* when to use it, and *use* it as an invaluable tool to achieve business goals. You may use different media to achieve these different promotional stages. Different user segments will be at different stages simultaneously.

When to Promote

There is a comfort in waiting to promote BusinessObjects XI only when you are finished with the first phase of your BI development. If you wait until then, however, you are starting too late and it will take you longer to achieve any measurable benefits. Users must be aware of BusinessObjects XI long before they sign up for a training class. Clearly, you need to manage user expectations and not promise more functionality than what you can deliver. In early promotions, emphasize the high-level benefits, implementation waves, and broad time frames. Battered IT departments who have been criticized for being late in the past may truly cringe at this approach. I understand. I myself have cringed at seeing the changing release dates for this book on Amazon. Can't they just wait until I'm done writing it before listing a date? However, in order to build demand and excitement, you must promote early, well before you are ready for deployment. Consider how much education Business Objects did early on about the new XI platform. High-level information and development plans were shared early in 2004, shortly after the merger with Crystal Decisions was completed. The company wanted you to be *aware* of what was coming. As the product went beta in summer 2005, more precise release dates and capabilities about XI Release 2 emerged so that you could start planning for migration *(knowledge).* With the product becoming generally available in November 2005, the company has been promoting training courses, migration strategies, and so on, all with the aim of increasing *usage.*

As a BI professional, you don't have to *like* promoting early, but you do have to do it.

Key Messages

When you promote your BI solution, develop key messages and mottos that emphasize the benefits, not just the features.

The key messages you develop depends on a lot on the situation analysis. If users currently have to wait months to receive a custom report, a key message may be "information now." If one of the goals is to retain customers, a key message may be "helping you know our customers." If users access paper-based reports and there is a low level of computer literacy, then a key message like "good-bye paper-based reports" may cause a panic. Look to emulate some of the most effective promotional campaigns, as shown in the following table:

Product	Benefit	Key Message
Ford Trucks	Rugged enough to go anywhere	"Built tough"
Dunkin Donuts	Their coffee and snacks give you energy	"America runs on Dunkin'"
Bounty Paper Towels	Clean spills fast with fewer towels	"The quicker picker upper"
Miller Lite	Drink more beer	"Tastes great, less filling"
7-Up	Clear, refreshing, different from cola	"The un-cola"
MasterCard	Using MasterCard makes you happy	"There are some things money can't buy; for everything else, there's MasterCard."
Business Objects	One version of the truth that will help improve business performance	"eXtreme Insight. Trusted Platform."

Promotional Media

Choose the media according to the desired promotional frequency and target user segment. Promotion is not something you do once, but rather, it requires repetition. Do you ever see a commercial one time? No, you see and hear the same messages in magazines, on TV, and on radio. Remember, the goal with promotion is to move people from *awareness* of BusinessObjects XI to *usage*. It will take a number of repetitions, with different messages and media to get there.

Recall from Chapter 3 that only a portion of BusinessObjects XI users may actually log in to InfoView; a larger majority of users may receive the benefit of BusinessObjects XI indirectly from analysts or via distributed e-mail reports. Therefore, if you use the InfoView sign-on page as your main communication medium, the message will not reach many user segments. You need several alternative media such as staff meetings, newsletters, or e-mail campaigns to reach these secondary users.

Time your promotion efforts to certain project milestones. For example, if you give shirts away as project awards, have the team wear their shirts when you release a new universe or complete a software upgrade. At a recent TDWI conference that emphasized bridging the gap between IT and business, Dave Wells, Director of Education, color-coded the name badges of IT people in red and business people in blue. He declared that the BI industry needed more "purple people," and as a way of generating awareness and excitement on this theme, people who bridged this gap wore purple shirts and badges.

- **Road shows**   When companies first start developing a business intelligence solution, many have corresponding information sessions about what is coming, when phase 1 will be available, and who will be trained first. The most successful "road shows" include business success stories and user testimonials on how BusinessObjects XI has had a measurable impact. For example, Blue Cross Blue Shield of North Carolina has an established data warehouse and BusinessObjects implementation. Even with a mature deployment, they still do two road shows a month for new groups of users. Their implementation is so successful that the project team is often now invited to speak at staff meetings to tell people about new functionality and how business units are benefiting from business intelligence.

- **Video / podcasts**   Some companies have created videos, Webinars, or podcasts to use at road shows or staff meetings. The video may show the CEO, the project sponsor, or a business user giving a testimonial as to how BusinessObjects XI helps the business. While a video or podcast may be difficult to produce at first, it helps reduce travel costs and logistic issues in always getting the right people together.

- **Company newsletters**   Existing corporate newsletters are excellent media for high-level messages to a broad audience. Given the readership of company newsletters, the primary purpose of these articles is to build awareness, not necessarily usage. These articles should include information about the business goals and project milestones. You do not need to get too detailed about functionality.

- **Industry journals**   Companies have a misconception that participation in user conferences and articles in industry journals help only the careers of the project staff and not necessarily the company. Not true! Owens & Minor has received a number of industry awards, something that helped create enthusiasm internally and helped them win new contracts. EMA also credits recent client wins to industry exposure. There are a number of ways to get your project into an industry journal. You can author an article. You can volunteer to be interviewed by Business Objects for a press release. Your company's public relations department can issue a press release either to technical journals such as *Computer World, DM Review, Intelligent Enterprise,* and *CIO Insight* or, if it has more of a business slant, to industry journals. Finally, consider submitting an application for industry awards. As a judge for TDWI Best Practices, I would encourage companies to submit an application for this prestigious award. In addition to taking time to reflect on their accomplishments, award winners enjoy additional exposure and speaking opportunities.

- **Training classes**   Training sessions should go beyond the straight how-tos and address the benefits and business application of the data and of sharing information. Some companies use a game-style approach to training to generate enthusiasm. For example, one company regularly holds group workshops in which they divide the group into two teams. There is a question and answer session in which the two teams compete to share tips and best practices.

- **Brown-bag lunches**   A brown-bag lunch is a casual information sharing session in which participants bring a bagged lunch and discuss effective usage of BusinessObjects XI or the data warehouse. Cingular Wireless, for example, refers to these as "lunch and learns" and will invite the vendor technical consultant to participate. A facilitator may start the lunch with a success story, tip, or project update. These provide a useful follow-up to training and another opportunity to raise awareness about best practices, success stories, and benefits. In the earlier SWOT analysis, Table 4-2, one of the strengths was that the data warehouse was mature and a number of initial ETL problems had been resolved. In this same company, the data warehouse project team communicated each resolution via e-mail. Users became desensitized to repeated e-mails and no longer trusted the integrity of the data warehouse. They were convinced that if they used BusinessObjects again, they would find still more errors. It took several face-to-face discussions during brown-bag lunches and a comparison of BusinessObjects reports with ERP-based reports to acknowledge the historical problems, explain how the problems had been resolved, and motivate the power users to trust the new reporting environment.

- **Internal user conferences**   Just as Business Objects and regional user groups host periodic user conferences, do the same in your own organization. Kick off the meeting with a review of the benefits, project milestones, and a key success story. Then ask users to share tips and techniques on both the how-to of BusinessObjects XI and how it has helped them achieve business goals.

- **T-shirt days**   Many project teams give away T-shirts, sunglasses, and other promotional items to reward staff for their accomplishments. As both a motivational technique and a promotion opportunity, get the entire team to wear their giveaway on milestone dates. This works particularly well if the T-shirt is brightly colored. Seeing 50 yellow T-shirts in the company cafeteria will generate interest and curiosity about what's new.

- **Intranet**   The Intranet and the InfoView portal may be useful for promoting to existing users and keeping them informed; however, they are poor media for secondary and potential users. Secondary and potential users do not log in to InfoView, so they will never see these messages. You can best reach these secondary users through staff meetings and company newsletters. For primary users, the intranet and InfoView home page are ideal places to repeat key messages and project goals.

- **Staff meetings**   Most departments and business units have regularly scheduled staff meetings. Ask for five minutes on the agenda each quarter to give an update on new deliverables, problem resolution, and how other departments are benefiting from BusinessObjects XI. A real sign of success is when the department invites you and requests 30 minutes!

Approaches to Training

As you define your user segments, tailor the training accordingly. For report authors, you may have classroom or Web-based training; for report consumers, training may consist only of a cheat-sheet with the quick steps to refresh a report. Following are some additional things to consider in developing a training approach:

- **Data vs. the tool**   A BI tool delivers no value without the underlying data users' wish to analyze. If you train users only on BusinessObjects XI with the sample databases, users may not be able to translate the skills to their own data sets.

However, training users on their own universes and reports may be a logistical challenge if you don't have a sufficient number of users with common universe needs to fill a class. In these cases, you may want to offer tool training separately from data training. The bottom line is that you must do both, particularly for users who will create their own reports. Users who only refresh reports may not need data training, as in their view, there is only one meaning for an object.

TIP *Brown-bag lunches are a good way to supplement classroom training on the tool with discussions about the data.*

- **Internal vs. third-party**   Business Objects and a number of certified training partners will train end users on the software. Some will customize the training material to include your universes, reports, and data in the screen shots. You also can buy the training material from Business Objects and incorporate your own screen shots.

- **Training method**   While classroom-style training is the most traditional, it can pose a logistical challenge when users are at different sites and have busy schedules. Some users may do quite well to read a book and then supplement that with computer-based training, on their own schedule and at their own pace. BusinessObjects Knowledge Accelerator allows you to integrate your own data with computer-based training.

Regardless of the formal training method, for a successful implementation you must supplement scheduled training classes with other means to share tips, techniques, and uses.

Customizing per Segment

Chapter 3 defines different ways of segmenting potential users; this chapter covers developing a marketing strategy for BusinessObjects XI. Now you need to tie the two together and tailor the marketing strategy to each user segment. Table 4-6 shows three potential user segments. Table 4-7 shows how you would customize the marketing mix according to these segments.

Segment Characteristics	Accountant	VP Marketing	External Customer
Computer literacy level	High	Moderate	Unknown
Primary or secondary user	Primary	Secondary	Primary
Job level	Mid	Upper	Unknown
Analytic job component	High	Low	Unknown
Spreadsheet user	Yes	No	Unknown
Amount of travel	Minimal	High	Minimal

TABLE 4-6   Possible User Segments with Different Characteristics

Marketing Mix	Accountant	VP Marketing	External Customer
Product(s)	Web Intelligence, Live Office	Dashboard Manager	InfoView
Product benefits to emphasize	Access to any information, ad hoc reporting	Monitor key indicators	Manage costs
Price	Overhead cost	Overhead cost	Per-report fee
Place	Browser	BlackBerry	Browser
Promotional media	E-mail, internal user conferences	Staff meetings, corporate newsletters	Fact sheet, site visit from salesperson
Training approach	Classroom, books	Reference card	Reference card

TABLE 4-7   Customized Marketing Strategy per User Segment

Summary

Applying a marketing strategy to your BusinessObjects XI implementation will help you speak the language of business users and speed your success. Marketing and promoting your efforts and accomplishments can be uncomfortable for many people, especially IT professionals. Enlist the help of your company's internal experts. Your best promoters will be the satisfied users themselves. Engage them to share their success stories in company newsletters, industry journals, and internal user conferences.

Under the Covers: Migrating to a New Architecture

The biggest change with XI Release 2 is its new architecture, although it, in some respects, is not entirely new: the XI architecture is largely based on Crystal Enterprise's architecture. Understanding high-level aspects of the new architecture will help you adapt your support organization and better plan your migration. Business Objects provides you with utilities that will help you migrate to this new platform. This chapter provides an introduction to the new architecture, migration approaches and tasks, and the migration utilities. It is not meant to be a comprehensive guide. System engineers who must configure and optimize server processes should refer to the vendor documentation for more in-depth information. Project managers and BI experts who must plan the migration should check discussion forums, consulting partners, and vendor white papers for more up-to-date and detailed migration strategies. Also note that this book has been written using the BusinessObjects Enterprise server on a Windows Advanced Server operating system; migration tasks may be different when using other operating systems such as Unix and Linux.

File-Based Repository

Business Objects was one of the first BI vendors to leverage a relational database for its metadata repository. The relational repository contained information such as universe definitions, security profiles, and corporate documents. The use of a relational database allowed for a central source of metadata that geographically dispersed users could easily access. Backups were easy, as DBAs could readily back up the database. The relational database approach also ensured the product was open, and many administrators learned to read the relational repository to manage their deployments. However, the relational repository also could be a bottleneck when binary files needed to be exported to or imported from the repository. If your company had a large universe, downloading changes to that universe, while automatic for users, could take several minutes. The same is true of publishing corporate documents. When a user published a report to Corporate Documents, the .rep file was stored as a BLOB in the relational database. When another user accessed that corporate document, the .rep file had to be extracted from the relational database and in a sense reconstructed on the file system. For large documents, this could take several minutes. The response time issues certainly affected users' behavior, as they avoided saving data with a corporate document, sometimes for security reasons but often because of long response times. Thus, full-client documents were more often shared outside the repository on local area networks.

BusinessObjects Enterprise XI continues to use a relational repository but uses the file system more extensively. In XI, the relational repository is significantly smaller. The relational database is used more as a method of maintaining pointers and relationships between universes, reports, and users. All of the universe definitions and reports are physically stored on the file system. The best thing about this approach is the performance improvement. For designers, exporting universes is pretty much instantaneous. For users, publishing and accessing corporate documents is as fast as saving them to disk.

For administrators, it's important to develop a backup strategy that includes both the relational database and the file system and to ensure those backups happen in a synchronized fashion. If your BusinessObjects 6 deployment contained multiple universe and document domains, these are now represented as separate folders within the XI repository and maintained via one Central Management Server (CMS).

NOTE *So where is my BOMain.key? The BOMain.key no longer exists! In the past, administrators and users might have chosen a different .key file whenever they needed to access a different security domain defined via Supervisor. With BusinessObjects Enterprise XI, you would specify a different CMS created during the installation process or specified in the Central Configuration Manager. If you want to see where the relational repository resides, follow these steps:*

1. *From within Windows, launch the Central Configuration Manager by selecting Programs | BusinessObjects XI Release 2 | BusinessObjects Enterprise | Central Configuration Manager.*

2. *Right-click the Central Management Server and choose Properties from the pop-up menu.*

3. *From the Properties tab, you see the database user name and password used to log in to the CMS database.*

4. *From the Configuration tab, you see the relational database used for the repository and auditing if enabled. In the example at right, this is a SQL Server database named BOE11. If you have a new deployment (not upgraded from XI.0), then the default database name may be BOE11.5.*

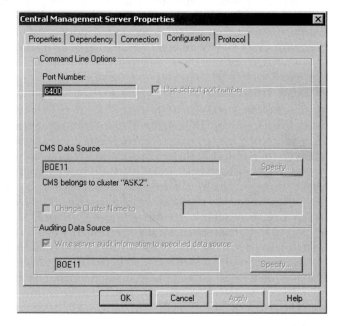

Optimized Processes

Another unique aspect to Crystal Enterprise's architecture was its optimized processes and plug-and-play components. Many of these same processes in Crystal Enterprise 10 continue to exist in BusinessObjects XI. However, there are additional processes dedicated to the treatment of Web Intelligence and Desktop Intelligence tasks. Although each of these processes is called a "server," this is conceptual only. They are not separate physical machines. Instead, they are processes potentially all running on one server or with multiple instances distributed across several machines.

Figure 5-1 provides a conceptual overview of the key components in a BusinessObjects Enterprise deployment. Your deployment will vary depending on which interfaces you have purchased, if you have licensed a premium or professional addition, or if your implementation includes Dashboard Manager and Performance Management.

The following services are shared across the suite. Even if you deploy only one interface, for example just Desktop Intelligence, your environment will use these services:

- The Central Management Server is the key component within XI, handling security and the routing of requests to other services. If the CMS is not running, then users will not be able to log in to BusinessObjects. If, however, the CMS is running but other servers are not, then users may in fact be able to log in to InfoView but will receive an error when they try to open or refresh a document. Which error appears and when depends very much on the task the user performs and which server is unavailable.

- The Input File Repository Server handles the process of writing the results of Report Servers to the repository. When users access a shared report in real time, the Input File Repository Server processes the request.

- The Output File Repository Server handles the process of serving requests for users accessing the results of a scheduled report, called an instance. When users schedule a report, a Job Server will send the results of the report to the Output File Repository Server, which stores the report in a compressed format.

- The Connection Server provides connectivity to the data sources such as Oracle, SQL Server, and Teradata.

For each end-user interface you deploy, you will have the following types of additional services. These services are optimized to process certain document types, depending upon whether they have been executed in real time or scheduled. A Job Server processes reports that have been scheduled to run. It will retrieve the definitions of the report from the Input File Repository Server, connect to a data source, execute the query, format the results, and save an instance of the report to the Output File Repository Server. Job Servers replace the functionality previously provided by the Broadcast Agent Scheduler. There is a Web Intelligence Job Server, a Desktop Intelligence Job Server, and Crystal Reports Job Server. There is also a List of Values Job Server for Crystal Reports lists of values, not for lists of values defined in universes.

Report Servers process reports that are executed on demand or built ad hoc. There is a Web Intelligence Report Server, a Desktop Intelligence Report Server, and a Crystal Reports Report Server.

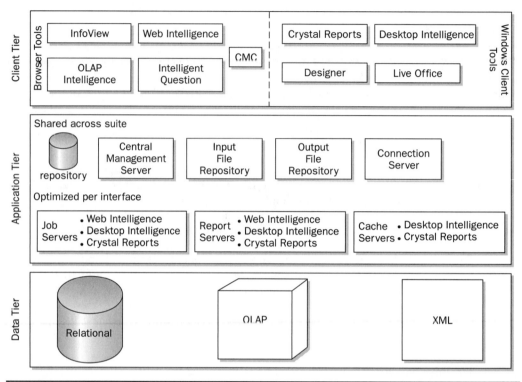

FIGURE 5-1   Conceptual overview of key components within the BusinessObjects Enterprise architecture

Cache Servers cache individual pages of reports for Desktop Intelligence and Crystal Reports users. When a user views a large report, the Cache Server sends a single page to the user's browser. The Web Intelligence Report Server has caching abilities as part of that process, so you will not see a separate Web Intelligence Cache Server.

If your deployment includes Crystal Reports for pixel-perfect reporting, then you will see additional server processes optimized for that report type: Crystal Reports Page Server, List of Values Job Server, Report Application Server, and Destination Job Server. Don't let the names of some of these servers mislead you to thinking they are not available for other report types; it's simply that the work is performed by a different server process. For example, the List of Values Job Server processes lists of values only for Crystal Reports documents; it does not process lists of values for Web Intelligence or Desktop Intelligence documents. Instead, the Web Intelligence Report Server and Desktop Intelligence Report Server handle the processing for those lists of values.

Administrators may start and stop services using the Windows Central Configuration Manager, or they may use the web-based Central Management Console, shown next. In the following screenshot, services that are running are indicated with a green up arrow and stopped services have a red down arrow:

Migration

Because so much has changed with the underlying architecture, migrating from BusinessObjects version 5 or 6 to XI demands careful planning. It is not an upgrade that involves a simple copy from one version to another. XI Release 2 contains two tools that will help with migration: an Import Wizard and a Report Conversion tool.

The Import Wizard allows you to

- Migrate users and content from one version of the platform to XI Release 2.
- Copy users and content from a development environment to a production environment.
- Consolidate content from departmental BusinessObjects and Crystal implementations to an enterprise implementation.

The Report Conversion tool allows you to convert full-client reports or Desktop Intelligence reports to Web Intelligence documents. Both of these tools are discussed more thoroughly later in this chapter.

Your migration project should have four broad phases: planning, test, implementation, and ramp-up. The length of each phase will vary significantly, depending on the size and complexity of your existing deployment and your consolidation approach. As you plan your project, use the checklist in Table 5-1. An electronic copy of this checklist may be available on the Osborne web site and BOB. Each of the items in Table 5-1 is described more fully in the following sections.

Category	Item	Lead Person	Start Date	End Date	Comments
Planning Phase	Understand key benefits you would like to obtain				
	Understand and identify licensing issues				
	Retain executive sponsorship and ensure incentives are in place				
	Ensure Crystal and BusinessObjects administrators work together				
	Take baseline of existing environment: FTEs to support, number of servers, defined users, active users, number of reports and universes				
	Read documentation (particularly Chapters 5 and 13 of *BusinessObjects XI: The Complete Reference*)				
	Train administrators				
	Inventory existing reports in repository, local networks				
	Identify shared reports that should be in repository				
	Identify opportunities for report rationalization and conversion to Web Intelligence				
	Develop/update security approach				
	Develop migration approach (consolidate or not)				
	Plan new architecture				
	Develop training strategy				
	Identify sample reports for benchmarking/testing (basic, complex); document current response times				
	Assess technical architecture readiness: Java application servers, standard browsers for Web Intelligence authors				
	Develop communication and implementation plan				
	Identify pilot users and content				
Development/ Test Phase	Install XI Release 2 software				
	Scan and repair version 5 or 6 repository				
	Back up version 5 or 6 repository				
	Back up version 5 or 6 reports not in repository				
	Plan groups and folders				
	Test the Import Wizard for users and groups, documents, stored procedures, universes, permissions				
	Understand and test new security				
	Test universe connections and/or define ODBC				
	Test sample reports and benchmark				
	Test server load and new architecture				
	Document new policies, procedures, support responsibilities				
	Identify and test manual tasks				
	Train pilot users and key support personnel				
	Identify possible user/group overlap between Crystal and BusinessObjects environments				

TABLE 5-1 Migration Planning Checklist

Category	Item	Lead Person	Start Date	End Date	Comments
Go Live	Freeze updates to old environment				
	Train users				
	Migrate full repository and reports				
	Complete manual tasks				
	Sunset old environment(s) to achieve cost savings				
	Measure new environment: FTEs to support, servers, defined users, active users, number of reports and universes				
Ramp Up and Redesign	Set up external authentication				
	Convert full-client reports to Web Intelligence				
	Optimize and/or redesign universes				
	Calculate ROI				
	Promote and extend to new users				
	Leverage new modules				

TABLE 5-1 Migration Planning Checklist *(continued)*

Planning Your Migration

The first and most important phase of your migration is the planning phase. With some IT projects, it may be acceptable to plan a little, test a little, and implement for a longer period of time. With your migration to XI, the planning phase of the project may be your bigger investment. Plan well and your migration will go more smoothly. Plan poorly and you can expect to face numerous challenges. Planning breaks down into a number of key actions, as described next.

Understand the Key Benefits You Would Like to Obtain

As with any upgrade, document the justifications for the upgrade. These may include cost savings if you are consolidating environments; increased scalability from the XI platform; or new features available in XI such as Intelligent Question, collaboration, and improved auditing for Sarbanes-Oxley compliance. There is also the issue of ongoing support and maintenance for versions 5 and 6. The vendor publishes Technical Support Lifecycle plans on its web site (http://support.businessobjects.com/programs/lifecycle/default.asp) and currently plans to end technical support for version 5.1.9 at the end of 2007 and for version 6.5 in June 2008, although product patches will cease earlier.

With some of these benefits, there may be licensing implications. In migrating to XI, the software upgrade is covered as part of maintenance for like-for-like functionality. However, XI has a number of modules that you may not previously have purchased. For example, Live Office and auditing capabilities are both provided as part of a Premium licensing bundle. Identify which capabilities may incur additional licensing costs, evaluate the benefits, and obtain the necessary budget.

Retain Executive Sponsorship

Many times a software upgrade is performed by the IT group as part of maintaining the BI infrastructure. However, if any of the goals of your migration project include BI standardization, consolidating departmental BI implementations, or leveraging new business features of XI

Release 2, then you need to ensure executive sponsorship before proceeding. Without this sponsorship, turf battles will impede your migration. The ability to provide additional business value is threatened.

Make Sure Crystal and BusinessObjects Administrators Work Together

In many organizations, there are separate Crystal Enterprise administrators and BusinessObjects administrators. Rarely do the different administrators talk to one another. They each have their own application responsibilities and user constituents, so why compare notes? However, as business intelligence becomes a strategic, enterprise resource, these administrators will ideally work within the same BI competency center and report to the same program manager. If that is not the case in your organization today, then at least begin a dialogue with one another to understand the environments, potential for overlap, and potential for synergy. BusinessObjects administrators have a lot to learn from the Crystal experts about the architecture and security. Crystal Enterprise administrators have a lot to learn from the BusinessObjects experts about the role of the universe, interactive reporting, and dashboards. Both need to understand product positioning and to develop a strategy for which product to use in particular applications.

Take a Baseline Inventory of Your Existing Environment

A baseline should include the number of full-time equivalent personnel (FTEs) to support the application and the number of servers, defined users, active users, and reports and universes. Many companies do not currently monitor active users and have not enabled auditing in their BusinessObjects environment. Even if you do not own an Auditor license, you can enable a degree of auditing on BusinessObjects version 5 or version 6 for logins that come through InfoView. This baseline is important in ensuring like-for-like performance in a version 6 and XI environment as well as understanding the cost/benefits of your migration. If you keep the hardware and support staff constant, yet have significantly increased your content, or active users, then you have achieved a measurable benefit.

NOTE *It was alarming to me to hear that some early migrators did this manually by counting items in various screens in Supervisor. Information on number of users, universes, reports, and more is readily available to you by running queries against the version 5 or version 6 repository tables. If you are not versed in the structure of these tables, use the ManagerO universe that has been available in the freeware directory in earlier versions of BusinessObjects.*

Read Available Documentation

A key part of any migration is to understand the areas that have the most significant changes. This includes any vendor-provided "What's New" papers and in this book, Chapters 5 and 13. However, if you are the type to embark on hooking up the new DVD player without first reading the manual or driving to a new destination without opening a map, then ignore this step at your company's peril.

Train Your BusinessObjects XI Administrators

BusinessObjects XI administrators should attend training sessions to learn how to install, configure, optimize, and maintain the server components and security. The vendor also provides training specific to migration tasks.

Inventory Shared Reports

Many BusinessObjects deployments have a multitude of reports on users' local disks and network folders. Many are not shared via Corporate Documents. It is possible to implement XI while leaving all these reports where they are. However, once an XI user saves the document or publishes it to the repository, it is converted to the latest release and version 6 users will no longer be able to open the report. If these documents are not being backed up on a regular basis, now would be a good time to do so. With XI, the concept of "Corporate Documents" is much more flexible. Folders (see Chapter 13) provide a powerful, secure way for users to share reports. As part of your migration planning, you want to inventory the reports stored in the repository, but also, understand the extent that reports are shared elsewhere. As part of this inventory, you may determine that a number of reports that were not in your 6.5 repository should indeed be shared via folders in the XI repository.

TIP *In addition to inventorying existing reports, be sure to clean up the repository by deleting unused documents and universes.*

Identify Opportunities for Report Rationalization and Conversion to Web Intelligence

This step will not be popular with full-client enthusiasts, people resistant to change, and people who hate cleaning out their closets. However, there are some significant advantages to a Web Intelligence document over a Desktop Intelligence document (discussed in the next section and in Chapter 24). As part of your migration planning, identify which documents are candidates for conversion or which documents will be left as is. As part of this planning step, you can use the Report Conversion tool to give you an estimate of the percentage of reports that will easily convert and the percentage of how many may be problematic. During this investigation stage, you may decide as part of your strategy that phase one will not include any conversion and that such conversions may happen only in a secondary phase. It's all a question of the trade-off between cost of converting versus benefits provided. Also consider if all the reports are necessary (accessing to auditing data is certainly helpful here!). If you have ten variations of one report with slightly different sorts or filters, consider if you can reduce the number of reports.

Develop/Update Your Security Approach

Security is discussed further in Chapter 13. Security in XI is much more granular than in previous releases of BusinessObjects. Now is the time to consider how granular you want the security, who will control resources, and what are the default permissions for various groups and applications.

Develop a Migration Approach and New Architecture

As I consider migration approaches, I can't help but think about pork barrel politics. You don't want your migration effort to get so bogged down in related redesign and consolidation efforts that it drags on indefinitely, and yet to migrate without some degree of cleanup is suboptimal as well. Figure 5-2 shows a typical departmental BI deployment. Each department has a different version of BusinessObjects, with its own repository and server infrastructure. The Finance group accesses both BusinessObjects version 5 and Crystal Enterprise. User IDs and passwords are duplicated in the two repositories. As you migrate to XI Release 2, the "fastest" migration with the least political impact is to continue to treat each of these siloed implementations separately and create three XI implementations. There are no issues of

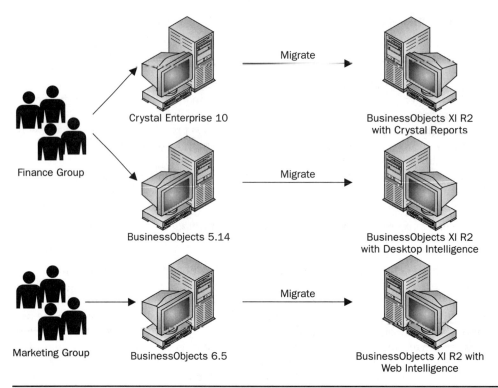

FIGURE 5-2   Simple migration approach with departmental BI implementations

overlapping user IDs and group definitions. However, you have done nothing to reduce your cost of ownership or to provide users with one source for all their BI content. Finance users still have to log in to two different InfoView portals. With this approach, your goal is to implement XI quickly and treat any cleanup, redesign, or consolidation efforts as a separate project.

Figure 5-3 shows an alternative approach to migration during which you consolidate the departmental implementations into one common XI implementation. You may externalize user authentication or continue to use BusinessObjects Enterprise's own authentication mechanism. Here, a Finance user is defined once. From a scalability perspective, you may choose to have the individual Report Servers (Web Intelligence Report Server, Desktop Intelligence Report Server, Crystal Report Server) run on separate physical machines; however, they are all controlled through one common CMS. With this approach, users access all BI content via a common InfoView.

Clearly, the approach in Figure 5-3 may offer the lowest cost of ownership for IT to administer. However, it requires a greater degree of coordination and planning and executive sponsorship. Importing rights for users who may have had different user IDs or replicated user IDs in previously departmental solutions will require some manual intervention. Consolidation is also *initially* more disruptive to users and support personnel. This disruption has to be weighed against the benefit of providing one common BI repository at a lower cost (although the end users may never see the BI support costs).

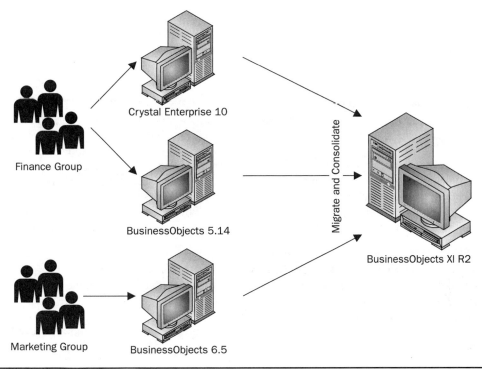

FIGURE 5-3   Migration and consolidation approach with enterprise-wide BI implementation

The best approach for any company is dependent upon the organization, available resources, and desired timeline. Even if you start by moving onto XI "as is" with separate server environments per department (Figure 5-2), do plan architecturally and organizationally for eventually consolidating environments (Figure 5-3) within a defined time period.

With some of the changes to the BusinessObjects Enterprise server architecture, you may also want to re-architect your deployment to distribute components across multiple servers. How you architect development/test/production environments also requires consideration (some options are discussed in Chapter 15).

The change in architecture is one aspect of the migration, the opportunity to "clean up" is another. With many initial BusinessObjects deployments, companies built huge universes not adequately aligned with the user needs. Users built powerful reports with way too many calculations that could have been defined in the universe to ensure one version of the truth and re-usability. The BusinessObjects XI universe has also evolved with features such as keys (see Chapter 9) and derived tables (see Chapter 11) that, when used appropriately, allow for a more scalable system that better leverages the power of the database. As part of your migration to XI, plan for some redesign time but perhaps in a secondary phase once you have reached steady state on the new platform. Failure to optimize universes and reports prior to increasing your deployment carries bad practices forward and may make it increasingly difficult to fix past problems.

> **NOTE** *Here too, you want to know how many users will be affected by any redesign efforts. Know how many users access any given universe. Ensure that your migration plan minimizes user disruption. In some cases, it may be wise to leave a poorly designed universe "as is" and provide an enhanced one separately.*

Develop a Training Strategy

As discussed in Chapter 4, training should be differentiated for the different types of users. So too should XI migration training. Report consumers who had already been trained on InfoView, for example, may only need an e-mail about new login procedures and a few highlights of what's new. Power users, on the other hand, may need web-based or classroom training or workshops that discuss the most significant changes. Training is not only determined by the type of BI user but also by your migration strategy. If you migrate to XI without consolidating environments or converting reports, less training may be necessary in the early phases of your implementation but more will be necessary as the users want to leverage some of the new capabilities.

Identify Sample Reports for Benchmarking/Testing

As with any major upgrade, it's recommended to establish a baseline for current response times to more easily diagnose and pinpoint problem areas. Identify some use cases and ensure you have documented response times. This may include times for certain tasks such as logging in and refreshing a simple report, accessing a corporate document with data, executing a complex report with complex SQL, executing a highly formatted report with a complex layout, and so on.

Assess Technical Architecture Readiness

If your current deployment is based primarily on BusinessObjects two-tier or client/server architecture, evaluate your intranet environment. While BusinessObjects offers an ASP interface that uses Windows as the application server, this lacks some of the interactive reporting capabilities for report consumers. The JSP interface provides report consumers with features such as sort and filter within a zero footprint browser, but to leverage this, your deployment must contain Java application servers. For Web Intelligence report authors and power users, you must ensure standard browsers to run Java applets.

Develop a Communication and Implementation Plan

As discussed in Chapter 4, part of a BI implementation is not just implementing the software but also helping users understand how to better leverage it and promoting its effective use. With an XI migration, you need to develop a similar communication strategy so that users know what will be changed, why, and when.

Tied to your communication plan is an implementation plan with the number of users added in phases. Your implementation may be phased by department, user group, or universes. Your approach will be influenced by how your BusinessObjects deployment was organized in the past. As you further test the environment, this implementation plan should be fine-tuned. As part of your implementation plan, I recommend you adopt a strategy of reaching "steady state" before leveraging the new capabilities in XI.

Identify Pilot Users and Content

As you prepare for your migration, identify which users will be part of the pilot. You may choose to select users of different profiles (power user, report consumer) from several business units, or using Figure 5-2 as an example, you may select just one department and subject area. This is a pilot and needs to be carefully controlled: you do not want to have to import a large number of user definitions, universes, and reports multiple times. The purpose of the pilot is to verify functionality, to check software configuration, and to understand what procedures and policies need to be modified.

Testing the New Environment

After thoroughly planning for your migration, you are now, finally, ready to get your hands dirty and start working with the software. I know: you may want to skip the planning and start working with all this cool stuff first. Indeed, evaluating XI before you initiate a project is one way to approach the migration. Arguably, a degree of evaluation time will better help you plan for your migration. But be very careful not to let your "controlled" evaluation evolve into a departmental implementation. There are a couple of areas in which you very quickly can impact some production users. The first of these is when you attempt to import or access reports.

Copy or Back Up the Version 5 or 6 Repository

During the XI Release 2 beta, when you used the Import Wizard to import reports, universes, or users to the XI repository, the Import Wizard updated the older repository to version 6.5. Certain tools, such as Designer, would then no longer be able to log in to the old repository. This practice changed in the production version, yet I still recommend that in testing the migration tools, you make a copy of the repository and generate a BOMain.key that points to the copied database. As part of your routine maintenance in version 6 or 7, you should be running a repository repair or compact on a periodic basis. If not, now is a good time to do so to delete any extraneous records from the repository tables.

NOTE *When using the Import Wizard, you will point the Import Wizard to the copy of the repository, thus ensuring production users are not affected.*

Back Up Version 5/6 Reports

When you publish a version 5 or 6 full-client report to the XI repository, Desktop Intelligence converts it to XI format. It is still a .rep file, but it can no longer be opened by an older version of BusinessObjects. Users will receive an error message that the file is corrupt. When you are still in the test phase, you do not want to render your existing full-client documents unusable to production users. Therefore, I recommend making a separate copy of any .rep documents that you may want to export to the XI repository.

CAUTION *Do not export a version 5 or 6 .rep file to the XI repository without first making a copy. If you skip this step, BusinessObjects full-client users may no longer be able to open their reports.*

Plan Groups and Folders

This topic and its importance are discussed in Chapter 13. It has a profound impact on how you structure security and on what security you import from your old repository. In version 6, access to individual documents had to be explicitly enabled or disabled. With XI, documents can be stored within folders, allowing administrators to control access at group and folder levels. This provides much more flexibility. You may then choose not to import what was a highly complex security scheme from your version 6 repository, but instead, to simplify the security in XI through groups and folders.

Test the Import Wizard for Users, Groups, Documents, Stored Procedures, Universes, and Permissions

The Import Wizard provides many options for importing content from previous versions of BusinessObjects and Crystal Enterprise to XI. During this test phase, you want to understand what gets imported and to where, what is the impact of merging environments, what is the impact of enforcing rights fidelity, and various other options. As part of your testing, plan to do the import multiple times and in multiple ways. The Import Wizard is very flexible, and you will find that doing an import of everything as it was may not be optimal.

> **NOTE** *You will want to test the Import Wizard multiple times, trying to import different content each time. Plan to spend days on this, not minutes or hours. This is not because the Import Wizard is particularly difficult but because you have different options as to how and what you import. The impact of certain settings is not immediately apparent until you also have a good understanding of the new security as well. Also, if you do not run a scan, compact, and repair as part of your routine repository maintenance, I recommend doing so before using the Import Wizard.*

Understand and Test New Security

Security in XI is much more granular than in earlier versions of BusinessObjects and leverages the Crystal Enterprise security model. This is discussed in Chapter 13. As part of the import process, importing users and groups is fairly straightforward. However, importing the associated permissions to documents and universes requires a greater understanding of the new options in XI Release 2. If you have poorly defined security in your version 5 or 6, you do *not* want to import it; instead, you will find it faster to redefine permissions at the group and folder levels.

> **NOTE** *Through several client and vendor conversations (and lively debates with the book's technical editors), I understand that the vendor does not officially recommend migrating security from older BusinessObjects deployments to XI. However, I think this recommendation is not so black and white and is highly dependent upon what you are trying to migrate and the effort involved in migrating versus rebuilding. Migrating user IDs, passwords, and universe permissions is straightforward and something I would recommend. Migrating profiles and complex permissions to individual Corporate Documents is significantly messier and something I would recommend to rebuild in the new environment. In any migration, evaluate your existing security and test the Import Wizard with multiple options.*

Test Universe Connections and/or Define ODBC

When you import a universe, the connection gets imported as well. However, if you use ODBC for certain connections, the system administrator must ensure that these same ODBC connections exist on the machine(s) running XI.

Test Sample Reports and Benchmarks

Assuming you took a baseline measurement of sample reports and use cases in your planning phase, you can now compare the performance improvements in XI.

Test Server Load and New Architecture

If you have re-architected departmental implementations to an enterprise implementation, run test scripts to understand the maximum load in the new environment for simultaneous logins, report viewing, query execution, and so on. Third-party tools such as Mercury LoadRunner can help you test server performance.

Document New Policies, Procedures, and Support Responsibilities

Given all the changes in the XI architecture, you will need to document and update a number of policies, procedures, and support responsibilities:

- **Backup of relational repository and file-based repository**   With earlier versions of BusinessObjects, your DBA backed up the repository that contained the universe and corporate documents. With the new XI architecture, the backup of the relational repository and the file-based portion must be synchronized.

- **Moving items from test to production**   How best to set up development, test, and production environments in earlier versions of BusinessObjects was widely debated, a debate that most likely will continue in BusinessObjects XI. You can use folders and copy items, or you can install a separate CMS and use the Import Wizard to create BIAR files (see Chapter 15). The important thing here is that your existing procedures will need modification.

- **Save to Corporate Documents**   With earlier versions of BusinessObjects, there was one area to share common reports within InfoView: Corporate Documents. This area was often tightly controlled by BusinessObjects administrators. In XI, you can have multiple folders. This flexibility will force you to re-evaluate who should be able to publish content to shared folders.

- **Prepare support staff**   Ensure support staff know what is coming and that they understand changes in responsibilities and procedures, new error messages, known problems, and migration plans.

Identify and Document Remaining Manual Tasks

While the Import Wizard will help you migrate a number of items within the BusinessObjects environment, there are a couple of things that you must define manually. As the Import Wizard is updated with subsequent service packs, check the vendor support site for remaining manual tasks. At the time of this writing, these tasks include

- **Broadcast Agent schedules**   Reports that were scheduled via Broadcast Agent Scheduler must be rescheduled. Calendars are new in XI Release 2 and require additional definitions. Web Intelligence reports that use the OpenDocument function are imported into the new repository, but the links need to be redefined as the file paths will have changed.

- **Train pilot users and key support personnel**   You planned an approach for training your pilot users; now you are ready to train them to begin using XI in a test environment. Ensure that key support personnel are part of the first wave of trained users.

Handle Consolidation Tasks

If you are also doing consolidation as part of your migration, be sure to identify possible user/group overlap between previously separate Crystal and BusinessObjects environments. Identify which user IDs and group names may have existed in multiple systems. For example, in Figure 5-2, the Finance group exists in both Crystal Enterprise and in BusinessObjects 5. Importing duplicate groups and users requires additional review of the merged rights.

Implementation Phase: Going Live with Your BusinessObjects XI Migration

You've *planned* your migration, you've *tested* the new platform; now you are ready to *implement* BusinessObjects XI and go live with your migration.

Freeze Updates to the Old Environment

Ideally, you will freeze any updates to any environments for BusinessObjects version 5 or 6. You may still run and support these environments, but if you can limit changes to universes and changes to corporate documents, you will not need to migrate the same content into XI more than once.

Migrate Full Repository and Reports

In the test phase, you may have imported only certain BI content into the XI repository. At this point, you import all users, groups (depending on external authentication approach and decision to migrate security or not), universes and their connections, stored procedures, and reports. Re-organize the reports to ensure that you are leveraging the new folder structure. Review the security settings and permissions to ensure that document access is defined at the group and folder levels.

Train Users

Depending on your migration strategy, you may migrate users to the new environment in phases according to department, groups, or subject area. Ensure you have an appropriate training plan and capabilities in place. Not all users will need to attend classroom training. Some may prefer to learn by doing; others may want to learn by workshops or Webinars. Plan classroom training for experts and power users.

Attain Steady State

Once all users have been granted access to the new environment and you have reached a level of stability in which users can perform the same tasks as in the old environment, you can plan to do the following:

- **Sunset old environment(s) to achieve cost savings**   Sunset the old server environment in phases, first by disabling logins, and then by shutting down the server.

- **Measure the new environment**   If one of your goals to migrating to XI is to reduce the cost of ownership for your BI environment, measure the new costs post-migration. Include FTEs to support the environment, hardware, and software. However, a BI environment rarely stays at the same level, so be careful to consider the costs relative to the number of active users, capabilities deployed, and applications.

Assuming you have the appropriate Premium licensing, Auditing is enabled by default in XI Release 2. Regularly monitor activity levels and response time in the new environment.

Ramp Up and Redesign

You've reached steady state, now ramp up: add more users, leverage new features, and add new modules. Be sure to

- Promote the availability of the new platform, intended benefits, and access to new users.

- Evaluate which new capabilities you will use: Collaboration, Encyclopedia, Intelligent Question, Process Tracker, Dashboard Manager, Live Office, and so on.

You may do some redesign as part of your migration, but I would advocate deferring such changes until after your initial wave of migration has reached a steady state on the new platform. Minimizing the number of changes can help you more easily pinpoint the root cause of a problem: is that query slower because of the new Connection Server or because you changed the universe? At the same time, you want to timebox the number of disruptions to users. You do not want users to feel they just went through a set of changes related to migration and then have to endure another set of disruptions as you optimize. In this regard, redesign should be planned for but done only after you have reached a stable environment on the new platform. Possible redesign tasks include the following:

- **Set up external authentication**   To ensure that users have a consistent user ID and password across your corporate applications, set up external authentication as part of the XI environment.

- **Optimize universes**   Ensure universes are aligned with business users' needs rather than the physical design of the data warehouse or source system, provide advanced objects that may previously had been created as individual report variables, and evaluate when to use new features such as derived tables and keys to provide better query performance.

- **Convert full-client reports to Web Intelligence**   Web Intelligence in XI Release 2 has many new features that previously only existed in the full client. For companies that have been waiting for more power in the thin client, you now have the opportunity to convert these full-client reports to Web Intelligence and still have powerful authoring capabilities.

Import Wizard

The Import Wizard is a utility that allows you to import repository content from earlier versions of BusinessObjects or Crystal Enterprise to XI. It is a desktop application and requires connectivity to both the old repository and the new repository. The wizard allows you to import everything from a repository or to select components of a repository such as users and groups, universes, documents, and stored procedures. As you import this content, you can merge the content (important if you are consolidating environments) or have the wizard append identifiers to determine from where the content was imported.

CAUTION *In earlier versions of BusinessObjects, it was an accepted practice for designers to copy universes via the file system and export the universe to relevant repositories. In XI, permissions are associated with a universe. In XI Release 1, sharing universe files outside the repository could render the universe inaccessible. This problem seems to be corrected in XI Release 2 as long as designers use the check box Save For All Users. However, when migrating universes from earlier versions of BusinessObjects to BusinessObjects XI, it is recommended to use the Import Wizard.*

NOTE *Before using the Import Wizard, ensure you have run a Repair and Compact on the old repository to delete any extraneous records in the repository tables. Also make a backup of the older repository database.*

In the following example, you will use the Import Wizard to import users and groups:

1. From Windows, select Start | Programs | BusinessObjects XI Release 2 | BusinessObjects Enterprise | Import Wizard.

2. At the Welcome Screen, click Next.

3. Specify the repository from which you want to import content. Under Source, use the drop-down menu to select the appropriate version. The required information will change, depending on the version of the source repository. In the following example, you are importing from a version 6.1 repository. For User Name, enter the General Administrator user name and password. Specify the network path for the BOMain.key. Click Next.

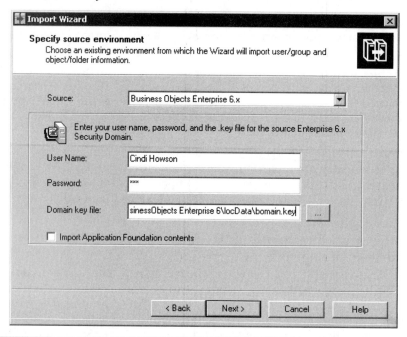

Note *For step 3 to work correctly, you must have a connection to the version 6 or earlier repository. Depending upon which database you used for this repository, you may need to make an ODBC connection on the computer on which you are using the Import Wizard.*

4. The wizard will display a warning informing you of which content it can import. Unfortunately, it does not tell you what content it will not import. Click Next.

5. Specify the XI repository that you want to import to. Enter the name of the Central Management Server as well as the administrator's user name and password. Click Next.

6. Specify the object(s) that you wish to import. As discussed elsewhere in this book, the term "object" here refers to any BI content, not to be confused with universe objects. By default all objects are selected. If you are testing the wizard and only want to import objects selectively, be sure that you have not inadvertently left any undesired objects checked. In this example, you are importing users and their group associations. If you only import corporate documents or universes and you want the rights associated with those documents and universes also imported, then you must also select users and groups. If you select users and groups, the wizard will later ask you to select which users and groups. If you select corporate documents, the wizard will later ask you to select document domains and individual documents. If you select universes, then all universes from multiple domains will be imported. This is one import option in which you will *not* later have the option to further narrow your selection.

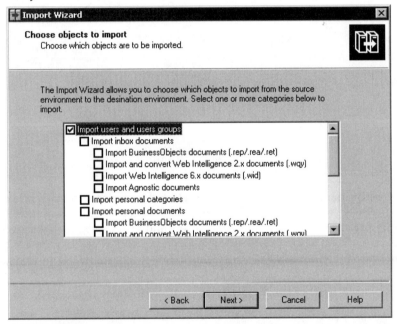

7. When importing users and groups, you are also prompted to choose a security option. If you wish to preserve the security from the source repository, select Yes. If you only want to import the user names and group assignments but not the associated permissions, choose No.

8. The wizard asks you if you wish to enforce rights fidelity. If you want the rights in the source environment to be identical to those in the destination environment, then check this box. However, if you are consolidating environments or if you are importing objects selectively, then do not check this box, as you will want rights from multiple sources to be merged.

9. The wizard asks you to choose an import scenario. Which scenarios are available to you will depend on whether or not you specified to enforce rights fidelity or to merge rights. You can either merge content or have objects renamed if they already exist in the destination system.

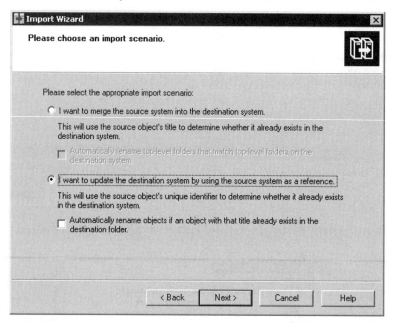

10. Depending on which objects you have selected to import, you may be prompted to further select elements. In this example, you selected users and groups. The wizard further prompts you to choose which users and groups. Figure 5-4 shows how the root or top level of the BusinessObjects 6.*x* repository (Plastics Express) becomes a group in XI. The left image shows the users and groups as they appear in Supervisor in version 6.1. The right screen shows the groups as they will be imported into the CMS. In this example, select the group Finance and click Next.

11. If you are importing users, the wizard will ask you if you wish to create database credentials for these users. If any of your universe connections want to use the BusinessObjects user ID and password as the same login for the data source, select the option "Yes, use the BusinessObjects account name . . . " and click Next.

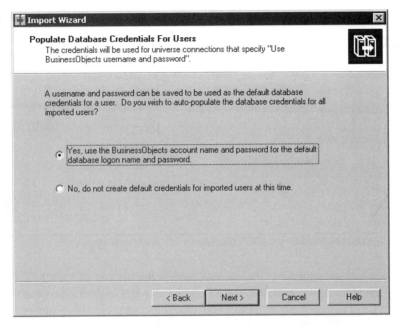

12. The wizard will provide a summary of the elements you intend to import. If these settings appear correct, click Finish to begin the actual import. If your selections appear incorrect, click Back to modify your selections.

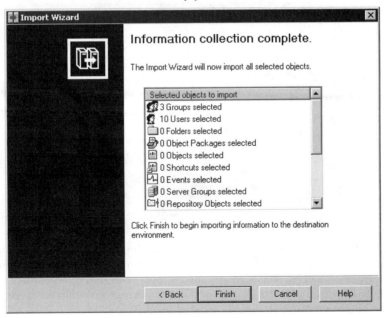

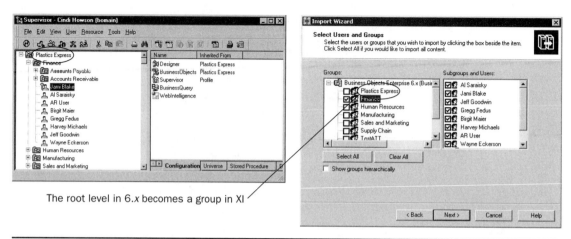

The root level in 6.*x* becomes a group in XI

FIGURE 5-4   Users and groups imported from a 6.5 repository into BusinessObjects XI

13. A thermometer will show you the progress of the import as it reads data from the old repository and copies it to the XI CMS. Once the wizard has completed the import, it displays a status of any warnings or errors. Warnings are informational; errors mean the item could not be imported. To investigate a warning, highlight the item from the list and click View Detail Log. In the following example, there is a warning for the group Finance:

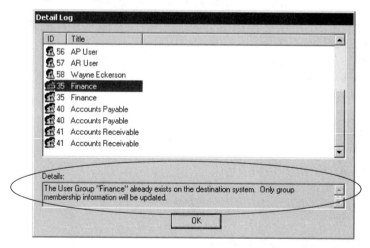

14. Within the detail log, scroll to the element with the warning. The following warning indicates that the group Finance already existed in the CMS. Because you chose to merge the rights in step 8, the Finance group from the 6.5 repository was not recreated, but rather users that existed in the Finance group in 6.5 have been added to the Finance group that already existed in XI.

15. Click OK to close the log and Done to close the wizard.

Once you have imported users, groups, documents, universes, and connections into the XI repository, test the various elements. Refer to Chapter 13 to understand how security settings in earlier versions of BusinessObjects are translated in XI.

Report Conversion

BusinessObjects began as a client/server application in which reports were authored in a Windows-based interface. In version 5, you may have published these full-client reports to Corporate Documents for other users to access them via a browser via the InfoView portal. Prior to version 6, Web Intelligence was quite limited in its capabilities as a web-based query and reporting tool. It lacked the rich report layout, complex queries, and advanced charting that existed in the BusinessObjects full client. Version 6 of Web Intelligence closed some of this disparity, and Web Intelligence XI Release 2 closes it even further. Lack of synchronized multiple data providers in the full client was one of the most often cited reasons for not using Web Intelligence. Web Intelligence XI Release 2 now has this capability. As well, the number of formula functions to create report-based calculations (see Chapter 22) is roughly double that of previous versions of Web Intelligence.

There are a number of additional benefits that a Web Intelligence document provides to end users over a Desktop Intelligence document, including:

- Greater scalability
- The ability to drill, filter, sort, and format a report from a zero-footprint browser with a simple right mouse click
- A context panel with help text and data lineage for individual objects that provide business users with essential metadata

One capability, however, that the Desktop Intelligence document continues to provide that is not available in Web Intelligence is disconnected analysis. End users can take a report with them and continue to access and analyze the data. The vendor plans to release an offline viewer for Web Intelligence in the near future. For a table comparing capabilities in the different interfaces, see Table 24-1 in Chapter 24.

For reports that you know only need to be accessed by InfoView users, Business Objects provides a report conversion utility that converts full-client documents to Web Intelligence documents.

NOTE *The use of this conversion utility is an entirely optional part of your migration. You can run full-client reports without modification in XI Release 2. Converting full-client reports to Web Intelligence reports is recommended only when there are certain Web-based capabilities you want users to be able to access.*

Expect the Report Migration tool to continue to be enhanced. The fact, for example, that there is a Free Hand SQL tab in the tool but that documents with this type of data provider do not convert suggests to me that the vendor has additional plans for improvement. However, for the initial version released with XI Release 2, according to Business Objects Product Management, if your document contains the following capabilities, the reports will not convert, as these capabilities do not exist in Web Intelligence, or they exist but involve capabilities that require reports to be rebuilt manually:

- Personal data providers
- Free-hand SQL
- Stored procedures
- OLAP data provider
- VBA data provider
- XML data provider
- Query on query
- Query filter based on calculation
- @script() function
- User-defined universe objects (not be confused with user-defined report-based variables)

If your full-client document contains the following capabilities, then the report will partially convert but then may need additional manual modification:

- VBA macros
- OLE objects/pictures
- Hide object
- Value-based breaks
- Breaks on multiple dimensions
- Complex report filters that use formulas in the filter
- Series in charts
- Multicube() function
- Fold/unfold
- User-defined hierarchies

In order to use the utility, the document must exist in the XI repository. It does not convert .rep files that exist on local or network drives.

To launch the BusinessObjects to Web Intelligence Conversion tool:

1. From Windows, select Start | Programs | BusinessObjects XI Release 2 | BusinessObjects Enterprise | Report Conversion Tool.

2. When prompted, log in to the XI repository that contains the full-client documents you wish to convert.

3. You can choose to perform the actual conversion or to preview which reports will convert successfully or not. To preview the conversion, choose Create An Audit Report Only. To perform the actual conversion, choose Convert And Publish Reports and then click Next.

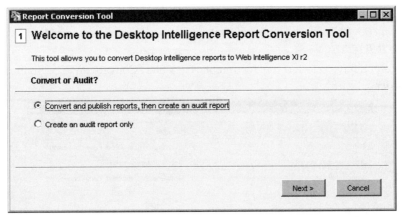

4. The tool displays a list of folders in the repository. To see just the full-client documents, check the box Show Reports Not Yet Converted. Folders that contain full-client documents appear in bold, with a count of the number of .rep files.

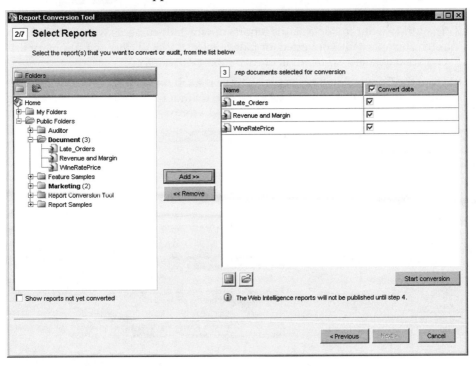

5. Highlight the reports you wish to convert and click Add so that they appear on the right under the column ".rep documents selected for conversion." If the documents also contain data, leave the Convert Data check box checked. If, however, your documents contain only query and layout information, and users must refresh the document upon opening it, then leave this box unchecked.

TIP *Converting documents without data will be faster. You need to consider the impact of re-running queries for however many reports you will be converting compared to slower conversion of reports that contain data.*

6. Once you have selected the documents, click Start Conversion to begin the conversion process.

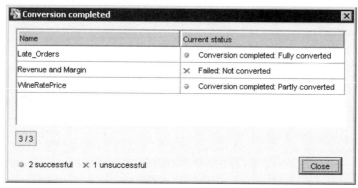

7. The utility will provide a status reports of which documents were successfully converted, partially converted, or failed. Select Close to close the summary list and see a detailed explanation of each report conversion.

8. From the Conversion Results panel, there is a tab for each type of conversion: successful, partial, or failed. Use these tabs to understand why a conversion may not have worked or to identify manual tasks for partial conversions.

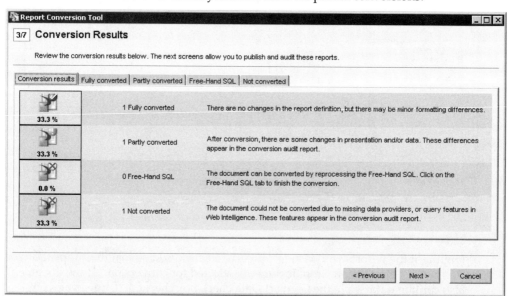

9. For successful and partial conversions, you can proceed to publish the newly created Web Intelligence documents to the repository. Click Next.

10. Choose the target folder for each report and click Next. In the following example, the .rep files and .wid files will remain in the same folder that they were originally imported from: Document. Note that the folder name, Document, was automatically created by the Import Wizard as the name of the Document Domain from the version 6 repository.

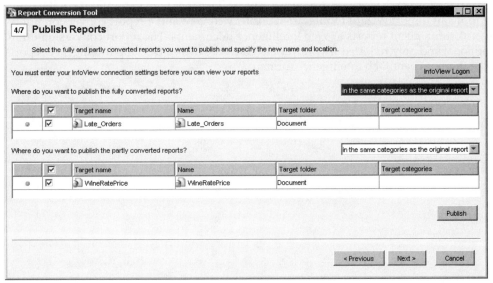

11. When you are satisfied with the settings for which reports to publish, click Publish.

NOTE *If you click Next without first clicking Publish, your reports will not be converted to Web Intelligence.*

12. The utility will provide you with a status list of converted and successfully published reports. Once you have previewed the list of reports, select Close.

13. You will be prompted whether to display an audit report of the conversion process or not. Click Next and then Finish to close the Conversion tool.

Once you have converted the desired reports, preview the converted reports within Web Intelligence and fine-tune the appropriate layout or query definitions.

Summary

Migrating to XI involves much more than a software upgrade. To properly leverage the capabilities of an integrated architecture, consider consolidating and merging previously disparate implementations. To do this requires careful planning and organizational readiness.

When there is no central BI competency center or when each implementation is departmentally controlled, you may want to migrate separate Crystal or BusinessObjects 6.*x* environments to separate XI server environments as a way of more rapidly moving to XI and gaining an understanding of key changes. Do realize, though, that this strategy may help you move onto the XI platform faster in the short term but does not help you realize the longer-term lower cost of ownership. Nor does it provide your users with one source for BI content. Thus, even if this is your short-term migration strategy, you should ideally plan for a consolidated environment in the long term, with the appropriate organizational support, security, and folder structure.

BusinessObjects XI Release 2 provides two utilities that help you migrate to the new platform: an Import Wizard to migrate repository content and a report conversion utility to convert full-client reports to Web Intelligence documents. The report conversion utility is optional and only required if you want to convert existing Desktop Intelligence reports to the thinner-client Web Intelligence format.

PART

II

A Better Universe

6

Universe Design Principles

Web Intelligence and Desktop Intelligence are a powerful ad hoc reporting and analysis tools. The single greatest component of either tool that will make your implementation succeed or fail is the universe. A *universe* is a business representation of your data warehouse or transaction database. It shields users from the underlying complexities of the database schema. Business Objects often refers to this as its patented semantic or metadata layer. In all your development efforts, you must stay focused on that purpose: *business* representation. If your universe becomes a glorified entity-relationship model, your project will fail. If your universe includes every data element any user may possibly want from now to eternity, your project will fail.

Universes can become unwieldy for end users. Poorly defined joins will result in unnecessarily slow queries. The universe is the most important component to get right. This chapter discusses concepts that will help you build a better universe and core universe components.

Keep It Simple

I have seen universes that include thousands of objects and every table in the data warehouse. Such universes are difficult and, more important, are overwhelming for even expert users. The result? End users create invalid queries and blame the tool for bad data. With such an overwhelming interface, users feel safer exporting the data to spreadsheets or MS Access databases, thus creating multiple versions of the truth and causing unnecessary data reconciliation.

To build a successful universe, keep it simple. The universe should be useful for a clearly defined group of users and should not have much more than 200 objects in it. Are there well-defined universes with more than 200 objects? Yes, but the target user group is much more sophisticated in their knowledge of both the data and the tool. The ideal number of universe objects will vary from organization to organization. Keep in mind that bigger universes are technically feasible but not user friendly. Having more universes to build and maintain may result in slightly higher maintenance costs but will significantly increase end-user productivity and satisfaction. As your target user group expands, constantly ask yourself if the needs are distinct enough to justify a separate universe. If some users need only a handful of additional objects, keep them in the same universe. However, if they need many additional objects, create a separate universe.

Figure 6-1 illustrates how different user groups will need access to different information. Human resources is one group of users that needs access to salary details but does not need product sales and order information. Therefore, a Salary universe will have information from only this one fact table. Marketing people may need information on sales but will rarely need information on the individual order numbers that customer service representatives need; however, customer service representatives need both order details and sales summaries. This is an example in which it may make sense to have one universe that meets the needs of both user groups (marketing and customer service representatives). A director of the marketing group is most likely a people manager and may need salary and employee details; the director would use two universes, as including three subject areas in one big universe would potentially be overwhelming for the majority of users who don't need this information.

Technical Realities

Keeping it simple is the most important aspect of designing a universe. However, there are some technical issues that may challenge this design principle. In earlier versions of Web Intelligence, each document could contain queries from only one universe. As a work-around to this limitation, designers would build bigger and bigger universes to ensure all possible business questions could be answered. With XI Release 2, this limitation has been removed as Web Intelligence now supports multiple synchronized data providers.

Another argument for a bigger universe is response time related, particularly with lists of values. Assume, for example, that the object *Product ID* is used in each universe. As there are thousands of products, this is a customized list of value so that users are first prompted to filter their pick list according to a product grouping. This pick list is refreshed and maintained for each universe, so it can be rather user-unfriendly to have to wait for a pick list to be generated for each universe. The answer, of course, is faster pick lists or, better yet, common

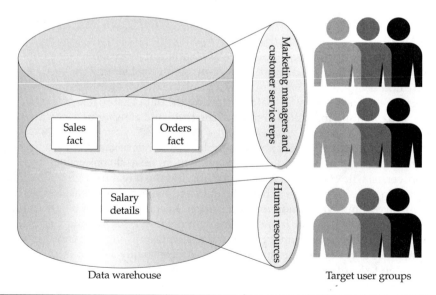

Data warehouse   Target user groups

Figure 6-1   A universe is a business representation of the database based on the needs of target user groups.

pick lists that can be shared across universes. List of values caching on the Enterprise server has improved response time for pick lists. For reusable pick lists, consider creating a linked universe (see Chapter 15) that contains common dimensions. In earlier versions of BusinessObjects, customized pick lists were not shared with linked universes. In XI, the definitions for the customization are shared but the resulting pick lists are not.

Align with Business Goals

As discussed in Chapter 2, a data warehouse or business intelligence deployment should be carefully aligned with business goals. As you develop a universe, compare how this universe helps achieve the business goals. Sometimes, companies build new reporting solutions simply because the data is available or because a certain report always existed. However, old reports may no longer be meaningful in today's business climate.

The process of determining universe requirements will vary depending on whether your implementation is based on an existing data warehouse, a new data warehouse developed in conjunction with a BusinessObjects XI implementation, or a transaction system.

Existing Data Warehouse

Just because information is in the data warehouse or data mart, that doesn't mean it needs to be in the universe. For example, data warehouses may contain dimension histories seldom used by end users. Likewise, data warehouses may contain only raw data elements that require a bit more intelligence in the universe. Likewise, just because users haven't specifically asked for something in a JAD session, that doesn't mean it shouldn't be in the universe. As an example, let's assume your company has a goal for on-time delivery performance. REQUESTED_DELIVERY_DATE and SHIP_DATE may be columns in an ORDER_FACT table. In evaluating how this universe is aligned with the company's business goals, a good universe designer will know to add an object called *Days Late* that calculates the difference between the requested delivery date and actual ship date. Users may not know what SQL functionality can be added to database columns. A universe designer must be well versed in SQL reporting capabilities that can make the universe more robust.

Herein lies one of the greatest challenges in designing a good universe: you must know both the business and SQL. SQL-certified experts may be proficient in creating tables, optimizing indexes, and loading volumes of data quite efficiently. This is not to say they know how to extract that same data into a report that provides business insight. This mixed skill set can be a challenge in identifying the best universe designer in a company (refer to Chapter 3 for a discussion on project roles). It's often a DBA who has the SQL technical skills. A universe designed by a DBA with little knowledge of the business may be technically robust but lack the business functionality required. Universes designed by power users trained in SQL may have more robust business functionality, but with suboptimal joins or objects that result in slow queries. Therefore, it's important that both a DBA and a power user jointly develop and review a universe.

New Data Warehouse

If you are building a new data warehouse or data mart in conjunction with your BusinessObjects XI implementation, ideally your development efforts are already driven by business goals. Requirements gathering in the development stage will drive the fact table design as well as the universe design. As discussed in Chapter 14, many of the issues at this stage will be where to put the intelligence—in the fact table or in the universe.

Transaction System

When your universe is based on a transaction system, some of your universe design choices will depend not only on the business goals and user requirements, but also on minimizing the impact on the source system. While users may want to search on customer name, a nonindexed field, such queries can cripple the source system (thus many organizations implement a data mart or data warehouse). If your company is not quite ready for a data warehouse, a quick alternative is to replicate the tables in the transaction system to a read-only instance of a database. This will better support detailed operational reporting requirements, without adversely affecting transaction processing. Even with this approach, a good designer needs to evaluate which business goals the universe is fulfilling. To follow on our supply chain example, customer phone numbers and contact details exist in the transaction system. This information is necessary for processing orders but useless for measuring on-time shipments. (If you are building a customer support system, then perhaps you need these details.) In building a user-friendly universe, the designer must constantly evaluate objects that fall into the category of "I might need it one day." In an initial universe, defer adding the object to the universe.

Deployments against a transaction system generally fulfill the operational needs of a company but not the strategic goals of the business, as the data is not aggregated. If the goal of the deployment is to provide a Windows- or Web-based, flexible, operational reporting environment, then your universe may indeed re-create fixed reports that exist in the source system. Another benefit of this approach is that the OLTP truly becomes the data entry/processing system, without detailed queries slowing down data inputs.

***

TIP   *As a way of ensuring your universe is fulfilling the business requirements, use the integrated auditing capabilities to monitor which universes and individual objects are most frequently used and which ones are never used. See Chapter 16 for more information on usage monitoring available through the Auditor product.*

Evolving the Universe

For designers used to a waterfall development approach, welcome to the realities of business intelligence: it's all iterative! The universe is never finished. Your first universe is version 1, which will evolve as you elicit user input, the business environment changes, the applications evolve, the source systems/data marts change, and the technology changes. Figure 6-2 illustrates how a universe evolves over time.

You normally update the universe as the first users see it. Ideally, pilot users will *preview* the universe as you are developing it to ensure it will fulfill the intended business goals and requirements. This can be in a formal joint application development (JAD) session or with one user looking over the designer's shoulder. It is not a pilot! Until you have done a thorough quality assurance review, users do not access the universe. As a result of the quality assurance review (see Chapter 16), you may make more changes, perhaps to correct errors, tweak performance, or make classes and objects more meaningful. Following quality assurance, the universe goes to a pilot phase. The goal of the pilot is to identify errors and opportunities for further improvement that you as the designer could not uncover yourself; the goal of the preview is to tell you if the universe development looks as users expect.

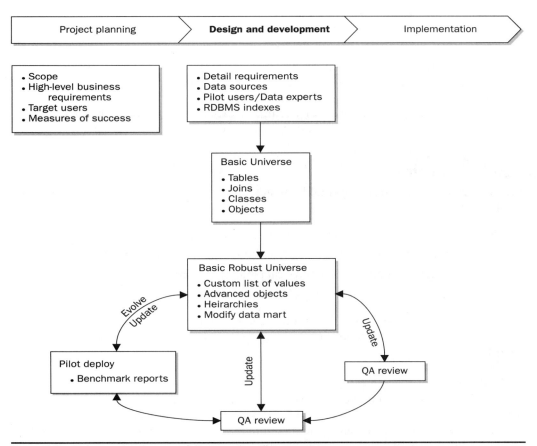

FIGURE 6-2 Universe development follows an iterative process.

Finally, users begin accessing the universe in a controlled way via a pilot. This is your first glimpse of payback for all your development efforts. If your company is new to ad hoc reporting, be sure to choose your pilot users wisely; casual users accustomed to fixed-screen DSS systems will be overwhelmed unless you provide them with parameterized reports. The pilot is typically a limited number of power users who understand the data and are fairly computer literate. For ad hoc access, these power users may be accountants or business analysts used to writing their own SQL or 4GL reports. The pilot uncovers more objects that you may need to build or modify, allows you to remove hiccups in the security restrictions, and so on. Modify the universe following the pilot period and before you move to full-scale implementation.

As you make major changes to the universe, it's helpful to document these in the Comments (File | Parameters | Summary and discussed in the next chapter). Once you implement the universe, expect to continue to evolve the universe as a wider user base accesses it. The best implementations keep a close pulse on how the universe is performing: if users are having to do too much processing in the reports via variables, multiple data providers, and so on, look for ways that the universe can simplify and enhance reports.

> **TIP** *The pre-built Auditor report User Activity Per Session is a useful document for understanding how people are using BusinessObjects XI. Chapter 16 provides an example of this report.*

At some point, the universe will reach a stable state. However, as often as the business environment changes, so should your universe. If the business agrees upon a new way of calculating customer profitability, then that new definition should get reflected in the universe. If the business acquires another company, expect the underlying data sources and/or data warehouse to accommodate the acquisition, again impacting the universe.

Universe Components

BusinessObjects XI administrators build universes using Designer. The key components of a universe are

- Parameters that define database connectivity and SQL options
- Classes and objects that users see when building queries and reports
- Tables that are pointers to the physical tables in the database
- Joins that define the relationships between the tables

These are the basic components of a universe. As you further enhance your universe, subsequent chapters discuss more complex components such as contexts, hierarchies, and security.

Parameters

The first step in building a universe is to define the universe parameters. At a minimum, the parameters define the name of the universe and the connection to the data source. Administrators also can adjust parameters to determine such things as the type of SQL users can generate and query limits. Chapter 7 explains the various parameters in more depth.

Classes and Objects

Classes and objects are the main items a business user sees when building a query, as shown in Figure 6-3. Objects become individual columns in a report; classes never appear in a report. *Classes* are a way of grouping individual objects; they do not necessarily relate to physical tables in a database. Some universe designers will mistakenly organize their classes to correspond to physical tables. This is rarely advisable. Instead, classes should represent business topics. In Figure 6-3, classes appear with a folder icon. For example, in the sample Efashion universe, the class *Product* is a more meaningful business term than *Article* and includes items from multiple tables ARTICLE_LOOKUP and ARTICLE_COLOR_LOOKUP.

Objects refer to columns of data. There are different types of objects (as explained further in Chapter 9) denoted with a square, sphere, or triangle icon in Figure 6-3. Objects can include a significant amount of intelligence and may not relate directly to one column in the database. For example, the object *Sold At (Unit Price)* includes a calculation of revenue/quantity. However, to avoid divide by 0 errors, it also includes an if-then-else statement to check for 0 quantities. This is one example of why universes are so powerful and a much better alternative to providing users with direct access to tables; if-then-else statements in SQL are implemented differently for each RDBMS and are not something most users would know how to write.

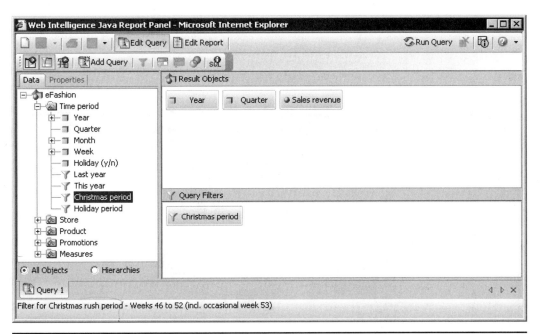

FIGURE 6-3   Users see classes and objects when building or modifying a query.

Tables, Joins, and Contexts

Report authors never directly see other core elements of a universe such as tables and joins (see Figure 6-4). Universe designers use *tables* to map data from fields to objects in the universe. *Joins* allow the use of more than one table in a report. A *context* is an optional component that resolves which join path to take when more than one path is possible. All three of these components are then combined to dynamically build SQL statements in the end user interfaces.

Another strength of the universe is its ability to support almost any physical table design. As shown in Figure 6-5, many data warehouses use star schemas to ensure fast queries. However, some use snowflake schemas to make for smaller dimension tables. OLTPs use normalized schemas to eliminate data redundancy and speed data inputs (but which can make for very slow queries). BusinessObjects XI supports all three of these designs, alone or in combination.

Tables

Tables are individual database tables that provide data. A table may be a physical table in the RDBMS, or it may be a view or synonym. Designer provides functionality to create *aliases* that are treated like tables. Further, Designer allows you to create *derived tables* that are SQL queries, as an alternative to a DBA creating a stored procedure or a view.

In a data warehouse or data mart environment, you will have two types of tables: 1) a *fact table* that contains numeric information and 2) *dimension tables* that allow a user to analyze the numeric data from different perspectives such as product, time, or geography. The fact table can have millions of detailed rows of data or can be smaller, with summary numbers. One fact table together with its associated dimension tables is referred to as a *star schema*. There can be multiple fact tables and star schemas within a universe.

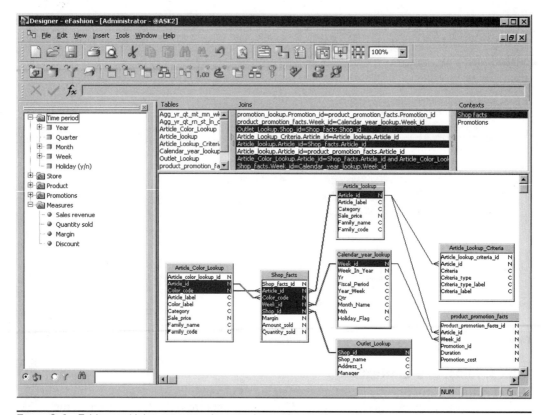

FIGURE 6-4 Tables and joins are core elements in a universe that only universe designers see.

Dimension tables are also referred to as lookup tables or reference tables. The dimension tables can be broken into more than one table; for example, detailed material IDs may reside in a MATERIAL_ID table. The groupings and product hierarchy for the material IDs may reside in a separate table such as PRODUCT_GROUPING. This type of structure, referred to as a snowflake design, is used in some data warehouses that have extremely large dimensions.

In a normalized OLTP, both the fact tables and the dimension tables may be spread across many tables. For example, order information may exist in both an ORDER_HEADER table and an ORDER_LINES table. Dimensions and hierarchies often do not exist in the OLTP (note in Figure 6-5 that there is no Time or Plant table, just the individual facility that produced the product). Only the individual material IDs, customer IDs, and so on are stored with detailed records. BusinessObjects XI does not allow a universe to point to two different databases, so when users want to analyze transaction details with reference data, it generally calls for a data warehouse or data mart. However, if this is not immediately possible, BusinessObjects provides a work-around in the end-user interfaces. You, as the designer, can create two separate universes: one that points to the OLTP and one that points to the dimension database. Users then would have to build two queries; however, as long as the detailed key information is named consistently between the universes, the results will be nicely displayed in one table, without the user having to manually stitch the two result sets together. This technique is discussed further in Chapter 23.

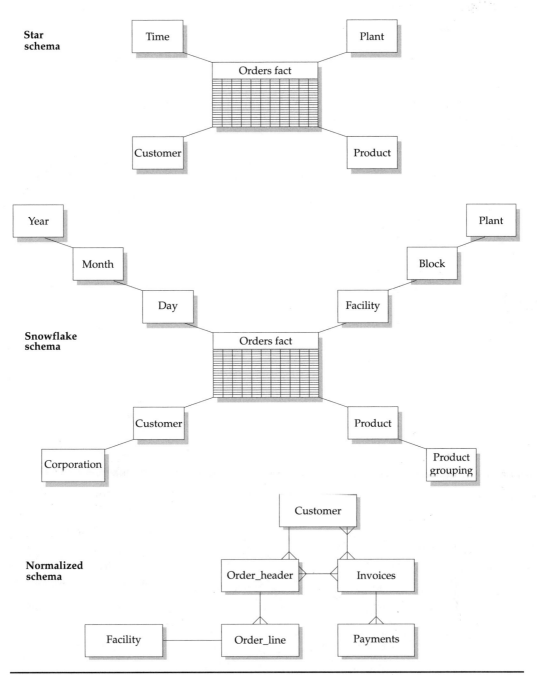

FIGURE 6-5   The universe supports star schemas, snowflake schemas, and normalized table structures.

When you build a universe, you are not replicating any data from these sources. Instead, you are basically creating pointers to tell the query where to find the data; no data is stored in the universe itself. This is a drastically different approach than a MOLAP database such as Hyperion Essbase or Microsoft Analysis Services. Data gets replicated only when a Desktop Intelligence or Web Intelligence user launches a report and the RDBMS sends results back to the report, populating a microcube in a .wid or .rep file on either the Enterprise server or the Windows client (for Desktop Intelligence).

Joins

Joins specify how tables, views, synonyms, or aliases relate to one another. Joins allow a user to combine information from two or more tables. For example, in the following diagram, there are joins between ORDERS_FACT and the dimension table PLANT as well as between ORDERS_FACT and the dimension table PRODUCTS. There are no joins to the SUPPLIERS table. Without this join, a user is not able to determine which suppliers provide various products. There are many types of joins; they are discussed further in Chapter 8.

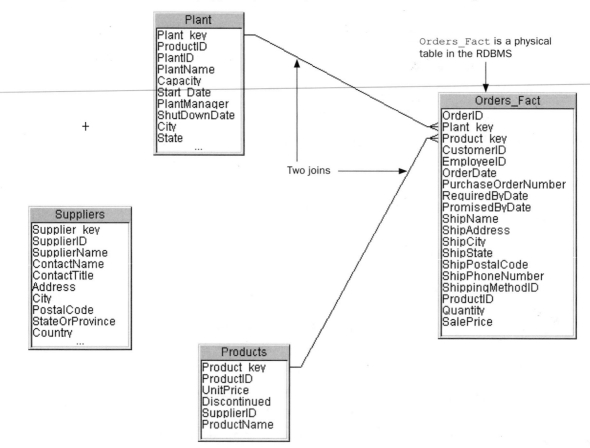

Contexts

Contexts group related joins. A context groups a set of joins together for each dimensional schema. Therefore, if your universe contains only one fact table or dimensional schema, it may not use contexts. Without contexts and when multiple dimensional schemas are involved, Web Intelligence and Desktop Intelligence would generate SQL that contained a loop. Loops generally result in incorrect queries with fewer rows returned than expected. Initial versions of BusinessObjects supported queries that contained only one context. As contexts were generally confusing for end users, they were best avoided in the earlier universe versions. Unfortunately, this legacy has carried forward unnecessarily into some current universe designs. Designers will use aliases unnecessarily to avoid contexts at all costs. For years now, both BusinessObjects classic and Web Intelligence allow one query to generate multiple SQL statements, one for each context, *without* prompting the user. This allows users to query multiple star schemas to create powerful business reports.

How Designer Works

Designer is a Windows client application that is installed on your PC. When you modify universes, you are working on a copy of the universe. When you are finished with your changes, you export your copy of the universe to a repository that end users can access.

In earlier versions of BusinessObjects, the universe was stored as a binary file within the repository. When users accessed the universe, the binary file was extracted from the database and stored as a .unv file on the file system. With BusinessObjects XI, the repository stores only pointers to binary files that are permanently stored on the file system. This results in much faster import and export times for both designers and end users.

Universe Storage During Development

When you first build a universe or after you have imported a universe from the repository, the universe is stored as a .unv file on your local workstation. Following is the default directory:

```
C:\Documents and Settings\username\Application Data\
Business Objects\Business Objects
11.5\universes\@BOE_repository
```

where *username* is the name of the Windows user, and *BOE_repository* is the name of the BusinessObjects Enterprise repository.

This folder structure is created automatically when you first save or import a universe and can be changed via Designer Options. Within the CMS repository, you also can have multiple folders for work groups or to separate test and production environments. Folders are similar in concept to universe domains in previous versions of BusinessObjects.

Universe Storage for Deployment

When you have finished designing and testing your universe, you export it to the repository. Exporting it to the repository is necessary to make the universe accessible to Web Intelligence and Desktop Intelligence users.

When you export the universe to the repository, several things happen:

- Entries are made in the related Central Management Server (CMS) tables in the repository to assign the universe a unique object identifier. From within the Central Management Console, you can see the file storage location for each universe as shown in the following screen:

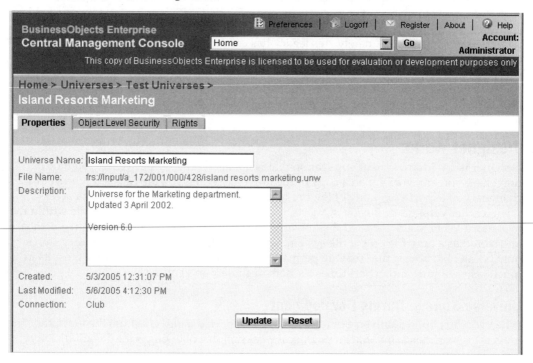

- The .unv file is compressed and saved to the BusinessObjects Enterprise (BOE) server file system under the Input folder. The last set of numeric folders is system generated from the object numbers assigned in the CMS.

```
C:\Program Files\Business Objects\BusinessObjects Enterprise
11.5\FileStore\Input\a_172\001\000\428
```

- The .unv file from the designer workstation is renamed with the long universe name and given a .unw extension. For example, the sample Beach.unv is renamed Island Resorts Marketing.unw. In earlier versions of BusinessObjects, files could only be saved to disk with the eight-character filename. This limitation has been removed in XI, so for new universes, your filename and universe name are often one and the same.

- Customized lists of values (see Chapter 10) files (*.lov) that are separate files during development become part of the .unw file when the universe is exported to the repository.

> **NOTE** *When users create documents, the .unw file is also cached on the WIReportServer, which can be on a different server from the repository. As you export universe changes, Web Intelligence checks the universe modification date and automatically updates the cached universe file.*

A Word about Backups

As you develop universes, consider how you will treat incremental design changes and backups. Clearly, in the event of a disk crash or other hardware failure, you need to ensure both your hard disk and the repository database and files are backed up on a regular basis. However, as you revise individual universes, there is no way to recover a particular version from the repository; therefore, I recommend you keep a separate backup copy of the *universe*.unv file before making major design changes.

Crystal Business Views

For long-time Crystal developers, the universe may seem like an unnecessary bottleneck if your immediate goal is to develop a report. The difference, however, is when to invest development time and the purpose of the metadata layer. Indeed, the start-up time is significantly longer to develop a universe than to develop a handful of reports. The benefits, though, are in the long-term maintenance and reusability. With a universe, measures are centrally defined and maintained. If they change, the administrator changes the calculation centrally and these changes are propagated to any report in which the calculation is used.

The concept of business views, introduced to Crystal Enterprise in version 10, shares some similarities and capabilities with universes. However, there are a few key differences, as shown in Table 6-1. One important difference is in the purpose of each. Crystal Business Views were under development *before* Crystal Decisions was acquired by Business Objects. The business views would have been a good competitive feature to a universe if the companies had remained separate. However, the intended user base of the two products was different before the acquisition and remains so today. Therefore, I see business views primarily as a way of providing developers with a library of reusable components. Such a library of reusable components existed in Crystal version 9 but is more advanced with business views. Universes, on the other hand, were always focused on business users who wanted to be shielded from underlying database and SQL complexities. Such a fundamental difference in purpose leads to different uses and capabilities. The vendor has stated a commitment to preserving customer investments in either the universe or the business view but recognizes that ultimately, these two metadata layers should be merged.

As part of BusinessObjects version 6.5, the universe became a new data source for Crystal Report developers. While it would seem, then, that Crystal developers would only need the universe, there are some features that require business views. (Two examples are view-time security and cascading pick lists.) Thus while the universe as a data source is a useful integration point, it is not a substitute for all Crystal Report developments. Also, when a Crystal Report accesses a universe as a data source, it does not inherit the full functionality of the universe. Crystal Reports cannot, for example, take advantage of such things as contexts; it can only generate a query that accesses a single star schema.

> **NOTE** *There is a new parameter available in XI Release 2 that allows for a Crystal Report to process multiple contexts on the database server but response time impact is variable. As well, once a Crystal Report developer builds a query against a universe, the developer cannot readily modify the query.*

Aspect	BusinessObjects XI Universe	Crystal Business Views
Accessible To	Crystal Reports, Desktop Intelligence, Web Intelligence, Performance Intelligence	Crystal Reports
Primary users	Business users	IT developers
Primary purpose	Act as a business view so that users can build reports without knowing SQL	Provide reusability to speed developer productivity
Usage	Required for most reports	Optional
History	Patented since BusinessObjects version 1, so more than a decade of evolution	New in Crystal Enterprise version 10, so only a couple years old
Data sources	Single	Multiple
Number of dimensional schemas	Multiple within a database, as contexts and other options can create multipass SQL	Ideally single
Query Governers	Rows returned, execution time, cost estimate	None

TABLE 6-1 Comparison of Universes and Crystal Business Views

Summary

The universe is core to the entire BusinessObjects XI suite:

- Web Intelligence and Desktop Intelligence users access the universe to build new queries using familiar business terms.

- Crystal Report authors may use it as an optional data source but will not be able to leverage the full capabilities of the universe.

- Dashboard Manager uses measures in the universe to create metrics.

In designing a better universe, understand who will be the query authors today and in the future. Ensure that the universe is simple enough not to overwhelm users, yet powerful enough to facilitate business insight.

Using Designer to Build a Basic Universe

I n Chapter 6, I discussed the importance of aligning the universe with business goals, outlined techniques to plan for iterative development, and reviewed the basic components of a universe. In this chapter, you will get much more technical and look at the Designer interface and key parameters that help you build the universe.

Launching Designer

BusinessObjects XI administrators use Designer to build universes. While much of BusinessObjects XI is managed via a web environment and browser-based tools, Designer must be installed locally on your PC. In previous versions of BusinessObjects, designers could work on a universe offline for when they did not have connectivity to the repository. With BusinessObjects XI, you must first log in to the CMS repository, even when you are working against a local copy of a universe file.

To launch Designer, follow these steps:

1. From Windows, select Start | Programs | BusinessObjects XI Release 2 | BusinessObjects Enterprise | Designer. Designer presents you with a login screen.

2. If your deployment has multiple CMS servers, for test and production, select the correct enterprise server from the System drop-down.

3. Enter your BusinessObjects Enterprise user name in the appropriate box. (Note: Administrator is a default user name created during initial installation.) BusinessObjects Enterprise user names are not case sensitive, but user names with other authentication systems in Step 5 may be.

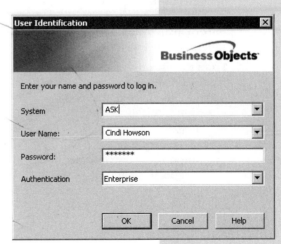

4. Tab to move to the Password box. The system administrator determines the minimum length and case sensitivity of passwords. (The Administrator user name initially contains no password.)

5. Select the Authentication source for your user name.

6. Click OK.

If you have entered the preceding information correctly, you will be presented with a Designer screen or wizard. If you entered an invalid user name, password, or authentication source, you will receive an error. As shown next, the error message does not clearly indicate if the error is related to an incorrect user name or password or if you chose the incorrect authentication source.

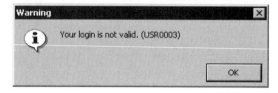

Within BusinessObjects Enterprise, user names can be authenticated against one or more security databases. The default authentication source is Enterprise. However, if your company uses Windows NT, for example, then your NT user name and password can be used to log you in to Designer. Authentication options are discussed more fully in Chapter 13.

Opening a Universe

Once you have logged in to the CMS repository, you can open a universe that you have saved locally or you can import a universe from the repository.

To open a universe from the repository, follow these steps:

1. From the pull-down menu, select File | Import.

2. From the Import Universe dialog, select the repository folder that contains the desired universe. If you do not see the universe listed, click the down arrow to navigate to a different universe folder.

3. From the list provided, select the name of the universe you wish to open. In the preceding example, eFashion is selected.

4. Select OK.

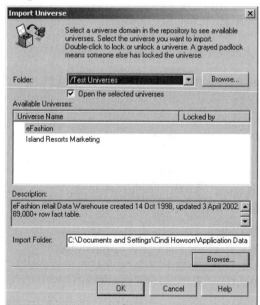

Designer imports the universe definitions from the repository and displays classes, objects, and the universe structure. During the import process, Designer also saves a copy of the universe definitions to your local computer under the following default directory:

```
C:\Documents and Settings\username\Application Data\Business Objects\Business Objects
11.5\universes\@BOE_repository
```

where *username* is the name of the Windows user and *BOE_repository* is the name of the BusinessObjects Enterprise repository.

As discussed in the preceding chapter, it's important to remember that during universe development, you are working on a local copy. Users will not be able to see your changes until you export the universe to the repository.

Folders and Domains

BusinessObjects XI uses the concept of *folders* to help you organize universes and to simplify access control. Earlier versions of BusinessObjects referred to these as domains. Domains, however, were separate physical databases, whereas folders are still within one CMS repository and file system. If you imported a previous repository into XI, these folders were created automatically according to the domain names you used in version 6.*x*.

Folders, like domains, can be used to separate test and production universes. Another way of separating test and production development is to have completely separate Enterprise implementation and server environments. The latter approach is clearly more resource intensive but better separates development, test, and production environments. The addition of an Import wizard and BIAR files further facilitates packaging of development content and moving to a production server. These two approaches are discussed more in Chapter 15.

Folders are created within Designer during the universe export process. However, it's preferable to plan your folder structure beforehand.

To create a new universe folder, follow these steps:

1. Select File | Export from the pull-down menu.

2. From the Export Universe dialog, select Browse.

3. Position your cursor at the appropriate level in the list and click the button Insert A New Folder. Note in the screen at right, ASK2 is the root or top level in the universe folder.

4. When prompted, enter the name of the new folder.

5. Click OK to close the folder dialog box.

6. Click Cancel to close the Export Universe dialog box.

Rename...	F2
Delete	Del
New Folder	
Expand All	
Refresh	F5

From within this folder list, you can right-click any folder to invoke a pop-up menu that allows you to rename or delete folders:

Designer Workspace

Figure 7-1 shows the Designer workspace that includes the classes and objects that users see, the physical tables you reference to build the universe, and the joins between the tables. As you focus on particular aspects of the universe design, you may decide to resize or close certain panes. The status bar displays messages or additional information as you add tables and change object definitions. In Figure 7-1, because the *Quarter* object is selected, the status bar displays the object description. How the universe initially appears to you and which panes are automatically displayed are controlled via settings in Tools | Options, discussed later in this chapter.

Designer Toolbars

As with many Windows applications, you can perform tasks by selecting options from the pull-down menus or from the toolbar. Figure 7-1 shows the Standard toolbar and the Editing toolbar. The Formula toolbar is discussed in a later chapter.

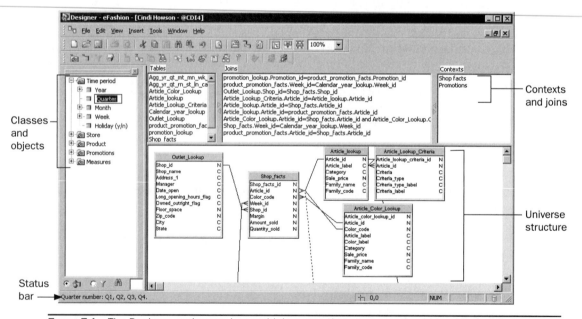

FIGURE 7-1   The Designer workspace has multiple panes that you expand or hide while building your universe.

To display, hide, or control toolbar options, select View | Toolbars from the pull-down menus.

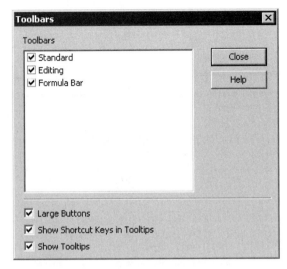

- Large Buttons controls the size of the buttons on the toolbar.
- Show Shortcut Keys In Tooltips will provide additional help text in the tooltips if there is a keyboard equivalent to performing a task, for example, CTRL-S to save a universe file.
- Show Tooltips displays help text for each button when you move your mouse over a button. The following shows the tooltip with a shortcut equivalent.

Table 7-1 describes the purpose of each button in the standard toolbar. Table 7-2 describes the purpose of each button in the editing toolbar.

Button/Key Combo	Name	Function
or CTRL-N	New Universe	Creates a new universe.
or CTRL-O	Open Universe	Opens an existing universe.
or CTRL-S	Save Universe	Saves the universe to disk in the .unv file. Does not export the universe to the repository.
or CTRL-P	Print	Prints the universe definitions and structure.
	Print Preview	Previews what definitions will be printed.
or CTRL-X	Cut	Cuts the selected item (table, join, object).
or CTRL-C	Copy	Puts the selected item into the MS Windows clipboard.
or CTRL-V	Paste	Pastes the selected item.
or CTRL-F	Find	Invokes a dialog to find an object or part of SQL. New in XI or 6!
or F3	Find again	Repeats the last search.
or CTRL-Z	Undo/Redo	Undoes or redoes the last action.
	Quick Design Wizard	Launches the Universe Design Wizard to build a new universe.
	Parameters	Modifies the universe parameters such as connection information, SQL settings, strategies.
	Hierarchies	Creates or modifies the universe hierarchies.
	Connections	Allows you to create or edit connections. New in XI and formerly within Supervisor.

TABLE 7-1   Designer Toolbar Buttons for the Standard Toolbar

Button/Key Combo	Name	Function
	Universe Window	Toggles to display classes and objects.
	View List Mode	Views the join and context lists in statements as well as in the ERD.
	Arrange Tables	Reorganizes the tables to make the structure pane easier to read.
100%	Zoom	Makes tables in the structure window appear larger or smaller.

TABLE 7-1   Designer Toolbar Buttons for the Standard Toolbar *(continued)*

Button/Key Combo	Name	Function
	Insert Class	Inserts a new class.
	Insert Object	Inserts a new object within a class.
	Insert Condition	Inserts a condition object.
or CTRL-SHIFT-H	Show or Hide Item	Hides an object or class from users.
	Table Browser	Shows a list of tables available to add to the universe.
	Insert Join	Inserts a join between two tables.
	Insert Alias	Creates an alias name for a table that already is used in the universe.
	Insert Context	Creates a context to prevent loops in a universe.
	Detect Joins	Checks the universe to determine if any tables are not joined.
1,00	Detect Cardinalities	Detects cardinalities, or relationships between tables.

TABLE 7-2   Designer Toolbar buttons for the Editing Toolbar

Button/Key Combo	Name	Function
	Detect Loops	Checks the universe to determine if there are any loops, and prompts for ways to resolve.
	Detect Aliases	Checks the universe to determine if any tables create a loop that an alias could resolve.
	Detect Contexts	Checks the universe for loops and determines if contexts would resolve the loops.
	Detect Keys	Detects keys for each physical table used in the universe to help Desktop and Web Intelligence generate more efficient SQL.
	Check Integrity	Performs multiple universe integrity checks.
	Create or Apply Access Restriction	New in XI is the ability to group multiple restrictions into sets. See Chapter 13.
	View Net Access Restrictions	Users can inherit restrictions through group assignments. This allows you to see the net effect.

TABLE 7-2   Designer Toolbar buttons for the Editing Toolbar *(continued)*

Universe Parameters

 The universe parameters provide information about your universe as well as allow you to change universe behavior such as how long a query can run and the complexity of the SQL generated. The parameters you enter here can be overridden by settings for individual users or groups. To modify the universe parameters, bring up the Universe Parameters dialog box by selecting File | Parameters.

Definition Tab

From the Definition tab, you see the name of the universe as well as the connection you specified when building the universe through the wizard. The Description appears to Desktop Intelligence users whenever they create a new report and select a particular universe; Web Intelligence users do not see the universe description. The Description box is a good place to provide users with information about the purpose of the universe and the target business user group, as well as timely information such as when data was last updated or if there are any data integrity issues.

This is the full-length name users see when creating a report (different from the universe filename)

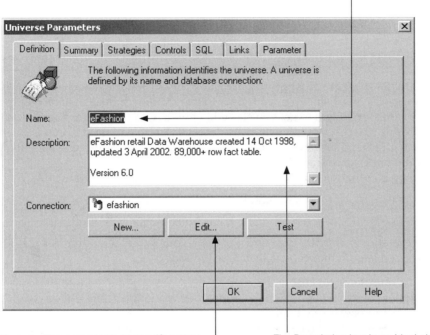

Edit connection parameters to specify source system login IDs, passwords, and disconnect time

The Description box is an ideal place to provide users with additional help text

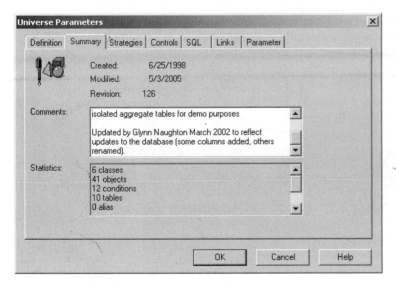

Summary Tab

The Summary tab of the Universe Parameters dialog box provides information about the universe, such as the number of classes, objects, and joins. Additionally, it provides a last modification date, the name of the modifier, and a revision number. The revision number is updated each time you export the universe to the repository, regardless of whether or not you made changes to it.

> **TIP** *The Comments section in the Summary tab allows an administrator to include additional technical notes on the universe. End users do not see these notes. This makes the Comments section an excellent place to store detailed revision notes for change control purposes.*

Strategies Tab

The Strategies tab of the Universe Parameters dialog box defines how the universe uses information from the data dictionary to help you build the universe. A *data dictionary* is a set of system tables that your RDBMS automatically creates and maintains about the objects (tables, views, synonyms, owners) in your data source. Although BusinessObjects provides some very powerful strategies to get you started, if you have a data warehouse or source system architecture that uses public synonyms (most do), you will need to create external strategies to ensure Designer can see those tables. The default strategies vary slightly for each type of database you are accessing.

The strategy information is used during a number of Designer activities:

- During the wizard's universe build
- If you use the Insert button or menu to insert tables, joins, or candidate objects
- In automatically creating joins and objects, if your database options use this setting (discussed later in the section "Database Options")

Although your source system DBA will generally help you customize these strategies, as a universe designer, the more you understand how they work, the better you can advise the DBA on the best approach to customization.

Strategies are SQL statements that read the data dictionary tables in your source system. The queries then use that dictionary information to present you with a list of initial classes, objects, joins, and tables. Thus if all your data warehouse tables start with DW, for example, then your initial proposed classes will also start with DW (such as *Dw Product*). If you do not want the user to see this DW (not recommended), then you can modify your strategy file to drop the DW from the proposed classes automatically. Without modifying the strategy file, you must manually modify each individual object.

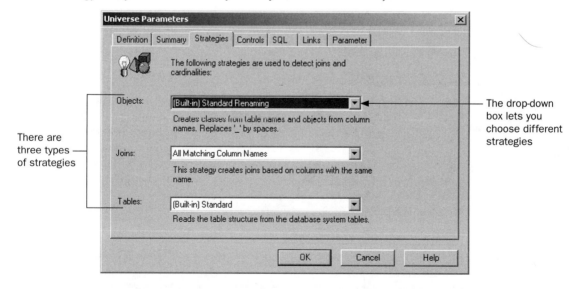

There are three parts of a universe that strategies interact with: objects, joins, and tables.

- **Objects**   The object strategy determines how Designer reads the table and column information from the data dictionary to come up with some initial classes and objects (either when using the wizard or when inserting tables). By default, the table names become the proposed class names and the individual columns within each table become the objects in your universe. The default object strategy also converts all names to initial caps and removes the underscore (_) from any table and field names.

- **Joins**   Designer has several built-in approaches to automatically create joins, listed next.

  - **Edit manually (none)**   Joins are not created automatically.

  - **Database keys matching names**   Joins are created automatically between columns that are indicated in the database as primary keys and foreign keys.

NOTE   *The database keys matching names strategy is not working in Service Pack 1.*

  - **All matching column names**   When the column names match between two tables, the joins are automatically inserted, regardless of whether they were designated as keys by the DBA when the tables were created.

  - **All matching numeric column names**   Joins are created automatically between columns that are numeric and have matching names. In the Oracle sample Sales History (SH) schema, the primary key in the TIMES dimension table is TIME_ID and is a date field. In the fact table SALES, TIME_ID is a foreign key and a date field. This strategy would not automatically propose a join because the field format is date. If you wish joins to be proposed when the field format is numeric, data, or character, select the preceding strategy.

- **Tables**   This part of the strategy is probably your most important part. If Designer cannot find your necessary tables, it can never move to the next step of creating objects and proposing joins. Information collected from the table part of the strategy is displayed in the structure window, such as the column name, data type (Numeric, Character, Date), and key.

In early versions of Designer, the SQL used to find the tables in the RDBMS was quite seamless and designers could easily modify it. As of version 4, Designer switched to this approach of built-in strategies and external strategies. Thus, the exact SQL of the built-in strategies is no longer viewable. However, Designer basically selects all physical tables owned by the individual user specified in the connection parameters. For example, if the owner of the tables in your Central Data Warehouse is CDW, then you must log in with the user ID CDW for Designer to find these tables. Usually, the DBA will also create synonyms so that users can access these tables without prefacing them with CDW.

You can change the OWNER parameter for the universe to N for No (see the "Parameter Tab" section in this chapter). This will drop the owner name from your table prefix and will cause the built-in strategies to look for public synonyms and views (for example, the user name specified in the connection parameters does not necessarily own the physical tables). However, setting OWNER to N without customizing an external strategy can also pick up a lot of clutter such as system tables. Therefore, you will still need to use or create an external strategy.

Automatically creating objects and joins can either be a productivity booster or a nuisance. The usefulness of this process is very much dependent upon your data source and how closely aligned it is with the business terminology. When the data source is a data warehouse with conformed dimensions, I find automatic join creation more helpful than automatic object creation.

External Strategies

External strategies are customized files that allow you to control how the data dictionary is read. It can be rather tedious to implement external strategies, yet there are several often-cited reasons when you must use them:

- Your database uses public synonyms.
- You want to extract column comments from your source system and use them as object descriptions.
- You wish to import metadata from a text file.
- Certain tables do not appear in the universe structure.

You also may use an external strategy to import metadata from a spreadsheet or text file. External strategies appear along with the built-in strategies under each of the drop-down options for objects, joins, and tables along with the built-in strategies. However, you create external strategies outside of Designer using an XML editor. In version 5.x, strategy files were text files. All related files are stored under

```
C:\Program Files\Business Objects\BusinessObjects Enterprise
11.5\win32_x86\dataAccess\ConnectionServer\RDBMS
```

where *RDBMS* is the data source type used for this universe connection.

There are three main steps to declaring and creating a strategy file. In order for Designer to recognize any changes to these files, you must make the changes before you launch Designer or restart Designer:

1. Reference the external strategy file.
2. Edit the external strategy file to specify the SQL to execute and the type of strategy. This is the "essence" of the file.
3. Specify the help text to appear within Designer. You edit this text in the *RDBMS_LANGUAGE*.STG file, for example ORAEN.STG for the Oracle English language file. This step is optional.

Steps 1 and 2 are described in detail in the following sections.

Reference External Strategy File

So that the external strategy file is active within Designer, you declare it in the *RDBMS*.SBO file. In version 5, this was declared in the *RDBMS*.PRM file. For example, if Oracle is the data source and Windows the operating system, you modify the following SBO file:

```
C:\Program Files\Business Objects\BusinessObjects Enterprise
11.5\win32_x86\dataAccess\ConnectionServer\oracle\oracle.sbo
```

Within this file, there are multiple parameters. The parameter that declares the external strategy file is

```
<Parameter Name="Strategies File">oracle</Parameter>
```

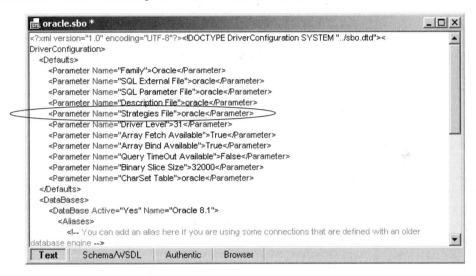

Business Objects provides a sample external strategy file for each database, named as *RDBMS*.STG. You can edit this file (make a backup copy first!) or change the preceding parameter within the SBO file to reference a different STG filename.

Edit the External Strategy File

The following screen shows a sample Oracle strategy for defining joins based on database constraints:

```
oracle.stg                                                      _ □ x
<?xml version="1.0" encoding="UTF-8"?><!DOCTYPE Strategies SYSTEM "../strategy.dtd"><Strategies>
    <Strategy Name="Constraints">
        <Type>JOIN</Type>
        <SQL>SELECT
INSTANCE1.TABLE_NAME,'|',
INSTANCE2.TABLE_NAME,'|',
INSTANCE1.TABLE_NAME || '.' || INSTANCE1.COLUMN_NAME
|| ' = ' ||
INSTANCE2.TABLE_NAME || '.' || INSTANCE2.COLUMN_NAME, '|',
' ','|'
FROM
    USER_CONSTRAINTS,
    USER_CONS_COLUMNS INSTANCE1,
    USER_CONS_COLUMNS INSTANCE2
WHERE
    USER_CONSTRAINTS.OWNER = USER
AND USER_CONSTRAINTS.CONSTRAINT_NAME = INSTANCE1.CONSTRAINT_NAME
AND USER_CONSTRAINTS.R_CONSTRAINT_NAME = INSTANCE2.CONSTRAINT_NAME
AND USER_CONSTRAINTS.CONSTRAINT_TYPE = 'R'
AND INSTANCE1.POSITION = INSTANCE2.POSITION</SQL>
    </Strategy>
```

As shown in the preceding example, these are the main components of the STG file:

Component	Purpose	Example
Strategy Name	Appears in the drop-down list of the universe parameters, Strategies tab.	`<Strategy Name="Constraints">` `</Strategy>`
Type of Strategy	Determines how the strategy is used in building the universe. The three types are OBJECTS, JOIN, STRUCT. STRUCT is used to build the list of tables.	`<Type>JOIN</Type>`
SQL Statement Output or Text File	Execute SQL to read from the data dictionary.	`<SQL>SELECT ... </SQL>`

The `SQL` section is the core of the strategy. This is where, for example, if you don't like `DW` appearing in each class name, you can use `LTRIM` within the SQL to cut it. If your source system uses `L33` for every column involving a customer, use `REPLACE` to replace `L33` with `CUSTOMER` to create automatically more meaningful object names.

Each strategy type requires a precise layout for the SQL output in order to function correctly. The Object strategy has nine output columns, as shown in Table 7-3, with a vertical bar (|) as a delimiter between each column. An external strategy for object creation can be helpful to read column comments from the dictionary tables. Unfortunately, the built-in strategies do not do this.

For example, the Oracle dictionary tables that would be used to create an object strategy are `USER_TABLES`, `USER_TAB_COLUMNS`, and `USER_COL_COMMENTS`. The dictionary table `ALL_OBJECTS` could be used in the SQL statement, particularly if public rather than user synonyms are used in the database; however, `ALL_OBJECTS` would also bring in too many unnecessary tables, including system objects, so a `WHERE` clause should be added to the SQL to filter the results.

Following is the SQL for the sample external strategy file ORACLE.STG that helps build object definitions:

```
SELECT
        U1.table_name,'|',
        U1.column_name,'|',
        translate(initcap(U1.table_name),'_',' '),'|',
        translate(initcap(U1.column_name),'_',' '),'|',
        U1.table_name||'.'||U1.column_name,'|',
        '  ','|',
        decode(SUBSTR(U1.DATA_TYPE,1,1),'N','N','F','N','D','D','C'),'|',
        SUBSTR(U2.comments,1,474),'|',
        'O','|'
FROM USER_TAB_COLUMNS U1,USER_COL_COMMENTS U2
WHERE
    U1.table_name=U2.table_name
```

```
and U1.column_name=U2.column_name
UNION
SELECT
      S.SYNONYM_NAME,'|',
      U1.column_name,'|',
      translate(initcap(S.SYNONYM_NAME),'_',' '),'|',
      translate(initcap(U1.column_name),'_',' '),'|',
      S.SYNONYM_NAME||'.'||U1.column_name,'|',
      '  ','|',
      decode(SUBSTR(U1.DATA_TYPE,1,1),'N','N','F','N','D','D','C'),'|',
      SUBSTR(U2.comments,1,474),'|',
      'O','|'
FROM ALL_TAB_COLUMNS U1, ALL_COL_COMMENTS U2, ALL_OBJECTS O, USER_SYNONYMS S
WHERE
      S.table_owner=O.owner
AND   S.table_name=O.object_name
AND   (O.OBJECT_TYPE='TABLE' OR O.OBJECT_TYPE='VIEW')
AND   O.owner=U1.owner
AND   O.object_name=U1.table_name
AND   U1.owner=U2.owner
AND   U1.table_name=U2.table_name
AND   U1.column_name=U2.column_name
```

Column	Output	Explanation
1	Table	Table, view, or synonym.
2	Column	Field from the object or table.
3	Class Name	The class name is converted from the physical table name, view, or synonym by applying all initial caps and converting underscores (_) to spaces.
4	Object Name	The object name is converted from the column name by applying all initial caps and converting underscores (_) to spaces.
5	SQL Select (Table.Column)	The table and column names are concatenated to form the SQL Select statement for each object.
6	SQL Where Clause	
7	Object Type	The object type is determined from the data type in the source data and converted to N for Numeric, D for Date, C for Character, or L for Long Text.
8	Description	The Object description is taken from the column comments.
9	Object Type (D, M, I)	The object type is D for Dimension, M for Measure, and I for Information.

TABLE 7-3   Format for Object Strategy File

In accessing the sample Oracle sales history owned by SH, the preceding SQL would create the following partial output:

```
SALES | PROD_ID       | Sales |Prod Id       | SALES.PROD_ID       || N | FK to the products dimension table                                           | 0 |
SALES | CUST_ID       | Sales |Cust Id       | SALES.CUST_ID       || N | FK to the customers dimension table                                          | 0 |
SALES | TIME_ID       | Sales |Time Id       | SALES.TIME_ID       || D | FK to the times dimension table                                              | 0 |
SALES | CHANNEL_ID    | Sales |Channel Id    | SALES.CHANNEL_ID    || C | FK to the channels dimension table                                           | 0 |
SALES | PROMO_ID      | Sales |Promo Id      | SALES.PROMO_ID      || N | promotion identifier, without FK constraint (intentionally) to show outer join optimization| 0 |
SALES | QUANTITY_SOLD | Sales |Quantity Sold | SALES.QUANTITY_SOLD || N | product quantity sold with the transaction                                   | 0 |
SALES | AMOUNT_SOLD   | Sales |Amount Sold   | SALES.AMOUNT_SOLD   || N | invoiced amount to the customer                                              | 0 |
```

A structure (<TYPE>STRUCT</TYPE>) or table strategy is used when you insert tables into the universe pane. It has six output columns as shown in Table 7-4, with each column separated by a vertical bar (|).

NOTE *Accessing USER dictionary tables can be a problem in strategies if the user name in the connection parameters is not the owner of the tables, views, or synonyms. Often synonyms are set up as PUBLIC. In such cases, use ALL_ dictionary tables to find synonyms and use WHERE clauses to find the appropriate database objects.*

The following table or STRUCT strategy was created by an oil and gas company that uses public synonyms in its data warehouse. This strategy file does a good job of limiting the information generated, thus making structure refreshes faster.

```
SELECT
        'REPT', '|',
        S.TABLE_OWNER, '|',
        S.SYNONYM_NAME,'|',
        U1.column_name,'|',
        decode(SUBSTR(U1.DATA_TYPE,1,1),'N','N','F','N','D','D','C'),'|',
        '','|'
FROM ALL_TAB_COLUMNS U1, ALL_COL_COMMENTS U2, ALL_OBJECTS O, ALL_SYNONYMS S
WHERE
     S.table_owner=O.owner
AND  S.table_name=O.object_name
AND  (O.OBJECT_TYPE='TABLE' OR O.OBJECT_TYPE='VIEW')
AND  O.owner=U1.owner
AND  O.object_name=U1.table_name
AND  U1.owner=U2.owner
AND  U1.table_name=U2.table_name
AND  U1.column_name=U2.column_name
AND  S.table_owner NOT IN ('SYSTEM', 'MDSYS', 'ORDSYS', 'SYS')
AND  S.DB_LINK IS NULL
UNION
SELECT
        'PRD5','|',
        S.TABLE_OWNER, '|',
        S.SYNONYM_NAME,'|',
        U1.column_name,'|',
        decode(SUBSTR(U1.DATA_TYPE,1,1),'N','N','F','N','D','D','C'),'|',
        '','|'
FROM ALL_TAB_COLUMNS@PRD5.WORLD U1, ALL_COL_COMMENTS@PRD5.WORLD U2,
ALL_OBJECTS@PRD5.WORLD O, ALL_SYNONYMS S
```

```
WHERE
     S.table_owner=O.owner
AND  S.table_name=O.object_name
AND  (O.OBJECT_TYPE='TABLE' OR O.OBJECT_TYPE='VIEW')
AND  O.owner=U1.owner
AND  O.object_name=U1.table_name
AND  U1.owner=U2.owner
AND  U1.table_name=U2.table_name
AND  U1.column_name=U2.column_name
AND  S.table_owner NOT IN ('SYSTEM', 'MDSYS', 'ORDSYS', 'SYS')
AND  S.DB_LINK = 'PRD5.WORLD'
```

Join strategies (<TYPE>JOIN</TYPE>) use five output columns as shown in Table 7-5, with each column separated with a vertical bar (|). It's rarely necessary to use external strategies for join creation.

For your external strategies to work, you must use the exact output layout. If you forget a column, mix up the order, or forget the delimiter, you will get unusual results or an error.

TIP   *If you have created business descriptions or other metadata inside a spreadsheet or other Office tool, you can read this metadata into the universe through the use of external strategies. The metadata must be saved in a text format with the appropriate layout and column delimiters described in Tables 7-3–7-5. Within the external strategy file (for example, Oracle.stg), instead of listing a SQL statement, you reference the text filename as in this example:*

```
<Strategy Name="Object Help Text">
 <FILE>C:\METADATA\OBJECT_HELP.TEXT</FILE>
</Strategy>
```

Database Options That Relate to Strategies

The settings on the Strategies tab also relate to the Designer's Database Options under Tools | Options | Database. For example, in the Strategies tab, even if you tell Designer to use Smart Matching based on the column names, Designer will automatically create the joins in the universe only if you check the box Extract Joins With Tables in Options. The main difference between Parameters and Database Options is that Parameters are specific to the individual universe, whereas the Options apply globally to Designer and, therefore, all universes created on the PC. Refer to the section "Designer Options" later in this chapter for other Designer options.

Column	Output	Explanation
1	Table Qualifier	Database name
2	Owner	Owner of the tables if OWNER=Y is set in the .prm file
3	Table	Name of table, view, or synonym
4	Column	Column name
5	Data Type	Data type to appear in structure window as C, N, or D
6	Null?	Indicator if the column can be null. Valid values are No or blank

TABLE 7-4   Format for Structure or Table Strategy File

Column	Output	Explanation
1	Table1	Table 1 forms the left side of the join statement.
2	Table2	Table 2 forms the right side of the join statement.
3	Join Operator	The Join operator, usually = but can also be >=, <>, and so on.
4	Outer_Type (L,R)	If the join is an outer join, then an indication if it is left outer join or right; otherwise blank if it is not an outer join.
5	Cardinality	An indication of the cardinality between the tables, such as one to one (11), one to many (1N), or many to one (N1).

TABLE 7-5   Format for Structure of a Join Strategy File

Controls Tab

The Controls tab of the Universe Parameters dialog box enables you to specify additional limits that will affect individual users' queries. These parameters are sometimes referred to as query governors:

- **Limit size of result set to**   Prevents the Enterprise server (for Web Intelligence), the user PC (for Desktop Intelligence), or the wide area network from becoming saturated with too many rows of data. It does not reduce the load on the source system database. Therefore, leave this box unchecked or increase it to a larger number such as 200,000 rows. If you use drill-down, the number of rows in the result set can be quite large, even if the initial summary report displays only ten rows of data, for example. However, larger result sets lead to slower report generation, particularly when you have complex formatting and variables.

TIP *If you are concerned about novice users incorrectly retrieving large result sets, you can use Restriction Sets (see Chapter 13) to tailor these settings for individual users or groups.*

- **Limit execution time to**   This is another check box to use carefully. This option limits the time the server connection or PC (for Desktop Intelligence) is tied up, but it will not limit the time the database is affected. So if an administrator sets the limit to 10 minutes, the database could actually try to run the query for 60 minutes. In the past, BusinessObjects Enterprise server supported only synchronous connectivity to the database, meaning users could not cancel a query and only received an error only *after* the query completed. With asynchronous connectivity, the database session becomes inactive after 10 minutes and users will receive an error message at that time. Desktop Intelligence will say "No Data to Fetch," while Web Intelligence will indicate only partial results have been retrieved (but no error). However, the query is still executing to completion on the database server, consuming resources there. Also, this option refers to the time for all of the SQL statements to execute. If your query contains multiple, synchronized SQL statements (which get created when there are multiple contexts in the universe), ensure this setting is high enough for all the statements to execute.

NOTE *If your queries are running this long, you need to do some serious index optimization, possibly modify your universe to generate more efficient SQL, or as a last resort, encourage users to schedule long-running reports.*

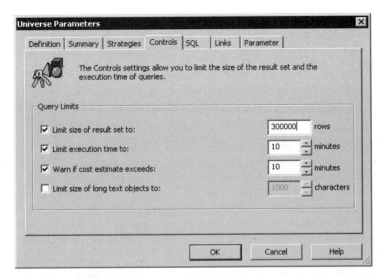

- **Warn if cost estimate exceeds**   Certain databases support the use of cost estimates when analyzing how long a query will take to execute. Although the preceding screen suggests this relates to the duration of the query, in reality, the cost is a relative measurement determined by the data source's I/O utilization, memory consumption, and CPU time. This setting was not available in XI Release 1 and is not currently working in XI Release 2; when you set this parameter, it has no effect on the query completion. However, in previous releases, if you enabled the cost estimate, you also had to ensure that each user had write access to the Oracle PLAN TABLE so that the cost estimate could be performed and then used to warn the users.

- **Limit size of long text objects to**   This parameter is useful for BLOB fields or for very long variable-length fields. Users can adjust their column widths if they do not want to see the full text. However, if you as the designer set this number too low, users cannot override it; they never can get to the data at the end of a long field.

SQL Tab

When deploying BusinessObjects XI directly against a transaction system, you may want to limit complex SQL queries so that they do not affect response time for inputting data. Otherwise, I prefer to leave complex SQL enabled in pure reporting databases or data warehouses. Casual users may not require these features and can ignore the options. However, if you disable advanced SQL, then power users may get frustrated. The following three options in the SQL tab of the Universe Parameters dialog box allow you to limit complex queries:

- **Allow use of subqueries**   Subqueries are a powerful type of query that allows users to nest one query within a main query (see Chapter 23). As these queries are complex and use additional RDBMS resources, administrators can remove this capability. By default, leave it enabled.

- **Allow use of union, intersect, and minus operators**   These operators allow advanced users to combine multiple SQL statements into one data provider. By default, leave it enabled.

- **Allow complex operands in query panel**   This option is similar to the preceding one but allows users to select the conditions from the query panel: Complex operands are "Both" and "Except." The operand "Both" generates an `INTERSECT` query, and "Except" generates a `MINUS` query.

The Multiple Paths options determine the kind of SQL generated behind the scenes. The users may not see the SQL, but these options do affect the performance and accuracy of any given query.

- **Multiple SQL statements for each context**   Contexts are explained in detail in Chapter 8. This option should be checked so that a separate SQL statement is generated for each context or star schema. If your universe has multiple contexts and you do not enable this box, users will receive an error message when trying to create a query that contains measures from two different contexts. In the Efashion universe, for example, one could not create a query that analyzes promotion costs and sales revenue for a given product without the use of contexts and this option.

- **Multiple SQL statements for each measure**   When you have measures that come from multiple tables within the same context, this box should always be enabled or queries from multiple fact tables may produce incorrect results. For example, in the Efashion universe, unit sales price and extended sales price are from two different tables within the same context. In order to produce correct results when these measures are used in the same query, Web Intelligence needs to issue two `SELECT` statements. It's also useful to check this option even if you think you have one central fact table. For example, you may later create measures such as number of days or number of products that go against dimension tables. Without this option enabled, Web Intelligence will create a Cartesian product and give incorrect information when the measures come from more than one table. The disadvantage of this option, though, is that certain queries could be processed more efficiently with one `SELECT` statement and still return accurate results. For example, if your query contains a `COUNT DISTINCT` (see Chapter 11) of products from a dimension table with sales from a fact table, as long as the count object uses `DISTINCT`, you will get correct results. However, it will take longer and significantly more resources to process the multiple `SELECT` statements generated by default with this option set than when using one `SELECT` statement without this option enabled. My recommendation, then, is that correct queries are more important than fast queries. Check this option by default but monitor how many queries users create that generate multiple `SELECT` statements unnecessarily.

- **Allow selection of multiple contexts**   Enables users to create queries on objects from multiple contexts. This box should be enabled. In the Efashion universe, it allows users to analyze sales and promotions in one report even though sales and promotions are two different contexts.

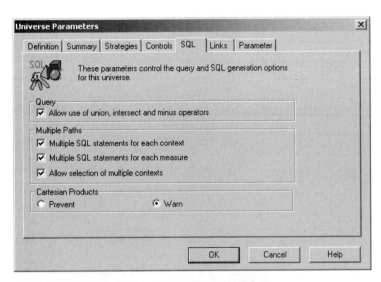

Understanding Multiple SQL Statements for Each Measure

The option Multiple SQL Statements For Each Measure has some nuances that are important to understand. First, even if this box is enabled, if the measures come from the same fact table, the query engine will issue only one SQL statement. This is a good thing, as it avoids tying up the database unnecessarily. Second, the query engine will issue only two SQL statements if the object is a measure (as discussed further in Chapter 9) and it contains an aggregate function (sum, count, and so on).

When SQL joins two tables together, it will repeat each row for each combination in the GROUP BY section. Figure 7-2 illustrates how this happens. The ARTICLE_LOOKUP table has only one row and shows a price of 114.55. The SHOP_FACTS table has six rows showing that this style blazer sold six times during week 8 of year 2000. When SQL joins ARTICLE_LOOKUP with SHOP_FACTS, the 114.55 unit price will get repeated six times and summed to 687.30—an incorrect result. Business Objects will refer to this problem as a "fan trap," but SQL experts and DBAs will generically refer to it as a Cartesian product.

BusinessObjects XI will prevent Cartesian products and this overstatement of results by issuing a SELECT statement for each measure coming from different tables. This is seamless to users.

NOTE *This example uses the object Extended Price object, which includes a SUM. As discussed in Chapter 9, unit prices should never be summed. If anything, they can be averaged or recalculated with revenue/quantity sold. If you wish to see another example of a fan trap, disable the option Multiple SQL Statements For Each Measure and include the two measures from two different tables, such as Store Details \ Extended sales floor size and Sales revenue. These measures must contain aggregate functions such as SUM or COUNT.*

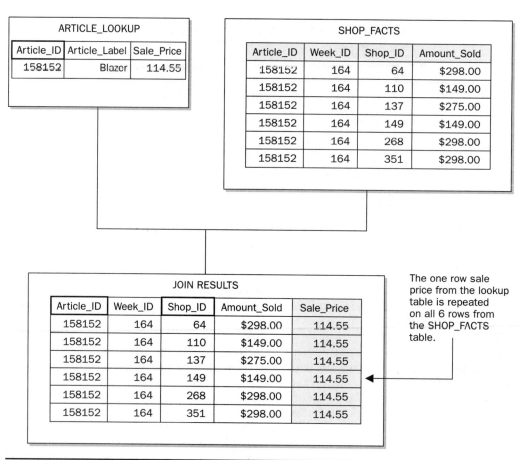

ARTICLE_LOOKUP

Article_ID	Article_Label	Sale_Price
158152	Blazer	114.55

SHOP_FACTS

Article_ID	Week_ID	Shop_ID	Amount_Sold
158152	164	64	$298.00
158152	164	110	$149.00
158152	164	137	$275.00
158152	164	149	$149.00
158152	164	268	$298.00
158152	164	351	$298.00

JOIN RESULTS

Article_ID	Week_ID	Shop_ID	Amount_Sold	Sale_Price
158152	164	64	$298.00	114.55
158152	164	110	$149.00	114.55
158152	164	137	$275.00	114.55
158152	164	149	$149.00	114.55
158152	164	268	$298.00	114.55
158152	164	351	$298.00	114.55

The one row sale price from the lookup table is repeated on all 6 rows from the SHOP_FACTS table.

FIGURE 7-2   Queries produce incorrect results when aggregates are used on multiple tables. Split the SQL statements to prevent this.

The reports in Figure 7-3 show how the results depend on which option is set in the SQL universe parameters. The top report shows the correct results as the SQL is split for each measure and each table. As a control, I have added an object to the universe that does not contain the SUM on price. Notice that both the *Extended Price* object that contains the SUM and the *Unit Price* that does not contain the SUM yield the same correct results: 114.55. For the middle report, only one SQL statement is generated, as the parameter "Multiple SQL Statements for Each Measure" was not selected in the universe. Notice how the *Extended Price* returns grossly incorrect results, 687.30. The results have been overstated by however many rows there are in the SHOP_FACTS table.

Multiple Measures, 2 SQL Statements

SKU number	SKU desc	Sales revenue	Extended price	Unit Price - No Sum
158152	Blazer	$970,977	$114.55	$114.55

Multiple Measures, 1 SQL Statements Wrong Results

SKU number	SKU desc	Sales revenue	Extended price	Unit Price - No Sum
158152	Blazer	$1,468	$687.30	$114.55

Multiple Measures, 2 SQL Statements but WRONG Results

SKU number	SKU desc	Year	Sales revenue	Extended price	Unit Price - No Sum
158152	Blazer	2001	$290,117	$125,775.90	$114.55
158152	Blazer	2002	$666,235	$257,508.40	$114.55
158152	Blazer	2003	$14,626	$19,702.60	$114.55

FIGURE 7-3 Splitting the SQL ensures correct results for reports with multiple measures.

Unfortunately, even with this setting to split the SQL, you cannot guarantee users will always get correct results as shown in the bottom report. Although there are two SQL statements for this report, the query contains an additional result object *Year* that forces a join to SHOP_FACTS and again overstates the results. Therefore, while splitting the SQL can help in many cases, it will not resolve all problems of having measures in multiple tables. The best way to prevent such problems is to have all measures in one fact table per context. Measures that contain counts are an exception and can be resolved differently as discussed in Chapter 11.

Links Tab

The Links tab of the Universe Parameters dialog box allows an administrator to create a master universe that is then linked to other universes. As this is an architecture and maintenance issue, links are described more fully in Chapter 15. By default, leave this tab blank.

Parameter Tab

The Parameter tab is new in XI. In the past, many database parameters could be set only by modifying the *RDBMS*.PRM file with a text editor. This file is still used for certain parameters. However, parameters you set here are specific to individual universes and no longer maintained in the *RDBMS*.PRM file. The universe-specific parameters are documented in the online help. Additional parameters that are database specific are available in the vendor documentation, specifically, in the *Data Access Guide*. Table 7-6 lists commonly changed parameters.

NOTE *You cannot add parameters that are used in the RDBMS.PRM file. For example, the parameter OWNER is still maintained in the RDBMS.PRM file and will be ignored if entered here.*

To change a database parameter,

1. Click Parameters from the toolbar or File | Parameters from the pull-down menu.
2. Select the Parameter tab.

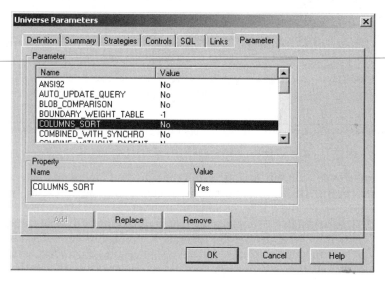

3. From the list of parameters, select the one you wish to change—in this example, COLUMNS_SORT.

4. In the Value box, enter the new parameter value, **Yes**.

5. Click Replace to update the parameter value and then OK to close the dialog.

Parameter	Options	Default	Explanation
ANSI92	Yes|No	No	Determines the type of SQL generated, either ANSI 92 compliant or not. See Chapter 8 for more information.
COLUMNS_SORT	Yes|No	No	Determines the order that columns are displayed in tables in the structure pane.
CORE_ORDER_PRIORITY	Yes|No	Yes	Determines the order in which classes and objects are sorted when universes are linked. Yes causes them to be sorted according to the master universe. No causes them to be sorted in the derived universe.
DISTINCT_VALUES =	GROUPBY DISTINCT	DISTINCT	Determines how the SQL for Lists of Values is generated (See Chapter 10). With the default settings, the LOV query uses SELECT DISTINCT, which can be slow against large tables.
MAX_INLIST_VALUES	*NN* up to 256	99	Specifies the maximum values users can select when using IN LIST in query conditions.

TABLE 7-6   Database Parameters Configurable Per Universe

Universe Connections

The universe connection determines how users connect to the data warehouse or data source when they build or refresh a query. The user name and password used for the universe connection can be the same as or different from the user name and password used to authenticate a user in the BusinessObjects Enterprise repository. Often they are the same if you use the database to control security. Certain databases, such as Teradata, also perform better when each database user has its own workspace, whereas others, such as Oracle, perform better with a "shared" database login as memory and resources are shared.

Connections can be defined in two places within Designer:

- When you access the universe parameters, Definition tab
- Via the Connections button on the toolbar or select Tools | Connections from the pull-down menu

This second option is new in XI and replaces the approach of defining connections via Supervisor in 5.*x* and 6.*x*. The Connection dialog in previous versions has now been replaced with a wizard that guides you through the process of adding and editing connections.

As discussed earlier, when you work with universes, you are working on a copy and changes appear to users only when you export the universe. The opposite is true of connections. As you make changes to connections, they are immediately saved to the repository when you click Finish from within the Connection Wizard.

Connection Types

Designer supports three different types of connections, each denoted with a unique symbol in the list of connections:

- *Personal* connections that users may create for freehand SQL or that universe designers create when testing new data sources. The definitions reside in C:\ Documents and Settings*User*\Application Data\Business Objects\Business Objects 11.5\lsipdac.lsi (personal data account.local security information), where *User* is the name of the network or NT user.

- *Shared* connections that are shared via work group folders on a LAN server for designers to share outside the CMS repository. The definitions reside in sdac.lsi (shared data account).

- *Secure* connections that reside in the CMS repository. In order to deploy universes to end users, you must use secure connections.

Two Approaches to Login Parameters

To understand how login parameters within the universe connections work, you must first understand how BusinessObjects XI is deployed and how security concerns in the various data sources, whether OLTPs or data marts, interact.

Scenario 1: Use Database Credentials

Let's assume that you are deploying an Orders universe directly against a transaction system. Users who enter Orders use BusinessObjects XI to create real-time reports against the same data source. Therefore, you want the same security in the source system to apply in BusinessObjects XI. You want BusinessObjects XI to pass individual database logins to the Orders data source. In order to do so, you create a set of database credentials for each individual user that will be passed on to the Orders data source. While it would be preferable for users to have the same user ID and password between different systems, this is sometimes not the case when different administrators are involved. As shown in Figure 7-4, the user ID and password to log in to BusinessObjects Enterprise is Cindi/ASK. However, the user ID and password to log in to the Orders Transaction system is completely different: U761358/ASK1. In order to pass this second user ID through to the universe data source, an administrator defines a set of database credentials for each user (see Chapter 13). These database credentials will apply to any universe or connection with the option "use database credentials" enabled.

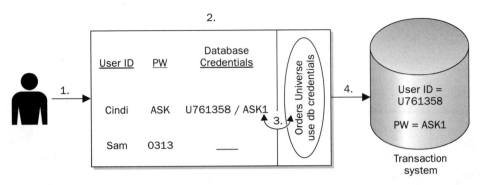

FIGURE 7-4   Database credentials can be different from BusinessObjects Enterprise login IDs and passwords.

NOTE *Database credentials are new in XI Release 2. In earlier versions of BusinessObjects Enterprise, there was a check box in the connection parameters "Use BusinessObjects User Name And Password." If you used the Import Wizard to migrate these universes to the new platform, you were prompted to create database credentials for each user.*

The following happens when a user tries to refresh a query:

1. The user supplies a BusinessObjects Enterprise user ID and password, in this example, Cindi/ASK.

2. The CMS validates the user ID and password against definitions in the BusinessObjects Enterprise repository and checks permissions.

3. When the user refreshes a document based on the Orders universe, the CMS checks which connection parameters to supply to the data source. For the Orders connection, the parameters are set to use database credentials. The database credentials for user Cindi are defined as U761358/ASK1.

4. When the Enterprise Connection Server connects to the orders data source, the user ID U761358 is passed through to the database.

CAUTION *If you enable the use of database credentials for the universe, then all users who access this universe must have a unique login ID to the data source and the credentials must be defined via the CMC (see Chapter 13). If this is missing, users will receive an error when trying to refresh a query. In Figure 7-4, the user Sam does not have database credentials defined and would receive an error.*

Scenario 2: Shared Login to the Data Warehouse

As shown in Figure 7-5, many companies use a data warehouse environment rather than accessing data directly in an OLTP. The CMS repository tables may be physically installed on the same machine as the data warehouse tables or on a separate server. However, the table owners and the database instance used are most likely different. As users execute queries against the data warehouse, the connection to the database uses the same user ID and password, BOEnterprise/BOEnterprise.

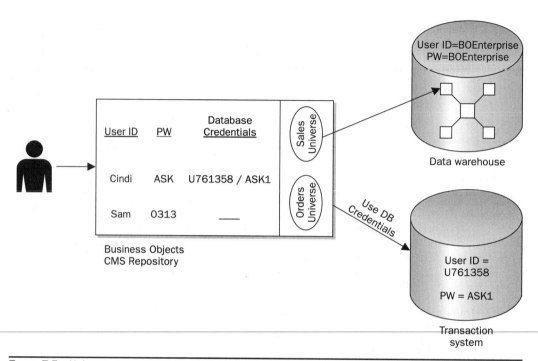

FIGURE 7-5 Universe connections can use a common database login for different BusinessObjects Enterprise users.

The workflow is similar to that in Figure 7-4; however, in step 3, the user name and password are stored as part of the universe parameters connection and shared by multiple BusinessObjects Enterprise users. Database credentials for individual users are not read.

Which Connection to Use in a Universe

When you specify the user ID and password in the universe connection parameters, the administrator must understand how these IDs and passwords interact and carefully consider ease of use, security, usage tracking, and cost.

- **Ease of usage**   If database credentials are not defined correctly or if they become out of sync with passwords in the source system, users will blame BusinessObjects XI for being too difficult to use or not working.

- **Security**   If you define row- and column-level security in the source system, you may want to use database credentials to leverage that security. If, however, you are only concerned about access to reports in the repository or if you use the tools in Designer to control row- and object-level security, then you may want to use a common data source login.

- **Usage tracking**   There are two levels of usage tracking in a BusinessObjects XI deployment: the first is within BusinessObjects Enterprise, and the second is at the database level. BusinessObjects Enterprise usage tracking will tell you which users access which reports and how long those queries are executing. However, you also may track usage at the database level to determine how frequently certain indexes are used and whose queries are most often doing full table scans. If you decide to use a shared login from BusinessObjects Enterprise to the source system database (Scenario 2, Figure 7-5), it makes it harder to control runaway queries. The DBA sees only one user ID (BOEnterprise) logged in to the database, even though it may represent hundreds of different end users. For this reason, many companies assign user IDs and passwords at both the BusinessObjects Enterprise and data source levels.

- **Cost**   Finally, another consideration in choosing between unique source system IDs or a shared one is your RDBMS licensing. If your license is by named user, then it may be more cost effective to use a shared database login for data access. You will still need to pay for the appropriate number of concurrent licenses. Designer also enables you to set how long a database connection remains active to keep concurrency against the data source low.

- **Performance**   Certain databases perform better when there is a shared login, while other databases, such as Teradata, prefer individual database credentials because of the way resources and memory are allocated.

TIP   *Always, always test your connection when changing a user ID, password, or database name. Just when you think you've typed it perfectly, you may find you've made a mistake, rendering everyone's universe unusable!*

Advanced Connection Parameters

The Advanced Parameters of the Connection Wizard provide additional options that affect users during query execution. These options and their defaults will vary depending on which database you are using.

The first three settings tell the Enterprise server what to do when a query is complete:

- **Disconnect after each transaction**   This option can make repeated querying for users appear unnecessarily slow as the login process is added to each data refresh. It does, however, keep the number of database connections open to a minimum.

- **Keep the connection active for *NN***   This allows you to specify a time limit. If no additional queries are submitted to the database during that time, then the connection is closed. A good balance is to allow the connection to be active for ten minutes, as shown in the following screen.

- **Keep the connection active during the whole session**   This means user queries are never slowed down for the source system/data warehouse login and logout process. This is great for users but can become expensive for RDBMS licensing and Enterprise server overhead.

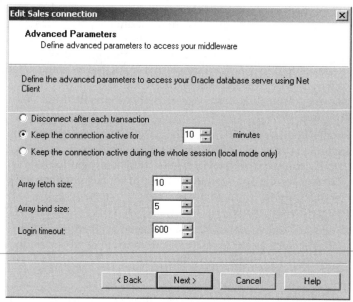

- **Array fetch size**   This option determines how many rows of data can be shipped back to the client or Enterprise server in one fetch. Increasing the fetch size causes query results to return faster to the user; however, higher settings consume more memory. Response times are more greatly affected by network utilization and query performance. If you are experiencing slow fetches, try increasing the number by increments of 10. For example, in one scenario, increasing the array fetch size from 10 to 100 caused query results to return 25 percent faster.
- **Array bind size**   This is a new setting in XI. This affects how much data can be held in memory before being written to the repository. When the bind array fills, it is transmitted to the database. This setting seems to have a smaller impact on performance than the array fetch size but a larger impact on memory used by the WIReportServer process.
- **Login timeout**   This is also a new setting in XI; it relates to the universe connection to the data source (not between users and InfoView). As the BusinessObjects Enterprise Connection Server connects to the data source, the user ID and password in the connection parameters are passed to the data source. Busy data sources may have slow login times. This setting allows you to increase the number of seconds the Connection Server will attempt to log in to the data source before returning an error.

Asynchronous Connections

Earlier versions of BusinessObjects allowed you to specify the connection mode as either synchronous or asynchronous. Earlier versions of Web Intelligence did not support asynchronous connections that would allow users to cancel their query. With XI, Web

Intelligence supports asynchronous connection to the data source by default; if a user cancels a query, that query gets cancelled (at an appropriate point) on the database.

Custom Connection Parameters

The Custom Parameters enable you to make additional changes that are database specific and rarely used. Your DBA may suggest changing certain custom parameters. In Oracle, for example, Hints can tell the Oracle optimizer a more efficient way of executing queries. For the most part, the cost-based optimizer will automatically figure out the best execution plan. However, when this is not working optimally, the DBA may recommend inserting Hints.

Creating a Connection Step-by-Step

To create a connection that you use in defining the universe parameters,

1. Select the Connections button on the toolbar or select Tools | Connections from the pull-down menu.

2. Click Add.

3. The Welcome to the Connection Wizard screen appears. Click Next.

4. You are presented with a list of Database Middleware types. For each type, you expand the folders to select a particular driver version. For example, to use Oracle 10, click + next to the Oracle folder, then Oracle 10, and then Oracle client. Click Next.

5. Enter the Login Parameters. For universes deployed through the CMS repository, the connection type is secured.

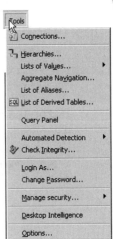

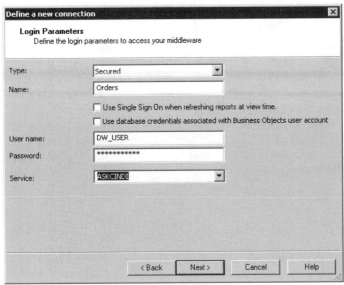

6. Tab to move to the Name box and enter a connection name. The name should be meaningful to other universe designers.

7. Enter the user name and password to be passed through to the data source as discussed earlier in "Two Approaches to Login Parameters." If you wish to pass through individual database credentials for each user, check the appropriate box.

8. Depending on the database type, select the name of the database and the name of the database server. Then click Next.

9. When prompted to test your connection, *always* select Perform A Test. This will tell you if you have incorrectly entered a login parameter. Click Next.

10. Confirm or modify the Advanced Parameters and click Next.

11. Confirm or modify any Custom Parameters and click Finish.

12. When you are returned to the list of connections, click Finish to close the Connection Wizard.

Designer Options

There are a number of options in Designer that determine the appearance of tables in the universe pane, how your universe definitions are saved, and printed reports. These options are discussed in various chapters as they are used.

Database Options

Settings on the Designer database options determine if your universe joins and objects are automatically inserted and interact with strategies as discussed earlier in this chapter. To access these options, select Tools | Options | Database from the pull-down menus.

- **Extract joins with tables**   As you insert tables into the universe structure, this option will insert joins according to the strategies you set in the universe parameters.

- **Detect cardinalities in joins**   When Designer detects cardinalities, it analyzes the number of rows in each table to determine where the one-to-one, one-to-many, and many-to-many relationships are. Checking this option for large databases can cause very slow structure creation (half an hour in some cases). As a default, I recommend leaving this option disabled and only explicitly detecting cardinalities while working on joins via Tools | Detect Cardinalities.

- **Create default classes and objects from tables**   This is helpful during rapid development and testing but less than ideal for larger schemas. As you insert a table into the universe structure, objects are automatically created based upon each field in the table. Clearly, users will not need access to a number of key fields. Additionally, your column names in your data mart must be based on business terminology, and even then, you will still need to delete a lot of extraneous objects and move them around to more meaningful classes. Therefore, leave this option disabled.

- **Table and column values**   This is a useful feature to show you a sample of the data in your tables as you build objects in the universe. As a default, Designer will present you with the first 100 values in your database.

Quick Design Wizard

Designer includes a wizard for building basic universes. Although you probably will not be able to use a universe created with the wizard "as is," it is a useful tool for creating a universe quickly and becoming more familiar with universe components.

In the following example, you will create a new universe based on the MS Access database Efashion.MDB that Business Objects provides as a sample.

   1. To invoke the Quick Design Wizard, start Designer and choose File | New or click Quick Design Wizard.

NOTE   *If the wizard does not appear, check that your default settings enable the wizard. From the Designer menu, select Tools | Options. On the General tab, click the check box File/New Starts Quick Design Wizard.*

2. The wizard will present you with a welcome screen that gives you an overview of the steps to build a universe. Click Begin to proceed.

3. Give your universe a meaningful name such as **Test Fashion**. This is the name that users will see when selecting a data source for a report.

4. Click New to create a new connection to a data source connection or use the drop-down list to select an existing connection.

5. Click Next to proceed to Step 2 of the wizard, Create Initial Classes and Objects. In this step, you select either the full tables or individual data columns that will become universe classes and objects, respectively. By clicking the + sign next to the table name, you can choose individual columns from the table that will become objects. You may find it easier initially to add all the columns and delete the individual ones you don't want. Hold down the CTRL key while clicking the following three tables: ARTICLE_ LOOKUP, CALENDAR_YEAR_LOOKUP, and OUTLET_LOOKUP. In this step, you only want to select dimension tables, not fact tables that are used for measure objects.

PART II

6. Click Add so that elements from these three tables become universe classes and objects as shown in the following example. If you click the + sign next to any of the individual classes, you will notice that Designer has added all the columns in each table with a blue box next to the item to denote a dimension. These symbols and object types are discussed further in Chapter 9.

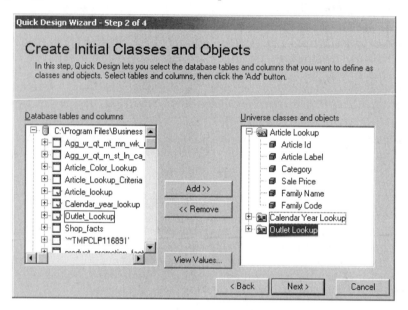

7. Click Next to proceed to Step 3 of the wizard, in which you select objects that become measures. A measure is often referred to as a "fact" in a fact table in a data warehouse. It is numeric data that business users wish to analyze by different dimensions. In BusinessObjects XI, measures generally include a SQL aggregate function such as COUNT or SUM. These are also discussed further in Chapter 9. For now, click the + sign next to the table SHOP_FACTS, select MARGIN, AMOUNT_SOLD, and QUANTITY_SOLD, and then click Sum. Notice that the wizard will add a measure object with a pink circle or sphere before each of these fields. At this point, you also could create Count objects to count products or customers.

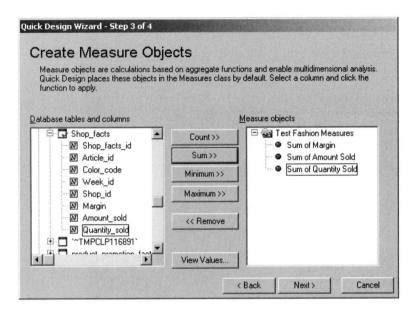

8. Click Next to proceed to Step 4 of the wizard. In this step, the wizard tells you how many classes, objects, and joins your initial universe contains. Click Finish to exit the wizard and view the universe in Designer.

9. Click File | Save from the pull-down menu or click the Save button on the toolbar to save your universe.

NOTE *In earlier versions of Designer, if your universe name was longer than eight characters or contained spaces, you would have been prompted for a filename different from the universe name. This is no longer the case in XI, which will automatically use the long universe name as the filename.*

10. For other designers or end users to see this universe, you must export it to the repository. From the Designer pull-down menu, select File | Export.

Congratulations! You have just completed your initial universe. If only a real business universe could be this easy!

Summary

This chapter introduced the Designer interface and parameters that affect how you build your universe. A number of the parameters determine what users can do when building queries and how the SQL is generated. Universe connections affect query performance and interaction with the physical data source. While universe parameters affect the current universe, connections apply to all universes that use that connection.

Universe Joins

J oins define how two tables relate to one another. In Designer, your strategies (under File |
Parameters) can automatically propose joins based on common names between two
tables. Alternatively, you can manually define the joins. Most of the complexities
around joins occur when your universe contains multiple star schemas or when you are
using BusinessObjects XI against a normalized transaction system.

Join Graphics

In Designer, you can change the appearance of the join lines and the symbols used to display
relationship cardinalities. You also can have Designer provide you with additional information
that will help you create or modify the joins more accurately. These settings will apply to
all universes (unlike parameter settings reviewed in Chapter 7 that are universe specific).
Figure 8-1 shows the database structure for a sample Oracle Sales History (SH) database.
A number of the graphic settings have been changed to make the structure easier to read.

To display this information in all universes, select Tools | Options | Graphics from the
Designer menu.

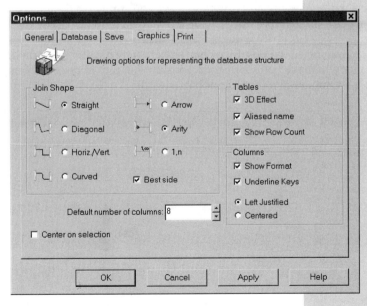

Arity or three-legged stool shows one to many relationship

An ellipsis indicates more columns

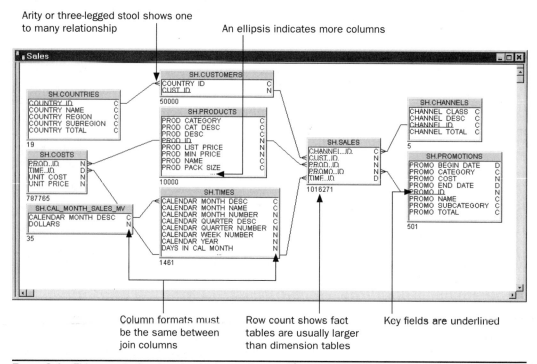

Column formats must be the same between join columns

Row count shows fact tables are usually larger than dimension tables

Key fields are underlined

Figure 8-1 This sample Oracle sales history universe shows table sizes, key names, and cardinalities, useful information in defining joins.

The Join Shape settings determine how you would like the join lines drawn. This is purely personal preference and does not affect your universe design. The Arrow join shape is the least helpful, as it does not provide any information about the cardinality of the join. Use either Arity or 1,n. Arity will give you a crow's foot for a many relationship, and 1,n will display numbers. The Best Side check box merely has the line drawn from the side of the table that will make your entity-relationship diagram appear less busy and easier to read. Table 8-1 summarizes other graphics options.

Note *Key info is not extracted for the sample MS Access databases, so changing your parameters or display option has little effect. It does, however, work correctly for Oracle and SQL Server databases.*

Option	Purpose
Default number of columns	For tables with many columns, Designer will display the first n columns in the structure pane and use an ellipsis to indicate that more columns exist in the table.
3-D Effect	Displays a shadow box around the table name.
Aliased Name	Aliases are described later in this chapter, in the section "Aliases." This check box will allow you to see both the alias name used in the universe and the physical table name in the underlying RDBMS.
Show Row Count	This option works only when you have separately extracted the row counts for each table (View I Number Of Rows In Table). The row count will display the actual or expected number of rows in each table, useful for determining join order and outer join issues.
Show Format	Show Format will display the format of the column: C for character D for date N for number T for long text L for lob—all large binary objects (blob, clob, bfile, nblob in Oracle) Join fields are either character, date, or number. Most databases do not allow you to join between two columns that are in different formats, even if the values are the same. For example, if the ARTICLE_ID in SHOP_FACTS is character and ARTICLE_ID in ARTICLE_LOOK_UP is numeric, the database will return an error during query execution and/or when you select Parse in editing the join statement. During the universe integrity check, quick parsing will not reveal this error, but thorough parsing will. Therefore, use thorough parsing.
Underline Keys	Joins between two tables are usually between key columns. For Designer to underline which columns are keys, check this box, and in addition, extract the key information via your strategies (see Chapter 7). Select the File I Parameters I Strategies tab. In the Join box, select All Matching Column Names. Note that the first join strategy does not include key info. If Designer does not underline the key names in the structure pane, refresh your database structure by selecting View I Refresh Structure.
Left Justified or Centered	Left Justified and Centered affect the appearance of whether the column names are left aligned or centered beneath the table name in the structure pane.

TABLE 8-1   Designer Graphic Options Used in the Structure Pane

Show Row Count

Extracting row count information requires a full table scan against each table. It can be slow to generate this information for fact tables that contain millions of rows of data, as it does a SELECT COUNT(*) against the table. Therefore, when you turn on the option to display the row counts, Designer does not automatically fetch these numbers. To fetch the numbers, ensure that your mouse is not on any one table, and then select View | Number Of Rows In Table. Designer will ask you if you want to set or detect row counts for all tables. Click OK. Select Refresh row count for all tables, as shown here:

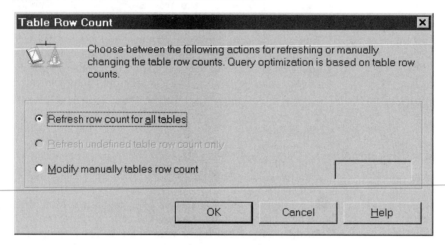

The Modify Manually Tables Row Count option allows you to enter manually the number of rows for an individual table. This can be useful if you are working with test data and you want to enter expected rows or if you know the approximate row counts for large fact tables and you do not want to wait for Designer to extract this information.

The row count information is used in two ways: First, it helps you as the designer understand when you are joining large tables together. Second, when generating the SQL for a query, the SQL generated will list the largest table first in the FROM section of a SQL statement to make queries run faster. Databases that do not have an optimizer will benefit from careful ordering of tables in the SQL statements. Databases such as Oracle and DB2 have an optimizer, so there is no need to spend time modifying row counts (unless you are using the rule-based optimizer).

The row count information works in conjunction with the REVERSE_TABLE_WEIGHT parameter in the *database*.prm file. By default, this parameter is set to Y to list tables largest to smallest. If you wish to have smaller tables appear first in the FROM section of the SQL statement, set this parameter to N.

Basic Joins

Once you have set your graphics options, you can begin modifying or creating basic joins. Displaying the joins in list mode can be helpful in determining the order of the tables in the join statement as well as seeing long join statements. Click the View List Mode button on the toolbar or select View | List Mode from the pull-down menus.

Referring back to the Test Fashion universe you created in Chapter 7, the universe has three basic joins:

- From SHOP_FACTS to CALENDAR_YEAR_LOOKUP
- From SHOP_FACTS to ARTICLE_LOOKUP
- From SHOP_FACTS to OUTLET_LOOKUP

The arity or three-lined "crow's foot" indicates that the relationship between SHOP_FACTS and ARTICLE_LOOKUP is one to many. For every one article in ARTICLE_LOOKUP, there may be one or many sales transactions in SHOP_FACTS (for example, blazers can sell one or more times). View List Mode gives an overview of all join statements, as you can see here:

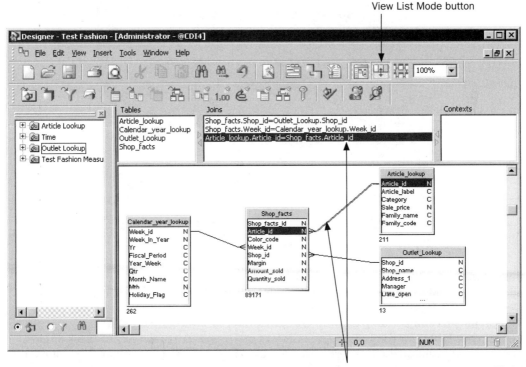

There are several ways to modify the join statement:

- Double-click the join line in the structure pane.
- Double-click the join line in the join list.
- Manually enter changes in the formula bar.

NOTE *To display the join statement in the formula bar, select View | Formula Bar from the pull-down menus.*

Modify the join between SHOP_FACTS and ARTICLE_LOOKUP. You are presented with the Edit Join dialog box. Keys are often used in joins. If your keys are not underlined in the structure pane, check File | Parameters | Strategies and refresh the structure.

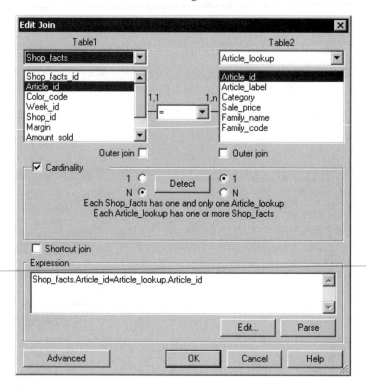

Table1, SHOP_FACTS, appears on the left-hand side, and Table2, ARTICLE_LOOKUP, on the right. In some RDBMSs, which table is right or left does not matter, but in others, it can affect how quickly a query is processed. When Designer proposes joins via the Quick Design Wizard, it puts the tables on the side in which they appear in the structure pane. Thus in the preceding example, Shop_Facts is Table2 for the join to Calendar_Year_Lookup but Table1 for the joins to Article_Lookup and Outlet_Lookup. This order may result in faster queries for certain databases, particularly for joins other than equi-joins (BETWEEN, >=, >!, =).

NOTE *When Oracle uses the cost-based optimizer, the order of the joins and the order of the tables in the FROM section of the SQL does not matter. However, if you are using the rule-based optimizer, it does.*

The first drop-down box lets you define the join operator:

Join Operator	Explanation
=	Equi-join. This is the most common and default join type. Two tables are related when every data value in the left table has an equivalent value in the right table
!=	Not equal
>	Greater than
<	Less than
>=	Greater than or equal
<=	Less than or equal

Cardinality

Above the join type, the cardinalities are indicated with 1,n = 1,1. Cardinality defines how many instances there are of each unique record in the related table: zero, one, or many. In a standard, single-star schema, all of your relationships will be one to many between the dimensions and the fact table.

If you remove the check from the cardinalities box, the 1,n and 1,1 are no longer displayed in the join panel beside the join operator. To change the appearance of the cardinality in the structure pane, select Tools | Database | Graphics.

Cardinality applies to each table in a join statement:

- **Table 1(1,n)**   Every item in the dimension table has one or more records in the fact table.
- **Table 2(1,1)**   For every record in the fact table, there is one and only one record in the lookup table.

According to the vendor-provided documentation, the sole purpose of cardinality detection is to warn you of possible loops. If you do not set the cardinalities and request Designer to detect loops, you will receive a warning that this feature works only after cardinalities have been set. In reality, though, the loop detection appears to work with or without cardinalities being set.

Also, cardinality detection does not correctly detect many-to-many relationships, nor does it detect zero relationships (which would be quite useful in defining outer joins). According to Business Objects product management, the detection algorithm counts rows to determine the cardinality and does not catch anomalies that may affect cardinality. This does not appear to have changed from versions 5 and 6 to XI.

If you skip cardinality detection completely, Designer will still correctly detect loops but will not propose contexts. Therefore, you may want to skip this process entirely if

- Your universe will have only one star or snowflake schema.
- The cardinality between tables is not typical of star schemas. A star schema typically has one dimension to many facts. If your tables have many-to-many relationships and Designer correctly detects this (it normally doesn't), then Designer will falsely tell you "No New Contexts Needed." For more accurate context detection, manually set the cardinalities.

If your data is clean, however, and if your universe will have multiple schemas, cardinality detection can be helpful in later detecting contexts.

Outer Joins

Outer joins are a special join type and one that requires careful consideration before use. An outer join is a relationship between two tables in which records from one table do not have matching records in the other. BusinessObjects does not provide a sample universe that contains outer joins, but you can create one using ARTICLE_LOOKUP and SHOP_FACTS.

In the ARTICLE_LOOKUP table, you add a new record, ARTICLE_ID 189480, a new sweatshirt for Leeds United Football Club. You know that there are no sales against this

	Article_id	Article_label	Category	Sale_price	Family_name	Family_code
+	185114	2 Row Pearl Necklace	Jewelry	$161.00	Accessories	F60
+	185125	Wool and Lycra Trousers	Long lounge pants	$182.00	City Trousers	F2
+	185203	Burlington Canvas Jacket	Boatwear	$136.00	Jackets	F45
+	185403	Starlet Jacket	Fancy fabric	$161.00	Jackets	F45
+	186108	Vivaldi Tunic	Long sleeve	$159.00	Shirt Waist	F20
+	186370	Flounced Collar Shirtdress	Long sleeve	$200.00	Shirt Waist	F20
+	187710	Africa Zipper Cardigan	Cardigan	$231.00	Sweaters	F25
+	187901	Fake Leopard Skin Gloves with Lurex Trim	Hats,gloves,scarves	$852.50	Accessories	F60
+	187904	Denim Front Button Dress	Casual dresses	$127.50	Dresses	F80
+	189479	Whisky Dancer T-Shirt	T-Shirts	$214.00	Sweat-T-Shirts	F36
+	▶189480	Leeds United Football Club	Sweats	$150.00	Sweat-T-Shirts	F36

Record: ⏮ ◀ | 1 | ▶ ⏭ ▶* of 212

New record in article table with no corresponding record in fact table

sweatshirt in the SHOP_FACTS table, because you just added it. If a user were to run a report for the sales category "Sweats," he/she would not see this sweatshirt listed if the universe contained a default equi-join. Therefore, you need an outer join on the ARTICLE_LOOKUP table.

To change the existing equi-join to an outer join, do the following:

1. Double-click the join line between SHOP_FACTS and ARTICLE_LOOKUP or right-click and select Join Properties from the pop-up menu.

2. Under Table2, ARTICLE_LOOKUP, select the Outer join check box.

3. Select Parse to ensure the join is valid.

4. Click OK to save the change to the join.

5. Click Save on the Designer toolbar to save the changes to the universe.

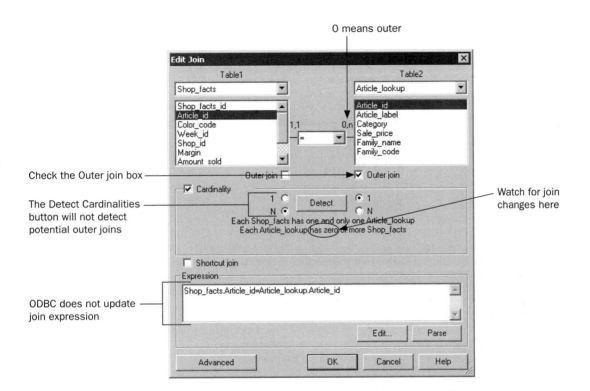

0 means outer

Check the Outer join box

The Detect Cardinalities button will not detect potential outer joins

ODBC does not update join expression

Watch for join changes here

NOTE *With the sample MS Access databases, the Expression in the Edit Join dialog box may still appear as if it were an equi-join, but when the SQL is generated in Web Intelligence, it will rewrite the expression as an outer join. When you are accessing other databases such as SQL Server or Oracle, the Expression does change to show the =* for SQL Server or + for Oracle (SQL 1 syntax). Likewise, if you have set the universe parameters to ANSI 92 (see the later section "About ANSI 92 or SQL 92"), the join statement in the Expression box also may not change, even though the correct SQL is generated at query execution. To verify that the correct SQL is generated, use Tools | Query Panel to build a small query that pulls two objects from the two related tables, and then select SQL to view the generated SQL statement.*

Now if you run a Web Intelligence report, you will see the Leeds United sweatshirt even though you have had no sales yet. The outer join allows this new ARTICLE_ID to appear in the report, even though there are no corresponding rows in SHOP_FACTS.

Outer Join Report

Article Id	Article Label	Sum of Amount Sold
167,731	Zipper Sweat Shirt	37,925.5
170,108	Loose-Fitting Turtleshell	28,425.9
179,739	Crepe Stitch Shirt	326,617
181,248	Hooded Velvet Sweatshirt	110,410.8
183,572	Crushed Velvet Sweatshirt	43,892
183,801	Missoni Stitch Shirt	44,604.6
183,869	Vivaldi Cotton Sweatshirt	72,082.4
184,352	Modigliani Zipper Sweatshirt	43,155.2
189,480	Leeds United Football Club	

New article ———————→ 189,480 Leeds United Football Club ←——————— No sales

The actual SQL syntax for outer joins will vary depending on which database and driver you are using. In the Edit Join dialog box, ODBC does not update the expression to show the outer join. Other RDBMSs will adjust the join expression in the dialog box. The Microsoft Access SQL uses the following default syntax:

```
{ oj Shop_facts RIGHT OUTER JOIN Article_lookup ON
Shop_facts.Article_id=Article_lookup.Article_id }
```

You may now be thinking that it makes sense to put outer joins on all lookup tables, since you often have inventory before items have sold. However, it's also possible to have items in a fact table that do not have a corresponding record in the dimension table. As an example, imagine a frustrated sales clerk who keeps trying to scan a trendy new scarf for an impatient customer. The scanner does not ring up the product at the register, so the sales clerk manually enters the article code from the scarf's tag (let's avoid the worst-case scenario, when the clerk rings it up under a different article with the same unit price, a common occurrence at my local department store). Why didn't the scarf scan? Who knows! Of course, the scarf should have been in inventory! And it should not have been on display without existing in the article master! But it happened, and unfortunately, it happens more than business people realize and more than data modelers wish.

In an ideal world, the sales transaction would automatically have added an entry in the article master. In an almost ideal world, the data warehouse will plug a number in the ARTICLE_ID such as 999 or XXX to say the article description is not found.

In reality (such as with a transaction system or poorly modeled data mart), you will need to use an outer join. Outer joins may not be a problem for small lookup tables, but they are best avoided for large lookup tables because the RDBMS cannot use the index to process the query because of lousy response times. Also, earlier versions of certain databases did not support outer joins.

Even when you use an outer join on a small lookup table, be sure to test the response time or analyze an explain plan in your RDBMS. If the response time is slow, train the users to understand that if they want full product listings, full customer listings, or a list of customers who have not bought this year, analyze that data separately. Use of subqueries (discussed in Chapter 23) may help them answer the same questions more efficiently.

About ANSI 92 or SQL 92

The American National Standards Institute (ANSI) develops a number of standards, including those that affect SQL syntax. With these standards, SQL is a universal language with common syntax that each RDBMS understands (in theory). In 1992, ANSI provided major revisions to SQL. These revisions are referred to as ANSI 92 or SQL 92. In reality, each RDBMS has its own SQL dialect with specific functions that may not be part of the SQL 92 standard.

The ability to understand the SQL 92 is dependent on the RDBMS and its version. For example, Oracle 9*i* supports ANSI 92, but earlier versions do not. Support within SQL Server 2000 for ANSI 92 is set via an RDBMS parameter. In addition to the RDBMS having to support ANSI 92, you also have to tell BusinessObjects XI to generate queries using SQL 92 syntax.

For example, the preceding outer join is in SQL 1 syntax. SQL 92 syntax is as follows:

```
Article_lookup LEFT OUTER JOIN Shop_facts ON
(Shop_facts.Article_id=Article_lookup.Article_id)
```

Oracle in SQL 1 syntax uses the + to indicate the outer join. The + always goes on the table that has fewer records (yes, it feels illogical to me, too!). As there are more article codes in inventory than have had sales yet, the + goes on the fact table:

```
SHOP_FACTS.ARTICLE_ID(+)=ARTICLE_LOOKUP.ARTICLE_ID
```

With ANSI 92, the Oracle syntax would be the same as the MS Access syntax:

Setting Universe Parameters for ANSI 92

If your database supports ANSI 92, you should set this parameter to YES for each universe.

1. Select Parameter from the toolbar or File | Parameters from the pull-down menus.

2. Select the Parameter tab.

3. From the list of available parameters, select ANSI92.

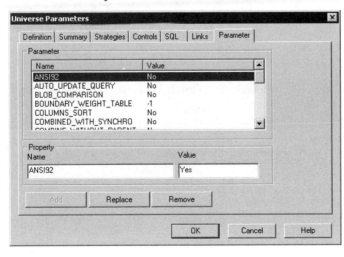

4. In the Value box, change the default No to **Yes**.

5. Click Replace to change the value.

6. Click OK to save the parameter changes.

CAUTION *if you accidentally click OK without selecting Replace first, the parameter will not be changed.*

Loops and Contexts

Loops occur when there are two different paths to accomplish one join. The following structure now includes PRODUCT_PROMOTION_FACTS in the Test Fashion universe. If users want to analyze articles versus time, there are now two join paths. BusinessObjects XI does not know which path to take, the one via SHOP_FACTS or the one via PRODUCT_PROMOTION_FACTS. Is the business question which products *sold* when or which products were *promoted* when?

The circular appearance of these four joins is a loop, which can give undesired SQL results, usually returning fewer rows than expected.

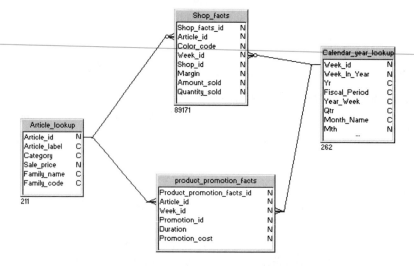

The query behavior between Desktop Intelligence and Web Intelligence is slightly different. If Desktop Intelligence users tried to create a query based on articles and time, prior to the administrator resolving this loop, they would receive the following error message:

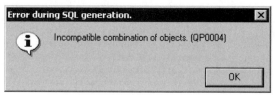

Web Intelligence users, meanwhile, would be allowed to create a query that contains the loop (see the later section "Are Loops a Bad Thing?"). Contexts help break this loop into two sets of join statements, so the desired join path is always clear and so business users can answer perfectly valid business questions.

Valid Business Questions That Demand Contexts

Following are two sample business questions that often involve multiple star schemas that would require the use of contexts (and that would otherwise cause a loop if you didn't use contexts).

Days Sales Inventory (DSIs)

How many days worth of inventory do you have according to the daily sales volume? As shown in Figure 8-2, this query would involve two contexts, one with all the joins for the star schema with a SALES_FACT table and a second context with all the joins related to INVENTORY_FACT. Although certain tables appear twice in this figure (Plant, Time, and Product), this is strictly for conceptual purposes; they exist only once in the physical database.

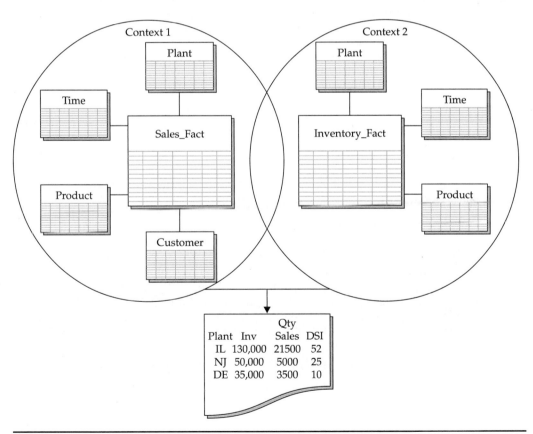

FIGURE 8-2 A context groups a set of tables into one star schema.

Account Balance vs. Debit/Credit

Most measures can be aggregated over time; other measures are valid at only one point in time. These are often referred to as *semi-additive* measures. Measures such as inventory, account balances, and number of customers are good examples of semi-additive measures (see Chapter 9, Figure 9-2 for further discussion). These measures are valid at only one particular point in time. Often, though, users will want to compare them with other measures that can be aggregated over time as shown in the following table:

Semi-Additive Measures	Measures Aggregated over Time
End-of-month inventory	Movements in and out within a month
Beginning-of-month account balance	Debits and credits within a month
Number of customers at start of month	Customers gained and lost within a month

OLAP tools such as MS Analysis Services or Hyperion Essbase allow an administrator to specify measures that relate to one point in time versus a period in time, but BusinessObjects XI does not currently support this. Contexts provide a work-around. For example, a user can run a query, selecting individual month-end balances from an ACCOUNT_FACT table and then requesting summaries for all 30 days from a DAILY_DEBIT_CREDIT_FACT table. With contexts, BusinessObjects XI will issue two SQL statements, and the results are again stitched together dynamically in the report.

Inserting a New Context

Designer can help you detect and resolve loops by using contexts. To enable this, you will first add a table PRODUCT_PROMOTION_FACTS to create a loop and then resolve the loop with a context.

1. From the pull-down menu, select Insert | Table or right-click in the structure pane and select Insert Table from the pop-up menu.

2. From the table browser, select the PRODUCT_PROMOTION_FACTS table and click Insert.

3. If your Database Options are set to extract joins with tables (check the Options dialog box reached by choosing Tools | Options, Database tab) and if your universe parameters are set to propose joins based on matching column names (in File | Parameters, Strategies tab—see Chapter 7), Designer will automatically add the join between PRODUCT_PROMOTION_FACTS and related dimension tables. If these are not set, then create the joins manually by drawing a join line between CALENDAR_YEAR_LOOKUP.WEEK_ID and PRODUCT_PROMOTION_FACTS.WEEK_ID and another between ARTICLE_LOOKUP.ARTICLE_ID and PRODUCT_PROMOTION_FACTS.ARTICLE_ID. This last join is what creates the loop and closes the circle as shown here:

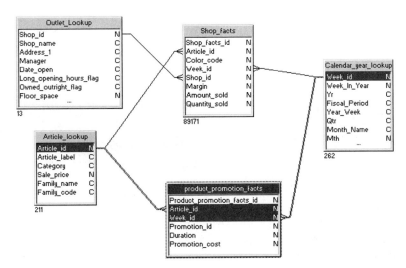

 4. Click the Detect Loops button on the toolbar or select Tools | Automatic Detection | Detect Loops from the pull-down menus. Designer will highlight all the joins that create the loop or circle.

5. If you had already defined a context, at this point Designer would propose a Candidate Context. This universe does not have existing contexts, so you need to detect them. From the Loop Detection dialog, select Candidate Context.

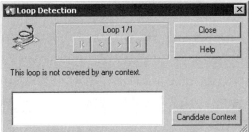

NOTE *Designer will detect contexts only when the cardinalities have been set. You can set them manually or click Detect Cardinalities. Designer will check the cardinality box in the join statement and show the relationships in the structure pane. If your data is not clean and the cardinalities do not follow the typical one-to-many for one dimension to many facts, Detect Contexts will not work correctly.*

6. Designer will present you with a list of names as proposed contexts. These contexts include all the joins in each part of the loop or one set of joins. The proposed context name comes from whichever table name is at the center of the join path, in this case SHOP_FACTS and PRODUCTION_PROMOTION_FACTS. Highlight both Candidate Contexts by CTRL-clicking and select Add to include the two new contexts in the universe.

7. Click OK to create the contexts and close the Candidate Contexts box. Designer will now confirm that the loop is resolved with the two contexts.

8. Select Close to close the Loop Detection dialog.

9. Click Save on the toolbar to save your universe changes.

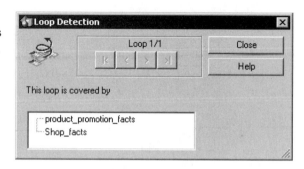

The universe structure pane and List Mode should now appear as shown in Figure 8-3. Note that when a particular context is highlighted in the Contexts list, the join statements that belong to that context are also highlighted in the Joins list as well as the structure pane.

Congratulations! You have resolved your first loop. Unfortunately, your real-world universe may not be so easy. If your universe contains aggregates or is a snowflake design,

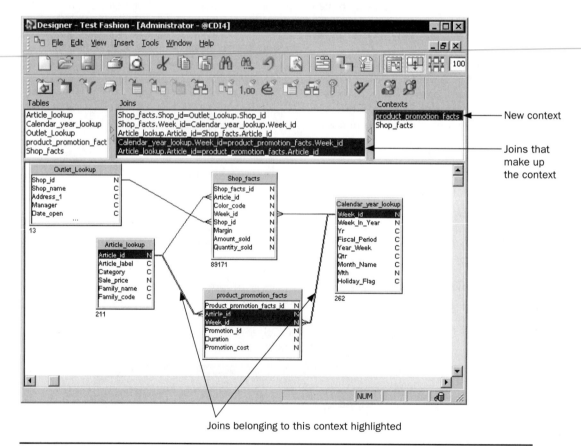

FIGURE 8-3   Contexts group related joins and allow users to answer valid business questions.

Designer may propose more contexts than necessary. Likewise, as you add new tables to your universe, your contexts may become incomplete. If you leave the context name at its default and if your cardinalities are typical, Detect Contexts works very well and will help you identify isolated joins that do not yet belong to a context.

Modifying a Context

As a general rule, leave the context name as the default until you have added all tables, loops, and contexts. This makes the universe designer's life easier, as Designer will automatically add the table to an existing context, when you use Detect Contexts. With this semiautomatic insertion, you may never want to rename contexts. However, it is not the friendliest situation for users. When users launch a query involving a potential loop, they will have to select a context. If the context name uses the default table name, it may not be user friendly. It's always better to make life harder for one designer than for hundreds of users!

In the following example, I have renamed the context "Product Promotion Fact" to "Promotion." You can rename a context either while initially defining the context or after you have added the context to the universe. To rename the context after it has been defined,

1. Select the Context from the list.

2. Use the pull-down menu Edit | Context Properties or right-click the context name and select Context Properties.

3. In the Context Name box, enter a business-oriented name; replace Product Promotion Facts with **Promotion**.

4. In the Description box, enter help text that will appear when users are prompted to select a context. For example, **BusinessObjects XI is not sure how to answer your question. If you want to know which articles were promoted in a certain time period, select the Promotion context. If you want to know which articles sold in a certain time period, select the Sales context.**

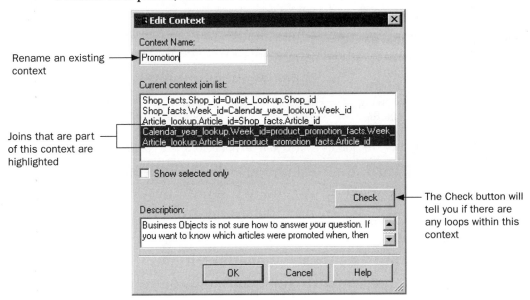

5. Click Check to verify that this particular context contains no loops; it does not check for other loops within the universe.

6. Click OK to close the Edit Context box.

Isolated Joins

Once you use contexts in a universe, you must keep using them and ensure they are complete. As you add new tables to your universe, the joins between the tables must be added to an existing context or included in a new context. In the following example, you will add the PROMOTION_LOOKUP table to the universe to create an isolated join. An integrity check will help you identify this problem. Then you will include it in an existing context.

1. From the pull-down menu, select Insert | Table or right-click in the structure pane and select Insert Table.

2. From the table browser, select the PROMOTION_LOOKUP table and click Insert.

3. If the join was not automatically created, draw a join line between PROMOTION_LOOKUP.PROMOTION_ID and PRODUCT_PROMOTION_FACT.PROMOTION_ID.

 4. From the toolbar, click Check Integrity.

5. Universe integrity is discussed in more depth in Chapter 16. In this example, I want to point out the isolated join you just created. Check the boxes for contexts, as shown here.

6. Click OK to run the Integrity Check. Designer will now go through and verify that any new joins belong to at least one context. The following screen shows that the newly added table

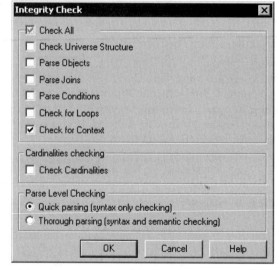

PROMOTION_LOOKUP and its related join do not belong to a context:

7. Click OK to close the Integrity Check Results box.

8. From the pull-down menu, select Tools | Automatic Detection | Detect Context or click Detect Context.

9. Designer will prompt you with the context product_promotion_facts, which includes the three joins to the fact table. If you did not rename this context "Promotion" in the last section and left it as the system-generated name "production_promotion_facts", Designer will ask you if you want to overwrite your existing context.

10. Click OK and then Save to include this new context or additional join in the existing context.

Once you have created a context, it is also possible to add additional joins without using the Detect Context command. You will need to do this if your cardinalities are atypical (or if detection is slow and you know to which context new tables need to be added). To modify a context, either double-click the context from the list pane or use the pull-down menus to select Edit | Context Properties.

CAUTION *Once you start using Contexts, you must ensure all joins are included in at least one context. If you fail to do this, user queries are split into multiple SQL statements that may lead to inaccurate results or messages such as "Incompatible combination of objects." What happens depends on the universe Parameters | SQL | Multiple Paths settings.*

How Contexts Are Used

Now that you have two contexts, all user queries will be affected in one of three ways, sometimes with user prompting and sometimes without prompting:

- When a user selects objects from tables purely within one context (CALENDAR_YEAR_LOOKUP, SHOP_FACTS, ARTICLE_LOOKUP), BusinessObjects XI is smart enough to know which context or join path to use to generate the SQL. The user is not prompted to choose a context.

- When a user selects objects from both contexts, for example, sales and promotion costs by article and month, both contexts need to be used and BusinessObjects XI will intelligently generate two separate SQL statements and seamlessly stitch the results together in one report. Some vendors refer to this functionality as Multipass SQL. As the administrator, you must make sure you have the correct Parameters | SQL settings (see Chapter 7) to allow this or users will see the error message shown earlier.

NOTE *The capability to generate multiple SQL statements and automatically stitch the results together is one of BusinessObjects XI's most powerful features and one that sets it apart from other BI tools. Prior to this technology, users would have to follow such a process manually.*

The left side of Figure 8-4 shows the first SQL statement Web Intelligence generates to retrieve sales amounts. Select1 uses the Shop_Facts context. The right side shows the second SQL statement Web Intelligence generates to retrieve the promotion costs for the *same year and article IDs*. This is very important. The dimensions form the GROUP BY section of the SELECT statement. If these are not exactly the same, the query still executes but with additional rows of data, as Web Intelligence is not clear how to synchronize the results. For example, if I added a result object *Radio Promotion* to my query, it would appear only in Select2. The beauty of this

Measures are unique to each subject

SQL statement number

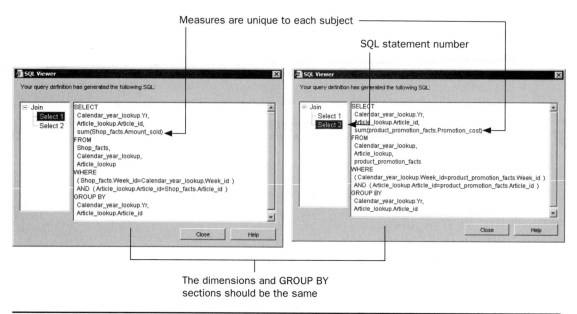

The dimensions and GROUP BY
sections should be the same

FIGURE 8-4   Web Intelligence automatically generates a SELECT statement for each context, without user
intervention.

synchronization feature is that users never see it; their business question is
answered automatically and correctly.

- When a user selects objects from the lookup tables without including objects from a
fact table, BusinessObjects XI
cannot determine automatically
which context to use. Therefore,
it prompts the user. In the next
example, I created a query that
includes Article Id and Year.
BusinessObjects XI cannot
determine if I want to know
which articles sold (Shop_Facts
context) within a certain year or
which articles had promotion
costs (Product_Promotion_Fact
context) within a certain year.
Note in the following screen
that users see the Description
added in the earlier section
"Modifying a Context."

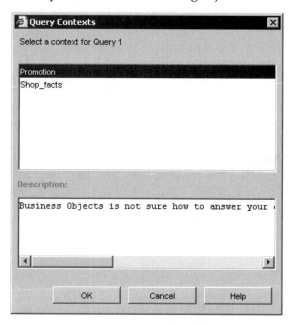

Processing Contexts on the RDBMS

BusinessObjects XI Release 2 includes a new capability that allows your contexts to be processed on the database server. In the preceding examples, when the query engine executes the separate SQL statements, each query is processed by the RDBMS sequentially. If your document contains several SQL statements, this can result in slow response times. As well, each SQL statement will return a result set that the Enterprise server then processes to present you with one merged report. If you have a summary report that calculates days sales inventory, perhaps you have 10 rows for sales and 10 rows of inventory data. The RDBMS, then, sends a total of 20 rows of data across the network and the Enterprise server synchronizes them to display 10 rows in your final report. For such small reports, the impact on the network and Enterprise server is not significant. For reports with thousands of rows (times thousands of users), though, the impact is naturally bigger.

The parameter JOIN_BY_SQL allows you to shift the processing from the BusinessObjects Enterprise server to the RDBMS. The RDBMS server does more of the work, but fewer rows travel the network and the Business Objects Enterprise server does less work. Whether this is a good thing or a bad thing depends on which aspect of your BI architecture is the bottleneck. If the load on your RDBMS is limited and it has greater processing power than the BusinessObjects Enterprise server, then the JOIN_BY_SQL parameter can improve performance. If, however, the RDBMS is often the culprit for poor query performance, then using this parameter will further degrade performance.

Another consideration in using this parameter is that it allows Crystal Report developers to build reports that access multiple contexts, a capability not previously possible. The bottom line, then, is that you have to test the impact of using the parameter in your own real-world implementation against production data sources.

NOTE *Desktop Intelligence has a slightly different query engine than Web Intelligence and these reports will not use this new parameter. Also note that if you use the Query Panel from within Designer (Tools | Query Panel), you will not see the new SQL syntax. You must build your test report in Web Intelligence to see the modified SQL. Finally, not all databases support this new parameter. If your database doesn't then the parameter is ignored and multiple SQL statements will be generated.*

The following SQL is generated from an Oracle-based universe with the parameter JOIN_BY_SQL set to Yes. Microsoft Access does not support this capability, so I cannot provide you with an equivalent of Figure 8-4. As you see here, the RDBMS still issues two SQL statements (or however many contexts are involved), but now, the statements are joined in memory.

```
SELECT
  NVL( F__1.Axis__1,F__2.Axis__1 ),          ─── Joined
  F__1.M__217,                                    result set
  F__2.M__82
FROM
    ( SELECT
        SH.PRODUCTS.PROD_DESC AS Axis__1,
        sum(SH.COSTS.UNIT_PRICE-SH.COSTS.UNIT_COST) AS M__217
      FROM
        SH.PRODUCTS,
        SH.COSTS,
        SH.TIMES
      WHERE                                    ─── This SQL
        ( SH.TIMES.TIME_ID=SH.COSTS.TIME_ID  )    comes from
        AND  ( SH.COSTS.PROD_ID=SH.PRODUCTS.PROD_ID  )  the first
        AND   SH.TIMES.CALENDAR_YEAR  In  ( 2005  )   context fact
      GROUP BY                                    table, COSTS.
        SH.PRODUCTS.PROD_DESC
    )
    F__1
    FULL OUTER JOIN
    ( SELECT
        SH.PRODUCTS.PROD_DESC AS Axis__1,
        sum(SH.SALES.AMOUNT_SOLD) AS M__82
      FROM
        SH.PRODUCTS,
        SH.SALES,
        SH.TIMES
      WHERE                                    ─── This SQL
        ( SH.TIMES.TIME_ID=SH.SALES.TIME_ID  )    comes from
        AND  ( SH.PRODUCTS.PROD_ID=SH.SALES.PROD_ID  )  the second
        AND                                       context fact
        SH.TIMES.CALENDAR_YEAR  In  ( 2005  )    table, SALES.
      GROUP BY
        SH.PRODUCTS.PROD_DESC
    )
    F__2
    ON ( F__1.Axis__1=F__2.Axis__1  )
```

When the query is based on an Oracle data source, the SQL generated will use NVL to display the dimensions common to both sets of queries. When the query is based on a MS SQL Server data source, the SQL generated will use COALESCE as NVL is not supported. The end result is the same.

To enable this parameter in your universe, follow these steps:

1. Click Parameters from the toolbar or File | Parameters from the pull-down menu.

2. Select the Parameter tab.

3. As this is a new parameter, it may not appear in the list and must be added. In the Name box, enter **JOIN_BY_SQL**. In the Value box, enter Yes.

4. In the Value box, enter the new parameter value, **Yes**.

5. Click Add to update the parameter list, then OK to close the dialog.

For more information on Parameters, refer to Chapter 7.

Are Loops a Bad Thing?

You have spent a lot of time identifying loops and getting rid of them with contexts. In many cases, a loop is unintended, caused by poorly written SQL against complex schemas. However, loops can be the result of a valid business question if users really want to know which articles and weeks are common between both the promotion fact table and the sales fact table.

Product Promotion Context

SKU number	SKU desc	Week
145404	Rounded Rectangle Brooch	30
165170	Modal Shirt	33
166544	Polo Collared T-Shirt	29
166550	Whisky Dancer T-Shirt	6
166583	Military Shirt	32
166583	Military Shirt	50
166699	Suede Stretch Dress	30
167042	Long-Sleeved Stitch Shirt	33
167695	Pomodore Lace T-Shirt	33
167695	Pomodore Lace T-Shirt	45
Count:		8

Loop - Fewer Rows

Article Id	Article Label	Year Week
145404	Rounded Rectangle Brooch	2002/30
165170	Modal Shirt	2002/33
166583	Military Shirt	2002/32
166583	Military Shirt	2002/50
166699	Suede Stretch Dress	2002/30
167042	Long-Sleeved Stitch Shirt	2002/33
167695	Pomodore Lace T-Shirt	2002/45
Count:	6	

Look at the following two Web Intelligence reports. The articles Polo Collared T-Shirt (166544), Whisky Dancer T-Shirt (166550), and Pomodore Lace T-Shirt (167695, week 33) had promotions but no shop sales, so they appear in the table labeled "Product Promotion Context" but not in the table labeled "Loop – Fewer Rows."

The first table, "Product Promotion Context," contains ten rows of data for eight distinct articles that had promotions during particular weeks. The second table, "Loop – Fewer Rows," contains only seven rows of data and lists six distinct articles and weeks that are common between *both* the promotion fact table and the shop fact table. There are fewer rows in this second table because not all products had both promotions and sales in the exact same week. Desktop Intelligence does not allow loops in universes; users cannot run queries that contain an unresolved loop. Web Intelligence, on the other hand, does allow loops.

The following SQL is generated for a report in which the Promotion Context is selected. Note that three tables are involved in the FROM portion of the query and two join statements:

```
SELECT DISTINCT
Article_lookup.Article_id,
Article_lookup.Article_label,
Calendar_year_lookup.Week_in_year
FROM
  Article_lookup,
  Calendar_year_lookup,
  product_promotion_facts
WHERE
  ( product_promotion_facts.Week_id=Calendar_year_lookup.Week_id )
  AND  ( Article_lookup.Article_id=product_promotion_facts.Article_id )
```

Compare the preceding SQL with the joins from a second query that contains a loop. Note that there are now four tables in the FROM portion of the query and four join statements:

```
SELECT
  Article_lookup.Article_id,
 Article_lookup.article_label,
 Calendar_year_lookup.Week_In_Year
FROM
  Calendar_year_lookup,
  Article_lookup,
  product_promotion_facts,
shop_facts
WHERE
  ( Calendar_year_lookup.Week_id=product_promotion_facts.Week_id  )
  AND  ( Article_lookup.Article_id=product_promotion_facts.Article_id  )
And
  ( Calendar_year_lookup.Week_id=shop_facts.Week_id  )
  AND  ( Article_lookup.Article_id=shop_facts.Article_id  )
```

The bottom line? Unintentional loops are a bad thing. In the past, Designer did not allow them and would force you to resolve them. With Web Intelligence, users can create queries that contain loops. Be sure to review your universe design carefully to avoid incorrect queries.

Chasm Traps and Contexts

Contexts allow a universe to contain multiple dimensional schemas and allow users to query these multiple schemas simultaneously. In addition, contexts prevent another possible join problem from occurring when you may have a common dimension table and two fact tables. Refer back to Figure 8-3. A loop exists when the dimension tables ARTICLE_ LOOKUP and CALENDAR_YEAR_LOOKUP are both referenced via either fact table. However, a loop is not present if CALENDAR_YEAR_LOOKUP is not part of the universe. The universe would pass an integrity check without its being in the universe; however, your users may get incorrect results if their query contains measures from both fact tables. Two things will go wrong.

First, promotion costs will be significantly overstated as the one-to-many join between ARTICLE_LOOK_UP and SHOP_FACTS essentially results in a many-to-many join and Cartesian product between SHOP_FACTS and PRODUCT_PROMOTION_FACTS. If you care to test this to understand what is going on, note that there are 529 unique rows in the SHOP_ FACTS table for the ARTICLE_ID=145404. When the join is processed via the PRODUCT_ PROMOTION_FACT table, the one row in this fact table is repeated 529 times.

Second, just as a loop will cause rows to be dropped from a query, so will accessing two fact tables via a common dimension table. Thus users will not get all sales for all products; instead, they will get only sales in which a corresponding ARTICLE_ID exists in the PRODUCT_PROMOTION_FACT table. The vendor refers to this as a *chasm* trap, as results appear to disappear into a chasm. Additionally, if there are multiple rows in the sales table, rows from the promotion table are overstated. Figure 8-5 shows how a chasm trap causes you to lose rows, as well as overstates rows. The table on the left shows the chasm trap. The two right-hand tables show the correct results when these individual facts are used in separate queries. At first glance, the results in the left-hand table seem to answer a valid

business question: "What were the promotion costs and revenues for all products?"
However, because relevant options were not set correctly in the universe, users will get
revenues only for those articles that had a promotion. So Promotion costs are overstated
(wrong value of 97,436,675 versus correct value of 60,975) and revenues for any products
that do not have a corresponding promotion disappear down a chasm (understated value
of 9,261,619 versus correct value of 36, 387,202).

The following SQL is generated when you don't use contexts and that will yield
incorrect results.

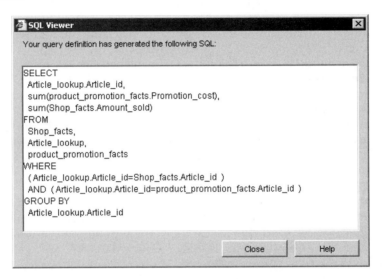

Thus, I strongly recommend you use contexts when your universe contains multiple fact
tables so that multiple SQL statements are generated for each dimensional schema. In
addition to contexts, the universe parameter "Multiple SQL Statements for Each Measure"
will also prevent this chasm trap (see Chapter 7).

Chasm Trap Results

Article Id	Promotion Cost	Sum of Amount So
145,404	5,025,500	435,145.8
165,170	1,320,000	474,172.3
166,544	10,348,000	4,967,526.8
166,550	11,704,000	622,943.4
166,583	10,385,650	604,034.6
166,699	41,314,000	1,412,632.5
167,042	15,142,050	511,546.7
167,695	2,197,475	233,617.8
Sum:	97,436,675	9,261,619.9

Correct Promotion Costs

Article Id	Promotion Cost
145,404	9,500
165,170	1,200
166,544	2,000
166,550	9,500
166,583	12,650
166,699	13,000
167,042	8,050
167,695	5,075
Sum:	60,975

Correct Sales

Sum of Amount Sold
36,387,202.8

FIGURE 8-5   Chasm traps produce incorrect query results.

CAUTION *The universe integrity check will never warn you of such potential chasm traps, so it's important you view all possible joins. Keep in mind that you are developing a reporting environment, not a single query in which you can precisely control the generated SQL.*

Fan Traps and Many-to-Many Joins

Many people get confused by "fan" traps and "chasm" traps. These are two types of join problems that lead to incorrect results. How they are different matters little. In fact, I don't even like to discuss them, because if you really follow the rules in the other sections, you should never encounter either. Further, if you use these terms with a SQL programmer, he or she will stare at you dumbfounded: *a what trap?* However, the vendor uses these terms in education courses and help text, so I'll describe them briefly.

As discussed in the last section, a chasm trap occurs when you lose results by joining two fact tables to a common lookup table. With a fan trap, the opposite happens: your results are overstated (spread like a fan) because a Cartesian product occurs when aggregates go across one-to-many joins. (See Chapter 7, Figure 7-3 for an illustration of how this happens.) A prime example of a fan trap is joining Order Header to Order Detail. This is typically a one-to-many join relationship. Freight exists on the Order Header table and Quantity exists on the Detail table. The Freight will be fanned or overstated by however many line items there are in the Order Detail table.

Contexts Versus Aliases

There seems to be a tendency for long-time BusinessObjects developers to avoid contexts at all costs. This might have been valid with the earliest versions of BusinessObjects, but it is not a valid concern with XI, or really anything later than version 4. As described earlier, users are rarely prompted to choose a context. The use of contexts prevents loops and, most important, allows users to formulate and answer valid business questions. In an attempt to avoid contexts, some designers will turn to aliases as a way of breaking a loop and avoiding a context. This is the wrong use of aliases. While it might result in valid join statements, it can create an unnecessarily complicated universe and more objects (that really mean the same thing). Instead, try to understand the data from the business perspective. Use contexts to group the related schemas and use aliases only when one table can have multiple meanings such as a Sold To Customer versus a Ship To Customer or a Manager who is also an Employee.

Composite Keys and Complex Joins

Most fact tables have several columns that uniquely identify one row of data. In the BEACH or Island Resorts Marketing universe, the two columns CUST_ID and INV_ID uniquely identify the records in the SALES table. The two columns together are called a *composite* key. Lookup or dimension tables also may have a composite key. None of the BusinessObjects XI sample universes contain lookup tables with composite keys, and recently implemented, well-designed data warehouses also should not require them. However, early data warehouses often used composite keys, and transaction systems still do.

For example, to track changes in customer reference data, the month and year often may be part of the composite key. To illustrate this concept, I have modified the CUSTOMER table

Composite key

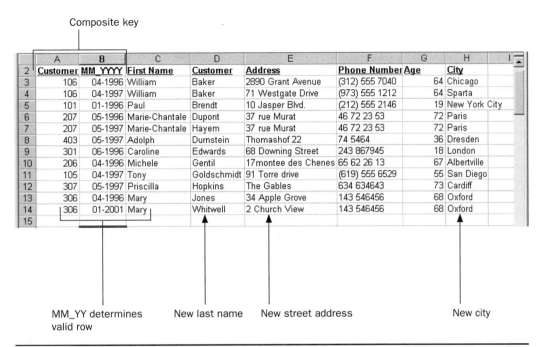

	A	B	C	D	E	F	G	H	
2	**Customer**	**MM_YYYY**	**First Name**	**Customer**	**Address**	**Phone Number**	**Age**	**City**	
3	106	04-1996	William	Baker	2890 Grant Avenue	(312) 555 7040	64	Chicago	
4	106	04-1997	William	Baker	71 Westgate Drive	(973) 555 1212	64	Sparta	
5	101	01-1996	Paul	Brendt	10 Jasper Blvd.	(212) 555 2146	19	New York City	
6	207	05-1996	Marie-Chantale	Dupont	37 rue Murat	46 72 23 53	72	Paris	
7	207	05-1997	Marie-Chantale	Hayem	37 rue Murat	46 72 23 53	72	Paris	
8	403	05-1997	Adolph	Durnstein	Thomashof 22	74 5464	36	Dresden	
9	301	06-1996	Caroline	Edwards	68 Downing Street	243 867945	18	London	
10	206	04-1996	Michele	Gentil	17montee des Chenes	65 62 26 13	67	Albertville	
11	105	04-1997	Tony	Goldschmidt	91 Torre drive	(619) 555 6529	55	San Diego	
12	307	05-1997	Priscilla	Hopkins	The Gables	634 634643	73	Cardiff	
13	306	04-1996	Mary	Jones	34 Apple Grove	143 546456	68	Oxford	
14	306	01-2001	Mary	Whitwell	2 Church View	143 546456	68	Oxford	
15									

MM_YY determines valid row   New last name   New street address   New city

FIGURE 8-6   This table shows that Customer_id and MM_YYYY together uniquely identify each record as customer names and addresses have changed over the years.

within the sample Island Resorts Marketing database to add the month and year column as MM_YYYY. Figure 8-6 shows multiple records for the customer IDs 106, 207, and 306.

- Customer 106, Baker, moved from Chicago, IL, to Sparta, NJ, in April 1997. The row from customer ID 106, MM_YYYY 04-1996 contains old data for the same customer.

- Customer 207, Dupont, divorced and reverted to her maiden name of Hayem in May 1997. The row from customer ID 207, MM_YYYY 05-1997 contains old data for the same customer.

- Customer 306, Jones, married and changed her name to Whitwell in January 2001. The row from customer ID 306, MM_YYYY 04-1996 contains old data for the same customer.

When analyzing reservations by city or by last name, the join between CUSTOMER and RESERVATIONS must now include MM_YYYY to RES_DATE, *in addition to* the CUST_ID. In much earlier versions of BusinessObjects, one could include these joins as separate line items (see Figure 8-7), since the query engine automatically connects multiple join statements with an AND. In fact, when you use join detection or if your database options are set to extract joins with tables, Designer will incorrectly propose multiple join statements. However, with the addition of loop detection, these compound joins must be done in one join statement or Designer will falsely detect a loop.

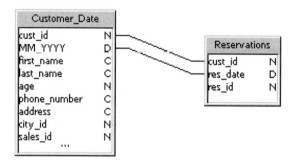

FIGURE 8-7 Designer will identify compound join statements created this way as a loop.

To correctly create a complex join, select the join on CUST_ID and double-click it to bring up the Edit Join box. Use a CTRL-click to select the additional join relationships between the two tables. Alternatively, in the Expression box, type **AND** at the end of the join statement. As soon as you enter AND, Designer changes the join type to Complex. Your join should read

```
Customer.cust_id=Reservations.cust_id AND Customer.MM_YYYY=Reservations.res_date
```

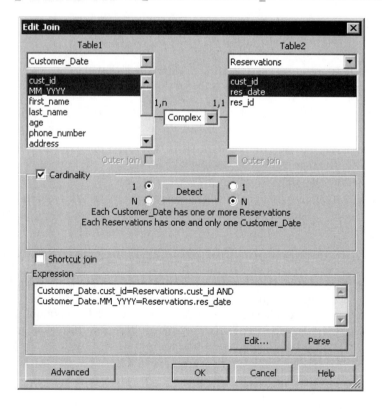

Aliases

When Designer sees two join statements between the same two tables, it often will propose an *alias* to resolve the loop. If your company has multiple SQL tools accessing a data warehouse, your DBA may have resolved many of these issues by creating synonyms or views in the RDBMS. For example, one physical `CUSTOMER` dimension table could be joined to a fact table two times as synonyms `SHIP_TO_CUSTOMER` or `SOLD_TO_CUSTOMER`. Synonyms in the source RDBMS appear to Designer as physical tables, even though they behave much like aliases. If such synonyms or views do not exist in your RDBMS, create an alias to use one physical table in different ways.

NOTE *Be careful not to confuse this type of join with composite keys in which more than one column uniquely identifies a record and that can be resolved only by creating a complex join. Designer will propose an alias in either circumstance, even though it is valid to use it only when the join between the fact table is to the same column on the dimension table.*

When you insert a table that already exists in the universe, Designer will force you to create an alias and prompt you to give a new name to the table. Alternatively, you can ask Designer to detect potential aliases, or you can consciously choose tables that you know you want to use in multiple ways.

Detecting Aliases

The sample Island Resorts Marketing (BEACH.UNV) universe contains information about resorts and customers who visit those resorts. Resorts can be located in different countries, and customers can be located in different countries. If you were building this universe from scratch, Designer would have detected a join between the following tables:

```
COUNTRY.COUNTRY_ID=REGION.COUNTRY_ID ─────────── which eventually joins to CUSTOMER
COUNTRY.COUNTRY_ID=RESORT.COUNTRY_ID.
RESORT.COUNTRY_ID=REGION.COUNTRY_ID ─────────── which you don't really want
```

Note in the following screen that these joins cause a loop:

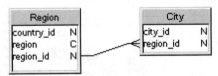

At this point, loop detection would suggest using aliases to resolve these loops. As you are a good data modeler who understands from the business rules that "country" has multiple meanings, you agree and can move directly to alias detection.

1. Create a new universe that includes the five tables shown in the preceding illustration: `CITY, COUNTRY, CUSTOMER, CITY, REGION, RESORT`. The `CUSTOMER` and `CITY` tables are not necessary to create the loop but are included to clarify how `COUNTRY` is used in two different ways, with two different business meanings.

 2. From the pull-down menus, select Tools | Automatic Detection | Detect Aliases or click the Alias Detection button.

3. Designer suggests that an alias should be created for COUNTRY called COUNTRY_
   REGION.

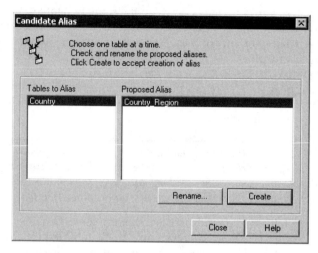

4. Click OK to confirm the Alias creation. Note in the structure pane that Designer
   has inserted what appears to be a new table with the physical table name indicated
   below the alias (see Figure 8-8), if you have set your Join Graphics as described
   earlier in this chapter.

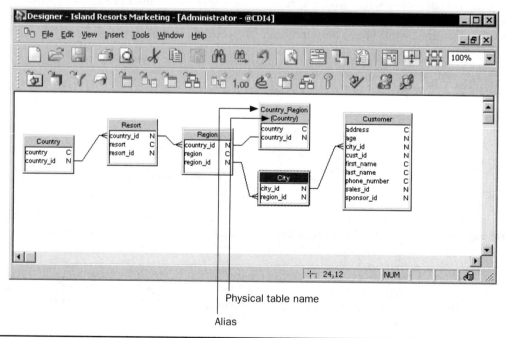

FIGURE 8-8 With aliases, the universe no longer contains a loop. The alias name replaces the physical
table name in parentheses.

NOTE *This exercise is intended to demonstrate loops and aliases. The joins created are not valid according to the business rules of our data model. There is no direct relationship between resorts and regions in which customers reside (even though the* COUNTRY_ID *in both tables is the same). The relationship is valid only when a customer makes a reservation or is invoiced, so even though Designer may automatically create the join between* RESORT *and* REGION, *you would have to delete them in order to build a valid universe. Meanwhile, the need for an alias for the* COUNTRY *table is valid, as it has two different purposes.*

Renaming the Alias

In the last section, you accepted the proposed alias name COUNTRY_REGION. This can get a little confusing, as clearly every region belongs to a country. However, the meaning and join relationship here really concern where the customers are located, and in which countries. To give the alias a clearer name, rename it to COUNTRY_CUSTOMER. Note that this is purely for your own purposes, as users will never see the alias name.

1. From within the structure pane, select the alias COUNTRY_REGION.

2. Right-click to invoke the pop-up menu.

3. Select Rename Table.

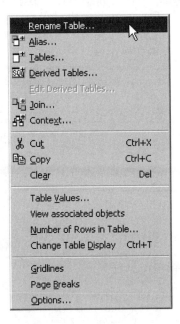

4. In the Table Name box, enter **Country_Customer.**

5. Click OK to close the Rename Table dialog.

TIP *Best practice is to name the alias using the first part of the underlying physical table to more easily keep track of related physical tables and aliases.*

Inserting Aliases Manually

You may want to insert an alias manually if Designer does not propose an alias that makes business sense or if you know your business meanings in advance. To create the same COUNTRY_CUSTOMER alias as you did in the last section manually,

1. Select the COUNTRY table from the structure pane.
2. Click the Insert Alias button or select Tools | Insert Alias.
3. When prompted, enter the name **Country_Customer** as the new alias name.
4. Add a join between REGION.COUNTRY_ID and the new alias, COUNTRY_ CUSTOMER.COUNTRY_ID.

Aliases in SQL

In generating the SQL, BusinessObjects XI will use the alias name in the column selection, join statements, and WHERE clause. In the FROM section, the query engine rephrases the physical table name with the new alias name. This is standard SQL syntax and is not unique to BusinessObjects XI. In the Island Resorts Marketing universe, the alias created was RESORT_COUNTRY (based on the physical table COUNTRY). Through the use of aliases, a user can ask the question "What are the sales for our customers in Germany who wish to stay in our resorts in the U.S.?" This generates the following SQL:

```
SELECT
  Country.country,
  Resort_Country.country, ──────────── Note here the use of the alias name
  sum(Invoice_Line.days * Invoice_Line.nb_guests * Service.price)
FROM
  Country,
  Country   Resort_Country, ──────────── Declaring the alias here allows it to be used
Invoice_Line,                            elsewhere in the query
  Service,
  Resort,
  Service_Line,
  Sales,
  Customer,
  City,
  Region
WHERE
  ( City.city_id=Customer.city_id  )
  AND  ( City.region_id=Region.region_id  )
  AND  ( Country.country_id=Region.country_id  )
  AND  ( Resort_Country.country_id=Resort.country_id  )
  AND  ( Customer.cust_id=Sales.cust_id  )
  AND  ( Sales.inv_id=Invoice_Line.inv_id  )
  AND  ( Invoice_Line.service_id=Service.service_id  )
  AND  ( Resort.resort_id=Service_Line.resort_id  )
  AND  ( Service.sl_id=Service_Line.sl_id  )
  AND
  (
  Country.country  =  'Germany'
  AND
```

```
      Resort_Country.country  =  'US'
    )
GROUP BY
  Country.country,
Resort_Country.country
```

Self-Joins and Aliases

Self-joins are a way of joining a table to itself. You may need to use one as a way of restricting rows in a table or because the same values are used in two columns in the same table. A classic example is that of employees. Employees have managers. Thus, the employee ID in one column is also used in the manager ID in another column.

The following example uses data from Oracle's HR sample schema. In this schema, every employee has a supervisor, except for the main boss, Steven King (thus, you need an outer join for this one employee). Managers may supervise one or more employees. As you see in Figure 8-9, the Employee Id is also used to indicate the Manager Id in the same table. So Employee ID 100, Steven King, manages Neena Kochhar (101) and Lex De Haan (102). Steven King, as the head boss, does not have a manager; to see this requires an outer join.

To implement the self-join, first create an alias for the EMPLOYEE called EMP_MANAGER, as shown here:

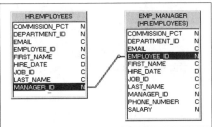

Employees and Their Managers

Employee Id	First Name	Last Name	Manager Id	Manager First Name	Manager Last Name
100	Steven	King			
101	Neena	Kochhar		Steven	King
102	Lex	De Haan		Steven	King
103	Alexander	Hunold	100	Lex	De Haan
104	Bruce	Ernst	102	Alexander	Hunold
105	David	Austin	102	Alexander	Hunold
106	Valli	Pataballa	102	Alexander	Hunold
107	Diana	Lorentz	102	Alexander	Hunold
108	Nancy	Greenberg	100	Neena	Kochhar
109	Daniel	Faviet	101	Nancy	Greenberg

FIGURE 8-9 Employees report to managers, requiring a self-join using aliases.

Next, create the join that uses the alias. By using the alias, you are self-joining the EMPLOYEE_ID field in one table to the MANAGER_ID field in the same table; the alias makes it appear as if you are joining two different tables. To get a list of any employees that do not report to a manager, include an outer join on the EMP_MANAGER alias.

This last part is tricky. If you left the universe the way it is now, it would work fine as long as objects from EMP_MANAGER were never used in a report by itself. For example, if you tried to create a report that listed managers only, all employees would be listed on this report, as the self-join would not be activated: David Austin (105) would appear on the report, even though he is never listed in

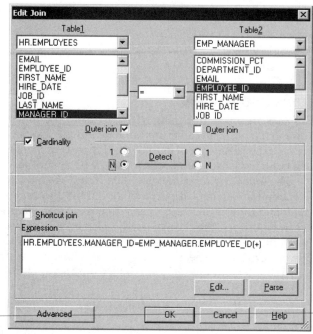

the EMLOYEE.MANAGER_ID column, as shown in Figure 8-9. To ensure that you get a list of managers only, you must force the self-join as described in the next section.

Forcing a Join

There are two ways to ensure the self-join is activated any time you select objects from the EMP_MANAGER alias. The first, most obvious way is to include the join as a WHERE clause in each object definition. The second, less obvious way is to force the join by selecting EMPLOYEE as a Table in any objects that reference EMP_MANAGER such as *Manager's Last Name*. This second way is preferable, as the join statement is added to the SQL statement once; with the WHERE clause in each object definition, the WHERE statement is added to the SQL statement multiple times according to how many objects contain the condition.

To force a join, modify the relevant object definitions (how to create and modify objects is explained in Chapter 9). From the Edit Properties dialog box, click Tables. Use a CTRL-click to select the two tables EMP_MANAGER and EMPLOYEE, and then click OK.

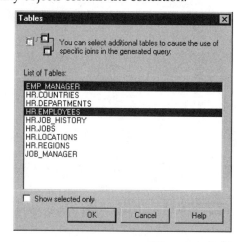

TIP *Forcing a join to a table is also useful for security purposes when the additional table contains permissions for which rows of data a user is permitted to see.*

Shortcut Joins

Shortcut joins are the best thing since chocolate chip cookies were invented (I know, the cliché is sliced bread, but I have a preference for cookies ☺). Shortcut joins allow you to define an alternative, faster join path between two tables. Without the use of a shortcut join, your query would have to go through a huge fact table to create simple reference lists. To the unsuspecting user, this query could take hours.

To help you understand shortcut joins, the following example uses the concept of orders, products, and plants. Products can be ordered, and plants manufacture products. Figure 8-10 shows an example of a shortcut join between the PLANT table and the PRODUCTS table (line 1). If the shortcut join were a normal join, Designer would detect a loop. If you did not define a shortcut join and users wanted a list of which plants made which products, their query would be forced to join three tables together (join lines 2 and 3) and unnecessarily go through the large 30-million-row ORDERS_FACT table. The shortcut join is a way of telling BusinessObjects XI that this is the fastest path to use for queries in which no objects come from the ORDERS_FACT table. Therefore, if users created a report to determine which suppliers ship to specific plants, the shortcut join is also used.

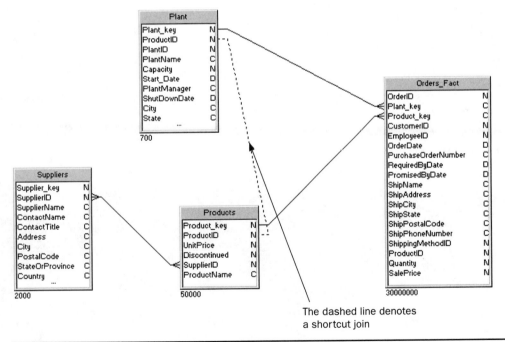

The dashed line denotes
a shortcut join

FIGURE 8-10 Shortcut joins provide BusinessObjects XI with an alternate, faster join path without creating a loop.

Summary

Joins can hardly be called an exciting, business-driven subject; however, if you correctly define the parameters covered in Chapter 7 and the joins covered in this chapter, you have built a sturdy foundation for a correct universe. The Classes and Objects covered in the next chapters become the familiar façade that users trust. If, on the other hand, you have made mistakes in the joins, then objects may not work with one another—or worse, they give users incorrect results. To define joins correctly, keep in mind the following guidelines:

- Define joins based on the actual data and not just the logical business model.

- If you start using contexts, you must keep using them and ensure all tables belong to at least one context.

- Use aliases to create multiple joins between the same two tables that have different business meanings.

- Use shortcut joins to provide faster paths between two tables that have a direct relationship, rather than forcing a join through a fact table.

Classes and Objects

C lasses and objects are the primary items a user sees when building a new query or working with an existing report. *Classes* allow you to organize objects into topics in much the way you organize documents into file folders. *Objects* correspond to columns of data in a database table. However, objects can be much more powerful than raw data lists, enabling you to add intelligence such as aggregations, transformations, prompts, and formatting. This chapter focuses on the basics of classes and objects, whereas Chapters 10 and 11 provide information to make your objects more robust.

The Universe Pane

 In Chapter 8, you mainly dealt with the universe structure that represented the joins and physical tables that users never see. In this chapter, you will work primarily with the universe pane, which provides information on the classes and objects. Unless an individual class or object is marked as hidden, Figure 9-1 shows what users will see when they create a new query or insert a table or graph into an existing document. While building the universe, you can choose to display the universe pane or just the structure pane. To view the universe pane, select the Universe Window button from the toolbar or select View | Universe Window from the pull-down menu.

Click the + sign to expand items in a class or the – sign to collapse the individual objects within a class.

You can have multiple levels of classes for classes that have a large number of objects such as *Store Details* as a subclass within the main class *Store*. These groupings are purely to ease navigation for the users. If you have a lot of detail information that is not used on a regular basis, placing these objects further within a subclass makes the universe appear less busy or difficult. However, if the information is used frequently, do not bury the objects.

In the EFASHION universe, the promotional media of *Print, Radio, Television,* or *Direct Mail* are details of the base object *Promotion (y/n)*. These details become organized in a separate folder within *Promotion (y/n)*, making the universe appear less cluttered. Specifying an object as a detail rather than a dimension also means it will not be available for multidimensional analyses.

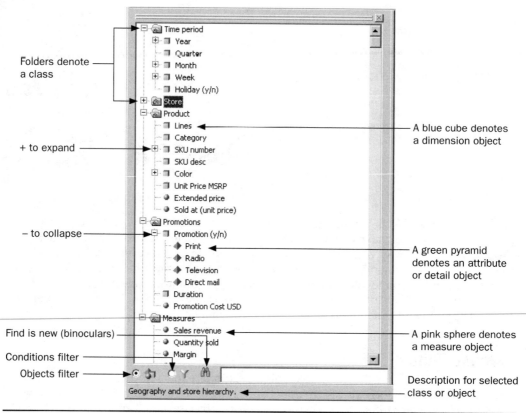

Folders denote a class

+ to expand

– to collapse

Find is new (binoculars)

Conditions filter

Objects filter

A blue cube denotes a dimension object

A green pyramid denotes an attribute or detail object

A pink sphere denotes a measure object

Description for selected class or object

FIGURE 9-1   The universe pane shows classes and objects as they appear to users when building a query.

In the bottom-left corner of the universe pane, you have two radio buttons that allow you to toggle the display between regular classes and objects or condition objects, which are special objects used to generate a SQL WHERE clause. The Find option, which is relatively new (introduced in version 6), allows you to search for objects when your universe is particularly large. The binocular icon in the bottom left of the universe pane relies on Find settings that you can set via the toolbar or Edit | Find to allow you to search object names, descriptions, or SQL.

NOTE *When you want to find database field names or other text within the SQL statements, first click in the universe pane. You cannot specify where to search when your mouse is positioned in the structure pane.*

Types of Objects

Objects can be one of three types: dimension, measure, or detail. Business Objects refers to these types as object qualifications.

Dimension

A *dimension* object, denoted by a blue cube, is typically textual information by which users analyze numeric measures, such as product, region, or month. A dimension object often comes from the lookup or reference tables within the universe. Dimensions are typically character or date information or numeric codes such as product numbers and customer numbers.

If your data warehouse uses keys for reference information, then your dimension objects will point to a lookup table. However, if your universe accesses a transaction system or if meaningful codes and IDs are stored in your fact table, you face a decision whether to point the dimension object to the dimension table or to the fact table. Some universe developers will mistakenly point the dimension object to the fact table, trying to reduce the number of joins for performance reasons. Others will duplicate the object for each occurrence in a different table. Don't do it. Create one dimension object that points to the lookup table. This makes for the simplest universe for users, who are your primary concern. Additionally, you may be able to specify keys for each object that can minimize the number of joins to process a query (see the section "Object Keys" later in this chapter).

TIP *Have one object point to the dimension table rather than multiple instances of similar fields / foreign key references pointing to multiple tables.*

Measure

A *measure* is a number that users wish to analyze; it is denoted by a pink sphere or circle. Measures often come from a fact table, but measures such as number of products or number of days could come from a dimension table. Measures are almost always aggregated in some form, such as sum, count, average, min, or max.

The only measure that is not aggregated is unit price. Price is a measure, but it applies to one particular product, and it is wrong from a business viewpoint to sum prices across multiple product lines. *Average* price across multiple product lines would be a more appropriate aggregation; however, the universe should then contain two distinct price objects to ensure users can query both unit price and average price.

Universe designers may get confused about measures that apply to one point in time such as inventory quantity, account balances, or number of customers. Measures that should not be aggregated by time (but that may be aggregated by other dimensions such as region or product) are referred to as semi-additive measures. Unfortunately, Business Objects does not provide a solution to ensure that users do not aggregate these measures across time; they are either aggregated or not. Certain OLAP tools such as MS Analysis Services and Essbase do provide capabilities to prevent incorrect aggregation by time. With such measures, then, many designers will think it too risky to allow users to make the mistake of aggregating ending inventory/balances across time.

How do users make this mistake? Figure 9-2 gives an example from my fictitious bank account. Using the data in Figure 9-2 as an example, assume that the universe references two fact tables: daily debits and credits and daily account balances. If a user builds one query that accesses both tables, the user will generally insert a condition where month equals September. Desktop Intelligence would tell the users that the ending account balance would be $129,955, rather than the correct number of $9,134. (If this were true, I would be vacationing in Florence rather than diligently writing this book!)

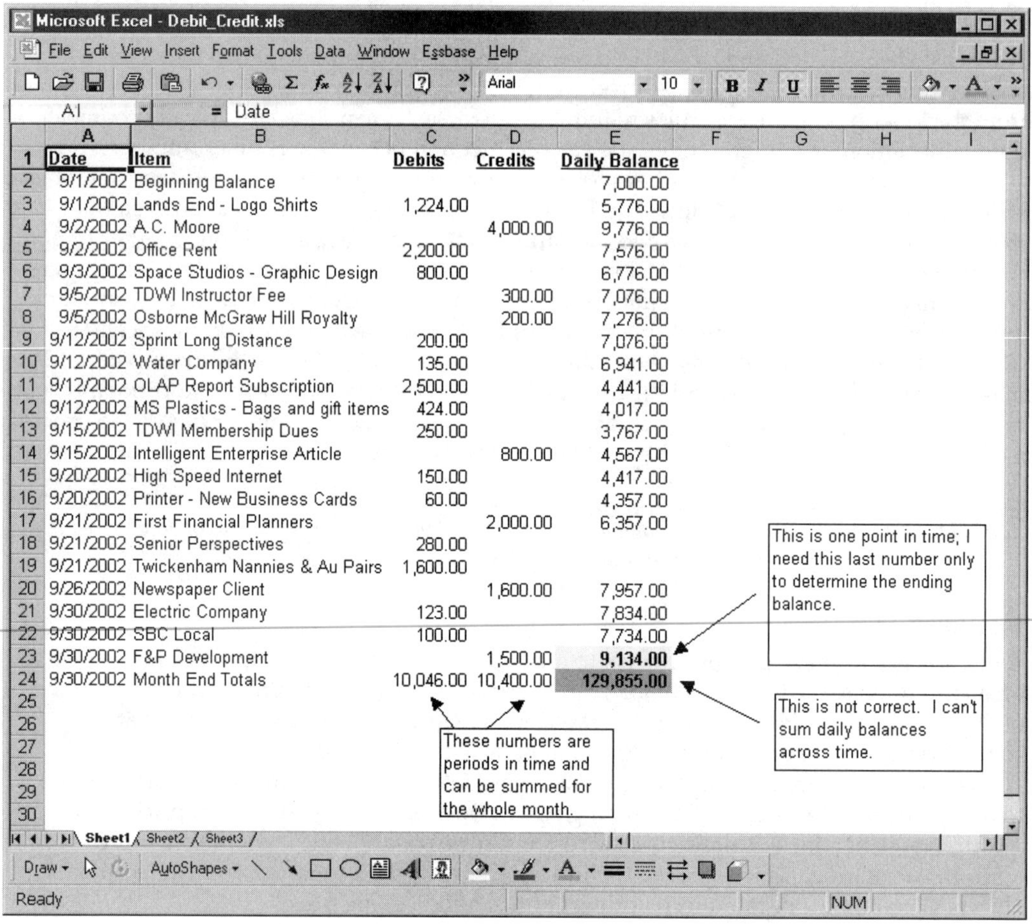

	A	B	C	D	E
1	Date	Item	Debits	Credits	Daily Balance
2	9/1/2002	Beginning Balance			7,000.00
3	9/1/2002	Lands End - Logo Shirts	1,224.00		5,776.00
4	9/2/2002	A.C. Moore		4,000.00	9,776.00
5	9/2/2002	Office Rent	2,200.00		7,576.00
6	9/3/2002	Space Studios - Graphic Design	800.00		6,776.00
7	9/5/2002	TDWI Instructor Fee		300.00	7,076.00
8	9/5/2002	Osborne McGraw Hill Royalty		200.00	7,276.00
9	9/12/2002	Sprint Long Distance	200.00		7,076.00
10	9/12/2002	Water Company	135.00		6,941.00
11	9/12/2002	OLAP Report Subscription	2,500.00		4,441.00
12	9/12/2002	MS Plastics - Bags and gift items	424.00		4,017.00
13	9/15/2002	TDWI Membership Dues	250.00		3,767.00
14	9/15/2002	Intelligent Enterprise Article		800.00	4,567.00
15	9/20/2002	High Speed Internet	150.00		4,417.00
16	9/20/2002	Printer - New Business Cards	60.00		4,357.00
17	9/21/2002	First Financial Planners		2,000.00	6,357.00
18	9/21/2002	Senior Perspectives	280.00		
19	9/21/2002	Twickenham Nannies & Au Pairs	1,600.00		
20	9/26/2002	Newspaper Client		1,600.00	7,957.00
21	9/30/2002	Electric Company	123.00		7,834.00
22	9/30/2002	SBC Local	100.00		7,734.00
23	9/30/2002	F&P Development		1,500.00	**9,134.00**
24	9/30/2002	Month End Totals	10,046.00	10,400.00	**129,855.00**

FIGURE 9-2 Account balances and other semi-additive measures should not be aggregated over time.

Hopefully, most users would recognize an inventory or account balance that is so blatantly wrong. However, good universe designers will take extra precautions in designing a universe to guarantee correct answers, no matter how users might construct a query. Some designers will remove the `SUM` aggregate from all semi-additive measures, ensuring users receive a correct value for every row for each day. However, this is not a good solution because now users cannot ask the question "What are my global inventories for a given product across all plants?" or "What is my total account balance across my various bank accounts?" As discussed in Chapter 8, the use of contexts is the first step to allowing users to pose this kind of business question. Chapter 11 discusses other ways to prevent users from constructing an inaccurate query, but the best practice is to include the `SUM`.

TIP *Always use an aggregate function on a measure object, unless that measure is a unit price or other similar number.*

Detail

A *detail* object provides additional information about a particular dimension. In Figure 9-1, *Print, Radio, Television,* and *Direct mail* are detail objects. Within a customer dimension, age, fax, phone number, street address, and notes are typical details. Details and attributes may supply users with additional ways to analyze the measures, or they may be purely informational. For example, users may want to analyze sales by customer age group but rarely by customers' individual street addresses. In this respect, the street address is purely informational. If you are using an OLAP database, Microsoft Analysis Services refers to details as member properties; Hyperion Essbase refers to them as attributes.

Classifying an object as a dimension or as a detail has no impact on the query or microcube size. An object may be classed as a detail rather than a dimension for primarily visual reasons, to ease user querying. The main limitation with detail objects is that in BusinessObjects XI, they are not hierarchical (for example, if age is a detail, then ranges within age such as Youth, Adult, Senior cannot be grouped). Differentiating between dimensions and details allows BusinessObjects XI to work more consistently with OLAP databases that do differentiate between these information types. For example, Hyperion Essbase distinguishes between a base dimension and an attribute. BusinessObjects XI understands this difference and correctly presents users with the two different types.

Object Ordering

If you use the Designer Wizard to build your universe, objects are added either in alphabetical order or in the order they are stored in the physical tables. In the universe parameters (File, Universe, Parameters), there is a parameter COLUMNS_SORT. The default is Yes, which means that columns in tables appear alphabetically in the table browser (shown in Figure 9-3

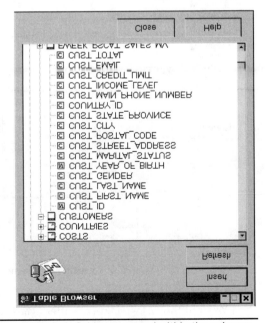

FIGURE 9-3 The universe parameter COLUMNS_SORT affects how fields are sorted within the universe structure and how automatically created objects are ordered.

on the left) and therefore are alphabetical in the universe the wizard builds. If you change this parameter to COLUMNS_SORT=No, then objects are sorted according to their physical order in the table (shown on the right). This is a much better sort order because join keys then appear at the top of the table browser, rather than being intermingled throughout the list.

NOTE   *In earlier versions of Designer, this parameter was controlled via ColSort in the* database *.sbo file. Also, note that the parameter COLUMNS_SORT is case sensitive. If you enter it in initial caps or misspell the parameter, the parameter is ignored.*

The order of the columns in the table browser and the order of the objects that users see are only partially related; if your objects are automatically added to your universe when you insert a table (use the pull-down menu Tools | Options, select the Database tab, and check Create Default Classes And Objects From Tables) or if you build your universe with the Quick Design Wizard, then the order of the tables and fields in the table browser will match the order of the classes and objects in the Universe pane. However, if you do not like this predetermined order, you can manually reorder the objects by dragging and dropping them. Notice in the following screen from the Test Fashion universe you created in Chapter 7 that objects in the *Calendar Year Lookup* class are in the same order as in the physical table CALENDAR_YEAR_LOOKUP:

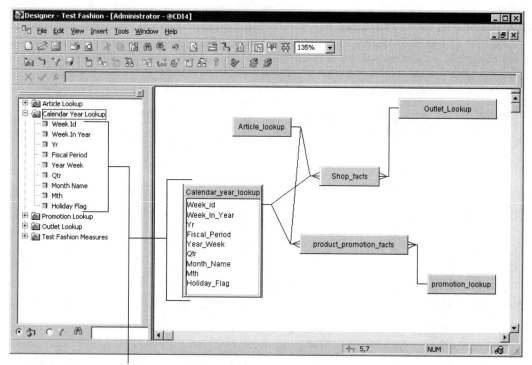

Users see objects in the same order as they appear in the physical table

This order is really not logical from a business viewpoint; *Week* is a smaller increment than *Year*, but then *Month* appears after *Quarter*. However, alphabetical is not logical either.

Therefore, you must manually re-sort the objects into incremental order by dragging and dropping. The following screen shows how you want the sort order to follow time increments, running from *year* to *month* to *week*. As explained in Chapter 12, for multidimensional analysis, the larger increment or grouping should always appear at the top, the most detailed at the bottom. This sort order facilitates drill-down.

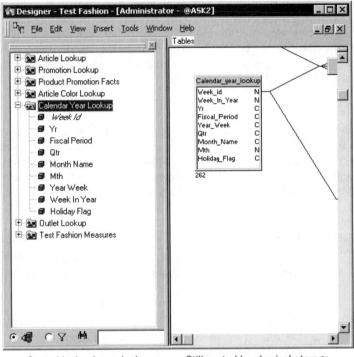

Sorted by business logic
or time increment

Still sorted by physical storage

The naming of these objects is not particularly helpful to the users. What is the difference between *Mth* and *Month Name*? (Naming conventions are discussed in the next section.) Also, users will never need to access the *Week Id* object that acts as a key to the `Calendar_Year_Lookup` table. Therefore, this object should either be hidden as shown in the preceding illustration or deleted altogether.

Naming Conventions

In creating your classes and objects, it's important to develop and follow a consistent naming convention, using the following four Cs as naming principles.

Customer Oriented

Your universe is for your internal and/or external customers, so you must use business terminology. Anything that reveals technical database-naming conventions does not belong in a universe.

Clear

The class and object names must be clear in their meaning. *Customer* is not clear if it could potentially mean *Ship To Customer* or *Sold To Customer*. Think back to the universe design principles discussed in Chapter 6. Who is the target user group for your universe? If these users know of only one type of customer, then *Customer* alone is acceptable as an object or class name. For example, supply chain personnel may only think of the ship-to customer, and accounting personnel may only think of the invoiced or sold-to customer. If these two groups of users will have separate universes, then *Customer* is acceptable; if they will share a universe, then the names must be clear and explicit. In the Test Fashion universe you have developed so far, the object names *Mth* and *Month Name* are not clear. For all a user knows, the object *Mth* could be Jan, 01, or January.

Consistent

Object names should be consistent in two respects. First, use the same name when you mean the same thing. Always refer to the customer as the customer, and do not mix in other terminology such as client or business partner. Second, use the same clarifiers consistently. If your universe has columns that are IDs or codes and columns that are names or descriptions, then append these clarifiers consistently, as Table 9-1 illustrates.

Initial Object Name	Potential Problem	Consistent Object Name
Article code	N/A. This object name is consistent, assuming "article" is the generally used business term. The code name qualifier makes it clear.	Article code
Article name	N/A. This object name is consistent, assuming "article" is the generally used business term. The code name qualifier makes it clear.	Article name
Article	It's not clear if this object refers to an article code or a description, unless all description fields have a name or description appended at the end of the object name and, by default, everything else is a code or a number.	Article code
SKU	Duplicate of Article code and not the generally accepted business term. However, it is concise, which would make for a nice column heading in a report.	Article code
Product	Duplicate of Article code or SKU. Also, not clear if this is a code or a description object.	Article code
Gmid	Gmid is the abbreviation for global material identification as used in the OLTP; data entry users know the term, but business users within the target universe group do not.	Article code

TABLE 9-1   Object Names Should Follow the Four C's: Be Customer Oriented, Clear, Consistent, Concise

Concise

Object names should be concise, as they become the default column heading in a report. The bad thing about this is that *Article code* can be a long column heading if most of your article codes are only four characters long. In such a scenario, the abbreviated form *SKU* or *Gmid* may make for shorter and better column headings.

It would be a nice feature if Designer allowed you to centrally rename a column heading (just as SQL does), but unfortunately, it does not. Column headings can be renamed and wrapped within individual reports. Therefore, you can consider clear business terms a higher priority than concise column headings.

Warning: Cutting and Pasting Objects and Object IDs

In early versions of BusinessObjects, object names within individual user queries and reports had to match object names within the universe. For example, in the Test Fashion universe, there is a *Mth* object. Unless users look at the data, users are not sure whether this is the month name, a number, or a three-character abbreviation. As a universe designer, you can rename *Mth* to *Month Number* in the universe and all the user reports will automatically reflect this new object name.

Often in renaming objects, a universe designer will make the mistake of cutting and pasting the original *Mth* object to a new object titled *Month Number.* This is a bad practice, as it creates a different object ID, an internal mechanism Designer uses to keep track of changes to objects. After testing the new *Month Number* object, the universe designer will then go back and delete the original *Mth* object. Once the original *Mth* object is deleted, all existing reports that previously used the *Mth* object will generate an error that the *Mth* object is missing. Users can still view the reports, but as soon as they attempt to refresh the report, they will receive this error. If the universe designer had modified the original *Mth* object, then the existing queries and reports would have automatically been updated with the new object name.

To minimize report errors, take these precautions:

- Modify existing objects when you really wish to change the name or underlying SQL; avoid re-creating new objects to replace old ones.

- Always make a backup copy of a universe. One client I worked with deleted a number of objects accidentally. The designer thought he had fixed the problem by simply re-creating the objects with the exact same object names (which didn't work). A backup version of the universe allowed us to more quickly access and restore the original object IDs.

Working with Classes and Objects

You have already seen how objects can be re-sorted within a class in the *Calendar Year Lookup* example. Classes and objects can also be renamed, deleted, hidden, and modified. In manipulating an object, you can access these actions in a number of ways:

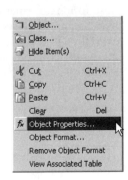

- Use the Edit pull-down menu to clear, hide, or modify properties and formats.

- Select the item and then right-click to choose from various actions on the pop-up menu.

- Double-click the item to bring up the object's Edit Properties dialog box.

The modifications described in the remainder of this section will generally use the right-click approach.

Rename an Object

Using the Test Fashion universe created in Chapter 7, you want to rename the class *Calendar Year Lookup* to *Time*.

1. Select the class *Calendar Year Lookup.*

2. Right-click and then choose Class Properties from the pop-up menu. The following screen shows the initial class definition:

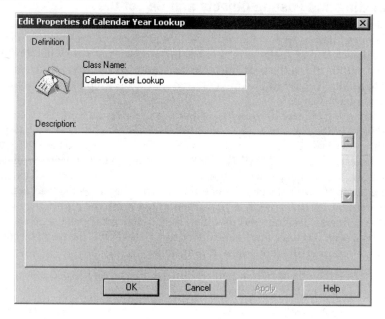

3. Once you are in the Edit Properties dialog box, replace the current name in the Class Name box with **Time**.

4. Click OK.

In the following screen, the *Calendar Year Lookup* class has been renamed *Time,* and class description information has been added. Classes as well as objects can contain meaningful help text in the Description box. Help text is an underutilized feature in many universes, even though it is fairly easy to extract via the universe strategies. Power users or subject matter experts can also provide description information via spreadsheet files and object strategies (see Chapter 7) that can be easily imported into the universe.

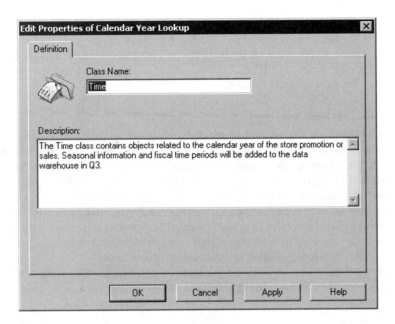

Delete an Object

To delete a class or object, you can use the same three selection methods described earlier or two shortcut keys:

Key	Menu Equivalent	Explanation
DELETE	Edit | Clear	This deletes the class or object. The only way to retrieve it again is to use the undo button.
CTRL-X	Cut	This cuts the class or object and puts it in the MS Windows clipboard. To retrieve the object again, use paste or CTRL-V.

Let's imagine the worst-case scenario: you accidentally deleted a class. When you delete a class, all the objects in that class will also be deleted. Designer warns you of this with the error message shown here.

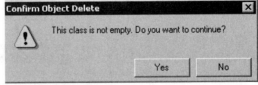

With Clear or DELETE, the contents are not placed in the MS Windows clipboard. Undo allows you to undo only the last action. As the Clear was several steps ago, the undo button no longer can help you. All is not lost. Recall from Chapter 6, the section "How Designer Works," that you are working on only a copy of the universe. There is still a universe, with all the old object definitions, stored in the repository. When you make a catastrophic mistake like this, you can re-import a copy of the universe from the repository, although you will lose all other changes you made during this Designer session.

Given that DELETE doesn't add items to the Windows clipboard, I suggest you use Cut as often as possible so that you have a better recovery process in case you accidentally delete something important. Keep in mind, though, that if you Cut an object and recover it with the Paste command, the object will be assigned a new object ID and will generate errors in any existing user reports that reference the object.

Hide

Hidden classes and objects are items that appear to you as the designer in italics but that users do not see when creating queries against this universe. Because the items still exist in the universe, they do take up space and will increase the size of the universe. Some designers will hide items so that all columns within the data mart appear to the designer but not to the user. I don't like this use of Hide because of the impact on universe size. However, Hide is useful when you want to hide "work in progress" or if you wish to remove an object but want a transition period to ensure that the removed object will not create problems for the users. You also may want to hide an object that users will never access directly but that you as the designer may reference in @WHERE or other object logic.

In the following example, I've added the table ARTICLE_COLOR_LOOKUP; Designer automatically added the corresponding class and objects. I don't want the users to see these items yet, as they are not in business terms, nor have I added my joins.

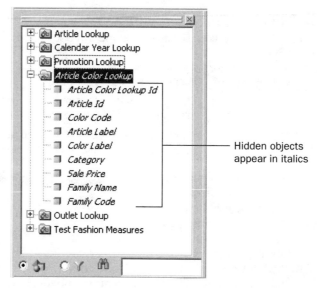

Hidden objects appear in italics

 To hide a class or object, select the item and then click the Hide/Show button from the toolbar. The Hide/Show button acts as a toggle. When you are ready for users to see this new class and its objects, unhide or show the items with the same button.

Modify a Dimension

If you have used the Quick Design Wizard to create your universe, or if you have made the setting to automatically create new classes and objects when you add a table to the universe (Tools | Options | Database), then much of your work now will be to modify those objects. In the next example, you will modify the dimension object *Mth,* in the renamed *Time* class.

Definition

1. Select the object *Mth* and double-click to bring up the Edit Properties dialog box. This dialog has several tabs: Definition, Properties, Advanced, Keys, and Source Information. The Definition tab contains the object name, type, SQL, and description or help text.

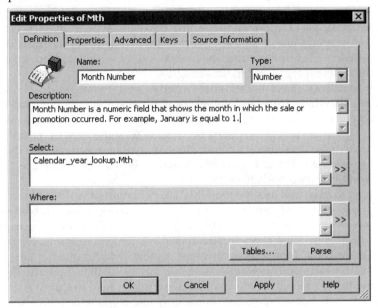

2. Change the object name from *Mth* to **Month Number**.

3. The object type relates to the field format in the source database as well as to how users will choose to manipulate the object's data in a report. Leave the Type as Number.

4. In the Description box, enter help text that is meaningful for users. If users will use a field as part of a condition, I like to give them an indication of the format. Enter the following help text: **Month Number is a numeric field that shows the month in which the sale or promotion occurred. For example, January is equal to 1.**

5. The Select statement is the SQL used to dynamically build the user's query. If you are creating a new object, it is best to use the arrow button to launch the SQL Editor to select tables and columns to ensure the SQL is accurate.

6. The Where box is used to generate the WHERE clause within a SQL statement. It's important to remember, though, that Desktop Intelligence and Web Intelligence append the WHERE clause to the entire query (assuming the particular object is used in the query). For example, if you have an object *Current Year Sales* with a WHERE clause of Year=2003 and a *Last Year Sales* where Year=2002 and a user selects both objects for one report, then no data will be returned; the two WHERE clauses are mutually exclusive. Therefore, this box is most often left blank or used for variable prompts as discussed in Chapter 11.

7. Click OK to close the object's Edit Properties dialog box.

Object Types vs. Database Field Format

In the preceding Step 3, you left the object type as numeric to match the data source field format. Normally, these are the same, and keeping them the same can prevent a number of errors. There is, however, one possible exception: when your source system is a number field that you will never use as a measure. For example, product ID and customer number may be numeric fields in the source system, but you will rarely want to treat them as numbers (unless the coding has some meaningful logic that you wish to manipulate). In this case, I have in the past recommended setting the object type to character to prevent any object misuse. However, some of the user interfaces will now generate errors depending on the type of mismatch. Therefore, setting the Object Format is a safer alternative. Table 9-2 summarizes the different types and their settings.

When you specify an object as a number (whether or not you specify it as a measure), certain functionality within Desktop Intelligence and Web Intelligence is available to end users. Users will be able to do sums, divisions, averages, and so forth, on these numbers. From a business point of view, these calculations make no sense against most ID fields. The only calculation that makes sense is a count: How many new products sold this month? How many customers do I have? The count calculation is available to all objects, regardless of their types (number, date, and character).

The only way to suppress this functionality is by changing the ID field from numeric to character type (even though it is physically numeric). At one point this was a good work-around for preventing object misuse, but with each version of the software, it checks for certain object mismatches, and changing the type can later lead to errors. For example, in the Test Fashion universe, from a business point of view, I would much prefer that *Month Number* be a date type object. This would allow users to use all the wonderful date functions within Web Intelligence formulas. However, it is a numeric field in the physical database, and if you specify it as a date type object in the universe, users will receive an error when executing a query. If users want to display a long month name within a report that is derived from the numeric month (so January instead of 1), they have to use multiple report functions to convert the numeric field to character and then to date.

In Web Intelligence:

```
=Month(ToDate(FormatNumber([Month Number N];"00") ;"MM"))
```

In Desktop Intelligence:

```
=Month(ToDate(FormatNumber(<Month Number> ,"00") ,"MM"))
```

CAUTION *If you change the object type to be different than the source data field type, certain formula functions within Desktop Intelligence will generate an error. Within Web Intelligence, the query may not run at all. Also, parsing the object or running a universe integrity check will give you an error.*

Clearly, having users do extra conversions for what should be a simple task is poor universe design. To prevent users from having to do extra conversions, a business-oriented universe designer may try to help users by converting the number field to a date field (or number to character, and so on) in the objects' SQL select statement. This might seem good in theory, but in practice, it can pose additional problems in terms of query performance.

Object Type	Explanation
Number	Any measure objects must have the object type of Number.
Date	Fields that are in date format in the data source should be set to date type in the universe.
Character	Fields that are character in the data source should be set to character as the object type. Numeric fields that are not measures and that will not benefit from calculations may also be set to character.
Long Text	Long text fields are generally used for comments and note fields. The length of the long text object returned in a query can be controlled and is specific to each universe; it is set under File I Parameters I Controls.

TABLE 9-2 Object Types Correspond to Physical Database Field Formats

With most RDBMSs, if you change the appearance of a field, the index will not be used when the query uses such an object as a condition. Therefore, work closely with the DBA or analyze an explain plan whenever you use SQL functionality to convert field types. (See Chapter 11 for more on creating advanced objects.)

CAUTION *If you specify a character database field as a number and attempt to use it as a measure, BusinessObjects XI will drop any rows that contain characters from your report.*

Properties

The Properties tab of the Edit Properties dialog box sets the object type or qualification, the aggregates if it's a measure, and settings for a list of values or pick list when users insert an object as a query condition.

To navigate to the Properties for the object *Month Number*:

1. Within the universe pane, double-click the *Month Number* object from the list of classes and objects.
2. Select the Properties tab.
3. The *Month Number* is a dimension, so leave this radio button checked.
4. By default, dimension and detail objects have an associated list of values. This check box is enabled and Designer provides a system-generated list name. Change the list name of the associated list of values to **MonthNN**. Lists of values and these settings are explained in more detail in Chapter 10.
5. Click OK to close the dialog.

Advanced

The Advanced tab controls who can access the object, where the object can be used in a query, and date formats.

On the Advanced tab, security access level settings interact with other settings discussed in Chapter 13. The Public setting allows all users to access an object and is the default.

For each object, you can control whether the object can be used as a result, a condition, or a sort as described in Table 9-3.

> **NOTE** *Concerned with response time issues, some DBAs may disagree with the recommendations in Table 9-3, but it provides the most user flexibility. You need to weigh the risk of users creating inefficient queries and affecting system response times versus modifying these options and having an overly restrictive deployment that prevents them from asking valid business questions.*

Can Be Used As A	Explanation
Result	A result is a column in a query or a report. Most often, all objects are results.
Condition	Conditions relate to the WHERE clause of a SQL statement. If your universe accesses an OLTP, you may want to disallow nonindexed fields as conditions, as they may result in slow queries and bog down the source system. If you are in a data warehouse environment, I recommend allowing all objects as conditions. It's true that you may want users to search on the indexed CUSTOMER_ CODE, for example, but what if there are several related customers that all start with the same first few letters, such as Deloitte & Touche? They could have the forms Deloitte Consulting, Deloitte & Touche Management Solutions, Deloitte Parsipanny office, etc. If you allow *Customer Name* as a condition, a user could select everything starting with Deloitte.
Sort	Sort allows users to sort results on the server rather than on the client. As with conditions, I suggest allowing this on all objects. In most cases, users will sort their results within the report once they see the data. However, if users want to select top 10 product sales, or top 100 customers, the sort must be processed on the server.

TABLE 9-3 Objects Can Be Used in Three Different Ways in a Query

Database Format applies only to date fields and will be dimmed for nondate fields. The date format can be very confusing, particularly when you consider that there is different behavior in XI versus earlier versions and between Web Intelligence and Desktop Intelligence. So proceed with caution!

As an American, it took me a while to realize that much of the rest of the world writes the date differently, and I humbly apologize to the international world for being so ethnocentric! I only learned this the hard way after living in Switzerland for a number of years and having an English husband: An American will refer to April 1 as 04/01. A European will write April 1 as 01/04. (You can imagine the confusion this causes when my husband and I attempt to confirm various appointments!)

The format displayed in the list of values and in the report comes from either the Control Panel Regional settings (for Desktop Intelligence) or the InfoView General Preferences, Locale (for Web Intelligence). Meanwhile, the query engine uses the date format defined in the *database*.prm file to generate the SQL syntax when a date is used in the WHERE clause. Thus the date you see in a list of values may be different than the date format in the SQL generated. The parameter files are located in the following directory on Windows:

```
C:\Program Files\Business Objects\BusinessObjects Enterprise
11.5\win32_x86\dataAccess\ConnectionServer
```

NOTE *In earlier versions of BusinessObjects, these settings were stored in plain text files in the .SBO file. With XI, they are XML files and the settings are in the .PRM files.*

You can change the database settings for an individual object in the Database Format box. This will affect the SQL generated but not the list of values. For example, the ODBC .PRM file has the following parameter:

```
<Parameter Name="USER_INPUT_DATE_FORMAT">{\d 'yyyy-mm-dd'}</Parameter>
```

Oracle uses the following default settings in the Oracle.prm file:

```
<Parameter Name="USER_INPUT_DATE_FORMAT">'dd-MM-yyyy HH:mm:ss'</Parameter>
<Parameter Name="DATABASE_DATE_FORMAT">DD-MM-YYYY HH24:MI:33</Parameter>
```

SQL Server uses the following default settings to generate the SQL where clause:

```
<Parameter Name="USER_INPUT_DATE_FORMAT">'mm/dd/yyyy HH:m:s'</Parameter>
```

If any of your date fields in your database do not follow the default format, you may need to modify the object properties to override the settings in the respective parameter file. It's important to note that

- These settings come into play only when a date field is used as a condition.
- You need to worry about such settings only when users get errors, no data is returned, or you suspect a mismatch in the way date fields are physically stored versus in a query condition.
- In Web Intelligence, they do not affect the list of values date format.
- In the BusinessObjects 6.1 full client, they *do* affect the list of values date format, but in Desktop Intelligence, they do not appear to.

In the Island Resorts Marketing universe, TIME.RESERVATION_DATE is stored in MS Access as YYYY-MM-DD. When a user places the *Reservation Date* object in the condition panel, the query engine will automatically take the user's input and convert it to whatever input format is set in the ODBC.PRM file (yyyy-mm-dd). Because this format is the same format for how the physical date values are stored, the user gets the correct results. However, if the object properties specified a precise time stamp that included hours and minutes or an incompatible date format, users would receive an error or no rows returned.

To ensure users get the correct results, specify a date format in the Object Properties dialog that corresponds with the date in the physical database. In this example, {\t\s 'yyyy-mm-dd HH:mm:ss'} would be the correct Database Format if the Reservation Date also included a precise time of day. As shown in the following screen, note that ODBC requires the brackets and \t\s parameters for time stamps; Oracle and SQL Server do not.

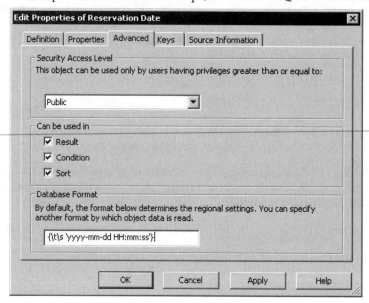

Now, if a user enters 1/12/2001 as a condition value, the hours and minutes are automatically appended to the condition as Web Intelligence converts the SQL using the format specified in Object Properties:

```
SELECT
  Reservations.res_date
FROM
  Reservations
WHERE
  Reservations.res_date  =  {ts '2001-01-12 00:00:00'}
```

TIP   Review the database.prm file to ensure it corresponds with the date values in your database.

Object Keys

The specification of keys was introduced in Designer 6.5 with the sole purpose of generating more efficient SQL. As discussed earlier in this chapter, when users add conditions to a query, it may be more efficient to filter from the fact table than the dimension table. At the time of this writing, I advise against the use of keys in the universe design. Web Intelligence generates various errors when users access objects that use keys. As well, sometimes it causes the database to return more rows of data than necessary, so ultimately it is not giving the performance benefits expected. In the expectation that these issues will eventually be resolved, I am documenting how the keys work. One thing that is sure, though, is that filtering on columns that contain distinct values and that are indexed columns will always be faster than filtering on columns that contain textual descriptions and that may or may not be indexed. In theory, there are two ways to accomplish this:

- Specify keys in the universe.

- Customize the list of values as described in the next chapter. In practice, this is the alternative that works as expected and consistently between Web Intelligence and Desktop Intelligence.

A primary key is a unique identifier for each row in a given table. A foreign key is when that same identifier in one table is used in another table. As shown in the following illustration, `Article_ID` is the primary key to the table `Article_Lookup`. `Article_ID` then becomes a foreign key in the `Shop_Facts` table. The primary key to `Shop_Facts` is `SHOP_FACTS_ID`. `SHOP_FACTS_ID` is not used as a foreign key elsewhere in this schema.

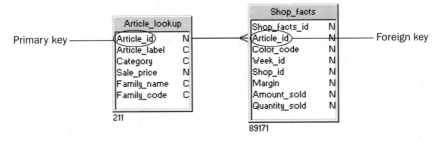

When you define these keys within the universe, you only want to define them for related description objects. It basically will tell the query engine that whenever users filter on a description object, to use the ID field instead. If you define keys on objects for other columns, it provides no benefit and may result in less efficient SQL.

For example, a user wants to analyze sales for Blazers or Article_ID 158152. The user has no idea what the article ID is and you have not customized the list of values. The following SQL would be generated by default:

```
SELECT DISTINCT
  Article_lookup.Article_label,
  sum(Shop_facts.Amount_sold)
FROM
  Shop_facts,
  Article_lookup
WHERE
  ( Article_lookup.Article_id=Shop_facts.Article_id  )
  AND  (
  Article_lookup.Article_label  =  'Blazer'
  )
GROUP BY
  Article_lookup.Article_label
```

Notice that the value 'Blazer' is used to filter from the lookup table. However, if you specify the primary and foreign keys on the *Article Label* object, the user builds the query in the exact same way but with the following SQL:

```
SELECT
  max(
Article_lookup.Article_label  ),
  Article_lookup.Article_id,
  sum(Shop_facts.Amount_sold)
FROM
  Article_lookup,
  Shop_facts
WHERE
  ( Article_lookup.Article_id=Shop_facts.Article_id  )
  AND
  Article_lookup.Article_id  In  ( 158152  )
GROUP BY
  Article_lookup.Article_id,
  Article_lookup.Article_id
```

Notice that the value '158152' is used to filter from the fact table (not the description Blazer and not from the lookup table as in the first SQL statement).

To specify the primary and foreign keys for the object *Article Label* object:

1. From the universe pane, expand the class *Article Lookup* by clicking the + sign.

2. Double-click the object *Article Label* to invoke the Edit Properties dialog.

3. Select the Keys tab.

4. For most databases, you can click the Detect button and Designer will automatically add the relevant primary key and foreign key to the object. With MS Access databases, you must do it manually. Click the Insert button. Designer will insert the Key Type Primary Key as shown in the following screen:

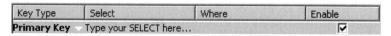

Key Type	Select	Where	Enable
Primary Key Type your SELECT here...			☑

5. Under the Select column, Designer displays a message "Type your SELECT here . . . ." The SELECT statement should be the table.fieldname of the primary key. Double-click the ellipsis character (. . .) to invoke the SQL Editor and select `Article_Lookup.Article_ID` or enter it manually. Click OK to close the SQL Editor and return to the Key tab of the Object Properties dialog.

6. Repeat Steps 4 and 5 to insert the foreign key as `Shop_facts.Article_ID`. Your settings should appear as follows:

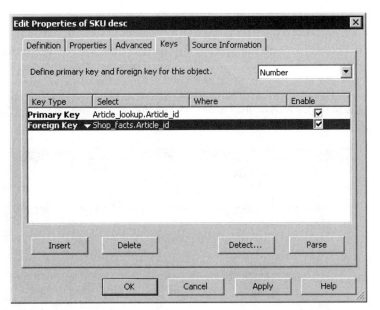

7. Click Parse to ensure your SELECT statements are correct. Note that Parse will not warn you of selecting the wrong columns.

8. Click OK to apply the key settings and close the Edit Properties dialog.

To verify the effect of these settings and see the SQL generated, use Tools | Query Panel to build a query that contains a condition on *Article Label*. Note that the Designer Query Panel may generate SQL that is different from that generated within Web Intelligence.

CAUTION *Support for keys was not available to Web Intelligence users in version 6.5 or XI Release 1 but is theoretically available in XI Release 2. However, the SQL generated is sometimes different between Desktop Intelligence and Web Intelligence. In XI Release 2, the SQL generated by either interface will correctly use the foreign key when the query involves a measure from the fact table and the filter value is chosen from a list of values. When the filter value 'Blazer' is manually entered, then the key field is not used. Also, when the query simply involves a dimension table for a list of products, for example, then Desktop Intelligence will use the primary key field to filter the query whereas Web Intelligence does not. I have encountered numerous problems in Web Intelligence with list of values for objects that use these key settings. Therefore, I do not recommend using this feature if your query environment will be Web Intelligence until the vendor has fixed in a service pack or hot fix later than SP1.*

Source Information

The Source Information tab is new in XI Release 2. Data Integrator populates the fields in this dialog to provide technical metadata, mapping of columns, and lineage from source systems. This information is displayed to Web Intelligence users in the context panel.

Modify a Detail or Attribute

You define detail objects in much the much the same way that you create a dimension object. The main difference is that you must associate a detail object with a dimension object. In the following example, the detail object *Street* is associated with the dimension object *Shop Name*. Once you have associated *Street* with *Shop Name*, *Street* and other related details will now appear in a separate folder under *Shop Name*. These objects will not be available when users are drilling within a report.

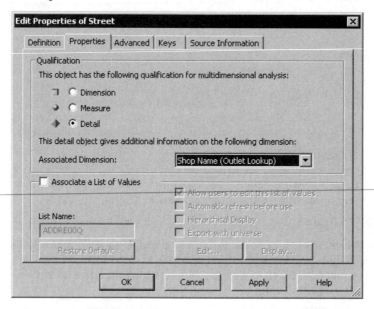

The object *Address_1* was created when you inserted the table `Outlet_lookup` into the Test Fashion universe. By default, Designer listed it as a dimension object. In the following example, you will rename the object as *Street* and change its type to detail:

1. From the universe pane, expand the *Outlet Lookup* class by clicking the + sign.

2. Select the object *Address_1* and double-click to invoke the Edit Properties dialog.

3. In the Name box, replace *Address_1* with **Street**.

4. Select the Properties tab and change the qualification from Dimension to Detail.

5. Once you select Detail, a new option will appear for you to associate the object with a dimension. Choose Shop Name from the drop-down menu.

6. Click OK to apply the changes and close the dialog.

Insert a Measure

The preceding section discussed modifying an existing object. You can also add new objects by clicking the Insert Object button or using the menu choice Insert | Object. In this section, you will add a measure object called *Promotion Cost*. This assumes that the table PRODUCT_ PROMOTION_FACTS exists in your Universe pane. Depending on your Tools | Options | Database settings, a dimension object *Promotion Cost* may already have been automatically created, in which case, modify that object.

1. Position your mouse in the *Test Fashion Measures* class. Click the Insert Object button.

2. Designer will present you with the same dialog boxes as when modifying objects. Enter the name **Promotion Cost** and set the object type to Number.

3. Enter the object description as: **Promotion Cost is the dollar value spent on a given radio, newspaper or other media promotion. Promotion costs are unique for each individual product but are allocated across all stores**.

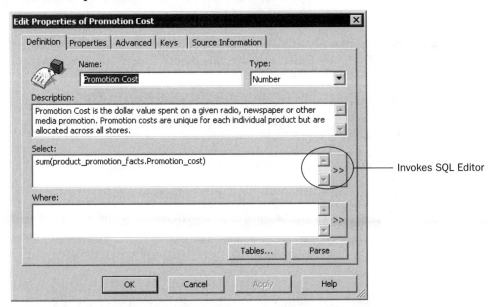

4. In the Select box, click the >> button to access the full Select statement and SQL functions. The functions here relate to your specific database. The SQL Editor and popular functions are discussed further in Chapter 11.

5. In the Functions column, click the + sign next to Number functions. Scroll to the Sum() function and double-click to add it to the Select statement.

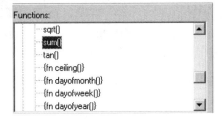

6. Ensure your mouse is positioned in the middle of the Sum parentheses in the top box. In the Tables and Columns box, click the + sign next to the table PRODUCT_PROMOTION_FACTS to find the column PROMOTION_COST.

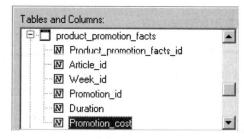

Double-click to add this field so that the SQL appears as follows:

```
sum(product_promotion_facts.promotion_cost)
```

7. Click Parse to check that your SQL is correct.

Tip *You can wait to parse all objects when checking the universe integrity, but it is easier to diagnose problems if you parse objects as you build them. Parse will verify that the SQL statement contains the correct syntax and that the object type matches the database field type.*

8. Click OK to save your Select statement and return to the Definition tab.

9. Select the Properties tab and verify that the object qualification is a measure. The default qualification is Dimension, but this should have changed automatically when you selected the Sum function.

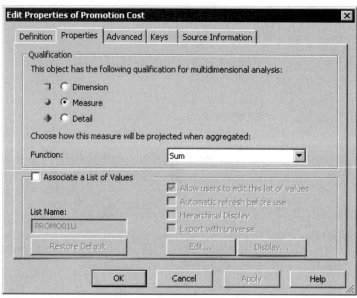

10. Verify that the projection aggregate is set to Sum. The default projection aggregate is interpreted from the SQL aggregate.

11. There is no reason to have a list of values for measure objects, so leave the option Associate A List Of Values unchecked.

12. Click OK to save your object changes.

 13. Click Save to save the changes made to the universe.

About Aggregates

Two forms of aggregates are involved in a measure objects: SQL functions and projection aggregates. Users can create a third aggregate called *calculations* within individual reports.

SQL Aggregates

SQL aggregates such as SUM, MIN, and MAX require a GROUP BY clause that the query engine automatically includes in each SQL statement.

Refer back to Figure 9-2. There are 23 rows of data in the sample fact table. If I select debits and credits without the SQL SUM function, then my report will display 23 rows. If I use the SUM function and request only debit and credits by day, SQL will group the debits and credits for each day. For example, there are four detail entries for September 12, 2002, in Figure 9-2. SQL sums these into one entry for September 12, as shown in Figure 9-4. With the SUM function, Figure 9-4 shows 10 rows of data compared to the physical 23 rows from Figure 9-2. Failure to use SQL aggregates correctly can unnecessarily cause millions of rows of data to be sent across the network.

In this example, the number of rows returned to the client workstation or to the Enterprise Server has gone from 21 to 10 through use of a SQL aggregate function. In a real-world example, this could be the difference between returning a few rows or millions of rows of data to a client.

CAUTION *Always use a SQL aggregate on a measure unless it involves a unit price or something similar; otherwise, you risk overloading your servers, network, and client PCs.*

SQL Aggregate

Month	Date	Debits	Credits
September	9/1/02	1,224	
September	9/2/02	2,200	4,000
September	9/3/02	800	
September	9/5/02		500
September	9/12/02	3,259	
September	9/15/02	250	800
September	9/20/02	210	
September	9/21/02	1,880	2,000
September	9/26/02		1,600
September	9/30/02	223	1,500
	Sum:	10,046	10,400

FIGURE 9-4   SQL Sum and GROUP BY aggregate individual rows by common dimensions, reducing the number of rows of data sent to the Enterprise Server.

Projection Aggregate

Month	Debits	Credits
September	10,046	10,400
	10,046	**10,400**

Projection Aggregate

The second form of aggregate is the *projection* aggregate, used in multidimensional analysis and when users remove dimension columns from a report or chart that still exist in the results set. In the following example, I have deleted the *Date* object from the report display but not from the query itself. There are still ten rows in my result set. In Figure 9-5, Web Intelligence now does the grouping in the report to yield one row of data for the entire month of September.

As a general rule, the SQL function you use will match your projection aggregate used on the individual object properties. As discussed earlier in connection with measures, price is one measure in which designers may not use a SQL aggregate; however, it would be useful to set the projection aggregate to Avg to allow further analysis. With inventory and ending balance, I recommend using the SQL SUM function but then setting the projection aggregate to None.

Object Formats

Object formats determine how data is initially formatted within a report display. Users can override any of the default formats by formatting individual cells within a report. Using object formats, the universe designer can centrally define a format that includes number, alignment, font, border, and shading. Object formatting is often overlooked, and the fact that the Object Format dialog is somewhat hidden in the pop-up menu rather than in the Edit Properties dialog makes it all the easier to forget object formatting. However, for certain objects and formats, you can save hundreds of users time by applying these formats once, rather than by each user in each report. Also, if you intend to display hyperlinks in a report (discussed further in Chapter 11), you need to format the object to read as HTML.

In the following example, you will change the object format for *Promotion Cost* to include dollar signs with no decimal places.

1. From the universe pane, expand the *Test Fashion Measures* class by clicking the + sign.

2. Select the object *Promotion Cost*.

3. Right-click to access the pop-up menu and select Object Format or choose Edit | Object Format from the pull-down menu.

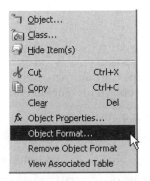

4. Select the Number tab and specify the desired format. For many numeric fields, in particular, key or ID fields, set the number format to drop the decimal place.

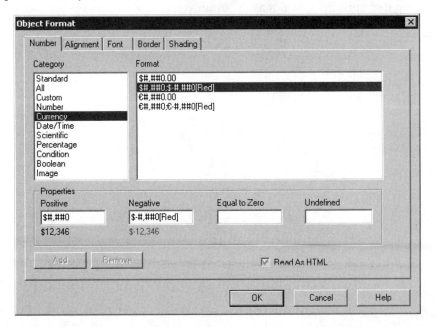

5. Click OK to apply the formatting changes and then close the dialog box.

Many of the formats you can apply in Designer are also available to end users within Web Intelligence and Desktop Intelligence. The various options are discussed further in Chapter 21.

Summary

Classes and objects act as the user interface to the physical columns in the data source. Designer provides three different types of objects (measures, dimensions, and details) to help users differentiate between types of information more easily. This chapter covered the basics of building different kinds of objects and highlighted some important design principles:

- Point dimension objects to lookup tables.
- Always use SQL aggregates on measure objects.
- Sort dimension objects from biggest to smallest to facilitate drill-down.
- Follow the four Cs in naming objects (customer-oriented, clear, consistent, concise).
- Ensure object types and data field types match the type in the physical database.

Following these principles will make your universe powerful yet ensure users consistently get correct results. In Chapters 10 and 11, you will add even more intelligence to the objects.

List of Values

The *list of values* is a powerful feature that allows users to select from a pick list when setting conditions in a query. You as a designer determine which objects have lists of values via the object properties.

Because users can select conditions from a list of values, they do not need to enter conditions manually and therefore do not need to memorize lists of codes or guess how many leading zeros there may be in a particular field. Designer allows you to customize the default list of values even further to present meaningful names with the codes or to shorten particularly long lists into a more manageable size.

How List of Values Works

When a user adds a condition to a query, BusinessObjects XI essentially launches a second query and returns a list from the dimension or lookup table in the RDBMS, as shown in Figure 10-1. In the following example, the user has a condition on City (1). To be able to pick from a list of city names, the Enterprise Server will query the data source for a list of valid cities (2). A list of cities is displayed to the user (3), and the user selects London (4). The list of values ensures the query condition is valid and in the correct syntax, such as London as opposed to LONDON.

When you are working in Designer, this list of values query file exists as an *object*.lov file, where *object* is the list filename specified in the object properties. This same file is used for Desktop Intelligence and is stored under

```
C:\Documents and Settings\user\Application Data\Business Objects\Business Objects
11.5\universes\Enterprise Server Name\folder\universe
```

When Web Intelligence users access a list of values, the .lov file is cached as part of the user session on the Web Intelligence Report Server. The name of the file is no longer *object*.lov but rather is a system-generated filename.

Designer automatically creates these query files whenever a universe designer enables a list of values on a universe object *and* the user requests a list of values for adding a condition to a query. Unless a designer customizes the list of values, the SQL generated is always

```
SELECT DISTINCT
  Table.column
FROM
  Table
```

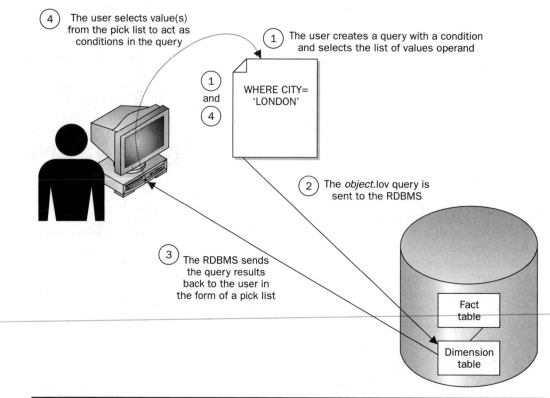

FIGURE 10-1   A list of values query is associated with an object in the universe. It queries the dimension tables to present users with a pick list for conditions.

Notice that the query engine adds a DISTINCT keyword to all list of values queries. This ensures that users receive only a single row for each distinct value. For example, a Customer dimension table may have multiple rows for each customer ID as changes to customer information are kept and time-stamped. In setting conditions in a query, users will need to see the unique customer ID only once. The use of the DISTINCT keyword is sensible from a user-functionality point of view, but it clearly has an impact on query response time when your list of values is directed to a large fact table.

TIP   *You can change the default setting for a list of values to use a* GROUP BY *rather than* DISTINCT. *This parameter is universe specific and is set by selecting File | Universe Parameters | Parameter tab. Set the value* DISTINCT_VALUES=GROUPBY. *See the section "Parameter Tab" in Chapter 7 for more information.*

While the file storage location is different, the process to generate the list of values in Desktop Intelligence is similar to that in Web Intelligence. When users add a condition to a query, they must select an operand, as shown here:

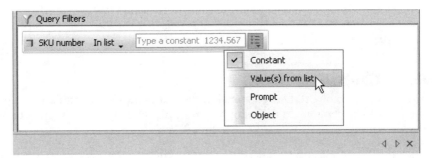

Users can either manually enter the value for the condition or select the operand Value(s) From List (Figure 10-1, Step 1). This operand will send the *object*.lov query to the dimension table in the RDBMS (Step 2). The RDBMS sends the query results back to the Web Intelligence Report Server (or client for Desktop Intelligence) (Step 3). Users then select which condition value(s) they want in the original query condition (Step 4). When the user launches the main query, the .lov query is no longer involved. Also, if a user selects the operand type Constant and manually enters a filter value, then the .lov query is not involved.

Once the user session has ended, the .lov file is no longer available, unlike in Desktop Intelligence, which permanently stores the *object*.lov file. For this reason, you as the designer must be particularly cognizant of long lists of values that are slow to generate. With BusinessObjects 6.5 and earlier, the way the repository was structured made exporting pregenerated lists of values to the repository exceedingly slow. A binary query file had to be extracted from the relational repository and rebuilt in the file system. With XI, when you export the universe and lists of values to the repository, it's primarily copying files to the file system, a significantly faster operation than in 6.5. With this change in architecture, then, long-time Business Objects customers have an opportunity to rethink their approach to lists of values.

Designers can customize the *object*.lov query to shorten long lists of values. For example, if you have millions of products, you may want to prompt users first to select a product category, in what is referred to as cascading lists of values. If the users do not know the codes or spellings of the product categories, for example, then BusinessObjects XI may first launch a prodcat.lov query. In this respect, Steps 2 and 3 may be repeated multiple times until the user finally selects values to add to the query in Step 4. The size of the *object*.lov files also may change over time as the number of products changes or as users select different product categories.

NOTE *If you are a long-time Crystal user, you will note that the approach to lists of values in the universe is quite different from the Crystal Reports approach. Crystal Reports historically has had static lists of values (parameters) that were stored with the report and could not be cascaded. BusinessObjects, meanwhile, has long had dynamic lists of values that are stored with the universe. Crystal Reports XI also now supports dynamic lists of values and cascades via Business Views.*

List of Values Settings

When you first create an object, Designer enables lists of values by default and assigns a name based on the object name. In the following example, you will explore the settings for the *Month Number* object that you used in Chapter 9:

1. Click the *Time* class and expand the folder by clicking the + sign.

2. Double-click the object *Month Number* to modify the object properties.

3. Select the Properties tab. Notice that the check box Associate A List Of Values is enabled. By default, this check box is enabled on all dimension and detail objects.

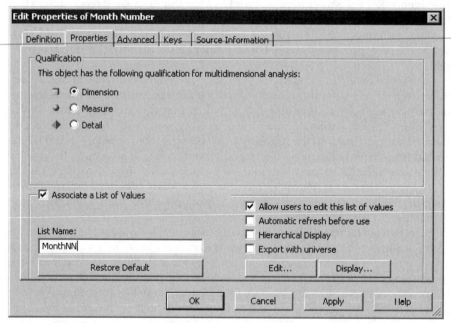

4. You can accept Designer's default List Name, or you can modify the name to be more meaningful. In this case, change the List Name to **MONTHNN**.

TIP *I prefer to change the List Name, as it helps when using the same list of values for multiple objects. It also helps when you need to use Windows Explorer to clean up the .lov files on your local disk or verify the file size of a customized list.*

---

5. The check box Allow Users To Edit This List Of Values is checked by default. Table 10-1 explains the purpose of each of these check boxes.

Option	Explanation
Allow users to edit this list of values	This is allowed by default. This option lets Desktop Intelligence users create their own custom lists, adding whatever filters, sorts, or personal data files they find most useful. I have rarely seen this used, even by power users. The main caveat here is that if the designer customizes and exports a .lov file, the universe .lov will overwrite the user's .lov, regardless of which is more recent.
Automatic refresh before use	This should rarely be checked and only for those objects in which the dimension information changes frequently. Otherwise, the users can easily refresh lists of values by request. Particularly with large dimension lists or slow RDBMS response times, it is important not to force an automatic refresh. However, if your company has recently gone through a major reorganization, or there have been a number of RDBMS changes that would cause old lists of values on Desktop Intelligence users' folders to be out of date, you may want to enable the automatic refresh for a defined period. For Web Intelligence users, the lists are always refreshed for each session.
Hierarchical Display	When you customize a list of values to display additional levels in a hierarchy, this lets users drill within the hierarchy to select their condition. When the list is cascaded, this option ensures a more intuitive interface.
Export with universe	This box should be checked only when the designer has customized the list of values with the universe, the list of values is slow to execute, or the acceptable values come from a personal data file or other source to which users may not have direct access.

TABLE 10-1   List of Value Settings

6. Click Display to see the same list of values that users will see when using them in a query.

7. Click OK to return to the Object Properties panel.

8. Click OK to close the Object Properties panel.

When to Disable LOVS

By default, lists of values are enabled on all dimension and detail objects, but there are instances in which it is better to disable them by removing the check from the check box Associate A List Of Values.

Nonindexed Fields

One would think that if you have disallowed an object to be used as a condition (select Edit | Object Properties and then click the Advanced tab), that would automatically remove the list of values functionality from the object. It doesn't. So for many of the same reasons that you disallow an object to be used as a condition, you also may not want to associate a list of values. If the field is not indexed, you may not want to associate a list of values.

For example, let's assume that *Customer Name* is an object whose source system field is not indexed. It is still allowed as a condition because you want users to be able to search for all customers that start with the name Deloitte & Touche. Ideally, you want *Customer Name* to be used only for wildcard searches and you would rather they use *Customer Code* as a condition, since it's indexed. In this case, allow the list of values on *Customer Code* and disable it on *Customer Name*.

"Unfriendly!" you say? Read the upcoming section "Simple Customization." You can still help users pick their customer codes according to customer name, but through a customized list of values that gives better query performance (user friendly!).

Details

Rarely will users want to use details as conditions in queries. For example, when users are looking for customer sales, do they use detail objects such as street address or phone number for the exact condition when it's unknown to them? No. If they know the phone number, they may use it as a condition, but then they are usually entering the phone number manually, *not* choosing it from a pick list.

However, if you look at the sample eFashion universe, it makes a lot of sense to allow a list of values for the object *ZIP code*, even though it is a detail object. I would recommend customizing it to display the state; I would also have *ZIP code* as a dimension object, not a detail (refer to Chapter 9) so that users can drill by it.

Simple Customization

A simple customization may involve adding a meaningful description next to the code or adding a prompt to shorten a long list. Each customization has three main steps:

1. Associate a list of values with an object.
2. Add additional information or conditions.
3. Export the customization with the universe.

NOTE *With XI Release 2, some of the customizations that you did before may no longer be necessary. For example, if you customized ID fields to include a description and forced query filters to use the ID fields for query performance reasons, the use of keys (as explained in Chapter 9) may be a preferred approach when the ID fields are not meaningful to the end users. Keys initially were leveraged only by Desktop Intelligence, but in XI Release 2, Web Intelligence also now takes advantage of them. As of Service Pack 1, however, use of these keys was problematic so do re-evaluate before using. Similarly, to create a cascaded list of values in earlier versions of Designer, you had to modify multiple lists of values. New in XI Release 2 is the ability to define the cascade in one place. With these changes, reconsider your design practices.*

Adding a Description Object to an ID Object

Some codes may have a logical meaning with which users are familiar. For example, many accountants know the meaning of certain account ranges. Power users also may know a number of account, product, and customer codes. However, in many cases, the codes are meaningless and users will only ever want to use names or descriptions as conditions. However, filtering queries on nonindexed description fields can result in slow queries. Customizing the list of values for ID fields meets both the users' need of seeing a description while also ensuring that the query is filtered on an indexed field. You also may want to include additional dimension objects in your list of values to facilitate sorting. Figure 10-2 shows that it may be meaningful to add *Country, Region,* and *City* to the *Customer Id* list of values.

Displaying additional information such as country can be useful

The region refers to a region within a country

Customer ID	Customer	Country of Origin	Region	City
201.00	Sartois	France	French Alps	Albertville
206.00	Gentil	France	French Alps	Albertville
204.00	Martin	France	French Alps	Grenoble
202.00	Michaud	France	French Alps	Lyon
207.00	Dupont	France	Paris	Paris
205.00	Piaget	France	Provence	Bordeaux
203.00	Robert	France	Provence	Marseilles
406.00	Tilzman	Germany	Bavaria	Augsburg
402.00	Schiller	Germany	Bavaria	Munich
405.00	Schultz	Germany	East Germany	Berlin
407.00	Reinman	Germany	East Germany	Berlin
403.00	Durnstein	Germany	East Germany	Dresden
404.00	Weimar	Germany	East Germany	Magdeburg
401.00	Diemers	Germany	Ruhr	Cologne
501.00	Arai	Japan	East Japan	Tokyo
504.00	Makino	Japan	East Japan	Tokyo
506.00	Oneda	Japan	East Japan	Tokyo
502.00	Kamata	Japan	East Japan	Yokohama
507.00	Okumura	Japan	West Japan	Kobe
505.00	Mukumoto	Japan	West Japan	Kyoto
503.00	Kamimura	Japan	West Japan	Osaka
301.00	Edwards	UK	England	London
305.00	Keegan	UK	England	London
306.00	Jones	UK	England	Oxford

Sort order by country, not by ID or name

FIGURE 10-2 Customers reside in cities that are part of countries. Displaying country information along with customer ID makes for a more meaningful pick list.

Associating a List of Values

In the following example, you will use the Island Resorts Marketing or BEACH universe. To ensure you do not affect the original universe, import the universe from the repository (choose File | Import and select Island Resorts Marketing). Then select File | Save As and enter the new name: **Test Island Resorts Marketing**. The sample universe includes a *Customer Name* object. You will create an object that accesses an ID field that is indexed, and then customize the list to include a description. Later, you will also customize this same list to display the customer's country and city.

1. Select the *Customer* class.

2. Select Insert | Object or click Insert Object.

3. Replace the default object name OBJECT1 with **Customer ID**. Complete the Description and SQL Select fields shown next:

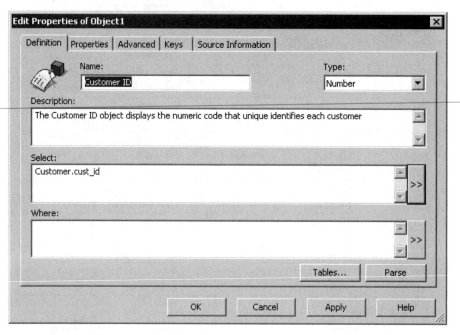

4. Click Apply.

NOTE *If you navigate to the Properties tab before selecting Apply, Designer does not update several settings and you may get an error with subsequent steps.*

5. Select the Properties tab.

6. Change the list name to **CUSTID**.

7. Click Display. If the list is blank, click Refresh. Note in the illustration that you are presented with a fairly meaningless list of codes to which you want to add the customer name.

8. Click OK to return to the Object Properties tab.

Adding More Information

Now that the object has an associated list of values, you can modify the .lov query file to include an additional column of information.

1. From Object Properties, select the Edit button to edit the list of values. Designer presents you with a standard query panel. For more information on using the query panel, refer to Chapter 20.

2. Click the *Customer* class to expand the list of objects.

3. Drag the *Customer* (CUSTOMER.NAME) object to the right of the new *Customer Id* object.

4. The *Customer Id* has no sequence that is meaningful to users, so add a sort on *Customer* so that the names are sorted in alphabetical order. While Customer is still selected in the Result Objects, click the Sorts icon. The final query definitions should appear as follows:

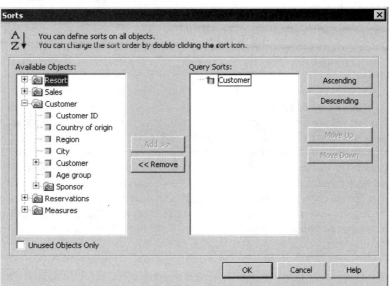

5. Click OK to return to the Edit Properties of Customer ID panel.

6. Click Display and then Refresh to see the results of your customized list of values. Set the view to Tabular View (these views are explained later under "Tabular vs. Hierarchical Views"). This is what users will see when accessing the list of values:

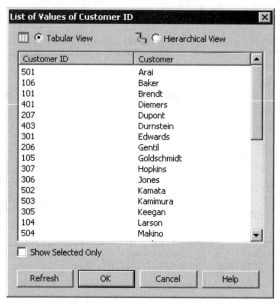

7. Click OK to close the list of values display and return to the Properties tab.

8. If you are satisfied with your customizations, enable the check box Export With Universe and click OK.

NOTE *When you enable the check box Export With Universe, the customized list of values is not immediately exported as a separate element of the universe. Instead, you only have told Designer to export the .lov query file to the repository along with the universe whenever you next choose File | Export.*

Purging Data from a List of Values

Now that you are satisfied with the customization, you are ready to export the list of values with the universe. When you clicked Refresh in Step 6 of the preceding section, your list of values query executed and the actual customer IDs and names became part of the .lov file. In earlier versions of BusinessObjects, exporting the data with the .lov file was generally a bad thing for performance reasons. With XI, the decision to include the data has more to do with relevance (particularly if it is a cascaded list of values as described in the next section) than performance. If you do not want this data exported with the query definition, follow these steps to purge the pick list data and ensure only the query file gets exported:

1. From the pull-down menu, select Tools | Lists Of Values | Edit A List Of Values.

2. Expand the *Customer* class by clicking the + sign.

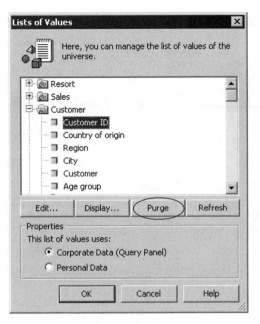

3. Select the *Customer ID* object and click Purge.

4. Click OK to close the dialog.

Cascading Lists of Values

The customer table in the Island Resorts Marketing universe is quite small (35 rows); however, for many real-world data warehouses and OLTP systems, the customer tables and product tables are fairly large. For this reason, universe designers should customize the list of values to shorten the number of rows presented to the user by adding a prompt. This is often referred to as a *cascading* list of values because two lists are linked to one another. There is no fixed limit to how many rows are reasonable; it's more a question of reasonable response time. For lists of values, aim for seconds, not minutes, or users may incorrectly assume the system is down.

NOTE *For Web Intelligence users, the list of values displayed is "chunked" according to the list of values batch size setting for Web Intelligence Report Server. For example, in Figure 10-3, the list of values batch size is set to 1000. This means that even if your list of values returns 2000 values, the user is presented with the first 1000; to get to the next set of 1000 values, they request the next page.*

When cascading your list of values, you must first be familiar with the dimension tables, how they relate, and which level of prompts will give a good response time without annoying the users. If a user is simply trying to find a customer code, the user does not want to be asked five questions in advance to arrive at the customer code; one or two levels of cascades should be the most you do. Whenever possible, strive to display more columns of information in the original list of values rather than adding a prompt as your first choice. The goal of the prompt is to shorten your list to guarantee a reasonable response time and navigable size; the goal is not to generate the smallest list possible.

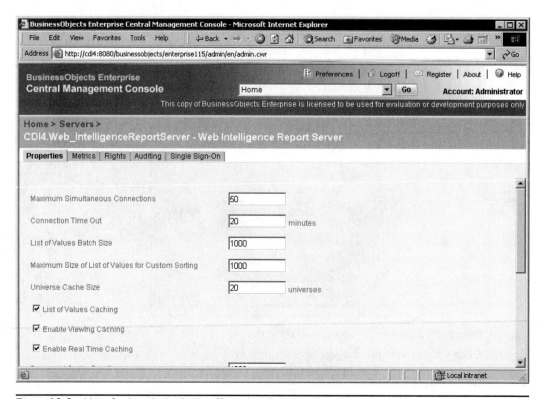

FIGURE 10-3 List of values behavior is affected by Designer customizations but also by Web Intelligence Report Server settings.

For customers, you may shorten the list by adding a prompt for customers beginning with a certain letter or a cascade for customers residing in a certain city or region. In looking at the sample data in earlier Figure 10-2, for example, you may want to prompt the users to filter the customer ID list according to customers who reside within a particular country. For individual products or SKUs, including a filter on product category or line of business brings the list of values to a more manageable size.

In the following example, you will continue to work with the *Customer Id* object. First, study the dimension data. In looking at earlier Figure 10-2, notice which city and country each customer resides in. Additionally, each country is divided into multiple regions within the country; if your business users had not specifically told you this or if you had not studied the dimensional data, you may have incorrectly assumed that *Region* referred to *World Region* (such as North America, Europe, and so on). Ideally, users will tell you which customizations they want, but for them, the choices may not be clear, and the business definitions may not be obvious; it's up to you as the universe designer to give them your best guess for the friendliest, fastest customization.

Next, look at the tables involved, as shown in Figure 10-4. If you decide to prompt the users on *Country of Origin,* then four tables will be joined together to present the shortened list of *Customer Ids.* In this demo example, the tables are small, so the joins are not a problem. In a production implementation, carefully evaluate the impact on response time when your list of values customization involves more than one table. At this point, also see if a shortcut join is available, for example, to shorten the list of product IDs according to which plants make the products (see Chapter 8). Prompting on *City* may result in a faster query, but it may not make sense from a business viewpoint if managers are organized by country.

To cascade the list of values from *Country* to *Customer ID*:

1. From the pull-down menus, select Tools | List Of Values | Create Cascading Lists Of Values.

2. When selecting values to cascade, position them from highest to lowest level of detail: in this example, from *Country* to *Customer ID.*

3. In the Available pane, expand the *Customer* folder and select *Country of Origin.* Click > to add it to the pane on the right.

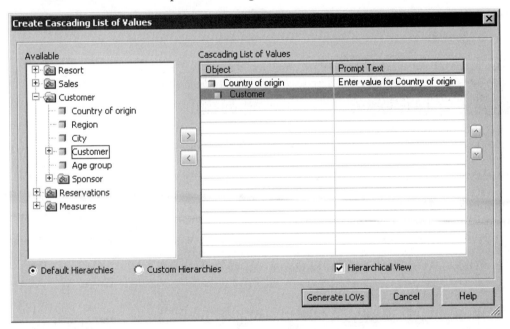

4. Select *Customer ID* and click >. Once you add an additional level in the hierarchy, notice that Designer automatically now includes Prompt Text for *Country of Origin.*

5. Click Generate LOVs.

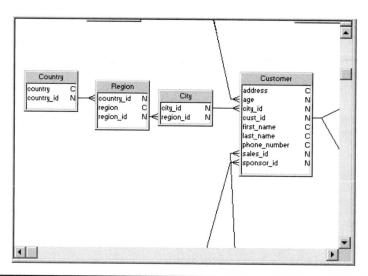

FIGURE 10-4   Adding *Country* as a prompt in the *Customer Id* list of values involves four tables.

TIP *Whenever you create a cascaded list of values, always check the Hierarchical view for a more intuitive list of values, described more fully in the later section "Tabular vs. Hierarchical Views."*

How the Cascade Works

If you go back and preview the *Customer Id* object, you will see that Designer has changed several settings. If your cascade also included other levels within the hierarchy such as region and city, the list of value settings for those objects also will have been modified. It's important to understand how the steps in the preceding section affect individual object settings, because if you ever wish to go back and change a cascade, you must do so manually, as described in this section. Further, if you implement a cascade *after* you have implemented other customizations, the cascade will overwrite those other customizations. Select the object *Customer Id* and double-click to bring up the Edit Properties box.

To manually modify the list of values for the *Customer Id* object:

1. Select the Properties tab.
2. Select Edit to modify the CUSTID.LOV query and display the query panel.
3. Notice the object *Country of Origin* in the Conditions box.

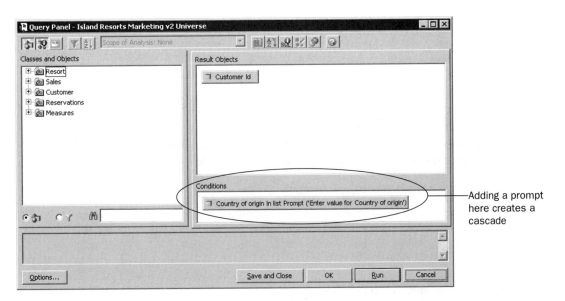

Adding a prompt here creates a cascade

4. Click OK to close the query panel.

5. From the Object Properties dialog, click Display in the bottom right and then Refresh from the List Of Values dialog. You will be prompted to choose a country before you can see the newly filtered set of customer IDs.

6. You may either click Values to choose from a list of countries or enter **France** and click OK. Notice how much smaller the list of Customer IDs is now compared to the list in Step 6 under the earlier heading "Adding More Information."

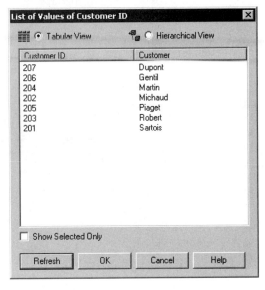

7. Select OK to close the list of values.

8. Once you are satisfied with your customization, verify that the check box Export With Universe is enabled. When you create a cascaded list of values through Tools | Lists Of Values | Creating Cascading Lists Of Values, this option is set for you.

9. Click OK to close the Object Properties dialog.

Tabular vs. Hierarchical Views

There are two check boxes for Hierarchical view, and they have different behaviors in Web Intelligence and Desktop Intelligence. Let's start with a simple recommendation.

TIP *Whenever you create a cascade, leave the option Hierarchical View enabled. Whenever you manually customize a list of values to either add a filter or add additional columns of information, choose the Object Properties Hierarchical Display as described in Table 10-1. For Web Intelligence users, the Hierarchical Display is most intuitive. For Desktop Intelligence users, there is little impact.*

Hierarchical Display in Web Intelligence

When a Web Intelligence user refreshes a query that contains a cascaded list of values, the list of values is grouped according to the hierarchy of the higher-level prompts as shown in the following screen. Users see only one prompt for Customer ID. When the list of values is exported with Hierarchical Display enabled, the cascade or initial prompt on Countries is embedded within the list of values. Users click the + to expand or collapse the individual countries.

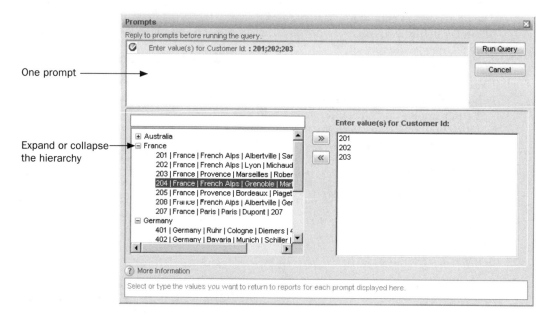

Without Hierarchical Display enabled, the prompting and list of values are far less intuitive. Compare the following screen with the former. Notice that without the Hierarchical Display there are two filters in the top prompt box. To see individual customer codes for any given country, users must first specify the value there and refresh the list of values for a country. Then they must position their mouse on the customer ID prompt and refresh that list to get a subset of the list of customer IDs within France. A similar workflow is followed with Desktop Intelligence reports that contain cascaded prompts.

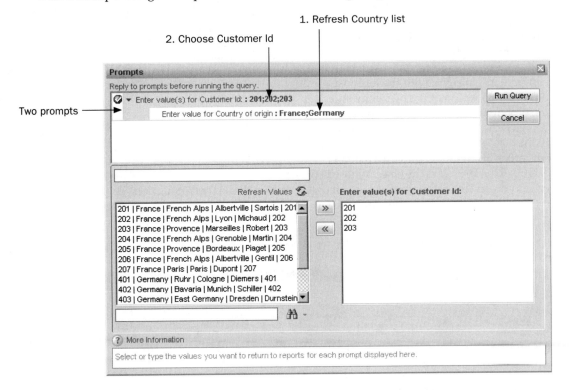

NOTE *The way Web Intelligence caches cascaded list of values is significantly different from how a regular list of values is cached. For example, in the preceding screen, each query refresh that uses the list of values for customers in France forces a regeneration of the list of values for those customers. Noncascaded list of values, however, use a cached pick list. Therefore, it's important to compare the performance impact between a long list of values that is cached and a short list of values that is not cached.*

Hierarchical Display in Desktop Intelligence

With Web Intelligence, the hierarchical display corresponds to the prompts. With Desktop Intelligence, it does not. Instead, it corresponds to the result objects that are part of the list of values. In both the preceding screenshots in Web Intelligence, there were additional result

objects in the pick lists. These were
displayed in a tabular format. However,
in Desktop Intelligence, users see the list
shown to the right.

In order for the hierarchical view to
work correctly in Desktop Intelligence,
the result columns must be in a particular
order. The list of values object must always
be the first column. If the object is an ID or
Code object, it would be intuitive if the
description were the second column; but it's
not! After the base object, the result objects
run from left to right, with the leftmost
object being the top of the hierarchy and
the description or most detailed object
being on the right side of the query. Each
of the objects should have a corresponding
sort order. To continue with the customer
example, *Customer Id* is the object whose list

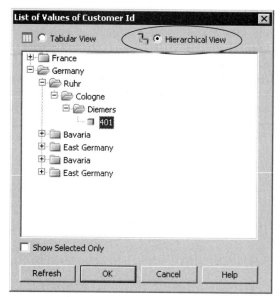

of values you are customizing. In the following screen, this is the leftmost object. *Country of
origin* is the top of the hierarchy and appears second. *Country of origin* is the primary sort order.

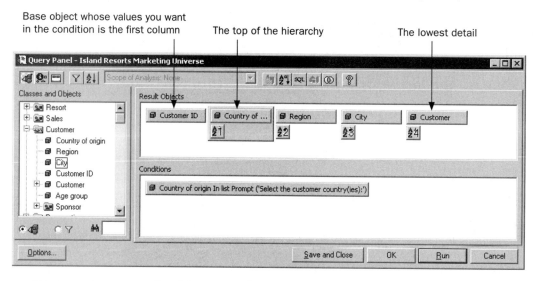

It is important to sort the objects according to the hierarchy levels, or the drill-down
may appear nonsensical. Now when users request to select a list of values, they can scroll
through the possible values by drilling down through a hierarchy. I have two complaints

with the Desktop Intelligence Hierarchy view: first, it does not work particularly well with code/description customizations. I would like it if the final drill-down displayed both the code and the description. Second, when you do this kind of "wide" customization, it is not easy for Web Intelligence users to see the wide list of values. They can only scroll to the right in a cumbersome way.

As with prompts, be careful that the Hierarchical view does not require too many extra clicks. In the preceding example, the country hierarchy alone would have been sufficient, and I would recommend leaving out the region and city columns for a real-world deployment.

Reusable Lists of Values

As mentioned throughout this chapter, lists of values are query files. As the files are stored separately from the object definition, it is easy to use one list of values query with multiple objects. I refer to this capability as reusable or shared lists of values. Giving the lists meaningful names will make this process easier to maintain.

You may want to share the same list of values for objects used in multiple alias tables, regardless of whether they have been defined as aliases within the universe or synonyms within the RDBMS. For example, customer number may be used in both *Ship To Customer* and *Sold To Customer*. Both objects use the same customer numbers. In the next example, there is a *Sending Plant Id* and a *Receiving Plant Id* for a company that has plant-to-plant transfers. The list of plant IDs remains the same. Sharing the list of values query across the objects will mean less customization for you as the designer. For users, it results in fewer list of values refreshes.

To share a list of values across multiple objects:

1. Select the object that contains the customization and double-click to edit the object properties.
2. Select the Properties tab.
3. Under List Name, assign a meaningful query name or note the system-generated name.
4. Customize the list of values query according to the instructions in the previous sections.
5. Ensure the box Export With Universe is checked.
6. Select the second object that will share the query definition for the list of values.
7. Under List Name, fill in the same query name as in Step 3. You do not need to check the box Export With Universe on this secondary object. Figure 10-5 shows how two objects can share the same list of values customization.

Two different object names

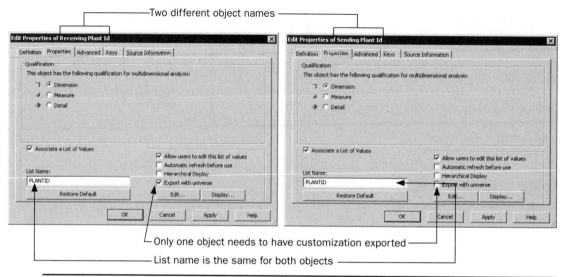

Only one object needs to have customization exported

List name is the same for both objects

FIGURE 10-5 Sending Plant Id and Receiving Plant Id share the same list of values query, PLANTID.LOV.

Incorporating Personal Data Files

Throughout this chapter, I've warned against exporting data with the universe list of values unnecessarily. However, there are several instances in which you may want to break this rule:

- The list is extremely small and it is faster for the repository to send the users a preexecuted query than it is for the users to execute the *object*.lov query themselves.

- The dimensional data in the data warehouse or OLTP is in transition; new groupings and codes are not available in a central RDBMS, but they are available through a spreadsheet or text file.

- A universe designer can incorporate personal data into the customized list of values and export it to the repository. Desktop Intelligence users may also do this on an individual basis.

Personal data files can be text, spreadsheet, or database files. Each file must follow a specific layout:

- The condition column or pick list value must be in the first column.

- The remaining columns may contain additional information. Unlike standard customized lists of values, these additional columns cannot be used for sorting once in Designer, so do the sorting first in the data file.

- It is okay to have column headings, but you must tell Designer they exist.

TIP *If your list of values is in a spreadsheet, create an Excel range name with just those columns and rows you want to appear as a list of values.*

Using the EFASHION universe as an example, let's assume that you want to regroup certain SKU numbers into different product lines, as shown in Table 10-2, which contains proposed product groupings that do not yet exist in the data warehouse or OLTP. The new groupings are

SKU Number	SKU Description	Category	Product Line	New Product Line Grouping
141406	Belted Tunic	Lounge wear	Accessories	Sweat-T-Shirts
150850	Zipper Vest	Lounge wear	Accessories	Sweat-T-Shirts
155576	Rudolph Shirt	Lounge wear	Accessories	Sweat-T-Shirts
159421	Striped Leggings	Lounge wear	Accessories	Trousers
160556	Spotty Leggings	Lounge wear	Accessories	Trousers
161363	Double Breasted Silk Jacket	Lounge wear	Accessories	Jackets
167119	Jacquard T-Shirt	Lounge wear	Accessories	Sweat-T-Shirts
182379	Lurex Leotard	Lounge wear	Accessories	Sweat-T-Shirts
182488	Chenille Leotard T-Shirt	Lounge wear	Accessories	Sweat-T-Shirts
182880	Diamond Cigarette Holder	Lounge wear	Accessories	Jewelry
183861	Lycra Culotte Shorts	Lounge wear	Accessories	Trousers

TABLE 10-2   Lists of Values Can Access Personal Data Files

available in a spreadsheet file that not all users can access. In the RDBMS, Lounge wear and Jewelry are currently grouped under the line Accessories. In the personal data file, they are regrouped into a newly created line, Jewelry. Other SKUs are moved into existing but different Proposed Lines such as 161363 Double-Breasted Silk Jacket from Accessories to Jackets, and Leggings to Trousers.

Once you have ensured your data file is in the appropriate format, you can associate this data file with the object list of values:

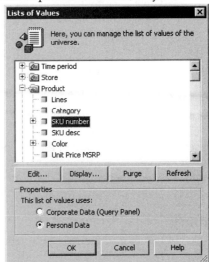

1. From the pull-down menu, select Tools | List Of Values | Edit A List Of Values.

2. This will present you with a list of all objects in the universe that have an associated list of values. Expand the *Product* class, then select *SKU number.*

3. Change the radio button from Corporate Data to Personal Data. When you change this option, you will receive the following warning message:

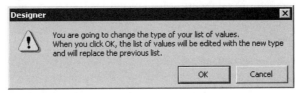

4. Click OK. Designer presents you with a Personal Data selection screen.

5. Specify the data file that contains your list of values and the format. If it is an Excel spreadsheet, you can specify a range name.

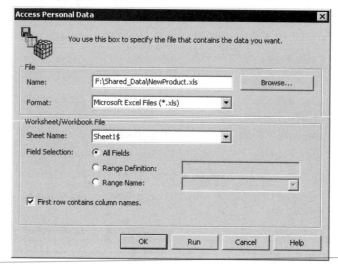

6. Click Run to have Desktop Intelligence access your personal data file and return to the List Of Values dialog box.

7. Click Display to see this new list. Change your view from hierarchical to tabular. Designer displays the customized list of values in the format that will appear to users when they request a list of values for a condition object.

8. Click OK twice to close the display list and List Of Values dialog box.

9. Modify the object properties for *SKU number* to mark the box Export With Universe.

When you click Run in Step 6, the data from the spreadsheet (or other personal data file) is dynamically added into the *object*.lov file. Designer exports this file with the universe definitions when you export the modified universe to the repository. If you skip Step 6 and users do not have access to the personal data file on a central server, they will receive an error message when trying to run the list of values. Similarly, if users ever click Refresh, they will need access to the data file or will receive an error message.

Summary

Lists of values and their customizations allow users to more easily filter their data. In the past, designers often had to weigh the disadvantages of increased universe size and import times against more usable lists of values. With the XI architecture, that is no longer a concern and designers can focus more on creating lists of values that improve query performance and ease of use.

Advanced Objects

In the previous chapters, you created some basic objects. In this chapter, you will add a significant amount of intelligence to columns of information. Designer provides two main categories of functionality to do this: internal Designer functions and SQL functions that are RDBMS specific. The first part of the chapter covers functionality that is specific to Designer but database independent. The second part of the chapter covers SQL commands that may be dependent on which RDBMS you use.

Reducing Maintenance with Base Objects and @Select

The `@Select` function is an internal function that allows you, as the designer, to reuse universe objects without forcing you to repeat the entire SQL syntax. For example, take an initial object *Sales* that provides information on revenue in U.S. dollars. You can add a number of forms of intelligence to this object: *Sales in Local Currency, Sales in Euros, Sales Adjusted for Inflation, Sales with 10% Projected Increase,* and so on. These additional objects are not columns in the database; they are objects you create by using SQL commands described in the second part of this chapter. However, they all reference the same initial column in the RDBMS, such as `Sales_Fact.Amount`, and then include further calculations to local currencies or forecasts. When building advanced objects with Designer, you can select either the RDBMS column or a universe object. Whenever possible, select the object. You will save time on universe maintenance. Imagine six months from now, the physical field for Sales (`Sales_Fact.Amount`) in the RDBMS is renamed. If all of the related sales objects explicitly referenced the RDBMS field, that is how many objects you now must modify manually. However, if all the related sales objects used `@Select`, you need to modify only the one base object.

The syntax of `@Select` is `@Select(Class\Object)`, where *Class* is the name of the class that contains the base object—for example, *Measures,* and *Object* is the name of the object that contains the base object—for example, *Sales.* When using `@Select`, you can still see the full SQL statement by enabling the check box Show Object SQL in the SQL Editor. In all the examples in this chapter, I use `@Select` whenever possible but display the full SQL syntax.

TIP *Whenever possible, use objects rather than individual RDBMS columns. This will save you work if ever you rename an RDBMS column, as you will need to modify only the SQL of the base object; Designer will automatically update the SQL for all other objects that use the base column.*

The @Where function is similar to @Select in that you can reuse a WHERE clause from an existing object.

The SQL Editor

When changing SQL statements, you can either enter the SELECT statements in the formula bar (to display, select View | Formula Bar), or you can use the SQL Editor to change either the SELECT statement or the WHERE clause. The SQL Editor also provides some help on Designer functions and SQL syntax.

Figure 11-1 shows the SQL Editor. You launch the SQL Editor by clicking the >> button from the Definition tab of the object properties. As you modify the SQL for an object, you can either point and click your way through it, or you can enter the functions, columns, and operators manually. Regardless of how you build the SQL statement, be sure to parse or validate (formula editor) each object as you go. Parsing validates that your statement is correct and won't produce an error when a user launches a query. Parsing will not catch all SQL errors and may be slower for objects that use @Select (as multiple SQL statements must be checked), but it will catch the majority.

In order to build a statement with point and click, you often start with the Functions box on the right. For example, to create the measure object *Revenue* from the Island Resorts Marketing universe, as shown in Figure 11-1:

1. Modify the Object Properties by double-clicking the object, in this example, *Revenue*. From the Select box, click >> to launch the SQL Editor.

2. Under Functions, expand the Number functions by clicking the + sign. Scroll to sum() and double-click. Notice that the mouse insertion point is correctly between the parentheses. If you had started with the Tables and Columns on the left, your mouse would be in the wrong place.

3. Under Tables and Columns, expand the INVOICE_LINE table by clicking the + sign. Double-click DAYS to insert INVOICE_LINE.DAYS into the statement.

4. Under Operators, double-click the multiplication sign (*). The list of available operators will change depending on whether you modify a SELECT statement or a WHERE clause.

5. Under Tables and Columns, double-click NB_GUESTS.

6. Under Operators, double-click * again.

7. Under Tables and Columns, scroll to the SERVICE table, click + to expand it, and double-click PRICE. The close parenthesis should still be in the correct place.

8. Click Parse to ensure you have built the SQL statement correctly with the functions, operators, and parentheses in the correct positions.

Some Caveats about SQL Functions

SQL contains a number of commands that are common to all databases. However, database vendors have added a number of extensions to make SQL more powerful. These extensions are not common for all databases. Some companies have development policies to keep the universe database-agnostic, particularly when they are contemplating migrating to a new

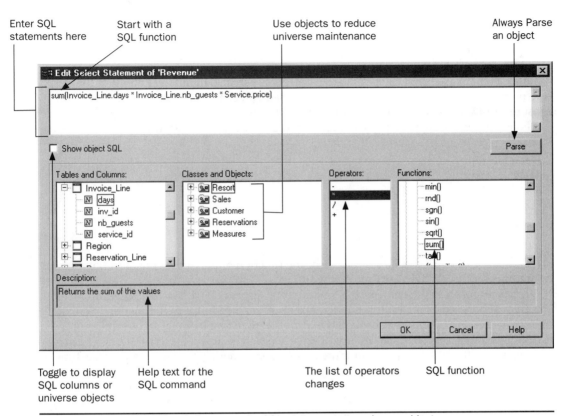

Enter SQL statements here

Start with a SQL function

Use objects to reduce universe maintenance

Always Parse an object

Toggle to display SQL columns or universe objects

Help text for the SQL command

The list of operators changes

SQL function

FIGURE 11-1   The SQL Editor helps you write SQL statements to enhance objects.

RDBMS. Analytic application vendors that use BusinessObjects XI as the reporting engine also may strive to keep their universes database-agnostic. However, when you avoid using database-specific SQL in the universe, you are generally forcing end users to do more work in the reports (see Chapter 14 for further discussion). My recommendation is to use your database SQL to its fullest. Your universe will be more powerful, and you will save users time.

SQL Parameters and the PRM File

The available database-specific functions are stored in the *database*.prm file (located under C:\ Program Files\Business Objects\BusinessObjects Enterprise 11.5\win32_x86\dataAccess\ ConnectionServer\oracle). The corresponding help text or function description as shown in Figure 11-1 is stored in a separate XML file that is language specific as *RDBMSLL*.PRM, where *LL* refers to the Language. For example, the English language help text for Oracle functions is stored in oracleen.prm. Business Objects provides you with a default *database*.prm file that you may want to modify. You may want to modify the *database*.prm file for the following reasons:

- To enable users to access SQL functions that have been disabled by default
- To improve the help text for frequently used functions, especially if your company has decentralized universe designers

- To add SQL functions that your RDBMS vendor has recently added but that Business Objects has not yet added in the *database*.prm file
- To add functions that your DBA may have created

If a command does not exist in the file, designers can also manually enter it in the SQL statement rather than changing the .prm file. When you change the *database*.prm file, you must restart Designer for the change to take effect.

Following is a section from the Oracle.prm file on the SQL UPPER function:

```
<Function Group="False"
ID="Uppercase"
InMacro="True"
Type="String">
<Arguments>
<Argument Type="String"></Argument>
</Arguments>
<SQL>upper($1)</SQL>
```

Function Group specifies if the use of the function requires the generation of a GROUP BY in the SQL. Upper does not, but SUM would.

ID corresponds to the name of the function that appears to you in the SQL Editor.

InMacro indicates if Desktop Intelligence users can access the SQL function to create their own objects. If you scroll through the .prm file, note that by default, users cannot access the Oracle DECODE function. If you want them to be able to, set IN_MACRO="True".

Type specifies if the output results are in an alphanumeric ("String"), date ("DateTime"), or numeric ("Numeric") format.

The Arguments section provides prompts when users create their own objects. The Argument Type indicates the format required. In the preceding example, users will be prompted to enter a String that then gets passed to ($1) as part of the SQL command. In the case of Upper($1), the string will be the universe object to convert to uppercase. If you were looking at an aggregate function such as SUM, the Argument Type would be "Numeric". The Arguments section and settings are similar to TRAD in earlier versions of the .prm file.

SQL shows the actual SQL syntax. The number of SQL parameters is indicated with ($1) and so on.

Help Text for SQL Functions

In previous releases of Designer, the description or help text for various SQL functions was stored in the same file as the function itself. To allow for multilingual deployments, the help text for the functions is now stored in a separate, language-specific XML file. Thus for each entry in the *RDBMS*.PRM file, there is a corresponding entry in the *RDBMSLL*.PRM file. For example, with the preceding Uppercase function, the ORACLEEN.PRM file contains the following settings:

```
<Function Name="Uppercase">
    <Message id="Help">Returns a character string in upper case</Message>
    <Message id="Name">Uppercase</Message>
    <Arguments>
       <Message id="1">String:</Message>
    </Arguments>
```

The Message id= "Help" message is what will appear to you as the designer when you select a function from the SQL Editor or to end users who create their own objects. In Figure 11-1, this is the text in the bottom left, "Returns the sum of the values."

The Message id within the Arguments section is what will appear to end users if additional parameters are required. In the preceding example and following illustration, the default argument message "String:" is not particularly helpful. Note that all messages within the Arguments section must end with a colon (:).

Default message ——————▶
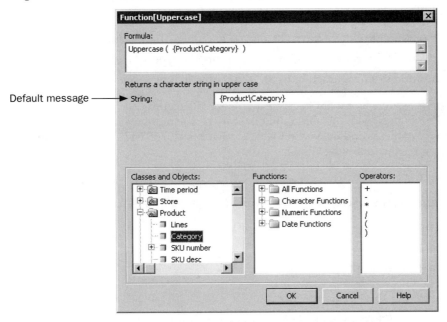

The dialog in Desktop Intelligence does not allow for a much longer message, but note in the following a clearer argument message, "Object to convert" versus the preceding "String":

Modified argument ——▶
message
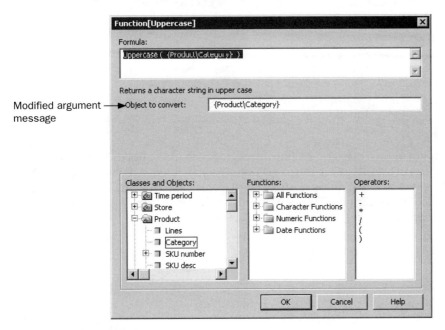

Multiple Arguments and Prompt Messages

Some SQL functions require multiple arguments. For example, SUBSTR displays a certain number of characters beginning at a certain position and counting forward so many characters (or until the end if this third argument is not supplied). So designers and users must specify at least two arguments and an optional third:

- The field or object to extract the text from, so Argument Type = "String"
- Which position to start extracting from, so Argument Type = "Numeric"
- Which position to stop extracting from, so Argument Type = "Numeric"

As an example, assume you want to create an object called *Area Code* from the object *Phone Number*. Poorly designed, the object did not store phone numbers numerically, and they do contain parentheses and dashes in the field such as (973) 555-1212. To extract just the area code requires the following SQL:

```
SUBSTR(Customer.Phone,2,3)
```

The Oracle.prm file would contain the following arguments and SQL:

```
<Arguments>
<Argument Type="String"></Argument>
<Argument Type="Numeric"></Argument>
<Argument Type="Numeric"></Argument>
</Arguments>
<SQL>substr($1,$2,$3)</SQL>
```

The help text in the ORACLEN.PRM file appears as follows:

```
<Function Name="Substring">
      <Message id="Help">Extracts a sequence of characters from a character
string</Message>
      <Message id="Name">Substring</Message>
      <Arguments>
         <Message id="1">String:</Message>
         <Message id="2">Initial position:</Message>
         <Message id="3">Number of characters:</Message>
      </Arguments>
```

Condition Objects

Condition objects are unique objects that allow users to access predefined conditions that the designer specifies in the WHERE clause. Condition objects are denoted with a filter symbol.

The Island Resorts Marketing universe, shown next, contains several predefined conditions. To access a condition object, click the Classes/Conditions filter in the lower-left corner. Click the + sign next to each class to see the Condition Objects.

Formula bar shows the `WHERE` clause

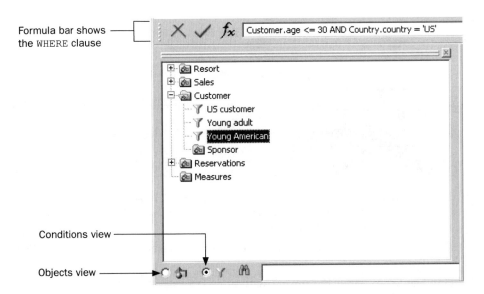

Conditions view

Objects view

Most of these conditions are fairly simple. In building condition objects, you, as the designer, must evaluate if the objects add clutter or value. If it saves the users time, create the object. If it defines some unique groupings that do not otherwise exist in the dimension tables, create the object. If it ensures a degree of consistency in how users filter the data, then create the condition object. Objects that contain one value such as *Year 1993* do not add much value; users probably could have added the condition themselves. The object *Young American*, on the other hand, contains two conditions (`Customer.age <= 30 AND Country.country = 'US'`). Nesting conditions can be confusing and cumbersome, so such an object would be very helpful to users.

In the following example, you will use the Island Resorts Marketing universe to create a condition object, *Platinum Customers*, for customers who generate more than $100,000 in revenue in any given year. Throughout this chapter, I will build upon this example to show a number of advanced object capabilities. In this sample universe, there are seven customers who had revenues of $100,000 or more. You will add each of these seven customer codes to the condition object.

NOTE *It is not possible to create condition objects based on measures (so you can't say* `Where Revenue >= 100,000`*), as doing so requires a different SQL clause. Condition objects will automatically use the* `WHERE` *clause, whereas filtering on measures requires use of a* `HAVING` *clause (explained in Chapter 23). If you try to build such a condition object, you will receive an error upon parsing. A work-around using a subquery in the condition is discussed in the next section.*

Customers With Revenue GT or Equal $100,000				
		FY93	FY94	FY95
Baker	106.00	128,362.00	150,666.00	162,566.00
Kamata	502.00	118,680.00	128,146.00	112,982.00
Larson	104.00		108,210.00	101,335.00
McCarthy	102.00	128,330.00	135,580.00	136,989.00
Oneda	506.00	120,198.00	143,984.00	122,906.00
Schiller	402.00	129,658.00	127,584.00	131,282.00
Titzman	406.00	123,606.00	145,300.00	126,090.00

1. Using the Island Resorts Marketing universe, set the Classes and Objects pane to display the condition objects. Position your cursor in the class where you want the new object to appear—in this example, *Customer*.

2. Click the Insert Condition button on the toolbar or select Insert | Condition from the pull-down menus.

3. In the Name box, enter **Platinum Customer**.

4. In the Description box, enter some meaningful help text, such as: **A platinum customer is a predefined list of customer codes with revenues of $100,000 or more in any given year.**

5. In the Where box, click >> to call up SQL Editor.

6. At this point, you could manually enter the WHERE statement shown in the next screen. These step-by-step instructions use point and click to build the condition object. Under Classes and Objects, scroll to the class that contains the object you want to use for the WHERE clause. In this example, click the + next to *Customer*.

7. For response time reasons, you want the WHERE clause on the indexed *Customer Id* object rather than the nonindexed *Customer*. Double-click *Customer Id* to have it added to the WHERE statement. Note that Designer uses the @Select function.

NOTE *The Island Resorts Marketing universe may or may not have Customer ID as an object, depending upon whether your universe was newly installed with XI Release 2 or imported from a previous version. If you do not see the object within Classes and Objects, then select the appropriate field from Tables and Columns and skip to Step 9.*

Click to view SQL syntax

If you select an object, Designer
uses its @Select function

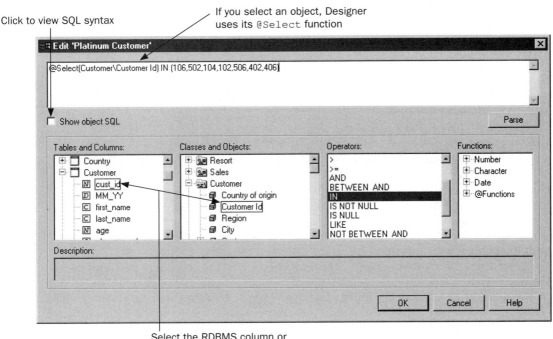

Select the RDBMS column or
the universe object name

8. To view the SQL syntax, click the Show Object SQL check box, shown next. Notice that Designer grays the SQL statement box and does not allow you to edit the statement.

SQL
syntax

9. In the Operators box, scroll to IN and double-click to add this to the SQL statement.

10. You do not need to transform your values, so you will not use any functions. Manually enter the list of customer IDs **(106,502,104,102,506,402,406)** generated by the preceding report. Because *Customer Id* is a numeric object,
it does not require single quotes around each condition value.

11. *Always* click Parse to test the validity of the SQL statement.

12. Click OK to close the SQL Editor. The condition object properties should now look like the illustration at right:

13. Click OK to close the Object Properties screen.

14. Click Save to save the universe changes. If necessary, export the changes to the repository with File | Export. When users build a query, they can now add the condition object to the condition panel.

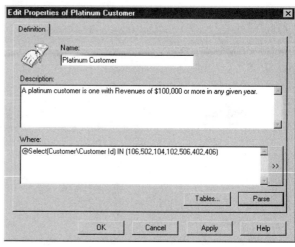

Condition Object with Subquery

The preceding object works perfectly fine and will provide the best query performance. However, what if your top customers change from quarter to quarter or year to year? In this case, you could add a subquery to the condition object so that the list of customers with a certain revenue level is generated dynamically. Subqueries are slow, so use them with care.

The following SQL would be used in the Where pane to create such an object:

```
Customer.cust_id in (
SELECT
  Customer.cust_id
FROM
  Customer,
  Sales,
  Invoice_Line,
  Service
WHERE
  ( Customer.cust_id=Sales.cust_id )
  AND  ( Sales.inv_id=Invoice_Line.inv_id )
  AND  ( Invoice_Line.service_id=Service.service_id )
GROUP BY
  Customer.last_name,
  Customer.cust_id,
  'FY'+Format(Sales.invoice_date,'YYYY')
HAVING
  sum(Invoice_Line.days * Invoice_Line.nb_guests * Service.price)  >=  100000)
```

TIP *Consider using @Prompt to allow users to specify the revenue amount dynamically when they use this object.*

Time Conditions

Condition objects involving time functions are popular. Additionally, BusinessObjects XI does not allow users to add calculations within the query panel, so condition objects become the only way in which users can create rolling reports. The following objects use SYSDATE, which returns the current date according to the RDBMS.

The following SQL creates a *One Year Ago* condition object. The comparison column is in a date format. Because `SYSDATE` is a date column including the day of the year, you subtract 365 days to arrive at the same date last year.

```
TIMES.END_OF_CAL_YEAR=SYSDATE-365
```

If the comparison column is not in a date format but is numeric, then you must also convert the `SYSDATE` calculation to numeric with `TO_NUMBER`. The following SQL creates a *Last Year* object in which the year is four digits. To extract only the four digits, use the `TO_CHAR` function.

```
TIMES.CALENDAR_YEAR=TO_NUMBER(TO_CHAR(SYSDATE-365,'YYYY'))
```

You can further nest date functions to create a *Current 3 Months* condition object. In the following example, `-3` shows that three months should be subtracted from the SYSDATE:

```
SH.TIMES.CALENDAR_MONTH_NUMBER BETWEEN TO_NUMBER(TO_CHAR(ADD_MONTHS(SYSDATE,-3),
'MM') ) AND TO_NUMBER(TO_CHAR(SYSDATE,'MM') )
```

NOTE *The* `WHERE` *statements from each condition object and the Row Restrictions set through the universe security restrictions (Chapter 13) are appended to the entire SQL statement. If users combine incompatible condition objects, they may get no rows returned.*

Objects with Prompts: Interactive Objects

Business Objects refers to objects that contain prompts as *interactive objects*. Each time a user accesses an interactive object, BusinessObjects XI prompts the user for additional information that you, as the designer, build into the object. Prompts can be useful but also annoying if the user always wants the same values. For example, if a user always wants current year data, it can be aggravating if the object prompts the user for the year each time the user refreshes the query. In such a case, the user is better off placing a fixed condition in a report. Objects with prompts should be reserved for items in which some sort of condition is required either to limit the number of rows returned or to guarantee correct results.

In Chapter 9, Figure 9-2, you looked at the risk of constructing a query that involved a single point in time (for semi-additive measures such as account balance, ending inventory, number of customers) and a period of time (debits and credits; movements in and out; customers acquired). One way to ensure users select one point in time for semi-additive measures is to prompt users to enter an individual date whenever they select month-end inventory, as shown in Figure 11-2. (It would be wrong to put the prompt on the *Day* object, because it would prevent users from analyzing movements in and out for more than one day.)

Notice in Figure 11-2 that the object or `TABLE.COLUMN` in the `SELECT` portion of the SQL can be different than the `TABLE.COLUMN` in the `WHERE` clause. In the preceding figure, the `DEBIT_CREDIT.BALANCE` is used in the select, but *Day* is used in the `WHERE` clause. Because these two columns can be different, the format types also may be different. The *Balance* object uses the Type=Number, yet the `@Prompt` uses *D* to indicate that the prompt answer will be in date format. Prompts are added in the `WHERE` clause of a new or existing

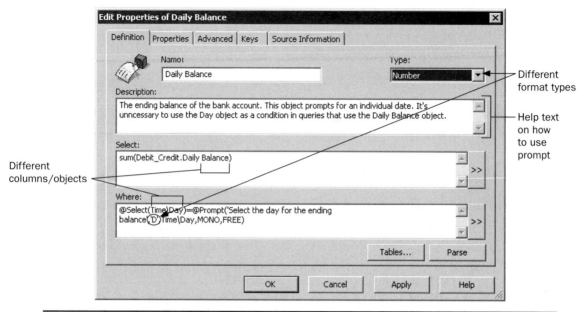

FIGURE 11-2 Create interactive objects with @Prompt.

object. Under Functions, double-click the @Prompt function to insert the syntax in the SQL statement, as shown here:

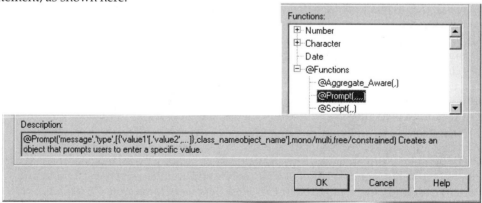

The @Prompt function uses the following syntax:

```
@@Prompt('Message','type','object or list of values',MONO/MULTI,FREE/CONSTRAINED)
```

where

- *Message* is the prompt you want users to see when they run a query that contains this object.

- *Type* is the object type or field format for the condition column. The query engine uses this to determine if the values require quotes or not. The base object and the

WHERE clause column may be two different types. In this example, *Balance* is numeric and *Day* is date. Acceptable values are

- *A* for alphanumeric
- *N* for number
- *D* for date

- The `'object or list of values'` parameter can be either the individual objects whose list of values you want to use or a list of values you enter manually in the prompt. When entering a predetermined list of values, you must enclose the values in single quotes, separated by commas, and the complete list must be enclosed by brackets. For example, suppose I wanted to restrict users to the most recent two ending balances: `{'09/30/02','10/31/02'}`.

- **MONO/MULTI**   If users can select only one value, use MONO. If users can enter more than one value, use MULTI. Note that the SQL operator must correspond to this setting. If users can enter more than one value, use the IN operator.

- **FREE/CONSTRAINED**   If users must select a value from the list of values, use CONSTRAINED. If users can either select from a list of values or enter their own value, use FREE.

TIP *The* @Prompt *function is very particular about commas, quotation marks, and matching object types. Be sure to Parse the object.*

When a user now constructs a query that uses the *Balance* object, BusinessObjects XI will always prompt them to **Select the Day for the Ending Balance**.

The following example illustrates how prompts can become user *unfriendly*. In the following query, the user wants to see daily account balances and correctly includes the *Day* object as a result object:

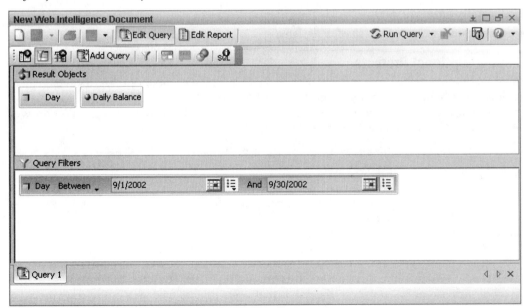

However, the *Balance* object also now includes the prompt to filter the query for one day (in addition to the user's condition on day). This generates the following SQL:

```
SELECT
  Daily_Balance.Date,
  Daily_Balance.Balance
FROM
  Daily_Balance
WHERE
( ( Daily_Balance.Date ) = @Prompt('Select the Day for the Ending
Balance','D','Time\Day',MONO,FREE)   )
  AND   (
  Daily_Balance.Date  BETWEEN  {d '2002-09-01'} AND {d '2002-09-30'}
  )
```

First, from the user's viewpoint it seems nonsensical that Web Intelligence will prompt for information that the user has already included in the conditions. Second, users will only ever be able to retrieve balances for one day at a time, whereas it is a valid business question for them to review daily balances over a period of time. In this respect, it is important in training and object descriptions to emphasize how these objects work and when to use them. As you build interactive objects, follow these guidelines:

- Use interactive objects only when the absence of a prompt could lead to inaccurate information or unacceptable query response times.

- If the prompts are for user friendliness or automation, have two objects, one without a prompt for unrestricted information and one with the prompt. Differentiate between these two objects with clear names—for example, *Balance* and *Balance-Date Required.*

- Provide usage information in the object description or in training.

CAUTION At the time of this writing, if the list of values for the prompt is long, Web Intelligence seems to hang in building the prompt page. If your prompt accesses a long list of values, verify if this problem has been resolved in the latest service pack before deploying.

Pseudo Optional Prompts

If you do not want the prompt to be mandatory to limit the number of rows, try the following technique, originally suggested by Walter Muellner of Mercury Business Solutions in Austria. The `Where` clause uses an `OR` statement to allow users to either answer **ALL** or choose individual values from the list:

```
'ALL'  IN @Prompt('Enter City or ALL','A', 'Customer\City',multi,)
 OR
City.city IN @Prompt('Enter City or ALL','A', 'Customer\City',multi,)
```

This is a very creative approach to balancing user friendliness with prompting. When users enter **ALL**, the first part of the condition SQL gets used (`'ALL'  IN  'ALL'`). Because the condition statement uses an `OR` clause, the second condition is not evaluated. Conversely, if users enter city names (or anything other than ALL), then the first part of the SQL is not true and so it does not get used, while the second condition does. Of course, if ALL is a possible data value in the City column, this poses a problem. The alternative is to use a symbol such as * or %—however, the risk is that users mix up true uses of these symbols (wildcards in certain databases). Finally, in order for this to work, the prompt in both condition statements must be exactly the same or users will be prompted twice.

Oracle Hints

Some designers have expressed concern that this approach causes the index not to be used. While I have not seen this problem in practice, it is true that the Oracle optimizer can sometimes get confused when there are many OR connectors. You can use Oracle Hints in your SELECT statement to encourage the optimizer to continue to use an index. I am not an advocate of building hints into universes, because it undermines the ad hoc nature of user queries, and in the end, Oracle still may ignore your hint. However, good response time is paramount to a successful deployment, so if you run into problems, incorporate hints where appropriate. The syntax for Oracle Hints for indexes is

```
/*+ Index(TableName IndexName) */
```

The following example uses the sample Oracle Sales History (SH) database and the detailed product ID. In defining the Object properties for the *Product Name*, the SELECT statement would be as follows:

```
/*+Index(SH.SALES_FACT SALES_PROD_BIX) */
SH.PRODUCTS.PROD_NAME
```

In earlier versions of Designer, the objects with hints did not parse. In Designer XI Release 2, the object will parse if you have entered the hint correctly.

Reusing Interactive Objects with @Variable

Designer allows you to reuse the prompt as a variable that you can then use in other objects. The variable can be one that you create with @Prompt, or it can be a system variable. BusinessObjects XI provides the following system variables:

- **BOUSER**   The BusinessObjects Enterprise user ID
- **BOPASS**   The BusinessObjects Enterprise password
- **DBUSER**   The database credentials used to connect to the data source
- **DBPASS**   The database password used to connect to the data source

As an example, let's assume that a hierarchical PRODUCT table contains both products and employees responsible for those products. So that users automatically see information for their products, the *My Product* object could contain the following WHERE clause:

```
PRODUCT.PRODUCT_OWNER = @Variable('BOUSER')
```

Reusing Interactive Objects with @Where

As mentioned previously, @Where allows you to reuse a WHERE clause in multiple objects. There are two benefits to using @Where: the first is decreased maintenance, and the second is decreased user prompting. If a query contains multiple occurrences of the exact same prompt, Web Intelligence and Desktop Intelligence will prompt the user only one time. For example, let's assume that users must filter Customer information by City to ensure only a limited amount of data is returned. The dimension object *City* contains a prompt. A designer could add @Where (Customer\City) to *Customer Name, Customer Id, Customer Age Group.*

Even if a query contains all four of these objects in a query, the user is prompted only once to select a city.

Prompts in Objects vs. Reports

Objects with prompts achieve a similar functionality as queries with prompts (Chapter 20, "Prompts"). In Chapter 14, you will look at the pros and cons of where to put this kind of intelligence. The main difference to consider with prompts is flexibility and maintenance. If you want to give the users flexibility, put the prompts in the query. If you want to minimize your maintenance costs, keep the prompts centralized in the universe objects. The following table summarizes some of the key differences between prompts in objects versus prompts in a query.

Universe Object with Prompt	Query with Prompt
Designer builds into universe	User builds in query
Centralized, so cost-effective to maintain because the designer creates the prompt once	Decentralized, so expensive to maintain because users must create the prompt in every document
Users cannot remove, so it can be inflexible, but error-proof, as it requires an answer	Users can remove, providing flexibility

Aggregate Awareness

An *aggregate table* is a summary table that DBAs build to execute queries faster. Aggregate tables are smaller than detail tables and can be aggregated in a number of ways. Most DBAs will strive for a certain compression ratio—for example, 10:1; the aggregate or summary table should be ten times smaller than the detail table, or for every ten detail rows, there is one summary row. Before you spend your time reading this section, talk to your DBA to determine if your database will automatically take advantage of aggregate tables. Newer versions of databases can automatically rewrite a query to leverage an aggregate table when it is available. The universe designer does not need to explicitly specify these aggregates. Unfortunately, though, it seems many organizations have been slow to take advantage of the database's query rewrite, so I am providing instructions here on how to use Designer's aggregate awareness. Given the choice, though, don't do this in the universe as it poses maintenance challenges; do it in the database. Alternatively, consider third-party solutions from technology partners such as HyperRoll or Netezza that are geared to improving query performance.

Figure 11-3 shows two sample dimensions, Time and Product. In the Time dimension, there are five years of history, with four levels going from Year to Day. Within a given year, there are 365 days. If the Time dimension contains five years of history, this results in 1825 rows of data. The Product dimension has four levels, ranging from Total Product to individual SKU. There are 210 SKUs (this is a very small product dimension).

A DBA may create an aggregate table summarizing data to any of these levels, across any dimension, as shown in Figure 11-4. The SALES_FACT_DAY table contains daily sales figures for five years, at the SKU level for all customers. The SALES_FACT_MONTH table aggregates sales by month and by product line. Customer is not aggregated in any way.

The following table shows the potential number of rows in such a fact table, if you have 30,000 customers. Typically, not every product sells daily, nor does every customer buy every product on a daily basis, so the potential rows represent strictly a worst-case scenario.

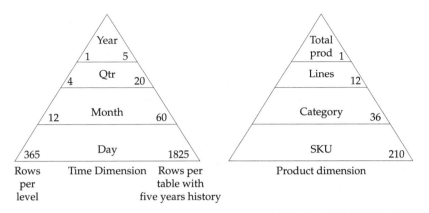

FIGURE 11-3   Two sample dimensions showing the number of potential rows at each level

However, the table illustrates the purpose of using aggregate tables for faster queries. If a user wants to analyze customer or product line sales only on a monthly or quarterly basis, the queries will run much faster against a 21.6 million–row table than an 11.497 billion–row table.

	Time	Product	Customer	Potential Rows
Day, SKU	1825	210	30,000	11,497,500,000
Month, product line	60	12	30,000	21,600,000

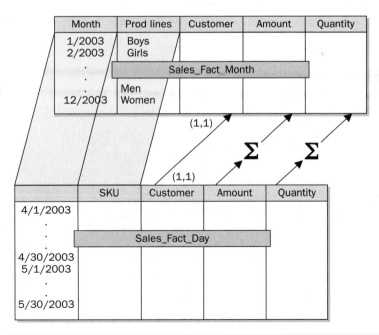

These symbols show that:

• The Month table is smaller than the Day table

• Month and Prod columns aggregate

FIGURE 11-4   Aggregate tables are summary tables that allow for faster queries.

The *existence* of aggregate tables does not help user queries. Users must *access* the summary tables, ideally automatically with awareness built into the RDBMS to force the query to be processed in the most efficient way. You most often will use aggregates with measures from fact tables as shown in Figure 11-4. For extremely large dimensions, you also may have a smaller dimension table, for example, that removes dimension details lower than month and product line (as shown in Figure 11-3). The following process outlines the key steps to enabling aggregate awareness:

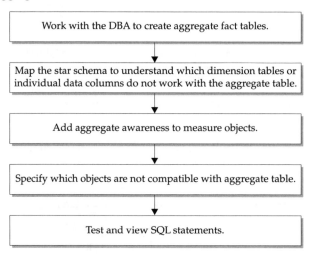

Work with the DBA to create aggregate fact tables.

Map the star schema to understand which dimension tables or individual data columns do not work with the aggregate table.

Add aggregate awareness to measure objects.

Specify which objects are not compatible with aggregate table.

Test and view SQL statements.

Creating Aggregate Fact Tables

Business Objects has provided two aggregate tables as part of the EFASHION.MDB. You will focus on the one table:

```
AGG_YR_QT_MT_MN_WK_RG_CY_SN_SR_QT_MA
```

The naming of the table is a bit cumbersome, so hereafter, I will refer to it as the aggregate fact table. The table name reveals some information on the contents of the table:

- **AGG** Aggregate
- **YR** Year
- **QT** Quarter
- **MT** Month Text
- **MN** Month Number
- **WK** Week
- **RG** Maybe region was intended but it is not in the final table
- **CY** City
- **SN** Store Name
- **SR** Sales Revenue

- **QT**   Quantity
- **MA**   Margin

I do have some concerns with the design of this table, as it has a fair bit of dimensional information that is typically stored in separate tables, but for demonstration purposes it will work fine. Notice that the number of rows for the aggregate table is 1982 compared to 89,171 in the detailed SHOP_FACTS table. Whenever possible, you want queries to run against the smaller AGG_YR_QT_MT_MN_WK_RG_CY_SN_SR_QT_MA rather than the larger, detailed SHOP_FACTS.

Identifying Dimension Tables Irrelevant to Aggregate Tables

In looking at Figure 11-5, you see that the aggregate table does not include any information on Articles. So the dimension tables ARTICLE_LOOKUP and ARTICLE_COLOR_LOOKUP will become incompatible with the summary objects. The fact table includes a lot of dimensional information. Time information is aggregated to the week level. You can retrieve dimensional information from either CALENDAR_YEAR_LOOKUP or the aggregate fact table. Outlet information is not aggregated; the aggregate tables contain details on the STORE_NAME, which is at the same grain as the OUTLET_LOOKUP but does not contain information about the store location.

Adding Aggregate Awareness to Measure Objects

You are now ready to define aggregate awareness to the individual measure objects *Sales Revenue, Quantity Sold,* and *Margin.* Aggregate awareness uses an internal function Designer:

```
@Aggregate_Aware(sum(smallest_table.column), sum(medium_table.column),
sum(biggest_table.column))
```

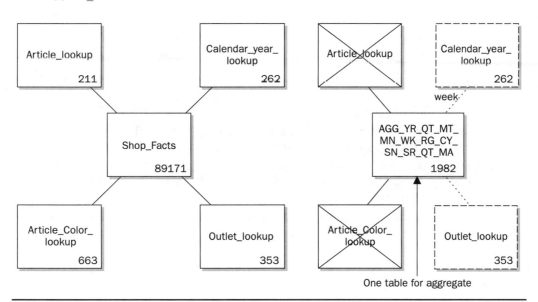

FIGURE 11-5   A detail fact table and a summary aggregate table may share some of the same dimension tables.

You can have multiple tables in the SELECT statement, with the smallest table first and the largest or most detailed table last. The @Aggregate_Aware function allows you to use any of the SQL Aggregate commands (SUM, COUNT, AVG, MIN, MAX); however, the aggregate command must be specified for each column as shown here.

Right:

```
@Aggregate_Aware(sum(Agg_yr_qt_mt_mn_wk_rg_cy_sn_sr_qt_ma.Sales_revenue),
sum(Shop_facts.Amount_sold))
```

Wrong:

```
@Aggregate_Aware(sum(Agg_yr_qt_mt_mn_wk_rg_cy_sn_sr_qt_ma.Sales_revenue,
Shop_facts.Amount_sold))
```

NOTE *If you normally have Designer automatically create objects when you add a table, turn this feature off before adding aggregate tables: Choose Tools | Options | Database. Remove the check mark from Create Default Classes And Objects From Tables. You do not want separate objects from these tables. Instead, you will point existing objects to access the aggregate tables.*

To follow the steps, use the Test Fashion universe created in earlier chapters.

1. Insert the aggregate table into the universe structure. Click the Table Browser button or use the pull-down menu to select Insert | Table | AGG_YR_QT_MT_MN_WK_RG_CY_SN_SR_QT_MA.

2. Expand the class *Test Fashion Measures.*

3. Select the object *Sum of Amount Sold* or *Revenue.*

4. Click the >> next to sum(Shop_facts.Amount_sold) to invoke the SQL Editor.

5. If you wish to avoid re-creating the SQL for the detail SHOP_FACTS table, ensure your mouse is positioned at the start of the SQL statement.

6. Under Functions, click the + sign next to @Functions to expand the group and display the Designer internal functions.

7. Double-click @Aggregate_Aware to insert the syntax in the SQL statement box.

8. Under Functions, click the + sign next to Number to display the SQL RDBMS functions. Scroll to sum() and click to insert the syntax into the SQL statement.

9. Under Tables And Columns, expand the aggregate table AGG_YR_QT_MT_MN_WK_RG_CY_SN_SR_QT_MA and double-click SALES_REVENUE to insert the table. column between the parentheses of sum().

10. Delete the right parenthesis and move it to the end to close the statement. Your SQL statement should appear as follows:

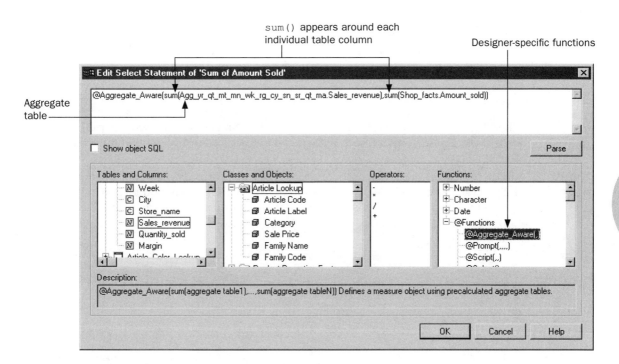

11. Click Parse to verify you have entered the correct syntax.

TIP *According to Business Objects, Parse on aggregate-aware objects only partially checks the SQL syntax. If you use* @Select *with* @Aggregate_Aware, *the parsing may be slower and less accurate. For complete universe integrity, be sure to test the objects by running queries and viewing the full SQL generated.*

12. Click OK to close the SQL Editor and then OK again to save the object definitions.

To enable aggregate awareness on *Quantity Sold* and *Margin,* repeat Steps 3–12, selecting the appropriate objects and columns.

At this point, there are no joins between the aggregate fact table and the dimension tables, nor is the aggregate part of a context. The aggregate table would normally have keys to join to the dimension tables that Designer may have detected; however, the design of this table is a bit unusual, so you must manually add the following two joins:

```
Agg_yr_qt_mt_mn_wk_rg_cy_sn_sr_qt_ma.Store_name=Outlet_Lookup.Shop_name
```

NOTE *I normally wouldn't recommend joining a description field from one table to a description field in another; the joins should be between indexed ID fields. If, however, users want stores within a particular state, for example, you have no choice with this model.*

```
Calendar_year_lookup.Yr=Agg_yr_qt_mt_mn_wk_rg_cy_sn_sr_qt_ma.Yr AND
Calendar_year_lookup.Week_In_Year=Agg_yr_qt_mt_mn_wk_rg_cy_sn_sr_qt_ma.Wk
```

1. Either draw join lines between the respective tables and columns or use the pull-down menu Insert | Join. Note that the second join is a complex join that must be entered manually.

2. Add these two new joins to a new context. If you have correctly defined the complex join, you can use the Detect Context button or use the pull-down menu Insert | Context to include the two joins in a new context. Complete the entries as follows:

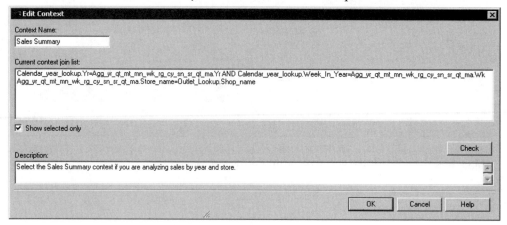

3. Click OK to accept the modified context.

4. From the pull-down menu, select File | Save or click Save to save the changes to the universe.

Specifying Which Objects Are Not Compatible with the Aggregate Table

The table now exists in the universe, and you have told Designer to use this table for certain measure objects. You now have to tell Designer that the aggregate table cannot be used when certain dimension objects exist in the query. This can be very confusing. Try to stay focused on two things:

- You are essentially telling Designer when to use the detail table.
- You need to worry about only one context or star schema.

Refer to Figure 11-4. Note that all article objects are incompatible with the aggregate table. If a user includes any article information in a query, it is not available in the aggregate table, and you must tell Designer to use the detail SHOP_FACTS table. You are only concerned with this one context and do not need to worry about the promotion objects. This second point is especially confusing, because when Designer detects incompatibility, it unnecessarily and incorrectly marks objects from other contexts. If you mark promotion objects as incompatible here, you prevent users from constructing a query that compares sales by store (using the aggregate table) with promotions by store. To define incompatible objects, follow these steps:

NOTE *You only need to mark objects as incompatible that exist in the one context or star schema.*

1. Open the pull-down menu Tools | Aggregate Navigation.

2. Highlight the table for which you will define incompatible objects, AGG_YR_QT_ MT_MN_WK_RG_CY_SN_SR_QT_MA.

3. Under Associated Incompatible Objects, you can select entire classes or individual objects. Click the *Article Lookup* class.

4. If you created a measure *Number of Article Codes* in Chapter 7, set this object to incompatible as well.

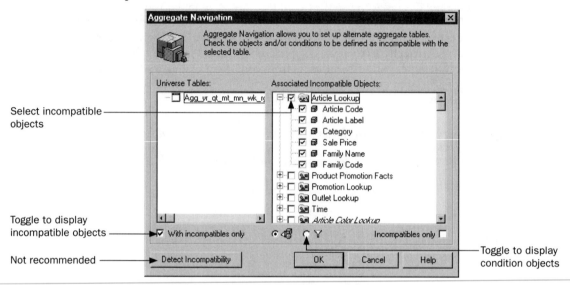

Select incompatible objects

Toggle to display incompatible objects

Not recommended

Toggle to display condition objects

CAUTION *If you toggle to display tables that contain incompatible objects, only aggregate tables should be displayed. If more than just the aggregates are displayed, you have a problem.*

5. You can now use the toggle check box Incompatibles Only to filter those objects that have been marked as incompatible against the aggregate table.

6. Click OK to close the Aggregate Navigation box.

7. From the pull-down menu, select File | Save or click Save to save the changes to the universe.

Testing and Viewing SQL Statements

Now that you have defined which objects are incompatible with the aggregate fact table, you need to make sure that the query engine generates the correct SQL. To test this, use Figure 11-4 to develop a test plan as shown in Table 11-1. Take each measure that contains @Aggregate_Aware and add a dimension object from each of the dimension tables to the query. As you create a query for each scenario, verify that the SQL generated uses the appropriate table.

To view the SQL statement, follow these steps:

1. Launch the query panel from Designer by selecting Tools | Query Panel.

Scenario	If Your Query Contains These Objects	BusinessObjects XI Should Use This Table
1	*Sum of Amount Sold*	`AGG_YR_QT_MT_MN_WK_RG_CY_SN_SR_QT_MA`
2	*Sum of Amount Sold, Month Name*	`AGG_YR_QT_MT_MN_WK_RG_CY_SN_SR_QT_MA`
3	*Sum of Amount Sold, Month Name, Shop Name*	`AGG_YR_QT_MT_MN_WK_RG_CY_SN_SR_QT_MA`
4	*Sum of Amount Sold, Promotion Cost, Month*	*2 SQL Select statements:* `AGG_YR_QT_MT_MN_WK_RG_CY_SN_SR_QT_MA` `PRODUCT_PROMOTION_FACTS`
5	*Sum of Amount Sold, Month Name, Store Name, Article*	`SHOP_FACTS`
6	*Sum of Amount Sold, Article Color*	`SHOP_FACTS`
7	*Sum of Amount Sold, Number of Article Code*	`SHOP_FACTS`

TABLE 11-1   Test Plan for Aggregate Awareness

2. Follow the test plan outlined in Table 11-1 to add the result objects to the query. The following screen shows a query based on Scenario 3 in Table 11-1:

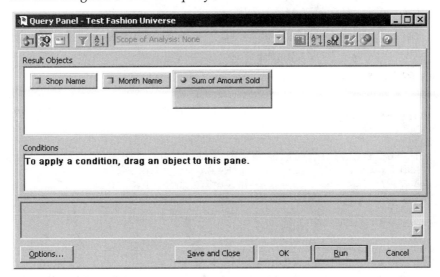

3. To verify that the correct fact table is used in the SQL, click the SQL button on the Query Panel toolbar. Note that for Scenario 3, the aggregate fact table was correctly used.

NOTE *When you view the SQL via the Designer query panel, it adds a DISTINCT to the query. This does not happen in either Desktop Intelligence or Web Intelligence.*

```
SELECT DISTINCT
  Outlet_Lookup.Shop_name,
  Calendar_year_lookup.Month_Name,
  sum(Agg_yr_qt_mt_mn_wk_rg_cy_sn_sr_qt_ma.Sales_revenue)
FROM
  Calendar_year_lookup,
  Outlet_Lookup,
  Agg_yr_qt_mt_mn_wk_rg_cy_sn_sr_qt_ma
WHERE
  ( Calendar_year_lookup.Yr=Agg_yr_qt_mt_mn_wk_rg_cy_sn_sr_qt_ma.Yr AND
Calendar_year_lookup.Week_In_Year=Agg_yr_qt_mt_mn_wk_rg_cy_sn_sr_qt_ma.Wk  )
  AND  ( Agg_yr_qt_mt_mn_wk_rg_cy_sn_sr_qt_ma.Store_name=Outlet_Lookup.Shop_name  )
GROUP BY
  Outlet_Lookup.Shop_name,
  Calendar_year_lookup.Month_Name
```

---

4. When you add *Article Code* to the query as in Scenario 5, the SQL engine automatically selects the `SHOP_FACTS` table without any user intervention.

```
SELECT
  sum(Shop_facts.Amount_sold),
  Calendar_year_lookup.Month_Name,
  Outlet_Lookup.Shop_name,
  Article_lookup.Article_code

FROM
  Shop_facts,
  Calendar_year_lookup,
  Article_lookup,
  Outlet_Lookup
WHERE
  ( Shop_facts.Article_code=Article_lookup.Article_code  )
  AND  ( Calendar_year_lookup.Week_key=Shop_facts.Week_key  )
  AND  ( Shop_facts.Shop_code=Outlet_Lookup.Shop_code  )
GROUP BY
  Calendar_year_lookup.Month_Name,
  Outlet_Lookup.Shop_name,
  Article_lookup.Article_code
```

For Scenario 4 in Table 11-1, BusinessObjects XI will generate two SQL statements and seamlessly stitch the results together in the report. This step can go wrong for two reasons: (1) if your File | Parameters, SQL tab, Multiple SQL Statements For Each Context setting is not enabled, or (2) if you used Tools | Aggregate Navigation | Detect Incompatibility; in the latter case, Designer incorrectly marked objects from other contexts as being incompatible with an aggregate table.

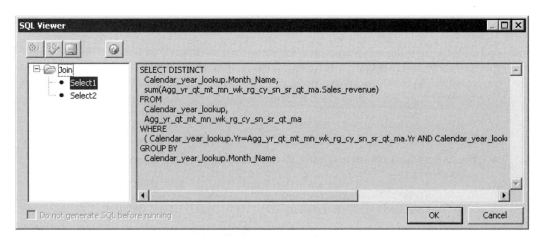

The most obvious error in this step of building aggregate awareness is if the wrong table is used in any instance. However, the ultimate goal is to get correct results. So as a final test, you should run a query to ensure that you get the same data when either the aggregate table or the detail table is used. In the preceding examples, Sales for September 2001 is $300,848, according to both the aggregate table and the SHOP_FACTS table.

There are a few reasons why you may not get the same result for an aggregate table as for a detail table:

- **One of the tables is incorrect**   If the DBA has not built the aggregate table correctly, you may not be able to fix it, but you must communicate this issue to both DBAs and end users. When something is wrong, BusinessObjects XI will always get the blame, because most end users don't know and don't care which component in the information flow actually has the problem. If the summary table is incorrect in all circumstances, don't include it in the universe design. If it is correct in most circumstances and the DBA is working to resolve one minor inconsistency, use the table but clearly explain in the object description when the data may be incorrect.

- **The aggregate table contains dimensional information that is different from details in the lookup or dimension tables**   As a general rule, I don't like when dimensional information is stored in the fact table. It's even worse when there is a difference between dimensional information in a fact table and a dimension table. Yes, in a perfect world the data is clean and consistent. However, I've yet to see a company that had such clean data. In the example of AGG_YR_QT_MT_MN_WK_RG_ CY_SN_SR_QT_MA, the store name exists in both this aggregate fact table and the dimension table OUTLET_LOOKUP. What if the fact table contained data for a store that did not exist in OUTLET_LOOKUP? Users would get different answers between queries that use the aggregate table and queries that use the detail table that joins to the dimension table that is missing information for a store.

- **The universe contains a mistake in the join or in a dimension definition**   An error in the design is completely within your control and must be resolved before deploying to end users.

Derived Tables

Derived tables are similar to views in the database, but as they are defined in the universe, they give universe designers more flexibility. A derived table is a query that can be referenced by you as a table. As it is a query and not a physical table, it's important to understand that the same performance issues that affect queries also affect derived tables:

- Do *not* use derived tables in place of aggregate tables. Aggregate tables must be physical tables built by the DBA to provide fast query performance.
- Do use derived tables that minimize the complexity of the queries users have to create themselves.
- Do use derived tables in place of views and stored procedures that in the past you would have asked a DBA to create.

Derived tables may be most useful when you want to UNION two queries together (for example, a supplier and customer table unioned to create a vendor table), when you want to include @Variable in the query logic, and in some cases, when you have different aggregation levels.

NOTE *If you use derived tables to create different aggregation levels, be careful to consider the impact on joins, contexts, and many-to-many relationships. If your database supports newer analytic and report functions (see the section "Ratio to Report" later in this chapter), these functions will give you much better response time than using derived tables.*

This example uses the Island Resorts Marketing universe. Earlier, in the section "Condition Objects," you created a condition Top Customers. A valid business question may be "How much of my business do the Top Customers account for?" To answer this, you need to get the total sales for all customers as well as the total sales for only the top customers and combine them in one query. Within the Island Resorts Marketing universe, the object *Revenue* is calculated from the `Invoice_Lines` table. To create an object *Top Customer Revenue*, you create a derived table:

1. From within the structure pane, right-click and select Derived Tables from the pop-up menu or select Insert | Derived Tables from the pull-down menu.
2. Within the Derived Tables box, replace the generic `Derived Table` name with a meaningful table name such as **Top Customers**.

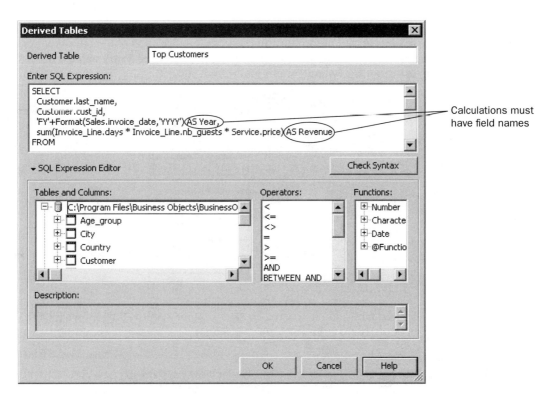

3. In the SQL Expression box, enter the desired SQL to create the derived table. If you have used Desktop Intelligence or Web Intelligence to create the initial SQL, you must ensure that each calculation is assigned a field name. For example, in the preceding screen, AS Year will create the field Top Customers.Year within the derived table.

4. Parse the SQL statement by clicking Check Syntax.

5. Click OK to close the Derived Tables dialog.

6. Add the necessary joins and include in relevant contexts. In this example, add the join `Top Customers`.cust_id=Customer.cust_id and include in the Sales context.

7. Create the object *Top Customer Revenue* as a measure with the following SQL that accesses the newly created derived table:

```
sum(`Top Customers`.Revenue)
```

Now, when a user creates a report that contains these two measures, Web Intelligence generates two SQL statements and automatically presents the results as one seamless report. Note in the following that any data not in the derived table appears as a null value. For example, Customer 101 did not have revenues greater than 100,000.

Customer ID	Revenue	Top Customer Revenue
101	8,420	
102	400,899	400,899
103	4,380	
104	301,545	209,545
105	18,715	
106	441,594	441,594
107	10,704	
401	10,976	
402	388,524	388,524
403	4,400	

With the use of derived tables, then, a user can easily create a report that shows that 78 percent of the total revenue comes from the top 7 customers.

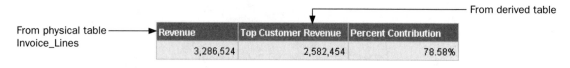

From physical table ——► Invoice_Lines

From derived table

Revenue	Top Customer Revenue	Percent Contribution
3,286,524	2,582,454	78.58%

HTML Links

You can embed links to web sites based on object values. For example, if an object returns a list of customers and you know the web site address for each customer, a user can click on the customer name in a report to link to that customer's web site.

CAUTION   If SQL tests your patience, combining HTML into your SQL may cause you to lose your patience entirely! Pay careful attention to quotes and note that the syntax is different for each database.

About HTML

The basic syntax for a link to a web site is

- **`<a>`**   An HTML anchor element
- **`Href`**   The hot spot reference where you will provide the web site address or URL. You may display the URL to users or display different text.
- **`</a>`**   Ends the HTML anchor element

Designer requires HTML elements to be enclosed in single quotes. (HREF uses double quotes for the URL.) So, if you want to create a simple list of authors who may be visiting your bookstore, the syntax would be as follows:

```
<a href="www.website.com">Text to display to users </a>
```

Following is an example with the author name and web site completed.

```
<a href="www.jodipicoult.com">Jodi Picoult </a>
```

In the object, you need to add the single quotes around the HTML elements, the <a> and </a>.

```
'<a href="http://www.jodipicoult.com">'Jodi Picoult'</a>'
```

At this point, your object would not parse, because it lacks a `table.column`. To have BusinessObjects XI display the results of a column, the data must be concatenated with the HTML statement. Concatenation symbols vary from database to database; MS SQL Server and MS Access use a plus sign (+), whereas Oracle uses two vertical bars (||).

Therefore, your basic HTML syntax for MS Server or MS Access is

```
'<a href="http://www.website.com">'+TABLE.COLUMN+'</a>'
```

and for Oracle it is

```
'<a href="http://www.website.com">'||TABLE.COLUMN||'</a>'
```

If you want the *website* portion of the `Select` statement also to be dynamic, you can either access a column that provides a web site address or transform data from another column to form a web address. Concatenating HTML commands with SQL data in addition to fixed strings can get messy pretty quickly. For all the concatenations to work correctly, you must use the RDMBS `CONCAT` function, rather than the + or || operators.

The following example is based on an MS Access database in which the web site address is a column in an `Author` lookup table:

```
{fn concat({fn concat('<A HREF='+ {fn char(34)}, '+Authors.Website+'+{fn char(34)}|
'>')},{fn concat(
Authors.Author, '</A>')})}
```

This second example is based on the sample Sales History database in which the web site address is derived from the `city` column. The web site address consists of three parts:

- The prefix, www.
- The city name, which comes from the SQL column `SH.CUSTOMERS.CUST_CITY`.
- The end of the web address, .co.uk. Commercial web site addresses in the U.S. end in .com or .net, while web site addresses in the U.K. end in .co.uk. For this object to work in a global deployment, one would need to add a `DECODE` or `CASE` function to test the Country as well.

```
Concat(concat('<A HREF=' || chr(34), 'www.'||SH.CUSTOMERS.CUST_CITY||'.
co.uk' || chr(34) || '>'),concat(
SH.CUSTOMERS.CUST_CITY , '</A>'))
```

In order for Desktop Intelligence to generate the SQL statement correctly as an HTML link, you must set the Object Format to Read As HTML. Select the object and right-click to bring up the following pop-up menu:

On the Object Format dialog, click the box Read As HTML.

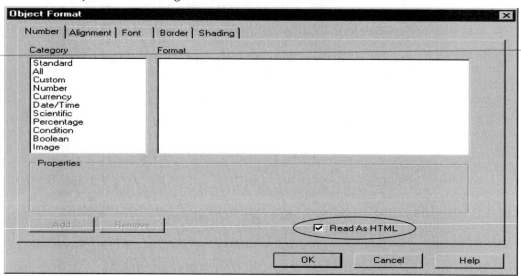

When users run a report, the object with the dynamic link to a web site address is displayed as a hyperlink. As long as you set the object format in Designer as Read As HTML, Desktop Intelligence users can access the web site by clicking the link. For Web Intelligence users, though, they must specifically format the cell to read the data as a hyperlink. In the screen shown here, you also see the correctly formatted web site address that will take you to the web site for the city of Leeds (www.leeds.co.uk).

Customer State Province	Customer City	City's Web Site
England - West Yorkshire	Bradford	Bradford
England - West Yorkshire	Halifax	Halifax
England - West Yorkshire	Keighley	Keighley
England - West Yorkshire	Leeds	Leeds
England - West Yorkshire	Wakefield	Wakefield

Popular SQL Functions

Take a deep breath. If the Designer internal functions have overwhelmed you, get a latte, have a glass of wine (at home, of course!), or do some yoga: SQL functions are ever more powerful and limited only by your creativity, but potentially, they are more overwhelming (especially if, like me, you have a nasty habit of putting commas and parentheses in all the wrong places). In the universe design process, this is when the power users, universe Designers, and DBAs must partner together to build a technically correct but business-robust universe.

There are entire books dedicated to SQL commands alone, so it is impossible to cover all of the functions here. What follows are just a few examples of some popular objects that use SQL functions to deliver business functionality.

Concatenated

Concatenated objects combine information from multiple fields. A common usage is to combine a customer or employee's *First Name* and *Last Name* into a new object, *Name*. Depending on your database, you have two ways to concatenate fields:

- The CONCAT function, which is database specific and allows you to combine two columns of data. One can nest CONCAT statements to combine multiple columns, but personally, I find the nested functions harder to read than an operator.

- An operator that allows you to combine several columns into one. Microsoft databases use +, and Oracle uses | |.

The following object uses the CONCAT function and Designer's @Select to reference existing objects in the universe:

```
CONCAT(@Select(Hr Employees\First Name),@Select(Hr Employees\Last Name))
```

The SQL statement will appear as follows:

```
CONCAT(HR.EMPLOYEES.FIRST_NAME,HR.EMPLOYEES.LAST_NAME)
```

Using an operator has the following syntax and allows you to combine more than two fields plus spaces between each column:

```
( HR.EMPLOYEES.EMPLOYEE_ID ) ||' '|| ( HR.EMPLOYEES.FIRST_NAME )||' ' || (
HR.EMPLOYEES.LAST_NAME )
```

Time Objects

If you look at any quarterly or annual report, it contains current period and Year-To-Date information as shown from the most current Business Objects 10Q filing, as in the following earnings statement:

	Three Months Ended September 30		YTD (Ended September 30)	
	2005	2004	2005	2004
Net license fees	120,308	105,705	360,317	337,380
Services	141,073	113,765	412,248	321,563
Total revenues	$261,381	$219,470	$772,565	$658,943

To create objects that include time period awareness or year-to-date functionality is a two-step process. First, you must determine what is the definition of "to-date": Is it whichever accounting month the books have closed? Is it the calendar day of today? The answer to this may depend on whether you are viewing accounting information or sales order information. Accountants may want *closed* accounting months, whereas salespeople will want the latest date possible. The second step involves grouping the information into columns of data as shown in the preceding table. Grouping information into columns of data is described in the next section, "If-Then-Else Logic with CASE."

If users want to run rolling reports, you can provide them with condition objects that let them select current time periods or a rolling period. If you are looking for a closed accounting month, the best practice is to store the closed accounting month as a flag in the time dimension table. If this is not available, create an interactive object that prompts for the closed accounting month.

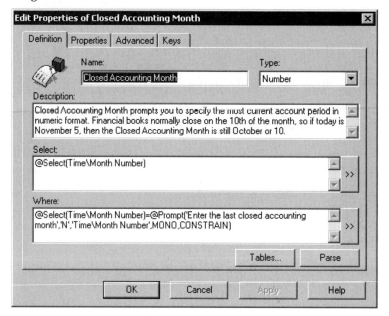

The prompt "Enter the last closed accounting month" can now be used as an @Variable in any Year-To-Date objects. For example, YTD Sales would include in the WHERE clause the following:

```
@Select(Time\Fiscal Month Number)<=@Variable('Closed Accounting Month')
```

If the interactive object *Closed Accounting Month* exists in the query or has been used during the report, then BusinessObjects XI will prompt the user and provide the list of values. If *Closed Accounting Month* is not in the current report, then when a user accesses *YTD Sales*, BusinessObjects XI will prompt the user for the *Closed Accounting Month* variable but will not know to link back to the interactive object to get the list of values. You can best resolve this quirk with user training and instructions in the Object Description.

So far, you have only asked the user to specify the month and not the year. You could include the accounting year in the prompt as well, or you could get the current year from the RDBMS's system date. Either users can include a *Current Year* condition in their query or you may have a compound WHERE clause in the object *Current YTD Sales*:

```
@Select(Time\Month Number)<=@Variable('Closed Accounting Month')
AND
@Select(Time\Year)=TO_NUMBER(TO_CHAR(SYSDATE,'YYYY') )
```

SYSDATE returns the system date on the RDBMS. It is a date field from which you want to extract just the year. TO_CHAR allows you to extract the four-digit year. However, your comparison object is numeric, so you must convert the character year to a numeric field using TO_NUMBER.

CAUTION *Be aware that with this type of object, the* WHERE *clause gets appended to the entire query and users will not be able to have* Last Year *objects in the same report. Refer to the next section for an alternative.*

To allow users to create a rolling three months, use the ADD_MONTHS SQL command to subtract three months from the SYSDATE. Note that in this example, you only need the month or MM from the TO_CHAR function.

If-Then-Else Logic with CASE

Oracle provides the CASE and DECODE SQL functions, both of which work like an If-Then-Else statement. The two functions have different syntaxes. DECODE has been around longer with earlier database versions, whereas CASE was introduced with Oracle 8, so many long-time developers still use DECODE. CASE statements are easier to write and more flexible; they also adhere to the ANSI standard.

This is the syntax for a simple CASE expression in Oracle 9*i*:

```
CASE @Select(Class\ Object) when @Select(Class\ Object)='a' then 'b' else 'c' end
```

where:

- @Select(Class\Object) can be either the object whose value you want to change or the RDBMS *TABLE.COLUMN*.
- *a* is the value in the data column you wish to compare and replace.
- *b* is the replacement value.
- *c* is the alternative if there is no match for a.

The syntax for DECODE is

```
DECODE (@Select(Class\Object),'if_a','then_b')
```

where @Select(Class\Object) can be either the object whose value you want to change or the RDBMS *TABLE.COLUMN*.

In the sample Oracle SH.CUSTOMER table, the CUST_GENDER column contains only two values: F for Female and M for Male. The gender description is not stored in a column. CASE or DECODE can help you create a description.

The syntax using `CASE` would be

```
CASE
    when SH.CUSTOMERS.CUST_GENDER ='F' then 'Female'
    when SH.CUSTOMERS.CUST_GENDER = 'M' then 'Male'
    else 'Not Listed'
    End
```

The syntax using `DECODE` would be

```
decode(SH.CUSTOMERS.CUST_GENDER, 'F', 'Female', 'M', 'Male')
```

Current Period

`CASE` is also quite powerful for creating *Current Period* and *Year-To-Date (YTD)* objects without the problem of conflicting `WHERE` clauses becoming appended to the entire query. To understand how to build this kind of object, first study the sample data in Figure 11-6. This is taken from the sample Oracle Sales History (SH) tables. The report shows sales amounts for this year and last, broken down by quarter. Assume the current quarter and year is third quarter, 2005. You want to create two objects, one that retrieves the current period sales = 66,772,321 and one that retrieves the cumulative year-to-date sales = 217,702,751.

To determine which quarter you are in, you again use the `SYSDATE` and `TO_CHAR` commands. This time you want the date to be in `YYYYQ` format. The sample `SH.TIMES` table has the Year and Quarter in two separate columns, so you will concatenate the two together to get the same comparison from your `SYSDATE`. You want to create a *Current Quarter Sales* object that says: If the current calendar quarter matches the accounting quarter, then, for the same period in the database, show the sales; else, return zero. The objects you are trying to design would look something like this:

Year	Current Quarter Sales	Current YTD Sales
2004	0	0
2005	66,772,321	217,702,752

Year	Quarter Number	Amount Sold	YTD Sales
2004	1	61,109,170	61,109,170
	2	62,312,131	123,421,301
	3	57,156,689	180,577,990
	4	69,232,579	249,810,569
2004	**Sum:**	**249,810,569**	

Year	Quarter Number	Amount Sold	YTD Sales
2005	1	73,956,184	73,956,184
	2	76,974,247	150,930,430
	3	66,772,321	217,702,752
	4	51,686,766	269,389,518
2005	**Sum:**	**269,389,518**	

Assume date = Q3 2005

Running totals

You want this value

FIGURE 11-6 Quarterly sales report

The corresponding SQL for a *Current Quarter Sales* object using CASE is

```
sum(
CASE
When SH.TIMES.CALENDAR_YEAR=to_char(sysdate,'YYYY')
Then (CASE When
 SH.TIMES.CALENDAR_YEAR||SH.TIMES.CALENDAR_QUARTER_NUMBER
=
to_char(sysdate,'YYYYQ' )
Then SH.SALES.AMOUNT_SOLD
End)
Else 0
End
)
```

You can build a similar object using DECODE. In this example, the date is fixed, rather than dynamically deciphered from the SYSDATE as in the previous CASE statement.

```
sum(decode(to_char(sysdate,'YYYYQ'),
'200503',DECODE(SH.TIMES.CALENDAR_YEAR||SH.TIMES.CALENDAR_QUARTER_NUMBER,'200503',SH
.SALES.AMOUNT_SOLD)))
```

When using CASE or DECODE in this way, it is important that the aggregate SUM function goes around the entire statement and is not nested within the CASE statement or between the DECODEs. The following table decomposes the DECODE portion of the SQL statement:

Part	Purpose	SQL Syntax
1	If the current calendar quarter	`decode(to_char(sysdate,'YYYYQ')`
2	Matches the accounting quarter	`'200503'`
3	Then for the same period in the database	`DECODE(SH.TIMES.CALENDAR_YEAR||SH.TIMES.CALENDAR_QUARTER_NUMBER,'200053'`
4	Show the sales	`SH.SALES.AMOUNT_SOLD`
5	Else null	

Cumulative To-Date

There are a number of ways to create a *Current Year-To-Date Sales* object that reflects the cumulative or running total for the current year (the last example just summed one quarter). While the comparison part of your SQL (parts 1–2) would remain the same, retrieving the values for a cumulative period in part 3 will be a bit more of a challenge. You can have three sums such as Q1+Q2+Q3, but if you ever try to create a *Current Week-To-Date* or *Current Month-To-Date* object, your SQL gets long and messy fast. What you really want is a way to retrieve a range of values or to test if the RDBMS accounting quarter is less than or equal to the SYSDATE quarter.

To create the *Year-To-Date* object, replace = 200503 with <= to get a cumulative total. The following SQL also contains a nested CASE statement to ensure that you add quarters from the same year:

```
sum(
    CASE
    When SH.TIMES.CALENDAR_YEAR=to_char(sysdate,'YYYY')
    Then (CASE When
SH.TIMES.CALENDAR_YEAR||SH.TIME.CALENDAR_QUARTER_NUMBER
        <=
        to_char(sysdate,'YYYYQ' )
        Then SH.SALES.AMOUNT_SOLD
        End)
    Else 0
    End
)
```

You can combine these automatic time period objects to create variances that compare sales trends between the two years or two quarters. For example, the following report uses several time period objects to determine that sales were 21 percent higher for the first three quarters of the year:

Automatic Dates				
Current Quarter Sales	Last Year Same Quarter	Current YTD Sales	Last Year YTD Sales	Variance
66,772,321.10	57,156,688.85	217,702,751.55	180,577,989.70	21%

One thing to be aware of with the *Current Year* and *YTD* objects is that users do not have to enter a *Year* as a condition. Everything is automatic. This can be great for users and for standard report maintenance, but it can be bad for the RDBMS if the queries result in a full table scan; the database will not use an index from any of the TIMES columns. If users will always select some other condition criteria such as *Product* or *Region*, then these indexes may be used to process the query. As a work-around, you may want to include a WHERE clause in the automatic objects that includes enough years for the results to be accurate, but also, for an index to be used. Alternatively, test the use of Oracle Hints if this is your data source.

For example, if you have automatic objects for *Current Year*, *Last Year*, and *2 Years Ago*, then include the following as a WHERE clause for each object:

```
@Select(Time\Year) IN ('2005','2004','2003')
```

To avoid having to update this each year, in theory you may be able to use <= SYSDATE-(365*3); however, this assumes that the base comparison year is also a date field. In the preceding example, it is not, in which case, you would need to convert the SYSDATE calculation using TO_CHAR. Once you add this kind of function to the SQL statement, the index is not used (unless the DBA creates a special function index).

Count

In Chapter 9, you looked at using the SQL COUNT function in measure objects to count the number of products or the number of customers. COUNT can get a little more complex than this, as (1) what you want to count is not always obvious, and (2) COUNT may give unexpected results.

What to Count?

The business user asks, "How many products do we have?" Easy, just count the unique PRODUCT_IDs in the dimension table! The following screen shows why this may not always be what the business user expects:

Prod Id	Prod Name	Supplier Id	Prod Min Price	Prod Pack Size	Prod Status
180.00	Potpourri Skirt	61.00	35.19	white paper bag	available, on stock
190.00	Potpourri Skirt	45.00	32.29	heavy duty box	available, on stock
195.00	Potpourri Skirt	77.00	32.29	brown envelope	available, on stock
200.00	Potpourri Skirt	77.00	32.29	heavy duty box	available, on stock
4,255.00	Potpourri Skirt	3.00	40.57	white paper bag	available, on stock
4,260.00	Potpourri Skirt	3.00	40.57	white paper bag	available, on stock
8,310.00	Potpourri Skirt	59.00	39.33	heavy duty box	available, on stock
8,315.00	Potpourri Skirt	105.00	39.33	heavy duty box	available, on stock
8,320.00	Potpourri Skirt	105.00	39.33	plastic bag	not available
8,325.00	Potpourri Skirt	105.00	39.33	heavy duty box	available, on stock
12,370.00	Potpourri Skirt	17.00	23.18	white paper bag	available, on stock
12,375.00	Potpourri Skirt	17.00	23.18	card box	ordered
12,390.00	Potpourri Skirt	17.00	33.53	white paper bag	available, on stock
12,395.00	Potpourri Skirt	47.00	33.53	water proof wrap	available, on stock
16,435.00	Potpourri Skirt	29.00	24.84	white paper bag	available, on stock
20,500.00	Potpourri Skirt	62.00	21.94	plastic bag	obsolete
20,515.00	Potpourri Skirt	62.00	40.99	heavy duty box	available, on stock
20,520.00	Potpourri Skirt	95.00	40.99	white paper bag	available, on stock
20,525.00	Potpourri Skirt	95.00	40.99	white paper bag	available, on stock
24,580.00	Potpourri Skirt	30.00	28.98	heavy duty box	available, on stock
24,590.00	Potpourri Skirt	93.00	36.43	plastic bag	ordered

A unique PRODUCT_ID is created for each combination of a product description, supplier, price, packaging, and availability. Note that the only difference between PRODUCT_IDs 195 and 200 is the packaging: brown envelope versus heavy-duty box. The business definition for number of products may in fact be according to the product ID, or it may be by product name. The SQL is different for each.

The object definition for counting product IDs is

```
COUNT(PRODUCT_ID)
```

The object definition for counting unique product names is

```
COUNT(DISTINCT PRODUCT_NAME)
```

Distinct Count

The COUNT function actually counts the number of rows returned; it does not count individual occurrences. In the preceding example, if you used COUNT(PRODUCT_NAME), you would get the same result as with COUNT(PRODUCT_ID). If you want "Potpourri Skirt" to count as one product regardless of the number of times it occurs in the database, you must use COUNT(DISTINCT *TABLE.COLUMN*).

Recall from Chapter 9 that a dimension object should always come from the dimension or lookup table and not the fact table, which will have multiple occurrences of the same product ID. With COUNT, this becomes even more important to guarantee correct results. There is a significant difference between counting the number of products versus the number of products sold in a particular period. The former must come from the dimension table; the latter must come from the fact table. The following report shows how each count yields different results:

COUNT - NUMBER OF PRODUCTS					
Product Category	Number of Products	Number of Product Names		Number of Products Fact	Number of Products Fact Dist
Boys	2,428.00	85.00		227,102.00	1,091.00
Girls	1,926.00	73.00		177,538.00	901.00
Men	2,594.00	193.00		238,860.00	1,278.00
Women	3,052.00	411.00		372,771.00	1,752.00

The following table shows the SQL used to generate each column of data:

Object	SQL
Number of Products	COUNT(DISTINCT PRODUCTS.PROD_ID)
Number of Product Names	COUNT(DISTINCT PRODUCTS.PROD_NAME)
Number of Products Fact	COUNT(SH.SALES.PROD_ID)
Number of Products Fact Distinct	COUNT(DISTINCT SALES.PROD_ID)

For the Boys' product category, there are 2428 unique product IDs or 85 different product names. These are both valid numbers. Users may want to see only one or both. If they want to see both, then the object name and the corresponding description must clearly convey what is being counted. Both columns come from the dimension table. The first object, *Number of Products,* includes the DISTINCT keyword, but only as a precaution; it is not strictly required. If the field you are counting is a unique ID or key field for the entire table, it is not required. Be careful about assuming that ID fields are always unique; some IDs may have an active/inactive flag or timestamp to indicate the latest record.

The next column in the report, Number of Products Fact, is misleading and meaningless. There are 227,102 occurrences of a PRODUCT_ID in the SALES fact table. When DISTINCT is used, there are 1091 distinct occurrences of a PRODUCT_ID in the SALES fact table. This number has a business meaning in that 1091 unique Boys' products were sold. Users may want to see one or all three types of counts.

NOTE *Always use* COUNT (DISTINCT TABLE.COLUMN) *when counting items in a fact table. Otherwise, only use* COUNT *against columns with unique IDs or keys.*

Rank

The RANK function is one of the newer analytic functions available in Oracle 8.1.6 or later and DB2 version 7.1 or later. At the time of this writing, a corresponding RANK function was not available in SQL Server 2000, but SQL Server 2005 is expected to have more analytic functions. The RANK function allows you to rank a dimension (customer, product, salesperson) according to any metric (sales, profit, commission, and so on). The ranked dimension is determined by the user as result objects in the query. You, as the designer, specify the metric for the ranking. The basic syntax of RANK is

```
RANK() OVER(PARTITION BY DIMENSION_TABLE.COLUMN ORDER BY AGG(FACT_TABLE.COLUMN)
   DESC
```

where PARTITION BY DIMENSION_TABLE.COLUMN is optional and is used to rank items within a subset of data.

AGG(FACT_TABLE.COLUMN) is the aggregated measure that forms the ranking. For example, products with the highest sales appear as SUM(SALES.REVENUE). Customers with the highest average order price would use AVG(SALES.ORDER_AMOUNT).

DESC is the sort order for the rank, either DESC for descending or ASC for ascending.

The next report shows how an object built with RANK appears to users. The Amount Sold column is not required in the report but is included to show how RANK works.

Prod Category	Product Name	Amount Sold	Sales Rank
Women	Stamped Knit Skirt Set	3,232,598	1
Women	Leather Boot-Cut Trousers	2,942,222	2
Men	Fagonnable Windowpane Blazer	2,807,726	3
Men	Wiesel Keetar Jean	2,560,431	4
Women	Ukko X-Track High	2,448,324	5
Men	Dr. Mortens 809243	2,398,941	6
Men	Fagonnable Cotton Drawstring Trc	2,360,721	7
Men	Joseph Abboud Microfiber Trousei	2,260,993	8
Men	Kahala Elastic Back Chino	2,188,582	9
Women	Aff Australia Ultra Short	2,001,247	10
Women	Kenny Cool Leather Skirt	1,912,233	11
Women	Four-Piece Cotton Knit Set	1,878,582	12

The SQL for the *Sales Rank* object is

```
RANK() OVER (ORDER BY sum(SH.SALES.AMOUNT_SOLD) DESC)
```

Note that this object did not use the PARTITION BY parameter. So in the preceding report, products are ranked regardless of the product category. The following report shows both the overall ranking and the ranking within a product category:

Men

Product Id	Product Name	Amount Sold	Sales Rank	Sales Rank within Product Category
415	Joseph Abboud Microfiber Trouser	2,273,292	6	1
1,960	Ukko Track High	2,204,930	7	2
4,800	Fagonnable Windowpane Blazer	2,194,745	8	3
930	Andrew D Yahoo Jacket	2,110,218	10	4
730	Fagonnable Windowpane Blazer	2,012,829	11	5

Women

Product Id	Product Name	Amount Sold	Sales Rank	Sales Rank within Product Category
1,805	Cole Huun Ashlyn	2,919,563.5	1	1
1,250	Laundry Slim Skirt	2,714,059.8	2	2
2,185	Laundry Ostrich-Texture Leather Skirt	2,566,398.7	3	3
1,065	Ukko X-Track High	2,339,010	4	4
585	T3 Faux Fur-Trimmed Sweater	2,329,816.5	5	5

If you want to see the rankings within a product category, the SQL would be as follows:

```
RANK() OVER (PARTITION BY SH.PRODUCTS.PROD_CATEGORY ORDER BY
sum(SH.SALES.AMOUNT_SOLD) DESC)
```

NOTE *When you use the* PARTITION BY *option, if your SQL settings are set to generate multiple SQL statements for each measure (File | Parameters | SQL), you will get two* SELECT *statements from the preceding report because both a dimension table and a fact table are involved in the SQL statement. Under normal circumstances, the query engine generates multiple* SELECT *statements only when the measures come from two different fact tables.*

For Web Intelligence users, you no longer need to create specific Ranks objects. See Chapter 19 for more information.

Ratio to Report

Certain calculations require different levels of aggregation. In the past this was very difficult to do in SQL, so many BusinessObjects users would do the calculations in the report. They might create variables using context operators to control the level of calculation, or they might use multiple data providers, with each data provider using a different GROUP BY. You also could use Derived Tables as described earlier, but with much poorer response time than from the built-in database function. The newer reporting functions allow you to provide such measures centrally, thus promoting one version of the truth and better scalability.

To understand how this function works, suppose you were analyzing sales figures for the year 2005. You want to know how much each quarter contributed to the total sales as shown in the following report:

Year	Quarter Number	Amount Sold	Grand Total	Percent of Total
2005	1	73,956,184	269,389,518	27.45%
2005	2	76,974,247	269,389,518	28.57%
2005	3	66,772,321	269,389,518	24.79%
2005	4	51,686,766	269,389,518	19.19%
	Sum:	269,389,518		100.00%

The following SQL will give you a grand total for the entire query:

```
sum(SUM(SH.SALES.AMOUNT_SOLD)) OVER ()
```

The OVER ( ) indicates it should be for the whole report. Note that there are two SUM functions in this statement. If you only use one SUM function, you will get incorrect results, although the object will parse. The additional SUM is working in conjunction with the OVER ( ) function.

With this new *Grand Total* object, you could use the regular *Amount Sold* object to create a *Percent of Total* object such as

```
@Select(Sales\Amount Sold)/@Select(Sales\Grand Total)
```

Alternatively, Oracle has a built-in RATIO_TO_REPORT function so that you do not need to first create a *Grand Total* object.

```
RATIO_TO_REPORT(sum(SH.SALES.AMOUNT_SOLD)) OVER ()
```

Summary

With Designer's internal functions and SQL commands from your RDBMS, you can build powerful objects that make your universe more robust and business-oriented. In this part of the universe design and build process, it's important for SQL-savvy designers to have a close dialog with the business users. Just because a user did not specifically request an object, that doesn't mean users don't need the object; they simply may not realize it's possible and so easy to build. Similarly, just because users can do powerful calculations in reports or more complex authoring in Desktop Intelligence, they shouldn't have to do so for routine and common business questions. Build a robust universe that promotes reusability, one version of the truth, and scalability.

While building advanced objects, you must constantly evaluate the impact on response time and user-friendliness. Certain objects may cause the RDBMS not to use a particular index to process a query. This is fine as long the RDBMS uses some other index. Objects with prompts, objects with built-in time-period intelligence, or objects that use derived tables may be incompatible with other objects and return unexpected query results. As the designer, be aware of these issues and take the necessary precautions to minimize the possibility of users building incorrect queries. As a last resort, ensure users understand when and how to use the objects to ensure accurate query results.

Multidimensional Analysis

If you have designed a logical, business-oriented universe, designers need to do very little to provide users with multidimensional analysis capabilities. Drill capabilities are automatically available to users; there is no need to explicitly build a cube. With robust measures, users can further perform rankings, top 10 queries, and so on.

New in XI Release 2 is the ability to create a universe on top of an OLAP database such as Microsoft Analysis Services, Hyperion Essbase, or SAP B/W. With the synchronized multiple data providers in Web Intelligence, users can create a report that spans both relational data sources and OLAP data sources. OLAP-based universes allow OLAP users to access the full range of Web Intelligence functionality including scheduling, discussions, and formulas.

What Is Multidimensional Analysis?

As discussed in previous chapters, a dimension is often textual or time information by which users analyze numeric measures. Dimensional information may come from a lookup or reference table. Dimensions often have different levels or groupings associated with them called *hierarchies*. Figure 12-1 shows two sample dimensions.

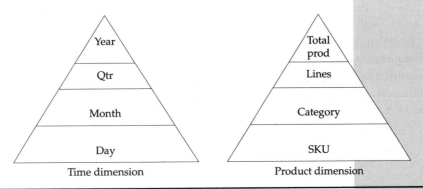

FIGURE 12-1 The time and product dimensions each have four levels that make up a hierarchy.

The levels or hierarchies allow users to analyze data by different groups. Some hierarchies, such as Time, are very clear-cut. As reviewed in the section "Object Ordering" in Chapter 9, time objects typically go from Year to Quarter to Month to Week to Day—a natural order. With multidimensional analysis, users may start by viewing sales for the year and then drill down to see details by quarter or month. Users may choose to further analyze data by another dimension altogether, such as sales by product, or in combination, such as sales by product for a particular month.

Like time dimensions, geographic hierarchies may also have a predetermined order, starting with Continent, Country, State. However, when the geography applies to a marketing region, each company may introduce its own variation. One company may group the Middle East and Africa together; another company may include Mexico as part of North America because it is part of NAFTA. Ideally, all these groupings should be agreed upon during your data warehouse design process and built into the dimension tables. However, as the universe designer, you may find that certain business units may want to view information according to different groupings. When the groupings change, do you provide users with the old grouping or the new grouping or both?

Time Hierarchy

Designer provides you with the capabilities of building a Time hierarchy, even if the upper-level groupings do not exist as columns in the dimension tables. As long as your table has a data column, Designer will create objects to calculate the year, quarter, and month. If, however, you have a Time dimension table in your data warehouse, skip this section; you are better off using physical columns from the dimension table rather than objects that contain SQL functions.

In order for the Time feature to be available, the database column and universe object must be in date format. As an example, use the Island Resorts Marketing universe, *Reservation Date.* (Note: Similar time objects already exist in this universe, so the following example is for instructional purposes only and is not intended to replace the existing time objects.)

1. From Designer, open the universe Beach.unv. Expand the class *Reservations* by clicking + next to the class name.

2. Select the object *Reservation Date* and double-click to bring up the Edit Properties screen.

3. On the Definition tab, ensure that the Object Type is set to Date.

4. On the Properties tab, click Automatic Time Hierarchy.

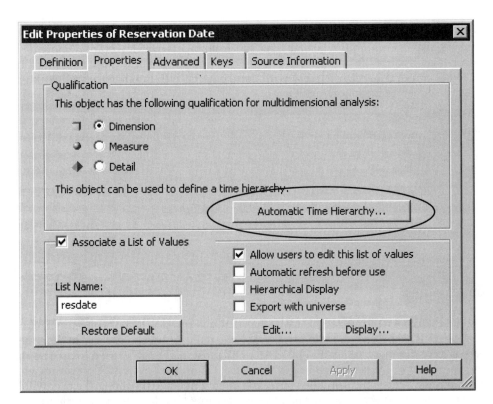

5. Designer presents you with an Automatic Time Hierarchy box, shown next. Click to choose which time levels you would like Designer to create. In the name box, enter

a name for each level. These become the names of the individual dimension objects.

6. Click OK to close the Automatic Time Hierarchy box and OK again to save the Object changes.

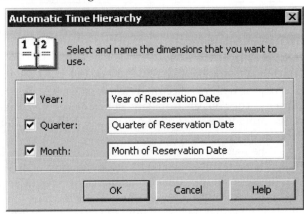

Designer creates the three dimension objects under *Reservation Date.* Once you Save and Export the universe, users can access the objects when building a query.

Limitations with Automatic Time Hierarchy

Chapter 19 discusses multidimensional analysis from the user's viewpoint in more depth; however, it is important for you, as the designer, to understand how these new time objects work. When a user constructs a query with these objects, Web Intelligence and Desktop Intelligence generate the following SQL:

```
SELECT
  DatePart('YYYY', Reservations.res_date),
  DatePart('Q', Reservations.res_date),
  DatePart('M', Reservations.res_date)
FROM
  Reservations
```

Using an Oracle data source, the SQL appears as follows:

```
SELECT
  TO_NUMBER(TO_CHAR(RESERVATIONS.RES_DATE,'YYYY')),
  TO_NUMBER(TO_CHAR(RESERVATIONS.RES_DATE,'Q')),
  TO_NUMBER(TO_CHAR(RESERVATIONS.RES_DATE,'MM'))
FROM
  RESERVATIONS
```

Notice that BusinessObjects XI is using the same advanced SQL that you learned about in Chapter 11. This poses two main problems: First, if a user tries to use one of the time objects as a condition, an index on RES_DATE will most likely not be used to process the query; Second, the SQL generated leaves the objects in numeric format. If a user tries to create a formula or variable using BusinessObjects' internal date functions, the user will first have to convert the object to date format. Designers cannot modify the object properties for these objects.

TIP *My recommendation is to build the Year, Quarter, and Month objects yourself as regular dimension objects.*

Custom Hierarchies

BusinessObjects has two types of hierarchies: *default hierarchies* that are based on the order of the objects within a class, and *custom hierarchies* that you, as the designer, specify. If you have ordered your objects from largest to smallest increments, as discussed in Chapter 9, you have provided users with a reasonable drill path. The benefit of custom hierarchies is that you explicitly control the drill path.

When setting up your custom hierarchies, you also need to consider how to treat code or ID fields. If users will rarely use ID fields and most often will drill on description fields, then leave the ID fields out of custom hierarchies altogether. If, however, your ID fields are meaningful to users, you may want two separate drill hierarchies, one for names and one for IDs. What you don't want is that users drill from *Product Category Name* to *Product Category ID*, for example.

In the following example, you will use the Test Fashion universe (TESTFASH.UNV) created in earlier chapters:

1. From Designer, open the Test Fashion universe.

2. From the pull-down menu, select Tools | Hierarchies or click the Hierarchies button on the toolbar.

3. Designer presents you with the list of classes and objects, as shown next. You will first build the drill path for Article. You can add either individual objects or entire classes. Select the *Article Lookup* class and click Add.

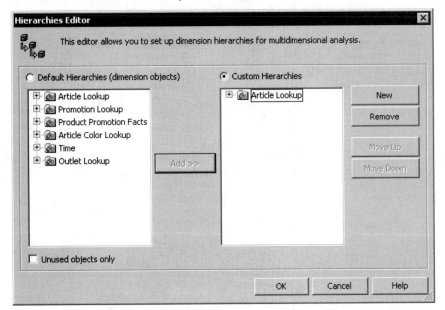

4. Under Custom Hierarchies, expand the *Article Lookup* class. Organize the objects so that they go from *Family Name* at the top to *Category* to *Article Name*. You can use drag and drop or select the objects and use the Move Up button.

5. In the drill path, it does not make sense to drill down from *Family Name* to *Family Code*, as they are at the same level. Therefore, remove *Family Code, Article Code,* and *Sales Price* by selecting each object and clicking Remove. The objects are only removed from the drill path. They still exist as dimension objects for query purposes.

6. Modify the hierarchy name *Article Lookup* to **Article Name** by clicking *Article Lookup* and typing over the name.

So that users do not drill from a name object at one level to a code object at the same level, create two hierarchies, one for name objects and one for code objects.

1. To create a separate hierarchy for the code objects, click New. Enter the hierarchy name **Article Code**.

2. Under Default Hierarchies, select the two objects *Article Code* and *Family Code* and click Add to add them under the new hierarchy, *Article Code*. You may CTRL-click to select noncontiguous objects.

3. The custom hierarchies should appear as follows:

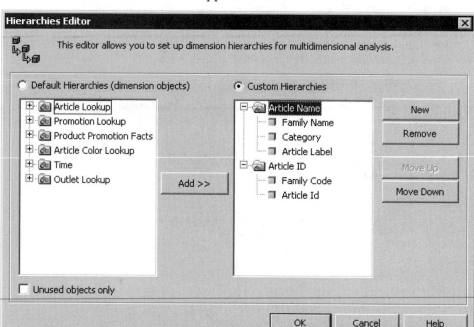

You can organize the hierarchies in any way that makes business sense. You may choose to follow agreed-upon corporate levels or incorporate groupings that are specific to various business units. For example, perhaps some business units want the drill path to be *Family* ⇒ *Category* ⇒ *Color* ⇒ *Article Name* ⇒ *Article Code*. It's perfectly reasonable for you, as the designer, to provide multiple drill paths. Users can also create the custom hierarchies per report. Therefore, you will want to reserve universe custom hierarchies for groupings that meet a broad set of users needs.

CAUTION *Once you begin using custom hierarchies, you must continue to use them for all dimension objects by which users will want to drill; otherwise, they will not be available for multidimensional analysis. For example, in the preceding example, a Time hierarchy has not yet been defined. When users begin drilling, the article objects will be drillable but the time objects will not, until you create a custom hierarchy.*

OLAP Universes

Within a BI deployment, OLAP databases provide a way of aggregating data to provide speed of thought analysis and complex, multidimensional calculations. Universes based on data residing in an OLAP database are new in XI Release 2. With an OLAP universe, users can use Web Intelligence or Desktop Intelligence to create formatted reports for information residing in a multidimensional database. They can also drill around, using the same analysis capabilities as those available to a relational data source. Business Objects also provides a separate interface, OLAP Intelligence, for more sophisticated member selection and server-based rankings. Another key benefit of an OLAP universe is that users can create one document that accesses multiple data sources and synchronize the data providers to create calculations that span relational and OLAP databases. For example, a user could have a sales query accessing an OLAP database and an inventory query accessing a relational database. As long as the product dimensions are similar in the two data sources, the user could calculate Days Sales Inventory by product.

To create an OLAP universe, you use an OLAP database in the universe connection parameters. The following example uses the Microsoft Analysis Services Foodmart database:

1. From within Designer, select File | New from the pull-down menus.

2. When prompted for the universe parameters, provide a name for the universe, **Foodmart**.

3. In the connection box, select New to create a new connection to the OLAP data source. This launches the Connection Wizard. Click Next.

4. Under Database Middleware Selection, expand the Microsoft folder by clicking +. Choose MS Analysis Services 2000 and then OLE DB for OLAP. Click Next.

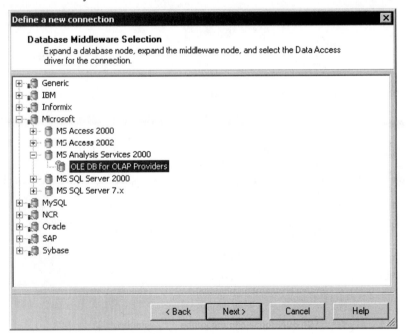

5. For login parameters, leave the default connection type as secure. Give the connection a name, **Foodmart**. Enter the user name and password for the OLAP database. Enter the server name on which the OLAP database is running. You can enter the name of the cube or click Next to select from a list of available cubes. Highlight the desired cube and click Next.

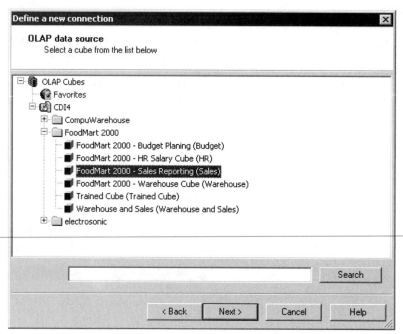

6. When prompted, test your connection.

7. Accept the default parameters and click Finish to finish creating the OLAP connection.

8. Designer returns you to the Universe Parameters dialog. Click OK to close this dialog. Designer displays the metadata from the cube as universe classes and objects. Note that the structure pane that normally would show the joins between the tables is empty.

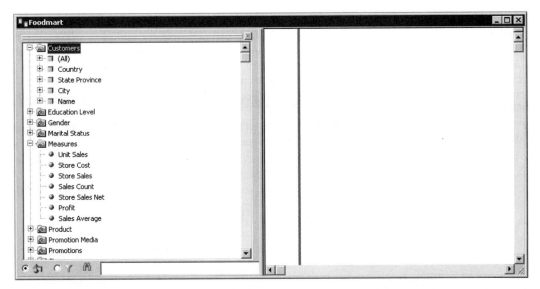

9. Choose File | Save and then File | Export to save your changes and export the new universe to the repository.

The screen to the right shows how the same information would appear within SQL Server Analysis Services Cube Editor. Within Designer and Web Intelligence, Analysis Services dimensions are displayed as universe classes, with members as the objects. Designer creates an object (All) within each class that allows users to retrieve the totals for all members within the class.

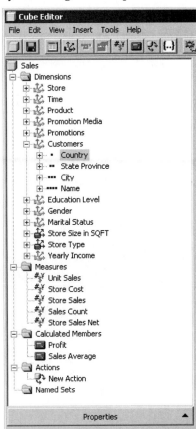

Summary

For standard multidimensional analysis within relational data sources, designers should create custom hierarchies that determine the users' drill path. These hierarchies should ideally separate code or ID objects from description objects. If you do not create these custom hierarchies, then the sort order of the objects within each class is used as the default drill path.

If you have data in an OLAP database, BusinessObjects XI now provides the ability to build a universe that accesses an OLAP data source.

Securing the System

I can only chuckle at the poetic justice of Chapter 13, unlucky 13, being dedicated to security. As readers of the last book and of some of my *Intelligent Enterprise* articles may know, security is one of my least favorite topics. It's not that I don't find security necessary; it is! But from a business perspective, I am discouraged when overly secure systems are barriers to business users leveraging BI successfully. Further dampening my enthusiasm is that security in XI has gotten ever more complex and involves a steeper learning curve than other aspects of the suite. The good news, however, is that security in BusinessObjects XI provides much of what many customers have long awaited: better integration with external authentication systems, web-based administration, and permissions granted per universe and more!

Security is a complex topic and requires that policies and procedures be firmly established yet flexible enough to accommodate a business' changing requirements. As you approach this chapter, then, don't dive in hoping to start clicking away. Instead, I recommend you first familiarize yourself with how security works in BusinessObjects XI and then develop a security approach that meets your company's needs. Given the complexity of this topic, I have specifically chosen to use simple scenarios throughout this chapter, rather than reflecting complex implementations.

The Enterprise Environment: What Needs Securing

Figure 13-1 provides an overview of a BusinessObjects Enterprise environment and the different phases of security. *Authentication* is the first phase. Authentication relates to user IDs and passwords—how BusinessObjects Enterprise recognizes you.

Authorization, the second phase of security, relates to what you are allowed to access and do once you have been authenticated. In order to make the process of maintaining authorization simpler, you may use groups.

This chapter is loosely organized according to the workflow in Figure 13-1. You will first define users and groups. Then you want to grant access to users and groups to be able to access reports contained in folders. Access to universes and their connections allows users to refresh the reports. You can further restrict access at the data source, limiting the number of rows returned or the dimensional values retrieved from the database.

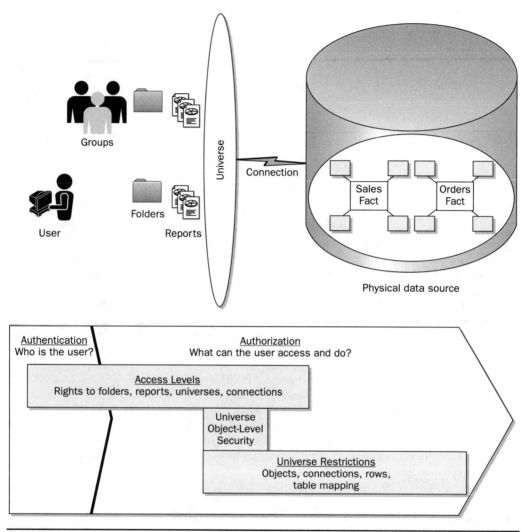

FIGURE 13-1   Security aspects of BusinessObjects Enterprise

Introducing the Central Management Console

In BusinessObjects 6 and earlier, security was handled through the Supervisor module, a client/server application. With BusinessObjects XI, security is predominately handled through the Central Management Console (CMC), a web-based application that allows for control of users and repository objects, as well as servers.

NOTE *Throughout this chapter, the term objects refers to BI content stored in the repository, not a universe object, as discussed in Chapter 9. A repository object could be a user, a group, a report, a folder, and so on.*

To access the CMC, do the following:

1. From the Windows menu, select BusinessObjects XI Release 2 | BusinessObjects Enterprise | BusinessObjects Enterprise Administration Launchpad | Central Management Console or enter the appropriate URL within a browser: **http:// BOEServer/businessobjects/enterprise115/admin/en/admin.cwr** where *BOEServer* is the name of your BusinessObjects Enterprise server.

2. You will be prompted to enter a user ID and password. During an initial installation, a generic ID of Administrator is automatically created with no password.

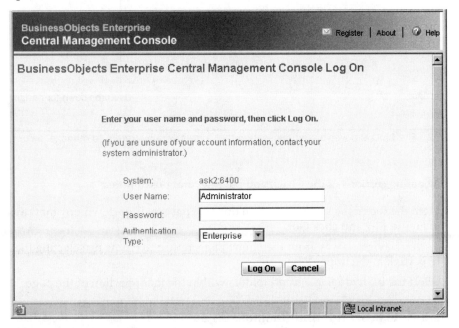

3. The default authentication type is Enterprise. Click Log On to continue. BusinessObjects presents you with the main console as shown in Figure 13-2.

As shown in Figure 13-2 within the CMC, administrators control access to reports and universes, calendars for scheduling reports (see Chapter 16), and server settings. In this chapter, you will be working primarily with the items in the Organize box. Other server settings are assumed to have been configured during installation.

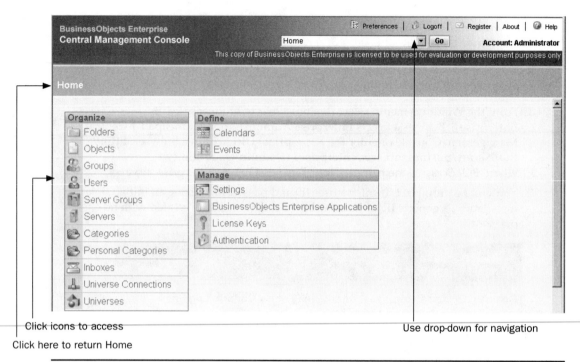

Click icons to access

Click here to return Home

Use drop-down for navigation

FIGURE 13-2 The CMC is a web-based application that allows administrators to manage security and servers.

In navigating sections of the CMC, you have several possibilities:

- From the top of the screen, select an option from the drop-down box that says Home in Figure 13-2 and click Go.
- As you navigate away from the Home page, return to Home by selecting the Home hyperlink in the upper-left corner.
- Select the individual icons and folders within the main portion of the page.

Transition Notes: Crystal and BusinessObjects

If you have upgraded from an earlier version of BusinessObjects, it's helpful to understand some background to former Crystal Enterprise's approach to security. If you have a Crystal Enterprise administrator within your organization, work together to develop an integrated security approach going forward.

Before version 10, Crystal Enterprise lacked a metadata layer, so administrators would grant users or groups access to folders or individual reports. This is a vastly different approach than BusinessObjects 6 and earlier, where many organizations organized access by universe. In Supervisor, administrators could control access to individual reports, but in reality, the universe was typically the primary level of security.

With Supervisor, BusinessObjects administrators would use command sets to control software capability for groups of users. For example, you may have a group of Report Readers who would have the ability only to refresh reports, not to author them. These users would not even see the menu options to create a new document. An often-cited limitation, though, with BusinessObjects 6 and earlier is that these command restrictions were global when customers wanted them to be universe-specific: for example, user Sam should be able to author reports for supply chain universes but only refresh reports for finance universes. With BusinessObjects XI, you now can control permissions specific to individual documents and universes.

BusinessObjects 6 and Crystal 10 also differed in how individual reports were organized. BusinessObjects used the concept of categories, allowing reports to be assigned to more than one category. Categories were strictly for organization purposes, not security. All shared documents were exported to one "folder" in version 6, Corporate Documents. Crystal, meanwhile, used folders and allowed subfolders; one report could belong to only one folder. Security was applied at the folder or individual report level. With BusinessObjects XI, you can use either approach or a combination of the two. Categories provide more flexibility, as items can be "cross-referenced," but when you add security to the mix, there is potential for confusion.

Row-level security and table mappings that are universe specific have remained relatively unchanged in XI. The main difference is that these commands are now defined within Designer and not within CMC, which has replaced most of the former Supervisor capabilities.

Object-level security (Private, Controlled, Restricted, Confidential, Public) that enabled only certain users to see individual columns within a universe is managed through membership of groups. As in earlier versions of BusinessObjects, these groups are not universe specific, however. Thus, if a user has access to Private objects in, say, the HR universe, that user also will have access to Private objects in the Sales universe (assuming the same user has access to both universes).

Finally, in BusinessObjects 6 and earlier, you often viewed security starting with the group or user. You might say, "Which universes and objects can Mary access?" With XI Release 2, you always view access by the content in question. For example, "Who can access the Marketing folder?"

The following table summarizes some of the old and new terminology:

BusinessObjects 6 Concept	BusinessObjects Enterprise XI Concept
Supervisor	Central Management Console plus Designer Security settings
Corporate documents	Folders
Categories	For cross-filing and searching but also security
Resources such as universes, documents, stored procedures	Objects
Command restrictions	Access levels and rights
Object-level security (Private, Controlled, Restricted, Confidential, Public)	Granted by adding users to groups

Given these differences, when discussing migration issues, the vendor seems to prefer that security from a BusinessObjects version 5 or 6 deployment is not migrated to XI. In reality, though, what you migrate depends entirely on the complexity of your existing security model. Migrating users and groups is very straightforward. Migrating complex permissions with extensive enabling/disabling is best redesigned through the use of folders.

Authentication

As the number of IT systems have expanded within organizations, users have been overwhelmed with multiple user IDs and passwords, different for the local area network, the ERP system, the data warehouse, and BusinessObjects. To address this issue, companies are increasingly trying to move to one central authentication system that the different applications rely upon. If your company has a directory server (such as Microsoft Active Directory, Sun ONE, or Novell eDirectory) or uses NT for networking, that same user ID and password can be used to log in to the BusinessObjects Enterprise suite.

In discussing this with customers, I often hear concerns, though, that the BusinessObjects Enterprise administrator does not want to rely on an NT administrator to grant access to corporate data. Clearly, there are a number of policy and organization issues that need addressing before you can leverage these capabilities. However, it's important to realize that we are only talking about externalizing the *authentication*. Access to data, reports, and universes continues to be controlled within the BusinessObjects XI environment even when authentication is centralized with network administrators or other security groups.

Enterprise Authentication

If your company does not have a centralized system for assigning user IDs and passwords, then you can use the built-in security with BusinessObjects Enterprise, referred to as Enterprise authentication. With this type of deployment, you assign user IDs and passwords that are internally maintained with the CMS repository. You also specify how secure the authentication should be in terms of password length, frequency to change passwords, and so on.

Before defining users, you should first set the desired restrictions:

1. From the main CMC page, select Authentication from within the Manage section of the Home page.

2. CMC presents you with a dialog of authentication approaches. Enterprise is the first dialog.

3. Table 13-1 describes each of the listed security settings. Change the settings as appropriate and click Update.

4. At the top of the page, click Home to return to the main CMC page.

NOTE *The restrictions in Table 13-1 are valid only for Enterprise user IDs and passwords. They do not affect external user IDs and passwords.*

Restriction Type	Option	Explanation
Password	Enforce mixed-case passwords	When this box is checked, users must use upper- and lowercase letters in the password. For example, "password" would not be accepted, but "Password" would be valid.
	Must contain at least N Characters	Specifies the minimum password length.
User	Must change password every N day(s)	Forces users to change their password every 90 days
	Cannot reuse the N most recent password(s)	It's hard for users to remember passwords, and when they like to use names of spouses, siblings, children's names, and so on, they often reuse them. Don't set this number too high; otherwise, users simply won't be able to log in.
	Must wait N minute(s) to change password	Determines how frequently a user can change his or her password.
Logon	Disable account after N failed attempts to logon	If the user specifies an incorrect password more than three times, the account is disabled and an administrator must manually re-enable it, or the user can try again after so many minutes.
	Reset failed log on count after N minute(s)	How long the system keeps track of the incorrect password attempts before setting it back to 0.
	Re-enable account after N minute(s)	When a user specifies an incorrect password, the account is locked for up to 100 minutes. If you don't want the account to be automatically re-enabled, set this value to 0.

TABLE 13-1   Default Restrictions for Passwords and User IDs

Adding a User

Once you have set the global restrictions for Enterprise authentication, you can begin adding users.

1. From the Home page of the CMC, select Users.
2. You are presented with a list of users. If you are working with a new installation, the installation procedure automatically creates the users Administrator and Guest.

3. In the top-right corner, click New User.

4. From the Authentication Type drop-down, leave the default type as Enterprise.

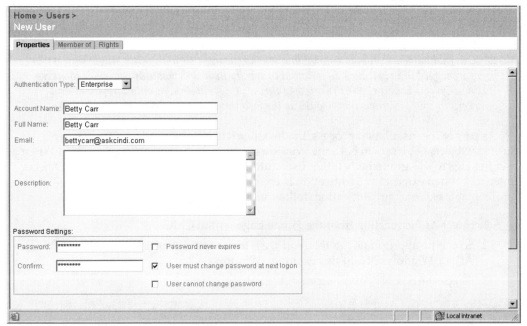

5. In the Account Name box, enter a login ID. In some organizations, this may be a numeric employee identification. This is the only required field to create a new user.

6. In the Full Name box, optionally enter a description for the login ID.

7. The Email address is used for scheduling reports to be automatically delivered via e-mail.

8. Description is optional.

9. Under Password settings, provide the user with a default password, or you may leave the password box blank and check the box to ensure the user enters a password on the first login.

10. Click OK to create the user.

The CMC will display the newly created user with the alias name. Because BusinessObjects Enterprise supports authentication against multiple directories, it uses aliases to map one BusinessObjects Enteprise user to different user IDs in other directories. In the preceding example, the user ID Betty Carr is given the same alias name.

PART II

External Authentication with Windows NT

External authentication allows companies to centrally maintain user IDs and passwords. As employees leave the company, their access can be centrally removed, preventing security breaches.

NOTE *External authentication is not synonymous with single sign-on. With single sign-on, once users are logged in to NT, they do not need to specify their user name or password to access BusinessObjects Enterprise. At the time of this writing, single sign-on is supported under only certain configurations that use IIS as the web server and BusinessObjects ASP.*

As part of the installation process, the installer will automatically create a group BusinessObjects NT Users in both the Windows Server environment and the CMC. When a user belongs to this group on NT, that user automatically gains access to BusinessObjects Enterprise when external authentication is enabled.

To enable external authentication, follow these steps:

1. Select Authentication from the Home page within CMC.

2. Select the appropriate tab that you wish to use for authentication: LDAP, Windows AD, or Windows NT. In this example, Windows NT.

3. Check the box NT Authentication Is Enabled.

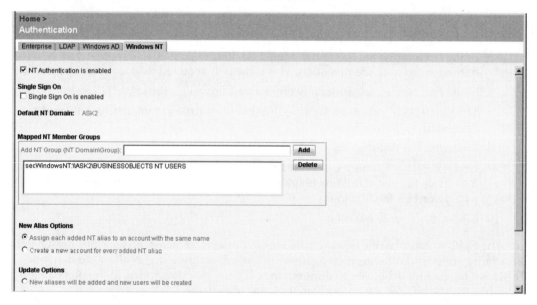

4. If necessary, enter the Windows groups that you wish to map to BusinessObjects Enterprise and click Add.

5. Click Update to enabled external authentication.

For each NT user that is added to the group mapped in Step 4, an alias is created within BusinessObjects Enterprise. The alias is either created automatically when the user is added to the BusinessObjects NT Users group on the Windows Server or when the user first tries to log in to InfoView. You control this by setting one of the following update options:

- **New aliases will be added and new users will be created**   Ideally, the text for this option should be modified slightly to say "... automatically within BusinessObjects Enterprise when they are added to the NT group." Use this setting with caution if your server uses a named-user license.

- **No new aliases will be added and new users will not be created**   Ideally, the text for this should be rephrased "... until users explicitly access InfoView."

With either option, user aliases are automatically created. The difference is in when they are created.

NOTE *When an account has been disabled within Windows Server, the user cannot log in to BusinessObjects Enterprise. The disabled status is unfortunately not reflected within the CMC. Also, if a user has been explicitly deleted from the Windows Server, the user alias remains in the CMC but the user cannot log in. To remove the user alias from the CMC, go to Authentication, Windows NT, and then click Update.*

Defining Groups

In a Windows environment, BusinessObjects Enterprise comes with three initial groups:

- Administrators, who can add users and control access to individual objects and folders
- Everyone, to which all users are automatically added and whose rights by default allow users to view reports in all public folders
- BusinessObjects NT Users, to which users with external authentication in Windows Server are added

You will most often want to grant access to groups at the folder and universe levels and specify exceptions only at the individual user level. Users can belong to more than one group, and new in BusinessObjects XI is the ability to give them more capabilities in one group and less in another.

To create a group, follow these steps:

 1. From the Home page of the CMC, select Groups.

2. You are presented with a list of the default groups or groups imported from a previous implementation.

3. Click the New Group button.

4. Enter a Group Name. In the following example, **Finance**.

5. Enter an optional description.

6. Click OK to create the group.

Once the group is created, you can add members to the group or create subgroups (for example, accounts payable and accounts receivable). You will want to define permissions for the group when you have exported universes and created folders.

Planning for Authorization

Defining users and groups is the easy part of security. Controlling access to the BI content is more complex and demands careful planning. Before you begin the task of defining users, folders, and groups, first consider

- How the company is organized; if you are using external authentication, you may be able to leverage groups defined in an external authentication system.
- How you want to organize reports in a way that facilitates decision-making and minimizes duplicate analyses and report creation.
- How tightly do you want to control access to BusinessObjects content.

This section first discusses concepts within CMC and then provides step-by-step instructions to implement the concepts.

Understanding Your Company's Organization

Table 13-2 provides a simple scenario in which members from different groups can access content created by other groups. This table is not exhaustive of all the functional groups you may have in your organization. I have specifically kept it simple to minimize confusion.

- **Finance Group**   Members of this group can access all reports contained within the Finance folder. There is a subfolder, \Finance\Internal, that everyone in the Finance group can save documents to. Documents in the top Finance folder are accessible to everyone else in the company and can be refreshed but not modified. Jami, as the Finance Director, is the only person who can modify reports in this top folder.

- **Marketing Group**   Members of this group can access, refresh, and create new reports in the Marketing folder. Megan, as the VP of the department, can also add new users to the Marketing Group.

- **Sam**   Sam is the Supply Chain Manager and occasionally may want to view some marketing and sales reports to understand order issues. He does not need to save reports to the marketing folder, so he won't be a member of the Marketing group. Also, no other members of the Supply Chain group need this access, so permission should be granted to the individual rather than to a group.

Access Levels

BusinessObjects Enterprise provides several initial access levels, starting with the most restrictive and progressing to the most permissive rights. Crystal administrators and vendor documentation will often refer to rights as they relate to "objects." These objects, however, are not universe objects (dimensions and measures), but rather collectively refer to any content, including folders, categories, reports, or spreadsheets. Table 13-3 describes the predefined access levels.

NOTE   *This is where BusinessObjects 6 and XI differ the most: access levels in XI are content-specific, whereas in version 6, command restrictions were global. A report reader in version 6 could never be a report author for specific universes. In XI, you can grant a user the permission to be a report reader in the Finance group, for example, yet a report author in the Supply Chain group.*

Employee	Role	Groups			Plus Individual Access
		Everyone	**Finance**	**Marketing**	
Jami	Finance Director	√	√		Full Control to the top folder \Finance
Betty	Manager Accounts Payable	√	√		
Megan	VP Marketing	√		√	
Sam	Supply Chain Manager	√			Can view marketing content explicitly but can't modify reports or publish new ones. Has full control over the Orders folder.

TABLE 13-2   Define Groups Within CMC That Match Your Company's Organization

Access Level	Rights
No Access	You would think this means that the user does not see the folder, report, or universe, but in reality, this access level sets all permissions to "Not Specified," which results in very different behavior when permission is granted elsewhere: the grant will take priority over the not specified. If you really want to remove access to something, do not use "No Access." Instead, use Advanced and explicitly deny the access.
View	The user can see the folder, report, or universe. If the report contains data, the user can open the report and interact with it. If the report does not contain data, the user cannot refresh the report. By default, the user can edit the report and save to a personal folder and refresh it there. You can explicitly prevent users from copying corporate documents to personal folders by setting an individual right that denies "Copy Objects to another folder."
Schedule	A user can schedule a report but cannot refresh it in real time.
View On Demand	A user can refresh a report in real time. When the report is a Web Intelligence document, the user also needs View On Demand access to the universe and universe connection to perform the refresh.
Full Control	A user can create new reports within a folder, modify existing reports, or delete items.
Advanced	When the preceding access levels do not meet your needs, you can provide more granular access by choosing advanced.

TABLE 13-3   Access Levels Are Granted to Groups and Individual Users

BusinessObjects Enterprise uses the concept of inheritance so that users inherit access by belonging to different groups. Alternatively, you may explicitly assign more permissive access or more restrictive access to a particular user or group and for a particular folder, category, or report.

NOTE *Explicit rights override inherited rights.*

CAUTION *The No Access level does not explicitly deny access, but rather, sets all permissions to "Not Specified." So only when this is the only access level inherited will access be denied.*

Use the following formulas as a guide to understand what happens when inheritance from multiple groups overlap:

Grant + Deny + Not Specified = Deny

Grant + Not Specified = Grant

Grant + Deny = Deny

Not Specified = Denied

To use the example from the first formula, if a user belongs to two groups and permission is granted in one and denied in another, then access to the repository object will be granted. However, explicit rights always prevail. So if the user has explicit permission to modify the object, then the inherited permission to deny this right is overridden by the explicit right to modify it. When in doubt, preview the final status as described in the later section "Checking Rights" and shown in Figure 13-3.

Folders and Categories

Folders and categories provide a way of organizing documents and BI content. *Folders* provide the physical storage location of a file as well as a means to navigate content. *Categories* provide navigation only. A file must be stored in a folder; it does not have to be assigned a category.

A *group* is a way of grouping users and granting access to folders or individual reports within folders. Groups will often be associated with particular folders. Thus, you may have a Finance group that has access to documents in a Finance folder. The Finance group may have subgroups such as accounts payable and accounts receivable that can edit individual reports within the Finance folder. At what point you create additional folders is dependent upon the number of reports you have and how easy it is to maintain permissions to individual reports versus folders. Because folders, categories, and groups are all interrelated, it's helpful to first plan how you want to organize documents and how you want to group users to maintain permissions before you begin the task of physically defining them.

BusinessObjects 6 did not use the concept of folders to organize documents. Instead, it used domains and categories. Many companies would have one document domain, or they may have established separate document domains based on geographic or organizational structure. Categories provide an additional means to organize. A key feature of categories is that one document can be assigned to multiple categories, a significant difference from folders, in which a document can reside in only one folder. With BusinessObjects Enterprise XI, you can use folders, categories, or a combination of the two. Permissions can be applied to folders, categories, and individual files. Users navigate within the InfoView portal using either folders or categories.

Folders and categories each have their merits, and I suspect that different administrators will be most comfortable with whatever approach they've used in the past. Folders are required; categories are optional—so you should provide a modest degree of folder structure before users can begin sharing content. I will say, though, that when you use a combination of categories and folders and grant different permissions to each, there is potential for confusion. Therefore, I recommend using categories only for navigation purposes, not security.

When you create a new folder, two sets of permissions are automatically assigned:

- Administrators are given the access level Full Control.
- Everyone is given the access level Schedule.

CAUTION *By default, when you create a new folder, members of the group Everyone are assigned an access level of Schedule, thus enabling all users to view, open, and schedule any reports saved in the new folder. For many companies, this default access level may be too permissive. In such a circumstance, whenever you create a new folder, be sure to explicitly set the access level for the group Everyone to No Access for the newly created folder. However, when you set the permission to No Access, members of the group Everyone will not even see that the folder exists, so you need to be careful that you will not later want to grant access to a report or subfolder at a lower level.*

Group	Folder	Access Level	Comments
Everyone	Top Level	View	Users can view all folders and reports and schedule them to run.
	\Finance	View On Demand	Users can view and refresh all reports in this folder. They cannot make changes to the reports. Jami, as the Finance Director, is the only individual who can save reports to this folder.
Finance	\Finance\Internal	Full Control	Members of the finance group can freely publish and modify content within this folder; other groups cannot see this content.
Marketing	\Marketing	Full Control	Members of the marketing group can freely publish and modify content within this folder. Other groups do not see this content.
	\Orders	View On Demand	Members of the marketing group can see reports and refresh reports within the Orders folder, but they can't save content or publish new reports. Only the individual user Sam, Supply Chain Manager, can save content to this folder.

TABLE 13-4 Use Folders or Categories to Organize BI Content and Grant Access

Table 13-4 provides some sample folders that an Administrator could define to allow the users and groups in Table 13-3 to share content.

NOTE *The Access levels you grant to a user also affect what options appear to a user from within InfoView. If the user does not have View OnDemand, for example, the user's toolbar will lack the menu option, Refresh Data.*

Creating Folders and Categories

To create the Marketing Folder, do the following:

📁 Folders   1. From the Home page of the Central Management Console, select Folders.

2. Click the New Folder button in the top right of the page.

3. In the Folder Name box, enter the name **Marketing**.

```
Home > Folders >
New Folder

 Properties │ Objects │ Subfolders │ Limits │ Rights

Folder Name: Marketing
Description:  Documents in this folder contain sales reports,
             price analysis, customer lists.



Keywords:
Folder Path:
                                              OK    Cancel
```

4. In the Description box, enter an optional description that users see when they navigate folders from within InfoView.

5. Click OK. The CMC does not give you a confirmation that the folder was created. However, the OK button changes to an Update button and the New Folder hyperlink at the top of the page changes to the name of the newly created folder.

You follow a similar process to create categories but select Categories from the CMC Home page (refer back to Figure 13-2).

Controlling Access to Folders

By default, the group Everyone is granted Schedule access to the Marketing folder. According to the notes in Tables 13-3 and 13-4, you want only Marketing users to be able to access and save content to this folder; users from other groups should not be able to see reports in this folder.

To change the access for the group Everyone, do the following:

1. Click the Rights tab from the page Home > Folders > Marketing. The Access Level column indicates if a group or user's rights have been explicitly defined for this

folder or if they have been inherited. In this case, the group Everyone inherited the Schedule access level from the top folder.

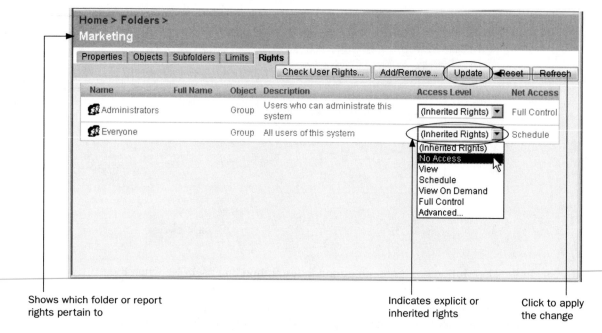

Shows which folder or report rights pertain to

Indicates explicit or inherited rights

Click to apply the change

2. Next to the group Everyone, go to the drop-down box under Access Level. Select No Access.

3. Click Update to apply the change.

4. Under the Net Access column, the previous access level of Schedule will change to No Access. From this same page, you now want to grant Full Control to the Marketing group so that they can freely update reports and save content to this folder.

5. Select Add/Remove.

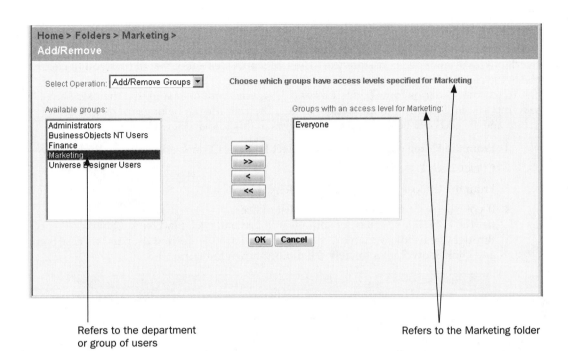

Refers to the department
or group of users

Refers to the Marketing folder

6. From the list of available groups, select the Marketing group.

7. Click the > button to add this to the list of groups with an explicit access level.

8. Click OK.

9. From the Access Level drop-down box for the Marketing group, change the access level from the default of Schedule to Full Control.

10. Click Update.

11. Your Rights should now appear as follows:

Name	Full Name	Object	Description	Access Level	Net Access
Administrators		Group	Users who can administrate this system	(Inherited Rights)	Full Control
Everyone		Group	All users of this system	No Access	No Access
Marketing		Group		Full Control	Full Control

If you want to grant access by categories, you follow a similar process.

Checking Rights

With users belonging to different groups and with inherited and explicit access, rights may overlap with unintended consequences. The CMC provides a tool that allows you to clearly check the rights for groups and individual users.

To use the scenarios from Tables 13-3 and 13-4, you want to ensure that the user Sam can save reports (Full Control) to the Orders folder. The user Megan belongs to the Marketing group and should only be able to refresh reports in this folder (View On Demand).

1. From the Home page of the CMC, select Folders, Orders, and then the Rights tab.

2. Click Check User Rights.

3. From the Choose From drop-down, select Users.

4. If your deployment contains a large list of users, use the Look For box to enter some search text and click Find Now. Otherwise, scroll through the list of Available Users until you reach the desired user, in this case Sam, and click Show Rights to view the dialog shown in Figure 13-3.

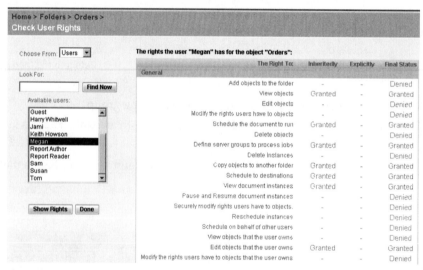

As shown in Figure 13-3, Check User Rights allows you to see the individual capabilities that are given within the access levels. The table is broken into multiple section parts:

- **General** permissions that relate to any BI content, including Excel documents the user may upload or that apply to Crystal Reports, Web Intelligence, and OLAP Intelligence documents

- **Desktop Intelligence Addin** for VBA

- **Desktop Intelligence Document** permissions that relate to this document type

- **Desktop Intelligence Template** for Desktop Intelligence templates

- **Report**, which relates to Crystal Report specific permissions

- **Text**, which provides access to BusinessObjects XI collaboration capabilities

- **Web Intelligence**, which relates to the ability to refresh a document, see the SQL, or export the data for Web Intelligence documents

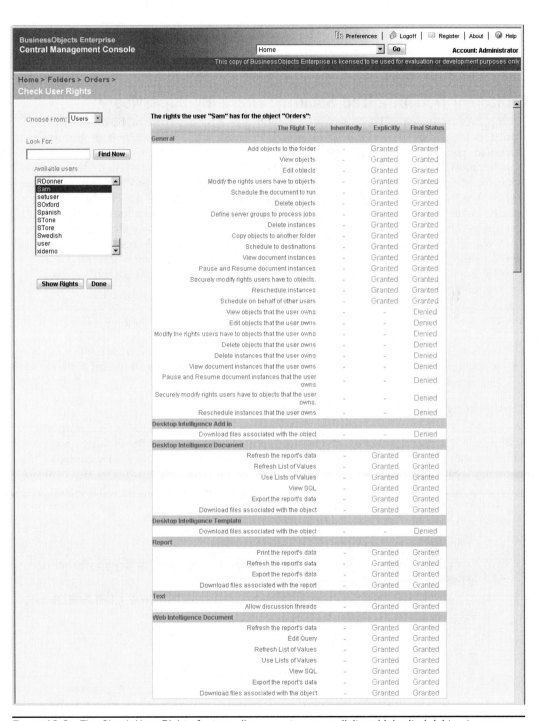

FIGURE 13-3 The Check User Rights feature allows you to see explicit and inherited rights at a more granular level than access levels.

NOTE *Default rights to all modules within BusinessObjects XI are set in the CMC by selecting Manage, BusinessObjects Enterprise Applications, and modifying rights assigned to the group Everyone for each application.*

Centralized or Decentralized Security: Who's My Supervisor?

Companies either centralize IT access or decentralize it by department, business unit, or function. Increasingly, user *authentication* is centralized, while *authorization,* or granting access to specific BI content, is decentralized.

BusinessObjects 6 and earlier used a profile of Supervisor to allow you to decentralize security, either for authentication or authorization. The Supervisor profile per se no longer exists in XI; however, the capabilities to decentralize administration do. For the sake of clarity, I will continue to use the term Supervisor. If you wish to allow individual work groups to control access to their BI content (which in my opinion, they should be able to), then you need to designate Supervisors. You must also determine if these Supervisors should also be able to reset passwords or create new users. The desire to grant these capabilities is highly dependent upon whether you are using external authentication or internal Enterprise authentication.

NOTE *In earlier versions of BusinessObjects, a Supervisor could add existing users to a group; in BusinessObjects XI, you must explicitly decide if such administrators should be able to change rights only for users they've added to the system or for any user defined in the CMC. I would recommend the latter approach. Also, in BusinessObjects XI, all users are created at the top level and cannot be created just within a group.*

Designating a Supervisor for a Group

As described in Table 13-2, Jami is the Finance Director. As the director of the group, she will decide who is a member of the Finance group. Adding users to the Finance group is the simplest way to ensure that all users in Finance will have access to necessary content. This content may include access to documents in the \Finance folder (which Jami also controls as described in Table 13-4), to relevant universes, or to folders owned by other departments.

To allow Jami to add users to this group, you will grant the user Jami the access level of Full Control to the group Finance (different from the folder Finance).

1. From the Home page of the CMC, select Groups.
2. From the list of Available Groups, click the name of group for whom you wish to designate a supervisor, and then select the Rights tab.
3. By default, you will see the Groups Administrators and Everyone. Click Add/Remove.
4. From the Select Operation drop-down, choose Add Users.

5. Highlight the user whom you wish to designate as a Supervisor and click the > button. In this example, Jami.

6. Click OK.

7. At this point you have simply added the user, Jami, for specific access to the Finance group of users. However, you have not said what additional rights Jami should have. Under the Access Level drop-down next to Jami, set the level to Full Control.

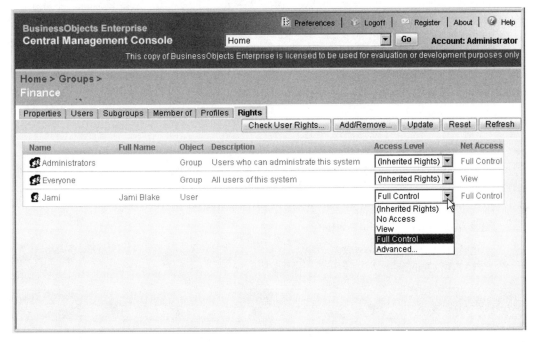

8. Click Update.

Allowing Supervisors to Add Users

Right now, Jami can add users to the Finance group only if she also creates the user. In many cases, you will want Supervisors to be able to grant access to existing users. In order to facilitate this, I suggest creating a group of users called Supervisors who have the ability to create users.

Recall from the earlier section "Transition Notes: Crystal and BusinessObjects" that you grant access according to the resource in question, not according to the user to whom you want to grant the access. The resource is All Users, and you want to allow Jami, as a member of the Supervisor group, to create new users (which are called objects in the rights screens).

To more easily control which people can create user IDs, create a group of Supervisors that have these specific rights.

1. Create a group called Supervisors: From the main CMC, select Groups, New Group, and enter the name **Supervisors**. Click OK.

2. Add Jami as a member of this group: From within the Groups, Supervisors page, select Users, Add Users, Jami, the > button, and OK.

To give the group Supervisors the right to create user IDs and set passwords:

1. From the main CMC, click Users.

2. Ensure that the page navigation says All Users and click Rights.

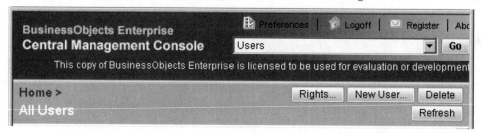

3. Click Add/Remove.

4. Under Available Groups, scroll to the Supervisors group and click >.

5. Click OK so that they appear under Home > Users > Rights. From the Access Level drop-down, change the default View to Advanced.

6. Under Explicitly Granted, click the following Rights:

   - Add Objects to the Folder
   - Change User Password
   - Edit Objects

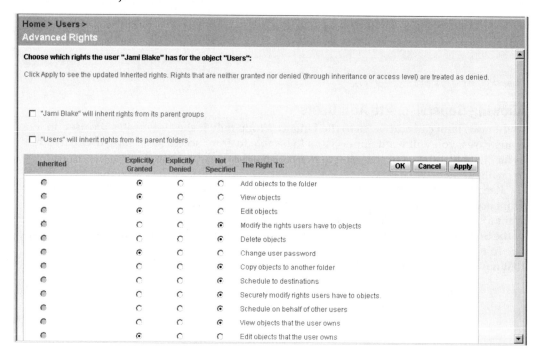

7. Click OK to update the rights.

8. Click Update to save the changes to the Advanced Rights.

The user Jami will now be able to create user IDs and reset passwords. She can add users to the group Finance, as Jami was granted Full Control to the Finance user group.

NOTE *Remember that creating the user IDs and granting access to folders are two different tasks. Supervisors will be able to add users to only those groups for which they have Full Control, and thus can grant access only to the folders that the relevant user groups access.*

Granting Access to Universes

So far, you've given users the ability to log in to InfoView, access content stored in folders, and in some cases, save content to these folders. This is the front portion of Figure 13-1. The question now, then, is where is this BI content coming from? Some of the content may be from Excel spreadsheets that get saved to the repository. If the content is from Web Intelligence or Desktop Intelligence documents, the users cannot *yet* refresh the data even if they have the right "Refresh the report's data." In order for users to be able to refresh reports or create new reports, they must also have access to a universe and a universe connection.

If you want users to be able to refresh reports at any time, assign the access level View On Demand to both the universe and the universe connection. Otherwise, users may only be able to:

- Create a query with no data (with the View access level).
- Schedule a query (with the Schedule access level).

Further, if you grant access to the universe and forget to include the universe connection, then users may successfully build a query and then try to execute the query, only to eventually receive an error message.

As with documents, you can choose to organize universes into folders and grant access to groups at the folder level. In particular, I would recommend having Test and Development folders for universes that only developers or pilot users can access (unless you have completely separated these environments as discussed in Chapter 15 in the section "Approaches to Development, Test, and Production Universes"). If you don't have dozens of production universes, you can store these universes in the top universe folder.

CAUTION *For the group Everyone, the default access to all universes and universe connections is View. This allows users only to see that the universe exists and to build a query without any data. It doesn't allow them to execute a query either on demand or scheduled. If a Designer chooses to export a universe to a specific group, then the access level is automatically changed to Full Control for the universe and Advanced for the universe connection. This potentially allows any user with access to the Designer application the ability to change a universe.*

In the following example, you will allow the Marketing group to access the Sales Summary universe and Sales connection.

1. From the main page of the CMC, select Universes.
2. Click the Sales Summary universe.
3. From the universe properties page, click the Rights tab.

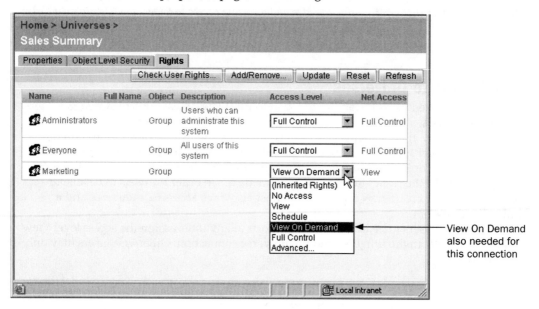

4. Click Add/Remove.
5. From the list of Available Groups, choose the Marketing group and click > to add it to the list of groups with an access level for Sales Summary.
6. Click OK.
7. Change the access level for the Marketing Group to View On Demand.
8. Click Update and ensure that the rights in the Net Access column change to View On Demand.

Repeat the preceding steps to grant access to the Universe connection.

TIP *If each universe has only one universe connection, consider granting the group Everyone, View On Demand to all connections. The connection alone does not provide access to the data; users need access to the universe to get to the data. If, however, your data is separated physically, for example, one Sales universe but with a connection to a European sales database and a North American sales database, then indeed you may want to control access at the connection level in addition to the universe level.*

As shown in the illustration accompanying Step 3 from the preceding steps, the Universe Properties page shows which connection the universe uses.

1. From the main page of the CMC, select Universe Connections.  Universe Connections

2. Click the Sales connection.

3. From the connection properties page, click the Rights tab.

4. Click Add/Remove.

5. From the list of Available Groups, choose the Marketing group and click > to add it to the list of groups with an access level for Sales connection.

6. Click OK.

7. Change the access level for the Marketing Group to View On Demand.

8. Click Update and ensure that the rights in the Net Access column change to View On Demand.

Further Securing the Data: Column- and Row-Level Security

In this chapter, you first created users and addressed user authentication. Through the use of folders and groups, you then managed access to reports within the folders and, ultimately, the universe and connections to allow users to refresh the reports or create new ones. This is the last phase of authorization or the right-most section displayed in Figure 13-1. BusinessObjects XI offers more granular security at both the column and row levels.

Object-Level Security

Object-level security, often referred to as column-level security, allows you to control access at the individual object level. Do not confuse object-level security with all the references to objects in the preceding sections. Remember that objects within the repository refer to users, reports, groups, and so on. Objects within a universe and to which I am referring in this section relate to dimensions and measures.

In earlier versions of BusinessObjects, object-level security was global to all universes and assigned to individual users. Thus if Jami, for example, was given the level Private, then Jami could access all Private objects in all universes she had access to. Within XI Release 2, these object levels can now be managed at the group level and are universe specific.

In Chapter 9, you left all the object definitions as Public. BusinessObjects XI offers five levels of column security: Private, Confidential, Restricted, Controlled, and Public (numbered 1–5 in Table 13-5). Private, priority 1, is the most restrictive and public is the most permissive. Table 13-5 provides some sample objects for which you may want to have an object-level restriction. For example, the user Peggy processes payroll, so she needs access to social security numbers, designated as Private. Salary objects have a security access level equal to Confidential. Users with an access level of Confidential or of a higher priority (Private) can access Salary objects. Profit-related objects are set to Controlled. Members of Finance and Marketing group whose security access level is set to Controlled (in this case, anyone who has been with the firm at least three months) can access the Profit objects, as can any users that have a higher-priority security level (Restricted, Controlled, Private).

Object Name	Security Access Level	Priority	User or Group
Social Security Number	Private	1	Peggy
Salary	Confidential	2	All Employee Managers
Bank Balance	Restricted	3	Finance Users (but not Marketing)
Profit	Controlled	4	Finance and Marketing users
Amount Sold	Public	5	All

TABLE 13-5   Five Levels of Object-Level Security

When you use object-level security, three things happen if a user does not have access to the object:

- When a user creates a new query, the user never sees the object in the universe.
- When a user tries to refresh a query that contains the private object, the user receives an error message. This error message is currently very user-unfriendly: "An internal error occurred while calling the Process DPCommands, Error WIS30270."
- When a user accesses a report that contains the private object, the user does see the object in the report and if data is available, he or she sees the data. In this way, object-level security is not entirely secure. Ways to overcome this breech include either publishing reports with no data or forcing a refresh on open.

You implement object-level security in two places:

- The universe's object properties, set within Designer
- The universe object-level security within CMC

These settings can be quite tedious to maintain. If you are not using them in your universe design or if you have implemented column-level security at the database level, leave all universe settings for objects as Public.

To set the security access level on a universe object, use Designer, select Edit | Object Properties, and click the Advanced tab. Choose the desired restriction level from the drop-down box. In this example, the Salary object has Confidential access:

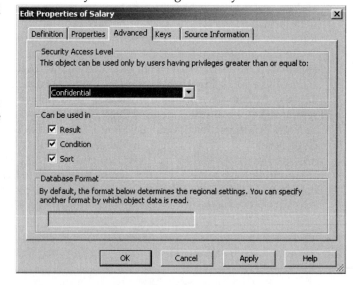

Within the CMC, you need to set the security access level for both the users or groups and the respective universes. You can do this either by individual universe or for all universes. In Figure 13-4, all object-level security is set for all universes according to group membership.

NOTE *If you used object-level security from an earlier BusinessObjects implementation and imported those users, the import utility automatically created groups such as Object Level Security – Private.*

To set the object-level security for all universes, follow this procedure:

1. From the Home page of the CMC, select Universes.
2. If you want to specify object-level security for an individual universe, user group, or user, then at this point click the desired universe. Otherwise, to apply the object-level security to all universes in the repository, select the Object Level Security tab.
3. Click Add/Remove.
4. From the list of Available Groups, choose the Object Level Security – Private group and click > to add it to the list of groups with an object-level security setting for all universes.
5. Click OK.

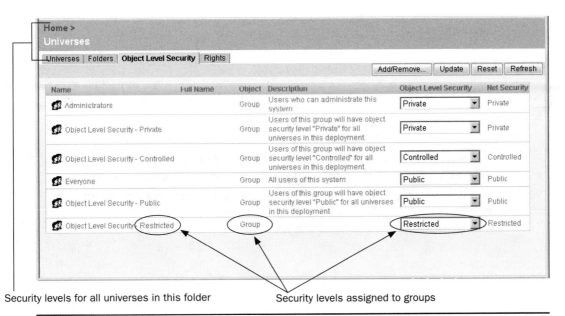

Security levels for all universes in this folder   Security levels assigned to groups

---

FIGURE 13-4 Special groups are created when object-level security is imported from earlier versions of BusinessObjects.

6. Change the default object-level security for this group from Public to Private. Note that the levels available are listed in order of precedence.

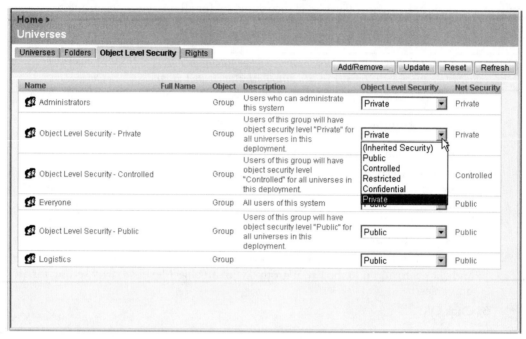

7. Click Update and ensure that the rights in the Net Security column change from Public to Private.

Object Restrictions

Object restrictions are similar to object-level security. They have the same impact on a user's ability to create new reports containing an object or to refresh a report. Some key differences:

- Object-level security has multiple levels; object restrictions are binary in that either you can see the object by default or access to the object has been removed.

- Object-level security is defined both in the CMC and the universe object definitions; object restrictions are defined only within Designer, Tools | Manage Security.

- Object-level security applies across multiple universes; object restrictions apply to a specific object within that one universe.

- You set object restrictions within Designer.

In the following example, the user Sam works in Supply Chain. He has access to a Sales universe, so he can see the orders; however, he should not be able to see the measure object *Margin*. In setting this restriction, you first set the restriction and then apply it to the user or group.

Create an Object Restriction

When you create a restriction, you must group multiple restrictions together. To create an object restriction,

1. Launch Designer and open the universe for which you wish to remove access to an object.

 2. From the pull-down menu, choose Tools | Manage Security | Manage Access Restrictions or select Manage Access restrictions from the toolbar.

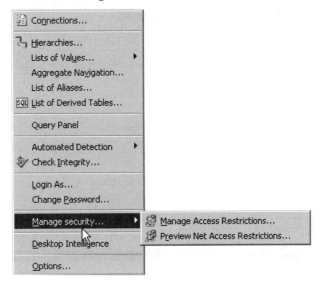

3. Designer will present you with a dialog that displays existing restrictions and groups to which they are applied. Click New.

4. For Restriction Name, enter **Margin Restriction**, and then select the Objects tab.

5. Click Add to insert an object.

6. Designer presents you with a New Restricted Object box. You can manually enter the *Class\Object* or click Select to use the Object Browser to expand any classes and select the individual object that you wish to restrict. In the next screen, I am adding a restriction on *Margin*.

7. Click OK to close the Object Browser and return to the New Restricted Object dialog box.

8. Click OK to add the object to the list of restricted objects.

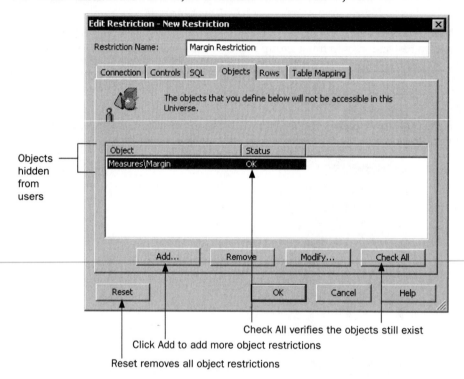

9. Click OK to close the Edit Restriction dialog and return to Manage Access Restrictions dialog.

At this point, you have defined which object(s) you want to restrict. You can now apply this restriction to the user Sam or to the group Supply Chain.

Apply an Object Restriction
To apply an object restriction, follow these steps:

1. From within the Manage Access Restrictions dialog, select Add User Or Group.

2. From the Select Users and Groups dialog, you can scroll to the individual user or, if you have many users, search for them. To search for the user, enter the name in the Search For Text box and click the binoculars icon.

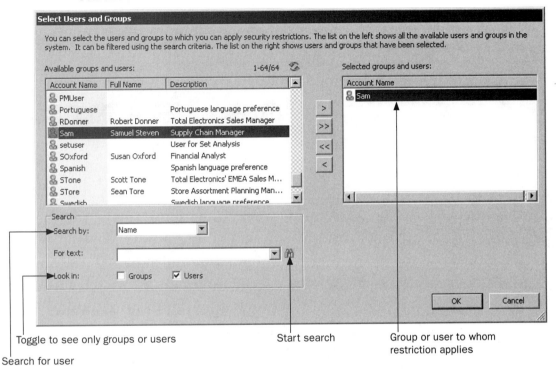

Toggle to see only groups or users   Start search   Group or user to whom restriction applies

Search for user

NOTE *All groups and users are displayed in this dialog, even though these groups may not have access to the universe. You only want to apply object restrictions to groups or users that have access to the universe.*

3. Select the user and click > to add the user or group to the right-hand side of the dialog, Selected Groups And Users.

4. Click OK to apply the change and close the dialog.

5. From the Manage Access Restrictions dialog, ensure that both the newly created restriction, Margin Restriction, and the user Sam are highlighted. Click Apply. In the following screen, under the Restriction column, <None> indicates the restriction

has not yet been applied to the user. Once you click Apply, this column will change to Margin Restriction.

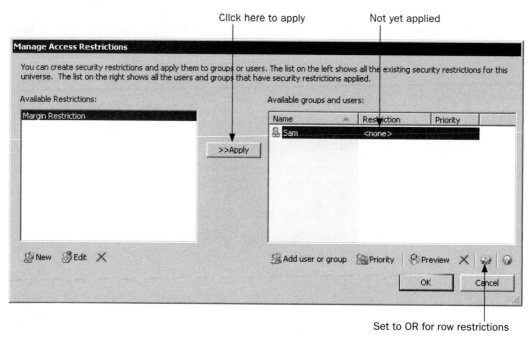

Click here to apply   Not yet applied

Set to OR for row restrictions

CAUTION *If you fail to click Apply in this last step, the restriction will not be implemented.*

6. Click OK to save the restriction definitions and close the dialog.

NOTE *Object restrictions apply to all instances of a user regardless of security access level and regardless of whether the restriction is inherited. If you have multiple instances of a user with different ways to inherit access to a universe, the objects will always be hidden, as the object restriction applies.*

When a user builds a query, the user will no longer see the restricted objects from the object list. If a user tries to refresh a query that contains a restricted object (or for which the user does not have sufficient security access), the user receives the error message shown here.

Many changes in Designer become available to users only when the universe is exported to the repository. However, with security restrictions, these changes are saved in real time to the repository.

Universe Parameter Restrictions: Connection, Controls, SQL

In Chapter 8, you set a number of parameters in the Test Fashion universe. You can override certain parameters by group or by user. For example, the default result set for a universe may be 100,000 rows; with Access Restrictions, you could increase this to 300,000 rows for certain power users. These are sometimes referred to as universe overrides because they override the default universe parameters. Keep in mind that these controls are universe-specific and would not, for example, allow power users to retrieve 300,000 rows of data from all universes.

You also can set a different database connection for certain users or groups. This is useful if your database is replicated on two servers (for response time or security reasons). For example, a European group could have a connection to a database with just European Sales data that is physically located in Europe. A North American group could have a connection to a database with North American sales, physically located in North America.

NOTE *In the last section, you created an object restriction. In the subsequent sections, you are creating controls and row restrictions. When you want these restrictions to apply to the same user or group, you must create them as a set. It is not possible to apply multiple restriction sets to the same user or group. For example, the Finance group can only have the Big Queries restriction set applied to them and not also a different connection parameter. If you want to have both applied to the Finance group, you would need to define both restrictions under the same set.*

In the following example, the group Everyone can access all the reports in the \Finance folder. However, you may decide that while the members of Everyone may be allowed to execute queries that return no more than 100,000 rows, members of the Finance group should be able to return queries with 300,000 rows of data and longer execution times.

1. From within Designer, choose Tools | Manage Security | Manage Access Restrictions or click Manage Access Restrictions from the toolbar.

2. Under Available Restrictions, click New to create a new set of restrictions.

3. In the Restriction Name box, enter **Big Queries**.

4. Select the Controls tab, shown next. Designer displays the default settings from Universe Parameters. (For a further explanation of the settings on these tabs, see Chapter 7.) Any changes you make for the specific user or group are highlighted

in red. To restore the universe defaults, click Reset. In the following example, increase the size of result set to 300,000 rows and the execution time to 10 minutes.

Settings different from default are red

Reset to default

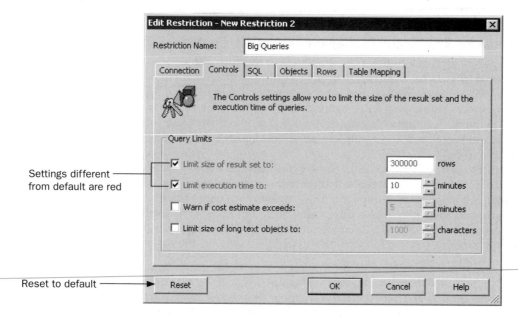

5. Select the SQL tab to control how SQL is generated and which operators the individual user or group can control.
6. Click OK to save your changes to this restriction definition.

Now apply the Big Queries restriction definition to the Finance group:

1. From within the Manage Access Restrictions dialog, select Add User Or Group.
2. From the Select Users and Groups dialog, scroll to the Finance group.
3. Select the group and click > to add group to the right-hand side of the dialog, Selected Groups And Users.
4. Click OK to apply the change and close the dialog.
5. From the Manage Access Restrictions dialog, ensure that both the newly created restriction, Big Queries, and the group Finance are highlighted. Click Apply.
6. Click OK to save the restriction definitions and close the dialog.

Row Restrictions

Row restrictions restrict the rows returned in a query by appending a SQL WHERE clause to every query a user runs. Multiple row restrictions are appended to the query with AND. New in XI is the ability to connect the restrictions with an OR. Row restrictions are useful for security purposes, but also for user productivity. They save users time by automatically filtering the data according to what they need to see. Companies that have complex security requirements may elect to implement row restrictions at the database level rather than through BusinessObjects.

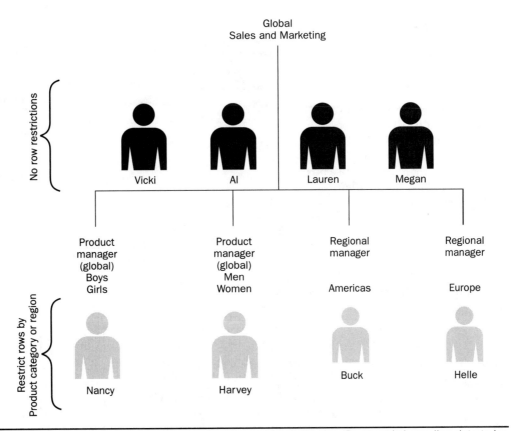

FIGURE 13-5   The Marketing group is organized by product and region. Row restrictions allow data to be filtered automatically.

Figure 13-5 shows a more detailed organization for the Marketing group. The group is organized by a combination of product managers who can view global information, and regional managers who can view sales information within their regions only. For example, Nancy is the Product Manager for children's clothes (product category = Girls, Boys). Nancy should be able to view all sales for these product categories, regardless of which country the customer resides in. Helle is the Regional Manager for Europe; she should be able to view sales for all product categories, but only where the region is Europe.

Figure 13-6 shows all data rows available in the source system. In order to restrict which rows of data Nancy sees, you will add a restriction for SH.PRODUCTS.PROD_CATEGORY IN ('Girls','Boys'). Helle needs the restriction SH.COUNTRIES.COUNTRY_REGION = 'Europe'.

1. From within Designer, choose Tools | Manage Security | Manage Access Restrictions or click Manage Access Restrictions from the toolbar.

2. Under Available Restrictions, click New to create a new set of restrictions.

3. In the Restriction Name box, enter **European Data**.

4. Select the Rows tab.

5. Click Add to insert a restricted table.

6. From the dialog at right, click >> to see a list of available tables. Choose SH.COUNTRIES.

7. Enter the WHERE clause **SH.COUNTRIES. COUNTRY_REGION = 'Europe'**. Alternatively, click >> in the Where Clause box to call the Where Clause Definition box.

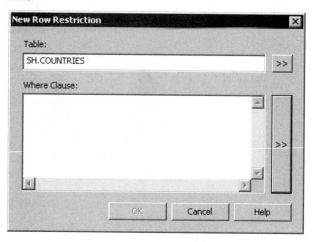

Helle, Regional manager of Europe, only sees these rows

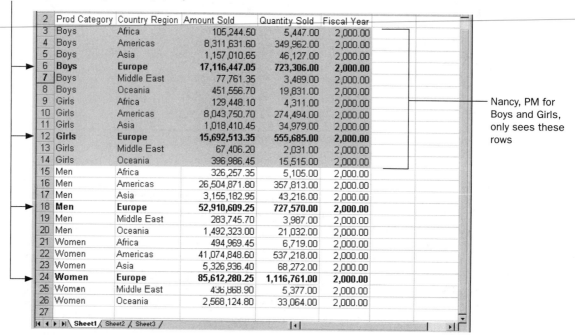

Nancy, PM for Boys and Girls, only sees these rows

FIGURE 13-6   Corporate users see all data available, but a WHERE clause will filter the data for Nancy and Helle.

8. Click OK to return to the Edit Restriction dialog box, shown here.

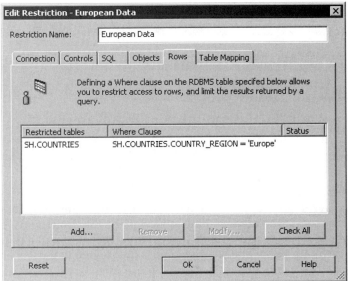

9. Click Check All to verify that the object still exists in the universe.

CAUTION *Check All only verifies that the universe object exists in the repository; it does not verify SQL syntax or valid data values. If you enter either of these incorrectly, users will receive an error or no rows when a report or query is refreshed.*

10. Click OK to close the restriction definition.

11. Apply the restriction definition to the user or group as in the previous sections.

Row restrictions can be quite powerful but also problematic if restrictions are applied against multiple groups. Row restrictions do not have priority levels; instead, all restrictions are used to generate the WHERE clause and by default are connected with AND. For example, if the Marketing group incorrectly contained a row restriction for REGION='Americas' and Helle's individual user restriction contained REGION='Europe', Helle would have no rows returned, since the two conditions are appended to the query with an AND connector. With BusinessObjects XI Release 2, you can override this default behavior and specify to use an OR connector:

 1. From within the Manage Access Restrictions dialog, select the cog wheel icon in the bottom right.

2. Choose the option "Combine row restrictions using AND within group hierarchies and OR between groups." Click OK.

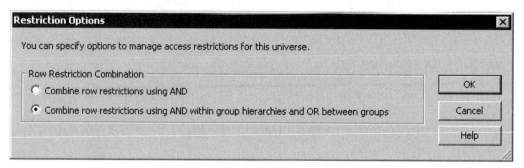

Database Views vs. Row Restrictions

Companies that have unique logins to the data source often create views for each user or group of users to accomplish the same thing as Designer's row restrictions. To implement this, the DBA would create a security table that contains each user and a column with the data values for each restriction. The security table is then joined to the fact or dimension tables to ensure users see only their own data.

There is no *best* solution for how to accomplish row-level security. Views may be easier to implement for many users with multiple security restrictions. Views are database-specific, so if your company uses more than one BI tool, the security model is open and independent of the tool. However, too many views may confuse a database optimizer, and queries may not be processed as efficiently. Unless the DBA creates an application to maintain the row restrictions, security becomes centralized with the DBA.

Simple WHERE clauses generated when security is managed through Designer will leverage the optimizer. However, the security settings are not seamless and can be more difficult to maintain for larger user groups.

Table Mappings

Table mappings provide another way to implement row-level security. Table mappings allow universe designers to remap the base table in a universe with a different table name. In this way, a corporate group of users may access data in a corporate fact table, whereas a regional group may access data in a regional table that contains less data. These "tables" do not necessarily need to be physical tables; they can also be database views. In order for table mappings to work, the column names from the original table used in the universe must be exactly the same as the column names in the mapped table.

To follow on the example in Figure 13-6, I could have multiple tables, either views or physical tables:

- SALES that contains all sales data
- CHILD_SALES that contains a subset of data for PRODUCT_CATEGORY IN ('Boys','Girls')
- EURO_SALES that contains sales for REGION='Europe'

To remap a table, create a new or edit an existing restriction set and then apply it to the group or user.

1. From within Designer, choose Tools | Manage Security | Manage Access Restrictions or click Manage Access Restrictions from the toolbar.

2. Under Available Restrictions, click New to create a new set of restrictions.

3. In the Restriction Name box, enter **European Data**.

4. Select the Table Mapping tab.

5. Click Add.

6. Use the Select button to launch the table browser or enter the default table name in the universe. This is the name of the table that you will be replacing. If you use the Table Browser, click OK to return to the New Table Mapping dialog box, shown next.

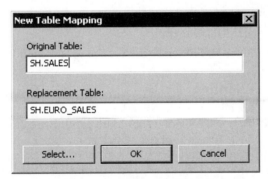

7. Position your mouse in the Replacement Table box. Use the Select button to select the new table or enter the new table name—in this example, SH.EURO_SALES.

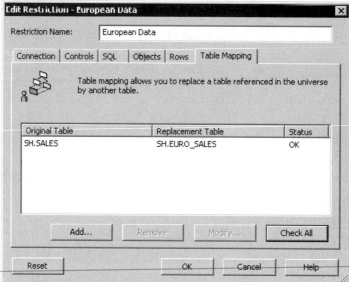

8. Click OK to return to the Edit Restriction dialog box.

9. Click Check All to verify that the table names exist in the universe structure.

10. Click OK to save the table mapping.

11. Apply the restriction definition to the user or group as in the previous sections.

Setting Restriction Priorities

While Row restrictions are all taken into consideration and connected with an OR or AND connector, for other restrictions, only one should be valid. For example, only one table mapping should take effect. You can specify which restriction should take precedence in the event that a user belongs to more than one group to which such a restriction has been applied. For example, in the earlier section, you increased the row limit for the Finance group. Let's assume that you also had a row restriction for the Marketing group that set the row limit to 200,000. If a user belongs to both groups, which restriction should take priority, the 300,000 row limit specified for the Finance group or the 200,000 row limit for the Marketing group?

By default, the priority goes according to the order in which the users or groups are listed in the Access Restrictions. You can change this by manually setting the priorities. Priority 1 takes precedence over Priority 2 and so on.

In the following example, you will set the Finance restriction to take priority over the Marketing restriction:

1. From within Designer, choose Tools | Manage Security | Manage Access Restrictions or click Manage Access Restrictions from the toolbar.

2. Note the Priority numbers in the following screen. You want to make Finance the top priority. Select Priority. If the Priority button is dimmed, be sure you have first selected a user or group.

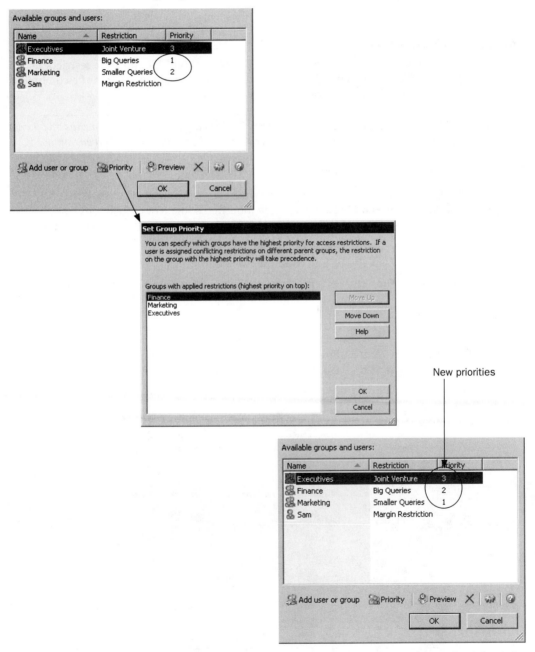

New priorities

3. From the Set Group Priority dialog, move the Finance group to the top by selecting the group and clicking Move Up.

4. Click OK to close the Set Group Priority dialog.

5. Note in the Manage Access Restrictions dialog that the priority numbers are now a 1 for Finance and 2 for Marketing.

6. Click OK to save the changes to the priority levels.

Previewing Net Restrictions

When a user belongs to more than one group or when you combine multiple restrictions into one set, it's helpful to see what the net impact is: how will the restrictions be combined. To see this net effect, Designer provides a Preview option.

NOTE *I recommend you use the Preview option from the toolbar or the pull-down menus and do not use the Preview button from within the Manage Access Restrictions dialog. When you use the Preview button from within the Manage Access Restrictions dialog, it does not immediately reflect all the restrictions. Also, you cannot readily check net restrictions for all groups and users.*

As an example, the user Sam was explicitly given an object restriction such that he cannot see the Margin object. He also may have inherited some row restrictions by belonging to the Marketing group. To preview his net restrictions, follow this procedure:

1. From within Designer, choose Tools | Manage Security | Preview Net Access Restrictions or click the button from the toolbar.

2. Scroll to the desired user or group or use the search capabilities to find the user or group.

3. Click Preview.

4. The Restrictions Preview dialog shows which restrictions affect the user, regardless of whether they were assigned via a group or an individual user. Note that only the tabs that contain restrictions appear in this preview.

5. Click Close to exit the preview and close again to exit the user list.

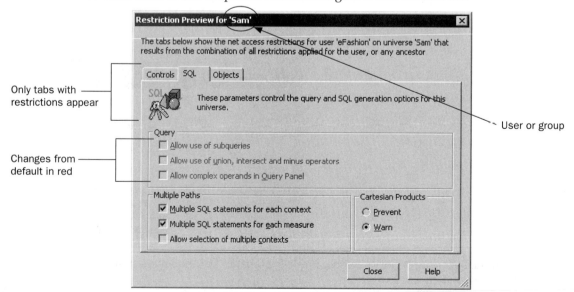

Summary

The security capabilities within BusinessObjects XI Release 2 have changed significantly from earlier versions of BusinessObjects. The options are more granular, providing more power but also risking confusion. In planning your implementation, first understand what is possible and then begin developing a security approach that fits your company security philosophy. Remember the following:

- Leverage external authentication and single sign-on when possible.

- Use Groups and Folders to simplify maintenance.

- With access-level security, the most restrictive rights apply when the rights are inherited through group membership. Thus if a user is granted view access in one folder through a group assignment and then *denied* the right to view an object (different from "no access" which translates to "not specified") via a different group membership, the more restrictive setting takes priority and the user will not see the folder.

- Access-level security affects which menu options appear to end users within InfoView and within the individual applications.

- Explicit access takes priority over inherited access. Thus if a user has inherited the right of denied to a particular report or folder and then the same user is explicitly granted the View On Demand right, the user will be able to view and refresh the document.

- With object-level security (Private to Public), the most permissive right applies. Thus if a user is granted Private in one place and Public in another place, then the Private access prevails.

- Restriction sets affect universe objects, rows of data, and SQL behavior. Group multiple settings together and apply them to different groups.

Design Principles: Where to Put the Intelligence

Y ou have built your universe, made it more robust with advanced objects and hierarchies, and developed a security strategy. You are off to a good start. As your universe evolves, you will face a number of choices about where to put the intelligence, specifically the *business* intelligence. This chapter focuses on the alternatives and the pros and cons of each alternative. My goal is to help you understand the cost/benefit implications of the choices as you deploy BusinessObjects XI.

What Is Intelligence?

Intelligence is information with a *business* context. QUANTITY may be a physical column in a table. Add a time period such as month, then a context to the time period such as order month, and multiply the column by a price, and you arrive at *Sales Revenue*, something with meaning and value to business users.

Users will rarely want to analyze straight columns of detailed data. If they did, the transaction or Enterprise Resource Planning (ERP) system would meet their needs just fine. To provide a business context, the raw data must be combined with other information, perhaps cleansed, transformed, and aggregated. Many transformations may be critical to the project's success and known to programmers and Extract Transform and Load (ETL) experts; however, they mean nothing to a business user. If a customer code is 306 in one system and 0306 in another system, the business person really doesn't care. The business person only cares and knows that this 306/0306 customer is Mrs. Whitwell. Transformations to make the data consistent are necessary to build the data warehouse or mart but are a given to the business user.

If the business user wants to do a promotion for newly married customers, then perhaps classifying these customers under a grouping such as Newlyweds would be a form of intelligence. At first glance, you may assume that this customer grouping should exist in a dimension table. A dimension table within the database is certainly one place to put the intelligence, but the customer grouping could also go in the universe or a user's report.

Following are a few more examples of items that I would consider to be more than just straight calculations or transformations; they provide business intelligence:

- Measures that include time periods, such as *Sales Year To Date* or *Days Late*
- Variance analysis that compares the difference between two numbers, such as *Current Year Sales versus Last Year Sales, Percentage of On-time Shipments*
- Ratios, such as *Market Share, Patient Visits per Diagnosis, Gross Margin*
- Dimension groupings, such as customer age, income level, product size or type

Places for Intelligence

There are a number of places to create and store this intelligence. Often, the decision of where to build the intelligence is based on one person's knowledge of how to do it; it's assumed there is only one alternative. For example, a universe designer may naturally assume that the universe should contain all the intelligence. Power users may want user objects and report variables to contain all the intelligence. Depending on how much disk space and time a DBA has, the DBA may want the intelligence to be in the table design so that it is tool-independent. This is where a good Program Manager or Project Manager will work with the different stakeholders and determine the best place for intelligence, considering a company's resources, time, and flexibility. Guidelines should become best practices and part of a quality assurance process. Companies can build intelligence into OLAP databases, the data warehouse, the universe, or user objects and reports. If you are using BusinessObjects XI directly against a transaction system, your alternatives may be limited to the universe and reports.

Figure 14-1 shows these different places and where the intelligence gets processed. In Chapter 11, you built an object called *Current Year To Date Sales* as part of the universe. Stepping through Figure 14-1, you could have used an OLAP database such as Microsoft Analysis Services to include the time period awareness in the sales column (place 1). The processing for this type of object is done on the OLAP server. The intelligence also could be a physical column in an aggregate fact table. The information is preprocessed by the RDBMS, so when a user runs a query, it is a simple fetch (place 2). If the object exists in either the universe or a user object, the RDBMS again does the work but does it upon query execution. The user may wait longer for the query to be processed, but the work is still done by the RDBMS. Larger-scale BI implementations will always strive to do more processing on the server, rather than on the mid-tier BI application server or, worse, on the user's desktop.

If a power user creates a report variable to calculate *Current Year To Date Sales*, then the RDBMS sends the detail rows to calculate that variable to either the Enterprise server in a Web Intelligence environment or the user's desktop if it is Desktop Intelligence. In a thin-client environment, the BusinessObjects Enterprise server must calculate the variable and present the results to the user in HTML format (place 3). With Desktop Intelligence, all the detail rows travel the network to the desktop PC that then calculates the report variable (place 4).

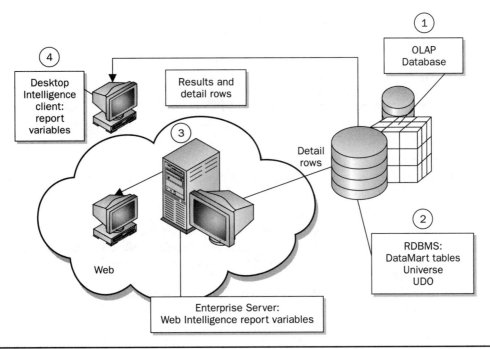

FIGURE 14-1   Intelligence can be built into a number of places in a BusinessObjects XI deployment.

Evaluating the Pros and Cons of Each Alternative

Occasionally, there is a single, clear-cut choice for where to put the intelligence. You are low on disk space, so you add it to the universe; the calculation is too complex for SQL, so you create a report variable. These are the easy answers. The not-so-easy answers are everything else in between. The best place for intelligence is as suggested by the consultant's annoying but valid answer "it depends." In the following sections, I offer examples of business intelligence that are better suited to one place than another. Each alternative will have a cost associated. The question you must answer is whether the benefits outweigh the costs and disadvantages. Building intelligence into the fact table provides faster response time and consistent results; is this a strong enough benefit to justify the cost of redesigning the table, modifying the load routines, and buying more disk space? In some cases, absolutely. In other cases, no.

OLAP Databases

In presenting this topic at user groups and conferences, the percentage of companies that integrate OLAP databases with the BusinessObjects Enterprise deployment remains small. There are a number of reasons for this.

OLAP Databases as Independent Applications

Companies often treat OLAP databases as separate applications for several reasons. First, each OLAP vendor provides their own access tools:

- Hyperion provides Web Analysis (formerly named Analyzer) and a spreadsheet add-in to access Essbase OLAP databases. As Hyperion has now entered the query and reporting space, Hyperion and Business Objects increasingly compete with one another.

- Microsoft uses Excel to access MS Analysis Services cubes and in Q2 2006 announced intentions to acquire ProClarity to provide visualization and dashboard capabilities to Analysis Services.

- Business Information Warehouse (BW) provides Business Explorer as a front end to BW (Net Weaver) Info Cubes.

Just as data marts and BI implementations can be implemented departmentally, so can OLAP databases. Unless a business sponsor and program management are in place to integrate the two, it seems rarely to happen. As these leading OLAP vendors offer their own front ends to their databases, customers often incorrectly assume that they must use the corresponding front end.

Furthermore, Business Objects' approach to OLAP access has gone through many transitions, so confusion and lack of awareness abounds. With BusinessObjects XI, the vendor now offers OLAP Intelligence, previously called Crystal Analysis, as a way of accessing third-party OLAP databases. Also, new in XI Release 2 is the ability to access OLAP databases through a universe.

Finally, BusinessObjects XI itself, with its microcube engine, is also considered an OLAP tool. Thus, many companies assume that they need only BusinessObjects XI and do not need another OLAP database. This assumption is reasonable. However, because of some of the inherent limitations with the dynamic microcubes, there are instances in which an OLAP database can provide some significant benefits—as long as the competing vendors do not encroach on each other's space within a customer organization.

One of the biggest differences between the OLAP capabilities via the BusinessObjects XI microcube and an OLAP database is the data volume. There is no hard rule as to the size of a BusinessObjects XI microcube; it could be 300,000 rows of data. It would not be 3 million, as is the case of an OLAP database. In this respect, it is much more appropriate to think of applications such as MS Analysis Services and Essbase as databases or data sources than as competing tools.

There also is a significant difference between drilling within a microcube and drilling against an OLAP data source. The goal with any OLAP deployment is to ensure that when users drill, it is at the speed of thought. Because an OLAP database is pre-aggregated, the response times are more predictable than relational query times. To ensure fast drilling times against a Desktop Intelligence or Web Intelligence microcube, report developers often cram too much information into a report. They are trying to get the microcube to act like an OLAP database. This approach is doomed to failure.

When users drill within either a Web Intelligence or Desktop Intelligence report, they are drilling within a subset of cached data, as shown in Figure 14-2. When a user drills from year to quarter, the details for quarter already exist in the report. If not, then the user can drill through to the details and send another query to the relational database. The results are fetched and stored in the microcube. Herein lies a challenge: if your relational database is well tuned, this drill through to detail could take a few seconds or a few minutes (hopefully

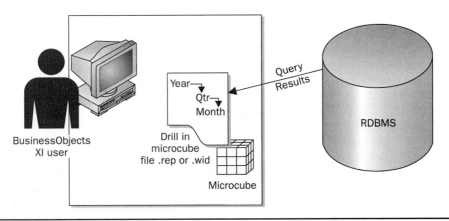

FIGURE 14-2   Users drill within reports.

not hours). And what if the majority of users never look at quarterly details? Then you have unnecessarily built a larger report than required!

Meanwhile, with an OLAP database such as Essbase or Microsoft Analysis Services, the cube is built in advance of the query. When a user drills from Year to Quarter, the drill goes against the highly tuned OLAP database as shown in Figure 14-3. This limits network traffic, as only the necessary results are sent to the BusinessObjects Enterprise server, as each user requests the details. The OLAP server performs sorts, nested rankings, cross-dimensional calculations, and more.

Advantages of Building Intelligence into OLAP Databases

Clearly, for this section to have any relevance, your goal is to integrate your OLAP database as another data source in your BusinessObjects XI deployment. The question becomes, then, when to build intelligence into the OLAP database. As shown in Figure 14-1, when the intelligence is put in an OLAP database, the server does the work (place 1), thus minimizing network traffic. In general, building intelligence into any server-based technology will also ensure consistent business definitions (compared to varying calculations in user reports and spreadsheets). Further, OLAP databases have a better understanding of business analysis than most SQL-based reporting tools, so a number of functions are built into the OLAP engine. For time period calculations, Essbase includes dynamic period-to-date calculations with a toggle. Period-to-date functions are native to MDX and MS Analysis Services, rather than the complex SQL `CASE` functions presented in Chapter 11. Recall the discussions on

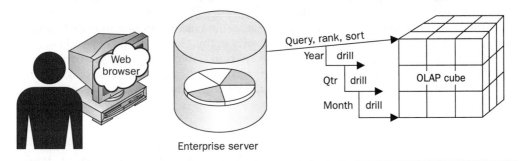

FIGURE 14-3   Drill within OLAP Intelligence is against the OLAP database.

semi-additive measures (from Figure 9-2) and the issue with comparing inventories and account balances (one point in time) with material movements and debit/credits (a period of time). BusinessObjects XI handles this through multiple SQL statements and user training; however, OLAP databases again are aware of these issues and allow you to flag with a simple setting that such measures may be aggregated by product, for example, but not by time.

OLAP databases also provide you with more control over the calculation order, something particularly important for ratios and percentages. As an example of calculation order, look at the calculations for profit as a percent of sales, as shown in Figure 14-4. To get sales and profit totals for quarter four, you correctly sum across the rows. However, for profit as a percent of sales, if you sum across, you get an incorrect percentage of 84. To calculate percentages and ratios, you need first to get the sums by quarter, and then calculate down to take profit/sales. This second calculation gives you the correct result of 28 percent.

Similar to this concept of a two-pass calculation are multidimensional and forward-looking calculations. As shown in the next screen, profit and sales are at two different levels within the accounts hierarchy. To calculate profit, one must first know the subtotals for Margin and Total Expenses. Profit is not a simple sum, but rather, an aggregation of Subtotal Margin – Subtotal Expenses. To calculate profit as a percentage of sales, you must know both levels of subtotals, as well as the detail Sales that is used to calculate the Margin Subtotal; the database must look "forward" to first calculate Profit before it can calculate Sales as a percentage of Profit.

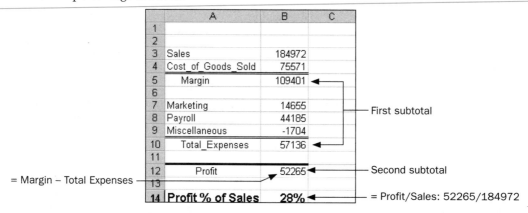

This is simple for an OLAP database, which understands dimension members and levels (just say Profit % Sales!), but not so simple for SQL. Are there ways of doing this in the fact table, universe, or report? Of course! It's all a matter of the time and cost to implement and maintain the intelligence.

An OLAP database is also an ideal place to store dimensional information that needs to be aggregated in different ways. As discussed early in this chapter, a customer dimension could have groupings by physical region (customers in California) or by type of customer (newly married). Users are viewing the same measures but by different groupings. OLAP tools allow dimensions to be aggregated in different ways, often without drastically increasing the size of the database.

Disadvantages of OLAP Databases

Before you rush out to implement the latest version of an OLAP database, note that they do have their disadvantages. First, they are another database and another data source. If your

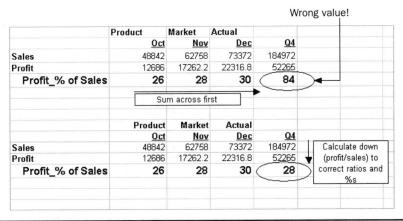

FIGURE 14-4   Percentages and ratios require a two-step calculation that OLAP databases easily handle.

organization is strapped for IT resources, you may be forced to limit which technologies you can support. As a separate database, it is another copy of the data, so there are latency and extraction issues. However, if the OLAP database is tightly integrated correctly with your data warehouse, I would argue that it is in fact another, smarter way to provide aggregate tables. OLAP databases are famous for ensuring consistent response times on precalculated data; however, this requires smaller data sets than what an RDBMS can handle. Some OLAP databases allow you to store data in relational tables (ROLAP) to increase capacity, yet this will have a performance impact. OLAP databases are not well suited for list analysis, and support for attribute analysis varies greatly. For example, if you want a list of customers above a certain age or a list of products packaged a particular way, OLAP databases generally do not support list-style reports.

The following table summarizes the key benefits and disadvantages to putting the intelligence in an OLAP database:

OLAP Database Benefits	OLAP Database Disadvantages
Understanding of semi-additive measures like inventory	Additional cost and expertise
Control over calculation order for ratios and percentages	Risk of duplicate, inconsistent data if not integrated with data warehouse
Multidimensional and multirow calculations	Expertise generally comes from IT
Aggregated, so fast, consistent response times	
Server-based, so consistent business definitions and minimal network traffic	
Built-in time period awareness such as year-to-date, year-over-year variances	

Relational Tables

Building the intelligence into relational tables provides many of the same benefits as OLAP databases:

- Tables are preprocessed and so are generally faster than the dynamic SQL that a universe or Desktop Intelligence user object would use.
- Tables involve server-based processing, so only limited data is sent across the network.
- Tables are server-based, so business definitions are consistent.

Again taking the example of *Current Year To Date Sales,* a DBA could build a fact table with the following structure:

product_key	customer_key	time_key	C_Month	LY_Month	C_YTD	L_YTD
123	111	102003	500	400	5000	3850
456	111	102003	200	180	2000	1800
123	333	102003	710	300	7100	3000
123	777	102003	900	1000	8000	10000

As the data is loaded into the fact table, each column represents a "bucket" of information with the time period intelligence built into each column. C_MONTH contains sales for just the current month; C_YTD contains sales for each month in the current year. If the month is October, it contains sales from January through October.

Data Integrator has a date generation transform, which generates the time periods needed (quarter, month, year, week, etc.). By using our special functions, we can aggregate fact data to these time periods and load the Fact tables in the warehouse with an appropriate indication of the "bucket" used. You can also create aggregations that manage running ytd, mtd, qtd fields. You use DI's stateful functions to do this.

Many analytic applications that build data marts (including SAP BW's Info Cubes) use this kind of structure. However, if your company designs and builds your own fact tables, the DBA must program this kind of intelligence into the load routines; unlike in OLAP databases, there may be no simple toggle to achieve time period intelligence (although newer data integration tools may assist with this). A robust ETL tool may help with the process. For example, BusinessObjects' Data Integrator has a date generation transform that will take an individual date value and create the appropriate year, quarter, and month hierarchies. Data Integrator also includes special functions to load data into fact tables to create running year-to-date measures, month-to-date measures, and so on. Even with an ETL tool, this kind of design requires more disk space and a stronger understanding of best practices in data warehouse designs. DBAs may not have the resources to implement this kind of design or the time. (Show me a DBA who is not overworked and overscheduled!)

Recall from the first section in this chapter that dimension groupings such as customer age, income level, and product size are also forms of intelligence. Analyzing data by dimensions is the bread and butter of most businesses. Providing alternative groupings can help reveal previously hidden patterns. For example, let's take a wine merchant. Users can analyze sales by type of wine and rating. Users also can see which customers buy the most wine. Now break that customer list down by corporate customers versus individual consumers, and the analysis will reveal which group of customers generates the most business. If the dimension table contained income information for each corporate customer, the wine merchant can better understand if large corporate customers are more profitable than small business owners. The same logic applies to product information: what are sales for soft drinks in plastic bottles versus aluminum cans? Unfortunately, this kind of dimensional information is often not captured, or when it is captured, it is stored in departmental databases and spreadsheets. While Desktop Intelligence users can incorporate personal data sources into their reports, I would advocate that more dimensional information be stored in sources that are accessible to more users. If companies use a star or snowflake schema in data marts, then a data mart can contain both a standard customer dimension and a customer dimension with business-specific groupings and hierarchies. BusinessObjects XI can handle multiple dimensions with alternate hierarchies in each. Further, dimensional information in relational tables allows users to create lists and easily do attribute analysis with the information, a type of analysis that not all OLAP databases support and that is not possible when such information remains in personal workspaces only.

TIP   If you do have dimensional information in a departmental database, different from the central data warehouse, this still may be accessible via Web Intelligence. It requires some creativity and some organizational issues, but here is a work-around: Web Intelligence in XI Release 2 allows for synchronized multiple data sources in a document. With this capability, the central data warehouse team does not have to load the departmental dimensional data into the central data warehouse to make it accessible to end users. They do, however, have to allow the department to build a universe off the departmental data source. End users can then easily combine the data from the central data warehouse universe with the dimensional data in the universe from the departmental data source.

When Not to Store Intelligence in Relational Tables

Relational tables are not a good place to physically store ratios and variances, as the ratio always needs to be recalculated with an aggregated numerator and an aggregated denominator. To follow on the earlier example, let's say you want to calculate the percentage variance between the current year-to-date sales (C_YTD) and last year's year-to-date sales (LY_YTD). For each row in the database, you can correctly store the variance.

product_key	customer_key	time_key	C_YTD	L_YTD	% Variance
123	111	102003	5000	3850	29.87%
123	333	102003	7100	3000	136.67%
123	777	102003	8000	10000	–20.00%

However, recall that Web Intelligence users will create reports that dynamically group information by dimensions. Thus a business user may ask for a variance analysis by product. In order to allow this, the universe designer includes the SQL SUM aggregate in the object definition. This incorrectly sums the individual variance rows, suggesting that sales are 146.54 percent higher than last year's sales. This is wrong!

product_key	customer_key	time_key	C_YTD	L_YTD	% Variance
123	111	102003	5000	3850	29.87%
123	333	102003	7100	3000	136.67%
123	777	102003	8000	10000	−20.00%
Subtotal for product 123:			20100	16850	146.54%

Wrong!

To arrive at a correct variance, you must get the subtotal for the C_YTD by product 123, and then the subtotal of L_YTD to arrive at a correct variance of sales being 19.29 percent higher than last year. OLAP databases allow an administrator to control the calculation order; SQL tools do not. To guarantee correct results, the universe designer would ignore the variance column in the fact table and dynamically calculate the variance using a SQL statement in an object. Refer to Chapter 11, under "Ratio to Report," for specific examples.

Summary

The following table summarizes when to store the intelligence in a fact table and when it poses disadvantages:

Relational Table Benefits	Relational Table Disadvantages
Precalculated in the table, so fast, consistent response times	Requires complex programming logic in the load routines
Server-based, so consistent business definitions and minimal network traffic	Fixed table design may limit flexibility IT/DBA must implement Requires additional disk space Not suitable for ratios and percentages

Universe

I confess I am biased: I prefer to put as much intelligence as possible in the universe. Of course there are exceptions, but let's start with the arguments for the universe. Intelligence in the universe offers much more flexibility than either an OLAP database or a relational table. When you add or modify an object, there is no need to restructure and recalculate a cube; there is no need to modify load routines and rebuild a table. The universe does not require the additional disk space that either OLAP databases or RDBMS tables require. Because the universe is centralized, it enforces consistent business definitions. Further, as shown in Figure 14-1, the processing is done on the database server, thus minimizing the impact on the network or BusinessObjects Enterprise servers that user report formulas can overload. The universe allows partial control of the calculation order, necessary for ratios and variance analysis, something relational tables cannot offer in an ad hoc reporting environment. In the preceding example, you cannot aggregate the variance stored in a relational table or you get incorrect results. Within the universe, one uses the following syntax to control the calculation order:

```
(sum(C_YTD)-sum(L_YTD)) /sum(L_YTD)
```

Alternatively, with databases that support newer SQL analytic functions, you can calculate ratios as

```
RATIO_TO_REPORT(sum(SH.SALES.AMOUNT_SOLD)) OVER ()
```

As users build queries that analyze the percent variance by different dimensions (product, time, geography), the variance for each row returned is always recalculated with the correct numerator and denominator. Problems may arise when users add breaks and subtotals within a report, but this can easily be corrected with report formulas.

Intelligence in the universe also does not necessarily require an overworked/understaffed IT department to implement. New intelligence can be added quickly, as is critical in a changing business environment. Responsiveness and flexibility are the two main reasons I am biased toward building intelligence into the universe. If the BI deployment cannot respond as quickly as the business requirements change, it will be less successful. Requirements change not simply because users "overlooked" something, but more often because they discovered a new or better way to explore information. Did anyone want to link click stream analysis with brick-and-mortar store sales before 1997? No.

The majority of companies put control of the universe in the hands of IT. This can be for the good, as IT staff have the skills to understand relationships between tables, joins, and index issues. They also can write complex SQL.

NOTE *Programmers and DBAs certified in SQL are not necessarily adept at SQL for business reporting; this is often a unique and hard-to-find skill set.*

However, unless the IT department has a close relationship with the business and an understanding of business reporting requirements, they may miss opportunities to add intelligence to the universe. Users do not know SQL and do not know what objects can be built with SQL; IT knows SQL but may not realize that the business would benefit from measures such as number of customers (COUNT function), number of late orders (COUNT and DAYS_BETWEEN functions), variance analysis ((SUM1-SUM2)/SUM2), and so on. Further, a recurring complaint about IT maintaining the universe is lack of flexibility. Users want something, and IT is either too busy to implement it or wants to keep the universe general.

This is when it makes sense to allow individual functions or business units to build and maintain their own universes. IT should still quality-assure these universes (see Chapter 16, under "Quality Assurance Check List"), but it may be easier to teach a power user how to build a universe than to get IT resources to build the universe the way the business wants.

When a universe designer fails to build enough intelligence into the universe to satisfy the common business needs, end users are forced to create their own objects or to build the intelligence in the report. This approach may be fine for individual needs, but it can be a disaster for reports that are widely shared, as it can significantly increase maintenance costs and the risk of inconsistent business definitions. While current Sarbanes-Oxley compliance efforts seem focused on ensuring the integrity of information on the data capture side, I would expect efforts to increase in the reporting environment. With BusinessObjects XI, there is no way to tell what has changed within a report. So if a user changes a report variable that suddenly calculates revenue in a slightly different way, there are no controls to document and identify this change. Changes in the universe at the object level are also not readily identifiable, but as a smaller group of developers are involved, they at least can be documented procedurally.

Disadvantages of Intelligence in the Universe

Even though I prefer to build a robust universe, there are times when the universe is not the best place for the intelligence. Advanced objects will generally use complex SQL or internal Designer functions to create the objects. This can result in unpredictable query response times, unless you have taken the necessary steps to ensure consistent performance. Also, as the universe becomes more complex, there is a greater risk that certain objects will not work well together. For example, if a universe contains the two objects *Sales* and *Current YTD Sales*, will the user receive accurate information if the user places these objects in the same query? The first object, *Sales*, does not include any time-period constraints. The user therefore adds *Month*=10 and *Year*=2005 as conditions in the report. This makes the *Current YTD Sales* information wrong (it's now one month of data versus year-to-date) as Web Intelligence appends the WHERE clause to the entire query. Hopefully, users will recognize query results that are blatantly wrong; it's the not-so-obvious ones that pose a problem. In either case, a perfect universe would include only those objects that can be accurately combined together; a real-world universe accomplishes this most of the time and supplements it with good object descriptions and training!

Universe Benefits	Universe Disadvantages
Designers (IT or power users) can implement, so it is flexible	Use of complex business SQL is a unique skill
Server-based, so consistent business definitions, minimal network traffic, and better scalability	Unpredictable response times compared to fact table or OLAP database, as SQL is processed at query run time
Ratios and variances are correct	Individual objects may not be correct when combined with other objects with conflicting definitions
Leverages newer RDBMS analytic functions	Database dependent

User Objects

Here is another bias: I prefer to avoid the use of user objects. User objects cannot be shared by other users. Rarely does only one person work with or view a report, so if the intelligence is lacking in the universe, either put it in the universe or put it in the report so that it can be shared.

NOTE *User objects are available only in Desktop Intelligence and have not been carried into Web Intelligence.*

The one problem that a user object solves and a report formula does not is that of too much data being sent across the network. If a user is using SQL for standard transformations (UPPER, TO_CHAR, and so on), then the same amount of traffic is sent across the network for a user-defined object as for a report formula. However, if a user builds an object that filters the query such as *Order Date – Ship Date < 5*, then the database server processes the query, generating less network traffic than a report variable that gets processed locally on the client or Enterprise server.

When users build objects with SQL functions, it may require a modification to the *database*.prm file, increasing ownership costs. Another concern about both user objects and report formulas is that the business definition may no longer be consistent. One user's definition of *Current Month Sales* may be based on the accounting month the invoice was sent; another may define it with the calendar month, and yet another, the date the product was shipped.

The following table summarizes the pros and cons of user objects:

User Object Benefits	User Object Disadvantages
Users can implement, so it is flexible	Use of complex business SQL is a unique skill
Server-based processing minimizes network traffic	Unpredictable response times, as SQL is processed at query run time
	Objects cannot be shared with other users
	May require modification to the *database*.prm file to access certain SQL functions
	Not centrally maintained, so increases risk of inconsistent business definitions and higher costs
	Not supported in Web Intelligence

User Reports

With robust calculations and formulas, Desktop Intelligence and Web Intelligence offers users the ability to overcome many limitations in SQL. The number of functions in Web Intelligence XI Release 2 is double the number of functions supported in earlier versions of Web Intelligence. Users are familiar with formulas from spreadsheets and are comfortable building some quite powerful ones within the Web Intelligence documents. In some cases, users may have no choice but to create a formula in a report for the following reasons:

- It's an individual reporting need.
- The intelligence cannot be built with SQL.
- It's immediate and avoids the politics that accompany other alternatives.

If the report really is for individual use and the formula is not a common business one, then the intelligence does indeed belong in a report. However, too often I see report-based calculations that were built there simply because there was little dialogue between the universe designer and end users.

SQL Limitations

SQL does have limitations. OLAP database vendors often emphasize their solutions as a way to overcome a number of limitations of SQL (forward calculations, time period versus point in time, and so on). However, IBM, Oracle, and Teradata in recent years have provided a number of SQL extensions that make SQL more robust. SQL Server 2005 reportedly will also have more analytic capabilities. Forward calculations such as rankings and percent market share are now possible with SQL.

But clearly, not everyone is on the most current database releases and not all intelligence can be solved with SQL; this is where many BI vendors have excelled. BusinessObjects XI in particular contains a number of formula functions that do not have a SQL equivalent. Variance Percentage (VarP), Percentile, and RunningSum are just a few. Long before database vendors added analytic functions to SQL, BusinessObjects offered a percent of sum calculation, as well as Rank and various running aggregate functions. Recall the particular problems that variance and ratio calculations can cause; the calculation order is very important to get the correct answer. With report formulas, users control the calculation order either by specifically inserting a formula at each break level or with Calculation Context Operators (explained in detail in Chapter 22). To use the earlier example of the variance between C_YTD and L_YTD, look how the percent variance is correctly calculated,

Desktop Intelligence - PCT_VAR.rep - [Administrator - @ASK2]						
File Edit View Insert Format Tools Data Analysis Window Help						
% Variance Analysis						
product_key	customer_key	time_key	C_YTD	L_YTD	% Var Prod	
123	111	102003	$5,000	$3,850	30%	
	333	102003	$7,100	$3,000	137%	
	777	102003	$8,000	$10,000	-20%	
123		Sum:	$20,100	$16,850	19%	
Report1						
		Last Exec: 11/21/2002 2:43			NUM	

even for the break level by product.

Desktop Intelligence and Web Intelligence automatically ensure the ratios are correctly calculated at each break level by using an extended syntax in the report formula. Within the individual rows, the full syntax for the ratio in Desktop Intelligence is as follows:

```
=((<C_YTD>-<L_YTD>)/<L_YTD> ForEach <product_key>) In (<product_key>, <customer_key>, <time_key>)
```

At the footer or subtotal level, the syntax is slightly different:

```
=((<C_YTD>-<L_YTD>)/<L_YTD> ForEach <product_key>) In <product_key>
```

In some cases, it may be technically feasible to build the intelligence into an object, but the user needs it immediately. IT may maintain the universe and be unable to create a new object quickly enough; the user creates a report formula for time expediency. The user also may want to avoid the politics of having to get common buy-in for a universe modification.

Disadvantages of Intelligence in User Reports

Too many report formulas can be problematic over time. First, report variables are stored within a document and therefore are not centrally maintained. As formulas change, there is no way to track how many versions of the report have been shared and modified. Multiple versions of the formula will now exist. This problem becomes worse when the original formula creator changes jobs or leaves the company. There once was a statistic about 75 percent of spreadsheets containing errors. I wouldn't be surprised if report formulas have an equally high number of errors, or at the very least, cause a number of misunderstandings. One of my clients spent hours each month reconciling differences between two inventory reports: they both accessed the same universe in the data warehouse, but each contained different formulas. We eventually standardized on one report that became published and centrally maintained in the repository.

Second, report formulas contain a significant amount of intelligence that could, and should, be leveraged across the company. If a company is to ensure business consistency and capture the power of user report variables, you must develop a process to review and maintain formulas. Figure 14-5 shows one possible process. A user creates a standard report that contains a number of formulas (Step 1). A report reviewer, who may be a power user or a universe designer, reviews the report and looks for formulas that are common needs (Step 2). When they fulfill common reporting requirements, the universe designer builds the intelligence into the universe (Step 3A). If it is not a broad reporting requirement but only fulfills the needs of a few users, then the intelligence will remain as a report formula. The report reviewer quality-assures the formula and saves the report to the public folders or corporate categories (Step 3B).

Users may balk at this additional level of quality control, and the last thing a company wants to do is add barriers to sharing information. An alternative is to let users freely save documents to the public folders or corporate categories but ensure a report reviewer and/or universe designer checks the shared reports periodically. I have gotten a fair degree

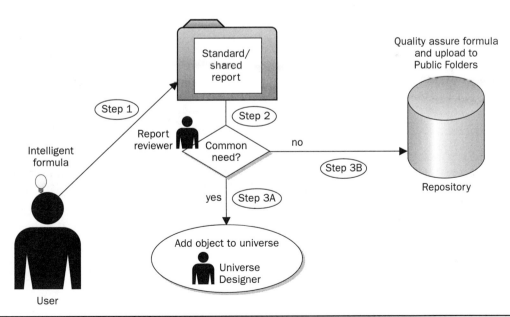

Figure 14-5   Creating a role of report reviewer can help companies minimize the risks of unnecessary and inconsistent report formulas.

of pushback from some BusinessObjects Enterprise administrators who wanted Corporate Documents (as the shared area was called in earlier versions) to be tightly controlled. With BusinessObjects full client, users could easily use the LAN file system to otherwise share the reports and may continue to do so in Desktop Intelligence in XI Release 2. In other words, if your deployment approach is an obstacle to sharing reports, users often will find their own ways to do so. When IT facilitates the sharing, though, IT can also provide some degree of control and quality assurance. With Web Intelligence, however, users can share documents only via the repository and not via the file system. My recommendation, then, is to actively facilitate sharing of reports. You may want to structure the categories and folders such that there is one super-controlled area and other areas with less restrictions, but making the whole repository too tightly controlled may make your deployment less successful in the long term.

Another major disadvantage of report variables is their effect on response time and system load. Overly complex reports can overload the Enterprise server. Formulas that require detail rows may cause too much data to be sent across the network. Let's look at the example of *Last Year YTD Sales.*

The following Web Intelligence report formula looks at the Enterprise Server's `CurrentDate` to determine which months are less than the current month. If it is less than the current month, then it displays the *Amount Sold,* else zero. The year must be one year ago.

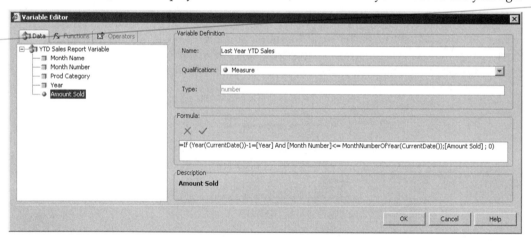

The report appears as follows (assuming the current date is July 2005). Notice that while there were sales in August, the rows for these months correctly display zeros, as it is greater than the current month.

NOTE *For a detailed explanation of these formula functions, refer to Chapter 22.*

Prod Category	Year	Month Name	Month Num	Amount Sold	Current Year YTD Sales	Last Year YTD Sales
Boys	2004	May	5	2,451,728	0	2,451,728
Boys	2005	May	5	3,207,527	3,207,527	0
Boys	2004	June	6	2,043,676	0	2,043,676
Boys	2005	June	6	2,443,540	2,443,540.1	0
Boys	2004	July	7	1,909,368	0	1,909,368
Boys	2005	July	7	2,344,933	2,344,933	0
Boys	2004	August	8	2,028,426	0	0
Boys	2005	August	8	2,368,214	0	0

Each year goes to a separate column

Report 1

Last Refresh Date: July 19, 2005 12:10:35 PM

Only months <= current month are used

Notice also that for every month, you need a row of data to be sent to the client. If you are analyzing sales for 20,000 products, then this kind of report requires 240,000 input rows (12 months times 20,000 products). You do not need the individual rows displayed in your final report, but as shown in the preceding report, Web Intelligence needs the detail month rows to process the formula.

TIP *Just because someone can build a complex formula in Web Intelligence or Desktop Intelligence, that doesn't mean it's the best place for it. Don't let someone's desire to show off their programming talents drive the report design process. Instead, stay focused on the business needs, one version of the truth, and scalability.*

The next table summarizes the advantages and disadvantages of putting the intelligence in a user report.

User Report Benefits	User Report Disadvantages
Users implement	Inconsistent business definitions
Flexible within an individual report	Increased maintenance costs, as reports and formulas are not centrally maintained
No politics to get defined centrally in the universe, RDBMS, or OLAP database	More rows than necessary shipped to client or Enterprise server, slowing response time
Easy to build!	Potential SOX compliance issues
Variables can span data providers	

Summary

I've presented different places in which to put the intelligence. As you can see, there is no clear-cut answer as to which place is best. I have said to end users, "What, are you crazy? That formula is much too complicated and important to be in a report!" I have also said to universe designers, "What, are you crazy? You can't build that object in the universe! It will conflict with other objects." It all depends on the benefits you are hoping to achieve (robustness, flexibility, consistent business definitions), your constraints (cost, skills, technology), as well as the trade-offs (time to implement, politics, maintenance effort, costs). Figure 14-6 is a scorecard that compares the different places with the trade-offs for each alternative.

If a box shows a "good" circle, then the place is good for that criterion in deciding where to put the intelligence; if it shows a "use with caution" triangle, then proceed with caution and be aware of the risks; and if it shows a "not recommended" square, there may be significant risks. For example, putting the intelligence in the RDBMS is great for consistency of business definitions ("good") but is not very flexible ("not recommended"); however, when compared to a universe, the maintenance effort may be somewhat higher because of the effort to redo load programs and rebuild tables ("use with caution" versus "good").

While it is important to consider these design principles in deploying BusinessObjects XI, it's much more important that you add the intelligence *somewhere*!

Summary of alternatives and trade-offs

○ Good
△ Use with caution
□ Not recommended

	OLAP	RDBMS	Univ.	UDO	Report
Consistent business terms	○	○	○	□	□
Fast queries	○	○	△	△	△
Flexibility/implementation time	△	□	△	□	○
User empowerment	△	□	△	○	○
Scalability	○	△	○	□	□
Politics	□	□	△	○	○
Cost to maintain	△	△	○	□	□
Skills required	△	□	△	△	○
Robustness	○	△	○ △	□	○

FIGURE 14-6   Deciding where to put the intelligence is a series of trade-offs.

Minimizing Universe Maintenance

A s the number of universes in your deployment increases, there are a number of ways you can minimize universe maintenance. As users access multiple universes, built by different designers, you need to ensure that the interface is as consistent as possible. Linked universes may help with this. For large-scale deployments, you will want to establish development and test environments that are separate from production. Finally, with so much metadata built into the universe, extracting metadata from metadata modeling or ETL tools may minimize your maintenance efforts while providing users with consistent terminology across a BI deployment.

Linked Universes

Linked universes allow a designer to build one master universe called the *kernel* that then is used to build a subsequent universe called a *derived* universe. Companies generally use linked universes in one of several ways:

- A central universe designer builds a reference universe that contains common dimension classes that then get linked to other universes. In the derived universes, a second designer can add universe-specific tables. For example, in Figure 15-1, the tables and corresponding classes and objects for *Time, Products,* and *Customers* exist in the kernel universe. The designer for the Sales universe links to the kernel to use these common classes and objects. The Sales designer hides classes that sales users do not need (*Accounts, Employees*) and adds new tables to the derived universe (SALES_FACT). This approach can drastically reduce implementation and maintenance efforts, while ensuring a consistent universe interface across multiple universes.

- A central universe designer maintains one kernel universe that contains all the star schemas in the data warehouse; business unit designers then create smaller *derived* universes that are focused on their individual user group (Figure 15-2). The business unit designer may hide many classes.

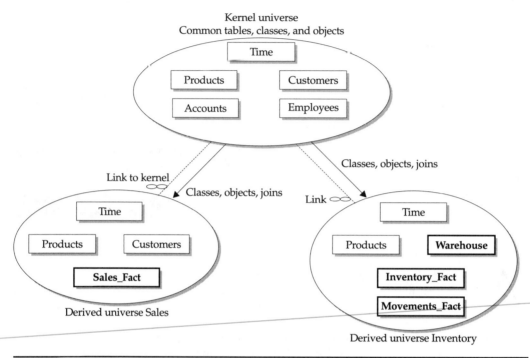

FIGURE 15-1   Linked universes ensure consistent dimensions across multiple universes.

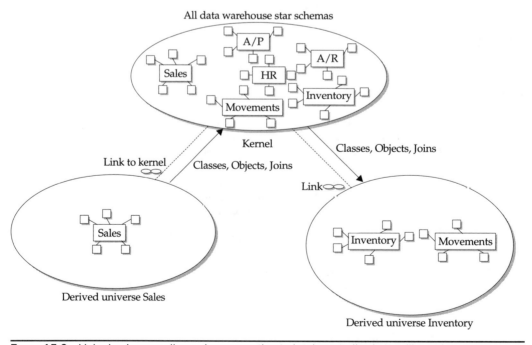

FIGURE 15-2   Linked universes allow universe creation to be decentralized yet still consistent.

- A derived universe can contain links to more than one kernel universe, so you may also have two small kernel universes that then link to larger derived universes. This approach is good for decentralized development, but unless your company follows some strict design principles, the derived universe may contain duplicates and/or you may find it hard to build a cohesive-looking derived universe. The problems faced with this kind of model are similar to the ones faced when trying to build a central data warehouse from independent data marts.

What Gets Linked

There are a few gotchas with linked universe, and the first one is that not everything is linked. Not linking everything is both a help and a hindrance. Universe parameters are not linked. Therefore, within the derived universe, you still need to set controls for query execution time and result-set size as well as SQL settings that determine if users can create complex queries or create queries that involve multiple fact tables.

NOTE *In earlier versions of BusinessObjects, customized lists of values did not get linked or work properly with linked universes. In XI Release 2, they do. The name of the list of value will not be the same, but the functionality provided by the customization is carried through. For example, if you rename the list of values on Customer ID to CUSTID, the derived universe shows a nonsensical name of ~00T0001.*

Join definitions are linked to the derived universe, but not the contexts. The vendor argues that this is the correct procedure, as the derived universe may contain additional joins and contexts. This is true; however, the current approach builds an incorrect universe that contains loops. I would like to see the contexts brought into the derived universe. A universe designer could then add new joins to existing contexts or create new contexts altogether. With the current approach, all contexts must be re-created in the derived universe.

Aggregate navigation settings are linked. If you add a new aggregate table within the derived universe, you can define additional incompatibilities; all the original incompatibilities are still preserved.

Custom hierarchies are not linked. However, as you build new custom hierarchies in the derived universe, when an object name changes in the kernel universe, the new name is included in the derived universe's custom hierarchy. The following table summarizes which components get linked or not:

Universe Component	Linked	Not Linked
Universe parameters		√
Classes and objects	√	
List of values customizations	√	
Joins	√	
Contexts		√
Aggregate navigation	√	
Custom hierarchies		√

How Linking Works

The linking works through the repository, so two key requirements for linked universes are that they use a *secure* connection and that the kernel universe must have been exported to the repository at least once. You then add the link within the derived universe. When you define a link, all the classes, objects, and joins get displayed within the derived universe; they appear gray to differentiate them from other items that you may add directly within the derived universe. The link is one-way and not bidirectional.

NOTE *Linking universes in XI has gotten better because of the new repository architecture in XI that makes more use of the file system. When linking universes in version 6, the size of the universes was a big concern because the user had to import both the kernel universe and the derived universe in what could be a slow process. Because the import process in XI is significantly faster, this hesitation to use linked universes is no longer justified.*

If, however, you are working with an existing universe or trying to combine two kernel universes into one bigger derived one, there are a few more caveats. First, class names must be unique. If the kernel universe contains a name that duplicates one in the derived universe, then Designer will rename this class upon linking. For example, if *Country* exists in both the derived universe and the kernel universe, it becomes renamed *Country2* in the derived universe. The object names within each class remain the same. The physical table, however, is another story. The table COUNTRY already existed within the derived universe structure. Upon linking, the table name remains the same, but unfortunately, the link table now takes priority and COUNTRY will appear dimmed. This will pose a problem only if you later decide you want to remove the link; you can't easily do this, as your existing *Country* class still needs the original COUNTRY table.

How to Add a Link

The following example uses Figure 15-1 as a model: the kernel universe contains common dimensions; the derived universe contains additional fact tables for a specific user group. For clarity, the kernel universe will be called Kernel and the derived universe will be called Derived. In an actual implementation, use the logical business names (for example, you may name your common kernel universe as Dimensions and the derived universe as Sales).

As discussed earlier, the kernel universe must contain a secure connection, and a designer must have exported the universe to the repository at least once. In the following example, assume that the kernel universe already exists.

1. Create a new universe by selecting File | New from the pull-down menu or clicking New Universe.

2. Designer displays the Universe Parameters. From the Definition tab, enter a universe Name and Description: **Derived**. In the Connection, select the same secure connection used in the kernel universe.

3. Select the Links tab from the Universe Parameters dialog box.

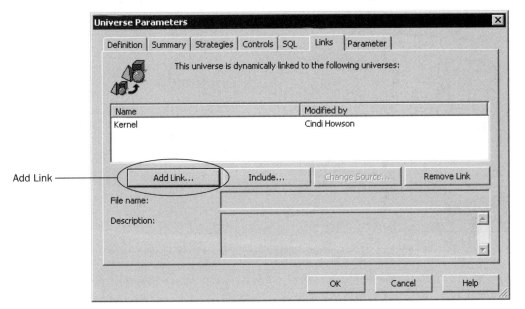

Add Link

4. Click Add Link.

TIP *If you have already created a universe, you can also use Insert | Universe.*

5. Select the *universe .unv* file to which you want to link. Click Open.

NOTE *If you have not yet exported the kernel universe to the repository, you will receive an error message. The kernel universe must exist in the repository prior to linking to it.*

6. Click OK to close the Universe Parameters dialog box. In the next screen, notice that any linked components are dimmed.

7. You can now re-create any necessary contexts and add new tables, joins, and objects. These items will not be dimmed but will appear as normal in the derived universe.

Nonlinked components added in the derived universe appear darker

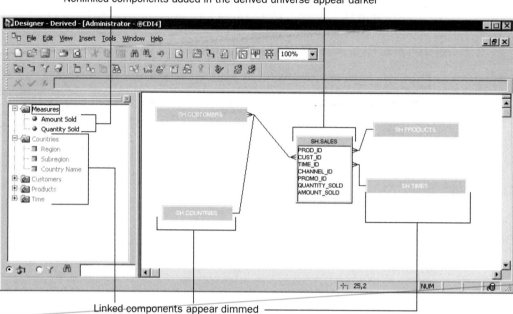

Linked components appear dimmed

NOTE *Even if strategies are set to create joins automatically between matching column names (set through File | Parameters, then selecting the Strategies tab), joins are not created automatically between tables in the derived universe and tables in the linked universe.*

8. For the link to become active, you must save the universe and export it to the repository. From the pull-down menu, select File | Save, then File | Export, and click OK.

Permanently Importing Universe Components

With some of the pitfalls of linked universes, you may decide it is better to maintain two separate universes rather than linking. You may decide to do this in an initial build, in which case the link helps save time only in the build process and not in universe maintenance, or you may decide to do this after a period of time. Either way, you are essentially importing certain universe components (classes, objects, joins, aggregate navigation . . . not custom hierarchies, contexts) into a new universe. After the initial import, there is no relationship between the derived universe and the kernel universe. To import a kernel universe into a derived universe, complete these steps:

1. Select File | Parameters | Links.

2. If this is a previously linked universe, highlight the Name of the kernel universe you wish to import. If this is an initial build, click Add Link, and then select the *universe*.unv file from which you wish to import components. Click Open.

3. Click Include.

All previously dimmed tables, classes, and objects now appear as regular components of the universe.

CAUTION   *Once you break the link by clicking Include, you cannot switch back to a link. The Undo button is not available. If you need to recover the link, do not save the universe.*

Removing a Link

Before removing a link, you must manually remove any newly created components from the derived universe that use a linked component. This may include

- Joins between linked tables and nonlinked tables
- Condition objects that use a linked object
- WHERE clauses in nonlinked objects that use a linked object
- Contexts that include joins from the kernel universe

To remove a link from a universe, use the pull-down menu to select File | Parameters, then select the Links tab. Highlight the link you wish to remove and click Remove Link. If you have not properly removed all the linked components that were integrated in the derived universe, Designer will give you the following error message:

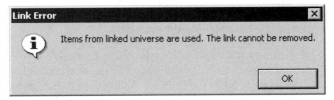

Object Sort Order

When two universes get linked, the initial sort order of the objects is the same in the derived universe and the kernel universe. If you reorder objects in the kernel universe, the sort order is not changed in the derived universe. If you add a class or an object in the derived universe, it stays in the order or position in which it was added.

If you want changes in the sort order in the kernel universe to be reflected in the derived universe, change the parameter in the derived universe, CORE_ORDER_PRIORITY=Yes.

To change this parameter:

1. Select File | Parameters from the pull-down menu or select the Parameter button from the toolbar.
2. Select the Parameter tab.
3. Scroll to the name CORE_ORDER_PRIORITY and select it.

4. In the Value box, change the default from No to **Yes**.

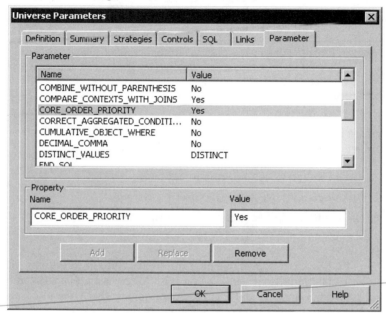

5. Click Replace.

6. Click OK to close the Universe Parameters dialog.

While this change helps synchronize sort orders, the downside is that it also adjusts the sort order for any new classes and objects added to the derived universe. New objects within a linked class get appended to the bottom of the class. New classes get appended to the bottom of any linked classes and cannot appear intermingled with the linked classes. This repositioning of objects does not appear immediately; it happens after you save and re-open the derived universe.

Approaches to Development, Test, and Production Universes

As business intelligence tools have matured, many companies are deploying them across the enterprise. However, all the version management that exists in a mainframe environment is still not quite as robust in the BI environment. In previous releases of BusinessObjects, there were several ways to implement development, test, and production environments. The process of moving content from one environment was manual, tedious, and error prone.

The Import Wizard in XI Release 2 provides richer capabilities for moving content from development to test to production. If you previously had multiple repositories and multiple BOMain.key files for development, test, and production environments, then in XI Release 2, a similar architecture is to have three Central Management Servers (CMS) running on three different servers. The Import Wizard and the use of Business Intelligence Application Resource (BIAR) files allow you to move content from one environment to the next. A BIAR file is a type of Zip or archive file that contains XML files for documents, universes, and other repository content. Because it is an individual file, you can incorporate the use of BIAR files with third-party version management software.

NOTE *With the initial release of XI Release 2, use of BIAR files for migrating objects from development to test to production was not considered stable. In Service Pack 1 (released March 2006), use of BIAR for straightforward migrations of universes and documents is acceptable. However, it requires a thorough understanding of the Import Wizard. Also, note that there is very little dependency checking. So you can inadvertently migrate reports without the updated universe. If you decide to use BIARs, check with technical support for the more recent version before proceding.*

If, in earlier versions of BusinessObjects, you established development/test/production environments via the use of one security domain and server installation but multiple universe repositories, refer to the later section "Test Folders."

Multiple CMSs and BIAR files

Multiple CMSs allow you to have the most robust development, test, and production environments. As shown in Figure 15-3, it allows you to separate:

- Hardware components
- Software versions
- Databases with smaller, test data sets
- All the BusinessObjects Enterprise repository content such as universes, reports, and user authentication

The disadvantage with this approach, though, is cost. You have to replicate hardware platforms, maintain multiple systems, and license the software to run on multiple servers. For smaller implementations, the robustness of such a development environment may not be required.

To promote content from a test environment to a production environment, you use the same Import Wizard that you may have used to migrate content as part of a migration from BusinessObjects version 6 to BusinessObjects XI Release 2 (see Chapter 5). The main difference here is that you will create a BIAR file that has packaged the related repository content into one file.

1. From Windows, select Start | Programs | BusinessObjects XI Release 2 | BusinessObjects Enterprise | Import Wizard.
2. At the Welcome Screen, click Next.

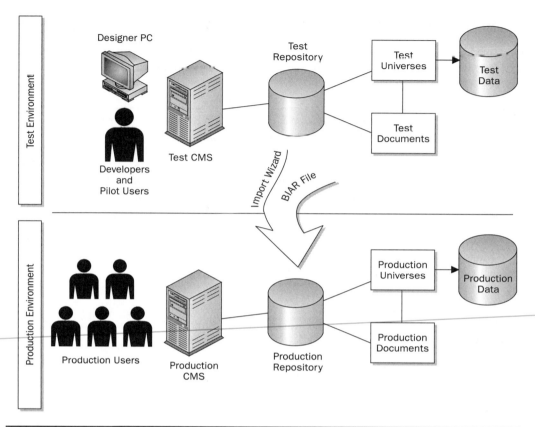

FIGURE 15-3 Multiple CMSs allow you to separate test and production environments.

3. Specify the repository from which you want to create content. For example, if you have been working in development, choose your development repository. Under Source, use the drop-down menu to select BusinessObjects Enterprise Release 2.

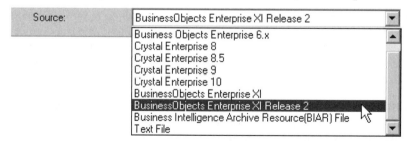

4. When prompted to select the destination environment, select Business Intelligence Application Resource File (BIAR) from the drop-down menu. Specify the path and name of the BIAR file, ensuring you include the extension **.BIAR**. Click Next.

NOTE *If you fail to include .BIAR in your filename, you will receive an error message.*

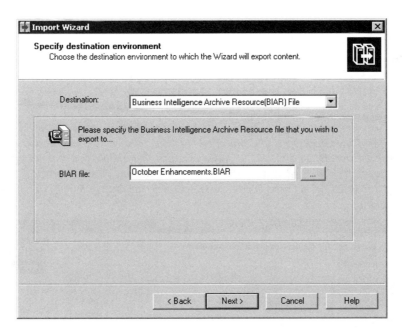

5. Specify the objects that you wish to copy from the test environment to production. By default all objects (BI content, not universe objects) are selected. In the following example, only certain folders, universes, and their connections will be moved to production. When you select "Import folders and objects" in this step, you will later be able to refine your selection to just certain folders or reports. Also, don't let the nomenclature in this dialog confuse you: at this point you are not really "importing"

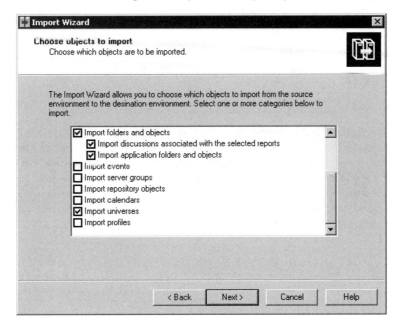

anything; you are copying items into a BIAR file that you will later import into production. Click Next.

6. When migrating universes, you will need the associated connections with those universes. It's unlikely that you will ever want to move all universes and connections in the repository. Select the desired option and click Next.

CAUTION   *If you only want to move certain universes to production, you must select the third option, "Import the Universes and Connections that the selected Web Intelligence and Desktop Intelligence documents use directly." If you select any other option, you will not later be prompted to select the desired universes to move to production. This is also true if you are only migrating universes but not associated reports. Granted, the description of this option can be a little misleading.*

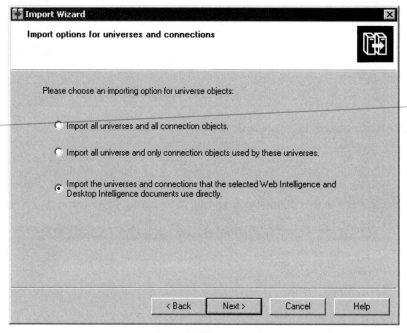

7. If you selected the third option in Step 6, you will be asked to choose which universes you want to migrate to production. If you also are migrating reports, then the wizard has automatically selected universes on which those reports depend. In the following screen, the Wine universe check box is grayed out because the import wizard selected it by default as certain reports use it. Additional universes in the Test Universes folder appear in black because I have explicitly selected them, and I am not moving reports associated with those universes.

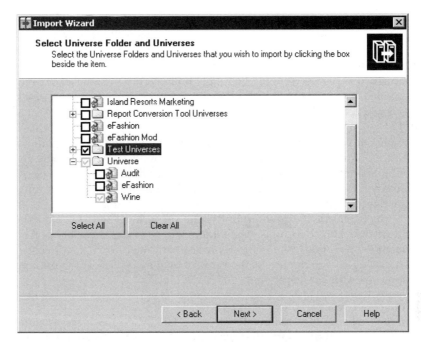

8. The wizard will provide a summary of the elements you intend to import to the BIAR file. If these settings appear correct, click Finish to generate the BIAR file. If your selections appear incorrect, click Back to modify your selections.

9. A thermometer will show you the progress of the import as it reads data from the test CMS to the BIAR file. Once this process is complete, the wizard will allow you to view the detailed log file. View this log to ensure that the documents, universes, and connections that you intended to move to production have been added to the BIAR file. Click Done to close the Import Wizard.

Once you have created the BIAR file, you now restart the wizard to import the contents of the BIAR file into your production environment. Follow the same steps as in the preceding section, but in Step 3 choose the BIAR file as the source, and in Step 4 choose your production environment as the destination.

Understand that the Import Wizard does not first read the contents of the BIAR file and then ask you the appropriate options. So, for example, if your BIAR file only contains one universe, you will still be prompted to choose whether or not and which users you want to import. It is a little confusing but eventually will be an improvement over the manual process that many companies were forced to rely on in earlier versions of BusinessObjects and as is described in the next section, "Test Folders."

Test Folders

In previous versions of BusinessObjects, the use of domains allowed an administrator to create separate domains for test, development, and production. With the new architecture in XI, the concept of universe domains has been replaced by universe folders (see Chapter 7, under "Folders and Domains"). While folders provide a logical grouping of universes, it is different from domains in that all the folders and universes within one CMS share the same repository. As the BusinessObjects community gains experience with XI, a number of best practices will emerge. How best to use test folders will be one of those areas. At this time, the main benefit to using folders over BIAR files is that folders are a lower-cost alternative to full-blown, multiple CMS deployments. While they may be closest to your approach in earlier versions, there are limitations.

How It Works

Assume you have a Sales universe in a test folder \TEST\SALES.UNW. Assume you have also developed a set of reports that access \TEST\SALES.UNW. You now copy that universe to production, \PRODUCTION\SALES.UNW. When a user accesses a report, the document will look for the correct data provider using a unique ID assigned to the universe. It looks for the universe initially stored in \TEST\SALES.UNW. If the production users do not have access to the TEST folders, then the universe is not found. Desktop Intelligence and Web Intelligence will then look using the *name* of the universe. As long as the document finds a universe with the same name, it will automatically access the new production universe. It's important to note that in XI Release 1, Web Intelligence did not behave this way and behaved differently than Desktop Intelligence. This has changed in XI Release 2, which once again checks data sources in terms of the universe name. In the longer term, checking based on universe naming can be a challenge, as the vendor supports multilingual universes. If the universe is not found, users will receive the error message shown here.

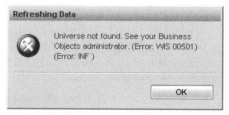

Therefore, I recommend you use a test folder approach only if

- You do not have the resources or licensing to implement multiple CMS environments.
- You use inheritance to grant access to universes at the folder level and not to individual universes.
- You do not intend to deploy universes in multiple languages.

To establish a test folder for universes, you create this via Designer when you export a universe.

1. From the pull-down menu, select File | Export.

2. Within the Export Universe dialog, click Browse to see a list of existing universe folders. It may be that you only see the top level or root. Position your cursor on the root and right-click to invoke the pop-up menu.

3. Select New Folder.

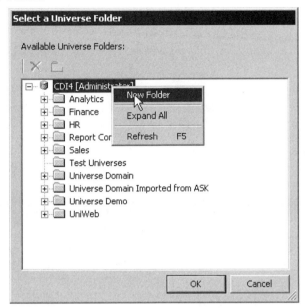

4. Enter a name for the new universe folder: **Test Universes**.

5. Click OK to create the folder and close the Select a Universe Folder dialog.

6. When you export a universe in development or test, be sure to select the appropriate folder from the Domain box.

Domain:	/Test Universes	▼

After you have developed and tested your universe, you move it to production by exporting it to a folder that production users can access. This may be the root directory, or it may be a subfolder for a particular group of users.

1. First, always export the universe to the folder \Test Universes to ensure you maintain a copy in the repository that you can continue to use for development purposes.

2. Re-export the same universe, but this time select the production folder. Designer will warn you that you are exporting the universe to a different location and will prompt you to either copy the universe or move it.

3. If the universe already existed in production, you will be warned that you will be overwriting an existing universe. Select Yes or No if you wish to proceed with the copy.

CAUTION *When you copy a universe, any universe-specific access restrictions are removed. This does not refer to the restriction sets; it only refers to access control lists defined in the CMC. Inherited restrictions defined at the folder level continue to be valid.*

4. Designer will confirm the universe was successfully copied. Click OK to close the dialog.

Documents in Test/Production Folders

When users create a report and there are two universes with the same name, the folder name gets reflected in [brackets] in Desktop Intelligence and as a folder within InfoView. For the most part, production users would have access to only one copy of the universe via a production folder. However, you may have developers or pilot users who might have access to both universe versions simultaneously. In the next screen, there are test and production copies of the Northwind Products universes:

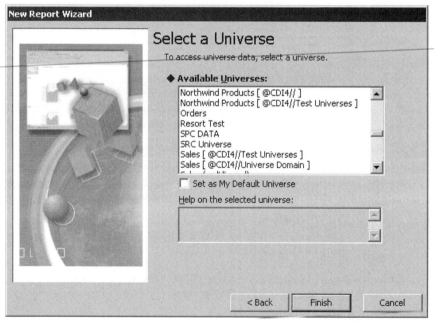

The Desktop Intelligence document references the unique universe ID and name of the universe, not the specific folder name. When a document finds only the production universe Northwind Products.unv, it automatically uses this universe.

If a developer or pilot user will continue to have access to both the test and production universes, that user must explicitly point Desktop Intelligence reports to the correct version of the universe. Report authors do this via the Data Manager.

1. From within Desktop Intelligence, select Data | View Data and the Definition tab.

2. Under the Definition setting, click the ellipsis button to modify which version of the universe the document should access:

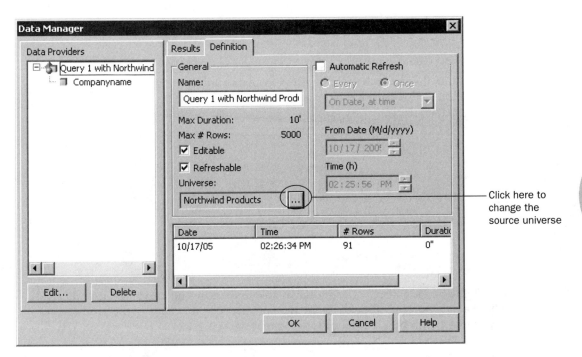

Click here to change the source universe

3. From the Change Universe dialog, scroll to the production version of the universe. In this case, it is Northwind Products, but from the root directory listed under the Repository with /. Note that you do not see the /Test Universes folder for Northwind Products, because this is the current version referenced in the document.

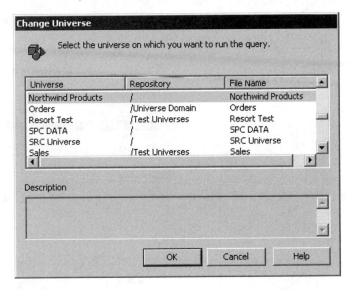

4. Click OK to specify the new universe source and OK again to close the Data Manager.

From within Web Intelligence, report authors can change which universe is accessed via the Java query panel.

1. Select Edit Query.

2. By default, the Data tab with the list of available universe objects appears on the left. Select the Properties tab.

3. Under the Universe section, click the ellipse.

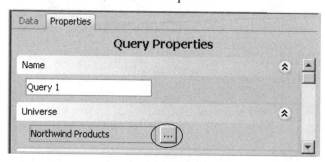

4. Web Intelligence displays a list of available universes. The universe currently used in the data provider appears in the top pane. Specify the name of the production universe you want to repoint the document to and click OK.

5. If any object names are different between the two universes, you will be prompted to remap them. Click OK to close the Change Source dialog and return to the query panel.

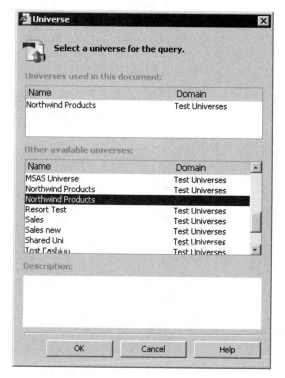

Multiple Designers

When working with a repository, Designer also allows universe development and maintenance to be distributed across several designers through a locking mechanism. As most development work is done locally on the designer's PC, it's possible for two designers to work on local copies of the same universe and overwrite each other's work when they export their changes. With the locking mechanism, each designer locks the universe for updates and unlocks it when he or she is finished making changes.

As an example, assume this is a global company with designers in Europe and the west coast of the U.S. There is a nine-hour time-zone difference between continental Europe and Pacific Standard Time. This essentially allows a company 16 hours of development time per day. The European designer imports the HR universe (File | Import). To lock the universe for updates from other designers, the European designer *must* double-click the universe name. The padlock symbol appears next to the HR universe to show it is locked, as shown here.

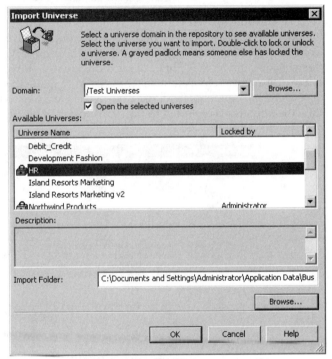

When any other designers log in to Designer and try to import a universe, a dimmed padlock appears next to the locked universe. In the Locked column, the name of the designer who has locked the universe appears under the Locked By column. In the next screen, Cindi Howson has locked the Debit_Credit universe, and Megan has locked the Development Fashion universe. The Administrator is logged in for this session and has a lock on the Northwind Products universe as indicated by the darker padlock. At this point, other designers may still import a copy of the universe, but they may not export changes to the universe.

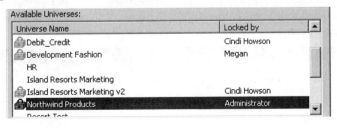

> **NOTE** *If multiple designers may make changes to the same universe, they must ensure they unlock the universe when their changes have been exported. This can be particularly aggravating when development occurs across multiple time zones. For example, if the designer in Europe finishes the workday and wants to allow the designer on the Pacific coast the ability to make additional changes, the initial designer must unlock the universe when exporting it to the repository. To unlock the universe, double-click the universe name; the padlock no longer appears next to the File Name. If the initial designer leaves for the day without exporting changes to the universe, the second designer cannot safely make any changes.*

In environments with multiple designers developing and/or maintaining one universe, the universe revision number becomes more important. To see the revision number, select from the pull-down menu File | Parameters | Summary tab. Notice in the next screen that the revision number is 9. For each revision, the two universe designers have entered notes in the Comments field as to what changes were made in each revision. To enter a new line of text in the Comments field, use CTRL-ENTER. Designer assigns a new revision number each time the universe is exported to the repository, not necessarily each time the universe has been modified.

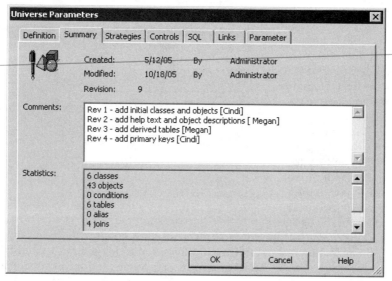

Designer provides a safeguard in the event that the second designer tries to make changes on an older version of the universe. With each export to the repository, Designer will assign a new revision number. In the past, a universe with an older revision number could not be exported to the repository. In XI, Designer will warn you but allows you to proceed with the export:

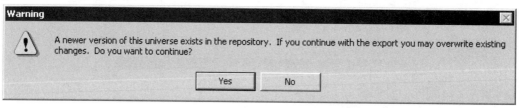

Metadata Integration

When your BusinessObjects XI implementation is part of an overall data warehouse initiative, you may be able to further minimize universe maintenance by integrating metadata from third-party modeling and ETL tools or from BusinessObjects Data Integrator. As BI systems become more complex and enterprise-wide, you as the designer must help ensure that users understand what they are seeing and that formation is consistently represented at different points in the BI architecture.

Figure 15-4 shows a BusinessObjects XI deployment and the various points in which metadata is most relevant. From an end-user perspective, they start with a report that displays Sales $. But what does this measure represent: is it gross sales or net sales net of discounts and returns? When was the data last updated? Did it come from the order system or the invoice system (which ideally is tightly integrated)? Is it based on the list price or the actual selling price? In an ideal world, the answer to these questions would be both obvious and consistent every time the user sees the measure Sales $. In reality, this measure can be interpreted differently, particularly when the measure may have been created within an individual report as opposed to the universe or when multiple universe designers create a slightly different object for each universe.

The integration of metadata is still relatively new in the BI industry. Metadata is often re-created and manipulated by a different tool for each different purpose. In Figure 15-4, you may have metadata created by

- A data modeler using ERwin or another design tool

- An ETL expert using Data Integrator or Informatica to extract, transform, and cleanse information from source systems and load into a data warehouse

- A DBA who may create his or her own tables in the data warehouse and add column comments to those tables

- A universe designer who creates classes and objects

- An end user who creates variables within a report

Metadata exchange between these different tools and constituencies often required proprietary interfaces that each vendor had to build and maintain. More recently, however, the Common Warehouse Metamodel (CWM) has been gaining industry acceptance. CWM uses a number of standards to determine how metadata can be exchanged between different tools. CWMI or XMI specifies how metadata can be exchanged via XML files. As with many standards, the use of CWM specifications allows for a degree of interchange but may not be as robust as tool-specific interchanges. For example, the CWM 1.0 standard does not include a business description, which clearly is something end users would want to see. Thus if a modeling tool exports to CWM 1.0 and you use this to build your universe, you may be able to share something like an object name but not a universe object description.

The other issue is that while a certain amount of metadata should be exchanged via the different components in a BI architecture, discrepancies arise when metadata is modified or extended within any component.

To address these issues, Business Objects plans to release a new module called Metadata Manager (due Q2 2006). Metadata Manager will allow you to incorporate metadata from third-party sources, build universes from them, monitor dependencies, and perform impact analysis between source systems through to the Web Intelligence reports.

Metadata in a BI architecture

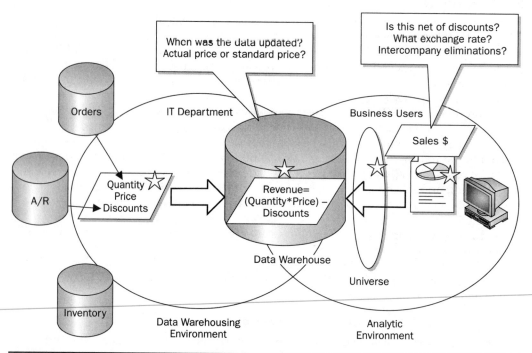

FIGURE 15-4   Metadata in a BusinessObjects XI environment

Summary

As the number of universes in your deployment increases, you need to look for ways to reduce the maintenance costs while ensuring consistency for users. Linking universes is a viable way to maintain a core set of dimension tables that multiple universes then access. As you develop universes and reports, you also need to establish development and test environments. With the XI release, the Import Wizard can facilitate this via BIAR files, also allowing you to integrate changes with third-party version control software. A more proven and cost-effective solution is to use test folders. When you have multiple designers modifying the same universe, Designer offers a good check-in/check-out capability to tell you when a universe is being modified by another designer. Finally, keep in mind that BusinessObjects Enterprise is only one piece of a BI environment. Metadata from related components of a BI environment should be incorporated as part of an enterprise solution.

Getting Ready for Production

This is a bit of a loose-ends chapter in which you finalize and quality-assure the universe, prepare universe documentation, and monitor system usage. If you have had close conversations with the business users and validated universe components as you added them, you may find that some of these steps are perfunctory. If, on the other hand, you built the universe in isolation and didn't test along the way, you will find this is an intensive time to revise the universe.

Universe Integrity

As you have built the universe, you have done a number of integrity checks. In modifying the SQL of individual objects, you should have parsed each one. The parse validates that you have entered the SQL correctly. In building joins, you have detected cardinalities and loops to create contexts and aliases.

The overall universe integrity check becomes a final chance to catch anything you may have missed in earlier stages. If you are using linked universes, it checks the integrity in both the kernel and derived universes. It also will determine if anything has changed in the data source structure that would make an existing object or join invalid.

To check the integrity of a universe, select the pull-down menu Tools | Check Integrity or select the Check Integrity button from the toolbar.

Designer presents you with the following dialog box:

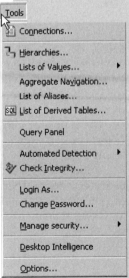

At this point, you can choose Check All to have Designer perform all possible checks, or you can choose to check the integrity of individual components. Table 16-1 explains the purpose of each check.

To perform the check, select the desired components and click OK. The following screen shows the results from Check All. Designer groups each warning according to the component tested, as listed in Table 16-1. Next to each component, Designer will display an OK or an Error count. Initially, any warnings and errors are collapsed. To see the full error, click the + sign next to the component.

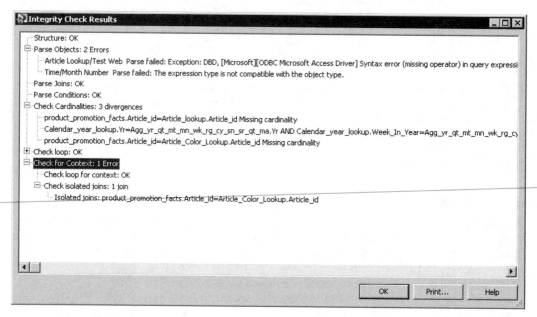

In the preceding example, there are several errors that need investigating. Under Parse Objects, the syntax may not be correct for the object *Test Web*. The object type for *Month Number* was set to character and does not match the numeric format in the database.

The status for Joins, Conditions, and Loops are all indicated with OK. Under Check Loop, you can expand this folder to display any loops and the contexts or aliases used to resolve them.

Under the Context check, you have a genuine error that can cause errors when a user executes a query. There is a join between PRODUCT_PROMOTION_FACTS and ARTICLE_COLOR_LOOKUP that does not belong to any context. Once you start using contexts, all joins must belong to at least one context. The exception is shortcut joins (see Chapter 8). By definition, these joins are most often used outside of fact tables and contexts. Therefore,

Option	Purpose
Check All	Checks all components within the universe, except for cardinalities, which must be explicitly selected.
Check Universe Structure	Compares the structure information in the Structure pane with the tables and columns within the RDBMS. If there is a difference between the two, Designer will give a warning. Tables within the Table Browser that have been removed or renamed but that are not in the Structure pane will not cause an error. If you regularly refresh your structure with View I Refresh Structure, this check should return no errors.
Parse Objects	Similar to the Parse button within the Object definition, this verifies that the SQL SELECT and WHERE syntax is correct and that the TABLE.COLUMN for each object is valid.
Parse Conditions	Similar to Parse Objects but checks predefined conditions only. This does not check the WHERE clause of regular objects.
Check Cardinalities	This will check if the cardinality has been defined for each join. It will not detect the relationship between the tables.
Check For Loops	This will detect any loops and inform you if they were resolved with an alias or context. Designer will list any loops that have not been resolved.
Check For Context	When you start using contexts, you must ensure that all joins defined belong to a context. The one exception is a shortcut join. These do not need to belong to a context but will generate an integrity check error if they are not defined to one; you can ignore this error, as it does not cause a problem during query execution.
Check Cardinalities	Ensures that the join cardinality (one to many, for example) has been set and is correct.

TABLE 16-1   Settings to Check the Integrity of the Universe Components

even if they produce an error during the integrity check, they still work correctly, as the shortcut join is used only when a user builds a query that involves only the two tables.

Checking as You Go

With the preceding two object errors, had you clicked Parse during the object modification, you also would have received an error. Hence a very important lesson: unless you like solving many problems at once, check the universe integrity as you make modifications. Designer allows you to set options that will force you to adhere to this practice. These options are global for all universes you develop from this particular workstation. From the pull-down menu, select Tools I Options and the General tab.

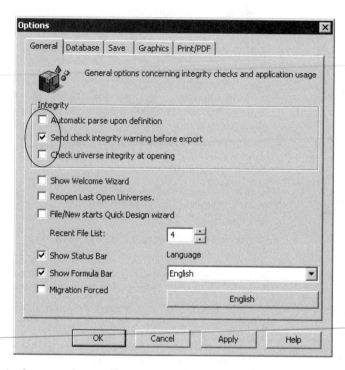

In the Integrity box, set the option Automatic Parse Upon Definition to have Designer check the SQL syntax whenever you add or modify an object or join. With this setting, you will not be able to add objects or joins that contain errors. Designer will not warn you about isolated joins when you create them, but it will prevent you from adding joins that contain an incorrect SQL statement (for example, if you define a complex join and skip a parenthesis or join operator). While this setting is fairly fail-proof, it can be aggravating when you are creating a complex object with long SQL syntax and it doesn't allow you to leave the partial SQL statement. Also, some readers of the first *Complete Reference* complained of intermittent problems parsing long DECODE statements against certain versions for Oracle, but I could not re-create this.

The second setting, Send Check Integrity Warning Before Export, will prompt you to do an integrity check prior to exporting the universe to the repository. Designer prompts you to check the universe integrity prior to export:

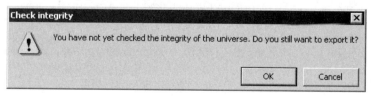

The last setting, Check Universe Integrity At Opening, forces an integrity check as soon as you open the universe. While this is a useful reminder to resolve errors, I personally find it annoying when used in conjunction with the first two settings.

Universe Documentation

Designer allows you to print a report to generate documentation on the universe. To select what information gets included in a particular printout, use the pull-down menu to set Tools | Options | Print/PDF.

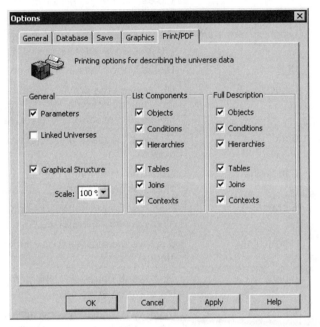

In general, elements under List Component will generate a simple list (refer to Table 16-2). Selecting elements under Full Description will give the complete SQL statements or Object Properties. When you select items from the Full Description, it's advisable to set your print options to landscape. Select File | Page Setup and then set the Orientation to Landscape. Sample reports are shown in Figures 16-1 through 16-3.

As shown in Figure 16-1, when you choose to print the universe parameters, you can save the output to PDF or send it to the printer. The parameters documentation displays all the universe information captured in File | Parameters, including the short and long names, the default connection name, SQL controls, strategies used to build the universe, and statistics on the number of objects.

Option Type	Option	Information Printed
General	Parameters	Universe-specific parameters such as the universe filename and description, revision number, total classes and objects, strategy settings, and SQL controls are set through File	Parameters. Refer to Chapter 7 for more information on these settings.
General	Linked Universes	When set, the name of the kernel universe is displayed plus all relevant objects, joins, and tables. Each is marked with the name of the kernel universe.
General	Graphical Structure	Displays the tables and joins as they appear in the Structure pane.
List Components	Objects	Displays the class and each object name.
Full Description	Objects	Displays all the properties for each object, including object type, SELECT statement, WHERE clause, list of values settings, and so on.
List Components	Conditions	Displays the class and object names for condition objects.
Full Description	Conditions	Gives the description defined for each condition object as well as the SQL statement.
List Components	Hierarchies	Displays the Class equivalent or dimension name of any custom hierarchies.
Full Description	Hierarchies	Displays the individual objects within the custom hierarchies.
List Components	Tables	Displays the physical table names that appear in the universe structure.
Full Description	Tables	Displays the columns and their field types for each physical table from the data source that appears in the universe structure.
List Components	Joins	Lists the simple join statements.
Full Description	Joins	Describes the cardinality between the tables and specifies whether or not the join is an outer join.
List Components	Contexts	Lists the names of the contexts, which are fairly meaningless without seeing which joins belong to which context (Full Description).
Full Description	Contexts	Displays the context name as well as each join that is included in the context.

TABLE 16-2   Print Options to Document the Universe

```
Universe:eFashion                                                    10/20/05
_____

    Universe Parameters

      Definition
        Name:                 eFashion
        Description:          eFashion retail Data Warehouse created 14 Oct 1998, updated 3 April :
                              89,000+ row fact table.

                              Version 6.0
        Connection:           eFashion

      General information
        Created:              6/25/98  by
        Modified:             9/20/05  by  Administrator
        Comments:             eFashion Data Warehouse Demo created by G.Bowman October 1998.
                              yright Business Objects 1998.        DB details: 89,000 line fact tabl
                              0 line promotions 2nd fact table, dual article lookup tables for performa
                              2 isolated aggregate tables for demo purposes

                              Updated by Glynn Naughton March 2002 to reflect updates to the datal
                              (some columns added, others renamed).
        Statistics:           7 Classes
                              43 Objects
                              10 Tables
                              0 Aliases
                              9 Joins
                              2 Contexts
                              3 Hierarchies
                              12 Conditions

      Strategies
        Join strategy:        Edit Manually (none)
        Table strategy:       (Built-in) Standard
        Object strategy:      (Built-in) Standard Renaming

      Controls
        Limit size of result set to:                         90000 rows
        Limit size of long text objects to:                  unchecked
        Limit execution time to:                             5 minutes
        Warn if cost estimate exceeds:                       unchecked
```

FIGURE 16-1   Parameters documentation displays universe definitions, controls, and so on.

Figure 16-2 shows a printout with the Full Description checked for Objects. With the Full Description box checked, you see the SQL statement, security settings (Public=0 to Private=4), whether the object can be used as a condition or result, and the default format.

Universe:eFashion   10/20/05

Object Properties

Class:	**Time period**
Description:	Time hierarchy

Object:	**Year**
Type:	Character
Description:	Year 1999 - 2001.
Select equivalent:	@aggregate_aware(
	Agg_yr_qt_rn_st_ln_ca_sr.Yr,
	Agg_yr_qt_mt_mn_wk_rg_cy_sn_sr_qt_ma.Yr,
	Calendar_year_lookup.Yr)
Where equivalent:	
Qualification:	dimension
List of values:	YEAR05D, editable, manual refresh, exportable
Security access level:	0
Can be used:	in result, in condition, in sort
Object status:	show
Format	Number
	Category = Standard
	Alignment
	Horizontal = Right

Object:	**Fiscal Period**

FIGURE 16-2 Object documentation displays information on classes and objects.

To save your documentation as an Adobe PDF file, rather than sending to the printer, you first set the options discussed here. Then choose File | Save As. In the Save As Type drop-down, select Portable Document Format.

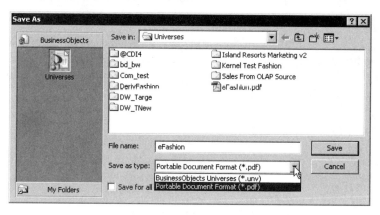

Quality Assurance Checklist

Before distributing the universe to the users, it is good to have a quality assurance session to review the universe. Table 16-3 provides a checklist that covers recommendations from the previous chapters. A spreadsheet version of this is available via various web sites (Publisher, BOB, and my consulting partners). A review session is different from an integrity check; the integrity check ensures that the universe is technically correct but does nothing to ensure that the universe follows best practices or will be successful with the users.

The following people should ideally be involved in a quality assurance review:

- **DBA**   The DBA will help verify the correctness of certain SQL statements, assess their impact on response time if there are advanced SQL functions, consider join strategies to generate the fastest queries possible, and identify opportunities to create aggregate tables and to tune indexes for popular condition objects.

- **Data modeler/architect**   The data modeler or architect will help identify any possible problems with joins that arise from missing data—for example, if a particular field is not required. This person can also review business terminology, object descriptions, customized lists of values, use of derived tables and aliases (CUSTOMER versus CUSTOMER_SHIP_TO versus CUSTOMER_SOLD_TO). A source system expert may also be helpful in this role.

- **Power user/report authors**   Power users and report authors will provide input on the overall appearance, organization, and functionality of the universe. Did you, as the designer, actually deliver what they hoped for? Will they be able to build the reports they need to build using the current design of the universe? Power users will also provide input on similar items to the data modeler.

- **Other designers**   If your company has multiple universe designers, it's useful to get an objective opinion from another designer on the universe. This is an excellent way to share tips and techniques and to provide a consistent user interface across universes (as an alternative to linked universes).

As companies increasingly deploy business intelligence as an enterprise solution, some have developed competency centers or centers of BI excellence. These competency centers would maintain and add to the quality assurance checklist to ensure best practices are documented and adhered to. With the competency center, individual business units may have their own universe designers but the competency center facilitates a quality assurance review to provide an additional level of expertise and quality control. Alternatively, designers may be staffed within the competency center, but the design review process ensures that all universe designers are adhering to best practices.

NOTE   *Oh, where, oh, where is ManagerO? Prior to printed reports, designers could get universe documentation only through another universe: ManagerO, a universe about universes that was available as freeware with version 5 and earlier. With printed reports directly from Designer, Business Objects had intended to eliminate ManagerO, but there were some things that ManagerO could tell designers that the printed reports could not. However, in XI, with the relational repository having been completely restructured, ManagerO has indeed disappeared and is no longer usable.*

Chapter	Category	Item	Date Reviewed	Comments and Exceptions
2 & 6 3	Overall Universe	• Subject area corresponds to business goal • Target user group identified • Number of objects appropriate for target user group		
7	Universe Parameters	• Universe description clear and complete • Connection synchronized with database user name and password • Controls adequate for query results • SQL settings generate correct results (recommend all enabled) • Query test for split SQL with multiple measures • Query test for split SQL with multiple contexts		
8	Joins	• Joined fields indexed • Join fields that contain nulls use an outer join • All loops are resolved with a context • Tables with multiple meanings have an alias • Joins belong to at least one context (exluding short-cut joins) • Joins with composite keys are entered as complex joins • Short-cut joins created for faster join paths not through fact table		
9	Objects	• Class names logical and meaningful • Classes sorted logically • Dimension objects point to lookup table • Objects not used for drill down marked as Detail objects • Column format and object type match • Measure includes SQL aggregate function • Separate measure provided for average unit price, etc. • Objects include description • Objects sorted logically within class (top to bottom for drill-down) • Object names are customer-oriented, clear, consistent, concise • Object format is set, particularly for numeric ID fields • Unnecessary hidden objects removed		

TABLE 16-3   Quality Assurance Checklist

Chapter	Category	Item	Date Reviewed	Comments and Exceptions
9 and 13	Objects *(continued)*	• Security access levels correctly set • Object uses are sensical (recommend all enabled) • Foreign/Primary Keys considered for better query performance		
10	List of Values	• List of values disabled for measure objects • List of values disabled for nonsensical detail objects • Long list of values are customized with prompt • Meaningless ID fields customized to include name or description or key enabled • List of values access dimension table not fact table • Object.lov file does not unintentionally contain data • Export with universe set only for custom list of values • Shared list of values used for common dimension objects		
11 14	Advanced Objects	• Condition objects created for common conditions, particularly time • Condition objects use index or give satisfactory query performance • Objects with prompts are not overly restrictive • Prompted field is indexed or gives satisfactory query performance • Count objects point to key field or uses Distinct • Ratios use SUM aggregate correctly SUM()/SUM() • Ratios in fact table recalculated in universe • Derived tables considered • Candidate objects for fact/dimension table insertion indentified		

TABLE 16-3 Quality Assurance Checklist *(continued)*

Chapter	Category	Item	Date Reviewed	Comments and Exceptions
11	Aggregate objects	• Aggregate table included in universe • Aggregate table has its own context • SUM function inserted correctly within Aggregate aware @ AGGREGATE_ AWARE(SUM(AGG1)), SUM(AGG2), SUM(DETAIL)) • Incompatible objects set • Incompatible objects include only relevant context • Query test to access aggregate table and detail table as intended • Query test verifies summary answers match answers from detail table		
12	Hierarchies	• Custom Hierarchies created • Hierarchies sorted from top to bottom • Separate hierarchies for ID and Description objects		
13	Universe Level Security	• Object level security matches universe object • Row restrictions do not cancel each other out • CMS Groups simplify access • Restriction sets group multiple universe restrictions		
16	Other	• Backup copy of universe available • Relevant documentation printed • Benchmark reports identified		

TABLE 16-3   Quality Assurance Checklist *(continued)*

Benchmark Reports

As you make changes to the universe and extend your implementation, it is important that either the designer or the power users develop standard reports that can be used to benchmark performance. Clearly, the universe is only one component that affects performance. However, if BusinessObjects XI is the interface that users see, it will get blamed entirely for performance issues. When a universe or report is poorly designed, or the Enterprise server overloaded, such blame may be appropriate. However, if the database is improperly tuned, users will still lament, "BusinessObjects is slow."

There are two purposes to designating benchmark reports. The first and simplest is to ensure that when you change your universe or server settings, you do not negatively affect performance. You want to know that a query that took ten seconds to run yesterday still takes ten seconds to run today even with all the underlying changes in the SQL settings (or better yet, maybe it now runs in one second!).

The second, more challenging purpose of identifying benchmark reports is to understand scalability. Some companies do a formal stress test during the pilot phase. Although BusinessObjects XI does not provide integrated load testing tools, these are available from third-party companies. For example, Mercury LoadRunner or Compuware's QALoad allow customers to simulate user load on the BusinessObjects Enterprise server.

Use Cases

To understand user load and performance tuning, also recognize that different types of reports and user interactions will stress different aspects of the system. If you have different BI content types (Crystal Reports, Desktop Intelligence, and Web Intelligence), you will want to test the processing power of each of these report types. Additionally, I recommend that you create use cases that represent the mixed usage patterns in your deployment:

- Concurrent users viewing static reports and/or the same report, for example, to simulate when you publish an income statement that many users wish to access simultaneously. Here, caching the report will help with performance.
- Concurrent users interacting (drilling, filtering, sorting) with different reports
- Concurrent users executing simple queries
- Concurrent users executing slow-running, complex queries
- Concurrent users generating and displaying reports with complex layouts, multiple data providers, numerous report-based calculations

Performance Bottlenecks

Figure 16-3 provides a conceptual overview of the phases of a user query, starting with the initial login and finishing with the presentation of a formatted report. The diagram is a simple deployment in which users access content via InfoView. Particular server processes can be distributed across multiple servers. If you are *modifying* reports using Crystal Reports or Desktop Intelligence, then a certain amount of processing occurs on the client PC rather than on the BusinessObjects Enterprise server. *Viewing* reports, though, shares the same performance bottlenecks. Table 16-4 explains the potential bottlenecks during each of these phases in accessing, refreshing, and interacting with a report.

Debugging performance is a complex task. In a BusinessObjects Enterprise environment, factors such as utilization of different server processes potentially distributed across multiple machines and a mix of Web Intelligence, Desktop Intelligence, and Crystal Reports users and processes make it harder to pinpoint bottlenecks. As the universe designer, the key aspect within your control is the query execution time, Phase 3 in Figure 16-3. While the RDBMS may largely affect this, the SQL generated is often the culprit of poor query performance. When your universe contains advanced objects as described in Chapter 11,

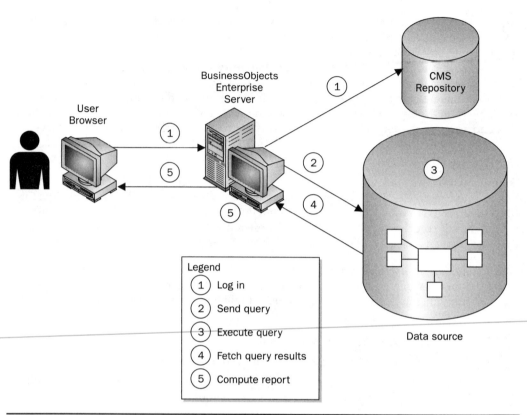

FIGURE 16-3 Performance bottlenecks can occur in multiple points of a BusinessObjects implementation.

you must understand how these affect query performance. If users filter their queries on objects that access nonindexed fields (because you did not define primary or foreign keys or because you added functions on all your dimension objects), their queries will be slow, and this is the fault of the universe designer. If your universe uses derived tables that generate complex subqueries, query performance here may also be affected.

As a way of identifying performance bottlenecks, use the SQL that Web Intelligence or Desktop Intelligence generates to isolate if the data source is the culprit for poor performance or if the culprit is load and settings within the BusinessObjects Enterprise server. First, evaluate if the SQL could have been written in a more efficient way; if yes, then modify your universe accordingly. Next, run an explain plan to see how the database is processing the query. Full table scans are an indication that either the SQL is not generated efficiently or the database is not tuned. Lastly, assuming the query runs equally slow when submitted directly to the database, your database is the performance bottleneck, not the Enterprise server.

Phase	Description	Potential Bottlenecks
1	Login	• CMS server load to process logins and permissions
2	Send Query, Connect to Datasource	• Universe complexity to generate the SQL, including use of restriction sets • Load on the BusinessObjects Enterprise Connection server to connect to the data source (Numerous slow-running queries will open numerous database connections, potentially becoming a bottleneck.) • Load on the data source to process logins
3	Launch Query: Analyzing and Executing	• Number of users concurrently logging into RDBMS • If using row-level security within data warehouse, complexity of security model and number of views to implement • If accessing source ERP, current load on system to update transactions • Ability of RDBMS to execute SQL efficiently, using indexes whenever possible; report and universe design comes into play here as certain SQL statements can be slow (subqueries, long CASE statements, filters with dimensions that contain functions)
4	Launch Query: Fetching	• WAN performance to deliver results from RDBMS back to the BusinessObjects Enterprise server
5	Display Report: Computing	• Specific Report Servers within the BusinessObjects • Enterprise server to convert query results to microcube, display charts, formatted tables, and convert to HTML or PDF

TABLE 16-4   Potential Bottlenecks That Affect BusinessObjects XI Response Time

As a designer, you can build a simple query within Designer to preview the SQL generated. However, to diagnose performance issues, you most often will want to see the SQL from a query a user has built.

To access the SQL from within Desktop Intelligence:

1. Select Data | Edit Data Provider and click SQL to launch the SQL viewer.

2. From within the SQL viewer, click Save to save the SQL to a separate text file.

From within the Web Intelligence, Java Report panel:

1. Select Edit Query from the menu bar.

2. Click SQL on the toolbar.

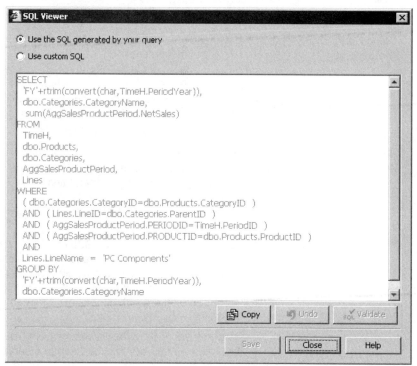

3. Click Copy to copy the SQL to the Windows clipboard and pull it into your own SQL diagnostic tools.

TIP *As a way of identifying query performance problems, use the prebuilt Auditor report Average Refresh Time.*

Monitoring User Activity

I have likened running an enterprise BI deployment without usage monitoring to driving at night with no headlights turned on and no dashboard information. It's dangerous and bound to lead to a crash. With a departmental deployment, you may not have the personnel to proactively monitor usage and system performance. You only know there is a problem when users start complaining. With critical deployments and enterprise deployments, you must be more proactive. You need to anticipate problems *before* they happen. Equally important, you must take care to evaluate that your design is meeting the needs of the users. If you've built reports and universes that are not widely used, you have a problem.

BusinessObjects Enterprise has had built-in monitoring capabilities for years, but they have not been widely used for a number of reasons, some technical and licensing-related but mostly arising from lack of awareness. With BusinessObjects XI, there are two different sets of auditing reports, depending upon whether you have a Crystal Reports deployment or Web Intelligence. If you use both interfaces, which format auditing report to use is strictly a matter of personal preference and degree of flexibility you want within a report. Both sets of reports access an Activity universe that provides access to data stored in an audit database. New in XI Release 2 is that Auditing can be enabled during the initial installation process (assuming you have an Enterprise license).

By default, activity is captured in a log file. In order to use the Activity universe, you need to capture the data to a relational database. The Auditing database is specified in the Central Configuration Manager (a Windows-based application on the BusinessObjects Enterprise Server), by selecting the Central Management System, Properties, and the Configuration tab.

You can determine which level of detail is captured in the audit database. To do so, you change audit settings in the Central Management Console. Select the server component for which you wish to capture activities, and then select the Auditing tab, as shown in Figure 16-4.

It's important to note that you can only capture a minimal amount of Desktop Intelligence activity. This was also the case in earlier versions, as much of the activity did not go through a central server. In XI Release 2, you can capture activity on the Desktop Intelligence Job Server for scheduled reports but not for real-time report actions. As Desktop Intelligence users log in to the CMS, session information such as login times is, however, captured.

Once you have configured auditing to a database and enabled auditing on the individual BusinessObjects Enterprise servers, ensure that the Activity universe contains the correct connection parameters to the Auditing database. As a way of understanding the auditing

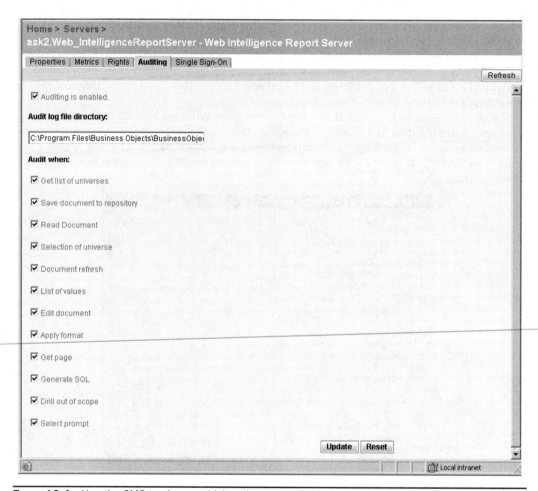

Properties | Metrics | Rights | **Auditing** | Single Sign-On

Refresh

☑ Auditing is enabled.

Audit log file directory:

C:\Program Files\Business Objects\BusinessObje

Audit when:

☑ Get list of universes

☑ Save document to repository

☑ Read Document

☑ Selection of universe

☑ Document refresh

☑ List of values

☑ Edit document

☑ Apply format

☑ Get page

☑ Generate SQL

☑ Drill out of scope

☑ Select prompt

Update Reset

Local intranet

FIGURE 16-4 Use the CMC to choose which actions to audit.

information available, I suggest you familiarize yourself with the prebuilt reports in the Auditor folder and described in Table 16-5. In the Type column, I've indicated when you might want to use a particular report. For example, if you want to get an overview of Usage, use the report Average Number of Users Logged In. If you want to better understand usage *style*, use the report User Activity Per Session (Figure 16-5). It displays a chart with the types of actions a user typically performs, so that you can better understand how users are using BusinessObjects XI.

As you run these prebuilt Auditing reports, you will find that the Activity universe could do with some tweaking. For example, the list of values on many objects is not

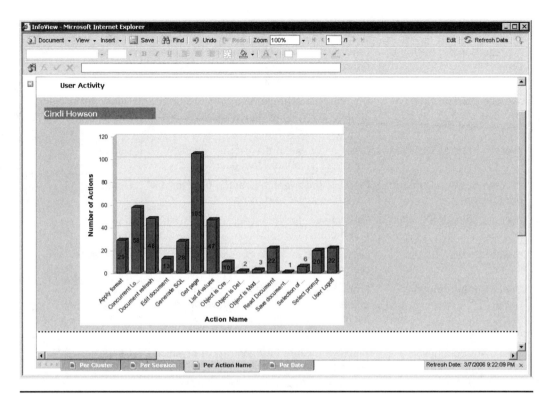

FIGURE 16-5   Sample audit report that shows activity type by user

properly sorted, which makes it difficult to respond to some of the query prompts. For example, the universe object *Object Name* can be a universe object or a repository object. When using this as a filter criterion, the list of available objects is not sorted alphabetically or by universe.

NOTE   *Many of the prebuilt reports only display content when data is available. All reports will initially display the message "No Information to Display" until you refresh the report.*

NOTE   *The Auditor product in BusinessObjects 6 and earlier included a security universe that allowed you to better understand who had access to which documents and belonged to which groups. This information was stored clearly in the repository tables. This level of detail is not available in BusinessObjects XI Release 2 as of SP1.*

Auditing is described more fully in the vendor documentation, BusinessObjects Enterprise XI Release 2 Auditor's Guide.

Report Title	Report Purpose	Type
Average Number of Users Logged In	Chart with the average number of users filtered by month and year. Contains a list report to show individual user logins.	Usage
Average Refresh Time	Displays the average query refresh time in seconds for individual documents, users, and servers.	Query Performance
Average Session Duration	Chart and table of the average session duration for an individual user.	Usage
Average Session Duration per Cluster	Displays the average session time for the CMS by quarter and by day.	Usage
Average Session Duration per User	For all users for year displayed by week and month.	Usage
Cluster Nodes	Lists the server or processes such as the Job Servers and Report Servers.	Information
Document Information Detail	Prompts you to select a document and tells you what actions have been performed such as refresh, apply formatting, etc.	Usage
Document Scheduling and Viewing Status	Displays a count for each report of which users viewed an individual document and how frequently it was viewed.	Usage
Job Summary	Charts the percentage of successful and failed scheduled reports.	Scheduling Usage
Jobs per Job Server	Displays a count of jobs processed by each of the job servers.	Scheduling Usage
Jobs per User	Displays jobs succeeded or failed (not pending) and the time it took for each.	Scheduling Usage
Job Servers on the System	Displays a list of job servers that handle refresh of scheduled reports.	Information
Last Login for User	Displays when an individual user last logged in to the system.	Usage
Least Accessed Documents	Ranking report that displays the ten least refreshed, edited, or viewed documents.	Usage
Most Accessed Documents	Ranking report that displays the ten most refreshed, edited, or viewed documents.	Usage

TABLE 16-5   Prebuilt Reports Based on the Activity Universe

Report Title	Report Purpose	Type
Most Active Users	Ranking report that shows the top ten users by refreshes and logins.	Usage
Most Popular Actions	Charts the most frequent actions such as logons or refreshes.	Usage Style
Most Popular Actions per Document	Similar to the Document Information Detail report, this ranks the actions filtered by individual document.	Usage Style
Number of User Sessions	Charts the number of user sessions by month and quarter for a particular year.	Usage
Number of Users in the System	Number of active users who have logged in at least once. This does *not* display all users defined to the CMC.	Usage
Password Modifications	Shows which users have changed their password within a defined period to identify possible security threats. This report does not include password changes made by an administrator in the CMC.	Security
Peak Usage	Displays a chart of the number of users logged in hourly, aggregated for the year.	Server Load
Refresh and Edit Activity	Displays a count of the total number of refreshes and edits for an individual user.	Usage
Rights Modification	Lists what BI content has had rights modified and by whom and how often.	Security
Total Users Logged in By Day	Displays hourly logins by individual user for one day.	Usage
User Activity	Displays the total number of logins for a time period.	Usage
User Activity per Session	Charts the type of activity performed by an individual user.	Usage Style
Users Who Logged Off Incorrectly	Counts total logins versus total logoffs. When there is not a logoff, then the session times out. It's an enlightening report: I fail to log off correctly 68 percent of the time!	Usage Style

TABLE 16-5   Prebuilt Reports Based on the Activity Universe *(continued)*

Summary

In the rush to meet your BI project deadlines, it's easy to skip the steps of documentation, quality assurance, and usage monitoring. So easy in fact, that it seldom happens! Yet for a mission-critical business intelligence solution, these tasks are essential. Quality assurance reviews help foster knowledge throughout the BI competency center and ensure a consistent design approach across development teams. Usage monitoring provides a mechanism for scaling your deployment in a controlled way and predicting potential performance issues.

Reporting and Analysis

PART

III

Navigating InfoView

Part I of this book lays the groundwork for implementing BusinessObjects XI, and Part II provides information for universe designers and administrators to build a business-oriented solution. Part III is for end users who need to access information to make decisions and improve business performance.

The chapters in this section of the book are organized by workflow, starting with decision-makers or report consumers who access published reports. If you are a power user or report author, then you may want to start with Chapter 20 to begin building new queries.

Logging In to InfoView

InfoView is Business Objects' portal solution. It allows you to interact with the BusinessObjects XI content and applications. The repository allows you to store BI content generated by one of the user interfaces (such as Web Intelligence, Crystal Reports, Desktop Intelligence, Dashboard Manager) or other documents such as Word, Excel, and PDF files, making it a powerful tool for managing business performance.

To log in to InfoView, you only need a browser and a web site address or URL. No additional software needs to be installed on your PC. You access InfoView by entering a URL or in some deployments, by selecting a link via a corporate intranet. The default URL for the JSP version is

```
http://servername:8080/businessobjects/enterprise115/desktoplaunch/InfoView/logon/logon.do
```

For the ASP version:

```
http://servername/businessobjects/enterprise115/InfoView/logon.aspx
```

where *servername* is the name of the BusinessObjects Enterprise server.

When you log in to InfoView, the server first validates your user ID and password. Your user ID and password may be specific to BusinessObjects XI or may be determined by another authentication source. These other authentication sources may be the same as your LAN login or a third-party directory server that you use for all corporate applications. Before beginning the login process, ensure you know the correct authentication source.

1. Under System, the default Central Management Server (CMS) will appear. If you have multiple BusinessObjects implementations, enter the name of the CMS in the System box.

2. Enter your user name in the box provided. When authenticating against BusinessObjects Enterprise, this is not case sensitive.

3. Enter your password. For security purposes, this is displayed as asterisk as you enter each character (*). Your password may be case sensitive and may be a combination of characters and numbers.

4. Choose the authentication source from the drop-down box. Enterprise is the default and refers to the BusinessObjects Enterprise repository. If your administrator has enabled authentication to be the same as your LAN login, choose Windows NT.

5. Click Log On.

The first time you log in to InfoView, you may be prompted to change your password, as shown in the following illustration. You also will receive this prompt if the BusinessObjects Enterprise administrator requires you to change your password on a periodic basis, for example, every 90 days.

Change Password

User Name:	Cindi Howson
Old Password:	
New Password:	
Confirm New Password:	

Submit

Password Expired
- Your account password has expired.
- Please update your password now.

NOTE *Some deployments may allow a guest login that does not require a user name and password. To log in as a guest, leave the user name and password boxes blank.*

If you need to change your password at some other point, choose Preferences from the Header panel (shown in Table 17-1), and then select the Password tab.

About Passwords

Password settings are determined by the BusinessObjects XI administrator (see Chapter 13) or, when using external authentication, by your company security administrator.

The administrator can require your password to be a minimum length. The system may also count back a certain number to prevent you from re-using the same password. When you enter the wrong password after so many attempts, your account will become disabled. Your account may be disabled permanently until you contact an administrator or disabled for a defined period of time.

If you enter the incorrect user name or password (or the right user name but against an incorrect authentication source), you will receive the following error message: **"Account Information Not Recognized: An error occurred at the server. Enterprise authentication could not log you on. Please make sure your logon information is correct."**

If you eventually remember the correct user name and password and the account has been disabled, you will receive the following error message: **"Account Information Not Recognized: An error occurred at the server. The user account has been disabled."**

PART III

The InfoView Panels

The InfoView portal consists of three main panels as shown in Figure 17-1.

The Header panel at the top of your screen is your main menu. This panel remains regardless if you are interacting with a document, changing portal options, or creating a new query. You can hide the Header panel by clicking the upward arrow from within the Workspace panel. You may want to hide the Header panel when you are working with a tall report and need a larger screen workspace.

If you hide the Header panel, a downward arrow appears within the Workspace panel. Click this arrow to have the Header panel restored.

The Navigation panel on the left-hand side of your screen provides a list of documents within the repository that you can navigate by selecting folders or categories. You can hide the Navigation panel by clicking the left pointing arrow or by clicking the Show Navigation Panel button. To restore the list of folders or categories, use the Show Navigation Panel button from the Header Panel toolbar.

The Workspace panel changes depending upon the content you have selected, usually a list of reports or an individual document. Figure 17-1 shows the default workspace. I recommend you customize this workspace to display your own reports, or My InfoView. Customizing the Workspace panel is described in Options.

As when working within a Microsoft Windows environment, you can manipulate the panels, or windows, by clicking the options in the upper-right corner:

The Header Panel

The Header panel acts as your main menu within InfoView. Table 17-1 describes the options available within this panel.

Navigation Panel

The Navigation panel helps you locate individual documents through folders or categories. Folders and categories provide a way of organizing documents and BI content. *Folders* provide the physical storage location of a file as well as a means to navigate content. *Categories* provide navigation only. A document must be stored in a folder; it does not have to be assigned a category. A key feature of categories is that one document can be assigned to multiple categories,

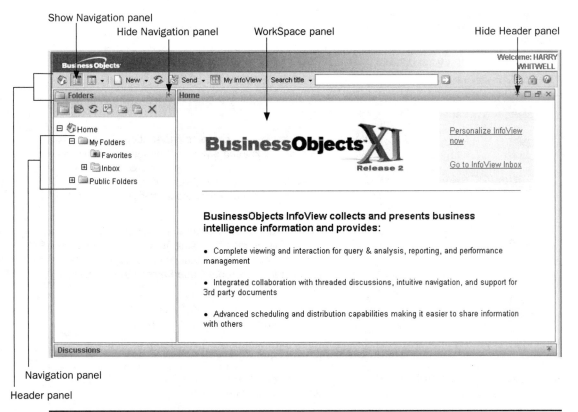

Show Navigation panel
Hide Navigation panel   WorkSpace panel   Hide Header panel

Navigation panel

Header panel

FIGURE 17-1   InfoView consists of three main panels.

making it easier to cross-reference documents, whereas with folders, a document can reside in only one folder. See Chapter 13, under "Folders and Categories," for more information.

Categories existed in previous versions of BusinessObjects but not in Crystal Enterprise. Crystal Enterprise users, meanwhile, are accustomed to folders. You as the user can decide if you prefer to navigate BI content by folders or categories. Figure 17-1 shows the default view of a user folder and public folders.

Table 17-2 describes the buttons available in the Navigation panel.

To change the Navigation panel to display categories, click the Show Categories button from the Navigation panel.

When you first log in to InfoView, you will see either the top-level folders (as shown in Figure 17-1) or the top-level categories, depending on your preferences. For folders, this is My Folders and Public Folders. For categories, this is My Categories and Corporate Categories. To expand the folders, click the + sign next to the folder or category. My Folders contains two standard folders: Favorites and Inbox. Documents in your Inbox are reports that other users have sent directly to you via the Enterprise repository. Documents in Favorites are documents that you create or modify that you do not wish to share with other users.

Button or Option	Name	Function
	Home	Returns you to your starting InfoView Home page.
	Show/Hide Navigation Panel	Toggles to display the list of folders or categories.
	Show/Hide Encyclopedia	The Encyclopedia contains information about individual documents and provides guided analysis.
New	New	Drop-down menu allows you to create New Web Intelligence documents, processes, folders, and so on.
	Refresh	Refreshes the Workspace panel to update the list of reports since initially logging in. If an administrator changed your security settings or if another user publishes a new report, use Refresh to see these changes.
Send	Send	Drop-down menu to send documents to other users via repository in-boxes, e-mail, or FTP.
My InfoView	My InfoView	Customizes the Workspace panel to display multiple reports.
Search title	Search Title	Drop-down menu to search for documents by title, author, date, folder, etc.
	Execute The Search	After entering the search options, click this arrow to perform the search.
	Preferences	Set InfoView preferences.
	Logoff	Log out of InfoView.
	Help	Launch contextual help.

TABLE 17-1   Buttons and Menu Options Available in the Header Panel

Button	Name	Description
	Show Folders	Display content organized by folders.
	Show Categories	Display content organized by categories that can optionally be assigned to each document.
	Refresh	Refresh the list of available folders and reports. When your access permissions change or new content has been saved, refresh the list to see the new items.
	Properties	Display the folder name and description.
	Move	Move the folder and its contents.
	Copy	Copy the folder and its contents.
	Delete	Delete the folder and its contents.

TABLE 17-2   Navigation Panel Buttons

Public Folders contains folders that may be organized by department or functional area. As shown in the following, there are folders for the Finance group and the Marketing group, as well as for the Plastics business unit. You will see only the folders for which you have been granted access. Public Folders replace the concept of Corporate Documents in earlier versions of BusinessObjects.

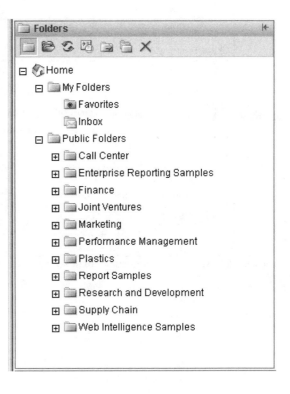

Accessing Documents

To see the contents of a folder, click the folder name within the Navigation panel. As shown in Figure 17-2, the Workspace panel displays the documents, a status of whether or not a document was run, and the document type, owner, and description if available. You can customize what information and options appear here by setting your InfoView preferences.

Beneath each document name is a list of available actions: View latest instance, History, Schedule, Modify, and Properties, as well as the document description. If you want to collapse this action line to allow you to display a longer list of documents in the same page, click the upward arrow next to the individual document or on the title bar to collapse the actions and descriptions for all documents.

NOTE   *The list of available actions for each document is also controlled by your permissions. If, for example, you do not have permission to modify the document, this option will not appear. Refer to Chapter 13 for more information on security settings.*

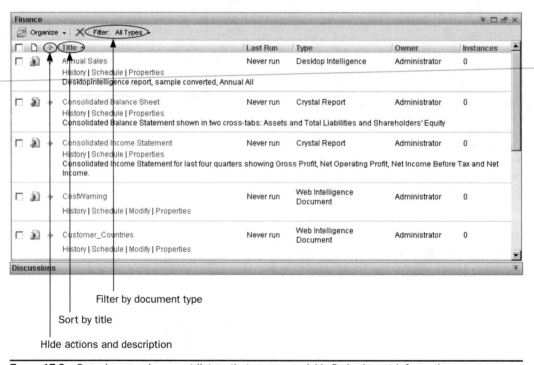

FIGURE 17-2   Organize your document list so that you can quickly find relevant information.

To view the document, click the document name. To see instances of a report that have been scheduled, select History. The Last Run column displays the date a report was refreshed through the scheduler, not the date it was last saved in the repository. Interacting with documents is discussed further in Chapter 18.

To filter the list of documents according to one type (see Table 17-2), select the Filter drop-down, shown to the right.

To sort the list of documents by Title, Owner, or Last Run date, click the column on the top bar as shown in Figure 17-2. A triangle appears next to the column providing the primary sort order. Which additional columns appear in this list (date, owner) are controlled through your InfoView preferences.

The BusinessObjects XI repository can contain several document types, each indicated with a different icon:

Icon	Document Type
	Crystal Report
	Desktop Intelligence
	Web Intelligence Document
	OLAP Intelligence
	Process Tracker
	Analytic

Organizing Documents

From within the Workspace panel, you can copy or move documents to other folders (assuming you have the appropriate access). You may want to do this when

- You want to use a document as a starting point but then modify it to add your own sorts, filters, and calculations. You want to save the modified report to your personal work.

- You want to provide access quickly to a document to another user that does not have access to the same folder. You can copy a document to a folder that the second user can access.

- You want to create a shortcut to a document as a way of simplifying your navigation, so all your important content can be found in one starting location.

For example, Figure 17-2 shows a list of reports within the Finance folder. The report Customer_Countries lists customer revenue and contact information by country. You want to modify the report so that you see only your individual country.

TIP *Prompts are another way to personalize a report when users want to see just their data. The report author could modify this report to add a dynamic prompt by country. See Chapter 20.*

To copy the report to your personal folder, follow these steps:

1. Check the box next to the document name.
2. From the Workspace Panel menu, select the Organize drop-down menu.
3. Select the desired task, in this case, Copy To New Folder.

4. InfoView presents you with a Copy dialog and asks you to where you want to copy the document.

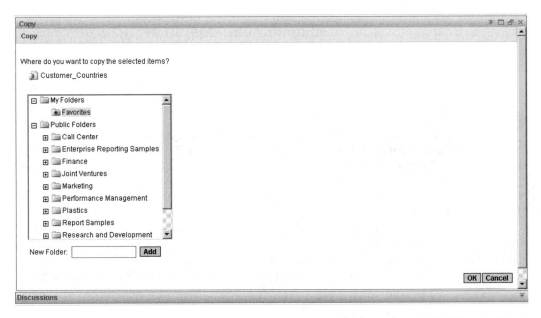

5. If you are copying the document to your personal folder, select My Folders and then the particular folder or Favorites.

6. Click OK in the bottom far right of the dialog.

7. InfoView will return you to the list of documents in the public folder. To see where you have copied the document, select My Folders from the Navigation panel.

NOTE *You can also copy the document to another public folder, assuming you have permission. If you do not have sufficient rights to copy the object to another public folder, InfoView will generate the following error message: "An error occurred at the server : Sorry, you do not have the right to 'Add objects to the folder' (id - 1) for 'Marketing ' (id - 20080). Please contact your system or permissions administrator if you require this right."*

About Shortcuts

InfoView shortcuts work much the same way as Microsoft Office shortcuts: they act as pointers to the original document. In this way, shortcuts may make your navigation to reports simpler, but they do not allow you to make changes to the report (unless you are also the owner of the public report).

In Step 3 in the preceding section, when you choose Add To My Favorites from the Organize drop-down, or when you choose Add Short Cuts To New Folder, InfoView creates a pointer to the original file:

```
☐  🗋  ✦    Shortcut to Customer_Countries
                  History | Schedule | Modify | Properties
```

You can view or refresh a shortcut, but you may not save changes to the underlying document. If the original document is later deleted, the shortcut pointer remains but the icon becomes a blank piece of paper.

InfoView Preferences

The first time you work with InfoView, you need to modify several options to ensure that you display and build reports in the desired format. To modify your default settings, select the Preferences button from top-right corner of the Header panel.

Some of the tabs that appear here will depend also on what interfaces your company has licensed.

General

Within the General page of the InfoView preferences, you set the defaults for your starting page, behavior when you open and close a document, how the list of documents appears, and so on.

```
Preferences                                                                                    ☀ ☐ ⊟ ✕
┌──────────┬──────────────────┬───────────────────────┬──────────────────┬────────────────┬──────────┬────────┐
│ General  │ Desktop Intelligence │ Web Intelligence Document │ OLAP Intelligence │ Crystal Report │ Password │ About  │
└──────────┴──────────────────┴───────────────────────┴──────────────────┴────────────────┴──────────┴────────┘

My initial view is ...

⦿ Home

○ My InfoView

○ Favorites

○ Inbox

○ the folder:   (unspecified)   [ Browse ... ]

○ the category:  (unspecified)  [ Browse ... ]


My default navigation view is ...

⦿ Folder

○ Category


On my desktop ...

Set the number of objects (max.) per page:  [ 10 ]


For each document, show me ...

☑ description

☑ owner

☑ date
```

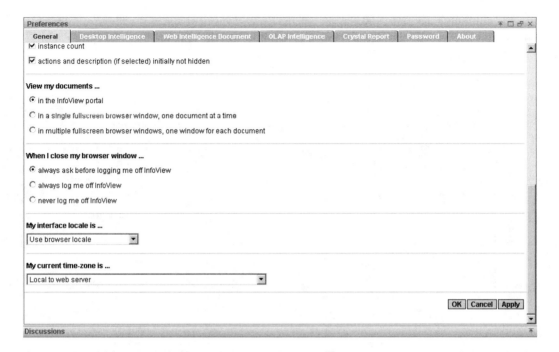

You set your initial InfoView display by choosing from

- **Home**   Displays the default screen as shown in Figure 17-1.
- **My InfoView**   Displays a customized layout with each portlet displaying a different document, URL, or list of documents.
- **Favorites**   Displays your personal documents or shortcuts to shared documents.
- **Inbox**   Displays documents that have been sent to you by other users or by the scheduler.
- **Folder**   Allows you to customize which folder contents initially appear in the Workspace panel.
- **Category**   Allows you to customize which category appears in the Workspace panel.

The option My Default Navigation View determines what appears in the left-hand pane as shown in Figure 17-1: folders or categories.

Set The Number Of Objects to appear in a given document list before you have to scroll to the next page. In the preceding illustration, 10 is the default. This setting also depends on whether or not you display the actions and document description as longer lists can fit on one page when these details do not appear.

For Each Document, Show Me determines how documents appear as shown in Figure 17-2. By default, all details for each document are displayed, including the description (when created by the report author), the owner or person who created the document, the date, the number of instances available for scheduled documents, and actions.

The following list of documents shows the same documents from the Finance folder as in Figure 17-2. The list appears less busy, as less information appears by default for each document.

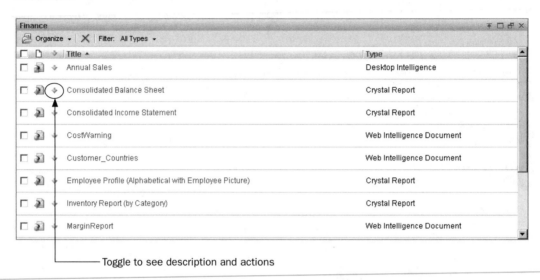

Toggle to see description and actions

TIP   *To simplify the initial list of documents, check only the description radio button and leave all the other buttons unchecked. Then use the arrow toggle next to the individual document to see the actions and description when necessary.*

Under the section View My Documents, you determine what you want to happen when you open a document:

- **In the InfoView Portal**   This displays the document in the same browser window as InfoView.
- **In a single fullscreen browser window, one document at a time**   When you select this option, your list of documents remains in one browser session. The report viewer opens a second browser session that displays the individual report. This option gives you a better workspace for viewing larger reports and then makes it easier to navigate to other reports.
- **In multiple fullscreen browser windows, one window for each document**   This option is recommended when you need to work with multiple reports simultaneously.

When you close a browser window, InfoView can either log you out automatically or prompt you. You are not prompted when you close individual document windows.

The interface locale refers to regional preferences for displaying date and time. This affects how dates appear in reports and in list of values.

Under My Current Time Zone Is, you can specify if you want times synchronized with the Web Server for the BusinessObjects Enterprise server, or if that server is located in another time zone, you can specify your time zone.

To make changes to your General InfoView preferences, do the following:

1. Select the Preferences button from the top-right corner of the Header panel.

2. By default, the General page appears first.

3. Click the desired option.

4. Scroll to the bottom of the page and click OK.

Document Options

From within the InfoView Preferences page, you can set the view options for each of the different document formats that you may access via InfoView and that your company has licensed.

Desktop Intelligence Options

For Desktop Intelligence documents, you can choose to view them in HTML format, Adobe PDF, or native BusinessObjects format.

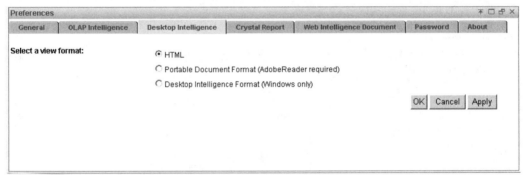

HTML viewing offers the fastest report display. However, when you view via HTML, your print options are limited. If you eventually want to print your document, then either PDF or Desktop Intelligence format offers the highest-quality presentation.

Within HTML mode, you can continue to navigate to different pages within the report; use the Find function; or convert to PDF, Excel, or CSV.

When viewing a Desktop Intelligence document in PDF format, you must have Adobe Reader installed on your desktop. One of the key benefits to PDF format is that you can take a report with you and work with it offline (assuming you have the appropriate permissions). Section headings are converted to PDF bookmarks for easy navigation. While viewing a report in PDF format, you can easily toggle to HTML format.

If you select Desktop Intelligence as the default viewing format, then a copy of the report is downloaded to your computer and Desktop Intelligence is launched. Therefore, you must have Desktop Intelligence installed on your computer.

Web Intelligence Options

For Web Intelligence documents, you can choose to view them as HTML, Interactive, or
PDF. Interactive viewing is available in the JSP version only when your company uses a
Java application server. The Interactive viewing option provides report consumers with the
most power, allowing them to sort, filter, and reformat reports via a right-mouse-click pop-
up menu. Interactive viewing is not available when BusinessObjects Enterprise is running
on a Microsoft Windows .NET application server.

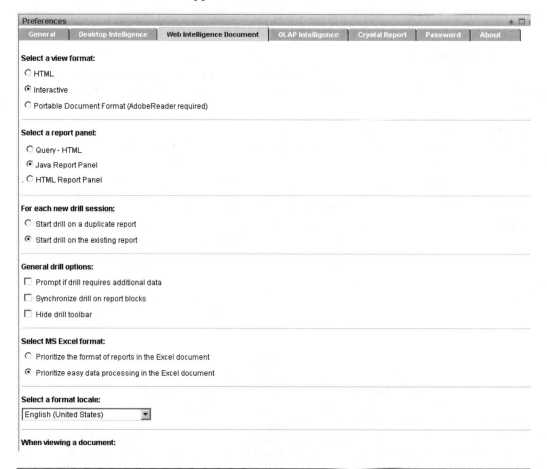

Tip   *To ensure you have the most power and ease of use when viewing Web Intelligence documents,
set your default viewing format to Interactive.*

Web Intelligence offers different report panels for authoring queries. Which default you
choose will depend on your Internet security, functionality requirements, and application
server platform. The naming of this section of options and the panels is not obvious. The

Query – HTML option does not in fact represent a *report* panel; it chooses a *query* panel so that when you choose to modify a document or choose Edit Query, you modify the query only, not the formatting. The Query – HTML panel requires no additional software, plug-ins, or applets. It is a zero-footprint authoring environment recommended when reports are authored across firewalls or via slow dial-up. Use the Query – HTML panel in conjunction with the Interactive viewer to do your formatting in the viewer.

The second report panel option, Java Report Panel, will download a Java applet the first time you launch it. It provides the richest Web-based authoring and report formatting capabilities. If you use the Interactive viewer, you also can choose the HTML Query panel as your default editor. In this way, you do all analysis and formatting via a zero-footprint viewer and then if you need to modify the query, you launch a separate zero-footprint query editor.

NOTE *If your Enterprise server is running on the .NET application server, then the Java Report panel is the only available report panel and this section of options will not appear in your InfoView preferences.*

The third report panel, HTML Report Panel, has both query design and report layout options. It uses a wizard-like interface to guide you through the query and report design process. It lacks some of the capabilities in the Java Report panel. For example, the HTML Report panel allows only one block style within a report; it does not allow you to have a crosstab and pie chart on the same page. When the HTML Report panel is set as your default editor and you attempt to modify a report that is too complex for it, you will receive an error. The Query – HTML (first option) panel is still zero-footprint but can edit these more complex layouts.

For drill options, you determine if you want Web Intelligence to make a copy of the report when you begin drilling or if the drill should occur in the same report page. Note that this refers to a report within one Web Intelligence document (.wid file) and does not make a duplicate file. I recommend you set this option to drill on a duplicate report copy, mainly as a way of preserving formatting and the initial view point. Drilling is discussed further in Chapter 19.

As you drill, you often will display additional levels of detail that may already exist within the document. However, in some cases, Web Intelligence may need to issue a new query to retrieve the additional details. By setting the option Prompt If Drill Requires Additional Data, you will be warned when a new query is executed. This is recommended when query response times are variable.

A Web Intelligence document can contain multiple blocks, for example, a chart and a crosstab. If you want a drill within a chart to be synchronized by the same drill within the corresponding crosstab, set the option Synchronize Drill On Report Blocks.

When you schedule a Web Intelligence document to run, you can choose the output format to be Excel. If you want the scheduled spreadsheet to preserve formatting, set the preference Prioritize The Format Of Reports In The Excel Document. If you want the scheduled output to contain data in text format, choose Prioritize Easy Data Processing In The Excel Document.

NOTE *This setting applies only to scheduled reports and does not relate to reports exported while viewing the document. Additionally, the easy data option had no effect on the output in the beta or initial production release.*

The next two settings regarding locales relate to one another. The format locale corresponds to regional settings that affect how dates and numbers are formatted in the report display, document filters, and query lists of values. For example, in Switzerland, a date is specified as DD.MM.YY and the separator for thousands is an apostrophe. The following report shows the format locale with Select A Format Locale set to German (Switzerland).

Swiss German Locale

Reservation Year	Reservation Month	Reservation Date	Revenue
FY2001	Jan	12.01.01	3'286'524

In the U.S., dates are written as MM/DD/YY and a comma is used as the separator for thousands. The same report just shown displays differently when the format locale is set to English (U.S.) and the option Use My Formatting Locale To Format The Data is set. If the option Use The Document Locale To Format The Data is set, then the report stays in the Swiss German format, as that is the locale that was used by the report author.

English U.S. Locale

Reservation Year	Reservation Month	Reservation Date	Revenue
FY2001	Jan	1/12/01	3,286,524

When you set the format locale for Web Intelligence to Use Interface Locale, it then takes the locale from the one you set in the General tab. You can in theory set the Web Intelligence locale to something different from InfoView, but frankly, I can't imagine a scenario when you would want to do that. Likewise, you most often will want the document to appear in your locale and not the report author's locale.

OLAP Intelligence Options

With OLAP Intelligence, you can set the option to use either an ActiveX viewer or a DHTML viewer. The ActiveX viewer requires Internet Explorer and will download ActiveX controls, which may not be permitted in some organizations for security reasons. When you export data to Excel, if you have used the ActiveX viewer, the link to OLAP Intelligence remains so that you can further drill and slice and dice. The DHTML viewer does not require any software or controls to be downloaded.

Preferences							
General	Desktop Intelligence	Web Intelligence Document	OLAP Intelligence	Crystal Report	Password	About	

View my reports using the ...   ○ ActiveX viewer.
          ● DHTML viewer.

OK | Cancel

Crystal Report Options

When viewing a Crystal Reports document, choose the default viewer that is most compatible with your browser and the functionality you want. All the viewers allow you to view, refresh, print, see the grouping tree, find, and export.

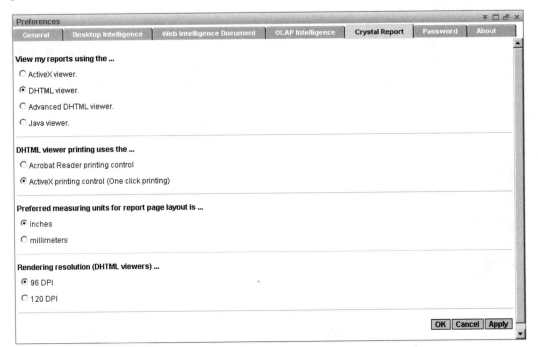

The ActiveX viewer uses ActiveX controls and requires Internet Explorer as the browser. If you use this as your viewer, you must ensure your browser security settings allow ActiveX controls to run. In addition to the standard viewing capabilities, this viewer also allows you to hover over a column and then freeze the panes for scrolling.

The DHTML viewer is a zero-footprint viewer; no controls are downloaded.

The Advanced DHTML option is supported in more recent browser versions and provides slightly more functionality than the basic DHTML viewer. Advanced DHTML includes an advanced Search panel that lets you interactively specify the search criteria, conditions, and results while viewing a Crystal Report.

The Java viewer requires that your browser use a Java Virtual Machine, similar to the Web Intelligence Java Report panel, and download a Java applet.

If you set the default viewer to DHTML, you also must specify how to print the Crystal Report, either by first converting to Adobe Acrobat or PDF format or by using the ActiveX printing control. The ActiveX printing is faster but, again, requires the correct browser security settings to allow the ActiveX control. Printing via Acrobat Reader requires that you have Acrobat Reader installed and is slower, as the report must first be converted to PDF.

When using the DHTML viewer, also set the resolution to either 96 dots per inch or 120. For wide reports, choose 96 to ensure the report fits within your browser screen. This setting has no effect if you are using the Java or ActiveX viewer.

My InfoView Dashboard

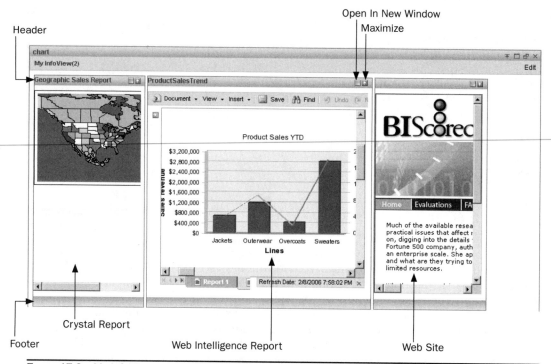 My InfoView is a dashboard or portal page that allows you to display the documents or web sites you most frequently access. Once you have customized My InfoView, you can set this as your starting page when you log in or you can navigate to it by selecting My InfoView from the Header panel.

Figure 17-3 shows an example of My InfoView.

Within the dashboard, you can maximize the frame so that it appears full screen within the Workspace panel. Alternatively, you can open the document in a new browser session by clicking the appropriate button within the individual frame as shown in Figure 17-3.

FIGURE 17-3   My InfoView acts as a personal dashboard.

To create a dashboard page, you first define how many items you want to appear on MyInfoView, and then you specify what content should appear in each frame.

1. From the Header panel, choose My InfoView, or when you first log in, you can choose Personalize InfoView now (shown in Figure 17-1).

2. InfoView displays a set of templates, or boxes that indicate how many frames you will use. In this example, there are two frames:

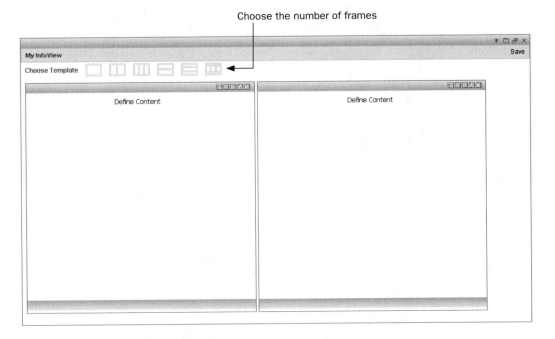

3. Once you select the template, you specify the content for each frame. Click Define Content within the frame.

4. You can either enter a web site address or select a report. As shown in the next example, the Web Intelligence Report, Annual Sales, will appear in the frame.

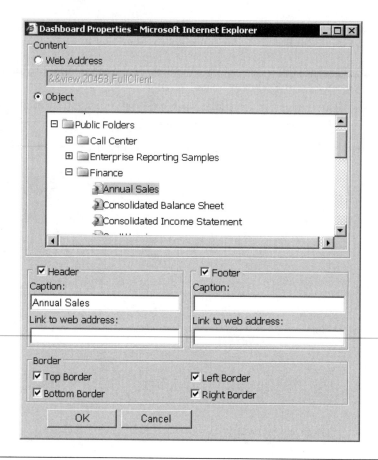

NOTE *In InfoView version 6, these frames were referred to as portlets and could also be document lists. With the new Navigation pane in XI, you no longer need to use space within a dashboard frame for such lists. Instead, simply toggle the Navigation pane as you wish to see specific report folders or categories.*

5. As shown in Figure 17-3, each frame can have its own caption on the Header or Footer. By default, this is the document name.

6. The borders indicate if you want a clear box drawn around each frame.

7. Click OK to close the Dashboard Properties dialog.

8. Define the content for the next frame.

9. Click Save in the upper-left corner to save your definitions. The dashboard is saved to your Favorites folder. To navigate to it at any time, click My InfoView from the Header panel.

To set My InfoView as the default start page:

1. Select Preferences from the Header panel.
2. Select the General tab.
3. Under My Initial View Is, select My InfoView.
4. Click OK.

Summary

InfoView is your portal to all the BI content and applications within a BusinessObjects Enterprise deployment. Understand the InfoView preferences that affect your report interactions and set the defaults accordingly. Customize My InfoView to create a simple dashboard of your most frequently viewed content.

Working with Documents

I f you are a long-time Business Objects customer and a reader of the original *Business Objects: The Complete Reference,* then you know that the full client (referred to as BusinessObjects classic in version 6 and earlier or Desktop Intelligence in XI) was the primary authoring interface for more than ten years. With the release of Web Intelligence version 6.0, web-based query and reporting made some inroads. With Web Intelligence XI Release 2, many of the advanced features that only existed in BusinessObjects classic have now been brought to the Web. For this reason, the primary emphasis in this version of the book is on Web Intelligence. Yes, I'm putting a stake in the ground that this will become the primary authoring environment for business users, despite the big investments existing customers have made in the full client.

Why this shift? First and foremost, Web Intelligence is more scalable. The documents are thinner and the services to process them less resource intensive than in Desktop Intelligence. Because the authoring environment is Web-based, usage can be more ubiquitous. Software does not need to be installed on users' desktops, nor are users forced to download large plug-ins. If that weren't reason enough, the Web-based interactivity of these documents (see Chapter 19) is something that really puts power into the hands of casual report consumers. Finally, the vendor has made it easy for you to preserve your existing investment by being able to run full client reports as is or optionally to convert them to Web Intelligence (see Chapter 5).

Chapter 18 introduces you to the basic tasks of viewing a document and understanding its structure so that you can more readily navigate its contents. As you view documents, you may need to refresh the data, answer prompts, and later, schedule it.

Opening a Document

Recall from the preceding chapter that your InfoView preferences determine which Web Intelligence viewer is used when you open a document and whether or not the document appears in a separate browser window or within the Workspace panel. This section assumes you are using the HTML viewer and that the document should open in a new browser section.

To open the document:

1. Locate the desired document within either a shared folder or a personal folder.

2. Click the name of the document.

Figure 18-1 shows a document in the HTML viewer, supported in all versions of Web Intelligence.

Show Left pane   Cross-tab block   Pie block   Refresh data

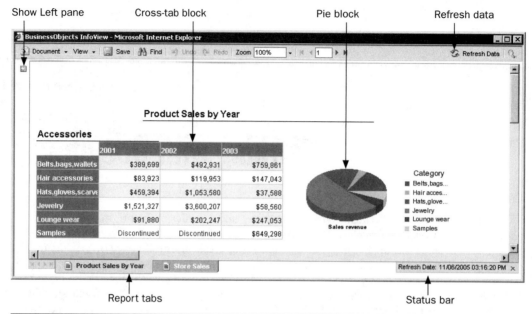

Report tabs   Status bar

FIGURE 18-1 A document in InfoView

View Modes

Figure 18-1 shows the document in page mode, as it would appear if you printed the report. You can change the view mode to either draft or PDF by selecting the appropriate option from the View pull-down menu.

The status bar appears in the bottom right of the document and displays the date the document was last refreshed. If only partial results are retrieved or if there is otherwise an error in running the query, it is displayed on the status bar. To display the status bar, select View | Status bar.

Printing a Report

In order to print a document, it must first be converted to PDF format. To print a report, do the following:

1. Select View | PDF Mode. Your report appears in an Adobe Acrobat Reader frame.

2. Click the Print icon from the toolbar.

3. Respond to the prompts for a printer and other settings and click OK.

4. Click the button "View In HTML Format" on the toolbar to return to the Interactive Viewer.

TIP *For a quick printout that prints only the current page and does not require high quality formatting, page breaks, and so on, use your browser's print capability.*

Navigation Map

The Navigation Map displays a list of the multiple reports within a document as well as individual sections within a master/detail report. The Navigation Map appears in the left panel (collapsed in Figure 18-1). To display the Navigation Map in the left panel, click the right-pointing arrow where the panel normally appears or select View | Left Panel from the pull-down menu.

In addition to navigating to different sections within a report or different reports within a document, you also can go to particular pages, use the Find button to search for text, and zoom to increase the size of the display.

When you click the Find button from the toolbar, the left panel and the Find dialog automatically appear. Find is useful when you want to find a particular item such as a customer name or individual product within a page.

In the Find text box, enter the text or numbers you want to search for. Check the appropriate box if you want your search to match on case or not. Then click Find Next. The matching string within the page is highlighted.

CAUTION *Find only searches for text within the page. This behavior is quite different from Find within a Crystal Report viewer, which will search through the entire document. Also, the Find does not work on text within a chart legend.*

TIP *If you want to search for text through the entire document, change your view to Draft mode (View | Draft mode). Note that for longer documents, it may take a minute to convert the display from page layout to draft.*

You also can navigate to individual pages within a document. Initially, Web Intelligence displays just the first page number. Use the triangles on the toolbar to navigate to the next page or the last page. Once you have navigated to the last page, Web Intelligence will change the page navigation to give you a total page count.

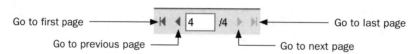

TIP *These are fairly basic report navigation features. For more robust analysis, use drill as well as the HTML Interactive viewer. These features are discussed in Chapter 19.*

Understanding a Document's Structure

Web Intelligence has a flexible document structure that allows you to view and interact with different data sets in multiple ways. A document is more than just a report and contains the following components:

- One or more universes that are typically SQL queries that extract information from a data warehouse or other data source. New in XI Release 2 is that these universes also include access to OLAP databases such as Hyperion Essbase, Microsoft Analysis Services, or SAP BW.

- A result set in which the results of the queries are stored as a microcube that allow for drilling and slicing and dicing.

- One or more formatted reports. Figure 18-1 contains two reports tabs: Product Sales By Year and Store Sales. Each report may be on a different universe or query, or they all may be based on the same query.

- Each report may contain multiple blocks such as a chart, table, or crosstab. These blocks can all come from the same query but provide different perspectives on the data, or they may come from different universes and queries. One report may have multiple report types. For example, the report "Product Sales By Year" shown in Figure 18-1 shows two blocks: a crosstab and a pie chart.

Figure 18-2 gives a conceptual overview of a document that is made up of two data sources: a universe that accesses a data warehouse and a second universe that accesses a departmental database. The document contains three reports, two that are tabular reports with a view to each result set and a third that displays a chart with data from both result sets. In many documents, you may have only one query, one result set, and one report. Alternatively, you may have one query, one result set, and multiple reports. Each report tab may contain a view with the full data set but in a different block type such as table, crosstab, or chart. Alternatively, each report may contain a limited number of columns or rows of data as you remove variables and apply filters. The structure of the Web Intelligence document allows you to explore information from multiple perspectives without ever having to requery the database. Similarly, the microcube technology allows you to seamlessly combine information from multiple data sources into one report, even if you don't have a central data warehouse.

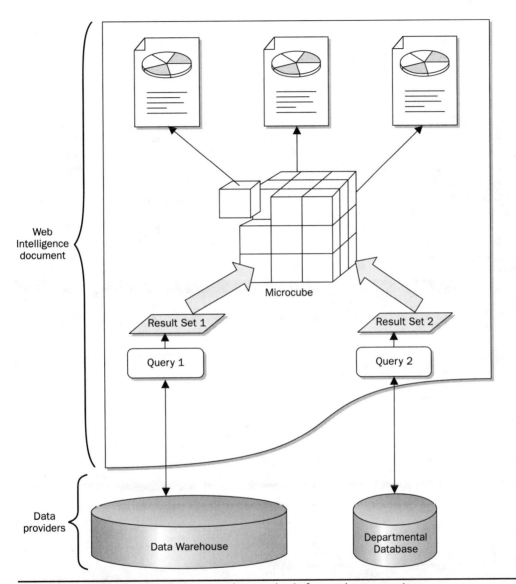

FIGURE 18-2 A Web Intelligence document is comprised of several components.

Components of a Report

A report is one tab within the Web Intelligence document, so in Figure 18-1, Product Sales By Year and Store Sales are two reports within the same document. You see these two reports either as tabs on the bottom of the document or in the Navigation Map. To navigate to an individual report, do one of the following:

- Click the report tab at the bottom of the main workspace.
- Open the Navigation Map (View | Navigation Map) and click the report name in the list.

Within a given report, you have several components: sections, blocks, and cells. As you explore information within a report, these components are not particularly important; as you try to format the report or add information to it, however, it's important to understand which component you are altering.

Sections

Every report has a main *section*. Within the main section, you can have a section header and a section footer; these are different from page headers and footers that appear in printed reports. Main section headers typically hold the title of the report but also may contain a picture or logo. Reports also may have subsections if you create a Master Detail report. In Figure 18-1, there is a section for each Product Line (Accessories, City Skirts, and so on) that contains a crosstab and pie chart for each line. These sections are indicated with a bullet point inside the Navigation Map shown earlier.

Note that these sections convert to bookmarks when you view the document in Adobe Acrobat PDF for printing or for sharing documents with users who do not have a BusinessObjects Enterprise login ID.

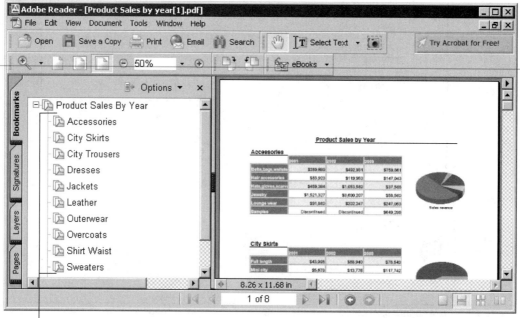

Sections convert to PDF bookmarks

Blocks

A *block* is a set of data that contains column headings, row headings, and data values. A block also may contain titles for an individual table or chart, different from a title that applies to the entire report (main section). Web Intelligence supports different types of blocks, such as a simple table, crosstab, or chart. A block is one component within a section. Two blocks can be related to each other or not. For example, you can have a crosstab block of sales with a corresponding pie chart to visually display the sales. Alternatively, you can have a crosstab of sales and a trend chart of employee satisfaction, populated from a different data provider. When viewing a report in interactive mode, you can easily change the block type without launching the full-blown editor or Report panel. This is discussed further in Chapter 19.

Variables and Cells

A *cell* contains either fixed text, formulas, or report variables. Cells that contain fixed text such as a title or a picture are referred to as *constants*; the contents of the cell never change, no matter which data you are viewing. A cell whose contents change may be either a formula or a report *variable*. Report variables are pointers to the columns of data. When a report author builds a query, the author selects *objects* from the universe. These objects become variables in a report. There are three types of report variables that correspond directly to how the universe designer defines an object:

- A *dimension* object is denoted with a blue cube and is typically textual information by which you sort and analyze numeric measures. In the reports shown thus far, *Lines, Category,* and *Year* are all dimension variables.

- A *measure* is a number that you want to analyze; it is denoted by a pink sphere or circle. *Sales Revenue* is a measure variable.

- A *detail* provides additional information about a particular dimension. You may want to see the information in a list report but will not want to use it to analyze measures by. Phone number and street address are typical detail variables.

Refreshing a Document

As shown in Figure 18-2, a document contains multiple components that deliver the formatted reports and analysis. When you want to retrieve new data from a data source, you are sending a query to a database.

 To refresh a query, select the Refresh Data button from the upper-right toolbar.

NOTE *Certain documents may force a query refresh as soon as you open the document. It is up to the report author whether or not a shared document initially contains data or is blank.*

One document may have one or more data sources. Depending on how the universe designer established the connection settings for each universe, a shared login may be used to connect you to the data source, or your individual database credentials may be used. Therefore, if you change your password in the source system, you may inadvertently cause your BusinessObjects Enterprise credentials to become out of synch with the data source.

When the two become out of synch, you will receive an error message similar to the following:

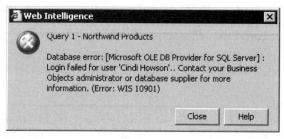

Contact your BusinessObjects Enterprise administrator to modify your database credentials (see Chapter 13).

When Web Intelligence refreshes a query, it refreshes the entire result set. For example, let's assume you have a document that shows year-to-date sales. The data source is from a data warehouse updated on a daily basis. A report author originally ran the query last week and sent you the results. Your version of the report is therefore out of date by a week. You refresh the query. This rebuilds the entire microcube (refer back to Figure 18-2); the microcube does not incrementally add one week of data. For smaller queries, this is not important, as the results may be returned in a few seconds. Other queries, however, may take quite a long time to run.

The status bar in the Report Window displays when a data provider was last refreshed and also displays if only partial results were returned.

Canceling a Query

While a query is refreshing, Web Intelligence displays a dialog that gives an indication of how long it should take the query to refresh. This is based on an estimate from the last query execution. If your prompt values or filter criteria change significantly from the last refresh, this can affect the execution time, as can changes in server load at different times during the day.

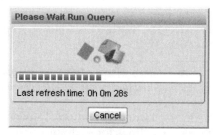

You may choose to cancel a query if you inadvertently select the wrong filters or if you decide it will take too long to refresh and you want to schedule the query. When you cancel a query using the HTML viewer, the query stops and you are presented with the last set of results. When you choose to cancel a query that you are refreshing from the Java Report panel, you have several choices of what to do with the results sent thus far:

- **Restore the results from the previous data retrieval**   Cancel the query and keep results from the last execution.
- **Purge all the data from the document**   Cancel the query and do not keep the results from the last execution.
- **Return the partial results**   Depending on what phase your query was in, you may be able to return partial results. Assuming the database has finished analyzing and processing the query, it may have begun the fetch phase in which the rows of data are shipped from the database to the Web Intelligence server. If you cancel the query at this stage, the status bar in the Java Report panel will display a yellow partial results warning in the bottom right. If you cancel the query from within the HTML viewer, no warning appears.

Time Limit Interruptions

If the universe designer has set time limits for query execution time, you also may receive only partial results of the query. When a time limit interrupts a query before any rows have been returned, you may receive an erroneous error message, "No Data To Fetch. Query 1." This is very misleading, as you receive the same error message when you construct an incorrect query, with mutually exclusive conditions.

Handling Prompts and Lists of Values

When you refresh a query, you may be asked to select additional information to ensure the correct data is returned to you. You can enter the values yourself, or in many cases, you can choose from a list of values. Choosing from a list of values ensures you have entered the possible values correctly (either uppercase or lowercase, with leading zeros or not) and therefore ensures you retrieve the desired results. Often, if you receive an error message "There is no data corresponding to this query," it is because you have entered invalid values in a query condition.

A list of values is a pick list generated from a query the BusinessObjects Enterprise server sends to the data source (for more information on how these are built into the universe, refer to Chapter 10). Because the list of values is specific to each universe, even if you have similar objects such as *Product* or *Customer* in multiple universes, you will have multiple list of values query files. Most often, these query files are initially empty and contain no values. Therefore, the first time a user accesses a particular list of values, the user may need to refresh the query associated with the pick list. Once the list of values has been refreshed and initially populated, the results are cached in a shared area on the Enterprise server. You should periodically refresh the list of values, as values in a dimension may change—for example, as new products or customers are added.

In the following example, when you click Refresh Data to refresh the query, you are prompted to choose a Year and Product Line(s). Follow these steps to make the appropriate choices:

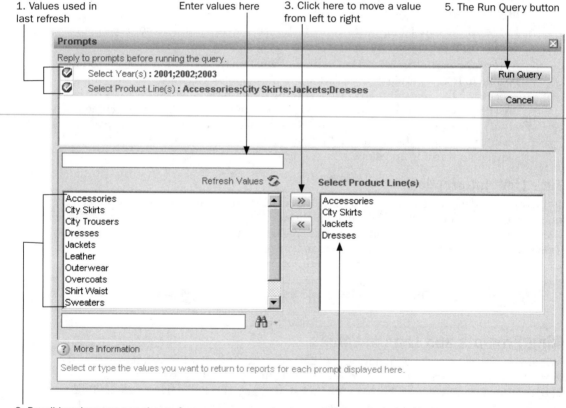

1. Values used in last refresh

Enter values here

3. Click here to move a value from left to right

5. The Run Query button

2. Possible values you can choose from

4. Filter criteria for this query

1. When you refresh a query, the last set of prompt values selected appears by default. You can select Run Query to accept the last values used or modify the filter criteria.

2. The first time you access a particular list of values, the possible list of values screen may be empty. Click Refresh Values to launch the list of values query.

3. For each of the prompts, select the prompt from the top of the dialog, and then select the desired values. For example, position your mouse on Select Product Line(s), labeled 1 in the preceding illustration.

4. In the possible values list, select an additional filter criterion, such as Sweaters, labeled 2.

NOTE *If you know the value with the correct use of uppercase, init caps, and so on, you also can enter it in the text box.*

5. Click the >> button (labeled 3) to add Sweaters to the right-hand box, Select Product Lines (labeled 4).

6. When you are satisfied with your selections, click Run Query, labeled 5.

Customized Lists of Values

For particularly long dimension lists such as customers or products, you may be prompted to further narrow the desired list of values. In such a case, the universe designer has customized the list of values query to include a prompt. If the dimension object displays an ID or code, the designer may customize the list of values to display the name or description in the list of values (refer to Chapter 10). For long lists of values, you can search to find a particular value or subset of values. For example, to find Customer Names beginning with N, enter **N*** in the list of values search box. The asterisk (*) acts as a wildcard for the list of values. Then click the binoculars icon to have the customers beginning with N appear in the list of values. Note in the following image that you can open the drop-down next to the binoculars icon to indicate if the search should be case-sensitive or not.

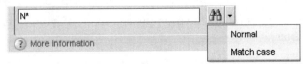

CAUTION *The wildcard in the list of values search box is different from the wildcard you would use in the actual query. When using Matches Pattern in a query filter, the wildcard character is %; for example, N% finds all names beginning with N.*

In the following example, the data source contains a long list of customer cities. In order to work with a manageable list of cities, you must first select a country in which the customer resides. The precise appearance of the prompt dialog depends entirely on how your universe designer built the list of values. If the designer did not cascade the list and set the Hierarchical Display option (see Chapter 10), the prompt dialog and which question to answer first is confusing at best. The following screen shows a correctly designed list of values. The last prompt value the query author used was city of Leeds. The + sign next to each country name indicates that the list of values for *Customer City* is cascaded or must first be further filtered by country. You can expand or collapse the list of cities for each country by clicking the + or −.

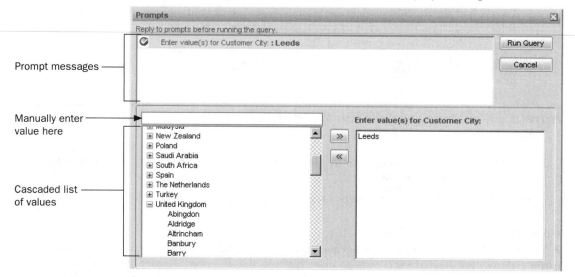

If you do not want to select from the list, you also can enter your value in the box provided. If the box does not appear, then the query author has set an option to force you to pick your value from the list.

1. Position your mouse on the prompt "Enter Value(s) for Customer City?" If your query contains only one prompt, then this row is highlighted by default.

2. Expand the country that contains your desired city, in this example, United Kingdom.

3. Highlight the city in the list and click >> to add it to the box on the right.

4. Once you have answered all the prompts and made all your filter criteria selections, select Run Query.

***

NOTE *When the list of values is cascaded, the list is not cached, so there may be a delay when you select an individual country before the list of cities within that country appear.*

Multiple Prompts

Sometimes when you refresh a query, you may need to answer multiple prompts. The report author should ideally sort in a logical order, for example, the year before the quarter. By default, Web Intelligence displays them in the order in which they have been added to the query. The default prompt message also gives an indication if you can select one value or multiple values. For example, "Enter Reservation Year" indicates you can choose only one year, whereas "Enter **value(s)** for Reservation Quarter," means you can select more than one quarter. In the following example, there are three required prompts. A green check mark next to the Reservation Year indicates a value has been selected. A red arrow next to the Quarter and Month prompts indicates that these values have not yet been selected. The Run Query button remains dimmed until all the prompts have been answered.

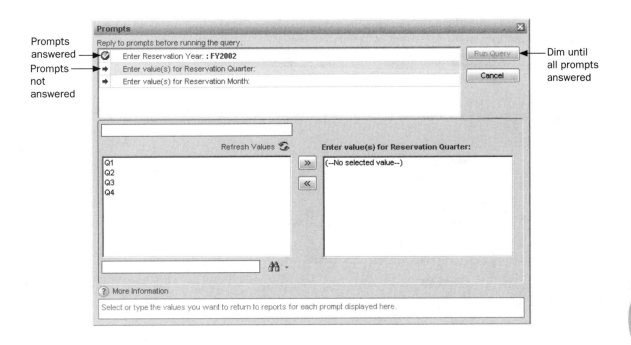

Prompts answered

Prompts not answered

Dim until all prompts answered

Saving Documents

One you have refreshed a document, you want to save the document with the new set of data. To save a document to the same place from which you opened the document, click the Save button on the toolbar. To close the document, select the Document | Close menu item or the X in either your browser toolbar or the Workspace panel.

If the Save icon does not appear on your main toolbar, you may not have permission to save the original document, particularly if it is stored in a public folder. In this case, use the Document pull-down menu and select Save As to save the document to another folder.

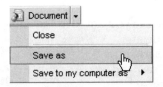

When you save the document to a different location and name, you are making a copy of the file; no link is maintained to the original report file. In the Save As dialog, enter a document title. This will become the name of the file as it appears in the list in InfoView. If you wish, enter a longer description. The description appears when you expand your document properties or display the Encyclopedia. Specify keywords if you wish to provide additional search options for locating documents. Refresh On Open will automatically force a query refresh when you open the document. By checking the box Permanent Regional

Formatting, you override users' personal InfoView locale settings so that formatting for dates and numeric values are stored with the document.

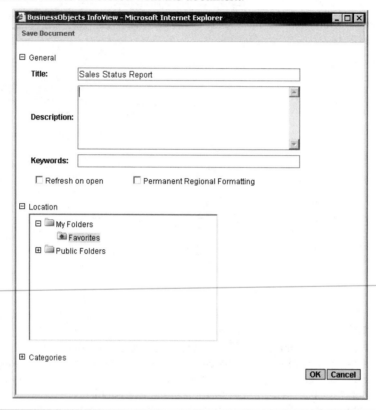

NOTE *If you check the box Refresh On Open, there is little point in saving the data with the document, particularly for large result sets with documents that have many pages, as the results are purged upon open.*

Under Location, the folders in which you can save a document depend on the rights the administrator has granted you. By default, your personal folder, Favorites, is selected. To see the Public Folders, click the + to expand the list of available folders. All folders for which you have view access appear in this list, however, you may not have create or edit rights that allow you to save a report to a public folder. If you do not have sufficient rights to save the document to a public folder, you will receive the following error message:

Save To My Computer As

Using Document | Save To My Computer As also allows you to select a different file format, including Excel, PDF, or CSV.

Excel

When you choose to save a document to Excel format, your browser will prompt you as to whether you want to open the Excel spreadsheet immediately or you want to download the file first.

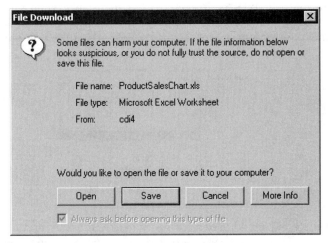

To download the file and specify a particular filename and path, select Save. By default, the Excel filename and Web Intelligence document name are the same. Web Intelligence will convert the document to spreadsheet format and, upon completion, will display a message "Download Complete." Select Open to open the spreadsheet. Note that if your document contained multiple report tabs, these convert to Microsoft Excel worksheets. Formatting is preserved and charts are converted to Excel charts.

Comma-Separated Values (CSV)

In some cases, you may not want the formatting preserved but just want the raw query results exported to Excel. If so, select Document | Save To My Computer As and either CSV or CSV (With Options). CSV With Options allow you to specify a different delimiter. When you save a document to CSV, all data is exported into one spreadsheet, including those from multiple report tabs.

Scheduling a Document

If you have slow-running queries or reports that you wish to refresh on a regular basis, you can schedule them. The scheduling features are available through InfoView and for all BusinessObjects Enterprise document types (Crystal Reports, Web Intelligence Desktop Intelligence).

From within your list of documents in InfoView, select Schedule.

NOTE *If you do not see the list of actions beneath the document name, click the down arrow to expand the actions.*

The Schedule dialog appears as shown in Figure 18-3. By default, the Instance title is the same name as the document title. An *instance* refers to a version of a scheduled report. The administrator determines how many instances are saved. For example, you may have ten versions of a scheduled report. You can give each of your schedules a unique instance name, a useful feature particularly if you need to keep track of an instance when a report is submitted to regulatory agencies, what the supplier shipping status is as of a point in time, and so on.

To schedule the report to run on a recurring basis or at a future point in time, click the drop-down next to Run Object.

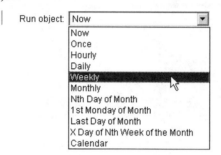

Once you have selected any kind of recurrence (weekly, monthly, and so on), the options in Figure 18-3 expand. You can now select which days to refresh the query and how long the schedule is valid for. Changing the start or end date is a bit quirky, as you cannot simply enter the new date in the box displayed. You must click the calendar icon, and then click a

```
Schedule                                                              ∓ □ ⌗ ×
Product Sales by year

Instance title: Product Sales by year

⊟ When
   Run object: Now  ▾

        Object will run now.
⊟ Destination
      Destination: Default Enterprise location ▾
⊟ Format
      Format: Web Intelligence ▾
⊞ Caching Options
⊞ Server Group
⊞ Events
⊞ Prompts




                                                          Schedule   Cancel
```

Figure 18-3   Use the scheduling capabilities for slow-running reports, or to refresh reports on a regular basis.

day in the display. Even if you only want to change the year, you must click a date within the calendar display. Use the single-arrow buttons (>) to navigate forward a month and two arrows (>>) to navigate forward a year. In the following example, the report will refresh every weekday at 8:53 P.M. for a year:

```
Schedule                                                                    ‑ □ ⊡ ×
Product Sales by year

 Instance title: Product Sales by year

 ⊟  When
    Run object: Weekly                          ▼

    Object will run every week on the following days.
    ☑ Monday              ☑ Friday
    ☑ Tuesday             ☐ Saturday
    ☑ Wednesday           ☐ Sunday
    ☑ Thursday

    Start Time:  8 ▼ : 53 ▼  PM ▼  11/14/2005          ▥
    End Time:    8 ▼ : 53 ▼  PM ▼  11/14/2006          ▥
 ⊞  Destination
 ⊞  Format
 ⊞  Caching Options
 ⊞  Server Group
 ⊞  Events
 ⊞  Prompts

                                                        Schedule   Cancel
```

Under Destination, you have the option of scheduling the output to refresh an instance within Web Intelligence, to send a report to another user's Inbox within the InfoView folders, or to a user's e-mail address.

If you leave the format as Web Intelligence and the destination as Enterprise Server, then you also can use the Caching Options to preload the document in HTML, Adobe PDF, or Microsoft Excel format. In this way, when you select View Latest Instance or a particular instance, you can very quickly toggle to access the document in either PDF or Excel format, as it has already been converted to these other formats.

NOTE *The cache here relates to the archived or scheduled instance. It does not correspond to the last saved version of the document as it may appear in the InfoView folders.*

Under Prompts, the last prompt values are used by default unless the document properties are set to Refresh on Open. You can override these values for the scheduled report.

E-Mail Recipients

To send a scheduled report via e-mail, under Destination, select Email Recipients from the drop-down. You can use the default settings established by the administrator by selecting Use Job Server. The e-mail settings are shown in Figure 18-4.

Specify the following settings:

- **From**   Enter your e-mail address using the full syntax; for example cindihowson@askcindi.com.

- **To**   Enter the recipient's e-mail address. The recipient does not need to be defined to the BusinessObjects Enterprise server.

NOTE *There is no drop-down menu of available e-mail addresses. Business Objects technology partner APOS Systems, however, has a product Address Book Gateway that integrates with the Enterprise server to provide this capability.*

- **Subject**   Here you can enter either static text or dynamic text that is populated according to the document title, refresh time, and BusinessObjects Enterprise login ID. To have the subject line filled in dynamically, select the desired text from the Add Placeholder drop-down. For example, the document title will appear here as specified by the placeholder %SI_NAME%.

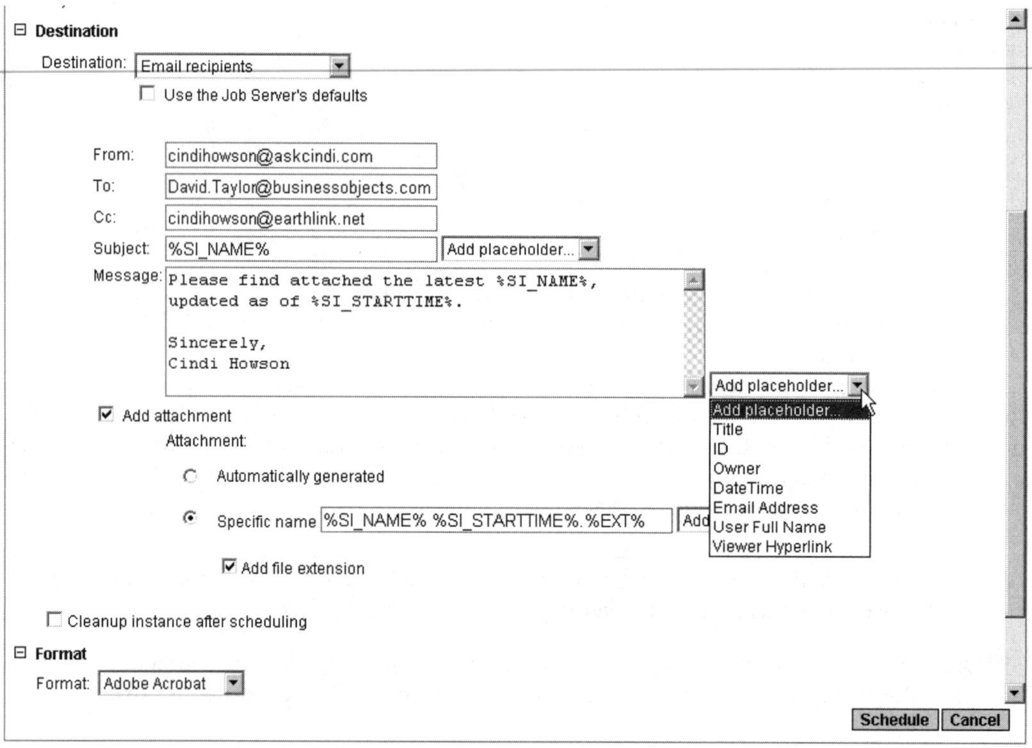

FIGURE 18-4   Schedule reports to be distributed via e-mail.

- **Message**   This is text to appear in the e-mail notification when the scheduled report is available. As shown in Figure 18-4, the placeholders Title (%SI_NAME%) and Date/Time the report was scheduled (%SI_STARTTIME%) have been inserted into the e-mail. Within the e-mail message, you can insert a hyperlink for the user to click to view the report via InfoView. To do so, select Viewer Hyperlink from the Add Placeholder drop-down that is next to the Message box.

When you specify a format such as Adobe Acrobat (PDF) or Excel, then you can send the report as an attachment. If, however, your output format remains the default of Web Intelligence, then the recipient must log in to InfoView to retrieve the report, or if you have inserted the Viewer hyperlink, the recipient can click the hyperlink to go directly to the scheduled report instance. Figure 18-5 shows the e-mail message generated by the Web Intelligence Job Server, according to the schedule settings shown earlier in Figure 18-4.

Events

When scheduling a report to refresh, you can also schedule this to be triggered by an event. There are three event types:

- When a file appears
- When a schedule succeeds or fails
- A custom event

By scheduling a report to run according to the status of another schedule, in XI Release 2, you can ensure that reports refresh in a particular order. This capability did not exist in the earlier Broadcast Agent.

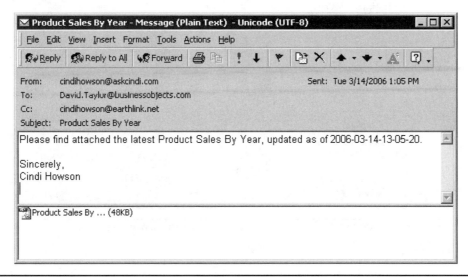

FIGURE 18-5   Users can schedule reports to be distributed via e-mail.

Scheduling a report to run upon an event requires two sets of tasks. The first involves an administrator defining an event in the Central Management Console. The second involves choosing the event to trigger and the event to wait for within InfoView.

Create Event

To define an event in the CMC as shown in Figure 18-6, follow these steps:

1. Choose Events from the main CMC page.
2. Click the New Events button.
3. In the Type drop-down, select Schedule.
4. Enter a name for the event that includes the name of the document for which you will associate this event; in this example, **Sales Query Completed**. This name will appear to users in InfoView when scheduling reports based on events.

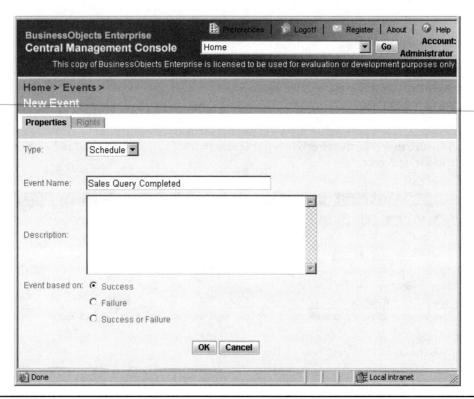

FIGURE 18-6 Use the CMC to create an event based on a successful query refresh.

NOTE *If this process seems confusing, it is! Part of the challenge is that the CMC was originally designed as an administrative tool, and yet, report scheduling is a user task. In order to schedule a query as dependent on another query refresh, you must ensure a unique name for the event, one that ideally indicates the name of the document with which it will be used. Without a unique name, the event can be used and triggered by other query completions, a situation that does not produce the desired dependencies.*

   5. Optionally enter a Description.
   6. Under Event Based On, choose Success.
   7. Click OK.

Schedule a Refresh Using the Event

You want to ensure that a second report runs only when the first one is finished. In scheduling the first report, you must tell it to trigger the event Sales Query Completed, as shown here:

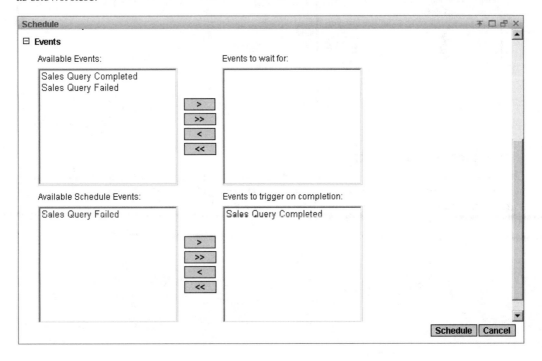

In scheduling the second, dependent report, you must tell it to wait for the event Sales Query Completed.

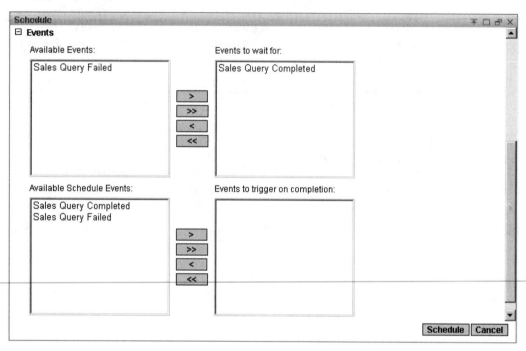

Viewing Instances and Status

Once you have scheduled a document to refresh, you can see the status and history of each schedule. From within the InfoView document list, select History. If you want to delete a particular instance, check the desired box and click the Delete button.

History							
Product Sales By Year							

☐ Show only instances owned by me
☐ Filter Instances By Time

Pause	Resume	Delete					Show all instances ▾

☐	🗋	Instance Time ▾	Title	Run By	Parameters	Format	Status	Reschedule
☐	🗐	3/14/2006 1:05 PM	Product Sales By Year	Administrator		Adobe Acrobat	Success	Reschedule
☐	🗐	3/14/2006 12:59 PM	Product Sales By Year	Administrator		Adobe Acrobat	Success	Reschedule
☐	🗐	3/14/2006 12:54 PM	Product Sales By Year	Administrator		Web Intelligence	Success	Reschedule
☐	🗐	3/14/2006 12:46 PM	Product Sales By Year	Administrator		Web Intelligence	Failed	Reschedule
☐	🗐	3/14/2006 12:39 PM	Product Sales By Year	Administrator		Web Intelligence	Failed	Reschedule
☐	🗐	3/13/2006 8:52 PM	Product Sales By Year	Administrator		Adobe Acrobat	Success	Reschedule
☐	🗐	3/13/2006 8:52 PM	Product Sales By Year	Administrator		Adobe Acrobat	Recurring	Reschedule
☐	🗐	3/12/2006 8:52 PM	Product Sales By Year	Administrator		Adobe Acrobat	Success	Reschedule
☐	🗐	3/11/2006 8:52 PM	Product Sales By Year	Administrator		Adobe Acrobat	Success	Reschedule
☐	🗐	3/10/2006 8:52 PM	Product Sales By Year	Administrator		Adobe Acrobat	Success	Reschedule

Pages: **1** 2

Logging Off

After a certain period of inactivity, your InfoView session may time out. For security reasons, though, it is best to log out when you are finished working with BusinessObjects XI. If your InfoView preferences have each document open in a separate browser window, first close these additional windows. Then, from the InfoView Header panel, select Log Off, the yellow padlock button (see Table 17-1 in Chapter 17).

NOTE *If your InfoView session times out or if you log out of InfoView before closing your documents, you will receive the following error message from within the document browser:*

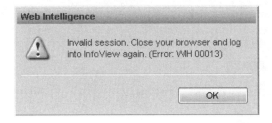

Summary

This chapter covered the basics of viewing a document and the document's components. A Web Intelligence document is much more than a report; it can contain multiple data sources and multiple report blocks to convey information from multiple perspectives. A document is a snapshot of the data. As data is updated, you will need to refresh your document. For reports based on continually changing data, you may wish to schedule your documents to refresh on a periodic basis. The next chapter highlights the more powerful capabilities of interacting within a document to analyze your data.

Analyzing the Data

In the last chapter, you viewed, refreshed, and navigated a Web Intelligence document. In this chapter, you interact with a report further to discover new insights. You are not creating a query from scratch, but rather, you are exploring data within an existing report to make it more meaningful. Such an analysis can range from viewing information in a different block style such as tabular or chart, to re-sorting, filtering, and drilling down into the details. This report-based analysis is aimed at report consumers, not just power users. Thus, many of the actions are available via right-mouse clicks. Also, all the analysis discussed in this chapter is available via a zero-footprint browser; you do not have to launch the full-blown Java Report panel.

However, while drill mode is supported in both the JSP and ASP versions of Web Intelligence, the HTML Interactive Viewer for on-report sorting and filtering is available only in the JSP version. If your company has not deployed the JSP version, you will have to modify the report to launch the Java Report panel to access some of the features discussed in this chapter.

The HTML Interactive Viewer

In order to open a document with the HTML Interactive Viewer, you must set your InfoView Preferences for Web Intelligence as shown in Chapter 17. Figure 19-1 shows the Product Sales Report in the Interactive Viewer. Compare this to the same report shown in Figure 18-1 via the standard HTML viewer. Note that with the Interactive Viewer, you now have an additional toolbar for formatting the report, an Edit button to modify the report or query, an Insert pull-down menu, and additional options in the Document and View pull-down menus. The Left panel in the HTML Interactive Viewer is called the *Context panel*. It has many more capabilities than the standard HTML viewer shown in Chapter 18, including the ability to see additional objects in the query (but perhaps not displayed in the report) and a data summary that displays a description of each object. The data summary is nothing short of excellent. Finally, report consumers as well as query authors can clearly see the universe object descriptions. If Data Integrator is part of your deployment, then the data summary

Report toolbar

Modify a report or query

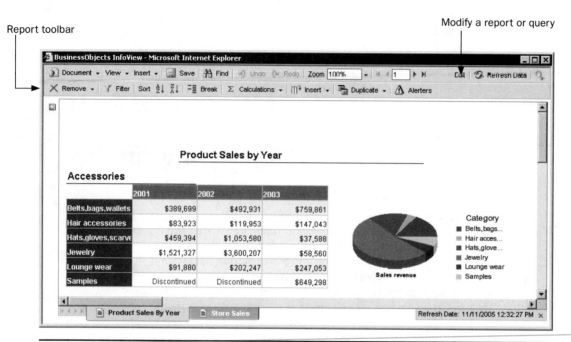

FIGURE 19-1   The Interactive Viewer allows you to fine-tune a report and analyze data further.

also displays source information that describes where the data originated, how it was transformed, and when it was last updated.

From the Document menu, you now have a Document | Properties option that displays the report author, document description, last modification date, and duration of the query refresh.

From the View menu, you have additional options to View Toolbars (Formatting, Report, Formula) as well as formatting and query preferences.

Table 19-1 describes the purpose of each button in the Report toolbar.

TIP *If you do not see the Report toolbar, select View | Toolbars | Report.*

Button	Name	Function
	Remove	Remove an entire cell or block, or invoke a drop-down menu to remove a row or column from a tabular block.
	Apply Quick Filter	Apply a filter to a dimension or measure within the existing block.
	Ascending Sort	Sort the data values in ascending order. To see the sort priorities, right-click the block and select Sort | Properties from the pop-up menu.
	Descending Sort	Sort the data values in descending order.
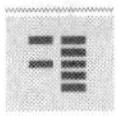	Insert Break	Insert a break to a dimension within the existing block.
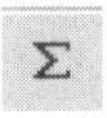	Calculations	Insert a sum, count, average, minimum, maximum, percentage to the table or crosstab.
	Insert Row or Column	Insert a row or column when you wish to add a new variable or formula to the block.
	Duplicate	Duplicate a block when you want to view the same data set in a different style.
	Alerters	Apply an alerter to the block. The alert must already be defined within the document. The ability to *define* an alerter exists only in the Java Report Panel.

TABLE 19-1 Actions Available via the Report Toolbar

Block Types

In Chapter 18, the different components of a Web Intelligence report were explained and the concept of a block introduced. A *block* is a set of data that contains column headings, row headings, and data values. BusinessObjects allows several block types: table, crosstab, form, and chart. A master/detail is a type of report but not specifically a block style. Within a master/detail report you specify a block style to appear in each section. A report can contain multiple block types. Figure 19-1, for example, has both a crosstab block and a chart block within each section of a master/detail report. Each block can be populated from the same query or a different query. Table 19-2 summarizes the different block types and when to use them.

Block Type	Use When . . .
Table	You want to detail information in a list or spreadsheet style. You may break the list into sections in a master/detail report or with breaks. Tables can contain additional columns for many dimensions, details, and measures.
Chart	You want to discover trends and patterns by exploring summary, not detail, numbers in a visual format. Charts are ideal for analyzing a limited number of measures by a limited number of dimensions.
Crosstab	You want to compare measures by different points within a given dimension. A crosstab is a particular kind of table layout that lets you compare actual sales with budget sales, for example, or to compare data from one period to the next.
Form	You want to see many details for a particular product, customer, or record. Instead of viewing a very wide report in which a lot of details are displayed on one row, a form lets you view the details vertically.

TABLE 19-2   Block Types

You can easily convert an existing block to another block style, or you can duplicate a block and then convert it to the new style.

Table

When you initially create a new query, Web Intelligence uses the default block type of table. A table is a spreadsheet-style block that lists data in rows and columns. In this example, you will change a chart to a table to further analyze the individual data values. Assume your report displays a horizontal, stacked bar chart. This is a good way to quickly identify that Texas, New York, and California stores have the highest revenues. However, you cannot readily tell from this chart who sold more: New York or California. Nor can you easily see the performance by individual year.

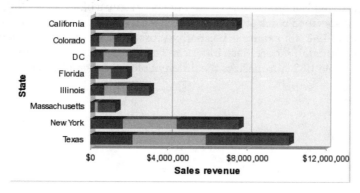

To convert the chart to a tabular block, do the following:

1. Click on the chart.

2. Right-click to invoke the pop-up menu. Select Turn Chart To.

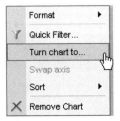

3. A Turn To dialog appears. Here you can either select a different chart style or, in this example, select Tables.

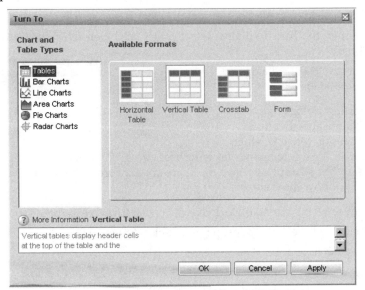

4. Within each Type, you will see several thumbnails that indicate a subtype. Select Vertical Table and then click OK to close the Turn To dialog. The horizontal chart now appears as follows, giving a clearer breakdown of the revenue per year. Also, you can more easily see that sales for New York are higher than for California in 2003 but lower for the other years.

State	Year	Sales revenue
California	2001	$1,704,211
California	2002	$2,782,680
California	2003	$2,992,679
New York	2001	$1,667,696
New York	2002	$2,763,503
New York	2003	$3,151,022

Crosstab

While the vertical table in the preceding section nicely displays the individual data values, comparisons are a challenge. A crosstab is the best block style for quick comparisons and transposes what may originally be rows in a tabular report to column headings. People frequently use crosstabs for the following types of analysis:

- Customer sales by year, quarter, or month
- Financial measures by actual and budget
- Product sales by region

To convert a block to a crosstab:

1. Select the block.
2. Right-click to invoke the pop-up menu. Select Turn Table To.

3. From within the Turn To dialog, select Tables, and then select the Crosstab thumbnail.
4. Click OK to close the dialog and see the crosstab.

	California	New York
2001	$1,704,211	$1,667,696
2002	$2,782,680	$2,763,503
2003	$2,992,679	$3,151,022

With converting a block to a crosstab, you cannot specify which dimensions appear on top and which appear in each row. Web Intelligence takes its best guess. You can easily swap the row and column headings. For example, to have the years appear across the top and the states appear vertically, follow these steps:

1. Select the existing crosstab block that you wish to convert.
2. Right-click to invoke the pop-up menu. Select Swap Axis.
3. The crosstab now appears as follows:

	2001	2002	2003
California	$1,704,211	$2,782,680	$2,992,679
New York	$1,667,696	$2,763,503	$3,151,022

TIP *To create stacked crosstabs and to use drag and drop to determine column and row headings, select Edit to launch the Java Report panel. See Chapter 21 for more advanced capabilities.*

Chart

Charts are a powerful way to uncover trends and patterns in your data. They can transform a dense page of numbers into a visual that quickly highlights opportunities and problems. Web Intelligence provides numerous chart styles. Advanced charting and formatting are discussed in Chapter 21.

Often when you want to chart data, you only need a subset of the data that may appear in a table. In such a situation, I recommend using the Duplicate button to first duplicate the table and then convert it to a chart.

1. Select the tabular block that you wish to graph.

2. From the Report toolbar, select Duplicate. If you wish the chart to appear to the right of the table, select To The Right. If you want the chart to appear beneath the table or at the end of the report, choose At The End.

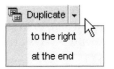

3. Modify the duplicated table to remove any extra columns or to further filter the data.

4. Select the duplicated table and right-click to invoke the pop-up menu. Select Turn Table To.

5. From the Turn To dialog, select the desired chart style, then click OK.

Insert a New Report and Block

I find the pop-up menus and Turn To the easiest, most intuitive way to view information in different block styles. Alternatively, from within the Interactive Viewer, you can also use the Left panel to insert new blocks or change the style of an existing one. When you insert a new block, you are not creating a new query. Instead, you are displaying data that already exists in the document in a new block style. This is discussed further in Chapter 21.

Master/Detail

A master/detail report is a particular kind of report in which a dimension value is used to separate different blocks. Master/detail reports allow you to analyze data within a particular subset. The report in Figure 19-1 is a master/detail report that contains a crosstab and a pie chart for each product line. Accessories is a section header. Compare the layout in Figure 19-1 to the layout of the crosstab in Figure 19-2, in which the product lines (Accessories, City Skirts, etc.) are another column in the crosstab.

		2001	2002	2003
Accessories	Belts,bags,wallets	$389,699	$492,931	$759,861
Accessories	Hair accessories	$83,923	$119,953	$147,043
Accessories	Hats,gloves,scarve	$459,394	$1,053,580	$37,588
Accessories	Jewelry	$1,521,327	$3,600,207	$58,560
Accessories	Lounge wear	$91,880	$202,247	$247,053
Accessories	Samples	Discontinued	Discontinued	$649,298
City Skirts	Full length	$43,095	$88,940	$78,543
City Skirts	Mini city	$5,679	$13,776	$117,742
Dresses	Casual dresses	$63,299	$145,319	$174,085
Dresses	Evening wear	$407,860	$711,590	$400,939
Dresses	Skirts	$21,277	Discontinued	$618,540
Dresses	Sweater dresses	$57,195	$100,487	$215,031
Jackets	Boatwear	$43,070	$18,950	$183,335
Jackets	Fancy fabric	$25,281	$53,404	$76,931
Jackets	Outdoor	$77,847	$154,384	$44,415

Click here to set as section →

FIGURE 19-2   This crosstab does not yet contain a section heading for a master/detail report.

To change an existing column in a report to a section header, click anywhere in that column and then right-click to invoke the pop-up menu. Assuming you have correctly selected a dimension column, the pop-up menu contains an option Set As Section.

In this example, the product line existed as a column in the crosstab. However, if it did not exist in the block, you can create a master/detail report by dragging an object onto the report page.

1. Display the Left panel by clicking the arrow to Show Left Pane or selecting View | Left Panel.

2. From the Left Panel drop-down, choose Available Objects. This shows you all objects that may be stored as part of the query results but that are not necessarily displayed in the block.

3. Drag the Lines object from the Left panel to the report. In order to create a section header, you must drop the object in the upper-left corner, just above the table. Pay careful attention to the shape and position of the mouse pointer.

Drag and drop

	2001	2002	2003
Belts,bags,wallets	$389,699	$492,931	$759,861
Boatwear	$43,070	$18,950	$183,335
Casual dresses	$63,299	$145,319	$174,085
Evening wear	$407,860	$711,590	$400,939

4. When you drop the object onto the report, if you do not get the desired results, click Undo and try again.

NOTE *The HTML Interactive Viewer has a multilevel undo, whereas the Java Report panel allows you to undo only the last action.*

Sort

Sorting data within a report allows you to rearrange the rows alphabetically, or if your sort is on a measure column, numerically. For example, you can use Sort to find stores with the highest sales. When you want to analyze data within a subset by using Breaks, the breaks take priority over the sorts. In the following example, you will sort revenue in descending order to quickly identify which stores have the highest revenues.

1. Select the column you wish to sort within the table.
2. Web Intelligence highlights the selected column with a gray box.
3. Click Descending Sort from the Report toolbar.

When you want to have multiple sorts within a table, use the pop-up menu to set the sort priority. To access the sort priorities, select the table and then right-click. From the pop-up menu, select Sort | Properties. For example, compare the priorities and results shown in Figures 19-3 and 19-4. In Figure 19-3, the data is sorted first in descending order of Revenue and then by State. In Figure 19-4, it is first sorted by State and then by Revenue. The sort priority in Figure 19-3 will tell you which state had the highest revenues for all years. The second figure will tell you what the highest revenues were for a particular state. The questions sound similar, but the insight provided on a larger set of data is quite different.

State	Year	Sales revenue
New York	2003	$3,151,022
California	2003	$2,992,679
California	2002	$2,782,680
New York	2002	$2,763,503
California	2001	$1,704,211
New York	2001	$1,667,696

FIGURE 19-3   Data is sorted first by Revenue and then by State.

State	Year	Sales revenue
California	2003	$2,992,679
California	2002	$2,782,680
California	2001	$1,704,211
New York	2003	$3,151,022
New York	2002	$2,763,503
New York	2001	$1,667,696

FIGURE 19-4   Data is sorted first by State and then by Revenue.

Breaks

A *break* will break the table into multiple pieces so that you can better analyze the data within a group. A master/detail report is somewhat similar, except that a break does not create a separate master cell. Also, a break column must exist in the table, whereas a section header in a master/detail report does not have to exist in the table. Finally, breaks give you additional options for keeping tables together for printing.

Once you create a break, you then use Calculations to generate subtotals. The first break column becomes the primary sort order. Often, this is the first column in the table, but it does not have to be.

Using the same sample table from the preceding section, add a break to the State column:

1. Select the State column.
2. Select Insert Break from the Report toolbar. Web Intelligence will insert the break and by default add the State as a break footer.

CAUTION   *The Break button on the toolbar acts as a toggle to add or remove breaks. If you inadvertently click this when what you really wanted to do was check the break properties, you will lose all your subtotals and other break settings. Use Undo to restore them and be sure to use the pop-up menu when you want to change Break Properties.*

Figure 19-5 shows a tabular data set with a break on State and a second break on Year.

In the table in Figure 19-5, it is now much easier to see that the data is sorted by state, compared to the data with a sort only in Figure 19-4. For each state, there is now a separate mini-table. Visually, you can now more clearly see the store performance from one quarter to the next.

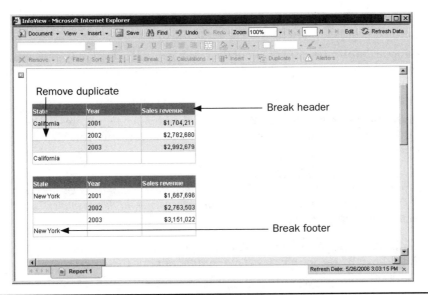

FIGURE 19-5   Use Breaks to group the data into what appears as mini-tables.

NOTE   *Although breaks make the data appear as if they are in separate mini-tables, in the strict sense, Web Intelligence still treats the table as one block, an important nuance when formatting the table. In Figure 19-5, the Format | Table options will be the same for both the California and New York mini-tables.*

Break Options

Figure 19-5 also shows the effects of certain break options, such as break header, break footer, and remove duplicates. To modify these options, right-click the table and from the pop-up menu, select Break | Properties.

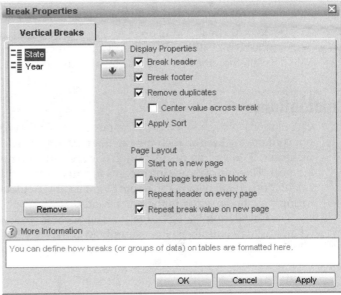

- **Break Header**   Repeats the column headings within each mini-table. If your table contains more than one break and you enable the Break Header for each break, certain mini-tables will contain multiple rows of column headings. To avoid this, set the Break Header only on the first break (or on the largest grouping for which you want to create a separate mini-table).

- **Break Footer**   Inserts a separate row beneath each mini-table. The calculation subtotals (not yet inserted) will appear in the break footer.

- **Remove Duplicates**   If you want the break value repeated only once in the first row of the mini-table, use this option. As shown in Figure 19-5, the state name California appears only in the first row of the table. Without this option set, California would be repeated in each row of the mini-table.

- **Center Value Across Break**   Works with the Remove Duplicates option so that the break value is centered within the rows of the table. (Note: This was not working as expected in SP1.)

NOTE *Do not confuse the term break "value" with calculation values that may appear in the row of a break footer. A break value is the value from the dimension—in this example, California, New York, and so on. A calculation value would be the subtotals.*

Chapter 21 discusses formatting a table to improve the layout when you print a report (see the "Page Layout" section). Breaks have similar options that affect the mini-tables when you print a report:

- **Start a New Page**   For each break level, print the mini-table on a new page. This print setting is useful when you intend to distribute each break level to a different person—for example, if you have different product managers and have a break on product.

- **Avoid Page Breaks in Block**   Use this option to force Web Intelligence to start the break or mini-table on a new page. For breaks that contain many rows of data, particularly long tables, it may not be possible to avoid a break in the middle of the mini-table. If the grouping of data is longer than a page and not the first grouping of data in the block, a page break will occur before the break and the mini-table will span multiple pages.

- **Repeat the Header on Every Page**   For each page break, repeat the column headings.

- **Repeat Break Value on New Page**   For mini-tables that span multiple pages, repeat the break value in the first row of each page. If you choose to repeat the header as well, then the row with the break value is repeated beneath the column headings.

Calculations

Calculations allow you to add subtotals to a table that contains breaks. If the table does not contain any breaks, then the calculations are grand totals for the entire block. In most instances, if you add a calculation to one measure, you will want them on all measures in a report. The subtotals are inserted as formulas in the break footer. Table 19-3 lists the calculations available via the Report toolbar or Calculation pop-up menu as well as the formula syntax inserted in the break footer.

The Calculation dialog box is somewhat context-sensitive, depending on the object type (character, date, number). For example, you may want to count the number of states in which you have stores, but this is not something you would sum or average.

Calculation	Explanation	Formula
Sum	Adds the values for a particular measure. SUM is the default calculation when you first apply a calculation to a variable. However, SUM may not make sense for certain measures such as ratios and percentages.	=SUM([*Measure Variable*])
Count	Counts the unique values within a break. Use this with dimension or detail objects.	=COUNT([*Dimension Variable*])
Average	Calculates the average based on the individual measures displayed in the table. If you hide certain rows of data through a filter, the values from the hidden rows do not, by default, affect the subtotal. Average is not a weighted average, so for things like average price, you may want to create a formula to get a weighted average or use extended syntax, as discussed in Chapter 22.	=AVERAGE([*Measure Variable*])
Minimum	Displays the minimum value for a particular measure within the break.	=MIN([*Measure Variable*])
Maximum	Displays the maximum value for a particular measure within the break.	=MAX([*Measure Variable*])
Percentage	Calculates the percentage contribution a particular break level makes to the grand total. In addition, it inserts a new column in the table that shows the percentage each row contributes to the individual break level. This calculation uses the Context Operator ForAll described in Chapter 22.	=PERCENTAGE([*Measure Variable*]) ForAll ([*Dimension Variable*])

TABLE 19-3   Calculations That Allow You to Create Subtotals

When inserting calculations, Web Intelligence automatically adds a grand total to the end of the report. Use the page navigation buttons to scroll to the last page to see the grand totals. The following report shows a sum calculation and percentage calculation in the break footer. Stores in Texas accounted for 27.17 percent of the total revenues ($8,096,124) for this report.

State	Year	Quarter	Sales revenue	Percentage
Texas	2001	Q1	$758,796	34.50%
	2001	Q2	$615,077	27.96%
	2001	Q3	$329,113	14.96%
	2001	Q4	$496,692	22.58%
Texas		Sum:	$2,199,677	
		Percentage:	27.17%	

		Sum:	$8,096,124	
		Percentage:	100.00%	

To add Total Revenues to the sample table in the preceding section:

1. Select the Sales Revenue column.

2. Click the Calculation drop-down from the Report toolbar.

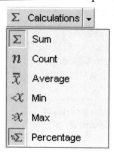

3. Select Sum.

TIP *Consider formatting the break footer row so that your subtotals stand out.*

NOTE *If you do not have your break options set to include a break footer, the calculations are inserted only as grand totals at the end of the report. Also, if you apply a break after you have inserted calculations, the calculations are not repeated in the break footer and remain as grand totals. To have them appear as subtotals in the break footer, first set the break, then insert the calculations.*

Filter

As you apply breaks, sorts, and calculations, you may find that you want to focus on one or more subsets within the report. Filters allow you to restrict the number of rows displayed in the report. They do not affect the query results; they affect only the data currently displayed in the block. It's important to understand that the calculations will also change to reflect only what is displayed. In Figure 19-5 shown previously, the table displayed several years of data. To focus only on the year 2003, insert a filter on Year.

1. Position your mouse in the table on the Year column.

2. Select Apply Filter from the Report toolbar or right-click to invoke the pop-up menu and select Quick Filter.

3. Web Intelligence displays a list of values available in the report. Note that this is only a subset of the list of values in the entire database. You can either enter the text to filter on or choose the year from the list. In this example, select 2003 and click >> to add it the box on the right.

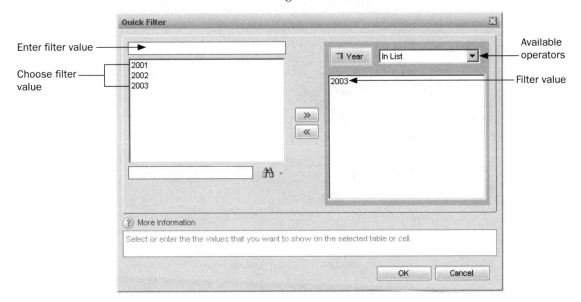

4. By default, Web Intelligence uses the In List operator to allow you to select multiple values. However, you can use the drop-down to choose Between, Not Null, and so on. Operators are discussed further in Chapter 20.

5. Click OK to see the effect of the filter.

Removing the Filter

To remove the filter, you must use the Left panel, Document Structure And Filters. You cannot use the Quick Filter button. For example, assume you want to remove the filter on Year 2003. If you invoke the Quick Filter dialog and simply remove 2003 from the right-hand box, Web Intelligence will attempt to filter the years for nulls.

1. Display the Left panel by selecting View | Left Panel, or click the arrow icon.

2. From the Left Panel drop-down, select Document Structure And Filters.

3. Here you see the underlying components of each report. The top row gives the name of the document. Immediately beneath this are the prompts or query filters. This is different from report filters that affect the display only. Here we are working with report filters. In this example, there is one report tab called Store Sales. There are two blocks, a table block and a pie block. Note the filter on the Table for Year In List 2003. Move your mouse to this filter until it is highlighted with a red box.

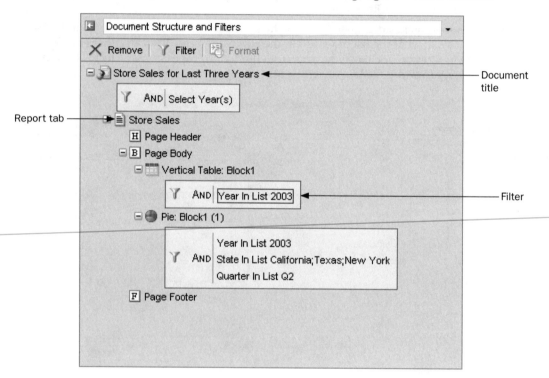

4. Right-click to invoke a pop-up menu and select Remove Filter.

Measure Filters

Filters in Web Intelligence XI Release 2 are simpler in many respects
from filters in previous versions of the full client. Measure filters used to require defining a formula as did nesting filters. Now, you easily filter on measures by entering a value to compare to. For example, to find which stores have revenues less than 700,000 per quarter, do the following:

1. Select the Revenue column.

2. Click Apply Filter from the Report toolbar or right-click to invoke the pop-up menu and select Quick Filter.

3. Note that a list of values is not available for measures. Enter the value in the left-hand box, in this case 700,000, and then click >>.

Enter value here

4. Change the operator from the default of Greater than to Less than or Equal to.

5. Click OK to apply the filter and close the dialog.

Report Filters

Report Filters are global filters that apply to all blocks in a report. In the section "Removing the Filter," you saw that the report Store Sales had both a tabular block and a pie block. Each block contained a separate filter on year for 2003. When you want all existing blocks and new blocks to inherit the same filter, apply them to the report via the Document Structure and Filters panel.

Select the component Page Body or the report tab (not the individual block) and right-click to select Quick Filter. This dialog now contains all the dimensions and measures for this report, as shown in Figure 19-6. Under the column Available Objects, these objects exist in the query but may not necessarily appear in one of your report blocks.

1. Drag the object for which you want to filter from the left panel, Result Objects, to the right, Report Filters.

2. To choose a filter value from a list, click Values.

3. To add a filter on a measure, enter the numeric value and then click Update Filter.

4. Select OK to close the Report Filter dialog.

Nested Filters

Nested filters within a report are new in Web Intelligence (see Figure 19-7). Previously, you could create a nested filter in a query but not within a report. You use nested filters when you need to group sets of conditions. For example, you have seen that stores in New York and California have the highest sales. They may be missing revenue targets only when sales are below 700,000 in a given quarter. For smaller stores, though, the revenue target would be much lower, at say 250,000 per quarter. To identify stores that are missing their revenue targets, you want to filter the report for (New York and California with revenue less than 700,000) or (stores in other states with revenue less than 250,000).

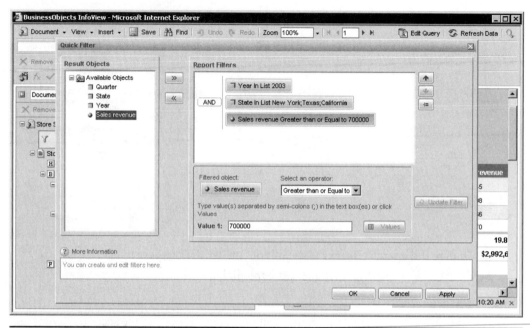

FIGURE 19-6 Report Filters apply to all blocks in a report.

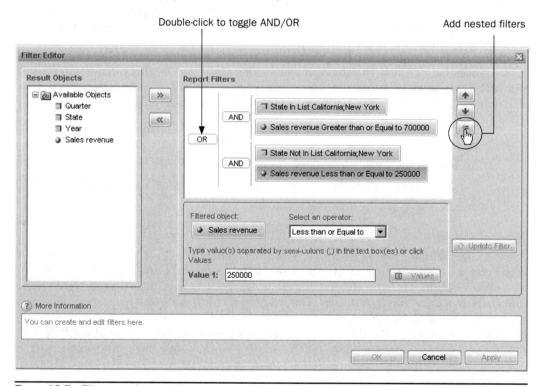

FIGURE 19-7 Filters can be nested.

Nesting filters can be rather tricky. First and foremost, you must have a clear understanding of what you want nested and what filters you wanted connected with an AND or OR.

1. To add a nesting or another AND / OR connector, select the block from within the Document Structure And Filters on the left, and then select Filter to call the Filter Editor. If you have selected just an individual column, your dialog will be different from that shown in Figure 19-7.

2. Click the Add Nested Filter button on the right of the Filter dialog. This will insert an AND connector leftmost.

3. Double-click the AND to toggle it to OR. Use drag and drop to reposition the connectors and filters.

4. Click Apply.

Ranking

Whereas filters limit the rows returned in accordance with specific selection criteria, *Ranking* enables you to limit the rows according to top or bottom values of measures.

NOTE *Ranking is only available in the Java Report panel; it is not available in the Interactive Viewer. To access the Java Report panel, your default InfoView preferences for Web Intelligence must be set to use the Java Report panel for modifying reports (rather than the Query-HTML or the HTML Report panel . . . not to be confused with the DHMTL Interactive Viewer that you have used so far ☺). Select Edit from the main toolbar to launch the Java Report panel.*

When you apply a ranking, you apply it in terms of the measure you are trying to analyze and whether or not the rank should be within breaks on dimensions. The following table gives some business questions that show which measure you would base the ranking on.

Business Question	Measure to Rank
Which business units have the highest expense variance?	Expense Variance
What are the top-selling products?	Sales Quantity
Which customers generate the most revenues?	Sales Revenue
Which warehouses have the most product on hand?	Inventory
Which wine producers produce the highest-rated wines?	Rating

A challenge with the Web Intelligence ranking feature is to understand that there are different ways to rank the data. I would argue that the generally accepted approach is to rank according to a percentage of the total. For example, suppose you want the top 10 percent of product sales. Earlier versions of BusinessObjects did not allow this. The ranking calculation mode of Cumulative Percentage is new in Web Intelligence XI Release 2. As shown in Figure 19-8, there are four calculation modes for ranking. The large table on the left shows the total data set for certain product lines in the Efashion universe. The four tables on the right show you the effects of ranking using different calculation modes.

- **Count**   Allows you to specify a certain number of rows such as the top or bottom ten rows. In Figure 19-8, I have selected the top 3 rows out of 20.

- **Percentage**   This percentage is based not on the total revenues, but rather, on the total number of rows. So if you select 10 percent and your original table contains 20 rows, the rank will return two rows as shown in the second table on the right in Figure 19-8. This has been the default behavior in the full client product.

- **Cumulative Sum**   This calculation mode looks at the running totals. So if you want to return the first four rows, the Top Cumulative Sum would be 10,000, as the running total through Evening Wear is $9,893,537.

NOTE *This ranking calculation mode was not working as expected in SP1.*

- **Cumulative Percentage**   I would suggest that this last calculation mode is the most useful, as it returns a cumulative percentage. So if you want to know which products account for 80 percent of your revenues, everything from Skirts up would be selected.

Category	Sales revenue	Cumulative Sum	% Sales	Cumulative %
Jewelry	$5,180,094	$5,180,094	36%	36%
Belts,bags,wallets	$1,642,492	$6,822,586	11%	48%
Hats,gloves,scarve	$1,550,563	$8,373,149	11%	58%
Evening wear	$1,520,388	$9,893,537	11%	69%
Samples	$649,298	$10,542,836	5%	74%
Skirts	$639,817	$11,182,652	4%	78%
Lounge wear	$541,179	$11,723,831	4%	82%
Casual dresses	$382,703	$12,106,534	3%	84%
Sweater dresses	$372,713	$12,479,247	3%	87%
Hair accessories	$350,919	$12,830,166	2%	90%
Outdoor	$276,646	$13,106,812	2%	91%
Boatwear	$245,354	$13,352,166	2%	93%
Full length	$210,578	$13,562,745	1%	95%
Long lounge pants	$179,563	$13,742,308	1%	96%
Fancy fabric	$155,616	$13,897,924	1%	97%
Mini city	$137,197	$14,035,120	1%	98%
Bermudas	$105,171	$14,140,291	1%	99%
Jackets	$78,503	$14,218,795	1%	99%
Shirts	$68,354	$14,287,149	0%	100%
Pants	$40,555	$14,327,704	0%	100%

Top 3 Count of Rows

Category	Sales revenue
Jewelry	$5,180,094
Belts,bags,wallets	$1,642,492
Hats,gloves,scarves	$1,550,563
Sum:	$8,373,149

Top 10 Percent of Rows

Category	Sales revenue
Jewelry	$5,180,094
Belts,bags,wallets	$1,642,492
Sum:	$6,822,586

Top Cumulative Sum

Category	Sales revenue
Jewelry	$5,180,094
Sum:	$5,180,094

Top 50 Cumulative %

Category	Sales revenue
Jewelry	$5,180,094
Belts,bags,wallets	$1,642,492
Sum:	$6,822,586

FIGURE 19-8   There are multiple ways to rank.

You can add a ranking to a table or chart:

1. Select the block you wish to rank.

2. Choose Ranking from the Java Report panel toolbar.

3. Web Intelligence displays the Rank dialog. Choose if you want to filter your data on the top-ranked items or bottom. In this example, select Top and enter a value such as **80.**

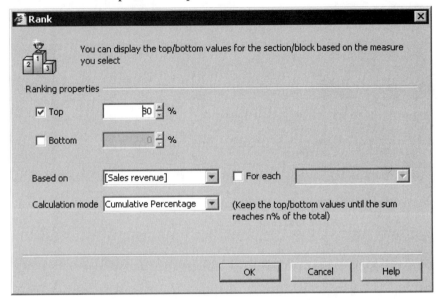

4. In the Based On drop-down, choose the measure on which you want the ranking based.

5. Choose the Calculation Mode as described earlier. In this example, select Cumulative Percentage.

6. If you are working with a large data set that has multiple break levels, check For Each and indicate the dimension on which to reset the ranking.

7. Click OK to apply the ranking.

NOTE   *This Ranking function works only on the rows within the local document, so it is a ranking within a subset of data. If you want a genuine ranking based on all the data in the source data, this must be set up at query time, as described in the next section.*

Server-Based Ranking

Server-based ranking is new in BusinessObjects XI Release 2 and requires that your database support the analytic function RANK. When your database supports this, an Add A Database Ranking button appears on the Query toolbar from within the Java Report panel, Edit Query, as shown in Figure 19-9.

Add a Database Ranking

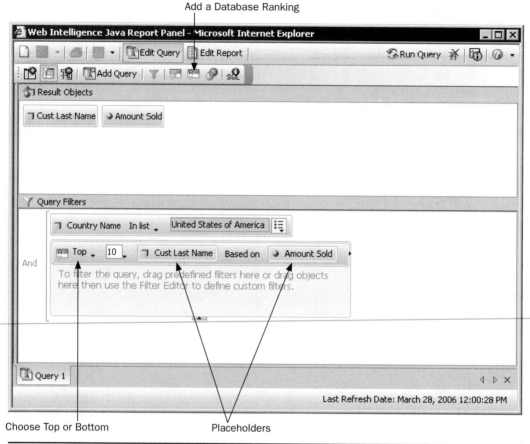

Choose Top or Bottom   Placeholders

FIGURE 19-9   Server-based ranking is performed in the query.

NOTE *This button is quite similar to the Add A Subquery button but is different in that it has a star.*

In the last section, you used the report-based ranking to rank data within a report. The server-based ranking is much more powerful in that you can rank data against the full data set. So you can answer questions such as

- Who are my top ten customers by revenue?
- What products did my top ten customers buy?
- What are my top ten products according to margin?

To perform a server-based ranking, follow these steps:

1. From the Java Report panel, select Edit Query.
2. Select Add A Database Ranking from the Query toolbar.
3. This will add a ranking row to the Query Filters section. Use the Top/Bottom toggle to select if you want the Top or Bottom ranking.

4. By default, the value of Top 10 is selected. You can change the constant of 10 or enter a prompt.

5. Drag the dimension for which you wish to perform the ranking onto the placeholder "Drop a dimension here." In Figure 19-9, this is *Customer Last Name*.

6. Drag the measure to base the ranking on to the placeholder "Drop a measure here." In Figure 19-9, this is *Amount Sold*.

7. Select Run Query.

The SQL generated will use the RANK function in the WHERE clause as follows:

```
WHERE
    SH.CUSTOMERS.CUST_LAST_NAME   In
      (SELECT
         View__1.Column__1
       FROM
       (   SELECT
           SH.CUSTOMERS.CUST_LAST_NAME AS Column__1,
           RANK() OVER( ORDER BY sum(SH.SALES.AMOUNT_SOLD) DESC  ) AS Rk__1
       FROM
           SH.CUSTOMERS,
           SH.SALES
       WHERE
         ( SH.CUSTOMERS.CUST_ID=SH.SALES.CUST_ID  )
       GROUP BY
           SH.CUSTOMERS.CUST_LAST_NAME )  View__1
       WHERE  View__1.Rk__1  <=  10     )  )
```

Drill

So far in this chapter you added many meaningful breaks, sorts, and calculations. With multidimensional analysis, you look at the same data but from different viewpoints. The viewpoints may be from different dimensions by drilling across or different levels of detail by drilling down.

A *dimension* is a kind of object by which you analyze numeric measures. Dimensions often have different levels or groupings associated with them called *hierarchies.* Multidimensional analysis is the process of analyzing data by different dimensions and levels within the dimensions. Within Web Intelligence, you can perform multidimensional analysis only with Dimension objects, not with objects the designer has created as Detail objects (see Chapter 9).

Hierarchies allow you to analyze data by different levels of detail. Some hierarchies are very clear-cut, such as Time, going from Year to Quarter to Month to Week to Day. There is a natural order. Geography hierarchies may also be predetermined, running from Continent to Country to State. When the geography applies to a marketing region, however, each company introduces its own variation. One company may group the Middle East and Africa together; another company may include Mexico as part of North America because it is part of NAFTA or will group it under a different management region such as Latin America. Many of these groupings are predetermined as part of your company's reference data and built into the ERP or data warehouse. The universe designer uses the hierarchies to build the default drill paths you use for multidimensional analysis.

With Web Intelligence, you can drill *down* within a hierarchy, for example from year to quarter to month. You also can drill *across* by analyzing the current year or the past year; you are at the same level of detail, year, but you are changing the selection value that you are analyzing. You can analyze data by one dimension at a time (Time) or by several at once (Time, Geography, Product). You can also drill against multiple report formats, including tables, crosstabs, and charts.

Fixed reports often deal with standard, recurring information needs and give you an overview of *what* is going on in your business. Multidimensional analysis is more exploratory and answers *why, where,* and *when.* For example, you may start with a standard management report that shows product sales for this year and last year. Sales for one product is lower this year than last year. You need to know *why.* So you begin to explore: were the sales bad for a particular region, salesperson, or quarter?

Understanding the Data

You can easily get lost when drilling within a report. Therefore, it's helpful to first understand how the different universe objects relate to one another and where you are drilling from and to. Figure 19-10 shows two sample hierarchies for the eFashion universe, Time and Product. Each has four levels.

It's also important to understand that most drilling occurs within a local microcube. You are not requerying the database. Figure 19-11 shows how this works. For simplicity, I will use an example of a Time dimension that contains Year, Quarter, Month. When you construct a query, you first specify which columns of data you want to retrieve from the database. Initially, the default report displays all columns of data. However, as you format the report, remove columns, and create objects, you may hide certain columns. These columns still exist in the query and therefore in the microcube, but they are not displayed in the report. In Figure 19-11, Quarter and Month exist in the microcube but are not displayed in the report. This allows you to drill from Year to Quarter to Month without having to execute a new query.

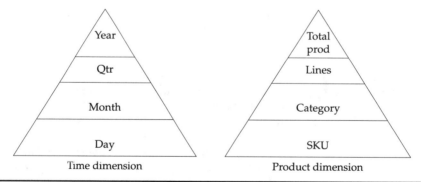

FIGURE 19-10   Understand the hierarchical nature of your dimensions before drilling within a report.

If, however, you want to drill down to a level of detail that does not exist in the document, to day for example, then new in Release 2 is the ability to drill through. Web Intelligence will issue a new query and seamlessly display the additional level of detail. This drill-through to detail had previously been possible in the full client but not in Web Intelligence.

How Is the Data Aggregated?

Web Intelligence aggregates measures in two ways: SQL functions and projection aggregates. SQL functions affect the number of rows returned in the initial query. When you drill within a document, Web Intelligence uses projection aggregates. Projection aggregates are set by the universe designer (see Chapter 9, in the section "Projection Aggregates," for more information). For the most part, you do not need to worry about projection aggregates if your universe has been designed correctly. However, I would caution you against drilling down on any kind of ratio or average. Figure 19-12 shows a summary table with sales revenue, quantity sold, and average selling prices by State and Quarter. The averages selling price for Q1 in Texas is listed as 143.11 in the top table in Figure 19-12. This selling price, however, is an average of other detail averages. It is not the revenue of 758,796 / quantity 5,278 as many users would prefer. The document or microcube contains additional details by individual Store Name and month. The bottom table in Figure 19-12 displays 12 rows of detail numbers for Texas stores that were used to calculate the one row in the summary table. For these particular objects, the universe designer specified a projection aggregate of Sum for Revenue and Quantity Sold, and Average for Selling Price. It would be blatantly wrong to use SUM, as the projection aggregate for Selling Price as 1,717.29 is wrong. The average of 143.11 is not completely correct either, as this is an average of the 12 detail averages. To get a correct aggregate, you would need to recalculate the ratio or the revenue of 758,796 / quantity 5,278 to display 143.77.

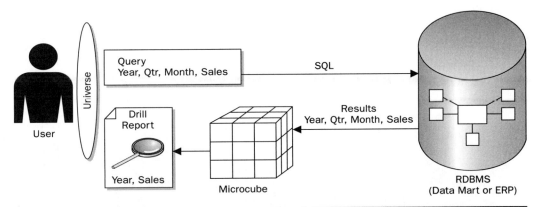

FIGURE 19-11   A document or microcube may contain more data than what appears in a report block.

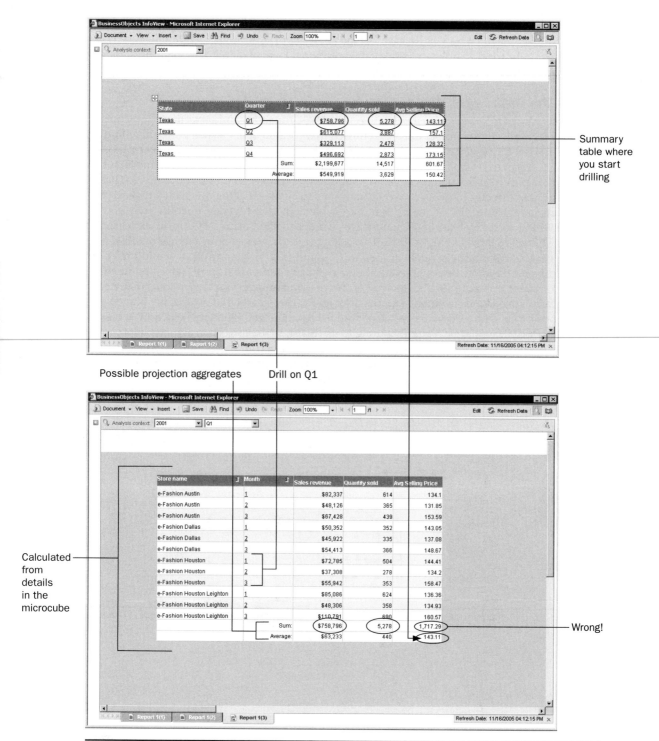

Drill Down

With *drill-down*, you are looking for lower levels of detail within an existing hierarchy. In the following example, you will use Drill to discover which cities and stores in Texas have the highest revenues.

NOTE *Be sure you have first set the desired drill preferences for InfoView, as described in Chapter 17.*

1. To begin drill mode, select Drill mode from the main toolbar.

2. As shown in Figure 19-13, Web Intelligence inserts another report tab, naming it *Report (1)*, where *Report* is the name of the first report tab (assuming this Drill option is enabled via InfoView preferences). You also now have several navigation icons embedded within the table or chart. A drill bar has been added to show that the current Analysis Context or slice is Texas. A drill-up arrow next to City indicates you can drill up to State. If you mouse over the City column, a navigation tip appears. Hyperlinks appear in each column for which drill-down is available.

3. From the Drill toolbar, you can use the drop-down box to filter the selection to All States or to an individual state. Selecting "Remove" will remove the filter so that details for all cities in all states appear in the table. To drill down from the city Houston to the individual stores in Houston, click Houston within the table block. City now appears as a drill filter in the drill toolbar.

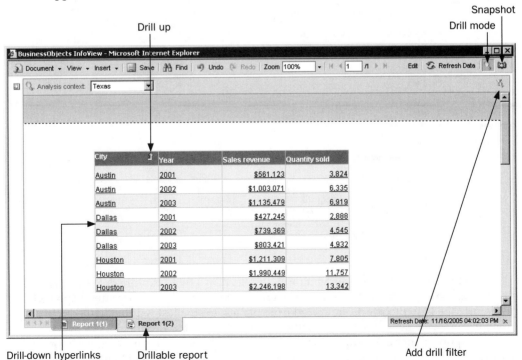

FIGURE 19-13 Drill within a report to explore the data further.

NOTE *In the full client, you could use the Drill toolbar option Move To Block so that State would reappear in the block. This is not available in Web Intelligence. As an alternative, use Drill By from the pop-up menu and select the desired dimension.*

TIP *As you drill around, you may reach an unexpected level of detail, an unwanted filter, or the like. Use the Undo button to undo the last drill.*

Drill Up

As you drill down, you may decide that the particular level of detail did not provide meaningful insight into the business trends or that you want to explore details by other dimensions. You can *drill up* to the preceding summary level.

To move back up the hierarchy by one level, click the up arrow next to the dimension. For example, in Figure 19-13, to drill from City back up to State, click the up arrow next to City. This will remove the detail column from the report and replace it with a column of data from one level up in the hierarchy.

Drill By

You also can right-click while hovering over the city column to call the Drill Down, Drill Up, or Drill By pop-up menu. This allows you to skip levels in drilling, for example, going immediately from Year to Month without first previewing Quarters. Your mouse must only hover over the city name rather than have the entire column selected for the correct pop-up menu to be invoked. By default, this mouse pointer appears in the shape of a hand, not an arrow.

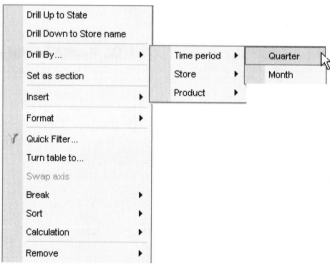

Using the same pop-up menu, you can also select Drill By to explore data by other dimensions that exist in the document or microcube but that are not currently displayed in the report. The Drill By objects are sorted from biggest to smallest within the hierarchy (Year to Month for the Time hierarchy or Product Lines to SKU in the Product hierarchy). In the preceding pop-up menu, Product Line would be an additional column of information that one can Drill By without generating a new query. Selecting Drill By to Quarter produces the same results as drilling down from Year to Quarter. However, setting Drill By to a dimension not yet in the report, such as Product Line, creates an entirely new perspective on the data. Web Intelligence will automatically move the current column to the Drill toolbar and replace it with the Drill By column.

The Drill By is contextual and becomes more powerful when more details and columns of data are available in the microcube but not displayed in the report. For this reason, many BusinessObjects deployments involve report authors creating ever larger microcubes (micro would not be an appropriate term here!), in an attempt to predict report consumers' drill paths. This is a bad practice. The multidimensional analysis in Web Intelligence is not a replacement for an industrial-strength OLAP database such as Microsoft Analysis Services or Hyperion Essbase (see Chapter 14 for further discussion on this topic). You want your initial report to contain only a minimal amount of data for response time and scalability reasons. If a certain dimension does not appear in the Drill By, users can still access it via Add Drill Filter or Scope Of Analysis.

The universe may contain still more columns by which to explore the data; however, if they do not exist in the local document, Drill By does not display them. Scope Of Analysis and Drill Through do.

Drill Across

Drill *across* is the process of moving within the same dimension level but changing your selection criteria or drill filter. You use the Drill toolbar to select different values to drill across. Dimensions get added to the Drill toolbar in several ways:

- As you drill down or choose to drill by different levels within the same hierarchy, the higher-level selection gets added to the Drill toolbar.

- You can also select the Add Drill Filter icon from the Drill bar and specifically select a dimension.

In the following example, you can drill across on State, City, or Year by using the drop-down menu for each. Note that the drop-down filters are linked. For example, as the State is currently filtered for Texas, the cities available from the City drill filter are only those cities in Texas (Austin, Dallas, Houston).

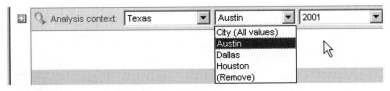

TIP *If you want to see these drill filters in a printed report, you need to insert a cell in the body of the report. From the Left panel, select Chart And Table Types, expand the cells folder, and then drag and drop Drill Filters to the report body.*

Snapshot

Snapshots allow you to save a picture of your drill at a particular level of detail or point within your exploration. Web Intelligence inserts a new report tab with drill turned off. To insert a snapshot, select Snapshot from the main toolbar.

Drill Through To Detail

As shown in Figures 19-13, the initial drill screen does not necessarily contain all the dimensions or levels by which you can drill; more data may exist within the microcube. Ideally, these additional drill-by details are still at a reasonably aggregated level for the most frequently performed analysis. With *Drill Through To Detail,* you can further expand the data in the microcube by expanding the scope of analysis. In this respect, drill through lets you expand the cube with still more detail rows or less frequently used drill-by dimensions than what was stored in the original cube. Expanding the scope of analysis modifies the query and retrieves a new full set of data; the microcube is rebuilt. Therefore, you want to reserve drill-through for retrieving less frequently used details and dimensions.

To invoke the Scope Of Analysis dialog, drill down to a level of detail not immediately available in the document. Web Intelligence indicates if your drill-down will generate a New Query in the pop-up menu. In the following example, you are drilling from Year to Quarter. Quarter does not exist in the microcube.

NOTE *You will be presented with the Scope Of Analysis dialog only if your InfoView Web Intelligence drill options are set to Prompt If Drill Requires Additional Data (see Chapter 17). Otherwise, Web Intelligence will automatically launch the query and retrieve the additional detailed data.*

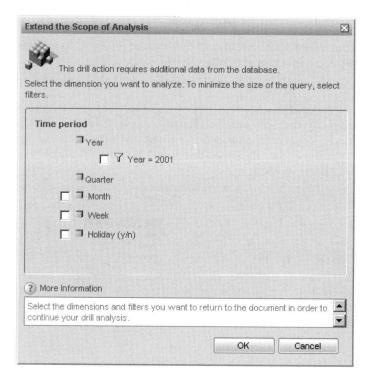

Because some drill-throughs can generate slow queries with enormous result sets, Web Intelligence gives you several options to minimize the number of times you must requery the database. In a highly tuned database in which your queries are instantaneous, these options are not that important. However, in many other databases in which query response time can vary from seconds to minutes to hours, pay careful attention to the scope of analysis options.

TIP *Multidimensional analysis is a powerful tool, and the microcube approach provides an enormous amount of flexibility. To maximize this value, ensure that drilling is fast—at the speed of thought. Leverage the capabilities in the database to provide consistently fast query times or investigate third-party solutions such as HyperRoll. HyperRoll acts as an intermediary cache between the document microcube and the physical tables in the data warehouse. As users drill, then, they are accessing a cache of aggregate tables to provide fast performance.*

When you modify the scope of analysis, you can choose whether or not the query should return all rows for all selections within the dimension or if the drill filters should get translated as a condition in the query. The current drill selections are marked with filter icons. The filter values come from either the Drill toolbar or the position of your mouse within the drill table. For example, this drill-down had the Year 2001 as the filter in the drill bar. In the drill, through, you can have the query results for the quarter details filtered for Year=2001 by checking the appropriate box in the Scope Of Analysis dialog. Also, Web Intelligence allows you at this point in time to retrieve details for Month or Week (or any other level of detail within this hierarchy) in case you will likely drill further.

CAUTION *Be careful about including too much data in your scope of analysis; use filters for large dimensions. Drilling times within a cube will vary, depending on your the BusinessObjects Enterprise server resources, but will become slower with larger result sets. Selecting the lowest level within a product or customer dimension without additional conditions may return millions of rows of data.*

Synchronized Drilling

While the previous sections showed drilling within a tabular block, you also can drill within charts. Further, if your report contains two block styles, such as a table and chart as shown in Figure 19-1, you can synchronize the drill between the two blocks. To synchronize drilling between two related blocks, set your InfoView preferences, drill options, as described in the next section. As you drill, pay careful attention to the chart style used. For example, while drilling in a tabular report from month to day may still yield a meaningful table, it most certainly will not yield a meaningful pie chart.

Drill Options

Web Intelligence allows you to specify several drill options via InfoView preferences, as explained in Chapter 17. Table 19-4 summarizes each option.

Option Type	Option	Explanation
New Drill Session	Start drill on a duplicate report.	When first enabling Drill mode, Web Intelligence will insert a new report.
New Drill Session	Start drill on the existing report.	If you do not want a separate Drill mode report inserted, check this option. Warning: When you enable Drill mode with this setting, Web Intelligence will remove all but the current block from the report. If your initial report has multiple blocks, do not use this option.
General Drill Options	Prompt if drill requires additional data.	As you drill through to details, check this box if you want the Scope Of Analysis dialog invoked to allow you to filter the data by drill filters and/or retrieve additional levels of detail in the same query.
	Synchronize drill on report blocks.	If your report contains multiple blocks such as a chart and a tabular set, drill actions performed in one are simulated in the other.
	Hide drill bar.	As you drill, drill filters are automatically added in a toolbar. If you don't want the toolbar to appear, then set this option.

TABLE 19-4 Web Intelligence Drill Options

Sharing Your Analysis: Discussions

The analysis you've performed throughout this chapter is only as good as the actions you take from the insight you've gleaned. As a way of fostering collaboration and insight, BusinessObjects XI provides a discussion capability through the InfoView portal. This is not a replacement for e-mail, but rather, a way of storing textual discussions as they relate to individual reports within the BI repository. When corporate e-mail systems are used to discuss BI content, the analysis becomes separate from the BI repository and a report may be sent as a static attachment. The discussion capability in BusinessObjects XI allows you to keep the textual commentary in the same place as the live reports.

Figure 19-14 shows a discussion thread around the earlier ranking report.

To initiate a discussion:

1. Select a report from the list within InfoView.

2. In the bottom-right corner of your browser, click the up arrow to expand the discussion pane so that it appears as in Figure 19-14.

3. Click New Message.

4. The right portion of the discussion pane displays a new message, inserting your name and date in the Subject box. Modify the Subject line.

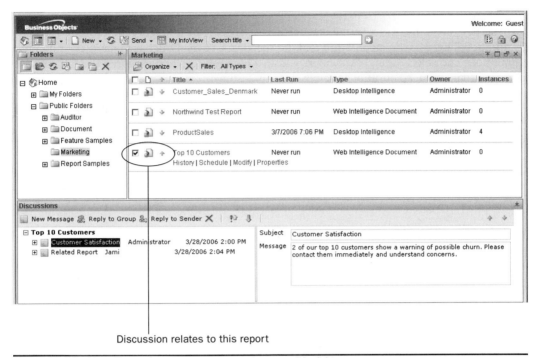

Discussion relates to this report

FIGURE 19-14   Use discussions to compare analyses and insights

5. Enter your text in the Message box.

6. Click Post.

As you view discussions, you can reply to just the sender of the message, or you can reply to the group, all users who have rights to view the message.

Summary

With the HTML Interactive Viewer, report consumers can analyze information in a report at the click of a mouse. Ideally, much of the formatting and breaks have been defined for you as a default in a shared report. You can fine-tune these options to suit your own analysis needs. You can change the block style from a tabular report to a chart to discover trends visually. You can resort the data, filter it, or insert subtotals to home in on particular patterns or problem areas.

Whereas a standard report may give you an overview of *what* is going on, multidimensional analysis helps you uncover why, when, and where. Use the drill functionality to explore data by additional levels of detail and different dimensions. Use the Drill bar to navigate different dimensions and select different members within a hierarchy. As you explore the data, you may find that you need additional details not within the microcube. Use Drill Through to retrieve additional information from the data source and re-execute the entire query.

Finally, use the discussion capability within InfoView to share the results of your analyses with other users.

Creating a New Query

W hether you are creating a new query or modifying an existing query to add a new result column or change a condition, you use the query panel. The query panel lets you select columns to display in a report and specify conditions to limit the rows returned, all without your knowing SQL. The universe's semantic layer displays business names and dynamically generates the necessary SQL behind the scenes. Chapter 6 gives a more thorough discussion of how the universe accomplishes this. This chapter provides a strategy for turning a business question into a query and how to use the Web Intelligence query panel.

Formulating a Business Question

Before you begin to create a new document through Web Intelligence, it's important to formulate the business question to help you construct a query that returns your desired information. If you do not do this, you may retrieve more data than necessary, making it difficult to uncover patterns and opportunities. You also may have to execute a query multiple times before you achieve the desired report. With large databases, this can be inefficient and frustrating. To formulate a business question in query terms, answer the following questions:

1. Where is the data?

2. What measures do I want to analyze?

3. By which dimensions do I want to analyze the measures? After viewing a high-level report, do I want to drill down or explore by other dimensions?

4. Do I want to see additional details for taking action on the information?

5. If the data source contains more data than I am interested in, how can I narrow my results to pertain to my area of interest or responsibility and ensure the query returns only the records I need?

As an example, assume you are a product manager. You want to analyze sales. "What are my sales?" is a fairly broad business question. Table 20-1 maps how you use these questions to refine a broad question into more specific details that help you formulate a query.

As you refine your business question following the guidelines in Table 20-1, you are ready to build your query when your question looks more like the following: "What are sales by product line by year for stores in New York for the most recent three years?"

Broad Question	Refined Answers	Query Component
1. Where is the data?	If you want to analyze sales for just your products, the data may be in a departmental data mart. If you want to compare your sales with other products, it may be in the central data warehouse. Actual sales may be in the central data warehouse; forecast sales may only be in a personal database.	Universe
2. What measures?	Sales could be stated in terms of revenues, quantity sold, and selling price.	Measure result objects
3. Which dimensions?	Do you want to analyze sales by product only or also by salesperson, region, customer, scenario (actual vs. budget), and time period?	Dimension result objects
4. Additional details?	If sales are falling from one quarter to the next, do you want the salesperson's phone number or e-mail address to follow up? Perhaps you want the customer web site address to view more information about new customers.	Detail result objects
5. Your area of interest?	A departmental data mart may already provide a number of conditions to limit the information returned to you. You may want to limit the data by time to the current three months, current year, and last year. If you are accessing a data warehouse, you may have to select your products only. You may choose to limit results according to new salespeople or to sales that are more than 10 percent lower than forecast.	Conditions

TABLE 20-1   Refine Your Business Question Before Constructing a Query

Choosing a Query Panel

Web Intelligence offers three different query panels:

- **The Query – HTML panel** (shown in Figure 20-1) lets you build a query and then use the Interactive viewer to modify the report layout.

- **The Java Report panel** downloads a Java applet to provide a richer interface. As an applet is downloaded to your computer, this is recommended only over fast networks and when security policies allow signed applets to be downloaded (see Figure 20-3).

- **The HTML Report panel** is a zero-footprint client that includes a wizard to step you through the process of building a report. This panel launches faster over dial-up lines and is recommended when your company does not allow applets to be

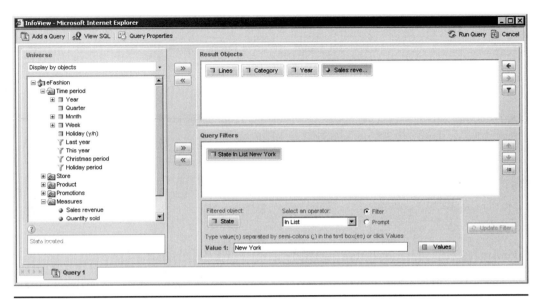

FIGURE 20-1   The Query–HTML panel

downloaded for security reasons (see Figure 20-2). However, queries and documents designed with this panel cannot be as complex as the first two.

You set your default query panel via InfoView, Web Intelligence preferences as described in Chapter 17.

Select a report panel:

○ Query - HTML

⦿ Java Report Panel

○ HTML Report Panel

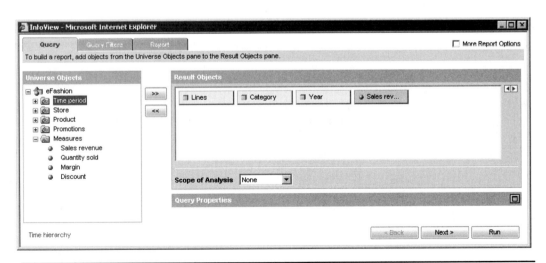

FIGURE 20-2   The HTML Report panel

Following is a partial list comparing the three panels:

Feature	Query–HTML panel	Java Report panel	HTML Report panel
Web interface	Thin-client DHMTL	Java applet	Thin-client DHMTL
Description	Query design only	Query and Report design	Wizard-like query and report design
BusinessObjects Enterprise platform	Available only on JSP, not supported in .NET	Available in .NET or JSP	Available only on JSP, not supported in .NET
Multiple blocks on a page	Yes	Yes	No
Multiple data providers	Yes	Yes	No
WYSIWYG formatting	No—use the interactive viewer	Yes	No

The Java Report panel allows for more complex documents and queries to be developed. Throughout this chapter, steps to build a query are demonstrated using the Java Report panel. The precise steps to build queries using one of the other panels will be slightly different, however, the concepts are the same.

To create a new document:

1. From within the InfoView portal, select New | Web Intelligence Document.

NOTE *The order of the drop-down menu is different depending upon whether your company uses the .NET version of BusinessObjects Enterprise or the Java version.*

2. InfoView prompts you to select a universe. Your company may have more universes, but only the ones to which you have access are displayed. Some companies have multiple universe folders for test and production environments or for each business unit. Select the desired universe and double-click to launch the query panel.

☐	Universe ▲	Owner	Folder
	Activity	Administrator	
	Advanced Objects XI v3	Administrator	
	eFashion	Administrator	
	HR	Administrator	
	Island Resorts Marketing	Administrator	

3. The first time you launch the Java Report panel, and depending upon your browser security settings, you will be warned that you are downloading a Java applet. Verify the digital signature and click Yes to download the applet.

NOTE *If your browser does not have a Sun Java Virtual Machine, you will be sent to a link to download and install this.*

The Query Panel

Figure 20-3 shows the query panel within the Java Report panel. Classes and Objects are displayed along the left side of the screen in the Data Manager. These are the objects that are available to use to display columns of information called *result objects* or to filter rows of data called *query filters*. Classes provide a logical grouping of objects. The objects in the Result Objects pane and those in the Query Filters pane can be different. For example, you can create a query to display a list of customers in NJ. *Customer* would be a result object, and *State* would be a query filter. In Figure 20-3, *Lines*, *Category*, *Year*, and *Sales Revenue* are the result objects. *City* is a query filter.

Within the Data Manager pane, each object type has its own icon. As described in Chapter 9, universes contain several object types:

- A *dimension* object is denoted with a blue cube and is typically textual information by which you analyze numeric measures, such as product, region, or year. These should be the first columns in your query result.

- A *measure* is a number that you wish to analyze; it is denoted by a pink sphere or circle.

- A *detail* object provides additional information about a particular dimension such as a phone number; it is denoted with a green pyramid.

- A *condition* object helps you filter your query results according to a predefined set of conditions. This type of object is denoted with a filter icon.

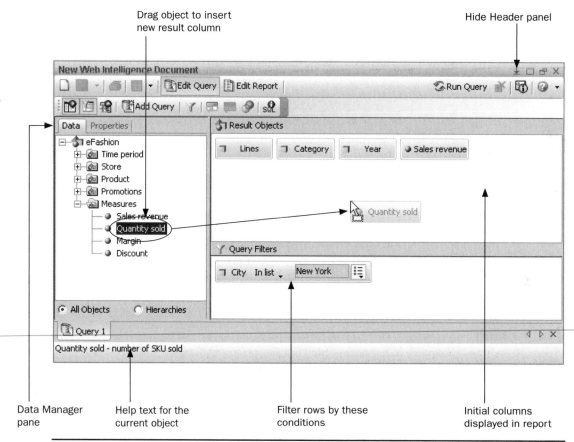

Drag object to insert new result column

Hide Header panel

Data Manager pane

Help text for the current object

Filter rows by these conditions

Initial columns displayed in report

FIGURE 20-3 The query panel within the Java Report panel

The query panel has its own buttons that allow you to modify the way the SQL is generated. Table 20-2 provides an overview of each of these buttons. The buttons in Table 20-2 are specific to when you are modifying the query and not formatting the report.

Table 20-3 shows the top row of buttons in the Java Report panel that you use while building a query. This row of buttons appears when you are editing either the query (Edit Query) or the formatted report (Edit Report). However, some will be grayed out, depending on which panel is active.

From the query panel, you build or modify your query definitions. You run the query to retrieve the results and display in a formatted document.

Button	Description	Purpose
	Show/Hide Data Manager	By default, the classes and objects are displayed. If you have a large query with many result columns, you may want to momentarily hide the classes and objects to see more result objects.
	Show/Hide Filter Pane	A toggle that hides the Query Filters pane to allow you to display more result objects.
	Show/Hide Scope of Analysis Pane	Modify the query to retrieve more levels of details in the microcube but display only summary levels in the initial report. Scope of analysis is discussed in Chapter 19.
Add Query	Add Query	Insert a new query as another data provider for this document.
	Quick Filter	A quick filter allows you to add a filter on the currently selected result object and presents you with a list of values. The object is then added in the Query Filters pane.
	Add a Subquery	Create a query within a query. In Desktop Intelligence, this is done by setting a condition equal to another query.
	Rank	Add a database ranking, different from a ranking within a report.
	Add a Combined Query	Create queries that are combined with the SQL operators UNION, INTERSECT, and MINUS. These are discussed in Chapter 23.
	View SQL	Launch the SQL Viewer, allowing you to view, copy, or modify the SQL query.

TABLE 20-2   Buttons in the Query Panel Toolbar

TIP *As you build your query, you may want to save your query definitions without executing the query. This is particularly true for complex queries or queries that you know may be better run scheduled rather than in real time. To do so, click Edit Report to go to the formatted report view and then select Save.*

Button	Description	Purpose
New Document icon	New Document	Create a new document or query off this same universe.
Edit Query button	Edit Query	When you are viewing the formatted report, select Edit Query to return to the query panel.
Edit Report button	Edit Report	To design the report layout, select Edit Report. Also, from here you can save your query settings and document without having first executed the query.
Run Query button	Run Query	Execute the query and retrieve the data. Once you run the query, you are automatically returned to the report layout. If your document contains multiple queries, this button becomes a drop-down menu that allows you to select which query to execute.
Purge Data icon	Purge Data	Once you have run the query, you can purge the data from the microcube. You may want to do this before publishing a corporate document to ensure users do not see data to which they do not have the appropriate permissions.
Show User Settings icon	Show User Settings	Display user settings for designing a report page either in pixels, centimeters, or inches using a grid.
Help icon	Help	Display online guide.

TABLE 20-3 Buttons in the Menu Toolbar

Building a Query Step-by-Step

You can build a simple query in as little as two steps: choose the result objects and run the query. However, for most reports and complex business questions, there is more involved. The rest of this chapter expands on options involved in each of these steps.

1. From within the InfoView portal, select New | Web Intelligence Document and choose the universe.
2. Choose your Result Objects that will become columns in a report.
3. Insert the appropriate Query Filters to retrieve only the data you want to analyze.
4. Select Run Query.
5. Apply the desired formatting. Basic formatting and analysis options are discussed in Chapter 19; advanced options are discussed in Chapter 21.
6. Save your document to the appropriate folder.

Result Objects

To see individual objects within each class, click the + next to the class. To add columns of data to the report, drag the individual object from the Data Manager pane to the Results

Objects pane or double-click the object name. When you drag an object, the cursor changes, as shown in Figure 20-3, in which *Quantity Sold* is being dropped into the Result Objects pane. You also can drag an entire class of objects to the results pane. Ideally, you should sort the order of the result objects from left to right by how you want them to appear in the initial report. This is typically from largest dimension to smallest dimension, with the measures rightmost. Once you execute a query, the order of the result objects and that of the variable columns in a report do not necessarily match.

To remove a result object, select the object and press DELETE. Alternatively, you can drag an object from the Result Objects window back to the Classes and Objects listing.

Scope of Analysis

As discussed in Chapter 19, in the section "Drill Through to Detail," the Scope of Analysis button enables you to retrieve additional columns of data for multidimensional analysis without immediately displaying the results in the report. The details exist in the microcube and become available when you select Drill By or Drill Down. To specify your scope of analysis settings, first ensure you understand the hierarchical nature of your data and the levels within each hierarchy. Refer to Figure 19-9 in Chapter 19 for a representation of the Time hierarchy and Product hierarchy. In setting the scope of analysis, you can either choose to include the next level for whichever result objects appear or you can specify a Custom analysis. For example, to enable drill down from Year to Quarter:

1. Drag Year from the Data Manager pane to the Result Objects pane.
2. Select Scope of Analysis.
3. From the Scope of Analysis pane drop-down, select One Level.

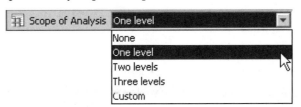

The data retrieved as part of the query corresponds to the result objects in your query. In this respect, the levels are relative and not fixed. If you change the scope of analysis to Two Levels, then the query will also retrieve results for *Quarter* and *Month*. If, however, your result object were Quarter, then the next two levels would be *Month* and *Day*. The following table shows how the levels are relative using the time hierarchy from Figure 19-9 in the previous chapter. For each example, assume that the scope of analysis is changed to Two Levels.

If the current result object is	Then the query also retrieves
Year	*Quarter, Month*
Quarter	*Month, Week*
Month	*Week, Day*
Week	*Day*
Day	No additional columns, as it is the lowest level of detail in the hierarchy

A Custom scope of analysis allows you to:

- Skip levels in a hierarchy such as *Year* as a result object with a direct drill to *Day*.
- Have different levels for each hierarchy, for example, three levels on the time hierarchy but only one level within the product hierarchy.
- Specify a drill-by dimension that is not included as an initial result object.

For example, note in the following settings that the store location or state appears in the scope of analysis but not in the Result Objects pane. Thus, when you are viewing the data and drilling, the initial table or chart will not display sales by store. However, with the Custom Scope of Analysis you can now drill from product sales by year into product sales by individual state or store location.

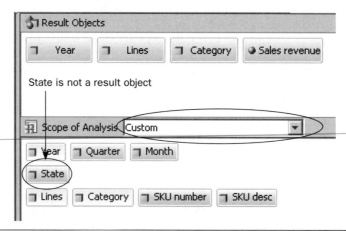

CAUTION *Scope of analysis is quite powerful and allows you to precache possible drill dimensions to enable you to have fast drill times. However, larger documents and larger result sets are more resource intensive, slower to refresh and navigate. You only want dimensions in the Scope of Analysis pane that are frequently accessed. If you are uncertain about retrieving a certain level of detail, you can still drill down by generating another query. If you are creating a report that other users will consume, then use the BusinessObjects auditing capabilities to monitor how often a user must drill beyond the initial scope of analysis. The standard activity report "Document Information Detail" provides this type of information.*

Query Filters

You use *query filters* to narrow your analysis to show information only for your particular subset of data. For example, if you are a product manager, you may limit your analysis to certain products. If you are a regional manager, you may limit your analysis to certain countries. If you are an employee supervisor, you may limit your analysis to the employees you manage. You limit your analysis by adding *query filters*. Query filters generate a WHERE clause in the SQL SELECT statement. In some cases, these filters may be applied automatically through security settings in your database or in the universe Designer Restriction sets (see Chapter 13). Usually, it is a combination of both. For example, if the transaction system or data warehouse contains information for multiple legal entities, the DBA may restrict your access to show you data only for the legal entity by which you are employed; you do not need to add an extra filter in your query. However, you will still need to add filters in the query to restrict your analysis to particular products, regions, employees, and so on, within your legal entity.

When you add a filter to the query, you need to consider the impact on response time, particularly if you are accessing a transaction system or a very large data warehouse. Ideally, it is better to apply filters to objects that have shorter values such as *Product ID* or *Product Code,* as these columns are more often indexed in the source database, rather than longer values such as *Product Name* or *Product Description,* which may not be indexed.

The query panel provides you with three ways to add a filter to your query:

- You can apply a simple filter by selecting a result object and then clicking the Quick Filter button. You are prompted to select from a list of values. By default, quick filters use only EQUAL TO or IN LIST operators. Once the filter has been added to the Query Filters pane, you can modify the operators. You apply quick filters only to dimension or detail objects that have an associated list of values, not objects that are measures.

- You can drag an object from the list of Classes and Objects to the Query Filters pane. This object does not need to be a result object and can also be a measure object. The object does not have to have an associated list of values.

- You can use a predefined condition object that is created by the universe designer (see Chapter 11) and includes the operators and possible values.

Adding a Query Filter

When you wish to use different operators or to add a filter on an object that is not in the result pane, use the Query Filters pane for more flexibility.

In the following example, you will use the eFashion universe and add a query filter on *State,* using the initial query displayed in Figure 20-3 as a starting point:

1. From the Data Manager pane, expand the *Stores* class by clicking +.

2. Select the *State* object and drag it to the Query Filters pane.

3. Web Intelligence uses the default operator In List. In this case, leave it as the default.

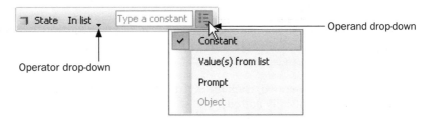

4. The default operand is a constant. You may enter the constant in the box, or you may change the operand to select Values From List. If you enter the constant, you must match the case exactly or you may not get any query results. For example, **New York** is not the same as **NEW YORK**. Use the drop-down in the preceding screen to change from Constant to Values From List.

5. Web Intelligence presents you with a list of States. Choose the desired store location and click the double arrow to add it to the pane Value(s) Selected. In this example, select New York and Texas.

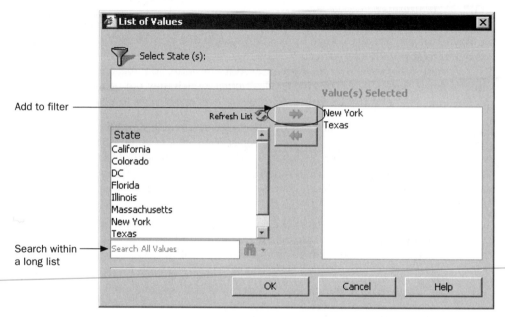

6. Click OK to close the List of Values dialog and return to the query panel.

7. Notice that in this dialog box, semicolons separate multiple values. The two conditions are connected with an AND in the SQL statement. In the SQL, the values are separate by commas.

NOTE *The Desktop Intelligence query panel uses commas to separate multiple values, whereas when answering a prompt, you use semicolons. Web Intelligence uses semicolons in both instances.*

CAUTION *When you enter multiple constants, there are no spaces between the semicolons and values. If you add a space, the SQL will contain a space in the value, for example, ' Texas' versus 'Texas', and no rows will be returned.*

 To view the SQL generated, click the SQL button from the query panel. Notice that Web Intelligence has automatically added a WHERE clause. Because the object type for *State* is character, the values are enclosed in single quotes automatically. If the filter had been on a numeric object, they would not use quotes.

```
WHERE Outlet_Lookup.State  In  ( 'New York','Texas'  )
```

Operators

Operators form the basis of comparison for the object and the values you specify. As you add an object to the Query Filters pane, click the down-pointing arrow next to In List to invoke the Operator drop-down menu (Step 3 in the preceding section). Table 20-4 lists the possible operators. Some SQL equivalents are different for specific RDBMSs. The SQL equivalents listed in Table 20-4 are Oracle-based.

Operator	SQL Equivalent	Explanation
Equal to	=	Exactly equal to one value
Not Equal To	<> or !=	Not equal to or different from one value
Greater than	>	Greater than a particular number, date, or character
Greater than or equal to	>=	Greater than or equal to a particular number, date, or character
Less than	<	Less than a particular number, date, or character
Less than or equal to	<=	Less than or equal to a particular number, date, or character
Between	BETWEEN	Records between and including the two values—for example, *Age* Between 20 And 30; *Price* Between 100 and 150; *Date* Between January 1 And January 23
Not Between	NOT BETWEEN	All values outside a particular range
In List	IN	Equal to multiple values, generally to select multiple character values in a noncontiguous list
Not In List	NOT IN	Different from multiple values
Is Null	IS NULL	Rows in which no value has been entered. Null is different from zero or blank spaces.
Is Not Null	IS NOT NULL	Records that do not contain a null
Matches Pattern	Like	This allows you to use a wildcard character such as % to find all records that contain or begin with a particular string. Use underscore (_) to match one particular space. For example, B% is everything that starts with B, %B% contains a B somewhere in the string, and _B% has B as the second position. Warning: this type of query filter means an index for the particular column will not be used.
Different from Pattern	Not Like	Does not match the pattern specified. Warning: this type of query filter means an index will not be used.
Both	INTERSECT	Retrieves records in which the two values overlap (discussed in Chapter 23)
Except	MINUS	Removes records from a main query (discussed in Chapter 23)

TABLE 20-4   Operators Available in the Query Panel

PART III

Operands

Operands allow you to specify the values to which you want to compare the object. The list of available operands may change, depending on the object and the operator you specify.

Constant enables you to manually enter one or more values. If you enter multiple values, connect them with a semicolon.

Value(s) from list allows you to choose one or more values from a pick list, if the universe designer has enabled a list of values for this particular object.

Prompt allows you to create a prompt for shared reports in which you want users to be able to enter different filters each time the query is executed.

Object allows you to set the filter to another object. For this operand, you may not use In List or Null operators. For example, you may create a query that filters orders in which the order date is equal to the ship date as shown in the following image:

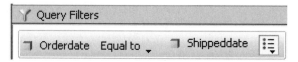

Filters on Dates

When you choose an object that is a date object, Web Intelligence adds a calendar icon next to the constant box.

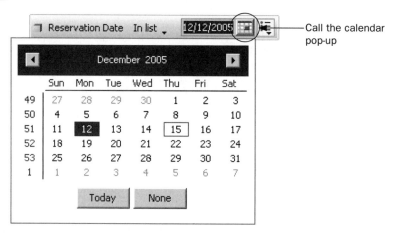

From within the calendar pop-up, you can click an individual date for the current month to add that to the constant. Today's date is highlighted with a red box. If you want to jump to a date for a different month or year, use the arrows to navigate through the calendar. Alternatively, you can enter the date in the constant box and then click the calendar pop-up to go directly to the earlier date.

NOTE *Even though the field contains date values, if the universe designer has set this object to a character type, the calendar dialog will not appear. As an example, in the eFashion universe, the object Opening Date of the store is set to character to match the field format in the data source.*

Predefined Conditions

As shown in Figure 20-4, your universe also may include predefined conditions, such as *Last Year* or *Christmas Period. Predefined conditions* are a particular kind of object that has built-in operators and values to restrict the number of rows returned and to display only the data you are interested in analyzing. For example, your universe may contain a predefined condition called *Current 3 Months* that automatically filters your data to retrieve the latest three months' worth of information. The conditions and SQL in a predefined condition can be quite complex, performing multiple SQL translations and comparisons. See Chapter 11, under "Condition Objects," for a more thorough discussion on how these are built.

Predefined conditions are denoted with a filter icon. To add a predefined condition to the query, double-click the predefined condition to add it to the Query Filters pane or drag the object to the Query Filters pane.

In Figure 20-4, the two predefined conditions have the same filtering effect as selecting Year = 2005 and Weeks Between 46 and 53.

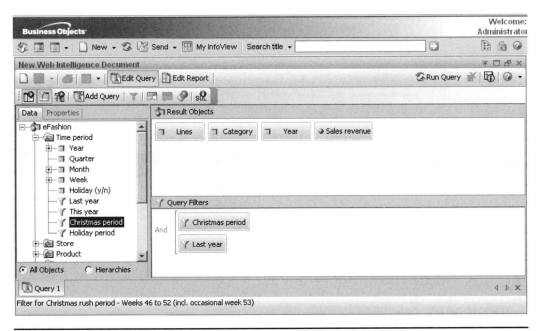

FIGURE 20-4 Predefined conditions are objects that apply complex filters.

Prompts

As seen in Chapter 18, under "Handling Prompts and Lists of Values," prompts allow you to refresh a query interactively. Prompts are useful when your query filters periodically change or if you are a report author creating a document for other users. When you set the operand to Prompt, Web Intelligence automatically creates a prompt for you, such as:

Enter value(s) for *Object*:

In developing prompts, follow these guidelines:

- If a list of values is available, start the prompt question with **Select**.
- If a list of values is not available, start the prompt question with **Enter**.
- Modify the default prompt to provide information on the format, particularly when a list of values is not present, such as **Enter Part Number as NNN-NN**.
- If a document will contain multiple queries with similar query filters, ensure you enter the prompt message exactly the same so that users are prompted only once. You can cut and paste your prompt message to ensure consistency. For example, in Figure 20-5, you have two queries within the same document that each contain a

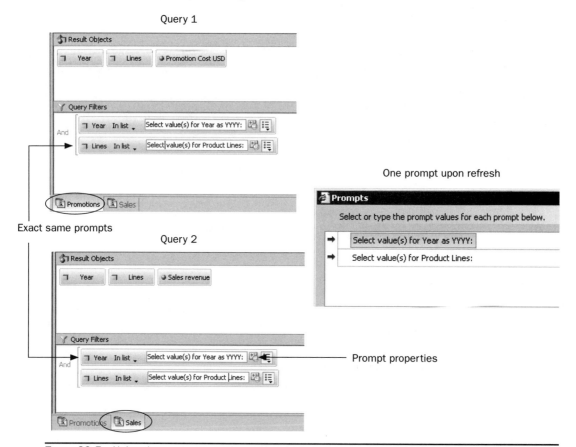

FIGURE 20-5   Using the same prompt in multiple queries passes the same filter value to each query while prompting the user only once.

query filter on *Year*; if you use the same *exact* prompt for each query filter, when you refresh a document, you will be prompted to select a year only one time. The prompt is case sensitive.

Compare the prompt box in Figure 20-5 with the following prompt box, in which the prompt message is not consistent. When you run the query, you have to specify the year twice and the product line twice (even though you really want the same query filters in each query).

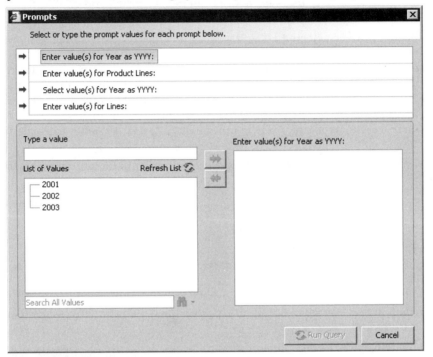

Prompt Properties

With Web Intelligence prompts, you also can specify several prompt properties. To invoke, click the Prompt Properties button next to the prompt message within the Query Filters pane.

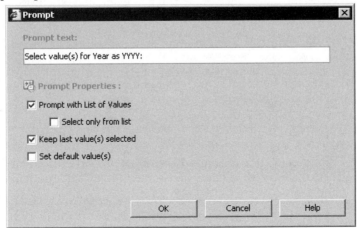

- **Prompt with List of Values**   This should be enabled by default whenever an object has an associated list of values. If you don't want users to wait for a long list of values, then you can disable this. This box should not be enabled if your query filter is on a measure.

- **Select only from list**   When users enter their own value, they may get no rows returned if they enter the filter value in the wrong format or case. For this reason, you may want to force users to choose from the list. When you do this, the prompt box changes slightly in that the box for "Type a Value" is removed.

- **Keep last value(s) selected**   The last prompt values used are stored with the query. The choice to use this setting depends very much on whether you are the only one who will run this query or other users will run it. If you are publishing the report to a shared folder, then I suggest that you uncheck this box. The filter values are reused for the current session or, if you are the report author, saved for reuse. If your filter is, for example, on a World Region and the default always reverts to North America, it can be very irritating for users in Europe. In this case, it's better to start with no value than the one last used.

- **Set default value(s)**   This prompt property is similar to the preceding one but explicitly sets a default filter value.

What's missing? An optional prompt! Unfortunately, this is still not available in XI Release 2.

Creating a Prompt

Using a similar query from the eFashion universe, to create a prompt on the *Year*:

1. Select the *Year* object and drag it to the Query Filters pane.

2. On the filter on *Year*, click the Operand drop-down menu as shown earlier and select Prompt.

3. Web Intelligence creates a default prompt message. Modify the message or accept the default.

4. Modify the prompt properties or accept the defaults.

A prompt generates the following SQL, which gets evaluated when you execute the query or schedule it via InfoView:

```
Calendar_year_lookup.Yr  In  @prompt('Enter value(s) for Year:','A','Time
period\Year',Multi,Free,Not_Persistent,,User:0)
```

Once you have executed your query and entered the prompt value, the SQL will show the `Where` clause as it is submitted to the data source.

Query Options

 To access Query Properties (shown in Figure 20-6), select Properties from the Data Manager. These options relate to the individual query and are used to override certain defaults.

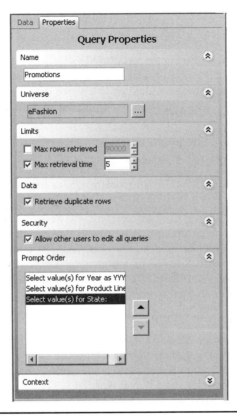

FIGURE 20-6   Query Properties

Use the up and down arrow buttons to expand or collapse the details for any given property.

Name refers to the name of the query. By default, Web Intelligence assigns the names Query 1, Query 2, and so on. If your document has multiple queries, you may want to specify a more meaningful query name. With more meaningful query names, you also can use the Run Query button to selectively refresh individual queries within a document.

Universe refers to the name of the universe used for this particular query. You can modify which universe the query accesses by clicking the ellipse next to the universe name. You should do this only when the object names between the universes are the same, or you will have to remap your query definitions. Changing the universe source is primarily used when repointing a report built in a test environment to a production environment.

TIP *You also can use this dialog to force Web Intelligence to load a new version of the universe if it has since been modified while you are building your query.*

Limits relate to the default settings specified by the universe designer for how many rows the query can retrieve and how long a query can execute. You may lower the limits for a particular query, but they may not be set higher than the default for the universe or group of users.

TIP *During query design and testing, use the limit settings to minimize the amount of data returned so that you are working with only a subset of data.*

Data properties affect how the SQL is generated when your query does not contain a GROUP BY or aggregate. If you are accessing dimensional data in which there are multiple rows for the exact same value, uncheck the box "Retrieve duplicate rows." For example, if you have a CUSTOMER or PRODUCT table in which there are multiple records with different valid to/from dates for the same customers or products, by default, you will receive multiple rows of information in a list report. Web Intelligence generates the following SQL by default:

```
SELECT CUSTOMER.CUSTOMER_ID, CUSTOMER.CUSTOMER_NAME FROM CUSTOMER
```

When you uncheck this setting, Web Intelligence modifies the SQL statement:

```
SELECT DISTINCT CUSTOMER.CUSTOMER_ID, CUSTOMER.CUSTOMER_NAME FROM CUSTOMER
```

Security settings are set by default by an administrator to determine which rights other users have for a particular folder or report. However, you as the report author can also restrict the ability to modify a query here. If users do not have the edit object permission set within the Central Management Console (see Chapter 13), then they will not be able to modify the query.

Prompt Order is determined by the order in which the query filters appear. This behavior has flip-flopped in different versions of BusinessObjects; at one point, it was alphabetical only. Here you can specify a different prompt order.

Context is used when the query path is not clear, usually when you access dimension tables without explicitly choosing a measure. When the join path is not clear, you are prompted to select a context. By default, you are prompted each time you refresh the query. If you do not want to be prompted each time and if you want to specify a default context, remove the check for Reset Contexts On Refresh.

Query Refresh on Open

When you save a document to a shared area of InfoView, you may want to force each user to refresh the query, particularly if the query contains prompts, so that each user sees only their relevant data. You will not, however, find this option in the query properties. Instead, it is in the document properties.

1. From the status bar, right-click on the report tab to invoke the pop-up menu.
2. Select Document Properties.

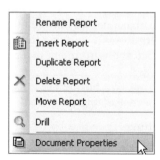

3. By default, the Document Properties panel will appear to the right of your report. Under Document Options, check the box Refresh On Open.

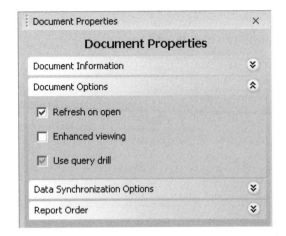

OLAP Access

In previous versions of Web Intelligence, accessing OLAP databases such as Hyperion Essbase or Microsoft Analysis Services was not particularly seamless and required a different user interface. This changes drastically in XI Release 2, with OLAP-aware universes.

If your administrator has built a universe against an OLAP database, you may not even realize that an OLAP database is the data source, as these universes look very similar to ones that access relational databases or a data warehouse. The dimensions, measures, and details all appear as classes and objects as they do in a relational data source. Figure 20-7 shows the sample Sales database in Microsoft Analysis Services.

There are several differences, however:

- Each class will have a new dimension object called (All). This is the top level within a hierarchy and represents a grand total such as All Products, All Customers.

- When filtering on a dimension, the list of values is automatically cascaded. This can be a little confusing, depending on which level in the hierarchy you are filtering on. For example, in Figure 20-7, the filter is on Country. To see the list of available countries, choose the operand Values From List, and then Refresh List. Web Intelligence first prompts What (All), since All Customers is the top of the hierarchy. You have to first click the ellipse (. . .) to see the All Customers value and then click the list of individual countries. If you place a filter on a lower-level dimension object such as City, the list of values is cascaded for each level: All, Country, and State.

- Lists of values on attribute or detail objects (indicated with a green pyramid) can be very slow to update, depending upon how the OLAP database has been structured, and distinct values are not displayed. So for example, Customer Gender, which is only M for Male or F for Female, will generate a very long list of values repeating M and F for every individual customer. Notice in Figure 20-7, in the object help text pane, the phrase for LOV_PROPERTIES. When this is not populated, the list of values generation is slow. Much of this has to do with the way the OLAP database has been designed. With Microsoft Analysis Services, the cube designer may make some of the member properties virtual dimensions that will give you better query performance in Web Intelligence.

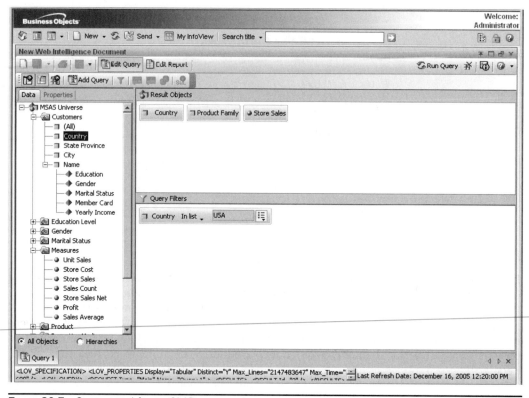

FIGURE 20-7   Query panel for an OLAP-aware universe

- There are no predefined condition objects.
- You cannot see the SQL (instead, MDX is generated).

Once you run an OLAP-aware query, you have the full set of Web Intelligence formatting and scheduling options available. You can even synchronize data providers between an OLAP data source and a relational data source (see Chapter 23).

Summary

The most important step in creating a new query is first formulating your business question in terms of what information you want to see, by which dimensions you want to explore the results, and which subsets of data you want to analyze. If the question is too broad, you may be overwhelmed by the amount of information returned. Query filters enable you to filter the information returned to you. Predefined conditions are set by the universe designer and enable you to select predefined groupings and complex conditions. Predefined conditions that involve time periods enable you to execute a query that automatically selects the most recent period, such as the last 90 days or current month. If you are building a report that will be refreshed by other users, use prompts to allow information consumers to select their own filters.

Advanced Report and Chart Formatting

A s you work with standard reports, you can format different report components to make your report easier to read and to better enable you to identify patterns and exceptions. Many of the formatting options in Web Intelligence are similar to those in Microsoft Office products. In Chapter 18, you were introduced to the components of a report. As you format a report, be sure to recognize to which component you are applying the formatting. In Chapter 19, you learned how to change basic block styles: table, chart, and crosstab. In this chapter, you will use some of the advanced formatting options to enhance the table, chart, or crosstab. You can apply a number of formatting options using the HTML Interactive Viewer. Use the Java Report panel for initial report design and formatting of large documents. This chapter first introduces you to routine formatting options using the HTML Interactive Viewer and then uses the Java Report panel for more advanced capabilities.

NOTE *The Java Report panel launches when you select Modify from the InfoView report list or when you select Edit while viewing a report. When you click the report name from the InfoView list, the HTML Interactive Viewer with formatting options launches only if this is set in your InfoView preferences, you have the appropriate permissions, and your deployment is using the JSP version of BusinessObjects XI.*

The Formatting Toolbar

While formatting reports in the HTML Interactive Viewer, display the Formatting toolbar. From the pull-down menu, select View | Toolbars | Formatting. Table 21-1 lists the formatting buttons. Most of the buttons in the HTML Interactive Viewer are the same as the formatting buttons in the Java Report panel.

Button	Name	Function
B	Bold	Formats the selected cell as bold.
I	Italics	Formats the selected cell as italics.
U	Underline	Underlines the text or numbers in the selected cell.
≡	Align Left	Aligns text and numbers to the left within a particular cell.
≡	Align Center	Centers the text and numbers.
≡	Align Right	Aligns text and numbers to the right. It is often easier to view numbers right-aligned. When you do this, be sure to align the corresponding column headings to the right as well.
	Merge or Split Cells	When you wish a column heading to span two columns, you can merge the two cells to create one wide cell.
	Background Color	Launches a color dialog box to allow you to change the background color of the current cell.
A	Font Color	Launches a color dialog box to allow you to change the font color for the current cell.
Thin	Border Size	Invokes a drop-down that lets you choose the border size from None, Thin, Medium, or Thick.
	Border Color	Launches a color dialog box to change the border color. The default border color is black.

TABLE 21-1   Buttons on the Web Intelligence Formatting Toolbar

Some of the commands are also available via the Format pop-up menu. To invoke the pop-up menu,

1. Select the cell or component you want to format and right-click.
2. Select Format | Cell.

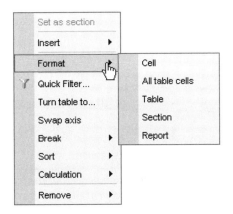

TIP *The Format dialog invoked from the pop-up menu has more extensive options than those in the toolbar. For example, to format numeric values to display a currency symbol, use the pop-up menu.*

What and How to Format

Within a Web Intelligence document, you can format individual report components ranging from a single cell to an entire block or a section. You can format the different report areas using the Formatting toolbar for common format changes. If you want to modify multiple formats at once, you may choose to use the formatting pull-down menus that display the full range of possible formats. When you are working with a large report, use the Java Report panel and apply the formats in Structure mode for better performance.

Formatting a Cell

An individual cell is the lowest level of detail in a Web Intelligence report. It may contain data values, a formula that calculates additional information, or a constant that shows a report title. Normally, you will format individual cells that are titles. Otherwise, it is more efficient to format the entire block or a section.

Formatting a Cell via Toolbar

By default, when you create a new query, Web Intelligence automatically inserts a free-standing cell with the contents Report Title, as shown next. The cell is centered to the page. The text is left aligned. The font is Arial 12.

Lines	Category	Sales revenue
Accessories	Belts,bags,wallets	$1,642,492
Accessories	Hair accessories	$350,919
Accessories	Hats,gloves,scarve	$1,550,563
Accessories	Jewelry	$5,180,094

TIP *You can either use the WYSIWYG formatting by selecting the report components in the report view, or you can select components in the Document Structure panel. To see the Document Structure, select View | Left Panel and then select Document Structure and Filters from the drop-down menu.*

To change the text from the generic "Report Title" to "Product Sales," double-click on the cell and enter **Product Sales.**

1. From the Formatting toolbar, use the Font drop-down box to change the font from Arial to Times New Roman.

2. Use the Font Size drop-down box to change the font from 12 point to 18 point.

3. Click the desired formats, shown at left, on the toolbar. In this example, Italic, Align Center, No Border.

4. The final cell format should appear as shown next. Notice that the left alignment applies only to the particular cell's contents and not to the cell's position in the report. To position a cell within a report, use Format | Cell and then select the Appearance tab, described in the next section.

Product Sales

Lines	Category	Sales revenue
Accessories	Belts,bags,wallets	$1,642,492
Accessories	Hair accessories	$350,919
Accessories	Hats,gloves,scarve	$1,550,563
Accessories	Jewelry	$5,180,094

The Formatting Dialog

The pop-up menu Format | Cell allows you to change formats in ways similar to those offered in the toolbar but provides more options. There may be fewer or more tabs than what appears in Figure 21-1 depending on what component you have selected. There are also a couple of idiosyncrasies about WYSIWYG formatting that require the use of the dialogs. Within the HTML Interactive Viewer, there is no drag-and-drop (this is available in the Java Report panel), so if you want to center the cell over the body of the report, use the Layout Properties tab. In this regard, while you can adjust the size of the cell from the right by dragging it, you cannot do so on the left, as the position of the cell is determined by the layout properties. As another example, currency symbols and decimals for numeric cells are also controlled via the settings in the dialog rather than via toolbar buttons.

Ideally, the BusinessObjects universe designer will have specified default object formats in the universe that make sense for most of the data values. If you find yourself often reformatting certain columns of data, ask the designer to apply a format to the object definition in the universe. Several of the tabs that allow you to format an individual cell serve the same purpose when formatting a table or a chart; common tabs are described only under the present section, "Formatting a Cell"; they are not repeated under "Formatting a Table" and "Formatting a Chart."

The General Tab

The General tab (shown in Figure 21-1) allows you to specify the size and contents of the free-standing cell. In the preceding section, you changed the default text of Report Title to Product Sales by double-clicking the cell contents. You also can change the text by specifying it here in the Name box. Within the General tab, you also specify the size of the cell. The measurement used (either centimeters or inches) is determined by your InfoView preferences. To wrap the text within the cell, check the box Wrap Text. If your cell will contain contents such as web site addresses, HTML formatting instructions, or image files, check the box Read Content As and select the appropriate option:

- Hyperlink
- HTML
- Image URL

The Number Tab

Within the Number tab, the currency types displayed are related to your InfoView preferences. For example, if your locale is set to English (United Kingdom), numbers with the £ symbol

| General | Layout Properties | Alignment | Font | Border |

Name: Product Sales

Size: ☑ Specify width: 10.63   cm

   ☐ Wrap text

   ☐ Specify height: 0.25   cm minimum (AutoFit cell to content if necessary)

☑ Read content as: Hyperlink ▼

Hyperlink
HTML
Image URL

FIGURE 21-1 General tab of the Format Cells dialog

appear. If your locale is set to English (United States), then $ symbols appear. Here you also control how many decimal places appear, the thousands separator, and formatting of negative numbers with a minus sign or parentheses. If the cell you selected contains date objects, then the Number tab provides several date formats.

NOTE *If you are looking for Boolean and Custom options similar to those in Desktop Intelligence, use the Java Report panel. These additional options are not available in the HTML Interactive Viewer.*

The Alignment Tab

Within the Alignment tab, you can position the text horizontally as left, center, or right aligned, as you can using the buttons in the toolbar. In addition, you can position text vertically along the top of the cell, the middle, or the bottom. By default, when you insert a new cell, the text is aligned on the bottom. Compare the following effects on vertical alignment. The cell Border has been set to Thick so that you can more clearly see the effect of changing the vertical alignment.

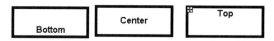

TIP *Wrap text is found in the Alignment tab of Desktop Intelligence and many Windows programs. In Web Intelligence, it's in the General tab.*

The Font Tab
When you want to change the font and font size for certain cells, you can use the Formatting toolbar as described earlier. Within the Font tab, you can make similar changes, but in addition, there are options to select a strikethrough format to put hatch marks over a particular cell.

The Border Tab
By default, Web Intelligence uses a thin border on the bottom of free-standing cells that you use as either titles or master cells in a master/detail report. The Border tab allows you also to specify a line format and a border color as grid lines within a table. While working within the Border tab, choose the default style you want applied to all borders: None, Thin, Medium, or as shown in Figure 21-2, Thick. You can then modify the border style for either the top, bottom, left, or right side of the cell.

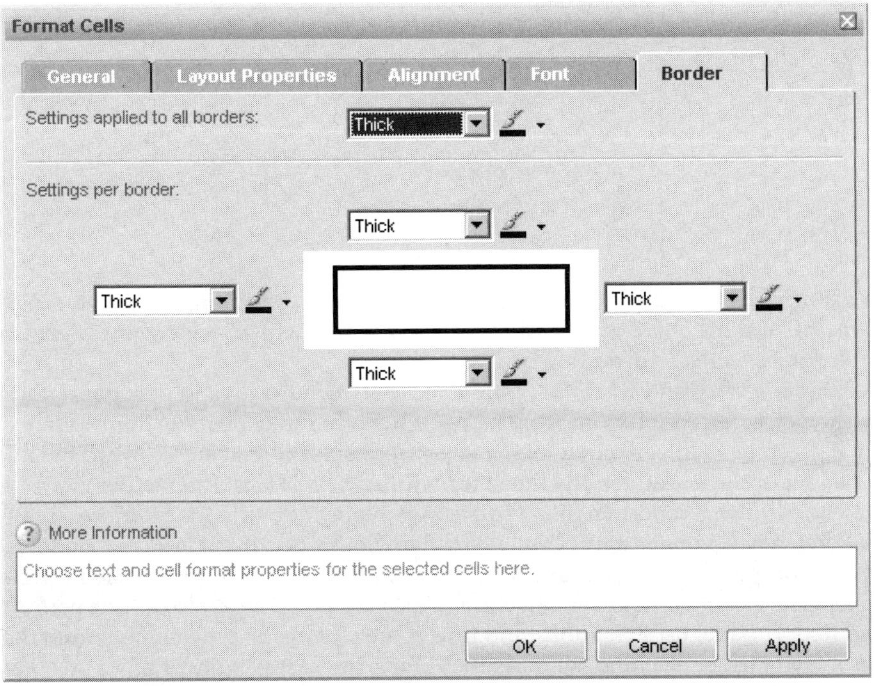

FIGURE 21-2   Border tab of the Format Cells dialog

Formatting in the Java Report Panel

In the previous sections, you performed simple formatting tasks using the HTML Interactive Viewer. When initially building a report or when applying more advanced formatting, use the Java Report panel. The remainder of this chapter uses the Java Report panel. Figure 21-3 shows the Report view from within the Java Report panel. Notice that many of the routine formatting buttons and options that are available in the HTML Interactive Viewer (Table 21-1) are also available here. However, the left panel looks somewhat different here, where it is called the Report Manager.

Table 21-2 compares the left panel in the HTML Interactive Viewer with the Java Report panel. Within the Java Report panel, you navigate to individual tabs to view or perform certain actions. Within the HTML Interactive Viewer, you select a view from a drop-down menu.

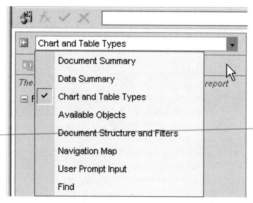

For example, within the Java Report panel, to insert an additional chart, you select the Templates tab and the chart style. Within the HTML Interactive Viewer, you select Chart And Table Types from the drop-down.

There are interface and workflow differences between the Java Report panel and the HTML Interactive Viewer. In some cases, one or the other may be more appropriate to perform a given task. In general, the Java Report panel is more geared toward the initial design of a report and used for advanced formatting. The HTML Interactive Viewer is geared to fine-tuning a report. In many respects, you may also find the interface a matter of personal preference. I prefer the HTML Interactive Viewer because it is more Windows-like. The Java Report panel has dialogs similar to those in Visual Studio and so may be preferred by developers. The difference in architecture of these two interfaces also affects performance. The Java Report panel uses an applet and thus more client-side processing within the browser's Java virtual machine, whereas the HTML Interactive Viewer relies on a Java application server.

In Figure 21-3, the Report Manager appears to the left of the Document pane and is expanded. You can configure how the Report Manager appears by opening the Configure View drop-down menu or clicking the pushpin/autohide button while viewing any of the tabs. In this way, each of the tabs becomes a collapsed option on the left, giving you more workspace for the data in the Document pane.

Tab Within the Report Manager of the Java Report Panel	Corresponding Drop-Down Within the Left Panel of the HTML Interactive Viewer	Purpose
Data	Data Summary	Lists the objects used in the report and a description of each object. In addition, the HTML Interactive Viewer displays the query execution time.
Templates	Chart and Table Types	Allows you to choose from a list of tabular report styles and chart types either to insert a new block or to change the format of an existing block.
Map	Navigation Map, Document Structure and Filters	Navigate to individual report tabs or sections in a master detail. View report filters (different from query filters).
Properties	Document Structure and Filters, Format menu	Format individual cells or components of a report, adjust page layout options. Within the HTML Interactive Viewer, these options are also available via a right-mouse click.
Properties, Document Properties	Document Summary	View the document name, owner, description, viewing options, and set refresh options.

TABLE 21-2 Comparison of Report Manager (Java Report Panel) and Left Panel (HTML Interactive Viewer)

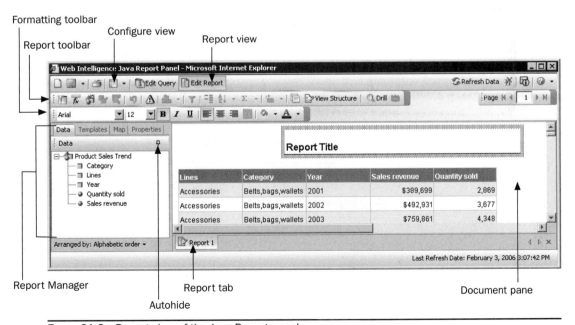

FIGURE 21-3 Report view of the Java Report panel

Adding or Removing a Report

A powerful feature within Web Intelligence is the ability to have multiple reports within one document (refer to Chapter 18, under the heading "Understanding a Document's Structure"). Each report can come from a different query, or it can simply be another way of viewing the same results of one query. Thus your first report may be a crosstab, and the second report may be a chart.

To insert a new report tab, do the following:

1. Right-click over the default report tab, Report1.

2. From the pop-up menu, choose Insert Report.

TIP *If you intend to use the same query and initial layout from Report1, then choose Duplicate Report from the pop-up menu.*

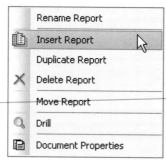

3. Web Intelligence inserts a blank report, named Report 2.

4. To change the name of the report, right-click the tab and select Rename Report from the pop-up menu.

5. Web Intelligence automatically opens the Report Manager and displays the Properties tab. In the Name box, change the default name of Report 2 to something meaningful, such as **Sales Trend Chart.**

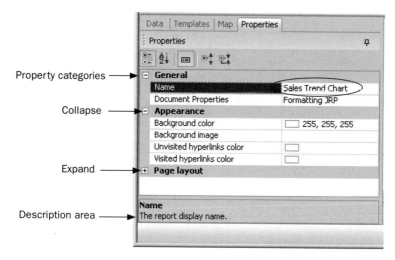

6. Press ENTER for the new name to appear in the Report tab. This new name will now also appear in the Navigation Map and as bookmarks if you convert the report to PDF format or worksheets if you save the report to Microsoft Excel format.

Navigating Properties Within the Report Manager

From within the Properties tab of the Report Manager, you have an additional mini-toolbar:

Button	Description
A↓Z↓	Lists all the items alphabetically. Thus Name (for report name) would be in the middle of the list of options.
▦	Show/Hide Description area displays a help text in the bottom of the Properties pane.
⊞↕	Expand the list of available options within the category.
⊟↕	Collapse the list of available options within the category.

When you access an individual option that has a submenu, an ellipse will appear next to the option. For example, to view the document properties, click the ellipse (...) next to the document properties. For other options, there may be a drop-down menu or an up/down arrow to increase/decrease sizes.

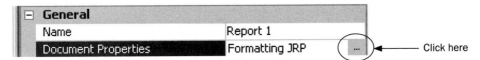

— Click here

Inserting a New Table

Within a blank report, there are several ways to create a new table. You can immediately begin dragging and dropping the universe objects directly onto the Report view, or you can first select the report style from the Templates tab and then choose the desired universe objects.

To build a vertical report similar to that in Figure 21-3,

1. Insert a new report as described in the earlier section.
2. Select the Data tab from the Report Manager.
3. Drag and drop the object *Lines* to the page area.
4. Drag and drop the object that you want to appear in the second column. Here, pay attention to the tooltip as you drop the object. You can replace the existing cell, insert a new column, create a crosstab, or create a section.

TIP *If in dropping the object your action does not produce the desired results, choose Undo from the toolbar. Note that the Java Report panel only undoes the last action, whereas the HTML Interactive Viewer has unlimited Undo.*

Alternatively, you may first choose the report style and then drag and drop the objects. For example, to create a crosstab report with Lines as a section heading,

1. Select the Templates tab from the Report Manager.
2. Expand the Tables folder by clicking the +.
3. Select Crosstab and drag and drop it to the Workspace pane.

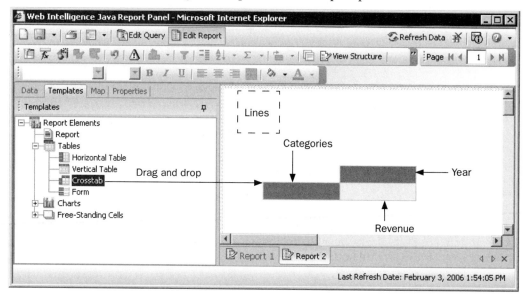

4. Select the Data tab. Drag *Categories* to the row headings and drop it when your tooltip says "Drop here to replace cell."
5. Drag *Year* to the column headings and drop it when the tooltip says "Drop here to replace cell."
6. Drag a measure such as *Revenue* to the body of the crosstab.
7. Drag *Lines* to the upper-left corner of the crosstab and drop it when the tooltip says "Drop here to create a section."

Your report should appear as follows:

Accessories

	2001	2002	2003
Belts,bags,wallets	2,869	3,677	4,348
Hair accessories	498	609	816
Hats,gloves,scarve	3,407	7,059	340

Removing and Inserting Columns or Tables
As you drag and drop data elements onto your tabular report, you may decide to later remove them. To delete a column,

1. Position your mouse on the column you wish to remove.
2. Right-click to invoke the pop-up menu.
3. Select Remove.

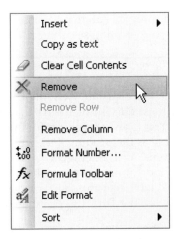

Insert	▶
Copy as text	
Clear Cell Contents	
Remove	
Remove Row	
Remove Column	
Format Number...	
Formula Toolbar	
Edit Format	
Sort	▶

You follow the same procedure to delete an entire table. The difference lies in being sure you have selected the entire table. As an example, in the following, the entire table is selected, as indicated by the gray box.

Year	Quantity sold
2001	53,078
2002	79,855
2003	90,296

Next, just the column Quantity Sold is selected. More precisely, the cell contents with the data values and not the column description is selected. When you remove an entire column, it's not particularly important if you have selected only the data values or the column heading. However, it would be important if you were trying to format a particular part of the column or clear the contents.

Year	Quantity sold
2001	53,078
2002	79,855
2003	90,296

When you drag an object onto a report, you automatically insert a new column as long as you drop it when your tooltip says "Drop here to insert a cell." In some cases, you may want to insert a blank column before you drop a data object. This is typically the case when you are making room for a text-based alerter or if you wish to insert a report variable (see Chapter 22).

To more precisely position where you insert a new column,

1. Position the cursor in the column next to where you want to insert a new one.

2. Choose the Insert Column button from the Report toolbar. Select the desired option from the submenu to insert a row or column either before your existing selection or after your selection.

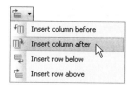

Formatting Crosstabs

When you convert a vertical table to a crosstab, Web Intelligence uses the first vertical column to pivot to column headings. This is not always the best guess. So, for example, if *Lines* is your first column and *Year* is your second column, you get a really messy pivot table, one far too wide to be usable as the product lines will become the column headings. If, however, *Year* is your first column, Web Intelligence will automatically pivot that to a column heading and use the second column, *Lines,* as the row heading.

To convert an existing vertical table to a crosstab, you can either drag the template style onto the existing vertical table or use the Turn To pop-up menu, as described next:

1. Select the vertical table. Be sure that a gray box appears around the entire tabular data set.

2. Right-click to invoke the pop-up menu.

3. Select Turn To. If Turn To does not appear in your menu, then you may have selected only one cell rather than the entire table.

4. From within the Turn To dialog, you are presented with several tabular formats. Select the image that looks like a crosstab report.

5. Click OK.

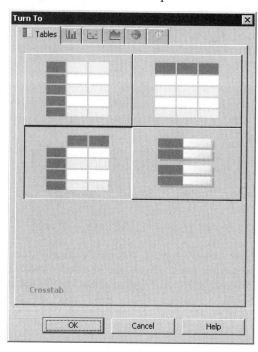

To pivot your column and row headings, drag the column heading on top of the row heading until your tooltip says "Drop here to replace the cell contents."

The following crosstab is not that easy to read. You have no idea which measure appears in which column. Visually, the column heading labels for the Years and Quarters are not that well aligned.

	2001		2002		2003	
	Q4		Q4		Q4	
Accessories	359	$65,919	851	$167,802	2,345	$370,144
City Skirts	158	$35,347	326	$78,494	149	$17,907
City Trousers	218	$45,671	491	$110,621	84	$9,117
Dresses	2,140	$289,066	4,825	$701,819	1,193	$192,677
Jackets	177	$33,694	394	$77,506	427	$72,556

Displaying Object Names Within a Crosstab

To more clearly identify which data values are in the crosstab, modify the table properties.

1. Select the entire table.
2. From Report Manager, select the Properties tab or right-click and select Edit Format.
3. Expand the Display category by clicking the + sign.
4. Select the option Show Object Name.

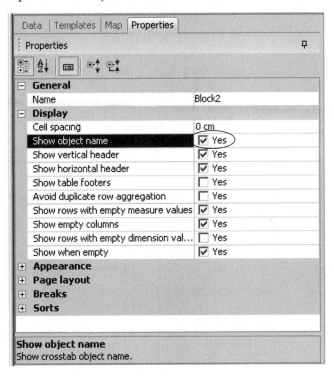

PART III

Merging Column Titles

You want the column label 2001 and Q4 to spread over both the *Sales Revenue* and *Quantity Sold* columns.

1. Use CTRL-click to select the first 2001 cell and the second empty cell to its right.

2. Right-click to invoke the pop-up menu and select Merge Cells.

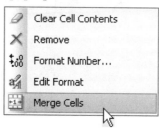

3. Repeat the same procedure for the *Quarter* column headings.

4. Center the column headings for both *Year* and *Quarter* by selecting Center from the toolbar.

Your final formatting should appear as follows:

Year	2001		2002	
Quarter	Q4		Q4	
Lines	Quantity sold	Sales revenue	Quantity sold	Sales revenue
Accessories	359	$65,919	851	$167,802
City Skirts	158	$35,347	326	$78,494
City Trousers	218	$45,671	491	$110,621

Structure Mode

Most of the formatting you've done up until this point has been with the data in WYSIWYG (what you see is what you get) mode. Formatting in WYSIWYG mode is helpful to immediately see the impact of your formatting changes. However, it can be slow when working with large reports or when applying multiple formatting changes at once. In these circumstances, you will have better performance if you format in Structure mode.

To see a report in Structure mode, click View Structure from the Report toolbar. As shown in the following screen, in Structure mode you see the cell contents rather than the data values. All of the same formatting options and Report Manager tabs that you have in WYSIWYG mode are also available to you in Structure mode.

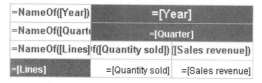

In Structure mode, each column heading will have the following cell contents by default:

```
=NameOf([Variable])
```

where *Variable* is the name of the universe object.
For example, the column heading for *Quarter* is

```
=NameOf([Quarter])
```

Each data row will have the following contents, where *Variable* is the universe object or report variable:

```
=[Variable]
```

For example, the data value for *Quarter* is

```
=[Quarter]
```

If your document contains more than one query with similar object names, then the query name precedes the object name, for example:

```
=[Query1].[Quarter]
```

For more information on report variables, see Chapter 22.

View Results   To return to WYSIWYG mode, select View Results from the Report toolbar.

Additional Tabular Formatting

Many of the formats you applied to individual cells can also be applied to a set of cells that make up the table block. Within a table block, there are three types of cells:

- **Header cells**   Column headings that usually are object or variable names
- **Body cells**   Values from the variables or universe objects
- **Footer cells**   Any subtotals

You can select the individual header, footer, or body, or else the entire table. To select a particularly large table, you may find it easiest to select the table within Structure view.

Column Headings

In formatting cells that are column headings, you can change the contents of the cell to shorten the column heading as well as format the headings. In a standard tabular report, the column headings are in the first row of the table. If you create a form-style table, the column names may also be in the first column.

Long Column Names

Sometimes the name of the variable is much longer than the values the column will contain. For example, if your product codes are only six digits and the object name is *Global Material Identification,* the column heading and width is unusually long for what would otherwise be a small column. Web Intelligence by default sets all column widths to 2.86 cm or 1.13 inches. It does not automatically adjust the column width to fit the cell contents or column name.

You can change the name of the column heading to show a smaller name.

1. Select the cell that contains the long column heading.

2. From the Report toolbar, click the Show/Hide Formula toolbar to ensure this is displayed.

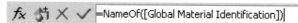

3. Type the shorter column name directly over the formula =NameOf([*Variable*]). In this example, enter **GMID**. Press ENTER or click the check mark to validate the entry.

If, however, you do not want to change the column heading description but would rather have it autosized,

1. Select the column whose width you want to adjust.

2. Right-click to invoke the pop-up menu and select Edit Format.

3. The Properties tab appears automatically. Within the Display category, check the box Yes for Autofit Width.

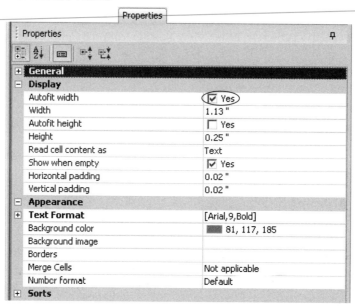

Column Height and Wrap Text

The column height and wrapping text work in conjunction with one another. When all the text fits in the normal column width, text is not wrapped. If you want the cell height to adjust automatically and wrap the text, you need to set both cell options.

1. Select the column whose height you want to adjust.

2. Right-click to invoke the pop-up menu and select Edit Format.

3. The Properties tab appears automatically. Within the Display category, check the box Yes for Autofit Height.

4. Within the Text Format category, click the ellipse (...) to call the Format Text dialog shown in Figure 21-4.

5. Check the box Wrap Text and click OK to close the Format Text dialog.

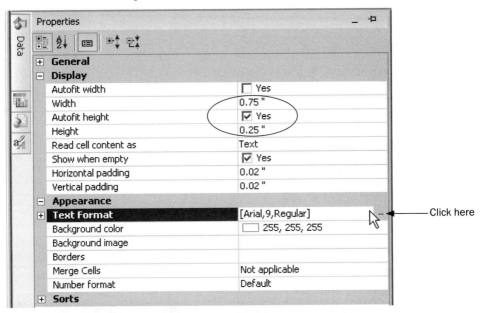

Figure 21-4 shows the Format Text dialog that you invoke from the Properties pane. Here you can change the font, set bold or italic, increase the size, and so on. In addition, you can apply effects of underline, strikethrough, and wrap text.

Data Values

Using the HTML Interactive Viewer, you worked with the Format Cells dialog as shown in Figure 21-1. With the Java Report panel, you have additional options to format numeric and date values. Although you apply most other formatting options via the Properties panel, you access the Number Format dialog only through the pop-up menu:

- Select an individual cell or column.
- Right-click to invoke the pop-up menu.
- Select Number Format. This menu option will not appear if you have selected an entire table.

Within the Number Format dialog, there are multiple format types such as Default, Number, Currency, Date/Time, Boolean, and Custom as shown in Figure 21-5. Under each type, you can further customize a cell's format. The available formats are different for each type. For example, Date/Time allows you to display a date object as dd/Mmm/yy (01/Jan/03) or as Mmm-dd-YYYY (Jan-01-2003), whereas Number allows you to choose thousands separators, to include the % symbol, or to specify the number of decimal places.

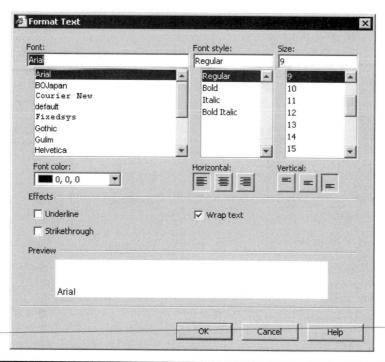

FIGURE 21-4 Format Text dialog

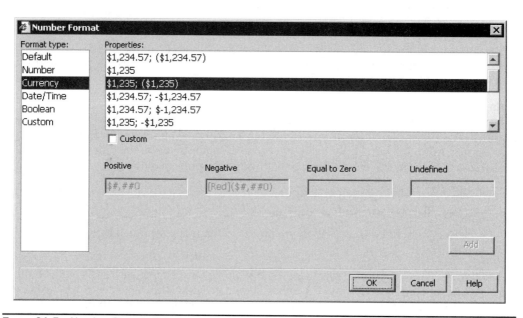

FIGURE 21-5 Number Format dialog

TIP *If you are spending an inordinate amount of time formatting each data column, work with the universe designer to provide meaningful defaults.*

The Custom category contains formats that you have added. The Number category contains settings for numeric fields that specify the number of decimal places, thousands separators, zero treatment, and negative values. For example, you can have positive numbers formatted in black with negative numbers formatted in red. To specify a color format, insert the color in brackets—for example, [Red] to display a negative number in red. Oddly enough, as a default, the only number type that displays negative values as red is Currency. Noncurrency values will display negative numbers in parentheses or with the minus sign, but not in red. To add red formatting to negative numbers as a Custom type, follow these steps:

1. Choose the desired initial format with the thousands separator and decimal places.
2. Check the Custom box.
3. In the Negative box, enter the text **[Red]** before the numeric placeholder.
4. Click Add.
5. The new type will now appear under the Custom type.

Within the Currency type, Web Intelligence provides U.S. dollars ($), Euros (€), and Yen (¥) as standard symbols. To create a format for British Pounds, enter the following in each box:

Positive	**£#,##0**
Negative	**£(#,##0)[Red]**

Note that you can use either the # symbol or a 0 as a placeholder for each digit. In the preceding example, there is a comma for a thousands separator and no decimal places. Negative values display in red and with parentheses around them.

Under the Boolean category, you can alter the format for cells that display 0's and 1's; unfortunately, the Boolean format does not work for cells that contain other Boolean types such as yes/no, true/false. The format provided will convert a cell containing 1 to True and 0 to False. The information in the data source may use a Boolean field to flag products as stock items or order items; valid or discontinued. While you could use an if-then-else formula to convert the 0's and 1's to more meaningful descriptions, it is easier to add a format to display Yes/No, Stock/Order, Valid/Discontinued, and so on.

Additional Table Format Options

In the preceding examples, you selected individual cells and components of a table. The Properties tab dynamically changes depending upon which elements of a table you have selected. In Figure 21-6, the entire table is selected. Notice that the Display options are different than in the preceding section, when just one column was selected.

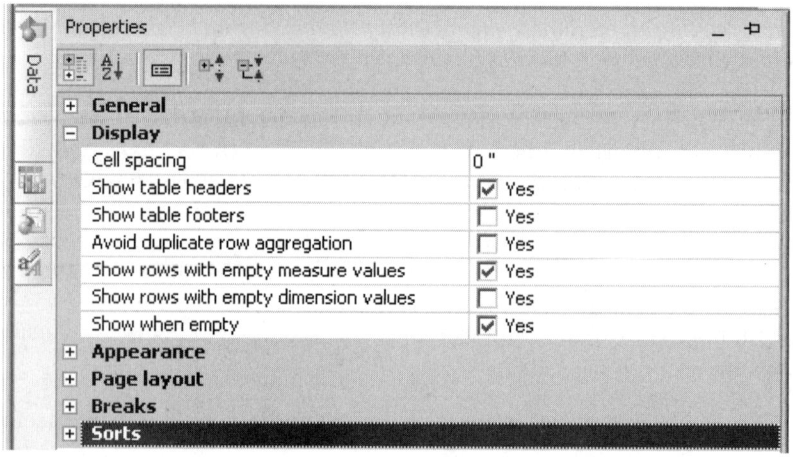

FIGURE 21-6   Display properties for a table

Display Properties

From within the Properties, Display category you can set the following options for the entire table:

- **Show table headers**   This box is enabled by default to display column headings for a tabular report.

NOTE When you insert a break on a table, the option to show table headers is automatically unchecked. So when a break section spans multiple pages, the column headings do not initially appear on the secondary pages. If you want the column headings to work correctly, you set this option not for the entire block, but rather, for each individual break level. To do this, select the break column and then check the box Page Layout, Repeat Header On Every Page. To be sure that you have selected a break column rather than the block, pay attention to the Name displayed under the Properties, General section. If Name, Block1 (the default) appears, you are setting options for the entire table. If something like Text = [Object_Name] appears, then you are setting options for that particular break level.

- **Show table footers**   When you add a calculation on a column (discussed in Chapter 19), this box is automatically checked and the table shows an additional row with the subtotals.

- **Avoid duplicate row aggregation**   When the universe designer sets an object to use a projection aggregate, Web Intelligence automatically shows the aggregate for the dimension and level of detail displayed in the table. You generally want to check this box only if you are trying to see the individual rows of a result set to identify calculation issues.

- **Show rows with empty measure values**   By default, if a row contains null values, Web Intelligence will suppress the row and corresponding dimension. In some cases, though, you may want the full data set to appear. In previous versions of

BusinessObjects, report developers would have to create their own solutions such as a ZeroTest variable and then filter the rows that were not 0.

- **Show rows with empty dimension values** This setting is particularly important when you are merging multiple data providers (see Chapter 23) and want to see rows from both queries.

- **Show when empty** Show the table even when no rows are returned.

Page Layout

Most of the options in the Page Layout category of the Properties tab (Figure 21-7) affect what happens when you print a report. To see the effect of these settings, click the View Page Layout button from the Report toolbar.

To change the position of the table, click the ellipse (...) on the Position line to invoke a Relative Position dialog. Here you can change the measurement of how far you want the table to be from another table, report title cell, or chart.

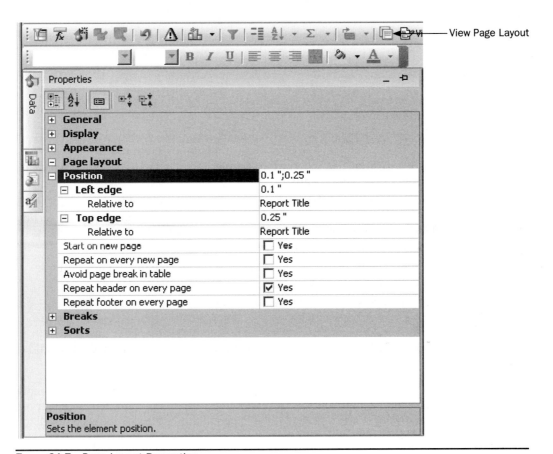

FIGURE 21-7 Page Layout Properties

NOTE *Within one report, you can have multiple charts and tables on one page. When you do, you must position these objects relative to one another, or else the contents from one table may run into the chart.*

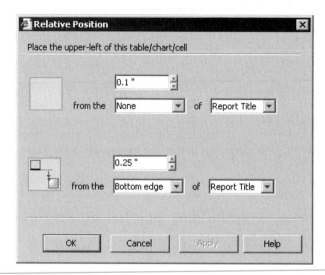

- **Start on new page** is useful only for very small tables. It will insert a page break between each table.

- **Repeat on every new page** repeats a small table on top of every new page. For example, if you have a small summary table at the top of a report and a long detail table beneath, check this box to have the summary table repeated at the top of each page as the details change beneath.

- **Avoid page break in table** is useful when you have multiple tables in a report. This option will force Web Intelligence to print the block on a new page so that the second table starts on a new page, or if possible, prints on one page. This option is unnecessary for reports that contain only one long table that spans more than one page.

- **Repeat header on every page** should be set to Yes when the table spans multiple pages. This is also the default. Headers refer to the column headings.

- **Repeat footer on every page** will repeat a grand total on every page (assuming you have inserted calculations, see Chapter 19). If you set this option, be sure to clearly label the grand total row; otherwise, the footer subtotal can appear mixed in with the smaller break tables. The footer refers to the additional row used for subtotal calculations.

    Remember that a master/detail report may appear to have multiple tables, but in reality, it is one table with multiple sections. If you want each new section in a master/detail report to start on a new page, then you must also set the Page Layout option for the section cell to start on a new page.

NOTE *Most of the preceding options are similar to the options that appear for individual break levels. Pay careful attention to what part of the report you have selected prior to setting these options. I find the process of formatting break levels much easier in the HTML Interactive Viewer, as described in Chapter 19, the section "Break Options."*

Alternating Row Colors

As demonstrated in multiple tables in this chapter, by default Web Intelligence will display alternating rows in gray and white backgrounds. This makes your report easier to read, similar to the legacy printed green bar reports. To remove or change this default,

1. Select the entire table.
2. Right-click to invoke the pop-up menu and choose Edit Format.
3. Within the Properties dialog, under the Appearance category, expand Alternate Row/Column Colors.
4. Set the Frequency to 1 and the Color to White.

⊞ **Footer cells**	
⊟ **Alternate Row/Column colors**	
Frequency	1

Alerters

An *alerter* is a type of conditional formatting you use to highlight rows of data. You can use different fonts and colors to highlight a row, or you can tell the alerter to display certain text. In Figure 21-8, there are two different types of alerters. The first highlights the column values, % Change, in green when the % Change is greater than 50% and in red when it is negative. The second alerter displays a text message Excellent or Decline based on the same criteria. Alerters are evaluated from top to bottom: if the first condition of > 50% is met, then this formatting/result applies; if the first condition is not met, then Web Intelligence proceeds to evaluate the second condition. If none of the conditions are met, then the cell content and format remain unaffected.

Working with alerters requires two steps: first, select the column(s) to which you will apply the alerter; then create the alerter. If you will be creating a text-based alerter, first insert the additional column in the table.

	2002	% Change	Sales Status	2003	% Change	Sales Status
Boatwear	$18,950	0%		$183,335	867%	Excellent
Fancy fabric	$53,404	0%		$76,931	44%	
Outdoor	$154,384	0%		$44,415	-71%	Decline
Sum:	$226,738			$304,680		

Alerter   Text alerter

FIGURE 21-8 Use alerters to highlight exceptions.

Creating the Alerter

To create the alerter as displayed in Figure 21-8, do the following:

1. Click Alerters from the Report toolbar.

2. The Alerters dialog box appears. In the following screen, two alerters already exist. The check box next to Sales Change Text indicates this is the alerter that is applied to the currently selected column. Click New to define a new alerter.

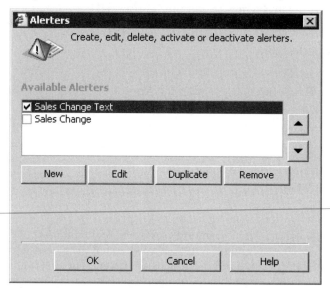

3. From the Alerter Editor, shown in Figure 21-9, enter a name and a description for the alerter.

4. Under Filtered Object Or Cell, select the variable that will determine if the row should be highlighted or not. This is most often a measure variable—for example, Revenue, or in this example, Year/Year Variance.

TIP *The default object is based on the column you selected when clicking the Alerters button. If this is not the correct object, click the ellipse (...) button to choose from a list of available objects.*

5. Under Operator, click the down arrow to specify equal to, greater than, and so on. In this example, select Less Than.

6. In the Operand(s) box, enter a value or click the drop-down box to select from a List Of Values. In this example, enter **0** to alter the format for products with negative revenue variances.

7. Click the Format button to open the Alerter Display dialog (see Figure 21-10). Under Text, choose the color red. In the Cell Contents box, the text turns to red.

Choose values or objects

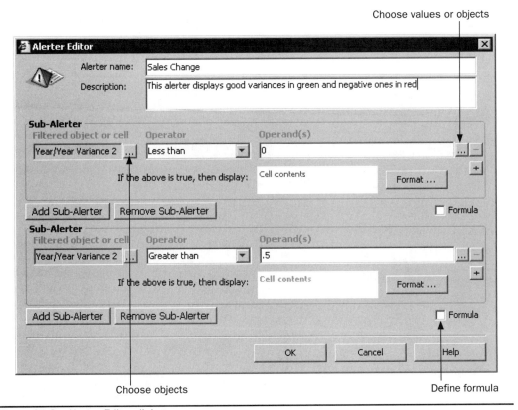

Choose objects   Define formula

Figure 21-9 Alerter Editor dialog

Click OK when you are satisfied with the format options and wish to return to the Alerter Editor.

8. To add a second condition, such as Year/Year Variance Greater than .5 as in Figure 21-9, select Add Sub-Alerter. Repeat Steps 5–7.

9. Click OK to close the Alerter Editor.

10. From the Alerters dialog box, the box next to your newly defined alerter should be checked. Click OK to apply the alerter to the currently selected column.

Textual Alerters

In the last section, you changed the color of the data values. Using the Alerter Display dialog shown in Figure 21-10, you also can change the font style, font effects such as bold, alignment, and borders. If you want your alerter to display a text message such as "Excellent" or "Decline" as in Figure 21-8, you define this in the formula Display box. If your alerter will display a text message, be sure to first insert a new, blank column within your tabular report.

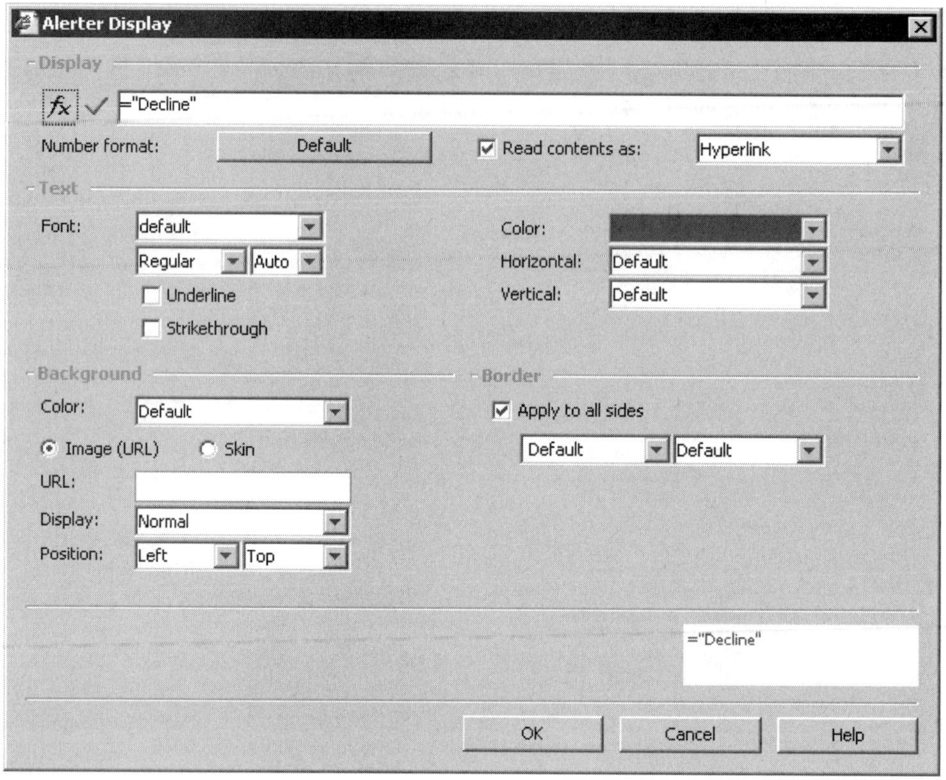

FIGURE 21-10 Alerter Display dialog

Formulas Within an Alert

In Figure 21-8, there is a specific column to show the Year/Year Variance. With Alerters you can define a formula within the alert. Thus, Revenue numbers appear in the report, but the alerter works off a variance calculation. In previous versions of BusinessObjects, you had to first define a formula or variable and then apply the alerter to the new variable. In Web Intelligence, you can define a formula as part of the alerter.

In the following example, the alerter calculates the number of days between an order's required date and ship date. If the difference is less than 0, the shipment is late and the format for that row of data will be different.

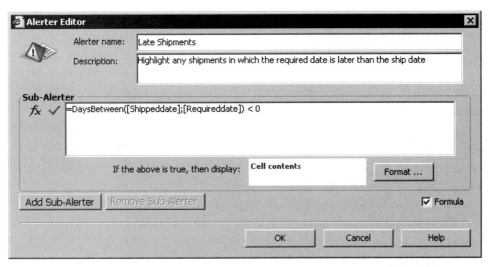

When you wish to embed a formula within an alerter, check the Formula box in the bottom right of the Alerter Editor (Figure 21-9). This changes the dialog to embed the formula editor rather than the individual objects, operators, and operands.

Formatting a Chart

Tabular reports are appropriate when you want to see the actual numbers. However, when you are trying to identify trends, patterns, and exceptions, then visually displaying your data in a chart is a more effective block style.

When you add a chart to your report, you do so in Structure mode. The procedure to add the chart is similar to that of adding a table, although in this case, you must first choose the chart style.

1. Select the Templates tab from the Report Manager.

2. Expand the Charts folder by clicking the + sign. Drag and drop the desired chart style to the report area. This can be either next to or below an existing table, or else it can be on a blank report.

3. Select the Data tab to see the available universe objects and variables. Drag and drop the objects to the appropriate part of the chart. As shown in Figure 21-11, measures must be placed on the upper left of a bar chart on the Y-axis. Dimension objects should be dragged and dropped to the X-axis.

4. Select View Results to see the chart with the data.

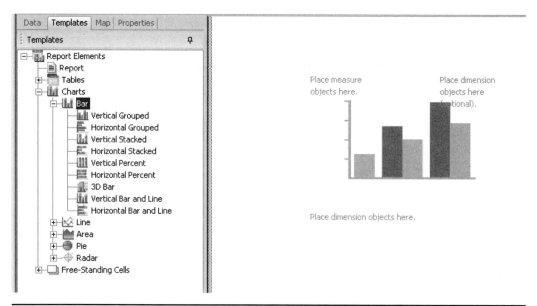

FIGURE 21-11   Charts are built in Structure mode.

Figure 21-12 shows how you would place dimension objects on a bar chart in Structure mode on the left and the corresponding effect on the right.

Chart Properties

As you graph your data, you can change a number of chart properties to make the chart more visually appealing and readable. In Figure 21-12, the X-axis labels for Product Line are truncated. The text is too long. You can choose to format the font for the X-axis. In this case, because there are many values, it is more appropriate to resize the chart using drag-and-

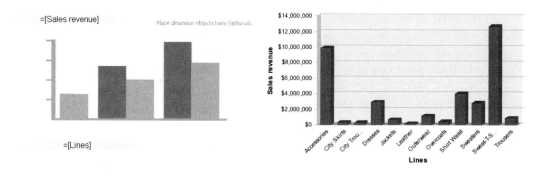

FIGURE 21-12   Change from Structure mode to View Results to see the data graphed.

drop or by modifying the chart properties. Alternatively, consider using a different chart style; horizontal bar charts are better when there is a long list of X-axis values.

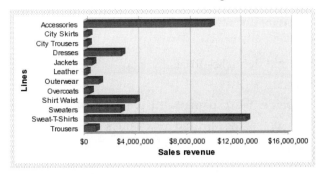

A Vertical Bar and Line chart allows you to have a dual Y-axis. This is necessary when you want to graph two different measures that have different scales. To change an existing chart style or tabular data set, you can either drag a template onto the existing block or

1. Select the block.
2. Right-click and select Turn To from the pop-up menu.
3. Choose the new chart type from the Turn To dialog.

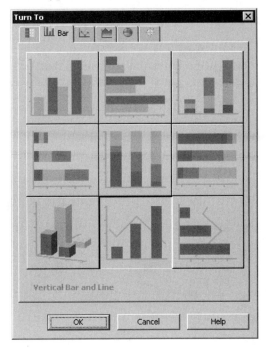

4. Click OK.

Figure 21-13 shows the different chart components. If you are used to charting data in either Microsoft Excel or Desktop Intelligence, the quantity sold in Figure 23-13 appears on the second Y-axis. However, within Web Intelligence, this is referred to as the Z-axis. This distinction is only important if you wish to change the font, scale, or gridlines for this axis.

To set the formatting for any axis,

1. Select the chart and right-click to call the pop-up menu.
2. Select Edit Format.
3. Within the Properties tab, expand the Appearance category and the Y-axis.
4. To change the scale, set the Min and Max values.

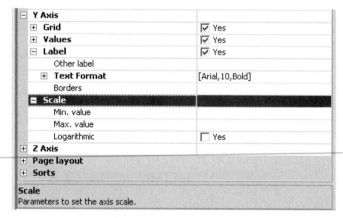

5. To change the font for the numbers that appear on the Y-axis, expand the Label group and click the ellipse (...) next to the Label to call the Format Text dialog.

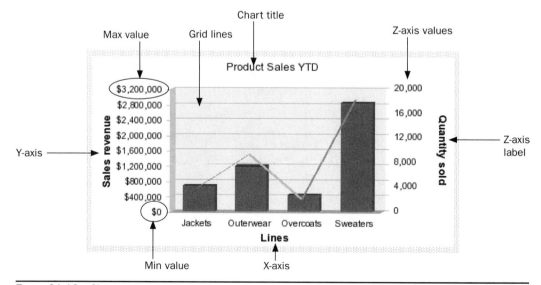

FIGURE 21-13   Chart components

Also, in Figure 21-13, the chart has a title. This title remains associated with the chart and is not a standalone cell.

1. To set the chart title from the Properties tab, expand the Appearance category.
2. Check the Title box to Yes.
3. This adds some new options, Text Format, Background Color, Borders, and Text. On the Text line, enter a title for the chart.

⊟ **Title**	☑ Yes
⊞ **Text Format**	[Arial,10,Regular]
Background color	☐
Borders	
Text	Product Sales YTD

The following pie chart shows some additional chart properties with the following options set under Appearance > Data > Values:

- Show data
- Show segment labels
- Show as percentages

A scatter plot chart type is helpful in visualizing the correlation between two measures. For example, if you discount products, do you increase your sales volume? As shown next, there are higher discounts on

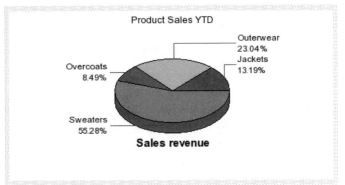

higher quantities sold for sweaters. However, even though overcoats had high discounts, volume sold is still lower than other product lines. This chart also shows some additional properties with data markers (Appearance > Data > Vary Data Markers). The legend is centered across the bottom of the chart (Appearance > Legend > Position=Bottom).

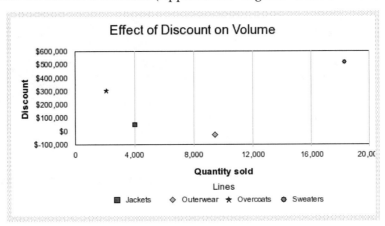

Chart Page Layout

Be sure to check the Properties for the Chart Page Layout, Avoid Page Break In Chart, if your report will have multiple charts and tables. You would think this would be the default, but it's not! Also, if you add a chart to an existing report that also contains a table, set the relative positioning as described earlier to ensure that as the number of rows in your table expands or increases, the chart placement moves with it.

Page Layout

You can view the layout of your report as it will appear in print form by selecting View Page Layout from the Report toolbar.

You set a number of layout options via the Properties tab such as the paper size and the report orientation (landscape or portrait). The Page Layout options appear, though, only when you have selected the entire report and not an individual report component (cell, table, or chart).

NOTE *You cannot select the entire report when you are in Page Layout view.*

To modify the Page Layout options,

1. Ensure you are not in Page Layout view. This button acts as a toggle, so if necessary, select View Page Layout from the Report toolbar to toggle back to Draft mode.

2. Then click anywhere on the margin so that a gray box appears around the entire report page (not around an individual block).

3. Select the Properties tab.

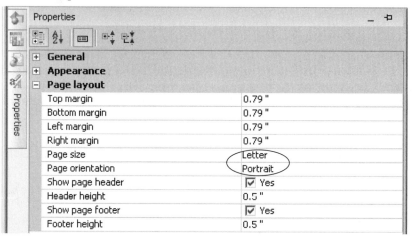

4. To change the page orientation from the default Portrait to Landscape, click the row Page Orientation.

5. A drop-down menu will appear on this row. Click the down arrow to set the orientation to Landscape.

6. Change your view back to Page Layout to view the effect.

NOTE *There are inconsistencies in PDF printing from the Java Report panel versus the HTML Interactive Viewer. Unfortunately, the Page Layout options you set here are not transferred to Adobe Reader when you convert your report to PDF for printing from the Java Report panel. You must explicitly choose the paper size and orientation for PDF. However, they are used when you print from within the HTML viewer.*

The default paper size and orientation are set for all users on the Web Intelligence Server via an XML file.

```
C:\Program Files\Business\Objects\Tomcat\webapps\businessobjects\enterprise115\
desktoplaunch\webiApplet\AppletConfig\defaultConfig.xml
```

To change the paper size to letter, replace A4 with LETTER:

```
KEY VALUE="page*default">
  <FORMAT NAME="A4" ORIENTATION="portrait" />
```

Special Fields

Web Intelligence allows you to insert *special fields* for commonly used document information such as document name, last refresh date, and page numbers. You can access additional document information through report formulas. With report formulas, for example, you can create a formula to display either the original document author (DocumentAuthor) or the user logged in to BusinessObjects Enterprise (CurrentUser). Refer to Chapter 22 for additional instructions on report formulas. In the following example, you will add two cells to display a last refresh date and a page number:

1. From the Report toolbar, select View Page Layout.
2. Scroll to the Footer area.

TIP *To more clearly see what is the Footer or Header area, view the report in Structure mode.*

3. From the Report Manager, select the Templates tab and expand the group Free-Standing Cells.

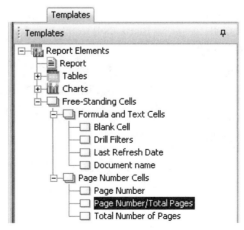

4. Drag the Template cell "Last Refresh Date" to the bottom-left corner of the footer. Notice that the formula for this cell is

```
=LastExecutionDate()
```

5. Select the Template cell "Page Number / Total Pages" and drag it to the bottom-right corner of the footer. Notice the formula for this cell is as follows:

```
Page()+"/"+NumberOfPages()
```

6. By default, Web Intelligence uses a thin line on the bottom border of any free-standing cells. You can remove the cell borders by selecting both cells in the Report window (use CTRL-click to select both footer cells), going to the Properties tab, selecting Appearance > Text Format > Borders, and removing the bottom border.

Figure 21-14 shows a formatted report with the default footer cells modified to include some additional text such as "Last Refresh Date" and "Page N of N." You can modify these cells as you would modify any formula. Ensure the Formula toolbar is displayed. Then select the footer cell and modify the formula.

```
fx  ⬚  X  ✓  ="Page "+Page()+" of "+NumberOfPages()
```

The default formulas in Figure 21-14 have been changed to

```
="Refresh Date "+LastExecutionDate()
="Page "+Page()+" of "+NumberOfPages()
```

Company Logo in Report Header

You may want to add your corporate logo within the report header. To do so, you insert a blank cell that then points to an image file. Within the Web Intelligence document, the cell format must be set to be read as an image file. The image file must be copied to the Enterprise Server in the following path:

```
C:\Program Files\Business Objects\BusinessObjects Enterprise 11.5\Images
```

1. Select View Page Layout from the Report toolbar so that a Page Header area appears at the top of your report.

2. From the Report Manager, choose Templates > Free Standing Cells > Formula And Text Cells > Blank Cell. Drag the Blank Cell to the Header portion of the page.

3. Choose the Properties tab.

4. On the General > Text line, enter the name of the logo file, preceded with **boimg://** (this is the virtual mapping to the image directory on the Enterprise Server). Alternatively, you can enter this in the formula bar.

5. Under Display > Read Cell Content As, change the default from Text to Image URL.

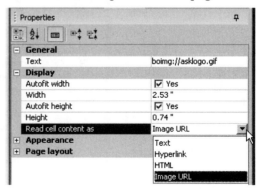

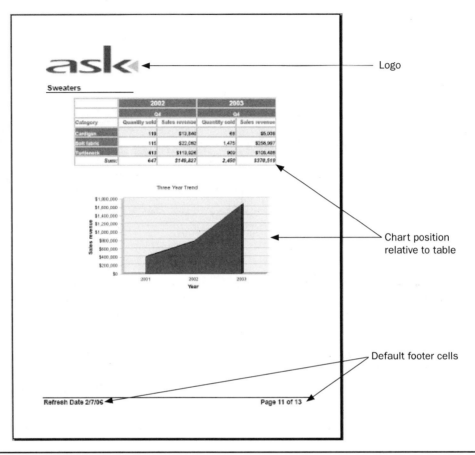

FIGURE 21-14   Formatted report in PDF

Formatting Master/Detail Reports

Master/detail reports are broken into sections. Formatting a section is not that obvious, as you clearly see the beginning and end of the section only when you are in Structure mode. Further, you see the properties for the section only when you have clicked that gray folder icon that says Section On as shown in Figure 21-15. At the bottom of the report on the right, you also have an End of Section On. As indicated in Properties > Display, the end of the section is 7.39 inches. This is a fairly large section as the result of adding a chart *below* the table. You would have a smaller minimum height if the chart were to the right, but the width of the table makes this impractical. The important thing is to ensure that your minimum height does not exceed the length of your page and takes into account your headers and footers.

When formatting a section, you have the following additional check boxes:

- **Show when empty** is set by default and ensures the section cell appears even if there are no values.

Click here

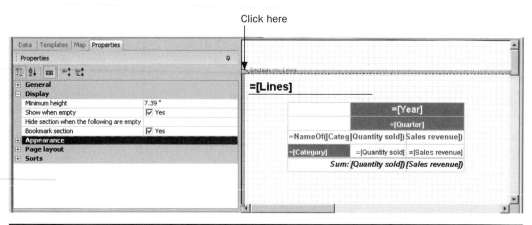

FIGURE 21-15   Use Structure mode to set section properties.

- **Hide section when the following are empty** has a drop-down menu for each dimension object that acts as a section header. With this box checked, if a particular section level has no corresponding data, all the tables and charts within that section are suppressed.
- **Bookmark section** converts section cells to bookmarks when the report is converted to PDF for printing and offline viewing.

User Settings

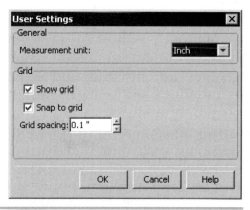

The Java Report panel user settings allow you to set the measurement in inches or centimeters, optionally display grid lines for positioning report components, and set snapping to grid. Figure 21-15 shows the report with grid lines. Note that these grid lines do not appear in a printed report; they are strictly for aiding in the layout. The User Settings button appears in the upper-right corner of the Java Report panel.

Summary

Web Intelligence offers several methods of formatting a document. Use the HTML Interactive Viewer when you wish to make changes to an existing report. Use the Java Report panel when you build a new report, require advanced formatting options such as alerters or custom numbers, or are formatting large documents in which Structure mode is faster.

Formulas and Variables

Until now you have displayed and manipulated objects returned from a data provider that are called *base report variables* or *universe object variables*. Formulas provide a powerful way to enhance your reports by transforming columns of data into more meaningful information. There are advantages and disadvantages to using user-defined formulas and variables that are created by the report designer. The key disadvantage to these user-defined formulas is that they are document specific. In other words, they cannot be shared with other users or other documents. You must re-create the formulas in each new document. This process can be error-prone and maintenance intensive. Differences in the way report authors create similar formulas can create multiple versions of the truth. Is it "revenue net of returns" or "revenue without returns"? For these reasons, ensure you work with the universe designer to evaluate if the formula should be a universe object that is then available to all users and documents.

However, it is not realistic or even possible for the universe designer to include every conceivable calculation in the universe. Formulas allow you to create one-time and unanticipated calculations that do not exist in the universe. Another advantage to using formulas is that Web Intelligence manipulates local report data using a syntax that can overcome many limitations of SQL. For more discussion on the pros and cons of report variables, see Chapter 14.

Web Intelligence Functions

The number of formula functions in Web Intelligence XI Release 2 is roughly double that of previous releases. Table 22-1 provides a comparison of the functions from each of the various interfaces and versions. Use this table to understand when you may have report conversion issues between Desktop Intelligence and Web Intelligence or in evaluating if a report must be built in Desktop Intelligence.

Function Category	Function	BusinessObjects 6.5	Web Intelligence 6.5	Web Intelligence XI Release 1	Web Intelligence XI Release 2
Aggregate	Average	X	X	X	X
	Count	X	X	X	X
	CountAll	X			
	Max	X	X	X	X
	Median	X			X
	Min	X	X	X	X
	Percentage		X	X	X
	Percentile	X			X
	Product	X			
	RunningAverage	X			X
	RunningCount	X			X
	RunningMax	X			X
	RunningMin	X			X
	RunningProduct	X			X
	RunningSum	X			X
	StdDev	X			X
	StdDevP	X			X
	Sum	X	X	X	X
	Var	X			X
	VarP	X			X
Numeric	Abs	X	X		X
	Ceil	X	X		X
	Cos	X			X
	EuroConvertFrom	X			X
	EuroConvertTo	X			X
	EuroFromRoundError	X			X
	EuroToRoundError	X			X
	Exp	X	X		X
	Fact	X	X	X	X
	Floor	X	X	X	X
	Ln	X	X	X	X
	Log	X	X	X	X
	Log10	X			
	Mod	X	X	X	X
	Power	X	X	X	X

TABLE 22-1   Comparison of Formula Functions in Various Product Versions

Function Category	Function	BusinessObjects 6.5	Web Intelligence 6.5	Web Intelligence XI Release 1	Web Intelligence XI Release 2
	Rank	X			X
	Round	X	X	X	X
	ServerValue	X			
	Sign	X			X
	Sin	X			X
	Sqrt	X	X	X	X
	Tan	X			X
	ToNumber	X	X	X	X
	Truncate	X	X	X	X
Character	Asc	X			X
	Char	X			X
	Concatenation	X			X
	Fill	X			X
	FormatDate	X	X	X	X
	FormatNumber	X	X	X	X
	Hyperlink	X			
	HTMLEncode				X
	InitCap	X			X
	Left	X	X	X	X
	LeftPad	X		X	X
	LeftTrim	X	X	X	X
	Length	X	X	X	X
	Lower	X			X
	Match	X	X		X
	Pos	X			X
	Replace	X	X	X	X
	Right	X	X	X	X
	RightPad	X		X	X
	RightTrim	X	X	X	X
	SubStr	X	X	X	X
	Trim	X	X	X	X
	Upper	X			X
	URLEncode				X
	WordCap	X			X

TABLE 22-1   Comparison of Formula Functions in Various Product Versions *(continued)*

Function Category	Function	BusinessObjects 6.5	Web Intelligence 6.5	Web Intelligence XI Release 1	Web Intelligence XI Release 2
Date/Time	CurrentDate	X	X	X	X
	CurrentTime	X	X	X	X
	DayName	X	X	X	X
	DayNumberOfMonth	X	X	X	X
	DayNumberOfWeek	X	X	X	X
	DayNumberOfYear	X	X	X	X
	DaysBetween	X	X	X	X
	LastDayOfMonth	X			X
	LastDayOfWeek	X			X
	Month	X	X	X	X
	MonthNumberOfYear	X	X	X	X
	MonthsBetween	X	X	X	X
	Quarter	X	X	X	X
	RelativeDate	X	X	X	X
	ToDate	X	X	X	X
	Week	X	X	X	X
	Year	X	X	X	X
Logical	Even	X			X
	IsDate	X	X	X	X
	IsError	X	X	X	X
	IsLogical	X			X
	IsNull	X	X	X	X
	IsNumber	X	X	X	X
	IsString	X	X	X	X
	IsTime	X	X	X	X
	Odd	X			X
Document	BlockNumber	X			
	DocumentAuthor	X	X	X	X
	DocumentDate	X	X	X	X
	DocumentName	X	X	X	X
	DocumentPartially Refreshed	X	X	X	X
	DocumentTime	X	X	X	X
	DrillFilters	X	X		X

TABLE 22-1 Comparison of Formula Functions in Various Product Versions *(continued)*

Function Category	Function	BusinessObjects 6.5	Web Intelligence 6.5	Web Intelligence XI Release 1	Web Intelligence XI Release 2
	GlobalFilters	X			
	LastPrintDate	X			X
	PageInSection	X			
	SectionNumber	X			
Data Provider	Connection	X			X
	DataProvider	X	X	X	X
	DataProviderSQL	X			X
	DataProviderType	X			
	LastExecutionDate	X	X	X	X
	LastExecutionTime	X	X	X	X
	NumberOfDataProviders	X			X
	NumberOfRows	X			X
	OlapQueryDescription	X			
	SourceName	X			
	UniverseName	X			X
	UserResponse	X	X	X	X
Miscellaneous	Application Value	X			
	ColumnNumber	X			X
	CurrentUser	X	X		X
	GetContentLocale				X
	GetLocale		X		X
	GetProfileNumber	X			
	GetProfileString	X			
	If		X		X
	LineNumber	X			X
	MultiCube	X			
	NameOf	X	X		X
	NoFilter	X			X
	NumberOfPages	X			X
	Page	X			X
	Previous	X			X
	RowIndex	X			X
	UniqueNameOf		X		

TABLE 22-1   Comparison of Formula Functions in Various Product Versions *(continued)*

Types of Formulas

A formula may contain any combination of universe object variables, user-defined report variables, functions, operators, calculation contexts, and numeric and string constants. Formulas can vary in complexity from basic calculations—formulas containing only universe object variables, basic operators and constants—to very advanced formulas using complex combinations of if-then-else logic, Boolean logic, other user-defined variables, and built-in functions that Web Intelligence provides. Formulas can perform calculations on any type of data, including numeric, string, date, time, and Boolean. Table 22-2 provides some samples of each type of formula.

Syntax Differences Between Web Intelligence and Desktop Intelligence

The samples shown in Table 22-2 and most of this chapter concentrate on creating formulas in Web Intelligence. If you are a long-time BusinessObjects developer or will also author reports in Desktop Intelligence, it is important to note three major syntax differences between the Formula Editors in Desktop Intelligence and Web Intelligence:

- Universe object variables and user-defined variables referenced in a formula are enclosed in square brackets [] in Web Intelligence but are enclosed by <> brackets in Desktop Intelligence. For example, the formula =[Revenue] * 1.10 would be used in Web Intelligence, but it would need to be created as =<Revenue> * 1.10 in Desktop Intelligence.

Type	Formula	Purpose
Numeric	=[Revenue]*1.10	Increases revenue by 10 percent
String	=[City] + ", " + [State]	Concatenates City and State separated by a comma into a single string
String	=Concatenation("Dear "; [Name])	Creates the salutation string that could be used for a form letter
Date	=ToDate("01/01/2005"; "MM/dd/yyyy") + 30	Converts a date string to a date data type and adds 30 days
Time	=LastExecutionTime()	The last time the report data was refreshed
Boolean	=[Revenue] < 100000	Will display true if revenue is less than $100,000 and false if revenue is greater than or equal to $100,000
String	=If([Revenue]<100000; "Low Revenue"; "High Revenue")	Distinguishes between "Low Revenue" sales and "High Revenue" sales

TABLE 22-2   Web Intelligence Allows You to Create Different Types of Formulas

- Function parameter lists are separated by semicolons in Web Intelligence but are separated by commas in Desktop Intelligence. For example the formula `=Concatenation("Dear ";[Name])` would be used in Web Intelligence, but it would need to be created as `=Concatenation("Dear ",[Name])` in Desktop Intelligence.

- When creating if-then-else logic in formulas, Web Intelligence provides the If function but Desktop Intelligence provides the If-Then-Else operators. For example, the formula `=If([Revenue]<100000; "Low Revenue"; "High Revenue")` would be used in Web Intelligence, but it would need to be created as `=If [Revenue]<100000 Then "Low Revenue" else "High Revenue"` in Desktop Intelligence.

Creating a Formula Step-by-Step

There are two ways to create a formula and display it in a block on your report. If you are new to creating formulas, you should start by using the Formula Editor. As you gain experience and get comfortable with Web Intelligence formula syntax, you can enter the formula or drag and drop the formula components directly into the formula toolbar.

Figure 22-1 shows the Formula Editor that is invoked by clicking the Formula Editor button on the formula toolbar in the Web Intelligence Java Report panel. Three tabs contain the components you will use to create your formulas:

- **Data tab**   Contains universe object variables and user-defined variables.
- **Functions tab**   Contains the many functions that can be used in formulas.
- **Operators tab**   Contains the operators used to perform numeric and comparison operations in your formulas.

To create a formula using the Formula Editor in the Java Report panel, do the following:

1. Insert and select a blank cell or table column in a report.

2. Click the Show/Hide Formula Toolbar button from the Web Intelligence report toolbar.

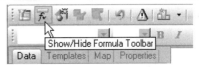

3. Click the Formula Editor button from the formula toolbar. The Formula Editor button will toggle the Formula Editor on and off.

4. In the Formula Editor, drag, double-click, or type the components (universe object variables, user-defined variables, functions, operators) into the Formula Editor as shown in Figure 22-1. From the Data tab drag the *Revenue* object for the formula text box on the right. Note that Web Intelligence automatically inserts the equal (=) sign at the beginning of the formula. Click the Operators tab and double-click the multiplication operator (*) from the list. String and numeric constants are not available in a list and must be typed in directly. To complete the formula, place

your cursor at the end of your formula in the formula text box by clicking after the multiplication operator and type in the numeric constant **1.1**.

5. Click the Validate button in the Formula Editor.

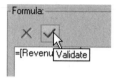

6. Click the Close button to close the Formula Editor and see the table with the new formula.

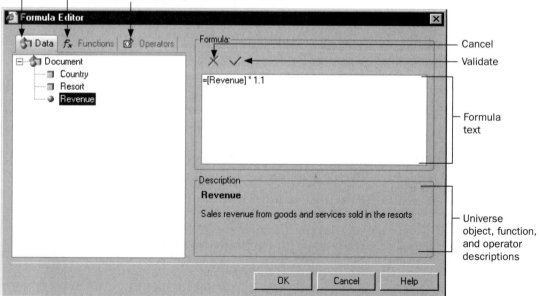

The Data tab displays the universe variables and user-defined variables that can be used in a formula

The Functions tab displays all of the functions that are provided by Web Intelligence

The Operators tab displays the operators used to perform numeric calculations and comparison operations in formulas

FIGURE 22-1 Web Intelligence Java Report panel Formula Editor

---

NOTE *If you open a report in drill mode, you must first turn off drill mode before you can display the Formula Editor.*

To create a formula using the formula toolbar, follow these steps:

1. Insert and select a blank cell or table column in a report.

2. Click the Show/Hide Formula Toolbar button from the Web Intelligence report toolbar.

3. Type the formula into the formula text box on the formula toolbar. Alternatively, you can drag the variables into the formula text box and type the remaining operators, functions, and constants to complete the formula.

Regardless of how you create formulas in the Web Intelligence Java Report panel, either by using the Formula Editor or by typing them directly into the formula toolbar, you must follow these guidelines:

- Always start the formula with an = sign.

- When you reference a base report variable or variable name, it must be enclosed in square brackets ([]). For example, the formula =[Revenue] * 1.10 contains a base report variable, [Revenue].

- Spaces between the components of the formula make the formula easier to read.

- Carriage returns can be added to formulas by using CTRL+ENTER or ALT+ENTER to make the formula easier to read.

- String constants in formulas are always surrounded by double quotation marks like "Year: ". For example, if you want to concatenate a label "Year: " to the year returned by the universe object variable, you would enter ="Year: " + [Year].

- Numeric constants are not surrounded by quotation marks.

- Numeric constants should be entered without any formatting such as dollar signs or thousands separators. For example, if you want to add $500,000.00 to the [Revenue] universe object variable, you enter =[Revenue] + 500000.

The HTML Report Panel Formula Editor

As discussed in Chapter 17, BusinessObjects XI has multiple report panels with slightly different interfaces and capabilities. You set your default panel in your InfoView Preferences. Regardless of your default report panel, the concepts behind creating formulas and using them in your reports remains the same; only the user interface is different. Following is a brief look at the HTML Report panel's Formula Editor. The remainder of this chapter uses the Java Report panel. Figure 22-2 shows the Formula Editor in the HTML Report panel.

To create a formula using the Formula Editor in the HTML Report panel:

1. Insert and select a blank cell or table column in a report.

2. Make sure the formula toolbar is displayed by clicking View | Toolbars | Formula from the report toolbar.

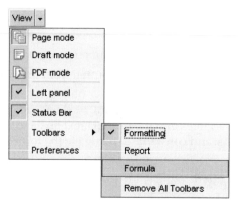

3. Click the Formula Editor button on the formula toolbar.

4. The Formula Editor will display as in Figure 22-2. Double-click the *Revenue* object from the list of Available Objects. Click the multiplication sign (*) from the Available Operators and complete the formula by entering **1.1** as the multiplier.

5. Click the Validate button. If there are no syntax errors, you will get a pop-up dialog box saying "The formula is defined correctly." Click OK.

6. Click OK in the Formula Editor to return to your report.

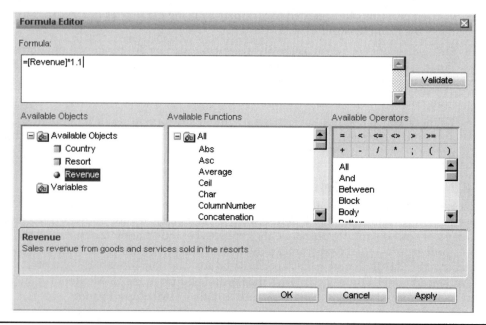

FIGURE 22-2   Web Intelligence HTML Report panel Formula Editor

NOTE *The HTML Report panel has both a Variables list and a Formulas list that allow you to add both Formulas and Variables to your report. The Java Report panel does not display a separate list of formulas; you can only identify them in the cell in which they were created.*

Saving Formulas as Variables

When you want to reuse a formula throughout your document, perhaps on a different report or within another formula, save the formula as a variable. A *variable* is simply a formula with a name and a qualification. Saving the formula as a variable also allows you to give the formula a meaningful name. It will be much easier to remember what the formula =[Revenue]*1.12 represents if it is defined as a variable with the name *Revenue w projected 12% increase*. You can either explicitly create the formula as a variable or convert an existing formula to a variable.

Creating a New Variable

To create a formula and save it as a variable:

1. Select the Show/Hide Variable Editor button from the Web Intelligence toolbar.

2. The Variable Editor will display.

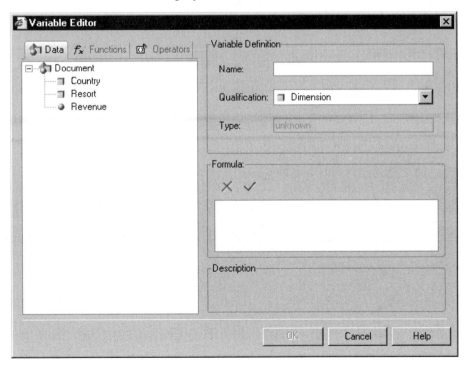

3. In the Name box on the right, specify a meaningful name. The variable name is used as the column headings in your reports and will be displayed in the variables folder on the data tab of your report.

4. Determine and select the qualification for your variable. Select Dimension for Character and Date fields; select Measure for numeric values that you will want to aggregate; select Detail for detailed information such as phone numbers and street addresses that provide descriptive data about other dimensions and that are not useful for drilling.

NOTE *You must select a qualification. Web Intelligence will always set the qualification to Dimension.*

5. Type your formula into the formula definition text box. You can also drag or double-click the components of the formula to enter them into the formula definition text box.

6. Select the Validate button to check if your formula has any syntax errors. If there are syntax errors, you will receive an error message.

7. Click the OK button to save your variable and return to your report.

8. Once a variable has been defined, you will see it listed in the Data tab of your report. You can now reference the user-defined variable in your report by dragging it into a table as a column, referencing the user-defined variable in other user-defined variables, using the user-defined variable to define filters and alerters, etc. This is the power of defining your formulas as variables.

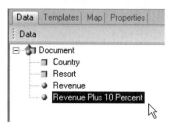

Converting an Existing Formula to a Variable

If your report already contains a formula, you can convert the formula to a user-defined variable.

1. Select the Show/Hide Formula Toolbar button from the Web Intelligence toolbar.

2. Select the cell in your report containing the formula that you wish to convert to a user-defined variable.

3. Click the Create Variable button on the Formula toolbar. The Create Variable dialog will display.

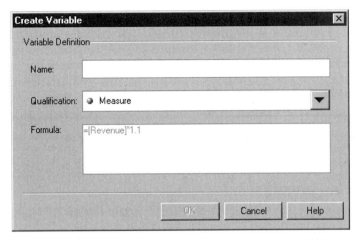

4. Type in a meaningful name, **Revenue Plus 10 Pct**, and select the qualification for your variable. Notice that the formula box is grayed out and cannot be changed here. If you want to change the formula, you can edit the user-defined variable after the variable is created.

5. Click OK to close the Create Variable dialog and return to the report. The results of the calculation in the report will not have changed; however, the cell formula has changed to =[Revenue Plus 10 Pct].

Editing a Variable

To make changes to an existing user-defined variable, within the left panel, right-click the variable on the Data tab and select Edit Variable from the pop-up menu.

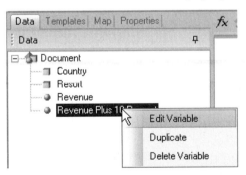

NOTE *When viewing objects in the Java Report panel, you cannot readily see which objects are report variables and which are universe object variables. The pop-up menu allowing you to edit, duplicate, and delete a variable will appear only when the variable is a user-defined variable, not when it is a universe object variable.*

Duplicating a Variable

Sometimes you need to create another user-defined variable that is only slightly different from an existing user-defined variable. An existing user-defined variable can be easily duplicated by right-clicking the variable and selecting Duplicate from the pop-up menu. Once the duplicate variable is created, you can edit the name and formula for the new user-defined variable.

Deleting a Variable

To delete a variable from your Web Intelligence document, right-click the user-defined variable on the Data tab and select Delete Variable.

Using Operators in Formulas

BusinessObjects XI provides many operators for you to use in your formulas. An operator allows you to perform mathematical operations, test for conditions such as whether one value is less than another, and link multiple conditional clauses together using logical operators such as AND and OR.

Mathematical

Mathematical operators allow you to perform the following basic mathematical calculations:

Operator	Description	Sample
+	Addition operator	=[Number of guests] + [Future guests]
–	Subtraction operator	=[Revenue] – 10
*	Multiplication operator	=[Revenue] * .06
/	Division operator	=[Revenue] / [Number of guests]

Conditional

Conditional operators allow you to perform comparisons between two components of a formula, returning a true or false value. Conditional operators are most commonly used in if-then-else logic; for example, = If([Revenue]>50000; "Good Revenue"; "Low Revenue").

Operator	Description	Sample
=	Equal to	= [Revenue] = 20000
>	Greater than	= [Revenue] > 50000
<	Less than	= [Revenue] < 15000
>=	Greater than or equal to	= [Revenue] >= 50000
<=	Less than or equal to	= [Revenue] <= 15000
!=	Not equal to	= [Revenue] != 20000

Logical

Logical operators allow you to connect multiple conditional clauses in your formulas, returning a single Boolean (true/false) value, or 1 for true and 0 for false. For example, = [Revenue] < 50000 AND [Year] = "FY1998" may return true or 1 for [Revenue] < 50000 and false or 0 for [Year] = "FY1998" if you were looking at revenues from a year other than 1998. The result for the formula = [Revenue] < 50000 AND [Year] = "FY1998" would then be evaluated as =true (for the revenue condition) AND false (for the year portion), which returns false.

Operator	Description	Sample
AND	True AND True returns True True AND False returns False False AND False returns False False AND True returns False	= [Revenue] < 50000 AND [Year] = "FY1998"
OR	True OR True returns True True OR False returns True False OR False returns False False OR True returns True	= [Year] = "FY1998" OR [Year] = "FY1999"
NOT	NOT True returns False NOT False returns True	= NOT(IsNull([Year]))

Where

The Where operator allows you to specify limiting criteria on data in a formula. The Where operator is used in a formula with the following syntax:

= [report object] Where (Boolean expression)

Examples include the following:

- The Where operator could be used to return the revenue if the invoice date is in the current year using the following formula: = [Revenue] Where (Year([Invoice Date]) = Year(CurrentDate())).
- The Where operator could be used to return the revenue if the country = "US" using the following formula: = [Revenue] Where ([Country]="US").
- The Boolean expression in a formula containing a Where operator can contain other operators including AND, NOT, and OR as in the following example: = [Revenue] Where ([Country] = "US" AND [Service Line] ="Recreation").

Context

Context operators are used with calculation contexts and extended syntax. See the section "Using Context Operators in Input Contexts" later in this chapter for a more thorough discussion of context operators.

Function Specific

Some functions can take specific operators as arguments. These operators are function specific and can be found in the next section.

Using Functions in Formulas

BusinessObjects XI provides many functions for you to use in your formulas. A function is an operation that takes zero or more input parameter values and generates a single output value. For example, `=Round(273.75;0)` returns 274. In this example, the Round function takes two input parameters, the number to be rounded (273.75) and the number of decimal places to round the number to (0) and returns the output value (274). Input parameters can be base report variables, numeric constants, or text literals.

Functions can be added to formulas by typing them directly into the Formula Editor or by selecting them from the list of available functions on the Functions tab when using the Formula Editor (see Figure 22-3). Until you are familiar with the function syntax, select the functions from the list of available functions in the Formula Editor. The Formula Editor provides you with a description of the function, the syntax for the function, the data types required as input parameters, and the data type returned as the output value. You can get a more detailed description of the function including examples if you click the link "More on this function."

As you build your formula, pay attention to the data types required as input parameters and the data type that will be returned as the output value. Providing incorrect data types as input parameters to a function will return an error when validating or saving the formula. For example, entering the formula `=Round("273.75",0)` will return an error because the first input parameter is expected as a number, not as a string. The quotes around 273.75 tell Web Intelligence to treat it as a string.

The available functions are organized into categories to help you find the appropriate function easily. The following illustration shows the categories collapsed. To see the contents of any one category, click + next to the category name.

All Functions

All functions allow you to find any of the functions found in Web Intelligence sorted in alphabetical order. The other categories that follow separate the functions by the type of data the function is intended to act on.

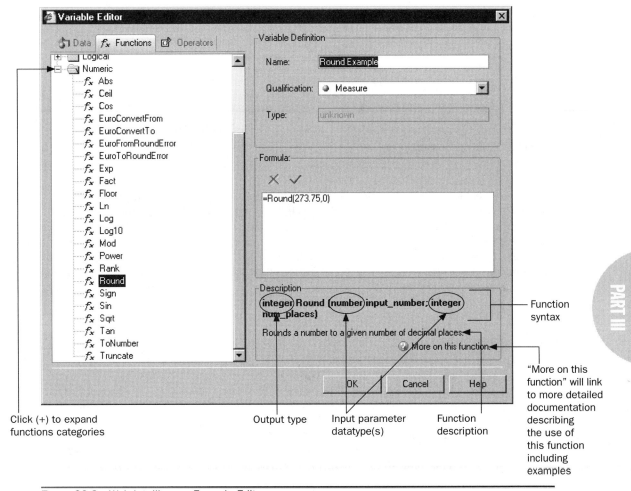

Click (+) to expand
functions categories

Output type   Input parameter
                   datatype(s)

Function
description

Function
syntax

"More on this
function" will link
to more detailed
documentation
describing
the use of
this function
including
examples

FIGURE 22-3   Web Intelligence Formula Editor

Aggregate Functions

Aggregate functions allow you to perform calculations over a collective grouping of data.
Subtotals and grand totals are examples of aggregate calculations. The aggregate functions
available in the Formula Editor are the same functions used when inserting standard
calculations on a report as discussed in Chapter 19.

All of the functions in the aggregate function category depend on the location or context
in which they are placed to determine their values. For example, the aggregate function Sum
placed in a break footer of a table will only sum values over that break or grouping of data,
representing a subtotal. If the aggregate function Sum were moved to the footer of the table,

all values in the table would be summed giving a grand total. For a more detailed discussion of contexts, see the section titled "Calculation Contexts and Extended Syntax."

Average

The Average function will return the average value over the numeric *report_variable* provided. The *report_variable* can be either a universe object variable or a user-defined variable.

```
number Average (number [report_variable]; [INCLUDEEMPTY])
```

`[INCLUDEEMPTY]` is an optional input parameter. By default, the Average function ignores nulls when calculating the average. If the `[INCLUDEEMPTY]` parameter is provided, the Average function will take nulls into consideration.

Examples:

`Average([Revenue])` will return 44,666.67 when the `[Revenue]` measure contains the values (45000; 37000; 52000; <Null>). By default, the Average function ignores nulls when calculating the average, so the calculation based on the preceding value is (45,000 + 37,000 + 52,000/3.

`Average([Revenue];IncludeEmpty)` will return 33,500 when the `[Revenue]` measure contains the values (45000; 37000; 52000; <Null>). When the optional IncludeEmpty parameter is provided, the average calculation becomes (45,000 + 37,000 + 52,000 + 0)/4.

Count

The Count function will return the count of items in a *report_variable* provided. The *report_variable* can be either a universe object variable or a user-defined variable.

```
integer Count(any_datatype [report_variable]; [INCLUDEEMPTY]; [DISTINCT/ALL])
```

`[INCLUDEEMPTY]` is an optional input parameter. By default, the Count function ignores nulls when counting the items in the *report_variable*. If the `[INCLUDEEMPTY]` parameter is provided, the Count function will take nulls into consideration.

`[DISTINCT/ALL]` is an optional input parameter. By default, the Count function only counts distinct items in the *report_variable*. If the `[ALL]` parameter is provided, the Count function will count all items in the *report_variable* whether they are distinct or not.

Examples:

Given the following sample report:

Country	Resort	Service Line	Revenue
France	French Riviera	Accommodation	563,250
France	French Riviera	Food & Drinks	107,400
France	French Riviera	Recreation	164,770
US	Bahamas Beach	Accommodation	673,664
US	Bahamas Beach	Food & Drinks	169,680
US	Bahamas Beach	Recreation	128,100
US	Hawaiian Club	Accommodation	981,210
US	Hawaiian Club	Food & Drinks	277,750
US	Hawaiian Club	Recreation	220,700
Count: 2			
Count All: 9			

`Count([Country])` returns 2. By default, the Count function will only count distinct items in [Country].
`Count([Country],All)` returns 9. The optional parameter of All instructs the Count function to count all items in [Country] whether they are distinct or not.
`Count([Country],IncludeEmpty)` would return 3 if the `[Country]` *report_variable* contained the values (France, US, <Null>).

Max
The Max function will return the highest value found in a *report_variable* provided. The *report_variable* can be either a universe object variable or a user-defined variable.

`any_datatype Max(any_datatype [report_variable])`

Examples:
`Max([Revenue])` will return 981,210 when the `[Revenue]` *report_variable* contains the values (128100; 981210; 277750).
`Max([Country])` will return "US" when the `[Country]` *report_variable* contains the values ("US", "France").

Median
The Median function will return the median value found in a numeric *report_variable* provided. The *report_variable* can be either a universe object variable or a user-defined variable.

`number Median(number [report_variable])`

Example:
`Median([Revenue])` will return 552,622 when `[Revenue]` contains the values (503356; 552622; 570630).

Min
The Min function will return the lowest value found in a *report_variable* provided. The *report_variable* can be either a universe object variable or a user-defined variable.

`any_datatype Min(any_datatype [report_variable])`

Examples:
`Min([Revenue])` will return 128,100 when the `[Revenue]` *report_variable* contains the values (128100; 981210; 277750).
`Min([Country])` will return "France" when the `[Country]` *report_variable* contains the values ("US", "France").

Percentage
The Percentage function returns the ratio of the numeric *report_variable* provided to the total sum of the *report_variable* in the current calculation context.

`number Percentage(number [report_variable];[BREAK];[ROW/COL])`

[BREAK] is an optional input parameter and seemingly irrelevant, as in multiple tests, the aggregate will use the break level regardless of whether or not this parameter is provided. According to the vendor's online help, the Percentage function uses the total for the *report_variable* over the entire table. If the [BREAK] parameter is provided, the total for the *report_variable* will be calculated over the break value in the table. [ROW/COL] is an optional input parameter. The Percentage function can be applied across either rows or columns.

Percentile
The Percentile function returns the percentile based on a numeric *input_parameter*, entered as a decimal, over a set of numbers in the *report_variable*.

```
number Percentile(number [report_variable];number input_parameter)
```

RunningAverage
The RunningAverage function will return the running average for the numeric *report_variable* provided.

```
number RunningAverage(number [report_variable];[ROW/COL];[INCLUDEEMPTY];
[(reset_dimension_variables)])
```

[ROW/COL] is an optional input parameter. The RunningAverage function can be applied across either rows or columns.
[INCLUDEEMPTY] is an optional parameter. The IncludeEmpty parameter tells the RunningAverage function to include null [*report_variable*] values as zeros.
The [*reset_dimension_variables*] are optional input parameters. Providing a *dimension_variable* or a list of *dimension_variables* tells the RunningAverage function to reset the average back to 0 whenever the *dimension_variable(s)* change values.

Examples:

```
RunningAverage([Revenue])
```

```
RunningAverage([Revenue];([Year]))
```

RunningCount
The RunningCount function will return the running count for the *report_variable* provided.

```
number RunningCount(any_datatype [report_variable];[ROW/COL];  [INCLUDEEMPTY];
[(reset_dimension_variables)])
```

[ROW/COL] is an optional input parameter. The RunningCount function can be applied across either rows or columns.
[INCLUDEEMPTY] is an optional parameter. The IncludeEmpty parameter tells the RunningCount function to include null [*report_variable*] values in the count.
The [*reset_dimension_variables*] are optional input parameters. Providing a *dimension_variable* or a list of *dimension_variables* tells the RunningCount function to reset the count back to 0 whenever the *dimension_variable(s)* change values.

Examples:

```
RunningCount([Country])
```

```
RunningCount([Country];([Year]))
```

RunningMax

The RunningMax function will return the running max value for the *report_variable* provided.

```
any_datatype RunningMax(any_datatype [report_variable];[ROW/COL]; [(reset_
dimension_variables)])
```

[ROW/COL] is an optional input parameter. The RunningMax function can be applied across either rows or columns.

The [*reset_dimension_variables*] are optional input parameters. Providing a *dimension_variable* or a list of *dimension_variables* tells the RunningMax function to reset the max value back to <Null> whenever the *dimension_variable(s)* change values.

Examples:

```
RunningMax([Country])
```

```
RunningMax([Revenue];([Year]))
```

RunningMin

The RunningMin function will return the running min value for the *report_variable* provided.

```
any_datatype RunningMin(any_datatype [report_variable];[ROW/COL];
[(reset_dimension_variables)])
```

[ROW/COL] is an optional input parameter. The RunningMin function can be applied across either rows or columns.

The [*reset_dimension_variables*] are optional input parameters. Providing a *dimension_variable* or a list of *dimension_variables* tells the RunningMin function to reset the min value back to <Null> whenever the *dimension_variable*(s) change values.

Examples:

```
RunningMin([Country])
```

```
RunningMin([Revenue];([Year]))
```

RunningProduct

The RunningProduct function will return the running product for the numeric *report_variable* provided.

```
number RunningProduct(number [report_variable]; [ROW/COL]; [(reset_dimension_
variables)])
```

[ROW/COL] is an optional input parameter. The RunningProduct function can be applied across either rows or columns.

The [*reset_dimension_variables*] are optional input parameters. Providing a *dimension_variable* or a list of *dimension_variables* tells the RunningProduct function to reset the product back to 0 whenever the *dimension_variable*(s) change values.

Examples:

```
RunningProduct([Revenue])
```

```
RunningProduct([Revenue];([Country]))
```

RunningSum

The RunningSum function will return the running sum for the numeric *report_variable* provided.

```
number RunningSum(number[report_variable]; [ROW/COL]; [(reset_dimension_variables)])
```

[ROW/COL] is an optional input parameter. The RunningSum function can be applied across either rows or columns.

The [*reset_dimension_variables*] are optional input parameters. Providing a *dimension_variable* or a list of *dimension_variables* tells the RunningSum function to reset the sum back to 0 whenever the *dimension_variable(s)* change values.

Examples:

```
RunningSum([Revenue])
```

```
RunningSum([Revenue];([Country]))
```

Country	Year	Revenue	Running Sum	Running Sum with Break
France	FY2000	259,170	259,170	259,170
	FY1999	280,310	539,480	539,480
	FY1998	295,940	835,420	835,420
France	**Sum:**	**835,420**		

=RunningSum([Revenue]) is not reset over a break

=RunningSum([Revenue]; [Country]) is reset over the [Country] break

Country	Year	Revenue	Running Sum	Running Sum with Break
US	FY1998	767,614	1,603,034	767,614
	FY1999	826,930	2,429,964	1,594,544
	FY2000	856,560	3,286,524	2,451,104
US	**Sum:**	**2,451,104**		

StdDev

The StdDev function will return the standard deviation for a set of numbers in the numeric *report_variable* provided.

```
number StdDev(number [report_variable])
```

StdDevP

The StdDevP function will return the population standard deviation for a set of numbers in the numeric *report_variable* provided.

```
number StdDevP(number [report_variable])
```

Sum

The Sum function returns the sum of the numeric *report_variable* provided.

```
number Sum(number [report_variable])
```

Example:
Sum([Revenue]) will return 835,420 when the [Revenue] *report_variable* contains
(563250; 107400; 164770).

Var
The Var function will return the variance for a set of numbers in the numeric *report_variable*
provided.

```
number Var(number [report_variable])
```

VarP
The VarP function will return the population variance for a set of numbers in the numeric
report_variable provided.

```
number VarP(number [report_variable])
```

Character Functions
The following Character functions allow you to manipulate and format string data.

Asc
The Asc function will return the ASCII value of a character value in the string *input_parameter* provided.

```
integer Asc(string input_parameter)
```

Examples:
Asc("J") returns 74.
Asc("K") returns 75.

Char
The Char function will return the character associated with the ASCII value indicated in
number *input_parameter*.

```
string Char(number input_parameter)
```

Examples:
Char(74) returns J.
Char(75) returns K.
Char(10) returns a carriage return.

TIP *This function comes in handy when you need to embed nonprintable characters in a character
string, most commonly a carriage return. For example, if you wanted to create a report header
cell with your report title followed by a carriage return and the date the report was executed, the
following formula would accomplish this:*

```
="Sales Revenue Report " + Char(10) + FormatDate(LastExecutionDate; "MM/dd/yyyy")
```

Concatenation

The Concatenation function will concatenate string *input_parameter1* with string *input_parameter2*.

```
string Concatenation(string input_parameter1; string input_parameter2)
```

Examples:

Concatenation([First Name]; [Last Name]) returns "JoeSmith" where [First Name]= "Joe" and [Last Name]= "Smith".

TIP *In many cases you will want to include a space (" ") between two strings when concatenating.*

Concatenation([First Name]; Concatenation(""; [Last Name])) returns "Joe Smith" where [First Name]= "Joe" and [Last Name]= "Smith".

Fill

The Fill function will return a string containing the string *input_parameter* repeated as often as specified by the *input_parameter*.

```
string Fill(string input_parameter; number input_parameter)
```

Example:

Fill(".";50) returns "..." This formula could then be used to create a table of contents, for example =Left([Section Title] + Fill(".";50), 50).

FormatDate

The FormatDate function takes a date *input_parameter* value and returns a string in the format specified by the string *date_format*.

```
string FormatDate(date input_parameter; string date_format)
```

Date Format	Description	Sample
D	The day number in the month with no leading zeros.	1; 9; 25
Dd	The day number in the month with leading zeros.	01; 09; 25
Ddd	The abbreviated three-character day name in proper case.	Mon; Tue; Wed
DDD	The abbreviated three-character day name in all uppercase.	MON; TUE; WED
Dddd	The full day name in proper case.	Monday; Tuesday; Wednesday
DDDD	The full day name in uppercase.	MONDAY; TUESDAY; WEDNESDAY

Date Format	Description	Sample
M	The month number in the year with no leading zeros.	1; 6; 12
MM	The month number in the year with leading zeros.	01; 06; 12
Mmm	The three-character abbreviated month name in proper case.	Jan; Jun; Dec
MMM	The three-character abbreviated month name in uppercase.	JAN; JUN; DEC
Mmmm	The full month name in proper case.	January; June; December
YY	The two-digit year.	87; 99; 05
YYYY	The four-digit year.	1987; 1999; 2005
hh:mm	The hour and minutes with leading zeros.	08:30; 09:21; 12:30
hh:mm:ss	The hour, minutes, and seconds with leading zeros.	08:30:27; 09:21:59; 12:30:00
hh:mm a	The hour and minutes with leading zeros and AM or PM after the time.	08:30 AM; 09:21 PM; 12:30 AM

NOTE *The values provided in the date value string are case sensitive. The string "mm" represents minutes, while the string "MM" represents month.*

Examples:
The FormatDate function is used to change the data type of a date variable to a string. This is used to

1. Use date variables in functions that require string variables:

   -Length(FormatDate([Invoice Date]; "M/d/YYYY")) returns 8 (the length of the string value returned) when [Invoice Date]= "1/1/1998" and returns 9 when [Invoice Date]= "12/1/1998".

2. Use date variables concatenated with other string data:

   ="Invoice Date: " + FormatDate([Invoice Date]; "Mmm dd, YYYY") returns "Invoice Date: Jan 01, 1998".

FormatNumber
The FormatNumber function takes a number *input_parameter* value and returns a string in the format specified by the *number_format* string.

```
string FormatNumber(number input_parameter; string number_format)
```

Number Format	Description	Sample
#	Displays a corresponding integer.	9999; <Null>; 1
0	Displays a corresponding integer unless there are no digits to display, in which case a 0 is displayed.	9999; 0; 1
#####	Displays a corresponding integer with no leading zeros.	9999; <Null>; 1
00000	Displays a corresponding integer unless there are fewer digits to display than indicated in the *number_ format* string, in which case leading zeros will display.	09999; 00000; 00001
#,###	Displays an integer with a thousands separator.	9,999; <Null>; 1
#,##0.00	Displays a number with a thousands separator and two decimal places.	9,999.00; 0.00; 1.00
+#	Displays an integer with a plus sign.	+9999; <Null>; +1
-#	Displays an integer with a minus sign.	–9999; <Null>; –1
#.0%	Displays a number with a percentage sign.	9999.0%; .0%; 1.0%
<space> 0.0 %	A space used anywhere within the *number_format* string will display in the number.	9999.0 %; 0.0 %; 1.0 %
<any alphanumeric character> $#,##0.00	Any alphanumeric character can be used in a *number_format* string.	$9,999.00; $0.00; $1.00
#,###[Red]	Indicating a color will display the value in the specified color. The valid colors are: [Red], [Blue], [Green], [Yellow], [White], [Dark Red], [Dark Blue], [Dark Green]	9,999; <Null>; 1

Examples:
The FormatNumber function is used to change the data type of a number variable to a string. This is used to

1. Use number variables in functions that are expecting string variables:

   =Length(FormatNumber([Revenue];"$#,##0.00") returns 11 when [Revenue]= 563250.

2. Use number variables concatenated with other string data:

   ="Your Region has revenue totaling: " + FormatNumber([Revenue]; "$#,##0") returns "Your Region has revenue totaling: $563,250" when [Revenue]=563250.

HTMLEncode
The HTMLEncode function takes a string *input_parameter* and returns the HTML encoded value.

```
string HTMLEncode(string input_parameter)
```

InitCap
The InitCap function takes a string *input_parameter* and returns a character string with the first letter of the string capitalized. It capitalizes only the first letter of the first word; it does not capitalize subsequent words in the same field. Use WordCap when you want each word capitalized.

```
string InitCap(string input_parameter)
```

Example:
`Initcap("jane doe")` returns "Jane doe".

Left
The Left function takes a string *input_parameter* and returns the leftmost *input_num_chars*.

```
string Left(string input_parameter; number input_num_chars)
```

Example:
`Left([First Name]; 1) + ". " + [Last Name]` returns "J. Doe".

LeftPad
The LeftPad function takes a string *pad_input_parameter,* an *output_length,* and a string *orig_input_parameter* and returns the *pad_input_parameter* padded on the left with the *orig_input_parameter*.

```
string LeftPad(string pad_input_parameter; number output_length; string
orig_input_parameter)
```

Examples:
`LeftPad("Character Functions"; 24; ".")` returns ".....Character Functions".
`LeftPad("Numeric Functions"; 24; ".")` returns ".......Numeric Functions".

LeftTrim
The LeftTrim function takes a string *input_parameter* and returns a string with all leading spaces removed.

```
string LeftTrim(string input_parameter)
```

Example:
`LeftTrim("  Jane Doe   ")` returns "Jane Doe   ".

Length
The Length function takes a string *input_parameter* and returns an integer representing the length of the character string.

```
integer Length(string input_parameter)
```

Examples:
Length("Hawaiian Club") returns 13.
Length([Country]) returns 2 when [Country]= "US".

Lower

The Lower function takes a string *input_parameter* and returns a character string converted to all lowercase.

```
string Lower(string input_parameter)
```

Examples:
Lower("Hawaiian Club") returns "hawaiian club".
Lower([Country]) returns "us" when [Country]= "US".

Match

The Match function takes a string *input_parameter* and compares it to a string *pattern.* If they match, the function returns a value of true; otherwise, false is returned.

```
boolean Match(string input_parameter; string pattern)
```

The string pattern can contain wildcard characters "*" to replace multiple characters and "?" to replace a single character.

Examples:
Match("Hello"; "He*") returns true (1).
Match("Hello"; "H????") returns true (1).
Match("Hello"; "H? ") returns false (0).
Match([Master Product Number]; [Supplier Product Number]) would compare two variables to see if the product numbers were the same.

Pos

The Pos function returns an integer representing the position in string *input_parameter* where string *pattern_input_parameter* is located.

```
integer Pos(string input_parameter; string pattern_input_parameter)
```

Example:
Pos("http://www.businessobjects.com";"/") returns 6.

Replace

The Replace function takes a string *input_parameter* and replaces all occurrences of string *input_replace* with string *input_replace_with.*

```
string Replace(string input_parameter; string input_replace; string input_
replace_with)
```

Example:
Replace("http://www.businessobjects.com"; "http:"; "https:") returns "https://www.businessobjects.com".

Right
The Right function takes a string *input_parameter* and returns the rightmost *input_num_chars*.

```
string Right(string input_parameter; number input_num_chars)
```

Examples:
Right([Social Security Number]; 4) returns "5555" when [Social Security Number]= "222-74-5555".
Right([Part Number]; 4) returns "7A56" when [Part Number]= "Controller Arm: 7A56".
Right("This String",4) returns "ring".

RightPad
The RightPad function takes a string *pad _input_parameter,* an *output_length,* and a string *orig _input_parameter* and returns the *pad_input_parameter* padded on the right with the *orig_input_parameter.*

```
string RightPad(string pad_input_parameter; number output_length; string orig_input_parameter)
```

Examples:
RightPad("Character Functions"; 24; ".") returns "Character Functions.....".
RightPad("Numeric Functions"; 24; ".") returns "Numeric Functions.......".

RightTrim
The RightTrim function takes a string *input_parameter* and returns a string with all trailing spaces removed.

```
string RightTrim(string input_parameter)
```

Example:
RightTrim(" Jane Doe   ") returns " Jane Doe".

SubStr
The SubStr function takes a string *input_parameter* and returns a substring starting at the position indicated by integer *start* for integer *length* number of characters.

```
string SubStr(string input_parameter; integer start; integer length)
```

Example:
SubStr("Part#7A59 Controller Arm"; 6; 4) returns "7A59".

Trim
The Trim function takes a string *input_parameter* and returns a string with both the leading and trailing spaces removed.

```
string Trim(string input_parameter)
```

Example:
Trim(" Jane Doe   ") returns "Jane Doe".

Upper

The Upper function takes a string *input_parameter* and returns a character string converted to all uppercase.

```
string Upper(string input_parameter)
```

Examples:
Upper("Jane Doe") returns "JANE DOE".
Upper([Country]) returns "UNITED STATES" when [Country]= "United States".

URLEncode

The URLEncode function takes a string *input_parameter* and returns the URL-encoded value.

```
string URLEncode(string input_parameter)
```

WordCap

The WordCap function takes a string *input_parameter* and returns a character string with the first letter of every word capitalized.

```
string WordCap(string input_parameter)
```

Example:
Wordcap([Customer Name]) returns "John Smith" when [Customer Name]="JOHN SMITH".

Date and Time Functions

The following Date and Time functions allow you to manipulate and format date and time data.

CurrentDate

The CurrentDate() function returns the current system date.

```
date CurrentDate()
```

Example:
CurrentDate() returns 02/01/2006.

NOTE *The CurrentDate() function will return the system date on the server adjusted to the InfoView user's time zone as specified in InfoView preferences.*

CurrentTime

The CurrentTime() function returns the current system time.

```
time CurrentTime()
```

Example:
CurrentTime() returns 1:44:19 PM.

NOTE *The CurrentTime() function will return the system time on the server adjusted to the InfoView user's time zone.*

DayName
The DayName function takes a date *input_parameter* and returns the name of the day of the week for that date.

```
string DayName(date input_parameter)
```

Examples:
DayName(CurrentDate()) returns "Wednesday" when CurrentDate()=02/01/2006.
DayName(ToDate("01/01/2006";"MM/dd/yyyy")) returns "Sunday".

DayNumberOfMonth
The DayNumberOfMonth function takes a date *input_parameter* and returns the number of the day in the month (1–31) of a date.

```
integer DayNumberOfMonth(date input_parameter)
```

Examples:
DayNumberOfMonth(CurrentDate()) returns 1 when CurrentDate()=02/01/2006.
DayNumberOfMonth(ToDate("01/28/2006";"MM/dd/yyyy")) returns 28.
DayNumberOfMonth(ToDate("02/30/2006";"MM/dd/yyyy")) returns #ERROR because 2/30/2006 is not a valid date.

DayNumberOfWeek
The DayNumberOfWeek function takes a date *input_parameter* and returns the number of the day in the week (1–7) of a date. Monday=1, Tuesday=2, Wednesday=3, Thursday=4, Friday=5, Saturday=6, Sunday=7

```
integer DayNumberOfWeek(date input_parameter)
```

Examples:
DayNumberOfWeek([Invoice Date]) returns 4 [Invoice Date]=01/01/1998.
DayNumberOfWeek(ToDate("01/01/2006";"MM/dd/yyyy")) returns 7.

DayNumberOfYear
The DayNumberOfYear function takes a date *input_parameter* and returns the number of the day in the year (1–365) of a date.

```
integer DayNumberOfYear(date input_parameter)
```

Examples:
DayNumberOfYear(ToDate("01/01/2006";"MM/dd/yyyy")) returns 1.
DayNumberOfYear(ToDate("12/31/2006";"MM/dd/yyyy")) returns 365.

DaysBetween
The DaysBetween function returns an integer representing the number of days between two dates: date *first_input_parameter* and date *last_input_parameter.*

```
integer DaysBetween(date first_input_parameter; date last_input_parameter)
```

Example:
DaysBetween([Invoice Date]; CurrentDate()) returns 5 when
[Invoice Date]=1/2/2006 and CurrentDate()=1/7/2006.

LastDayofMonth
The LastDayofMonth function takes a date *input_parameter* and returns the last day in the month for that date.

date LastDayofMonth(date *input_parameter*)

Examples:
LastDayOfMonth(CurrentDate()) returns 1/31/2006 when
CurrentDate()=1/16/2006.
LastDayOfMonth([Invoice Date]) returns 4/30/2006 when
[Invoice Date]=4/1/2006.

LastDayofWeek
The LastDayofWeek function takes a date *input_parameter* and returns the last day in the week (Saturday) for that date.

date LastDayofWeek(date *input_parameter*)

Examples:
LastDayOfWeek(CurrentDate()) returns 1/21/2006 when
CurrentDate()=1/16/2006.
LastDayOfWeek([Invoice Date]) returns 4/1/2006 when
[Invoice Date]=4/1/2006.

Month
The Month function takes a date *input_parameter* and returns the name of the month for that date.

string Month(date *input_parameter*)

Examples:
Month(CurrentDate()) returns "February" when CurrentDate()=2/1/2006.
Month([Invoice Date]) returns "June" when [Invoice Date]=6/15/2005.

MonthNumberOfYear
The MonthNumberOfYear function takes a date *input_parameter* and returns the number of the month (1–12) for that date.

integer MonthNumberOfYear(date *input_parameter*)

Examples:
MonthNumberOfYear(CurrentDate()) returns 2 when CurrentDate()=2/1/2006.
MonthNumberOfYear([Invoice Date]) returns 6 when [Invoice Date]=6/15/2005.

MonthsBetween

The MonthsBetween function returns an integer representing the number of months between two dates: date *first_input_parameter* and date *last_input_parameter.*

```
integer MonthsBetween(date first_input_parameter; date last_input_parameter)
```

Examples:
```
MonthsBetween(ToDate("01/01/2006"; "MM/dd/yyyy");
ToDate("02/22/2006"; "MM/dd/yyyy")) returns 1.
MonthsBetween(ToDate("01/01/2006"; "MM/dd/yyyy");
ToDate("04/10/2006"; "MM/dd/yyyy")) returns 3.
MonthsBetween([Invoice Date]; CurrentDate()) returns 17 when
[Invoice Date]=1/2/2005 and CurrentDate()=6/7/2006.
```

Quarter

The Quarter function takes a date *input_parameter* and returns the number of the quarter (1–4) for that date.

```
integer Quarter(date input_parameter)
```

Examples:
```
Quarter([Invoice Date]) returns 3 when [Invoice Date]=8/2/2005.
Quarter(ToDate("12/1/2006"; "MM/dd/yyyy")) returns 4.
```

RelativeDate

The RelativeDate function takes a date *input_parameter* and returns a date that represents that date plus the *number_of_days* specified.

```
date RelativeDate(date input_parameter; number_of_days)
```

Examples:
```
RelativeDate(CurrentDate(); 30) returns 9/1/2005 when
CurrentDate()=8/2/2005.
RelativeDate([Invoice Date]; 45) returns 7/16/2005 when
[Invoice Date]=6/1/2005.
```

ToDate

The ToDate function takes a string *input_parameter* that represents a date according to the string *date_format* supplied and returns a date.

```
date ToDate(string input_parameter; string date_format)
```

NOTE *If no day is provided in the string* input_parameter, *the default is 1. If no month is provided in the string* input_parameter, *the default is 1. If no year is provided in the string* input_parameter, *the default is 1970.*

Examples:
ToDate ("01/01/2005"; "MM/dd/yyyy") returns 1/1/2005.
ToDate ("Sep 1, 2005"; "Mmm d, yyyy") returns 9/1/2005.
ToDate ("12";"MM") returns 12/1/1970.

Week

The Week function takes a date *input_parameter* and returns the number of the week (1–53) for that date.

```
integer Week(date input_parameter)
```

Examples:
Week (ToDate ("01/03/2005"; "MM/dd/yyyy")) returns 1.
Week (CurrentDate ()) returns 31 when CurrentDate ()=8/2/2005.

Year

The Year function takes a date *input_parameter* and returns the number of the year for that date.

```
integer Year(date input_parameter)
```

Examples:
Year (ToDate ("01/03/2005"; "MM/dd/yyyy")) returns 2005.
Year ([Invoice Date]) returns 1998 when [Invoice Date]=1/1/1998.

Document Functions

Document functions allow you to access and display data related to a Web Intelligence document. Some of these functions are useful to insert in separate cells in a document header or footer as discussed in Chapter 21.

DocumentAuthor

The DocumentAuthor function returns the BusinessObjects Enterprise logon ID for the user who created the Web Intelligence document.

```
string DocumentAuthor()
```

Example:
DocumentAuthor () returns "Elizabeth Newbould".

DocumentDate

The DocumentDate function returns the date the Web Intelligence document was last saved.

```
date DocumentDate()
```

Example:
DocumentDate () returns 2/1/2006.

DocumentName

The DocumentName function returns the name of the Web Intelligence document.

```
string DocumentName()
```

Example:
DocumentName () returns "Resort Sales" if the document is saved with a title of
"Resort Sales".

DocumentPartiallyRefreshed
The DocumentPartiallyRefreshed function returns true if the document is partially refreshed
and false if the document is fully refreshed.

boolean DocumentPartiallyRefreshed()

DocumentTime
The DocumentTime function returns the time the Web Intelligence document was last saved.

time DocumentTime()

Example:
DocumentTime() returns 12:32:00 AM if the user last saved this document at 12:32:00 A.M.

DrillFilters
The DrillFilters function displays drill filters applied to the report and will only work when
your report is in drill mode. When your report is in structure mode, the cell will appear empty.

string DrillFilters(*any_datatype report_variable*; string *string_separator*)

TIP *Use this when you are printing a report in drill mode so that you can more readily see how the
report has been filtered or which level of drill it is at. Also, because you cannot invoke the Formula
Editor while in drill mode, add this cell by selecting the left panel, and then Templates | Free-
Standing Cells | Formula and Text Cells | Drill Filters.*

LastPrintDate
The LastPrintDate function returns the date a document was last printed. The value will
be empty if the document has never been printed. At the time of this writing, this function
returned no value even when documents were printed.

Date LastPrintDate()

ReportFilter
The ReportFilter function takes a *report_object* and returns the filter values applied to that object.

string ReportFilter(*any_datatype report_object*)

Example:
ReportFilter([Year]) returns "FY2000" if there is a filter on [Year] restricting values
to "FY2000".

DataProvider Functions

Connection
The Connection function takes a *data_provider_object* and returns the connection information
associated with that data provider.

string Connection(*data_provider_object*)

Example:

```
Connection([Query1])
```

DataProvider
The DataProvider function will return the name of the data provider for the *report_variable* provided.

```
string DataProvider(any_datatype [report_variable])
```

Examples:
DataProvider([Country]) returns "Query 1".
DataProvider([Query 2].[Revenue]) returns "Query 2".

DataProviderSQL
The DataProviderSQL function takes a *data_provider_object* and returns the SQL string associated with that data provider.

```
string DataProviderSQL(data_provider_object)
```

This function can be useful to return the SQL string that is generated by the data provider. This SQL string can be used to troubleshoot issues and perhaps tune a report to run faster.

LastExecutionDate
The LastExecutionDate function will return the last date a string *data_provider_name* was refreshed, or if no string *data_provider_name* is provided, this function will return the last date the query was refreshed.

```
date LastExecutionDate(string data_provider_name (optional))
```

Examples:
LastExecutionDate() returns 2/10/2006 if the user last refreshed this document on 2/10/2006.
LastExecutionDate("Query 1") returns 2/10/2006 if the user last refreshed Query 1 within the document on 2/10/2006.

LastExecutionTime
The LastExecutionTime function will return the last time a string *data_provider_name* was refreshed, or if no string *data_provider_name* is provided, this function will return the last time the query was refreshed.

```
time LastExecutionTime(string data_provider_name (optional))
```

Example:
LastExecutionTime() returns 12:32:00 AM if the user last refreshed this document at 12:32:00 A.M.

NumberofDataProviders
The NumberofDataProviders function returns a count of the data providers in a document.

```
integer NumberofDataProviders()
```

NumberofRows
The NumberofRows function returns the number of rows returned by the *data_provider_object* provided.

```
integer NumberofRows([data_provider_object])
```

UniverseName
The UniverseName function returns the name of the universe on which a *data_provider_object* is based.

```
string UniverseName([data_provider_object])
```

UserResponse
The UserResponse function will return the value entered by a user into the specified string *prompt_name* in the specified string *data_provider_name*.

```
string UserResponse(string data_provider_name (optional); string prompt_name)
```

Example:
UserResponse("Enter Country: ") returns "US" when a user enters "US" into a prompt named "Enter Country: ".

Miscellaneous Functions

ColumnNumber
The ColumnNumber function returns the number of a column in a table starting with 0 as the leftmost column and incrementing to the right.

```
integer ColumnNumber()
```

NOTE *The ColumnNumber function does not work in the first column of a table. The value that is displayed is blank.*

CurrentUser
The CurrentUser function will return the name of the user who is currently logged in to InfoView and working with the Web Intelligence document.

```
string CurrentUser()
```

Example:
CurrentUser() returns "Cindi" when Cindi is logged in to Web Intelligence.

GetContentLocale
The GetContentLocale function will return the locale settings for the current document.

```
string GetContentLocale()
```

Examples:
GetContentLocale() returns "en_US" if the document content is English – US.
GetContentLocale() returns "fr_FR" if the document content is French.

> **NOTE** *There are two locale settings available: the user session locale and the document locale. The locale is important for how dates and currencies are formatted.*

GetLocale
The GetLocale function will return the user session locale settings. This is a system setting in InfoView.

```
string GetLocale()
```

Examples:
GetLocale() returns "en_US" if the locale setting is English – US.
GetLocale() returns "fr_FR" if the locale setting is French.

> **NOTE** *There are two locale settings available: the user session locale and the document locale. The locale is important for how dates and currencies are formatted.*

If
The If function will evaluate a *boolean_expression*; if the *boolean_expression* is true, it will return the *anytype value_if_true*, or if the *boolean_expression* is false, it will return the *anytype value_if_false*.

```
any_datatype If(boolean_expression; anytype value_if_true; anytype value_if_false)
```

Examples:
If([Country]="US"; [Resort]; "") returns the value in [Resort] when
[Country]= "US" and "" when [Country]<> "US".
If([Year]=2006; [Revenue]; 0) returns the value in [Revenue] if the
[Year]=2006.

LineNumber
The LineNumber function returns the number of a row in a table starting with 1 as the header column and incrementing down the table.

```
integer LineNumber()
```

> **NOTE** *The LineNumber function is not working as documented in the online help. The LineNumber function returns the number of the row in a table starting with 2 and incrementing by 2.*

NameOf
The NameOf function returns the display name of the *report_variable* provided.

```
string NameOf(any_datatype [report_variable])
```

Example:
NameOf([Query 1].[Country]) returns "Country". This is the default formula used in all column headings.

NoFilter

The NoFilter function tells Web Intelligence to ignore any filters that have been applied when performing a *calculation*.

any_type NoFilter(*calculation*)

Example:

NoFilter(Sum([Revenue])) returns the sum of all revenues even if there were a filter excluding Austria from the table.

All Sales

Sales Person	Revenue
Fischer	233,886
Galagers	743,139
Ishimoto	644,883
Nagata	4,700
Sum:	1,626,608

Top 2 Sales People

Sales Person	Revenue
Galagers	743,139
Ishimoto	644,883
Sum	1,388,022
Sum with No Filter	1,626,608
Top 2 Pct of Total	85%

NoFilter(Sum([Revenue])) returns the total of all [Revenue] without the 'ranking' filter applied

NumberofPages

The NumberofPages function returns the total number of pages in the current report.

integer NumberofPages()

Example:

NumberofPages() returns 57 if the current report contains 57 pages.

NOTE *This function can be found in Templates | Free-Standing Cells | Page Number Cells and is most commonly used in the header or footer of a report.*

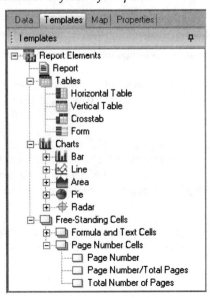

Pages

The Pages function returns the current page number in the report.

```
integer Pages()
```

Example:

`Pages()` returns 3 if the current page is 3 (of 57 pages, for example).

NOTE *This function can be found in Templates | Free-Standing Cells | Page Number Cells and is most commonly used in the header or footer of a report.*

Previous

The Previous function will return the value of the *object* in the previous row of the table.

```
any_type Previous(any_datatype [object];(reset_dimension_variables))
```

The *reset_dimension_variables* is an optional input parameter that allows you to reset the previous function to null.

Example:

```
=Previous([Revenue])
```

NOTE *This function can be used to calculate year-to-year variances in a format different than a crosstab.*

Year	Revenue	Prior Year Revenue	Year over Year Variance
FY1998	1,063,554		
FY1999	1,107,240	1,063,554	43,686
FY2000	1,115,730	1,107,240	8,490

=Previous([Revenue])   =If(Not(IsNull(Previous([Revenue])));[Revenue]-Previous([Revenue]))

RowIndex

The RowIndex function returns the number of a row in a table starting with 0 as the first row and incrementing on each subsequent data row.

```
integer RowIndex()
```

NOTE *The RowIndex function is different than the LineNumber function in that it only counts the rows of data and does not include the headers and footers for the table. You will receive a #MULTIVALUE error if you place this function in a header or footer.*

UniqueNameOf

The UniqueNameOf function returns the display name of the *report_variable* provided. If there are multiple queries on the report containing the same *report_variable*, the UniqueNameOf function will return the display name of the *report_variable* along with the query name that returned the *report_variable*.

```
string UniqueNameOf(any_datatype [report_variable])
```

Examples:
UniqueNameOf([Query 1].[Country]) returns "Country(Query 1)".
UniqueNameOf([Query 2].[Country]) returns "Country(Query 2)".
UniqueNameOf([Revenue]) returns "Revenue".

Logical Functions

Even
The Even function will return a 1 for true if the number *input_parameter* is an even number and 0 for false if the number *input_parameter* is an odd number.

```
boolean Even(number input_parameter)
```

Examples:
Even(2) returns true (1).
Even([License_Number]) returns true (1) when [License_Number] is an even number and false (0) when [License_Number] is an odd number.

IsDate
The IsDate function will return true if the *any_datatype input_parameter* is a date type report variable or constant.

```
boolean IsDate(any_datatype input_parameter)
```

Examples:
IsDate([Country]) returns false (0).
IsDate([Invoice Date]) returns true (1).
IsDate(LastExecutionDate()) returns true (1).
IsDate([Year]) returns false (0) where [Year]="FY1998".

NOTE *The IsDate function is used to determine if the data type of an object is of a date type or not. This is important because many functions require date type objects as inputs. If a string or numeric type is provided to a function expecting a date type object, as in* =FormatDate([Year]; "yyyy")*, you will receive an error as follows:*

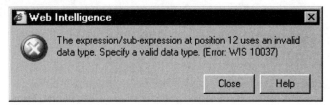

IsError

The IsError function will return true if the *report_variable* provided returns an error and false if the *report_variable* provided does not return an error.

```
boolean IsError(any_datatype [report_variable])
```

Examples:

IsError([Revenue]) returns false.

IsError([Average Revenue]) returns true if the [Average Revenue] variable is trying to divide by 0, causing a #DIV/0 error to be returned.

IsLogical

The IsLogical function will return true if the *any_datatype input_parameter* is a boolean data type.

```
boolean IsLogical(any_datatype input_parameter)
```

Examples:

IsLogical("any") returns false (0).

IsLogical(0) returns true (1).

IsLogical([any Boolean field]) returns true (1).

IsNull

The IsNull function will return true if the *any_datatype input_parameter* is null.

```
boolean IsNull(any_datatype input_parameter)
```

NOTE *The constant string "" is not interpreted as a null.*

Examples:

IsNull([Address 2]) returns true (1) when there is a value populated in [Address 2] and false (0) when there is no value populated in [Address 2].

IsNull("Hello") returns false (0).

IsNumber

The IsNumber function will return true if the *any_datatype input_parameter* is a numeric data type.

```
boolean IsNumber(any_datatype input_parameter)
```

Examples:

IsNumber([Country]) returns false (0).

IsNumber(125) returns true (1).

IsNumber([Revenue]) returns true (1).

IsString

The IsString function will return true if the *any_datatype input_parameter* is a character data type.

```
boolean IsString(any_datatype input_parameter)
```

Examples:
IsString([Country]) returns true (1).
IsString("Hello") returns true (1).
IsString(LastExecutionDate()) returns false (0).

IsTime
The IsTime function will return true if the *any_datatype input_parameter* is a time data type.

boolean IsTime(*any_datatype input_parameter*)

Examples:
IsTime([Country]) returns false (0).
IsTime(LastExecutionTime()) returns true (1).

Odd
The Odd function will return true (1) if the number *input_parameter* is an odd number and false (0) if the number *input_parameter* is an even number.

boolean IsOdd(number *input_parameter*)

Examples:
Odd(2) returns false (0).
Odd([Revenue]) returns true (1) when [Revenue] is an odd number and false (0) when [Revenue] is an even number.

Numeric Functions

Abs
The Abs function will return the absolute value of the number *input_parameter* provided.

number Abs(number *input_parameter*)

Examples:
Abs(-5) returns 5.
Abs(8) returns 8.

Ceil
The Ceil function will return the number *input_parameter* provided rounded up to the next whole number. This is different from the Round function, which will round a number either up or down.

integer Ceil(number *input_parameter*)

Examples:
Ceil(3.999) returns 4.
Ceil(5.1) returns 6.

Cos
The Cos function will return the cosine of the number *input_parameter*.

number Cos(number *input_parameter*)

Example:
Cos(90) returns –.45.

EuroConvertFrom

Although the Euro has been an active trading currency for many years, the European Union fixed the exchange rates for all participating countries January 1, 1999. The Euro coin and notes went into circulation later, on January 1, 2002. Not all members of the European Union agreed to participate in the Euro currency; for example, Greece only began participating in mid-2001, and Great Britain still uses pounds as the official currency. If you are accustomed to seeing measures stated in a local currency, it may not be easy to identify trends or fluctuations when viewing data in the relatively new Euro. Because the exchange rates for Euros are fixed, Web Intelligence can convert data to other currencies using this fixed, internal exchange rate table.

TIP *If you want to view the fixed exchange rates, you can do this via Desktop Intelligence (Data | Euro | Display Conversion Rates); however, a similar capability does not exist in Web Intelligence.*

The EuroConvertFrom function will convert an amount provided in number *euro_amount_input_parameter* to another currency indicated by string *currency_code* rounded to a number *decimal_places*.

```
number EuroConvertFrom(number euro_amount_input_parameter; string currency_code;
number decimal_places)
```

String Currency Code	Description
BEF	Belgian franc
DEM	German mark
GRD	Greek drachma
ESP	Spanish peseta
FRF	French franc
IEP	Irish punt
ITL	Italian lira
LUF	Luxembourg franc
NLG	Dutch guilder
ATS	Austrian schilling
PTS	Portugese escudo
FIM	Finnish mark

Example:
EuroConvertFrom(200;"DEM";2) returns 391.17.

EuroConvertTo

The EuroConvertTo function will convert an amount provided in number *othercurrency_ amount_input_parameter* to euros when the original currency is indicated by string *currency_ code* and the result is rounded to number *decimal_places*.

```
number EuroConvertTo(number othercurrency_amount_input_parameter; string
currency_code; number decimal_places)
```

Example:
`EuroConvertTo(391.17;"DEM";2)` returns 200.00.

EuroFromRoundError

The EuroFromRoundError function will return the amount that is rounded off when converting an amount provided in number *othercurrency_amount_input_parameter* to euros when the original currency is indicated by string *currency_code* and the result is rounded to number *decimal_places*.

```
number EuroFromRoundError(number euro_amount_input_parameter; string
currency_code; number decimal_places)
```

Examples:
`EuroFromRoundError(200;"DEM";1)` returns .03 because 391.17 will be rounded to one decimal place, making it 391.2 with a rounding error of .03.
`EuroFromRoundError(201;"DEM";0)` returns –.12 because 393.12 will be rounded to 393 with a rounding error of –.12.

EuroToRoundError

The EuroToRoundError function will return the amount that is rounded off when converting number *euro_amount_input_parameter* to another currency indicated by string *currency_code* rounded to a number *decimal_places*.

```
number EuroToRoundError(number othercurrency_amount_input_parameter; string
currency_code; number decimal_places)
```

Examples:
`EuroToRoundError(393.12;"DEM";2)` returns 0 because 201.00 will be rounded to two places with a rounding error of 0.
`EuroToRoundError(500;"DEM";1)` returns –.05 because 255.65 is rounded to 255.6 with a rounding error of –.05.

Exp

The Exp function will return a number raised to a power.
`number Exp(number.power)`

Example:
`Exp(3.7)` returns 40.45.

Fact

The Fact function will return the factorial of the number *input_parameter* provided.

```
integer Fact(number input_parameter)
```

Example:
Fact(6) returns 720.

Floor

The Floor function will return the number *input_parameter* provided rounded down to the nearest whole number.

```
integer Floor(number input_parameter)
```

Examples:
Floor(3.999) returns 3.
Floor(5.1) returns 5.

Ln

The Ln function will return the natural logarithm for the number *input_parameter* provided.

```
number Ln(number input_parameter)
```

Log

The Log function will return the logarithm for the number *input_parameter* provided for the number *log_base* provided.

```
number Log(number input_parameter; number log_base)
```

Examples:
Log(10;2) returns 3.32.
Log(16;2) returns 4.

Mod

The Mod function will return the remainder resulting from number *input_dividend* divided by the number *input_divisor.*

```
number Mod(number input_dividend; number input_divisor)
```

Examples:
Mod(10;3) returns 1 because 10/3 = 3 with 1 remaining.
Mod(5;3) returns 2 because 5/3 = 1 with 2 remaining.
Mod(10;2) returns 0 because 10/2 = 5 with 0 remaining.

Power

The Power function will return a number *input_parameter* raised to a power provided in number *power.*

```
number Power(number input_parameter; number power)
```

Examples:
Power(4;2) returns 16.
Power(2;5) returns 32.
Power(2;6) returns 64.

Rank

The Rank function will return the ranking for a numeric *report_variable* as it is rolled up by the dimensions provided in the *dimension_variable* list.

```
integer Rank(number [measure_variable]; ([dimension_variable] list); TOP|BOTTOM;
([reset_dimension_variable] list))
```

TOP|BOTTOM is an optional parameter that allows you to indicate the ranking order for the measure as either ascending – TOP or descending – BOTTOM.
reset_dimension_variable list is an optional parameter that allows you to reset the ranking back to 0 when the values in the *reset_dimension_variable* list change.

NOTE *The Rank function by default resets the ranking over a table break or section.*

TIP *For easy ranking, use the Ranking button from the toolbar. Use the function when you wish to display the ranking position as a column in a report.*

Round

The Round function will return a numeric *input_parameter* rounded to a specified number of decimal places provided in number *decimal_places*.

```
number Round(number input_parameter; number decimal_places)
```

Examples:
Round(4.499;2) returns 4.50.
Round(4.499;0) returns 4.
Round(4.75;1) returns 4.8.

Sign

The Sign function will return the sign of the number *input_parameter* provided: –1 is returned to indicate a negative number; 0 is returned to indicate a zero; 1 is returned to indicate a positive.

```
number Sign(number input_parameter)
```

Examples:
Sign(-23) returns –1.
Sign([Revenue]) returns 1 when the value in [Revenue] is positive.

Sin

The Sin function will return the sine of the number *input_parameter*.

```
number Sin(number input_parameter)
```

Example:
Sin(90) returns .89.

Sqrt

The Sqrt function will return the square root of the number *input_parameter* provided.

```
number Sqrt(number input_parameter)
```

Examples:
Sqrt(4)=2
Sqrt(25)=5
Sqrt(15)=3.87

Tan
The Tan function will return the tangent of the number *input_parameter*.

number Tan(number *input_parameter*)

Example:
Tan(90) returns –2.

ToNumber
The ToNumber function will return the string *input_parameter* as a number data type.

number ToNumber(string *input_parameter*)

NOTE *The string* input_parameter *provided must be a numeric value containing only numeric characters, including a decimal point. No formatting characters such as currency signs () or thousands separators ($, euro) can be provided in the string* input_parameter.

Examples:
ToNumber("23") returns 23.
ToNumber("125.75") returns 125.75.
ToNumber("$2,250") returns #ERROR.
ToNumber("ABC") returns #ERROR.

Truncate
The Truncate function will return the number *input_parameter* truncated to a number of decimal places provided in the number *decimal_places*. This function is different than the Round function in that it simply removes any numbers to the right of the decimal places specified. Truncate does not round the number.

number Truncate(number *input_parameter*; number *decimal_places*)

Examples:
Truncate(5.999; 1) returns 5.9.
Truncate(5.999; 2) returns 5.99.
Truncate(5.11; 1) returns 5.1.

Calculation Contexts and Extended Syntax
When a measure object is displayed in a block on your report, it is evaluated in the *context* of the dimensions to which it is being associated. By default, the *calculation context* will include all of the dimensions in the block. This is called the *default calculation context* (as shown in Figure 22-4) For example, a table that contains the dimension objects [Year] and

Year	Quarter	Revenue
FY1998	Q1	131,636
FY1998	Q2	116,096
FY1998	Q3	143,244
FY1998	Q4	112,380
FY1999	Q1	142,776
FY1999	Q2	148,508
FY1999	Q3	150,076
FY1999	Q4	129,270
FY2000	Q1	138,099
FY2000	Q2	143,093
FY2000	Q3	145,084
FY2000	Q4	126,346

Year	Revenue
FY1998	503,356
FY1999	570,630
FY2000	552,622

When the [Quarter] object is removed from the table, the default context automatically changes to [Year]

The default context contains the [Year] and [Quarter] dimensions

Figure 22-4 Default calculation contexts

[Quarter] and the measure object [Revenue] will evaluate the measure object in the context of [Year] and [Quarter]. If the [Quarter] dimension is removed, the calculation context is automatically changed to [Year].

Typically, you will not be concerned with the calculation context of a measure object or formula. Usually the default calculation context is the context you will want to use. However, in certain circumstances, you may want to control the calculation context by using extended syntax. A measure's or formula's context is made up of an input context and an output context.

An *input context* defines the dimension(s) that go into the formula. In other words, an input context defines at what level of granularity the records will be when the formula is applied. An *output context* defines which dimension(s) go into the output of the calculation as if the calculation were placed in a break header or footer based on the dimensions specified. Think of an output context as a break. A formula including extended syntax is written as follows:

```
=function([report_variable] In (InputContext)) In (OutputContext)
```

Using Dimensions in Input and Output Contexts

Input and output contexts may be specified by providing lists of dimension objects. In the following example, the default input context for the [Revenue] measure is ([Year], [Sales Person]). However, if you wanted to calculate the percentage of [Revenue] that each [Sales Person] represents in the total [Year], you must be able to change the *input context* for [Revenue] from the default as follows:

```
=Sum([Revenue] In ([Year]))
```

The default input context of [Revenue] is
([Year];[Sales Person]) for each detail row

Year	Sales Person	Revenue		
FY1998	Fischer	78,826	503,356	15.66%
	Galagers	220,362	503,356	43.78%
	Ishimoto	199,468	503,356	39.63%
	Nagata	4,700	503,356	0.93%
FY1998	Sum:	503,356		
FY1999	Fischer	78,330	570,630	13.73%
	Galagers	258,876	570,630	45.37%
	Ishimoto	233,424	570,630	40.91%
FY1999	Sum:	570,630		
FY2000	Fischer	76,730	552,622	13.88%
	Galagers	263,901	552,622	47.75%
	Ishimoto	211,991	552,622	38.36%
FY2000	Sum:	552,622		

Extended syntax allows you to
change the default input context:
=Sum([Revenue] In ([Year]))

Extended syntax allows you to
perform complex calculations
including the percentage of
revenue for each sales person
over the total year

Sum ([Revenue]) has a default
input context of [Year] when the
formula is placed in the footer of
a [Year] break

Output contexts are best demonstrated by the min and max functions. In the following example, the default output context for the [Revenue] measure is ([Year], [Sales Person]). However, if you wanted to display the highest [Revenue]-generating [Sales Person] for the [Year] alongside each [Sales Person] and that person's [Revenue] total for the [Year], you must be able to change the *output context* for [Revenue] from the default as follows:

```
=Max([Revenue]) In ([Year])
```

Year	Sales Person	Revenue	
FY1998	Fischer	78,826	220,362
	Galagers	220,362	220,362
	Ishimoto	199,468	220,362
	Nagata	4,700	220,362
FY1998	Max:	220,362	
FY1999	Fischer	78,330	258,876
	Galagers	258,876	258,876
	Ishimoto	233,424	258,876
FY1999	Max:	258,876	
FY2000	Fischer	76,730	263,901
	Galagers	263,901	263,901
	Ishimoto	211,991	263,901
FY2000	Max:	263,901	

=Max([Revenue]) In ([Year])

Both input and output contexts can be combined in a single formula. The following example represents [Revenue] calculated by [Year] and [Quarter] and the largest of those values output by [Year].

```
=Max([Revenue] In ([Year];[Quarter])) In ([Year])
```

Year	Quarter	Sales Person	Revenue	
FY1998	Q1	Fischer	18,240	143,244
		Galagers	56,596	143,244
		Ishimoto	56,800	143,244
	Q1	Sum:	131,636	
	Q2	Fischer	25,346	143,244
		Galagers	43,200	143,244
		Ishimoto	42,850	143,244
		Nagata	4,700	143,244
	Q2	Sum:	116,096	
	Q3	Fischer	21,800	143,244
		Galagers	61,892	143,244
		Ishimoto	59,552	143,244
	Q3	Sum:	143,244	
	Q4	Fischer	13,440	143,244
		Galagers	58,674	143,244
		Ishimoto	40,266	143,244
	Q4	Sum:	112,380	
FY1998		Max:	61,892	

=Max([Revenue] In ([Year];[Quarter])) In ([Year])

Using Context Operators in Input Contexts

In previous examples you have used the *In* context operator to specify dimension(s) to include in the input and output contexts. BusinessObjects XI provides two additional context operators that can be used in extended syntax:

- **ForEach**   The ForEach context operator allows you to add dimensions to the current default input context. For example, if a table contains the dimensions [Year] and [Quarter] and the measure [Revenue], the default context is [Year]; [Quarter]. In the following example, the ForEach context operator is used to add the [Sales Person] dimension to the context (without adding [Sales Person] to the table):

    ```
    =Min([Revenue] ForEach ([Sales Person])) In ([Year])
    ```

    This would be the same as explicitly listing all of the dimensions as follows:

    ```
    =Min([Revenue] In ([Year];[Quarter];[Sales Person])) In ([Year])
    ```

- **ForAll**   The ForAll context operator allows you to remove a dimension from the current default input context. For example, if a table contains the dimensions [Year], [Quarter] and [Sales Person] and the measure [Revenue], the default context is [Year]; [Quarter]; [Sales Person]. In the following example, the ForAll context operator is used to remove the [Sales Person] dimension from the context (without removing [Sales Person] from the table):

    ```
    =Min([Revenue] ForAll ([Sales Person])) In ([Year])
    ```

This would be the same as explicitly listing all of the dimensions as follows:

```
=Min([Revenue] In ([Year];[Quarter])) In ([Year])
```

Using Keywords in Input and Output Contexts

BusinessObjects XI provides keywords to help you specify the dimensions to include in the context of a formula. The use of keywords provides two benefits. First, it is a shorthand method of specifying dimensions, eliminating the need to type out the list of dimensions to include in the context. Second, the use of keywords allows you to add or delete dimensions to a report without having to change the extended syntax in your formulas. Since the context does not contain a hard-coded list of dimensions, the formula will continue to work.

The keywords that can be used in extended syntax are Report, Section, Break, Block, and Body. Table 22-3 describes what data will be included when using keywords in extended syntax in different areas of a table or report.

Some Popular Formulas

Web Intelligence provides dozens of functions allowing limitless formula combinations. The next section provides a few examples of multiple functions used together.

If-Then-Else

The If function allows the creation of complex formulas and powerful alerters. The following formula nests multiple If functions to return "Revenue Goal Exceeded" if [Revenue] exceeds $1,000,000, "Revenue Goal Met" if [Revenue] is between $850,000 and $1,000,000, and returns "Revenue Goal Not Met" if [Revenue] <= $850,000.

```
=If([Revenue]>1000000; "Revenue Goal Exceeded"; If([Revenue]>850000 And
[Revenue]<=1000000; "Revenue Goal Met"; "Revenue Goal Not Met"))
```

Keyword	When a Keyword is placed in...it refers to the following data:			
	A Block	**A Block Break**	**A Section**	**Outside Any Block or Section**
Report	All data in the report	All data in the report	All data in the report	All data in the report
Section	All data in the section	All data in the section	All data in the section	Not Applicable
Break	Data in the block delimited by a break	Data in the block delimited by a break	Not Applicable	Not Applicable
Block	Data in the entire block, ignoring breaks, but respecting filters	Data in the entire block, ignoring breaks, but respecting filters	Not Applicable	Not Applicable
Body	Data in the block	Data in the block	Data in the section	Data in the report

TABLE 22-3   Data Included When Using Keywords in Different Areas of a Table or Report

Whenever a formula performs division, it is a good idea to test the denominator for zero values; otherwise, you will receive a divide by 0 error (#DIV/0). The following formula uses the If function to test the denominator for 0.

```
=If([Number of guests]<>0;[Revenue]/[Number of guests])
```

Year-to-Date Measures

The following formula will create a Last Year Sales variable. If the year of the current date minus 1 (last year) is equal to the report variable representing the year, then display the revenue amount, else return 0.

```
=If(Year(CurrentDate()-1)=[Year]; [Revenue]; 0)
```

To make the year-to-date formula more precise, you can include a month comparison as well.

```
=If(Year(CurrentDate())-1=Year([Invoice Date]); [Revenue]; 0)
```

Concatenation

In some circumstances you will want to combine two strings together into a single string variable by using *concatenation*. This can be useful for formatting, for example, when you need a first name and a last name variable combined into a single name field for a form letter. This can also be necessary to combine multiple fields to create a single unique field for the purpose of counting distinct values.

Concatenation only works on string variables or string literals. If you need to include numeric values, date values, or other data types in the concatenation function, they will need to be converted to string types prior to concatenation. The following example displays a label "Total Revenue " concatenated with the sum of the revenue.

```
=Concatenation("Total Revenue "; FormatNumber(Sum([Revenue]);" $#,##0.00"))
```

Concatenation will not automatically trim blanks from fields or add spaces between concatenated fields to make the combined fields legible. For example, you will have to remember to include a space between the first and last names. To concatenate more than two strings, you will need to nest the concatenation functions.

```
=Concatenation([First Name]; Concatenation(" "; [Last Name]))
```

An alternative syntax for concatenation is the addition (+) operator. The addition operator allows you to concatenate multiple strings together without nesting concatenation functions. This method is easier to read. The preceding formula would be written using addition syntax for concatenation as follows:

```
=[First Name] + " "  + [Last Name]
```

Cumulative Aggregates

Cumulative aggregates will incrementally aggregate each row of data as the data is ordered in the report. By default, the running aggregate will continue tabulating through break levels to the end of the report without resetting back to zero.

```
=RunningSum([Revenue])
```

If you want to reset the cumulative aggregate after each break, you must specify the reset context (dimension variable) in the function. The following formula specifies a reset context of [Year]:

```
=RunningSum([Revenue]; ([Year]))
```

Year	Sales Person	Revenue	Running Sum No Reset Context	Running Sum with Reset Context
FY1998	Fischer	78,826	78,826	78,826
	Galagers	220,362	299,188	299,188
	Ishimoto	199,468	498,656	498,656
	Nagata	4,700	503,356	503,356
FY1998				
FY1999	Fischer	78,330	581,686	78,330
	Galagers	258,876	840,562	337,206
	Ishimoto	233,424	1,073,986	570,630
FY1999				
FY2000	Fischer	76,730	1,150,716	76,730
	Galagers	263,901	1,414,617	340,631
	Ishimoto	211,991	1,626,608	552,622
FY2000				

=RunningSum([Revenue]; ([Year])) resets the running sum across the [Year] break

=RunningSum([Revenue]) does not reset the running sum

Creating Variables in Desktop Intelligence

In earlier versions of Web Intelligence, the number of functions was much more limited, so this was an often-cited reason for authoring reports in BusinessObjects classic rather than Web Intelligence. Web Intelligence in XI Release 2 contains nearly all of the capabilities of Desktop Intelligence.

To create a variable in Desktop Intelligence:

1. Right-click any variable in the Data tab of the data manager and select New Variable.

2. The Variable Editor dialog box will appear. In the Variable Editor, drag, double-click, or type the components of your formula into the formula text box.

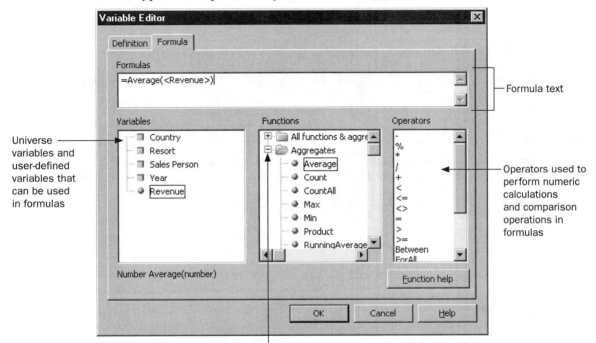

Universe variables and user-defined variables that can be used in formulas

Formula text

Operators used to perform numeric calculations and comparison operations in formulas

Functions provided by Desktop Intelligence. Click (+) to expand the list of functions by category

3. Click the Definition tab and specify a formula name and a qualification.

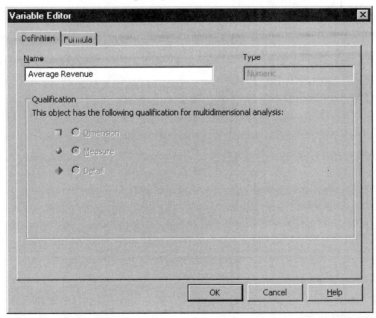

4. Click OK to save the variable.

5. The variable is now listed in the Data tab of the data manager and can be used on your report.

NOTE *When creating formulas in Desktop Intelligence, you must specify report variables surrounded with < > rather than [ ] as in Web Intelligence. For example, in Desktop Intelligence the formula would be* =<Revenue> * 1.10, *whereas in Web Intelligence the formula would be* =[Revenue] * 1.10.

Summary

Formulas provide a powerful way to take your reporting and analysis even further. However, formulas and variables are document specific, potentially posing a maintenance issue. If you are creating a formula that many documents and users will require, work with the universe designer to incorporate these formulas as universe objects.

Complex Queries

One of Web Intelligence's greatest strengths is the ability to create complex queries and answer complex business questions, *easily.* The powerful semantic layer via the universe lets you create complex SQL statements, without your ever having to know or write SQL. I use the term "complex query" to refer to any query that

- Generates SQL that is more than a straightforward SELECT and GROUP BY.
- Leverages features that you may not necessarily use on a routine basis.
- Potentially has an adverse effect on response time.
- May lead you to incorrect results if you lack a clear understanding of the functionality or logic.

You may not always realize when you generate a complex query; it's quite simple to add result objects to the query panel that, unbeknown to you, come from two different star schemas. In other cases, you may struggle to define conditions in a way that gives you the desired results—for example, you may be forced to use nested conditions or subqueries in which building the query with the attendant thought process and tasks *feels complex.*

Multipass Queries

For certain business questions, you may need to issue multiple queries to arrive at your desired result. Web Intelligence's ability to generate multiple SQL statements and present them to you as one report is referred to as *multipass SQL.* In some cases, you as the query author may explicitly create two distinct queries. In other cases, Web Intelligence will do this for you automatically if your universe contains contexts or derived tables.

Even when Web Intelligence creates multiple SELECT statements automatically, from the user perspective, there is only one data provider; it appears you are building one query. Web Intelligence generates multiple SQL statements and dynamically stitches the results together, often unbeknown to you (unless you view the SQL). This capability is one of the features that allow you to use Web Intelligence against complex data models such as those in a transaction system or against data warehouses that contain multiple star schemas. As long as your dimensions or GROUP BY clause for the two queries are exactly the same,

Web Intelligence will automatically display the result set in one table. If, however, your dimension objects are unique to a particular star schema, your report may not appear as you intended.

Following are some sample business questions for which Web Intelligence may generate multiple SQL statements to answer. Notice that most of these involve two different metrics that may reside in two different fact tables or be stored at different levels of granularity.

Information Requirement	Explanation
Debits, Credits, Month End Balance	Debits and credits are aggregated over a period of time, while balances are one point in time.
Movements In/Out, Inventory	Material movements are aggregated over a period of time, while inventory is one point in time.
Days Sales Inventory (DSI)	Sales are aggregated over a period of time, while inventory is one point in time.
Product Sales, Promotion	Sales come from one fact table, while promotion costs come from another fact table.

In order for multipass SQL to work correctly, the universe designer must set specific SQL parameters and define contexts for each set of joins that make up a star schema. These options are discussed in Chapters 7 and 8, respectively. From a user viewpoint, you only need to worry about multipass SQL if you think you are getting incorrect results or if Web Intelligence splits the results into two tables. For example, in Figure 23-1, there are two queries yet one table that displays *Sales Revenue* and *Promotion Costs* by *Year* and *SKU Description*. In Figure 23-2, there are two tables. The dimension object *State* (store location) was added to the query results. *State* relates only to *Sales Revenue* and not *Promotion Costs*. So while Web Intelligence continues to issue two SELECT statements to the data source, it now cannot join those results in the microcube and display them in one table.

TIP *Web Intelligence documents can take advantage of a new universe parameter JOIN_BY_ SQL=Yes that causes one SQL statement to be generated and processed on the server. However, initial tests show a variable impact on response time.*

Year	SKU desc	Sales revenue	Promotion Cost USD
2002	Long-Sleeved Stitch Shirt	$265,788	$8,050
2002	Long-Sleeved Torn Stitch T-Shirt	$252,853	
2002	Military Shirt	$125,554	$12,650

FIGURE 23-1   Multiple SELECT statements can produce one tabular result set.

Year	SKU desc	State	Sales revenue
2002	Long-Sleeved Stitch Shirt	New York	$46,447
2002	Long-Sleeved Stitch Shirt	Texas	$85,678
2002	Long-Sleeved Torn Stitch T-	New York	$39,085
2002	Long-Sleeved Torn Stitch T-	Texas	$77,473
2002	Military Shirt	New York	$27,340
2002	Military Shirt	Texas	$33,239

Year	SKU desc	Promotion Cost USD
2002	Long-Sleeved Stitch Shirt	$8,050
2002	Long-Sleeved Torn Stitch T-Shirt	
2002	Military Shirt	$12,650

FIGURE 23-2 Multiple tables appear when the SELECT statements do not have the same GROUP BY.

Figure 23-3 shows the two SQL statements used to generate the undesired report in Figure 23-2. The problem appears in Select 1. The dimension object *State* (OUTLET_LOOKUP .STATE) applies only to sales; it does not apply to promotions and is not defined as part of the promotion star schema or context. Therefore, OUTLET_LOOKUP.STATE does not appear in either the SELECT or GROUP BY sections of Select 2 in Figure 23-3. When a dimension does not apply to both measures, Web Intelligence automatically creates a report with two tables. In Desktop Intelligence, the impact is similar although it will also create a master detail report using the common dimensions as section headers (so somewhat more cumbersome).

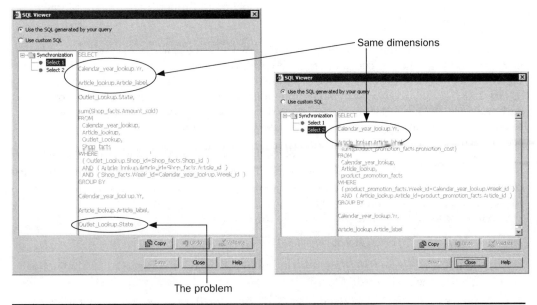

FIGURE 23-3 One query generates two SQL statements. Select 1 has an extra result and GROUP BY dimension.

Multiple Data Providers

Web Intelligence does a virtual join of result sets by common dimensions automatically when you have one data provider; the multiple SQL statements are issued because you have multiple fact tables within the same universe. You can, however, also have multiple queries within a document that come from different universes or that come from the same universe but with different filter criteria. The ability to synchronize these multiple data providers is a key feature new to XI Release 2. However, if you are used to authoring such complex reports in the full client, it's important to understand that the behavior is slightly different in Web Intelligence.

- With earlier versions of BusinessObjects, joining of multiple data providers happens automatically across universes as long as the object names are the same.

- With Web Intelligence and Desktop Intelligence, when the dimension object names are the same and come from the same universe, they are automatically merged. When they come from different universes, you must explicitly map them to one another, in a process called *merging*.

- Missing rows between the queries is treated differently; Desktop Intelligence will do a full outer join automatically so that all rows from each query result are displayed in the merged table. In Web Intelligence, the outer join is performed in only one direction unless you set the Document Properties to Extend Merged Dimension Values.

As an example, within the eFashion universe, Sales is one star schema and Promotions is in a second star schema. They both share common dimensions such as Time and Articles. However, let's assume they are in two separate universes; you can no longer build one query or one data provider to create the report shown in Figure 23-1. You need to create a query for each universe. In Web Intelligence, you must define how the dimensions in each query map to one another. In Desktop Intelligence, you need to do this only when the dimension names are different.

In the following example, I have purposely used different object names to make the different data sources clearer. However, ideally, your universe designer will ensure that common dimension names follow the same naming conventions across multiple universes. Ideally, the designer may link universes to ensure such conformity.

To link these multiple data providers, do the following:

1. Create a query from the first universe.

2. To insert a second data provider, from within the Web Intelligence query panel, select Add Query.

3. When prompted, select the universe to use as the data source and click OK.

4. Web Intelligence will display a blank query panel. Note at the bottom of your screen that there are now two queries.

TIP *You can assign the queries names instead of the generic Query 1 and Query 2 by modifying the Query Properties.*

5. Select Run Queries from the upper-right toolbar.

6. If you already ran the first query, Web Intelligence asks you what you want to do with the additional query results. As you ultimately want to display the measure Promotion Cost in the same report as Revenue, for now, select "Include the result objects in the document without generating a table." If you did not run the second query, then Web Intelligence will automatically create one report with only the first query results.

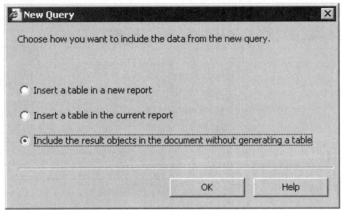

At this point, you have query results from both queries, but you see the data from only one of them. In order to display the two measures together, you must synchronize your data providers.

Synchronizing Data Providers

You can theoretically add the second measure to your existing table; however, the results displayed will not be correct.

Year	SKU desc	Sales revenue	Promotion Cost US
2003	Jet Pearl Bracelet	$4,944	$60,975
2003	Jet Pearl Choker	$7,164	$60,975
2003	Johnny Walker Turt	$58,536	$60,975
2003	Large Rectangular	$2,075	$60,975
2003	Large Rose Patterr	$166	$60,975
2003	Large Silver Bracel	$576	$60,975
2003	Leather Gloves	$215	$60,975
2003	Leather Trousers	$2,228	$60,975
2003	Long Lace Skirt	$54,965	$60,975
2003	Long-sleeved Crew	$4,241,803	$60,975

For correct results, you must first synchronize the common dimensions as shown in Figure 23-4, which shows the Merge Dimension dialog with two query providers. If your

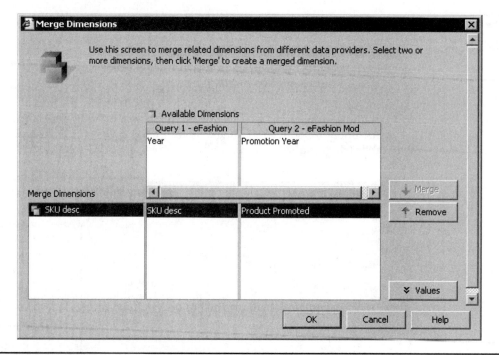

FIGURE 23-4   Merge dimensions from multiple data providers.

document contains more than two query providers, a column appears for each data provider.

1. From within the Report panel, select Merge Dimensions from the toolbar.

2. Under Query 1, select *SKU Desc*. Under Query 2, select *Product Promoted*.

3. You can preview the data values for each of these objects by selecting Values. If you have correctly mapped the two dimensions, select Merge.

4. A Create Merged Dimension dialog appears. Here you can change the name of the dimension, or Web Intelligence will use the object name and properties from the first data provider.

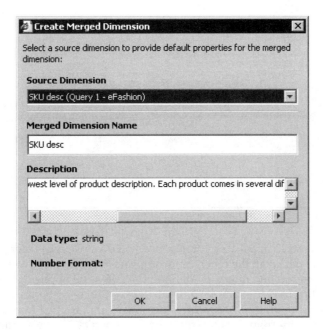

5. Select OK to close the dialog. Merge *Year* with *Promotion Year.* When you have merged all the dimensions, click OK to close the Merge Dimensions panel.

Figure 23-5 shows the results of the merged dimensions. Within the left-hand pane, you see on the Data tab when dimensions have been merged. Click the + sign next to any merged dimension to see the result objects from the original query. Also notice in Figure 23-5 that two dimensions have not been merged: Lines and State (Store location). These exist within Query 1 but not in Query 2. As a best practice, your dimensions between the multiple data providers should be the same. In practice, though, your query can have more objects in one than in the other as long as you do not add it to the tabular block. For example, Web Intelligence allows you to add Lines to the tabular report. When you do so, though, the virtual join goes from being an outer join to being an inner join: products (such as Long-Sleeved Torn Stitch T-Shirt) that do not have a corresponding promotion cost are dropped from the table. As promotion costs are associated only with products and not with individual store locations, Web Intelligence will not allow you to insert State into the tabular report. It warns you, "Cannot drop here. Incompatible object."

Merged dimensions

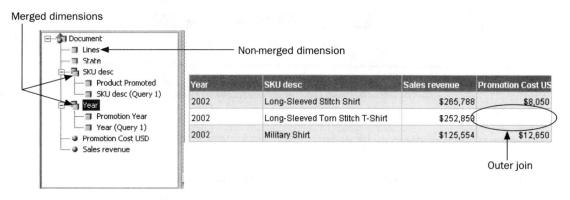

Non-merged dimension

Outer join

FIGURE 23-5   Synchronized multiple data providers

Also note in Figure 23-5 that Web Intelligence will do a pseudo–outer join when one query contains more data than the other. A null appears in the measure column for data that does not appear in the second query. By default, the outer join applies to only the second query and not the first. So for example, if there were products with promotions (the second query) and no corresponding sales revenue, these rows are dropped from the merged table. This is different behavior from Desktop Intelligence, in which all rows from both query results are automatically displayed in the table. If you want all results displayed from both queries, you must set this option in the Document Properties.

Data Synchronization Options

To set the Document Properties so that dimensions from the same universe are automatically merged,

1. Select the report tab on the bottom and right-click to call the pop-up menu.
2. Select Document Properties.

NOTE   *You also can invoke the Document Properties through the left-hand properties tab, but I find this process far less obvious. To do so, select the entire document in the report pane. A gray box will surround the entire pane and the Document Properties options will appear in the left-hand Properties tab. Click the ellipse next to the document name.*

3. This displays the Document Properties pane on the right.
4. Scroll to the section Data Synchronization Options.
5. Check the option Auto-Merge Dimensions to have Web Intelligence merge query results with common dimension names from the same universe.
6. Check the option Extend Merged Dimension Values; this will perform a double outer join or display results from both queries even when only one query contains a particular dimension value.

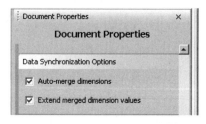

Measure Conditions/Having Clause

When you place a condition on a measure object that uses an aggregate function, Web Intelligence does not generate a straightforward WHERE clause, but rather, it generates a HAVING clause. The RDBMS first performs the aggregations and GROUP BY and then returns only those results that satisfy the HAVING condition. In the following example, the query returns rows for which the SUM of SHOP_FACTS.MARGIN is less than or equal to 0:

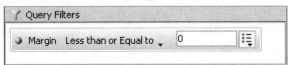

```
SELECT
  Calendar_year_lookup.Year,
  Article_lookup.Family_name,
  sum(Shop_facts.Margin)
FROM
  Shop_facts,
  Calendar_year_lookup,
  Article_lookup
WHERE
  ( Article_lookup.Article_code=Shop_facts.Article_code )
  AND  ( Shop_facts.Week_key=Calendar_year_lookup.Week_Key )
GROUP BY
  Calendar_year_lookup.Year,
  Article_lookup.Family_name
HAVING
  ( sum(Shop_facts.Margin)  <=  0  )
```

The problem here is that many users are deceived into thinking this is a simple query, as it returns few results. It is true that there may not be many article families/lines that have a negative margin for a particular month. However, to answer the query, the database must do a full table scan on the fact table. In the sample database, the fact table is quite small, however, in real-world databases, the fact table can be millions of rows of data. To minimize the risk of this, consider adding conditions on any other dimension objects that will generate a WHERE clause. For example, a condition on *Year* in addition to *Margin* will allow the database first to select only those rows for a particular year. The database then performs the GROUP BY and HAVING on a smaller set of data (possibly retrieved via an index).

TIP *If you use measures as conditions, ensure you include other conditions on dimension objects to improve the query processing time.*

Complex Query Filters

To understand how the AND, OR, UNION, INTERSECT, and MINUS operators work, it's useful to review a bit of set theory. Figure 23-6 shows a Venn diagram with three sets of criteria: Gender, Income, and Marital Status. When you add query filters to your query, the filters are joined by a default operator, AND. All conditions must be met for the query to return results. You can say this is the intersection, or solid triangle, in Figure 23-6 where all three sets of criteria are met. For example, if you set the conditions as shown in the following screen, the query will return information only for customers who are Female, Single, with incomes between $110,000 and 189,999 (levels F through I).

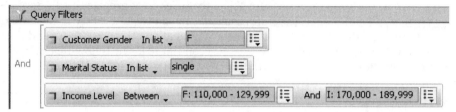

If *any* of the conditions could be met (an OR connector), then you can think of it as a nonoverlapping circle from Figure 23-6. If you wanted all Females, regardless of income or marital status, it's the full circle. If you are trying to filter your data for Females with a certain marital status, it's the overlap between the two criteria or smaller ellipse with the squares.

OR Operand and Nested Conditions

The complexity arises when you want to join one set of conditions with an OR and the other with an AND. For example, study the sample table in Figure 23-7. In some cases, sales segmented by marital status are drastically different for married customers versus single customers. In others, the income level shows higher sales, and for others, the differences are bigger by gender. Figure 23-7 shows that sales to single women in the salary levels of F through I are the highest, whereas sales to men in level F are highest regardless of marital status.

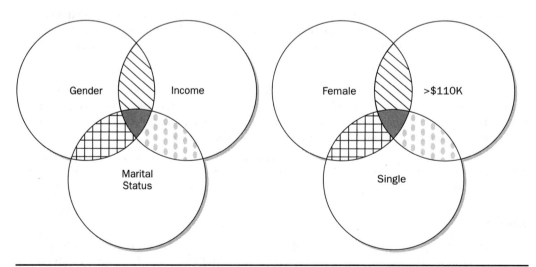

FIGURE 23-6   Intersection of multiple filter criteria

	F	F	M	M
	married	single	married	single
A: Below 30,000	838,016.45	1,828,867.95	2,123,201.55	1,855,278.8
B: 30,000 - 49,999	1,139,274.35	954,278.2	2,442,577	2,442,685.05
C: 50,000 - 69,999	2,747,839.15		3,237,100.3	
D: 70,000 - 89,999	3,524,997.9	2,901,261.05	6,267,553.75	4,418,348.7
E: 90,000 - 109,999	3,061,705.05		7,352,761.15	
F: 110,000 - 129,999	4,736,341.2	7,964,851.75	11,393,432.45	11,137,096.9
G: 130,000 - 149,999	2,549,879.65	4,756,429.2	6,684,283.2	7,367,284.25
H: 150,000 - 169,999	492,025	7,612,727.55	115,639.9	18,634,171.8
I: 170,000 - 189,999	492,307.75	6,981,267.85	661,204.6	12,678,978.5
J: 190,000 - 249,999	1,510,414.15	1,252,580.2	1,503,383.45	1,615,371.1
K: 250,000 - 299,999	1,980,190.5	1,087,277.85	1,849,512.2	2,119,613.6
L: 300,000 and above	1,265,383.05	998,722.9	1,918,524.25	1,989,219.5

Figure 23-7   Total sales by customer segments

If you want to analyze information according to these two segments, you need to group your conditions in a way that is often called *nesting*. Failure to nest your conditions properly will lead to incorrect query results. In this case, you want to nest your query filters as two segments:

- Female, Single, with income between $110,000 and 189,999 (levels F through I)
- Men, income level $110,000 to 129,999 (level F) and any marital status

To retrieve the circled items from Figure 23-7, your query filters should be nested as follows:

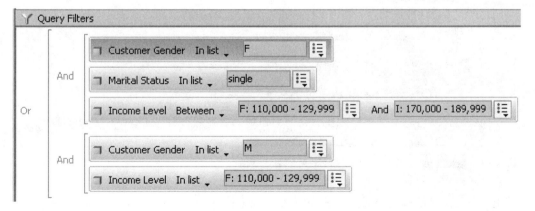

To nest your conditions, pay careful attention to the drag-and-drop indicators so that your query filters are correctly positioned. Normally, when you want everything connected with an AND (just the intersection of the criteria), Web Intelligence displays a line with two triangles to indicate how the new query filter will be appended.

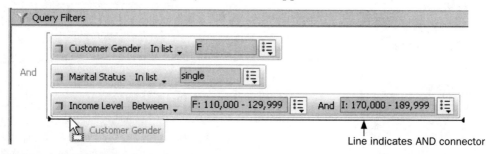

If, however, you drag the new query filters slightly to the left of the existing filters, no line appears and Web Intelligence will automatically switch to an OR connector.

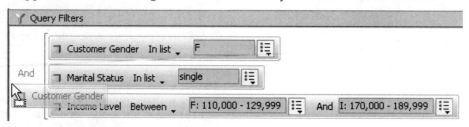

So to create the second group of criteria,

1. Drag *Customer Gender* to the Query Filters pane, ensuring the mouse is positioned just to the left of the criteria for female customers.

2. Select the Value = M.

3. Drag *Income Level*, positioning it on top of the Customer Gender = M so that your mouse appears as follows:

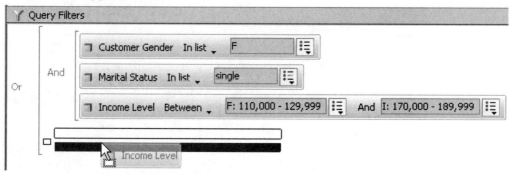

If you can't drag and drop your filters to produce the desired results, don't panic! Simply double-click the AND to change your connector to an OR and reposition the criteria accordingly. I also find it helpful to view the SQL (by clicking the SQL button from the toolbar) to ensure the parentheses appear in the correct places.

```
WHERE
  (
  (SH.CUSTOMERS.CUST_GENDER  In  ( 'F'  )
    AND
    SH.CUSTOMERS.CUST_MARITAL_STATUS  In  ( 'single'  )
    AND
    SH.CUSTOMERS.CUST_INCOME_LEVEL  BETWEEN  'F: 110,000 - 129,999'  AND  'I: 170,000
- 189,999')
   OR
   ( SH.CUSTOMERS.CUST_GENDER  In  ( 'M'  )
    AND
    SH.CUSTOMERS.CUST_INCOME_LEVEL  In  ( 'F: 110,000 - 129,999'  )  )
  )
```

In the preceding example, the OR operator allowed you to nest or group multiple sets of criteria. You also can use OR to search for the same value across multiple fields. For example, in SAP, the bill of lading may appear in several fields. With the following conditions, the OR operator allows you to search in multiple fields. By using the exact same prompt for each of the conditions, you need to enter only one bill of lading number, and it is filled in each of the conditions.

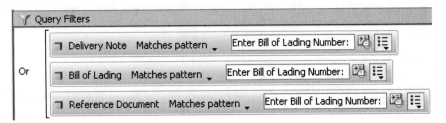

Combined Queries

In some cases, nesting the conditions will still not give you the desired results. This often happens when you want to test for multiple values against the same dimension object. For example, let's say you are looking for customers who bought two products together: a plasma TV, for example, along with a TV stand (or is everyone nowadays mounting them to the wall?). If you use the In List operator, you will get a list of customers who buy *either* a TV *or* a TV stand. If you create two conditions and join them with AND, you will get no rows returned, as the conditions in the WHERE clause are mutually exclusive.

To retrieve the desired results, you need to create two queries within one data provider, leveraging the RDBMS's set operators: UNION, INTERSECT, and MINUS. Table 23-1 explains the different operators and their purposes. In order to use these operators, the number of result columns and the data type for each of the columns must be the same. Often when using INTERSECT, the result objects are exactly the same and only the conditions change between the two queries. Chapter 8 discussed some of the problems with queries that contain loops; INTERSECT is a better alternative to answer a query that otherwise would contain a loop. For UNION and MINUS, you may want to change the measure column. It's possible to do this, but in the report, Web Intelligence will use the variable name from the first query. MINUS is also useful for determining if there are data quality issues between a fact table and dimension table, rather than using an outer join (see Chapter 8). For example, if you want a list of products for which there are no corresponding sales transactions, the main query would contain products from the dimension table and the minus query would

Operator	Explanation
UNION	Combines the results of multiple queries. When the query contains a measure, the common rows are aggregated.
INTERSECT	Selects the rows that intersect or overlap between the two queries. This is not recommended for use with measures as a result object. When the query contains a measure object, unless the measure values are exactly the same, there is no intersection.
MINUS	Subtracts the rows in the second query from the main query.

TABLE 23-1 Set Operators to Combine Queries

contain products from the fact table. The result set is a list of products for which there are no records in the fact table.

The following example uses the Island Resorts Marketing universe to identify customers who have stayed in both the Hawaiian Club resort and the French Riviera resort.

1. When creating a combined query, first evaluate the result objects in your main query. If you are using INTERSECT, ensure that it does not contain any result objects for dimensions that you will use as a condition. In this example, select *Customer Origin* and *Customer* as result objects.

2. Insert your query filter as *Resort* In List **Hawaiian Club**.

 3. Select the Combine Query button from the toolbar.

4. Web Intelligence opens a Combined Query pane as shown in Figure 23-8. By default, the operator is a UNION. Double-click UNION to change it to INTERSECT.

5. Ensure that you are positioned within Combined Query 2. Insert your query filter as *Resort* In List **French Riviera**.

6. You can continue to add additional queries to identify customers who have stayed at all three resorts by selecting the Combined Query button. If at any point you need to remove a Combined Query, select the particular Combined Query from the pane, right-click and select Remove. When prompted, click Yes to confirm that you wish to remove the combined query.

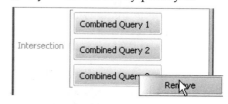

7. Once you are satisfied with each of your combined queries, select Run Query.

Note that the dimension for which you want to retrieve multiple values, *Resort*, should appear only in the query filters. If it appeared in the result objects, no rows would return, as these values are mutually exclusive. Also, if you do not have the same result objects when running an intersection query, you will receive an error message:

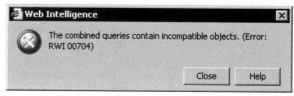

Combined Query button

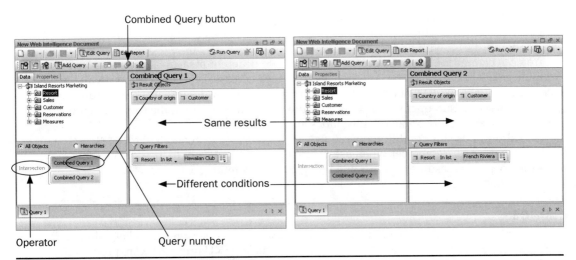

FIGURE 23-8   Combined query using INTERSECT

Figure 23-9 gives sample records to show how the different set operators work. The intersection between the two queries, as shown in Figure 23-8, consists only of customers Schiller, Titzman, and Weimar.

In the preceding example, if you change the operator to MINUS, and the first query filter to Resorts Bahamas Beach, the first query returns a list of customers who stayed in Bahamas Beach (all customers in Figure 23-9) and then removes the rows for those who also stayed in French Riviera (Schiller, Titzman, and Weimar).

Country of origin	Customer	Age group	Resort
Germany	Diemers	18-30	Bahamas Beach
Germany	Durnstein	30-60	Bahamas Beach
Germany	Reinman	Over 60	Bahamas Beach
Germany	Schiller	18-30	Bahamas Beach
Germany	Schiller	18-30	French Riviera
Germany	Schiller	18-30	Hawaiian Club
Germany	Schultz	30-60	Bahamas Beach
Germany	Titzman	Over 60	Bahamas Beach
Germany	Titzman	Over 60	French Riviera
Germany	Titzman	Over 60	Hawaiian Club
Germany	Weimar	30-60	Bahamas Beach
Germany	Weimar	30-60	French Riviera
Germany	Weimar	30-60	Hawaiian Club

FIGURE 23-9   Sample data for customers in Germany

Using the UNION operator in this example has the same effect as using IN List as the condition. With queries that contain multiple OR statements that are nested, you may find the query runs faster with UNION.

You can change the result objects to aggregate two different measures using UNION. For example, you could use a UNION query to aggregate fixed cost + variable cost or if you have sales figures for two different companies that come from two different fact tables. However, when you use a MINUS operator and the measure objects are different, the rows from the second query are simply removed; the values are not subtracted.

You also can use the condition operators BOTH or EXCEPT to generate the INTERSECT and MINUS queries. Remember when using BOTH / INTERSECT not to include the same condition objects as result objects, or you will get no rows returned.

Subqueries

A subquery is a query that the main SELECT statement calls to determine the filter values. For example, in the eFashion universe, certain clothing articles (SKU number) were promoted during various months in the year 2002. You would like to know sales for these articles by store in 2003. Did the promotions increase sales in the following year? The store in which the product was sold does not directly apply to product promotions, so if you tried to retrieve all this information in one query, the results would be split into two separate tables. The solution is to use a subquery to retrieve a list of articles that were promoted in 2002 and see the effect on sales in 2003.

Creating a Subquery

You create a subquery by defining a query filter in a particular way. This can get a little confusing, so be sure to think carefully about which conditions apply where. In this example, you want to know:

- Sales for stores in New York for the year 2003. The filters for Year=2003 and for Store location in New York go into your main query.

- But only for products that had a promotion in 2002. The filters for Year=2002 and promotion=yes are part of your subquery.

In Figure 23-10, the subquery is on the *SKU number*. Notice that the year conditions in the main query and subquery are different. The subquery looks for products that were promoted in 2002, but the main query displays sales for the products for a particular state in the subsequent year as well. Notice in the following SQL that there is another SELECT statement nested within the main query:

```
SELECT
  Outlet_Lookup.State,
  Calendar_year_lookup.Yr,
  Article_lookup.Article_id,
Article_lookup.Article_label,
 sum(Shop_facts.Amount_sold)
```

```
FROM
  Outlet_Lookup,
  Calendar_year_lookup,
  Article_lookup,
  Shop_facts
WHERE
  ( Outlet_Lookup.Shop_id=Shop_facts.Shop_id  )
  AND   ( Article_lookup.Article_id=Shop_facts.Article_id  )
  AND   ( Shop_facts.Week_id=Calendar_year_lookup.Week_id  )
  AND   ( Calendar_year_lookup.Yr  In  ( '2003','2002'  )
  AND  Outlet_Lookup.State  In  ( 'New York'  )
  AND Article_lookup.Article_id  In
      ( SELECT
        Article_lookup.Article_id
      FROM
        Article_lookup,
        Calendar_year_lookup,
        promotion_lookup,
        product_promotion_facts
      WHERE
        ( promotion_lookup.Promotion_id=product_promotion_facts.Promotion_id  )
        AND   ( product_promotion_facts.Week_id=Calendar_year_lookup.Week_id  )
        AND   ( Article_lookup.Article_id=product_promotion_facts.Article_id  )
        AND
        ( Calendar_year_lookup.Yr  In  ( '2002'  )
        AND
        promotion_lookup.Promotion_flag  In  ( 'y'  )          )
  )  )
GROUP BY
  Outlet_Lookup.State,
  Calendar_year_lookup.Yr,
  Article_lookup.Article_id,
  Article_lookup.Article_label
```

Subquery

To create a subquery as in Figure 23-10, use the eFashion universe:

1. Select the result objects *Year, Store Name, SKU number, SKU desc, Sales Revenue.*

2. Insert the query filters *State* In List **New York** and *Year* In List **2003; 2002.**

3. Position your mouse on the *SKU number* object within the Classes and Objects pane. Select Add A Subquery from the toolbar.

4. Web Intelligence will automatically insert the query filter *SKU number* In List *SKU number.*

5. Drag *Year* to the Subquery box and set the filter to Equal to **2002.** Drag *Promotion y/n* to the subquery box and set the filter to Equal to **y.**

6. Run the Query.

Subqueries are a powerful feature in Web Intelligence. Combining them with multiple data providers, you can answer a fairly complex business question: Were the promotions effective? Notice in the following table (which displays data for both years and uses two

PART III

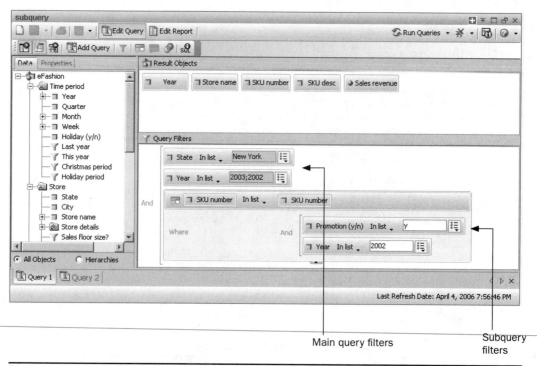

Main query filters

Subquery filters

FIGURE 23-10   A subquery selects conditions based on the results of another query.

separate data providers in addition to a subquery), they were not! In fact, it looks as if any products that were promoted had dramatically lower sales in the following year. Products, however, that were not promoted had much higher sales. Well, this is fictional data, so we don't really know what's going on here (maybe the promotions were part of an effort to clear out inventory for products to be discontinued).

Year	Non Promo Sales	Promotional Sales
2002	$1,937,593	$825,910
2003	$2,763,255	$387,767

To create this kind of report, you would use several advanced features discussed in this chapter:

- A subquery to get sales for products promoted in a prior year
- Multiple data providers in one document to display sales for products that were not promoted at all
- Synchronization of the two data providers to present the results in one report

Object Equal to Another Object

Setting an object equal to another object is a powerful capability but one that you again need to monitor query performance, as it creates a join between the tables that reference the objects (or creates a self-join when the two objects refer to the same table). You may use this capability to answer questions such as:

- Which orders shipped the same day the order was placed?
- Which customers traveled to the same country in which they reside?
- Which invoices have the same ship to customer ID and sold to customer ID?

The following example looks for orders that shipped later than the required delivery date.

1. Drag the object for which you want to filter your results to the Query Filters pane, in this example, *Shipped Date.*
2. Select the operator, in this case, Greater than.
3. From the Operand drop-down, select Object.

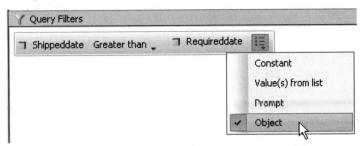

4. Web Intelligence will present you with a list of objects from the current universe. This list of objects is not narrowed by a type that corresponds to the object you selected in Step 1. However, in order for your query to be valid, the objects must be of the same type and field format. Select the object, in this case *Required Date,* and click OK to close the dialog.

Summary

Much of the power in Web Intelligence lies in its robust query capabilities. It can handle complex database schemas by allowing you to generate multiple SQL statements to present one seamless report. In some cases, such as multipass SQL, you may never realize this happens. In other queries, you may explicitly create separate queries and merge them. As you create complex queries, be aware that queries may run slower, and you should ideally test your query logic with small data sets. In some cases, there is no way around the performance issues; it's a complex business question answered with complex SQL. In other instances, you may be able to construct the query in ways that help the processing, or the DBA may be able to do some additional tuning in the data source.

Desktop Intelligence

It seems odd that the most prominent and long-standing aspect of the BusinessObjects suite has now been relegated to one chapter in this *Complete Reference*. BusinessObjects classic, the vendor's initial and long-time desktop product, has been rebranded Desktop Intelligence in XI Release 2. With the improvements in Web Intelligence in XI Release 2, the expectation is that Web Intelligence will become the primary authoring tool for business authors. Within the XI suite, Crystal Reports is the authoring tool best suited for IT developers. Desktop Intelligence is still part of the platform but primarily as a way of ensuring support for existing deployments. There are a few capabilities that are available in Desktop Intelligence that are not available in Web Intelligence, but for the most part, the capabilities of Web Intelligence exceed that of Desktop Intelligence. This chapter, then, discusses when you would want to use Desktop Intelligence instead of Web Intelligence. How-to instructions for advanced capabilities unique to Desktop Intelligence are included in this chapter.

Why Desktop Intelligence

Table 24-1 compares some of the major differences between Desktop Intelligence and Web Intelligence. Use this as a guide for determining when you might need to author a particular report in Desktop Intelligence, instead of Web Intelligence. For example, if a user decides he or she needs disconnected access to a report, then this would be one situation for when a report might better be created as a Desktop Intelligence report. However, for each situation, also consider what capabilities you will be losing:

- Users will not have interactive-access via the right-click to sort and filter the report via a web browser, nor will they be able to drill within a report.
- Users will not have access to the Context panel to display additional information about how metrics were calculated or where the data came from.

Given the trade-offs, also consider if there is a viable work-around. For example, with disconnected access, consider if providing the report via a PDF format or spreadsheet format is a viable alternative. Also, note that for this particular requirement, the vendor is working on a capability to provide disconnected access to Web Intelligence reports. As another example, if the report calls for user-defined objects (not available in Web Intelligence), consider if the universe designer should create these objects centrally. Alternatively, the SQL within Web Intelligence could be modified.

Even if you initially author a report in Desktop Intelligence and later decide it would better be created in Web Intelligence, you can use the conversion utility to convert a report (assuming the capabilities are available in Web Intelligence). However, the reverse is not true: if you author a report in Web Intelligence and later decide to deploy in Desktop Intelligence, you must re-create the report.

NOTE *This chapter assumes that you are a current BusinessObjects classic user and considers when a report is best authored in Desktop Intelligence versus Web Intelligence. It does not consider the broader issue of whether or not a report should be authored in Crystal Reports rather than Web Intelligence. See Chapters 1 and 4 for a greater discussion of product positioning.*

The following table provides a summary of some key differences between Desktop Intelligence and Web Intelligence. Some of these items are important features but do not affect many users. Other items, however, will have a greater impact on your deployment and should be given more consideration.

While Table 24-1 compares features, many things are common to both Desktop Intelligence and Web Intelligence documents: document components (described in Chapter 18), the microcube approach and drill capabilities (Chapter 19), block styles (described in Chapter 21), formula capabilities (described in Chapter 22), and more.

Online Mode vs. Offline Mode

There are two modes of working in Desktop Intelligence, online and offline. *Online mode* is the default mode and means you are connected to the BusinessObjects Enterprise repository; *offline mode* means you are not connected to the repository.

With online mode, you can interact with the repository to retrieve new universe definitions and documents as shown in Figure 24-1. As the designer changes the universe or creates new ones, you can access these changes via the repository in online mode. You can export reports to the repository so that they are available for viewing and scheduling in InfoView.

With offline mode, you do not interact with the repository, so you will not be able to do the following:

- Receive new or updated universe definitions.
- Export reports to the repository.

In order to use offline mode, you must have successfully logged in to Desktop Intelligence at least once, from the PC you currently are using. Each time you log in, Desktop Intelligence updates local files with security information:

```
C:\Documents and Settings\user_name\Application Data\Business Objects\Business Objects
11.5\lsi
```

Feature Category	Feature	Desktop Intelligence	Web Intelligence	Web Intelligence Work-Around
Suite	Live Office integration		√	
Suite	Report bursting via publishing	√		Leverage universe row restrictions, although the Web Intelligence query will execute multiple times
Suite	Greater scalability		√	
Suite	OLAP database access via a universe		√	
Analysis	Interactive viewing and personalization via Web		√	
Analysis	Synchronized multiblock drilling		√	
Analysis	Metadata display via Context panel		√	
Analysis	User-defined hierarchies	√		
Analysis	User-defined groups	√		Create a report variable
Analysis	Server-based ranking		√	
Formatting	Conditional block display	√		
Formatting	Additional chart controls	√		
Formatting	Formatting templates	√		
Portability	Disconnected analysis	√		PDF or Excel
Query	User-defined objects	√		Create object in universe Modify SQL
Query	Query on query	√		Subquery
Query	Additional data providers types	√		Derived tables in universe, ODBC connection to Excel

TABLE 24-1   Comparison of Desktop Intelligence and Web Intelligence

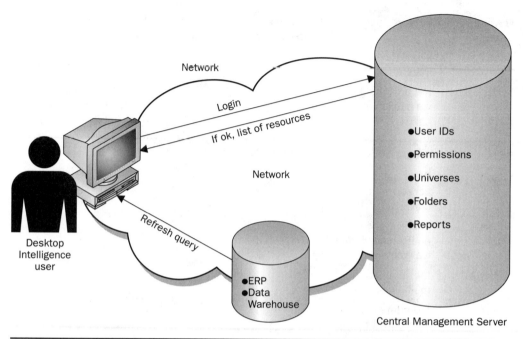

FIGURE 24-1   Users interact with the repository in online mode.

These files allow you to log in to Desktop Intelligence in offline mode while still maintaining secure access to documents. Note that the repository does not actually connect you to a data source. Therefore, you can in theory still refresh reports and build new queries while in offline mode. This may be useful if the repository is unavailable due to maintenance or network problems. In order for you to work with universes and create new documents, however, the universe definitions must be stored on a local disk or accessible network drive, and you must still have connectivity to the data source.

In reality, you most often will use offline mode with notebook computers while you are traveling and not connected to the network. In this respect, you do not interact with either the BusinessObjects XI repository or the data sources.

To work in offline mode, when you launch Desktop Intelligence and log in to the repository, check the box Use In Offline Mode.

Types of Data Providers

Desktop Intelligence enables you to create documents based on one or more data providers just as Web Intelligence does. However, in Desktop Intelligence, in addition to universes, a data provider can access data from the following sources:

- **XML Data Provider**   XML is increasingly the way to share data between applications. When you select XML Data Provider as the basis of a query, Desktop Intelligence launches an XML editor to allow you to select the location of the XML data source, define objects, and then add them to a query.

- **Freehand SQL**   This enables you to create your own SQL statements against data sources for which no universe has been built. The SQL Editor from this panel is quite basic and requires in-depth knowledge of SQL syntax.

- **Personal data files**   These enable you to access Excel spreadsheet, text, and dBase files and then analyze the results using the full set of Desktop Intelligence functionality. This is a powerful feature that enables you to access departmental data in a spreadsheet, for example, and combine it with corporate data from a universe. Note that a universe can access personal files via ODBC, but this approach uses the file system.

- **Stored procedures**   These are sets of SQL statements defined by the DBA.

- **Visual Basic for Applications Procedures**   These are programs that a BusinessObjects developer builds with the Software Development Kit (SDK). A Visual Basic procedure can perform many functions—for example, refresh data, build reports, and then e-mail the results to multiple users. When using Visual Basic procedures as a data provider, you can either create a new procedure or select an existing one.

TIP *If Web Intelligence does not provide you with the required access to a particular data source, this is a situation in which Crystal Reports may be a more appropriate tool, assuming it is part of your XI deployment. Crystal Reports provides access to a greater number of data sources than Desktop Intelligence.*

NOTE *In earlier versions of BusinessObjects, you could access an OLAP database such as Microsoft Analysis Services or Hyperion Essbase as another data provider. This capability is no longer available in Desktop Intelligence. Instead, Web Intelligence users access OLAP databases via a universe that is mapped to the OLAP database. If you as a Desktop Intelligence user try to build a query off such a universe, you will receive the error message "You are not authorized to use this universe." Alternatively, OLAP Intelligence (which you launch from InfoView) can access OLAP databases directly.*

To access an alternate data provider, do the following:

1. Select File | New from the drop-down menu, or New Report Wizard from the toolbar.

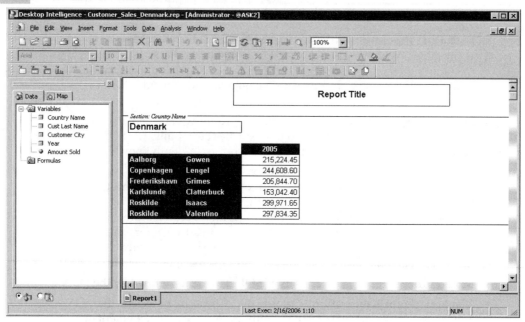

2. When prompted to specify data access, select Others. This will present you with a drop-down list of additional data providers.

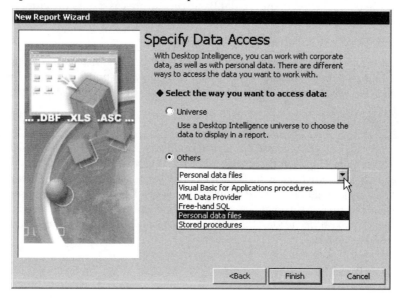

Combining Personal Data Files with Corporate Data

Let's assume you have data in a spreadsheet that you want to combine with a document based on a universe that accesses a corporate data warehouse. You can combine data from your spreadsheet with a standard report. You use the capabilities of multiple data providers, merged dimensions (both of which are available in Web Intelligence), and personal data providers (available only in Desktop Intelligence). Personal data files can be text, spreadsheet, or database files. Your data file may have column headings, but you must tell Desktop Intelligence they exist.

TIP *If your data file is a spreadsheet, use Microsoft Excel's capability to create a named range first.*

In the following example, customer sales comes from the data warehouse. A count of customer visits is stored in a spreadsheet. You would like to analyze whether or not increased customer visits affect customer sales.

1. From the Desktop Intelligence pull-down menu, select Data | New Data Provider.

2. Choose Access New Data In A Different Way and click Begin.

3. In specifying data access, select Others and then from the drop-down list, choose Personal Data File. Click Finish.

4. Specify the data file and indicate if the first row contains column headings as shown here:

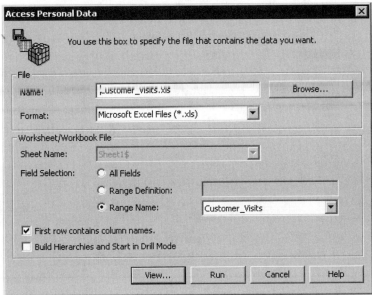

5. Click Run to have Desktop Intelligence access your personal data file.

At this point, the data has been returned to the microcube, but the results will not appear in your report until you synchronize the data providers and add the information from your spreadsheet to the existing tabular report.

Synchronizing Data Providers

When you insert a new data provider, Desktop Intelligence does not automatically affect the data displayed in the report or current table block; the data has only been retrieved into the local microcube. In order to display the results in the table, you insert the new variables via the Report Manager or the Slice and Dice panel. In order to ensure the data is correctly displayed, you must first synchronize the common dimensions via the Data Manager shown in Figure 24-2.

To access the Data Manager, select Data | View Data or select View Data from the standard toolbar and then select the Definition tab. Under Data Providers, the name of each data provider is assigned according to the type of data provider (Query from a universe, PD from a personal data file, and so on) and a sequential number. In Figure 24-2, note the link symbol next to Cust Last Name and Customer. This indicates that the two variables represent the same dimensions and content, even though the variable names are different. When you select a variable that is not linked, the Unlink button becomes a Link button.

Even if you display only one dimension in your report, you must link all dimensions to ensure you continue to get correct results. If you fail to do this correctly, you will get incorrect results in any block that accesses both data providers. If you are working with a personal

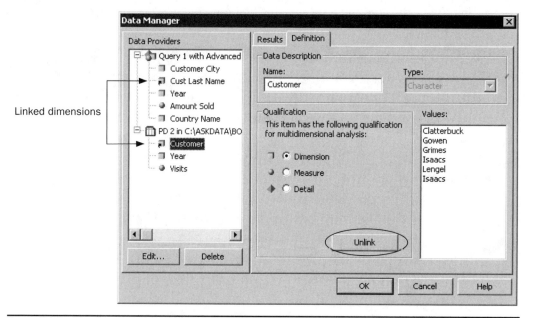

FIGURE 24-2   The Data Manager allows you to link common dimensions.

data file, freehand SQL, or another data provider that does not accurately qualify dimension objects, you also must first modify the qualification (dimension, measure, detail) for the object. For example, if Year in one data provider is a dimension object and in the personal data provider it is a numeric column, Desktop Intelligence will automatically treat it as a measure. You cannot link these two measures until they are the same qualification. Using the Definition tab shown in Figure 24-2, you can change the object qualification for any personal data providers, but you cannot change them for objects that come from a universe.

Once you have corrected the object qualifications, you continue to use the Data Manager to link the dimensions:

1. Select the variable in the first data provider. In this example, Query 1 Cust Last Name.

2. Click Link To.

3. The Define Link Between Dimensions dialog box displays a list of dimension objects from the second data provider (in this case, from a personal data file). Note that only the dimensions that do not have an existing link appear. Select the common dimension, Customer, and click OK.

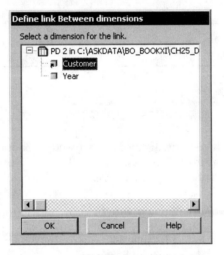

4. Repeat this process for all dimensions that are common to both queries.

5. Click OK to close the Data Manager.

6. Use the Report Manager to drag the new measure from the second data provider to the report table.

Figure 24-3 shows the combined results. Notice that data from the two sources has nicely been merged into one table and a XY scatterplot that seamlessly combines data from both queries. In answering the business question, the results show some relationship between higher customer visits and sales increase!

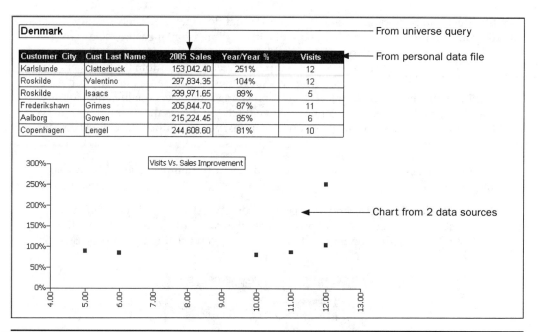

FIGURE 24-3   Report from corporate and personal data sources

Complex Queries

Building complex queries in Web Intelligence is discussed in Chapter 23. Many of the same concepts apply to queries authored in Desktop Intelligence. However, there are some additional capabilities that are unique to Desktop Intelligence.

Query on Query

Desktop Intelligence allows you to use the results of one query as a filter list in another query. At first glance, this sounds a lot like a subquery! In some respects it is, but the query-on-query capability is ever more powerful because

- Your filter list can come from an entirely different data source, whereas with a subquery, you access the same data source.

- Subqueries can cause slow performance, whereas query on query is often better. This does depend, though, on how many values you are comparing. If your filter list is thousands of rows, this data travels the network between the database and your desktop, whereas a subquery utilizes the database server completely. Also, certain databases have an upper limit for how many items can appear in a WHERE clause.

To understand subqueries, first review the section on subqueries in Chapter 23. Assume you want to know how sales are doing for products that were promoted in a particular period. In this example, you first build the query to get a list of those products. This list of products is your first data provider. As a second step, you use the list of promoted products (the first data provider) as a filter in your second query. The workflow and SQL generated are quite different from those of a subquery, as compared in the following table.

	Subquery	Query on Query
Workflow	Build the main query, then specify the subquery in your conditions.	Build an initial query that returns a list, and then specify the results of this query in your condition.
SQL generated	Two SQL SELECT statements are nested within one another and processed by the data base server.	Condition values are inserted directly into the WHERE clause of one SELECT statement.

With a subquery, if you were creating a subquery, you would build your main query and then specify the conditions as a subquery.

Figure 24-4 shows the query definition and the corresponding results to this query. In the second query, you will use the results from this query as a list of filters.

1. Specify your query result objects as shown in Figure 24-5. Note that these result columns are slightly different from those as shown in Figure 24-4. Here you are asking for *sales* information for certain products. In the query in Figure 24-4, you were asking for *promotional* information only.

2. Drag the object *SKU number* to the Conditions pane in the Query panel.

3. When prompted to <select an operator>, choose In List.

4. When prompted to <select an operand>, choose Select Query Result. When you choose this Operand, Desktop Intelligence will prompt you to select the data provider that you want to use as a query condition. This document contains only one other data provider, so the objects from Query 1 are listed.

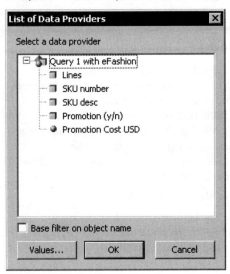

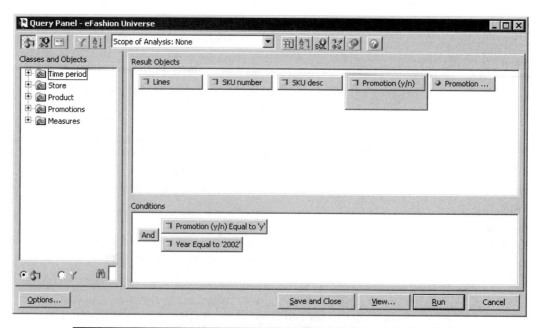

Product Line	SKU Number	SKU Description	Promotion (y/n)	Promotion Cost
Accessories	145404	Rounded Rectangle Brooch	y	$9,500
Dresses	166699	Suede Stretch Dress	y	$13,000
Shirt Waist	165170	Modal Shirt	y	$1,200
Shirt Waist	166550	Whisky Dancer T-Shirt	y	$9,500
Shirt Waist	166583	Military Shirt	y	$12,650
Shirt Waist	167042	Long-Sleeved Stitch Shirt	y	$8,050
Sweat-T-Shirts	166544	Polo Collared T-Shirt	y	$2,000
Sweat-T-Shirts	167695	Pomodore Lace T-Shirt	y	$5,075

FIGURE 24-4   Query settings and results to use as a condition in another query

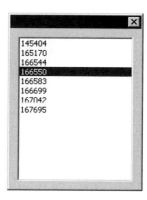

5. In many cases, your filter list will be based on values from one object from the same universe but coming from a different data provider. To see just the object with the same name, check the box Base Filter On Object Name. You will now see only the SKU number. Select this object. To preview a list of the values from the original data provider, click Values. These are the values that will be used in your query conditions.

6. Click the X to close the Values dialog.

7. Click OK from the List Of Data Providers dialog to close this dialog and have the SKU number from Query 1 added as the operand to your condition.

8. Run the query.

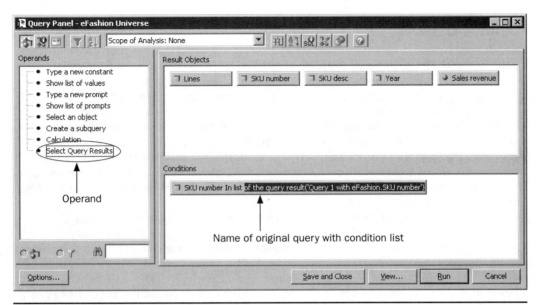

FIGURE 24-5   Query on query

The SQL generated for this type of query is as follows:

```
WHEREt
   (@dpvalues('Article_lookup.Article_id',9,2)@dpend)
```

When submitted to the database, the values from the data provider get translated as follows:

```
WHERE
Article_lookup.Article_id  IN  (145404, 166699, 165170, 166550, 166583, 167042,
166344, 167695)
```

Compare this to the subquery syntax as shown in Chapter 23.

Following are some additional sample business questions for which you may want to use the query on query capabilities:

Question: *Who are my new salespeople? How do their sales compare to more senior sales staff?*
Solution: Create a query from a Human Resources universe that lists the newer salespeople (Query 1). Create a second query from a Sales universe that displays total sales by salesperson (Query 2). Filter the salesperson according to the results of the first query. Create a third query (Query 3) that displays the total sales, but this time set the condition to Sales Person NOT IN LIST Query 1. Finally, create a report that displays the sales from both Query 2 and Query 3 as separate columns.

Question: *One of the manufacturing facilities had an unexpected closure. How much can we service the orders from another facility?*
Solution: Run a query to retrieve products and open orders for the out-of-order plant (Query 1). Create a second query of available inventory by product, filtering the list of products based on Query 1.

User-Defined Objects

User-defined objects (UDOs) are objects that a user creates and that get processed on the database server, different from variables that get processed in a report via the BusinessObjects Enterprise server or on your desktop. UDOs are available only for the particular user and from the PC in which the objects were defined. The definitions for user-defined objects are stored in a local file in the universe folder as *universe*.udo, where *universe* is the name of the universe to which the objects belong. Because the objects are stored in a local file, they cannot be shared with other users and you cannot schedule documents that contain UDOs via the scheduler. For this reason, I recommend keeping user-defined objects to a minimum and prefer that the universe designer create a common object or that you use a report formula or variable (see Chapter 14 for a discussion of where to build the intelligence).

A user-defined object gets converted to SQL, so any transformations or calculations are performed on the server. With report formulas and variables, the transformations and calculations occur on the local PC. For this reason, if the universe designer has not included certain objects in the universe, you may need to create a user-defined object to minimize the number of rows of data sent across the network. For example, let's assume you want to get a count of the number of orders for each month. To use the BusinessObjects CountAll function in a report, you would need to retrieve all the individual orders. For companies with high order volumes, this may be millions of rows of data and, therefore, not possible. If you use the SQL COUNT function, then the server counts the number of orders and returns only one row per month.

You create a UDO by either selecting User Objects from within the Query panel or selecting Tools | Universes and then selecting User Objects. Once you create a UDO, the objects are stored in a separate class, *User objects*. As the objects are universe-specific, you can reuse UDOs in multiple documents.

Similar to Report Variables and the Variable Editor (Chapter 21), the User Object dialog box has two tabs, a Definition tab, in which you define the object name, type, and qualification, as well as a Formula tab, in which you apply the calculation or transformation, as shown in Figure 24-6. If you will be creating UDOs, I recommend reading Chapters 9 and 11 to understand some of the options here. If you designate an object to be a measure, you specify two aggregates: the projection aggregate that is used in the report calculations and the SQL aggregate that is used on the server. The projection aggregate is the function on the Definition tab. The SQL aggregate is the numeric function on the Formula tab. Also note that the list of SQL functions here are database dependent.

From the Formula tab, if you select the option Get Assistance On Functions, Desktop Intelligence will prompt you to enter any required parameters.

Advanced Formatting Capabilities

This section describes three advanced formatting capabilities within Desktop Intelligence: how to hide a block, create templates for formatting documents consistently, and creating user-defined hierarchies and groups for drilling and subtotals.

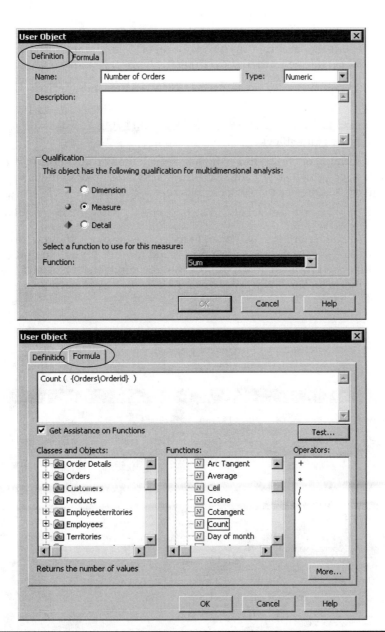

FIGURE 24-6 User-defined objects are processed on the database server.

Hiding a Table

The Appearance tab, shown in Figure 24-7, allows you to position a block within a page or to hide it entirely. The Hide Cell option will change to a Hide Block or Hide Section Header, depending upon which component you selected, and allows you to specify a formula to conditionally hide the block. This option is quite powerful for multiblock reports and master/detail reports. For example, if you have a report that contains a chart for trend analysis and a detail table beneath to show budget variance, you may only want to show the detail table when the total variance exceeds a certain value. To conditionally hide the block, do the following:

1. From the Table Format dialog box, select the Appearance tab.

2. Check the box Hide Block.

3. Enter a formula or click Edit Formula to launch the Formula Editor. You do not need to specify an If statement. For example, to hide a block when the total variance for the block is greater than 95 percent, enter = **\<Variance\> > .95**.

4. Click Apply to see the effect of this setting, and then OK to close the dialog box.

In a master/detail report, you will want to hide both the block and the corresponding section header, so be sure to use the same options and formula for both report components.

The Hide Block setting evaluates the entire table or minitable in a master/detail report. It will not hide individual break levels or rows. To hide these, you need to use Filters, which are explained in Chapter 19.

NOTE   *Web Intelligence allows you to conditionally display a block if the contents are empty or not; however, it does not allow you to control the display according to a formula as in Desktop Intelligence.*

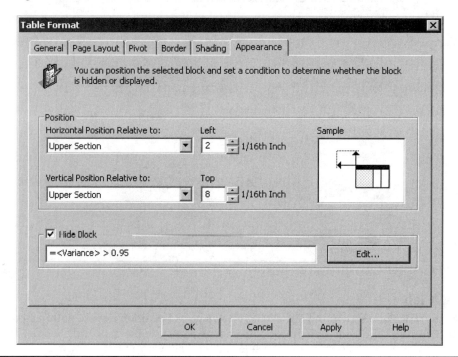

FIGURE 24-7   Conditionally hide blocks

Templates and Standard Report Styles

Templates and standard report styles allow you to format documents with predefined headers, footers, subtotals, break settings, and other formatting options. A *template* is a particular kind of file within Desktop Intelligence that allows you, for example, to include a company logo, the document title, default table and chart settings, and so on. Templates have a .ret extension and are stored in C:\Documents and Settings*User_Name*\My Documents\My Business Objects Documents\templates*LL*, where *LL* is the language, such as EN for English or DE for German. Templates also allow you to specify an initial block type and formatting options when creating a new document.

Standard report styles exist within a global template file, $default$.ret. They control the formatting of the different report components (section headers, table block, crosstab block). Unless your administrator has provided you with a modified $default$.ret file, the settings in this file create the standard white table with blue column headings. Once you are comfortable formatting the various components of a report, modifying the standard report styles is the best way to apply a consistent format to all reports you create. When you modify standard report styles, Desktop Intelligence automatically saves the changes to $default$.ret.

NOTE *If you are the BusinessObjects XI administrator and want the standard report styles applied to all users' reports, you must modify your $default$.ret file and ensure the modified version is installed for all Desktop Intelligence users.*

Templates and standard report styles are complementary. A template allows you to specify default headers, footers, and block styles when you create a new document. However, if you want all the new blocks that you add to a report to have a similar style, then modify the standard report styles.

Templates

In the following example, you want to specify the following defaults as part of the template:

- A header with the document name, centered
- A footer with the refresh date and page numbers

In developing a template, you can work with an existing document or create a new one with a small set of data. In the following sections, you will first define default headers and footers, and then save the definitions in a template to ensure consistent formatting in new documents.

Default Header

In the following steps you will create a default header that displays the document name.

1. Open an existing document by selecting File | Open or clicking the Open button from the toolbar.

2. Be sure the Report Manager is open and in Map/Structure mode. Select Report Manager from the standard toolbar, and then click the Map tab. From within the Map tab, select the Structure icon.

3. Select the report tab that contains the desired block layout. Select View | Page Layout so that you see the Page Header and Page Footer.

4. Select Insert | Cell.

5. The mouse cursor becomes an insert cell icon. Position it in the Header section and drag it to create a cell the approximate size of a document name.

TIP *You can follow a similar technique to add a logo in the header using Insert | Picture. When adding a logo, the size of the cell is important in preserving the shape of the logo. There is no way to preserve aspect ratios as other graphics programs do.*

---

6. The default cell format includes a border. Click the No Border button from the formatting toolbar.

7. Use the formula editor to insert the following formula into the blank cell:

```
=DocumentName()
```

8. Center the cell within the Page Header by selecting Format | Cell and the Appearance tab. From the Horizontal Position Relative To drop-down, select Center Across The Page.

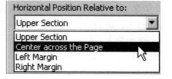

Default Footer

In the following steps you will create a default footer that displays the date the document was last refreshed and the number of pages in the report.

1. Within the Report window, scroll to the Page Footer. Alternatively, from within the Report Manager, in Map/Structure view, select Page Footer.

2. From the pull-down menu, select Insert | Special Field | Date And Time | Last Refresh.

3. The mouse pointer becomes an insert cell cursor. Position your cursor to the left-hand side of the footer and drag the mouse to the desired cell size.

4. Select Insert | Special Field | Page Numbers | Page # of #. The mouse pointer again becomes an insert cell cursor. Position the

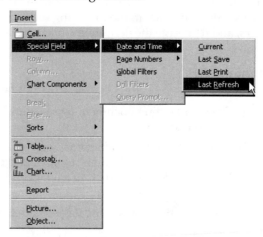

cursor to the right-hand side of the footer. Your footer should now appear as follows:

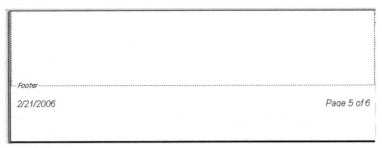

5. You can remove the cell borders by selecting both cells in the Report window (use CTRL-click to select both footer cells); from within the Report Manager, you can select and format only one cell at a time.

6. From the toolbar, click the No Border button.

TIP *If your template contains a tabular block with subtotals, then subtotals will also appear in any subsequent reports to which you apply this template.*

Save As Template

Once you have included the desired headers and footers, save the document as a template to be applied to other reports.

TIP *If you have included subtotals in your crosstab, then subtotals also will be included in the template. You also can set desired break settings.*

1. From the pull-down menu, select File | Save As.

2. Give the template a meaningful name and save it as a Desktop Intelligence Document: **Crosstab with Standard Footer**. Click Save.

TIP *When you save a report as a template, you cannot go back and modify the template. Therefore, save one copy as a .rep file and a second copy as the .ret file. This way, if you need to modify the template, you can do so by applying the changes initially in the .rep.*

3. Select File | Save As again, but this time, click the drop-down menu Save As Type and select Desktop Intelligence Templates.

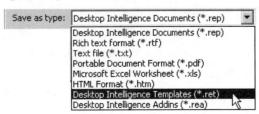

4. Click Save.

NOTE   *To have the template appear in the New Report Wizard, Select a Template step, you must save the template to the default template directory C:\Documents and Settings\User_Name\ My Documents\My Business Objects Documents\ templates\LL. file.*

Apply Template

You can apply the template to existing reports by selecting Format | Report | Apply Template. Additionally, when you create a new document, you can have Desktop Intelligence ensure that you select a template. To enable this option, follow these steps:

1. Select Tools | Options.
2. Select the New Document tab.
3. Check the box Select A Template.
4. Click OK to close the Options dialog box.

Standard Report Styles

Templates and standard report styles are similar in some respects. A standard report style includes default settings for the different block types. It does not, however, include default headers and footers that templates do. When your template includes an initial block style such as a crosstab, then the formatting settings you apply to that crosstab will get reflected in the first crosstab within your new document. However, if you create new reports and new crosstabs, the template settings do not come into play; in these circumstances, the standard report styles do.

TIP   *As a precaution, make a backup copy of the $default$.ret file before you make changes to the standard report styles.*

To modify the standard report styles, select Tools | Standard Report Styles (see Figure 24-8). Under Report Components, Desktop Intelligence displays the different block types and sections of a report. The tabs General, Page Layout, Border, and Shading are similar to those for individual cells and tables.

For example, assume that you want all column and row headings in any crosstabs to not contain the default blue background and white text. You want the column and row headings to have black text, bold, with a white background.

1. Select Tools | Standard Report Styles.
2. Under Report Components, select Crosstabs, Header, Top, as shown in Figure 24-8.
3. Select the Font tab and choose Color, Automatic.
4. Select the Shading tab and choose Fill, None.
5. Repeat Steps 3 and 4 for the Crosstabs, Header, Left cells.
6. Click OK to close the Standard Report Styles dialog.
7. To apply this new style to an existing crosstab, select Format | Report | Apply Standard Style.

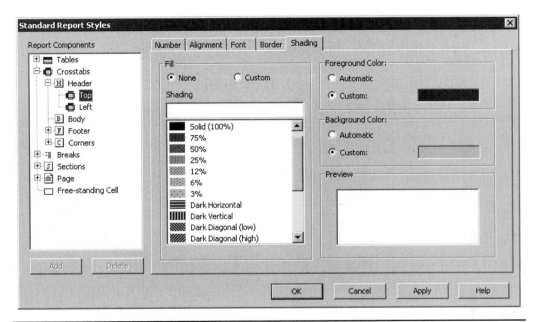

FIGURE 24-8   Standard report styles

TIP   *If you routinely change the page break options for master/detail reports or breaks, set the*
Standard Report Style to avoid page breaks within a block, to repeat headers on subsequent
pages, and so on.

User-defined Hierarchies

Desktop Intelligence contains similar drill capabilities to Web Intelligence. In addition, it
contains a Hierarchy Editor (see Figure 24-9) that allows users to override the universe default
hierarchies. As an example, the eFashion universe has two items that are not part of any
hierarchy: *Zip Code* is not part of a hierarchy because it is classified as a detail object. To enable
it to be a drillable dimension, you can create a variable to reclassify it as a dimension object
and then add it to the Product hierarchy. Likewise, *Color* is not part of a hierarchy. Yet, it's a
reasonable analysis to compare sales of products by color. Do black suits outsell blue suits?

1. From the pull-down menu select Analysis | Hierarchies.

2. Under Available Dimensions, click the + sign to expand the folder and see all
   dimension objects within the specified query. Under Available Hierarchies, Desktop
   Intelligence displays the custom hierarchies the universe designer created.

3. To add objects that appear in the query but not in a hierarchy, select the object under
   Available Dimensions. Then select the Hierarchy name to which you want to add
   the object and click Add.

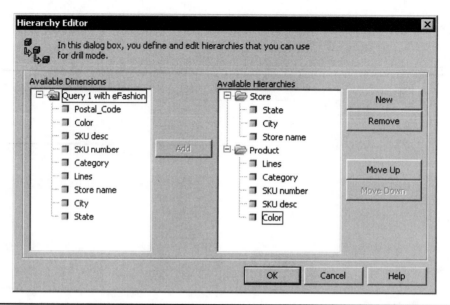

FIGURE 24-9   Hierarchy Editor

4. To move *Color* further up in the hierarchy to below *Category*, select *Color* under Available Hierarchies, and then click Move Up until it appears immediately below *Category*.

5. Click OK to close the Hierarchy Editor and save all changes to the Hierarchies.

6. Note that these changes are relevant for the current document only and do not affect other users or new documents.

User-Defined Groups

User-defined hierarchies allow you to specify a dimension to be part of a hierarchy, whereas user-defined groups allow you to classify individual rows of data into a group or dimension that does not yet exist.

For example, the following table shows a list of Jewelry products and their prices. You can group these products by price as Expensive or Value.

Category	SKU desc	Unit Price MSRP
Jewelry	Stole and Feather Boa Set	$40.90
Jewelry	Chain and Pearl Necklace	$69.30
Jewelry	Large Silver Bracelet	$69.30
Jewelry	Bell Necklace	$69.90
Jewelry	Pendant Earrings	$69.99
Jewelry	Ball and Chain Necklace	$79.20
Jewelry	Rigid Twisted Knot Bracelet	$83.50
Jewelry	9cm Gold Brooch	$99.00
Jewelry	E-Watch	$110.60
Jewelry	Large Rectangular Brooch	$116.10
Jewelry	Diamond Pendant Earrings	$118.50
Jewelry	Jet Pearl Bracelet	$118.50
Jewelry	Mini Pearl and Tubes Necklace	$118.50
Jewelry	Silver Hoop Earrings	$118.50
Jewelry	Thick Silver Bangle	$129.00
Jewelry	Pearl and Flower Necklace	$129.99
Jewelry	Pearl and Diamond Necklace	$133.00
Jewelry	Goldset Pearl Necklace	$134.10
Jewelry	Tortoiseshell Brooch	$135.00
Jewelry	Jet and Pearl Necklace	$135.20
Jewelry	Pearl and Diamond Necklace	$135.20

To create a new Group, follow these steps:

1. Select the column that contains the values you want to base the new group on, in this case, the *Unit Price.*

2. Choose Data | Variables from the pull-down menu. Click Group.

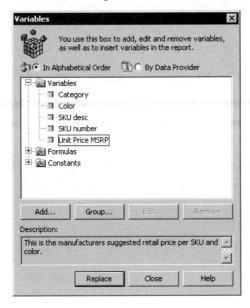

3. Desktop Intelligence displays the current values in the report. In the Name Of The Variable box, enter **Price Category**.

4. Click New to enter a new group of values. Desktop Intelligence will provide a generic Group 1 in the right-hand pane. Provide a meaningful group names such as **Value**.

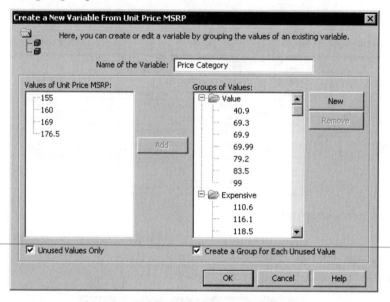

5. Click New again and overtype Group 2 with **Expensive**.

6. Select your newly created group, Value. Then select the prices on the left that are < $100 and click Add.

7. Repeat this to add items > $100 to the Expensive group.

8. Click OK to close the New Variable dialog and Close to close the Variables dialog.

9. Insert an additional column in your report with the new grouping variable, Price Category.

TIP *For groups that are based on values from measures, consider creating a variable that uses if-then-else statements and ranges to provide more flexible definitions.*

Publishing to the Repository

When you work with Desktop Intelligence documents, you routinely save your work to your local computer. If you want other people to access the document and refresh it, then you need to save it to the repository. This allows report consumers to view reports via InfoView and to schedule them.

To save your report to the BusinessObjects Enterprise repository,

1. Select File | Export To Repository.

2. Desktop Intelligence presents you with the Export dialog as shown in Figure 24-10. Choose the folder to export the document to. If this is a document that only you will access, choose Favorites. If you want others in your work group to access it, choose a Public Folder. For more information on Folders and Categories, refer to Chapter 17.

3. If your users navigate documents by categories, assign them by clicking the Categories button.

4. Click OK to begin the export process. Desktop Intelligence will confirm when the export to the repository is complete with a message "Export Successful." Click OK to acknowledge the message.

To schedule a Desktop Intelligence document to refresh on a periodic basis, you use InfoView. The steps to schedule a Desktop Intelligence report are the same as the steps for a Web Intelligence report. Refer to Chapter 18 for more information.

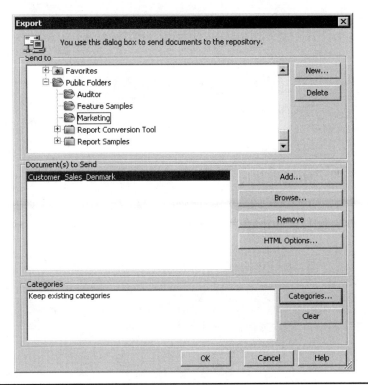

FIGURE 24-10 Export documents to the repository for users to access in InfoView.

Summary

Desktop Intelligence allows power users to author reports on the desktop, whereas Web Intelligence provides a Web-based authoring environment. Both types of reports can be accessed via InfoView. However, only Web Intelligence allows users Web-based drill, analysis, and report formatting. Desktop Intelligence has certain capabilities such as additional data provider types, disconnected analysis, templates, and custom hierarchies that are not available in Web Intelligence. Before developing a report, consider the intended target audience and their requirements.

Bibliography

BusinessObjects Enterprise XI Release 2 Auditor's Guide. Business Objects, 2005.

"BusinessObjects XI Keeps the Information Buzzing at Burt's Bees" (Business Objects Press Release). August 23, 2005.

Chang, Dr. Daniel T. "CWM Enablement Showcase: Warehouse Metadata Interchange Made Easy Using CWM." *TDWI What Works, Volume 11.*

Eckerson, Wayne. "Analytic Applications: Build or Buy." TDWI Business Intelligence Strategies Program, November 2002.

Eckerson, Wayne, and Cindi Howson. "Enterprise Business Intelligence: Strategies and Technologies for Deploying BI on an Enterprise Scale." TDWI Report Series, July 2005.

Groff, James. *SQL: The Complete Reference*. McGraw-Hill/Osborne, 2002.

Hope, Jeremy. *Reinventing the CFO*. Harvard Business School Press, 2006.

Howson, Cindi. "Marketing the BI Application." TDWI, August 2005.

Loney, Kevin. *Oracle 9i: The Complete Reference*. McGraw-Hill/Osborne, 2002.

McKnight, William. "How to Justify a Data Warehouse Using ROI." TDWI, February 2003.

Meta Integration (www.metaintegration.net).

Mishra, Sanjay. *Mastering Oracle SQL*. O'Reilly, April 2002.

Morris, Henry, et al. "The Financial Impact of Business Analytics, an IDC ROI Study." December 2002.

Object Management Group (www.omg.com).

Pense, Nigel. The OLAP Survey 5 (www.survey.com/olap).

Powell, Thomas. *HTML: The Complete Reference*. McGraw-Hill/Osborne, 2001.

Schauer, Val. "Business Objects." *DM Review*, January 2003.

Stoller, Don. "Turning Your Business Intelligence Investment into a Profit Center." TDWI Business Intelligence Strategies Program, November 2002.

Vesset, Dan. "Trends in the Market for Business Intelligence Software." *DM Review*, August 2001.

Watson, Hugh, et al. "Current Practices in Data Warehousing."

Wu, Jonathon. "Measuring the Value of Your Business Intelligence and Data Warehousing Initiatives." Knightsbridge Solutions, April 2004.

Zurich North America (www.zurichna.com).

Index

References to figures and illustrations are in italics.

G